REPRESENTATIVE GOVERNMENT IN MODERN EUROPE

THIRD EDITION

Michael Gallagher
Michael Laver
Peter Mair

Boston   Burr Ridge, IL   Dubuque, IA   Madison, WI   New York   San Francisco   St. Louis
Bangkok   Bogotá   Caracas   Lisbon   London   Madrid
Mexico City   Milan   New Delhi   Seoul   Singapore   Sydney   Taipei   Toronto

McGraw-Hill Higher Education

*A Division of The **McGraw-Hill** Companies*

REPRESENTATIVE GOVERNMENT IN MODERN EUROPE: INSTITUTIONS, PARTIES, AND GOVERNMENTS, THIRD EDITION

Published by McGraw-Hill, an imprint of The McGraw-Hill Companies, Inc., 1221 Avenue of the Americas, New York, NY 10020. Copyright © 2001, 1995 by The McGraw-Hill Companies, Inc. All rights reserved. Previously published under the title of *Representative Government in Western Europe.* Copyright © 1992 by McGraw-Hill, Inc. All rights reserved. No part of this publication may be reproduced or distributed in any form or by any means, or stored in a database or retrieval system, without the prior written consent of The McGraw-Hill Companies, Inc., including, but not limited to, in any network or other electronic storage or transmission, or broadcast for distance learning.

Some ancillaries, including electronic and print components, may not be available to customers outside the United States.

This book is printed on acid-free paper.

1 2 3 4 5 6 7 8 9 0 QPF/QPF 0 9 8 7 6 5 4 3 2 1 0

ISBN 0–07–232267–5

Vice president and editor-in-chief: *Thalia Dorwick*
Editorial director: *Jane E. Vaicunas*
Sponsoring editor: *Monica Eckman*
Editorial coordinator: *Hannah Glover*
Marketing manager: *Janise A. Fry*
Project manager: *Sheila M. Frank*
Senior media producer: *Sean Crowley*
Production supervisor: *Enboge Chong*
Coordinator of freelance design: *Michelle D. Whitaker*
Freelance cover designer: *Sheilah Barrett Design*
Cover illustration: *Richard Tuschman*
Senior photo research coordinator: *Carrie K. Burger*
Photo research: *Feldman & Associates, Inc.*
Compositor: *York Graphic Services, Inc.*
Typeface: *10/12 Times Roman*
Printer: *Quebecor Printing Book Group/Fairfield, PA*

Library of Congress Cataloging-in-Publication Data

Gallagher, Michael, 1951–.
   Representative government in modern Europe / Michael Gallagher, Michael Laver,
   Peter Mair. — 3rd ed.
       p. cm.
   Includes bibliographical references and index.
   ISBN 0–07–232267–5
   1. Representative government and representation—Europe—Case studies.   2. Political parties—Europe—Case studies.   3. Europe—Politics and government—1945–.   I. Laver, Michael, 1949–.
II. Mair, Peter.   III. Gallagher, Michael, Ph. D. Representative government in Western Europe.   IV. Title.

JN94 .A91 G35   2001
321.8′043′094—dc21

00–032896
CIP

www.mhhe.com

ABOUT
THE AUTHORS

MICHAEL GALLAGHER is associate professor in the Department of Political Science at Trinity College, University of Dublin; he has also taught at New York University. He is coeditor of *Candidate Selection in Comparative Selection* (London, 1988), *The Referendum Experience in Europe* (Basingstoke, 1996), and *Politics in the Republic of Ireland,* 3d ed. (London, 1999). His current research interests include a study of the backgrounds, attitudes, and roles of members of political parties.

MICHAEL LAVER holds the chair of Political Science at Trinity College, University of Dublin. He previously taught at Queens University, Belfast; the University of Liverpool; and University College Galway, and has been a visiting professor at the University of Texas at Austin, Harvard University, and Duke University. Recent books include *Private Desires, Political Action* (London, 1997); *Playing Politics: The Nightmare Continues* (Oxford, 1997); and (with Kenneth A. Shepsle) *Making and Breaking Governments* (New York, 1996). He is currently working on the impact of intra-party politics on inter-party coalition bargaining, and on the development of more dynamic models of government formation.

PETER MAIR holds the chair of Comparative Politics in Leiden University in the Netherlands and previously taught at the University of Limerick; the University of Strathclyde, Glasgow; the University of Manchester; and the European University Institute, Florence. He is the author (with Stefano Bartolini) of *Identity, Competition, and Electoral Availability* (Cambridge, 1990), which was awarded the Stein Rokkan Prize, and of *Party System Change* (Oxford, 1997). Recent coedited books include *How Parties Organize* (London, 1994), and *Parteien auf komplexen Wählermärkten* (Vienna, 1999). He is coeditor of the *European Journal of Political Research* and is currently engaged in a project on the long-term development of elections, parties, and governments in Western Europe over the period from 1950 to 2000.

CONTENTS

LIST OF TABLES
AND FIGURES

PREFACE

This is the third edition of *Representative Government in Modern Europe*. The need for a new edition arises, as before, from the relentless passage of time, and the timing of the new edition is especially appropriate. Writing as we are at the start of a new millennium, we can define "modern" Europe very neatly as the Europe that left the twentieth century and went into the twenty-first. It is a different Europe in many ways from the one that we wrote about for the first edition, a mere nine years ago. The two really striking changes have to do with Eastern Europe and with the European Union.

As far as Eastern Europe is concerned, the changes in the final decade of the twentieth century were truly astonishing. We completed the first edition at a time when the end of Communist rule in what people then still thought of as the Soviet Union and its Warsaw Pact allies had occurred no more than a year or two previously. Whatever they might have said at the time, nobody, if they were honest, had any real idea whether this was a temporary blip on an essentially authoritarian trajectory for the countries involved, or an irreversible political sea-change of historic proportions.

Nine more years of political history have given us the hindsight to know, first, that the changes in Eastern Europe really were of massive proportions, but, second, that the political consequences of these changes will take at least a generation to work their way through the system. The transition to democracy seems secure in many postcommunist states. At the same time, the appalling events in the disintegrating former Yugoslavia—in the geographic heart of Europe—have shown us in brutal terms that we can take nothing for granted. Shocking images beamed around the world have sharply reminded people—and many did indeed need to be reminded—what happens when politics fails, even in modern Europe.

While, with some notable exceptions, the transition to democracy seems broadly secure, the economic transformation that is following in its wake has proved difficult, less of a panacea than might have been expected, and extremely varied in its effects. On one hand, the former East Germany has integrated with West Germany into a unified state, allowing us to observe a remarkable experiment in social and political engineering but reminding us how huge and complex the unification project is. And some other European countries from the "near East" of Europe—notably Hungary, the Czech Republic, Poland, and Slovakia—seem to be moving steadily towards the West in many ways. On the other hand, there are certain Balkan states and parts of the former Soviet Union that are clearly struggling, both politically and economically, and for which the future is far from clear.

For these reasons we have retained our separate treatment of Eastern European states in this revised edition (very much revised, of course). While we might have expected nine years ago to be fully integrating our treatment of Eastern and Western Europe into a single unified whole, it has turned out to be both difficult and unwise to do this at present.

The other major changes over the past nine years have arisen as a result of developments in the European Union (EU). Certainly, the trend towards European integration has maintained a strong momentum. Countries at the heart of the EU project have set up a common travel area, to allow free movement between countries without passports, customs, or immigration controls. Another large subset of EU countries has set up a common currency, the euro, bringing about the end of the German deutche marks, French francs, Italian lire, and Spanish pesetas that have so much defined postwar European trade and travel. As an inevitable result of this, many aspects of financial policy, once at the heart of national politics for European states, have been "harmonized" to leave little scope for independent national policy making. European law has replaced domestic law for EU member states on many other important matters, once more taking important issues out of national politics.

These are huge changes and they not only affect our treatment of the EU, which has been very substantially revised, but have a bearing upon almost every chapter in this book. This creates an intriguing paradox. As the impact of the EU on its member states gets ever larger, it becomes ever more difficult to separate discussion of EU politics from discussion of the politics of its member states. In a few years' time, if this momentum keeps up, it may even undermine the rationale for a separate treatment of EU and national politics. For the moment, however, and almost certainly following the instincts of most European citizens, we have retained the distinction between the two.

We have of course also retained the fundamental philosophy that has guided this book through its various editions. We discuss the full range of European countries, large and small, and we organize our discussion of these in terms of the major themes that structure the study of representative government. This has become a much more popular way of doing things than when we wrote the first edition, and all reviews and discussions have stressed this as one of the book's main virtues. Thus we no longer have to defend analyzing European politics thematically, rather than taking the country-by-country approach that was once so common.

Our main task in this edition has thus been to improve, deepen, and modernize our discussion of representative government in modern Europe rather than to change it utterly. Reviews of the book have stressed its value in introducing readers to current debates among those who analyze European politics, and this edition sets out to keep our discussion of these debates as up-to-the-minute as possible. We have also updated and often completely recalculated the data in most tables, taking advantage of the opportunity, where possible, to include data relating to the beginning of the twenty-first century. Since the political science profession is nothing like as huge as its potential subject matter, however, not everything is researched all the time. This means that there are some areas for which somewhat "older" research remains the most current, and in these cases we have tried to be careful not to throw out the baby with the bathwater. But our overall intention has certainly been to make sure that our treatment of modern Europe is as modern as possible.

When all is said and done, what has encouraged us to produce a third edition is that we remain every bit as intrigued and enthused about the study of modern European politics as we were when we wrote the first edition nine years ago. We have been encouraged no end by the reviews and comments that we have received and the uses to which earlier editions have been put. And we have been fortified in producing this third edition by advice and assistance from many, many friends, colleagues and anonymous reviewers—far too many to list here. Those who have helped us know who they are. We thank them for their generosity, and hope that we have not done too much violence to their ideas. The debate, of course, is far from over.

Michael Gallagher
Michael Laver
Peter Mair

INTRODUCTION

European politics is as fascinating and exciting now, at the beginning of the twenty-first century, as it has been at any time in the past thousand years. The long-lasting postwar division of Europe into East and West has now ceased to have any real political meaning, with formerly communist European states holding multiparty elections and expressing the intention to join their Western neighbors as part of a united Europe. At the same time, the unique experiment of European integration continues to forge ahead, with European law superseding national law in increasingly many areas and with the introduction of a single currency creating a common means of exchange and a common monetary policy across most of the member states of the European Union.

But despite the apparent erosion of traditional political and cultural boundaries in modern Europe, it is still vitally important to have a reliable feel for the national politics of European states. The transitions to democracy in postcommunist Europe were informed crucially by the Western European experience. Western European states sometimes provided models for the postcommunist transitions, but they also indicated the pitfalls that were to be avoided. And despite all the ballyhoo about a future United States of Europe, the process of European integration is still essentially driven by political interests and demands that are shaped at the national level. Member states retain important veto powers—ultimately, they can even opt out of the entire process, albeit at massive cost. Both the collapse of the Soviet Union and the process of European integration, while changing the face of modern Europe, emphasize the vital importance of a solid understanding of the politics of the individual European states.

OUR APPROACH

We set out in this book to discuss modern European politics. We do so from a distinctive point of view. First, we concentrate on the politics of representation, focusing especially on institutions, parties, and governments. Second, our approach is wholeheartedly comparative. We organize our discussions around particular important themes in the politics of representation, not around particular important countries.

We are convinced that the benefits of our approach far exceed the costs. By restricting ourselves to the politics of representation, we give ourselves the space to take seriously the large body of comparative research and writing on this that can be found in the recent literature. By insisting on a comparative rather than a country-by-country approach, we give ourselves the opportunity to bring a much larger amount of evidence to bear on the problem at hand.

We feel strongly that many of the most important features of the politics of representation in modern Europe are overlooked by the still-too-common tendency to concentrate on only a few "important" countries. The smaller European democracies are often the sources of the most suggestive evidence on matters as diverse as the nature of party systems, the patterns in voting behavior, the importance of electoral laws, and the dynamics of coalition bargaining. If we want to find out about differences between urban and rural voters, for example, Scandinavia is one of the first places we should start looking. If we want to find out how proportional representation electoral systems work, we do well to begin with the Netherlands. Comparing Ireland and Denmark is a good way to begin to understand what makes some minority governments stable and others not. The list could be extended indefinitely. Confining ourselves to a few big countries is not the way to come to grips with some of the most important and exciting features of the politics of representation in modern Europe.

Our way of doing things does have costs, of course, and it is well to be aware of them. The most obvious has to do with depth. In a book of a certain size, when we broaden our coverage across a very wide range of countries, then our treatment of each is bound to be less detailed. In our view, the benefits of being comprehensive across Europe are greater than the benefits of adding more detail on a small number of countries, but others may come to the opposite conclusion about this inevitable trade-off. There are plenty of other books for these people to read, so we need not feel too sorry for them, but we should remember that they do have a point. In taking several steps back to expand our field of view, we may lose sight of important detail—but we may also gain a better sense of perspective.

Another potential cost has to do with consistency. Obviously, we cannot, discuss every European country in relation to every theme that we select. But if we choose specific countries to illustrate particular points, the reader may not get a clear sense of what is going on in any particular European country. We adopt a three-pronged approach to this problem, which we hope allows us to get the best of both worlds. First, we concentrate in the text on those examples best suited to help us explore particular themes. We do this to maximize the benefits of our broadly based approach. Second, although some of our information comes from authors who studied only a limited subset of European countries, we do our best in tables summarizing particular themes to include entries for every European country with which we are concerned. We do this to ensure consistency and completeness at least at the level of basic information.

Finally, we have selected a group of seven countries on which we lavish somewhat greater attention. These are France, Germany, Italy, the Netherlands, Spain, Sweden, and the United Kingdom. We have selected these countries because together they provide considerable variation on most of the important dimensions of politics that we wish to consider. They give us a wide geographic spread, from far north to deep south. They include large and small countries; rural and urban countries; Protestant, Catholic, and "mixed-religion" countries; richer and poorer countries; countries with stable and with unstable governments; new and old democracies; the countries with the most and the least proportional electoral systems; and so on. No matter which examples we have used in the main text, we pause in our discussion at key points to present a short box that summarizes key information for each of the seven countries in our core group. In this way we allow interested readers to follow this core group through our entire discussion, reaping many of the benefits of the more restricted country-based approach while paying none of its costs.

MODERN EUROPE

We have had a difficult decision to make about how to incorporate the rapidly unfolding developments in postcommunist Europe. Although politics in the four countries we deal with here—the Czech and Slovak republics, Hungary, and Poland—is becoming increasingly comparable to that in the West, these countries are still undergoing formative processes of democratic development. They obviously lack the long history of postwar democratic experience on which we frequently draw in the Western European examples to emphasize how some features of representative government remain the same and how other features change. For these reasons, we feel that we still cannot integrate them fully in the overall thematic approach. In addition, lack of a detailed body of research accumulated over time means that there is sometimes insufficient information available on the various topics that we discuss in relation to the other European states, while rapid change means that much of the information we might gather might be correct at the time of writing but could quickly go out of date and thereby become misleading. Our solution to this problem has been to prepare a stand-alone chapter on the four postcommunist states we consider. This treats many of the themes covered in the rest of the book while providing some general historical background on their transitions to and consolidation of democracy.

We should also say a word about our coverage of Western Europe's largest state, the Federal Republic of Germany. Before 1990, this state was familiarly referred to as West Germany, but after the absorption of the former communist East German state (the German Democratic Republic) this name ceased to be appropriate. In the following chapters, therefore, we have referred to "Germany" when discussing features of the current German state, but we also occasionally use the term "West Germany" when referring to events or patterns prior to unification.

Another country for which terminology is in some sense ambiguous is the United Kingdom. Formally, the United Kingdom of Great Britain and Northern Ireland includes England, Wales, and Scotland (all three of which make up what is known as Britain or Great Britain), as well as Northern Ireland. In the tables and displays that follow, we always use the term United Kingdom, or UK, for the sake of consistency. In the text, for stylistic reasons, we refer sometimes to Britain and sometimes to the United Kingdom.

PLAN OF CAMPAIGN

In this book we describe representative government in modern Europe in terms of an arena in which the hopes and fears of citizens are transformed by complex political interactions into the public policies that affect their everyday lives. At the end of this chapter we provide some basic information about modern European countries that should help set our subsequent discussions in context. In the remainder of the book, we concentrate on two basic aspects of representative government. The first concerns the institutions and "rules of the game" that create the arena for politics in modern Europe. The second concerns the political behavior that actually takes place in that arena.

Although every European country is obviously unique, the institutions of politics in most modern European states share some fundamental similarities and are collectively quite distinct from those to be found in the United States, for example. This makes politics in Washington a different business from politics in London, say, or in Paris, Brussels, Stockholm, Rome, or Madrid. This is because modern European states are almost all run according to the principles of "parliamentary government," a set of institutions that gives a particularly important role to political parties and parliamentary elections. Constitutionally, these rules have to do with the relationships between legislature, executive, and judiciary—that is, between parliament, government, and the courts—and with the role of the head of state.

In the next five chapters, therefore, we look at five different features of the institutions of representative government in modern Europe. We look in Chapter 2 at the role of constitutions and at that of the courts in interpreting these constitutions. Here we also draw attention to the two quite different legal traditions that can be found in modern Europe, and at the way in which the judiciary can have an important political role, despite popular notions that it is "above" politics. In Chapter 3 we look at the executive, and specifically at the head of state, the prime minister, and the cabinet—in a constitutional setting in which the head of state is typically far less important than in the United States of America. In Chapter 4 we examine the role of the legislature, which is typically responsible not only for legislating but also for generating and maintaining a government. Chapters 5 and 6 present the more general context of national politics in modern Europe. In Chapter 5 we look at supranational politics and in particular at the European Union (EU), now such an important feature of the political landscape of modern Europe and such an integral part of the domestic politics of most member states. In Chapter 6 we consider both the civil service and subnational systems of local and regional administration.

Every one of the institutional features discussed in Chapters 2 through 6 has a fundamental impact on the context of representative government in modern Europe, shaping the political behavior that is the focus of the rest of the book. In Chapters 7 through 14 we move on to trace the behavior that transforms individual interests into public policies through a number of stages. We begin in Chapter 7 by looking at the "party systems" that determine the choices offered to voters at election time. Here we introduce the party systems in the seven countries to which we pay special attention, and we puzzle over whether we can speak of a "typical" Western European party system. In Chapter 8 we present the "families" of parties that make up the cast of characters in most European elections, including communist parties, social democratic parties, liberal parties, Christian democratic parties, conservative parties, ecology parties, and the extreme right. We focus particular attention on the long-term patterns in the aggregate electoral development of these separate families across the past half-century. In Chapter 9, we consider the traditional cleavage structures that underpin party choice, as well as how these patterns might be now be changing, and whether, at the end of a century of mass politics, national electorates and party systems themselves are in a state of flux. In Chapter 10, we step inside parties to examine some of their workings: how they organize, how they choose their leaders and candidates, and how they raise money.

Chapters 7 to 10 thus take into consideration the politics of representation from the bottom up, from the perspective of voters, elections, and parties. Chapters 12 and 13 look at politics from the top down, from the perspective of legislatures and governments. Chapter 11 examines the key institution that links the two levels, the electoral system that turns votes cast by the electorate into seats won by legislators. Many different electoral systems are used throughout Europe, which is the world's premier laboratory for all who are interested in the workings of electoral law. Having examined how European legislatures are produced, we move on in Chapter 12 to look at what they do. The most important thing they do, as we will have seen in Chapters 3 and 4, is to produce and support a government. Because few European parties win a majority of seats in the legislature, forming a government typically involves forming a coalition. In Chapter 13 we explore whether the formation of different governments with different party memberships actually makes a difference in the policies that eventually emerge. If governments do not make a difference, after all, it is difficult to see why we should take an interest in the parties, the elections, the coalition bargaining, and all of the other steps in the political process by which European governments are selected.

In Chapter 14 we acknowledge that the formal institutions of representative government are not the be-all and end-all of politics in modern Europe, and we look at politics outside the party system. Many political decisions—most of those to do with the vital area of economic policy, for example—are taken by governments without recourse to the legislature. These decisions may well be strongly influenced by those who set out to apply pressure to the government, whether as part of the political establishment in an alternative institutional setting or as political outsiders using the tried-and-tested techniques of pressure politics.

Finally, in Chapter 15 we present politics in four former members of the former Eastern bloc: Hungary, Poland, the Czech Republic, and Slovakia. We try as far as possible to touch base for these countries on each of the major themes we have discussed in the earlier chapters, although limitations in the material available to us do not always make this possible. Because these countries are in one important sense also new actors on the stage of modern European politics, we also provide some general historical background, and we conclude by assessing the extent to which they and the long-established democracies in Western Europe may now be converging.

Notwithstanding the trend toward European integration and the role model provided by Western European states for the emerging states of the former Eastern Europe, the cast of characters in modern European politics remains a collection of countries with intriguingly different cultures, traditions, and political styles. There is no such thing as a "typical" European country, which is why it is so important to look at the group of European countries taken as a whole rather than at individual European countries one at a time. When we look at European politics in this way, distinct patterns do emerge. It is the search for such patterns that is the guiding purpose of this book. Before moving on to do this, however, we devote the rest of this chapter to providing some basic information about the group of countries with which we will be dealing.

MODERN EUROPE IN VITAL STATISTICS

Even though the modern Europe that we deal with in this book is divided into more than twenty independent countries, it is still quite small physically when compared with North or South America or with Asia or Africa. However, although the area covered by modern Europe is less than one-half of that covered by, say, the United States, some of the distances involved can still be quite large. A journey from one of the most northerly capitals, Oslo in Norway, to one of the most southerly, Valletta in Malta, would require you to travel some 2,700 kilometers, which is roughly the same as the distance between the northern shore of Lake Superior and Miami in the United States, and almost a third as much again as the distance between Toronto in Canada and San Antonio in Texas (see Figure 1-1). Along the east-west axis, however, the distance between Dublin, one of the most westerly capitals, and Warsaw, one of the most easterly, is just 1,800 kilometers, which is roughly the same as the distance between San Francisco and Kansas City and less than half that between the Canadian cities of Vancouver and Halifax.

Despite this relatively small area, the total population of modern Europe, at about 440 million, is more than half as big again as that of the United States. As Table 1-1 shows, population density, on average about four times greater in the European Union area than in the United States, is highest in Malta and the Netherlands. Indeed, the area around the Netherlands and northern Germany is a very heavily populated region where the concentration of major cities and industrial infrastructure supports a population of more than 350 persons per square kilometer. In the more peripheral areas of modern Europe, by contrast, with the exception of Malta, population density is relatively low; there are only some 20 persons per square kilometer in the vast but unevenly populated country of Sweden and 62 persons per square kilometer in the harsh and inhospitable landscape of Basilicata in southern Italy. In the peripheral Irish

FIGURE 1-1   Modern Europe.

Republic, for example, a land area of some 70,000 square kilometers supports a population of some 3.7 million; the more centrally located Netherlands, on the other hand, has an area of some 41,000 square kilometers, little more than half that of Ireland, but supports a population of more than 15 million, more than four times that of Ireland.

Modern Europe is an immensely diverse area, riven by many cultural, religious, and linguistic boundaries. Despite an overwhelmingly Christian culture, for example, a marked source of diversity is created by the balance between Roman Catholics and the various Protestant denominations. Table 1-1 shows that in some places Roman Catholics are an overwhelming majority—for example, in the southern and western parts of Europe, as well as in Poland. In Greece the vast majority formally adhere to the Greek Orthodox Church, which is quite close to Catholicism. In a second group of countries Roman Catholics tend to be very thin on the ground, particularly in the Scandinavian

TABLE 1-1 GENERAL AND DEMOGRAPHIC DATA ON EUROPEAN DEMOCRACIES (OECD FIGURES)

	Capital	Total area (× 1000 sq. km.)	Population 1997 total (× 1000)	Population 1997 (per sq. km.)	% Catholic, ca. 1995[a]	Gender empowerment index, 1998[b]
Austria	Vienna	84	8,072	96	75	0.686
Belgium	Brussels	31	10,181	334	88	0.600
Czech Republic	Prague	79	10,304	131	39	0.527
Denmark	Copenhagen	43	5,284	123	1	0.739
Finland	Helsinki	338	5,140	15	1	0.725
France	Paris	549	58,608	107	76	0.489
Germany	Berlin	357	82,061	230	34	0.694
Greece	Athens	132	10,498	80	1[d]	0.438
Hungary	Budapest	93	10,155	109	63	0.491
Iceland	Reykjavik	103	272	3	1	0.723
Ireland	Dublin	70	3,661	52	92	0.554
Italy	Rome	301	56,868	189	82	0.521
Luxembourg	Luxembourg	3	424	163	95	0.649
Malta	Valletta	0.3	373	1180	99	–
Netherlands	Amsterdam[c]	41	15,609	383	32	0.689
Norway	Oslo	324	4,393	14	1	0.790
Poland	Warsaw	313	38,650	124	91	0.494
Portugal	Lisbon	92	9,550	108	92	0.547
Slovakia	Bratislava	49	5,343	109	60	0.516
Spain	Madrid	505	39,323	78	67	0.617
Sweden	Stockholm	450	8,848	20	2	0.790
Switzerland	Bern	41	7,087	172	46	0.654
United Kingdom	London	245	59,009	241	10	0.593
United States	Washington D.C.	9,372	266,792	28	21	0.675
EU-15	Brussels	3,240	373,474	115	–	–

[a] Source: Encyclopedia Brittanica
[b] Source: Human Development Report
[c] The seat of government is in The Hague
[d] 95 percent Greek Orthodox

countries—Denmark, Finland, Iceland, Norway, and Sweden—where the overwhelming proportion of the population is at least nominally affiliated to one of a variety of Protestant denominations. Indeed, it is really only in the central spine of Europe—in Germany, the Netherlands, and Switzerland, as well as in the former Czechoslovakia—that we find some sort of even balance between Catholics and Protestants, with Catholics forming a significant minority of the population. Even in these countries, Catholics often tend to cluster in areas where they constitute an overwhelming majority—areas such as Limburg in the south of the Netherlands or Bavaria in southern Germany.

Catholics also constitute a substantial minority in Northern Ireland, which forms part of the United Kingdom, and where a virtual civil war between Catholics and Protestants persisted for more than twenty-five years. Note, however, that the nominal affiliations listed in Table 1-1 exaggerate the numbers of active adherents, with the proportion of nonpracticing Catholics being particularly pronounced in France and southern Europe, for example.

Table 1-1 also includes the index of gender empowerment devised by the *Human Development Report.* This measures the degree of women's representation in key areas of political and economic life, taking account of the number of women in national parliaments (see also Chapter 11), women's share of earned income, and their levels of occupancy in a range of professions. Variation here is also quite marked, ranging from relatively high levels in the various Scandinavian countries to relatively low levels in the new postcommunist democracies and in southern Europe. Two factors seem to be important here, and we come across this patterning throughout our discussion of representative government: on the one hand, there is the evident difference between the newer and the older democracies, with women tending to play a stronger public role in the latter group; on the other hand, there is the difference between Catholic and Protestant Europe, and again it is in the latter group of countries that women have tended to achieve the greater success.

Cultural diversity involves much more than religious or gender differences, of course. Virtually every modern European country has its own language, the only major exceptions being Austria, a German-speaking country; Ireland, an English-speaking country; Belgium, where some 57 percent speak Flemish (or Dutch) and some 42 percent speak French; Luxembourg, where the native language coexists with both French and German; and Switzerland, where some 74 percent use German, some 20 percent use French, and some 5 percent use Italian. In addition, a variety of countries have small linguistic minorities—including the Basque and Catalan minorities in Spain; the German-speaking minority in northeast Italy; the Swedish-speaking minority in Finland; the Hungarian minority in Slovakia; the Welsh in Britain; and a small number of Gaeli speakers in both Ireland and Scotland. Across modern Europe as a whole, German is the most widely used native language, being used as a mother tongue by roughly 95 million people, followed by French (64 million) and English (63 million), and then by Italian (57 million) and Polish and Spanish (both just less than 40 million). There is then a large drop to Dutch (just over 20 million).

Germany also enjoys the strongest economy in modern Europe. Even before unification in 1990, West Germany's gross domestic product (GDP) was more than one-quarter again as big as that of France, the next biggest; now it exceeds that of France by half (see Table 1-2). In general, however, the individual European economies are dwarfed by that of the United States. The combined GDP of the four largest economies—Germany, France, Italy, and the United Kingdom—actually totals to only about 75 percent of that of the United States.

The highest levels for GDP per head of population can be found in Denmark, Luxembourg, Norway, and Switzerland, at levels exceeding the equivalent figure for the United States. Before these figures can be used to compare real standards of living, however, they must be adjusted to take account of the relative cost of living in each country. Thus, Table 1-2 also lists GDP per capita for European countries at purchas-

TABLE 1-2 GROSS DOMESTIC PRODUCT IN EUROPEAN DEMOCRACIES (OECD FIGURES)

	Total 1998, $ billion (current exchange rates)	$ Per Capita (current exchange rates)	$ Per Capita (purchasing power parities)*	Per Capita OECD = 100 purchasing power parities)*
Austria	211.9	26,210	23,985	114
Belgium	249.3	24,432	24,097	115
Czech Republic	55.3	5,371	13,137	62
Denmark	174.8	32,934	26,280	125
Finland	126.2	24,484	21,659	103
France	1,435.5	24,398	22,091	105
Germany	2,142.1	26,056	22,835	109
Greece	119.3	11,366	14,463	69
Hungary	47.5	4,693	10,524	50
Iceland	8.1	29,820	26,296	125
Ireland	82.3	22,287	22,509	107
Italy	1,171.8	20,323	21,739	103
Luxembourg	16.5	38,616	34,536	164
Malta	3.6	9,636	–	–
Netherlands	378.3	24,107	23,082	110
Norway	145.5	32,853	27,497	131
Poland	150.6	3,894	7,986	38
Portugal	105.4	10,574	15,266	73
Slovakia	18.2	3,410	–	–
Spain	556.3	14,129	16,740	80
Sweden	228.8	25,852	21,213	101
Switzerland	262.4	36,869	26,576	126
United Kingdom	1,362.3	23,006	21,170	101
United States	8,178.8	30,514	30,514	145
EU-15	8,360.9	22,285	21,286	101

* Purchasing power parities refer to the rate of currency conversion that aims at eliminating the differences in price levels between countries, so that a given sum of money when converted into different currencies at these rates will buy the same basket of goods and services. This gives a much more realistic picture of the different levels of GDP per capita.

ing power parities (PPP), that is, adjusted so that a fixed sum buys the same bundle of goods and services in every country. Table 1-2 shows that when purchasing power is taken into account, the GDP per capita in the United States is higher than every European country with the exception of Luxembourg.

Differences within Europe, however, are even more marked. In 1998, levels of GDP per capita, taking purchasing power into account, ranged from highs of $34,536 in Luxembourg and $27,497 in Norway to west European lows of just $14,463 in

Greece, $15,266 in Portugal, and $16,740 in Spain. Falling behind these again are the three former communist countries for which comparable data are available: $13,137 in the Czech Republic, $10,524 in Hungary, and just $7,986 in Poland.

Here again, the imbalance is clearly related to different levels of economic modernization (within Western Europe) and to the communist legacy (in Eastern Europe). With some exceptions, it is an imbalance that also tends to be organized in terms of geographic division between richer countries in northern and central Western Europe and poorer countries in the Mediterranean south, and, of course, in the east. Indeed, this difference is strikingly evident in terms of regional disparities within the boundaries of a single country, Italy. The very prosperous northern part of the country enjoys one of the highest standards of living in modern Europe, contrasting sharply with the southern part of Italy, one of Western Europe's poorest regions. This social and economic tension is now also being exacerbated by a regional political divide, with the increasingly popular Northern League mobilizing in favor of greater political autonomy for northern Italy. Lower levels of prosperity also tend to be quite strongly associated with a continuing reliance on agriculture as a major source of employment, as well as with poorly developed industrial and service sectors.

Differences in sectoral development across modern Europe are less marked than was once the case. For example, as Table 1-3 shows, Greece, Iceland and Ireland were the only countries in Western Europe in 1997 where the contribution of agriculture (including fishing) to GDP exceeded 5 percent. Indeed, Ireland is now just on the edge of this category, whereas in Iceland and Greece, agriculture remains quite prominent. The agricultural sector is also important in postcommunist Europe, although precisely comparable figures are not available for 1997. In all Western European countries, without exception, the service sector now contributes most to GDP, accounting for an average which now runs close to the balance in the United States. In no single Western European country does this sector now fall below 55 percent, the Irish figure. Perhaps surprisingly, in view of its traditional image as one of the most agricultural of the Western European economies, Ireland in these figures emerges as having the single biggest industrial sector. This is largely due to the enormous economic growth Ireland has enjoyed in recent years, with the so-called "Celtic Tiger" phenomenon pushing Irish per capita GDP (measured in purchasing power) from 51 percent of that in the United Kingdom in 1960, to 62 percent in 1980, and now to 106 percent in these most recent figures.

In line with the generally increasing prosperity which modern Europe has enjoyed since the mid-1990s, unemployment levels have begun to fall. Despite this, however, levels remain substantially above those in the United States (Table 1-3), being particularly high in Spain, Finland, France, Belgium, and Italy. Across the European Union as a whole in 1997, unemployment was more than double that in the United States. Perhaps surprisingly, unemployment levels in the Czech Republic and also Hungary in 1997 were substantially less than those in many of the more advanced Western European economies, although levels in Poland were above those in the EU as a whole. In those countries with lower levels of unemployment and with larger service sectors, there are also higher levels of female participation in the labor force,

TABLE 1–3   SECTORAL, LABOR FORCE, AND PUBLIC SECTOR DATA ON MODERN EUROPEAN
DEMOCRACIES (OECD FIGURES)

	Sectoral contribution to GDP, 1997 (%)			Current government expenditure, 1996 (% GDP)	Government employment, 1996 (% total employment	Unemployment, 1997 (% total labor force)
	Agriculture	Industry	Services			
Austria	1.4	30.4	68.2	47.2	22.8	4.2
Belgium	1.1	27.6	71.3	49.9	18.7	12.7
Czech Republic	4.1	37.5	58.4	40.3	–	4.6
Denmark	3.6	24.3	72.1	59.6	30.5	6.1
Finland	3.5	30.2	66.3	56.2	25.1	14.3
France	2.3	26.2	71.5	51.6	25.1	12.4
Germany	1.1	29.1	69.9	45.8	15.3	9.8
Greece	12.0	20.0	67.9	52.1	–	10.3
Hungary	–	–	–	–	–	8.7
Iceland	9.4	21.6	69.0	34.0	19.8	4.1
Ireland	5.1	39.3	55.6	36.3	12.6	10.3
Italy	2.6	30.5	66.9	49.4	15.8	12.2
Luxembourg	1.0	24.0	75.0	45.0	11.3	2.7
Malta	–	–	–	–	–	–
Netherlands	3.1	27.1	69.8	49.9	13.5	5.5
Norway	2.0	32.1	65.9	42.4	30.6	4.1
Poland	–	–	–	–	–	11.1
Portugal	3.9	35.2	60.9	41.1	16.7	6.7
Slovakia	–	–	–	–	–	–
Spain	3.5	25.6	70.9	41.1	15.3	20.6
Sweden	2.0	27.5	70.5	62.9	30.7	8.0
Switzerland	3.0	33.5	63.5	33.9	14.0	4.2
United Kingdom	1.7	27.5	70.8	41.4	14.1	7.1
United States	1.8	26.8	71.4	33.7	13.2	4.9
EU-15	–	–	–	–	–	10.6

suggesting that women find it easier to become economically active when there is a more restricted pool of labor that is at the same time more flexibly organized.

Table 1-3 also highlights the different levels of government expenditure relative to GDP in the different Western European countries, as well as the levels of public employment. These figures relate to spending and employment on public welfare programs such as health, education, employment, and housing as well as the defense forces, police, administration, and publicly owned companies. The figures are not always easily comparable, however, since different state traditions use different definitions and categorizations for what are functionally equivalent activities. According to these figures, which apply to 1996, governments in Denmark, Finland, France, Greece, and—most notably—Sweden spend more than 50 percent of GDP, with Belgium falling marginally below this level. The lowest levels of spending are reported by Iceland, Ireland, and Switzerland, each of which borders close on the more limited American figure. Levels of public employment also vary significantly, exceeding 30 percent of the total employment in the three Scandinavian countries—Denmark, Norway, and Sweden—and falling below 15 percent in Ireland, Luxembourg, the Netherlands, Switzerland, and the United Kingdom.

It is evident that when we take all of these factors into account, we cannot talk about modern Europe as though it were constituted by a homogeneous group of countries. We are talking about a collection of places with quite distinctive social and economic profiles. Whether these differences are large or small depends on your point of view. As we have suggested, to travel within Italy from prosperous north to poor south is to see quite a striking social contrast. Even to cross the border from the now independent and relatively successful Czech Republic to the now independent and economically troubled Slovakia is to see a strong social contrast. Yet, even the poor southern part of Italy or the more impoverished parts of Slovakia are in no sense whatsoever among the world's poor regions; their levels of prosperity are far above that of virtually every Third World state, whether we measure this in terms of money, life expectancy, literacy, or indeed any other aspect of the quality of life.

For all their diversity, therefore, the countries of Western Europe constitute the world's largest collection of successful capitalist democracies, and a number of the countries of postcommunist Europe are trying to join this club as quickly as possible. Many of the Western European countries are tied together in an ever more powerful political union, the European Union, which we discuss in detail in Chapter 5, and most of those that are not already members of this union are now busily preparing their applications for entry, including the four postcommunist countries that we look at in Chapter 15. But the differences that we have highlighted must be kept in mind in the comparative discussions that follow; we are, after all, talking about a collection of different countries, and that is one of the things that makes the study of modern European politics so interesting. Nevertheless, these differences must not be exaggerated. This is why it makes sense to analyze politics in the collection of European countries in terms of their underlying similarities as well as their distinctive features. This is the main purpose of the chapters that follow.

2

CONSTITUTIONS, JUDGES, AND POLITICS

Books on United States government and politics invariably stress the important role of the courts and the constitution. Books on European government and politics, in contrast, often say nothing about either, something that might give students of the subject the impression that courts and constitutions make little impact on the political process in Europe. Such an impression would be quite wrong. The "rules of the game" play a large part in determining a country's government and politics, and these are generally set down in a country's constitution and laws. These rules may impose significant constraints on actors such as political parties, parliaments and governments. Although some of the rules may sometimes be inconvenient to politicians and political parties, and some of them may be sufficiently vague to allow politicians some leeway, in the last resort they are there to determine how things are done. These rules ensure that, in western Europe, government is limited government, with, for example, a "private" sphere into which not even a democratically elected government can intrude. European constitutions contain a number of common features but also exhibit some significant variation. In later chapters we look in detail at the contents of constitutions regarding such important matters as the powers of governments, presidents, and parliaments, as well as electoral law and the decentralization of power, but in this chapter we concentrate on constitutions per se, along with the authorities who interpret and apply constitutions.

If there is some doubt or dispute as to exactly what course of action the laws or constitution spell out (or rule out) in some specific situation, there is a need for someone to act as a referee or umpire. This is where the courts come in. Although the judicial system is sometimes seen as quite separate from the political system, and many Europeans still see it as "above politics," such a view does not reflect the reality of Europe today. In recent years, there has been a clear trend toward the "judicialization" of politics and the "politicization" of the judicial system, with what has been termed "the global expansion of judicial power" (Tate and Vallinder). In this chapter, therefore, we examine European constitutions, looking at their origins and contents and discussing some European constitutional traditions.

We consider the way in which judicial review—the process by which either the regular courts or a special constitutional court can constrain political actors, for example by striking down legislation that is not compatible with the constitution—has become a central fact of political life in several European countries. Once again, there is significant variation across the continent. We then look at the interaction between the judiciary and politics, examining both the politicized manner in which judges are appointed and the opportunity that judges in some countries have to *make* law as opposed to merely *applying* laws.

EUROPEAN CONSTITUTIONS

The Origins of Constitutions

The political turbulence in much of Europe in the nineteenth century and in the first half of the last century means that most European countries have adopted more than one constitution during the past two hundred years (Bogdanor; Johnson, 1993). There have been various "waves" of constitution making. One occurred in those countries regaining independence at the end of the Napoleonic wars, and there was a second following the 1848 revolutions. After the First World War, a number of countries, especially the successor states to the Austro-Hungarian empire, drew up new constitutions. Most of the constitutions drawn up in these first three waves have failed to survive. A more durable set of constitutions was promulgated in the aftermath of the Second World War, when those countries emerging from occupation adopted new constitutions, which in some cases were modified versions of their pre-war constitutions. More recently, new constitutions were adopted by countries moving from autocratic to democratic forms of government: Greece, Portugal, and Spain in the 1970s, and the postcommunist regimes of central and eastern Europe in the late 1980s and early 1990s.

Constitutions, then, are often adopted as part of a "fresh start"—either a change of political regime or the achievement of national independence. Just as the United States drew up a new constitution in 1787, so Finland in 1919 and Ireland in 1922 had to devise constitutions when they embarked upon independent statehood. Dramatic changes of regime led to new constitutions in Italy in 1948, Germany in 1949, Portugal in 1976, and Spain in 1978. On other occasions, new constitutions may be adopted in order to reform existing liberal democratic systems: examples here are France in 1958, Denmark in 1973, Sweden in 1974, and Belgium in 1989. There has been widespread agreement in Italy that fundamental constitutional amendment is needed to recast the country's political system in the wake of the upheavals of the 1990s, though, as yet, no agreement has been reached on precisely what changes should be made (Fusaro). Sometimes, however, major political changes do not lead to a new constitution. The German constitution (known as the "Basic Law") of 1949, which originally applied only to West Germany, envisages its own demise when the reunited German people choose a new constitution; Article 146 states, "This Basic Law … shall cease to be in force on the day in which a constitution adopted by a free decision of the German people comes into force." In the event, the reunification of Germany in 1990 took place under the terms of Article 23 of the Basic Law, which allows new units to join the Federal Republic. The Basic Law, though originally seen as only an interim document pending reunification, is thus still in operation with no great popular demand that it be replaced. The changes made to the Basic Law following reunification proved to be minor indeed (Benz).

If nothing dramatic happens in a country's history, there may seem to be no need for a new constitution. This is part of the reason for the absence in Britain of any document called "The Constitution." Britain has not been invaded for several centuries, and has not experienced a regime change since 1688; the emphasis since then has been on continuity and evolution, with no "clean break" with the past. This is not to say that no changes have taken place. On the contrary, major changes can be made under the general impression of continuity—for example, the establishment of a Scottish parliament and a Welsh assembly in 1999—without this explicitly requiring the adoption of a new constitution.

Britain is, in fact, unique among European democracies in having no formal codified constitution. In consequence, it is hard to be certain about what exactly makes up the British constitution, which has been seen as deriving from four sources (Norton, pp. 5–9). The first is statute law: some very fundamental pieces of legislation, such as the 1707 Act of Union that brought Scotland into the United Kingdom while preserving a separate Scottish church and legal system, are part of the British constitution. These pieces of legislation could, at least in theory, be amended or repealed by parliament in just the same way as any other law, although the political fallout would be immense if any attempt were made to do this in the absence of widespread consent. The fact that statute law is part of the British constitution shows that the common view that Britain has an "unwritten constitution" is not entirely true; the constitution is at least partly written. Sartori (p. 862) comments that the British constitution is not "unwritten" but "written differently." The second source of the constitution is common law, including some customs such as the supremacy of parliament and major judicial decisions. The third source is convention, which dictates that certain things—such as the appointment of a prime minister who does not hold a seat in the House of Commons, or any refusal on the part of the monarch to consent to a measure passed by parliament—cannot now be done simply because it is generally accepted by the political elite that they cannot be done. Finally, "works of authority" written by scholars of the constitution also affect perceptions of what exactly the constitution consists of.

Despite the stress usually laid by constitutions on popular sovereignty, most new constitutions are brought into being by representative organs, following the American precedent. Only in a few cases have the people of a country been given the opportunity to vote in a referendum on whether they wish to adopt a document as their country's constitution. In France, when the wartime leader of the Free French, Charles de Gaulle, was invited in 1958 to return to power, he had a constitution hastily drawn up, and this was put to and passed by the people in a referendum, thereby bringing into existence the Fifth Republic. Other examples of a constitution being adopted by referendum are Switzerland in 1874, Ireland in 1937, Denmark in 1953, and Spain in 1978; in the first three of these cases, the element of popular sovereignty is strengthened by the requirement that any subsequent change to the constitution requires the consent of the people at a referendum.

Constitutions, of course, vary from country to country, but there are certain near-universal features (Finer et al; Murphy). Constitutions regulate the organization of the government, stipulating, for example, whether government is parliamentary or presidential, what power the legislature has to constrain the executive, the role of the judiciary, and how power is divided between national organs of government and state or provincial bodies. In addition, they usually declare a number of rights, though sometimes what they say is primarily aspirational (as, for example, when a constitution speaks of citizens' "right to work").

Constitutional Traditions

The fact that both the United States and most European countries possess a document called "The Constitution" should not mislead us into assuming that all constitutions enjoy the same status in the eyes of the people who live under them. Ulrich Preuss contrasts the American pattern of constitutional authority with that in France. In the United States, he suggests, the constitution has priority not only over the government but also over the will of the people themselves. The constitution has a crucial place in history, in creating the United States of America: "It is the sanctity of the founding act by which the polity has been created which imputes to the constitution the authority of the supreme law. The supremacy of its authority over all other laws flows from the inherent significance and uniqueness of the act of nation building" (Preuss, pp. 20–22). Interpretation of the constitution is thus very important, leading to "the almost obsessive passion" of Americans with questions of constitutional interpretation. Regarding rights, the constitution gives the impression that government and parliament are more likely to be a source of endangerment than a defender of these, with its repeated prescription: "Congress shall make no law. . . ."

In France, in contrast, the genuine spirit of constitutionalism is encapsulated not in the constitution but in the constituent power of the nation; this constituent power cannot be bound by any constitution (Preuss, pp. 22–24). The creation of the constitution was not the founding act for the French nation; the French nation is seen as having existed long before the first French constitution, let alone the current one. The constitution is one of the emanations of the nation, which is prior to every institution. The nation has power to "constitute and reconstitute its sovereign power and give it its appropriate institutional shape at will." This helps to account for the relatively large number of constitutions in France over the past two hundred years, and the lack of veneration for any one that is comparable to the veneration accorded to its American counterpart. Political actors are seen as more important than the constitution and as the appropriate actors to rectify wrongs.

Most European countries might fall somewhere on the spectrum between France and the United States, while being much closer to the French position than to the American one. It would be fair to say that no European constitution inspires the kind of reverence that many Americans feel for their own constitution. Many Europeans have never seen a copy of their country's constitution, and have only the most general notion of what it contains. Europeans tend to evaluate their constitutions in pragmatic and instrumental terms, with no compunction about amending or replacing an existing constitution if it prevents a favored course of action from being followed. Partly for this reason, the relationship between constitutionalism and democracy, which has been so extensively explored in the American context, has generated far less agonizing in Europe (Bellamy; Holmes; Kommers, 1994, p. 488).

Amending a Constitution

The extent to which a constitution, promulgated by people or parliament at one point in time, binds successive generations in a manner that can be seen as "rule by the dead" depends partly upon how easy it is to change it. A constitution that is very difficult to amend or replace clearly constrains a nation in a way that a less rigid document does not. Certain constitutions can be changed only by referendum; as we have already pointed out, the constitutions to which this applies—those of Denmark, Ireland, and Switzerland—were brought in by referendum in the first place. In some other countries, such as Austria, Iceland, Malta, and Spain, minor changes can be made by parliament, but major changes require the consent of the people in a referendum. In Germany proposals for change must be passed by votes of two-thirds in both the directly elected Bundestag and the Bundesrat, which represents state (Land) governments. Thus any change needs agreement between the government and the opposition in the national parliament, as well as the consent of most of the Land governments. Moreover, certain provisions are declared unamendable, such as the federal and democratic nature of the state.

The French constitution can be amended in one of two ways (Carcassonne; Morel). Article 89 outlines a procedure under which the agreement of both houses of parliament is needed for any proposed change. Unless a joint meeting of both houses then approves the proposal by a 60 percent vote, it goes to a referendum. The French Senate is dominated by conservative rural members, which means that changes proposed by the left face an uphill struggle if they are to be passed by the parliamentarians, though several proposed by the right have been passed this way without the need for a referendum. However, constitutional change in France has often followed a different route: use of Article 11, under which the government may propose a change and the president can then refer it direct to the people in a referendum. (In practice, the president usually tells the government what to propose to him; de Gaulle sometimes announced the referendum before he had formally received the government's proposal.) This is not really the way the constitution seems to envisage amendment taking place, but it has become accepted that this is a valid method. The French public has shown little sign of objection, evidently feeling that it does have the right to change the constitution in this way, in line with the general attitude to the constitution identified by Preuss.

When it comes to amending the British constitution, there are no firm rules, as we would expect. There is nothing that says that those pieces of statute that are regarded

BOX 2–1

CONSTITUTIONS

France

France has had a number of constitutions over the course of the last two hundred years. The current constitution, the Constitution of the Fifth Republic, dates from 1958, when it was approved by the people in a referendum. Some subsequent changes have been made by parliament, but others have been made by referendum, including the most important, the 1962 amendment that introduced the direct election of the president. It has been argued that French political culture values the constituent power of the nation far more highly than it values any specific constitution.

Germany

The German constitution, known as the Basic Law, dates from 1949. The constitution cannot be amended without the consent of two-thirds majorities in both houses of parliament, so in practice any change requires the consent of both the national opposition and most of the state governments. Although in 1949 it was assumed that the Basic Law would be replaced by a new constitution when German unity was achieved, in the event unification took place within the framework of the Basic Law. The Basic Law stands high in the esteem of Germans, especially those living in the former West Germany.

Italy

The Italian constitution was promulgated in 1948 and, in reaction to the dictatorship of Mussolini, it provided for checks and balances to a degree that critics say has hampered the achievement of effective government in postwar Italy. The political upheavals of the 1990s led to calls for a new constitution, or at least a fundamental revision of the existing one, but the political elite was unable to reach a consensus on the amendments that should be made, so not very much has been changed.

Netherlands

The Dutch constitution dates from 1814, though it has been subjected to a number of major overhauls, most notably in 1848 and most recently in 1983. In most countries the constitution can be seen as a "basic law," with a status superior to that of any ordinary law, but in the Netherlands the constitution scarcely has this position. It states explicitly that the courts cannot review the constitutionality of acts of parliament and, unlike most constitutions, does not provide any real constraint on the behaviour of parliament.

Spain

After the long Franco dictatorship, a new constitution was drawn up and was approved by the people, with a 92 percent vote in favor, in a referendum in 1978. It provides for a constitutional monarchy and recognizes the multinational nature of Spain, while simultaneously asserting the indivisibility of the country. Although it has been criticized for vagueness or ambiguity in this and other areas, it has provided the framework for a successful transition to democracy.

Sweden

The current Swedish constitution was adopted in 1974 and asserts that the country is a democracy in which all public power "emanates from the people," in contrast to previous constitutions, which had stressed the importance of the monarch. The constitution can be amended by simple majority vote of parliament; though there must be two such votes to make any specific amendment, one before and one after a general election.

United Kingdom

Unlike every other country in Europe, the United Kingdom does not have a document called "The Constitution." It is not the case, though, that its constitution is therefore unwritten; some central elements of it are contained in Acts of Parliament, some of them several centuries old. The principle of parliamentary sovereignty is strong, and although in recent years there have been calls for the adoption of a formal constitution setting out the limits on the powers of government and parliament, such attempts at reform have made little headway.

as constitutional in nature cannot be changed just like any other statute. After all, these statutes came into being in the first place simply by being passed by parliament. Yet there are powerful political cultural constraints in existence; for example, it is generally felt that the House of Commons could not simply repeal, against the wishes of the

Scots, the laws that preserve Scotland's separate judicial system, something guaranteed under the 1707 Act of Union. Other major aspects, though, certainly can be changed by Parliament; examples are reductions in the powers of the House of Lords, which occurred twice in the twentieth century.

Constitutions regulate the power of political actors, in relation both to each other and to civil society. The referee or umpire whose role it is to decide whether the rules have been broken is usually the judiciary, and the power of a court to declare a law or regulation to be in conflict with the constitution of a country and hence to be invalid is one aspect of judicial review. Judicial review can also entail "the power of a court to declare a statute, an act of the executive, an administrative regulation, or another court's decision legally null and void because it conflicts with a statute or other law" (Shapiro and Stone, p. 401). The importance of judicial review varies across Europe, according to the stipulations of different countries' constitutions and to legal traditions, and it is this variation that we now explore.

JUDICIAL REVIEW

Judicial review may take one or both of two forms. *Concrete* judicial review refers to a challenge to a law arising out of some specific case before a court, and *abstract* judicial review involves the consideration of a law without reference to any specific case. Whereas concrete judicial review can be initiated by any defendant in a court case who feels that the law under which he or she is being prosecuted is unconstitutional or is otherwise null and void, abstract review can usually be initiated only by a designated set of political authorities (such as the head of state, the prime minister, or a fixed percentage of members of parliament). Abstract review itself can take two forms: in some countries it can be initiated only for a short period (typically up to three months) after a law has been passed (this is known as *a posteriori* abstract review); in Portugal, it can also be initiated *before* a bill has become law; in France and Ireland, abstract review can be initiated *only* before a bill becomes law (this is known as *a priori* abstract review).

In some European countries judicial review simply does not exist, and in countries where it does exist, it may be wielded either by the regular court system or by a special constitutional court (or by both, as in Portugal). We need also to remember that for the fifteen countries of the European Union (EU), the Court of Justice of the European Communities, which is based in Luxembourg, can exercise the power of judicial review, because it can declare any law of a member state to be invalid if it conflicts either with the constitution of the EU or with an EU law (for a fuller discussion, see Chapter 5).

Strong Judicial Review

First, we shall look at countries where there is express provision for a judicial body to strike down legislation as unconstitutional; Markku Suksi (p. 135) finds that 75 of 160 constitutions around the world contain such provision. There are two models here. One employs a dedicated constitutional court, separate from the regular court system, a model that was designed by the Austrian jurist Hans Kelsen. Such constitutional courts exist in Austria, Germany, Italy, Malta, Portugal, and Spain; a similar body, the Constitutional Council, fulfils this function in France. The second model is to allow the ordinary court system to exercise this power; this is the approach in Ireland (and also in the United States). When the "new democracies" of Central and Eastern Europe drew up constitutions in the wake of the collapse of communism in the late 1980s and early 1990s, many of them (including all the countries that we discuss in Chapter 15, along with Bulgaria, Croatia, Estonia, Lithuania, Romania, and Slovenia) established constitutional courts (Suksi, p. 118). When we examine the record of specific countries, we shall see how significant the role of the courts can be in a country's politics.

Of the main constitutional review bodies, the French Constitutional Council is the most likely to find its decisions interpreted in partisan political terms. It was established by the 1958 constitution, but made little public impact until the early 1980s. In 1974, the right to refer bills to the Council, hitherto reserved for a few figures who were likely to be government supporters and thus unlikely to want to test the constitutionality of legislation, was extended: any group of sixty deputies (or sixty senators) was given the power to refer a bill to the Council. After 1981, when the Socialist Party entered government for the first time, it became routine for the parliamentary opposition to refer every budget, and nearly every major piece of legislation, to the Council (Stone, 1996, pp. 64–65). The government drew up wide-ranging plans for the nationalization of a number of private companies, which the right-wing opposition parties referred to the Council. To the government's dismay, the Council ruled that the compensation arrangements provided for were in conflict with the constitution, and it in effect elaborated a new compensation formula, which would raise the cost of the nationalization program by about 25 percent. The government duly drew up a new law incorporating this formula, and the Council pronounced this bill constitutional (Stone, 1992, pp. 140–72). The Socialist government's plans fell foul of the Council on other occasions, too, as the opposition parties, having been outvoted in parliament, achieved total or partial victories in the Constitutional Council.

After 1986, when the right won power, the roles were reversed. Now the Socialists began to refer many bills to the Council, and the right-wing parties complained about the power of the Council in terms even more bitter than those used by the Socialists between 1981 and 1986. One ruling was described by leading right-wing politicians as "a veritable attack on national sovereignty" and an "amputation of the power of parliamentarians" (Stone, 1992, p. 3). Relations between the Council and politicians were relatively quiet during the next spell of Socialist government (1988–93), as from 1989 onward, a majority of Council members were Socialist nominees. But when the right returned to power after the 1993 elections, conflicts began again. In August 1993 the Council struck down some of the new government's anti-immigration legislation, and in January 1994 it declared unconstitutional the central aspects of a bill that would have led to a great increase in the amount of public money being spent on private, church-run schools.

Given the important role played by the Constitutional Council, it might come as a surprise to learn that judicial review as such is explicitly prohibited in France. This has been the case since the French Revolution and owes partly to the feeling that any check on parliament would be a check on the "general will" of the people. The idea that the United States has "government by judges" and that this is highly undesirable is part of political discourse in France (Provine, p. 185). The Constitutional Council is not a truly judicial body at all, being detached from the court system, so the power that it exercises is not, strictly speaking, that of judicial review, although it clearly has very much the same effect. The prohibition on judicial review means that the Council's power is confined to legislation in abstract form; once a bill has become law, its constitutionality cannot be challenged. Although in principle the role of the Council is "to impose stable and fundamental values" rather than to be swayed by short-term political factors (Bell, p. 40), its decisions are often interpreted in political rather than purely constitutional terms. One reason for this is that bills go to the Council immediately after their passage through parliament; this means that the Council is invariably judging bills that have very recently been the subject of partisan political battles on the floor of the National Assembly, and so it is sometimes seen as being akin to a decisive third chamber of parliament (Shapiro and Stone, pp. 403–8).

By contrast with the French Constitutional Council, other European constitutional courts are generally seen as "above politics," even though they often have to give decisions with political consequences. The most significant constitutional court is the Federal Constitutional Court (FCC) of Germany, which has been described as "an institution of major policy-making importance" (Kommers, 1997, p. 1). The FCC can exercise both abstract review (bills can be referred to it by a third of the members of the Bundestag or by a Land government) and concrete review (a law can be referred to it for a definitive verdict on its constitutionality by an ordinary court during the course of a case, and citizens themselves can write directly to the FCC complaining that their constitutional rights have been violated). Ordinary courts cannot judge the constitutionality of laws; if a question of constitutionality arises, it must be referred to the FCC. The great majority of the cases reaching the FCC are "constitutional complaints" from individual citizens (although 99 percent of these complaints are not substantial enough to warrant the Court's examining them in any detail), with about 2.9 percent consisting of cases of concrete review and 0.1 percent consisting of these involving abstract review (Kommers, 1997, pp. 11, 15).

From 1951 to 1990 the FCC declared 198 out of the 4,298 bills passed by the Bundestag to be invalid (Landfried, p. 113). Some of its decisions have had major political overtones. In the 1950s it banned a communist and a neo-Nazi party, and in September 1990 it complicated the process of German reunification by declaring unconstitutional the electoral system originally proposed for the first all-German elections in December of that year. In 1993 it heard a challenge to Germany's acceptance of the Maastricht Treaty, a major step of European integration that we discuss more fully in Chapter 5. The FCC rejected the challenge, in effect because it held that the Maastricht Treaty did not extend the powers of the European Union so far that the German people's right to self-government was undermined. However, in its judgment it affirmed that it would treat as invalid any EU action that went beyond the EU's authority, and for good measure declared that Germany had the right to withdraw from the EU at any time (Currie, pp. 99–100). This claim that it was a domestic court rather than the EU's own supreme court, the European Court of Justice, that had the ultimate authority to decide whether the EU was acting beyond its powers caused some disquiet across the EU. In 1995 it made a controversial decision in a case concerning church and state: when the parents of a child in Bavaria objected to the presence of a crucifix in the classroom, the FCC ruled that the crucifix should be removed because its presence violated freedom of religion. This prompted widespread protests, especially in Bavaria, a strongly Catholic region of Germany (Kommers, 1997, pp. 472–84).

Perhaps most controversial of all have been the decisions that the FCC has made on the subject of abortion. In 1975 it struck down legislation passed by the center left majority in parliament that had made abortion legal within the first three months of pregnancy. The FCC decided that this proposed law would not give adequate protection to life, and so it gave the Bundestag instead a fairly detailed (and much more restrictive) prescription as to how abortion legislation should be framed, which the Bundestag duly incorporated in revised legislation. In the early 1990s, it declared unconstitutional some key aspects of a new abortion law that parliament had passed to bridge the gap between the fairly restrictive West German law of 1976 and the relatively liberal East German law of the same year. The FCC rejected the new law, requested the Bundestag to enact a fresh one, and presented an interim regulation that would be valid until such a fresh law was passed (Kommers, 1997, pp. 335–56; Johnson, 1995, pp. 138–40). In addition, the FCC arbitrates in disputes over the jurisdiction of various organs of government, sometimes giving judgments that protect the rights of the Land governments and parliaments against threatened encroachment by their central (federal) counterparts, and on other occasions giving decisions that favour the federal government.

Generally speaking, Germans have a high regard for the FCC. Polls have found it to enjoy substantially more public trust than any other major institution, including parliament, the churches, the trade unions, and universities (Kommers, 1997, p. 56–57). With a mixture of pride and sarcasm, newspapers refer to the judges on the FCC as "kings" and to their pronouncements as "divine ordinances" (Kommers, 1994, p. 486). The general esteem in which the court is held arises partly because of individuals' right to send "constitutional complaints" directly to it, which makes it seem accessible and approachable, and partly because it is seen as "above politics" (Kommers, 1994, p. 489). Although, as we shall see, the main political parties control nomination to the court, commentators do not feel that the party affiliations of individual court members have much bearing on their judgments. The FCC has sometimes been criticized by the left, however, with the argument that it serves as a brake on social change, and Kommers agrees that "the court has often used its power . . . to invalidate reforms regarded as progressive and liberalizing by large segments of German society" (Kommers, 1997, p. 56).

The court's ultimate legitimacy in the German system "rests on its moral authority and the willingness of the political arms of government to follow its mandates" (Kommers, 1997, pp. 54–55), and the FCC has developed its own techniques to preserve this moral authority. Sometimes, when faced with a politically sensitive issue, it delays making a decision until the controversy has died down or the matter is settled by political means. It also has the power to distinguish between laws that are null and void as a result of being in conflict with the constitution and laws that, although unconstitutional, are not actually void. In the latter case, parliament is allowed a period of grace to put matters right, and during this period the law remains in operation. Although this has been described as a "rather dubious practice" (Holland, 1988, p. 99), the reason for its existence is that it enables the court to avoid "a possible vacuum in the legal order" that would result if the law were nullified with immediate effect (Brewer-Carías, p. 214). For the same reason, the court may uphold a statute while warning that it could soon become unconstitutional (Currie, p. 29).

Overall, the FCC occupies a very powerful position in the German legislative process. Just as U.S. Chief Justice Charles Evans Hughes declared that "the Constitution is what the judges say it is," so a German law professor was able to say, "The Basic Law is now virtually identical with its interpretation by the Federal Constitutional Court" (Abraham, p. 356; Kommers, 1997, p. 55). The fact that it has struck down only about 5 percent of laws passed by the Bundestag does not give an accurate reflection of its impact. For one thing, a number of laws have received conditional approval by the court; using the approach of "interpretation in conformity with the constitution," the court can declare that a law is constitutional provided that it means what the court interprets it to mean. This interpretation may not always coincide with the original intentions of parliament and, indeed, such a declaration by the court may be merely a less hurtful way of striking down the statute (Currie, pp. 28–29). For another, parliament, when drafting legislation, goes to great lengths to try to ensure that laws will not be found to be unconstitutional, including seeking the advice of legal experts (whose role has sometimes been compared with that of astrologers or soothsayers) as to how the FCC will react to specific laws. The Bundestag has been seen as legislating "in the shadow" of the court and as being excessively cautious for fear of displeasing it (Landfried, pp. 116–19; Kommers, 1997, p. 56).

The Constitutional Court of Italy is also fairly highly regarded by that country's citizens—no mean feat, given the general disdain with which many Italians regard their political institutions. In its early years in the 1950s, the court struck down legislation dating from the fascist era despite the claim of the government that it had no power to do this. These were difficult years for the court because the government did not always obey its rulings, while the ordinary courts, still in many cases staffed by judges appointed during the fascist regime of Mussolini, were hostile to it and refused to refer cases up to it. In the 1970s the court showed itself willing to stand up to the power of the Catholic Church at a time when most of the political parties were not doing so. In 1971 it invalidated fascist-era laws prohibiting contraception; between 1970 and 1974 it gave six decisions affirming the constitutionality of laws that allowed divorce; and in 1975 it nullified the portion of the penal code that made a woman's consent to an abortion a criminal act (de Franciscis and Zannini, p. 74; Volcansek, 1990, p. 134). The court has been characterized as generally a defender of civil liberties and has not slavishly followed the wishes of the government of the day, but it would be wrong to exaggerate its independence. The court collectively does not deviate too far from the sentiments of the mainstream political elite, and individual members may be receptive to the views of the party that secured their nomination (de Franciscis and Zannini, p.78; Volcansek, 1994). Italians do not see the court as completely independent of the political parties, but at least they perceive it to be less controlled by the parties than are most other Italian institutions.

Austria had the world's first constitutional court, which was created in 1920. It was suppressed during the Nazi period but was reestablished in 1945. Since then, like its counterparts elsewhere, it has grown more powerful (see Müller, pp. 115–18). Like the FCC, it can consider bills referred to it by a third of the members of parliament, and individuals can ask it to consider the constitutionality of laws and government decrees that affect them. Up to the mid-1980s, it interpreted the constitution in a formal and legalistic way and rarely struck down legislation, and when it did so the political background of the judges was important. Since then, however, it has moved to a more "substantive" approach, changing some of its own previous judgments and becoming generally less predictable. It has made a number of important decisions: it has forced parliament to introduce a widowers' pension and has struck down laws regulating the opening hours of shops and fixing different pension ages for men and women. The reasons for its increased activism include a generational change on the bench, with younger appointees taking a different approach from that of their predecessors, and a weakening of the stranglehold that the main parties used to enjoy on virtually every aspect of life in Austria. New members of the Constitutional Court feel less duty-bound to the party responsible for nominating them, and the court has felt confident enough to tackle topics that politicians had avoided because they affected the vested interests of powerful groups (Müller, p. 118). If the court strikes down a law, parliament has the option of reenacting it by a qualified majority as a constitutional law (thereby amending the constitution). However, although this was routinely done in earlier decades, it is now more rare, because the public would regard this as "party misbehaviour" (Müller, p. 118).

Constitutional courts were brought into existence in Spain and Portugal after the establishment of democratic regimes there in the 1970s. The Spanish constitution originally provided for abstract review in both a priori and a posteriori forms along with concrete judicial review. Abstract review can be initiated by a group of fifty deputies or fifty senators, among others, and individuals can write to the court requesting that their constitutional rights be protected; over 90 percent of referrals come from individuals (Heywood, pp. 105–9; Newton, pp. 26–28). As in a number of other countries, the court has been dragged into controversy by its decisions concerning abortion (Barreiro). Despite allegations that the court is frequently subjected to political pressure, some of its key judgments in the 1990s constituted rebuffs to the government of the day. As in France, the opposition tends to have recourse to the court when it has lost a battle in parliament and, like the French Constitutional Council, the Spanish Constitutional Court is sometimes seen as a third chamber of parliament (Lancaster, p. 327). The Portuguese Constitutional Court can review the constitutionality of legislation if requested to do so by a tenth of the members of parliament. The president has the power to refer bills to the court, and he or she is obliged to sign the bill into law if the court declares it constitutional or to veto it if the bill is declared unconstitutional.

Finally, we look at the case of Ireland, which differs from all other European countries in that judicial review is exercised not by a special constitutional court but by the regular court system, as in the United States. The High Court and the Supreme Court in Ireland—rather than every court as in the United States—are empowered to pass judgment on the constitutionality of laws, and they can exercise not just concrete review, as in the United States, but also abstract review (the a priori form only). However, the right of referral of bills to the courts for abstract review is much more restrictive than in the other countries we have looked at: only the president of Ireland may refer bills to the Supreme Court for this purpose. Since the Irish constitution came into force in 1937, only twelve bills have been so referred (six have been found by the Supreme Court to be constitutional and the other six to be wholly or in part unconstitutional). As in other countries, the number of actual referrals understates the significance of abstract review, for the very existence of this presidential power has no doubt made parliament particularly careful not to pass legislation that might prove to be in conflict with the constitution.

More significant in Ireland has been concrete review. Again, as in other countries, the courts in Ireland have become more active since the 1960s in exercising the power of judicial review, and lawyers have been more inclined to challenge the constitutionality of statutes (Gallagher). As in Austria, and for some of the same reasons (such as generational change on the bench), the courts have moved from a literal approach to interpreting the constitution to what is termed a "creative" approach, which implies that the judges do not feel limited by the actual words in the constitution but move beyond them to consider what they claim to be its overall spirit and tenor. The courts have made a number of important decisions as a consequence. In 1973, the existing law banning the sale or importation of contraceptives was declared unconstitutional as it violated the right to marital privacy; this right was "inferred" by the courts from the constitution, which makes no mention of any such right. In a very Catholic country, with at that time few signs of opposition to the influence of Catholic values on the body of laws, this decision was inevitably controversial, and it spurred the political parties, which had been fearful of losing votes on the issue, into belated action to legalize contraception. In 1987, the Supreme Court decided that the government was not entitled under the constitution to ratify the Single European Act (which marked a major step toward integration within the European Community), and as a result a referendum had to be held to change the constitution in order to allow the act to be ratified.

Perhaps most controversially of all, in 1992, the Supreme Court decided by four votes to one that the constitution conferred a right to have an abortion on a woman whose life would be threatened (perhaps by the risk of suicide) by the continuation of a pregnancy. This decision was based on a section of the constitution that had been added by referendum in 1983. The aim of the sponsors of the 1983 amendment (known as the "pro-life amendment") had been to ensure that abortion could not be legalized either by parliament or by the Supreme Court, should it deliver a judgment similar in its consequences to the 1973 judgment in the United States in Roe v. Wade. Consequently, anti-abortionists were angered by the 1992 decision, and one of their leaders criticized the very concept of judicial review, declaring that "it is unacceptable and indeed a deep affront to the people of Ireland that four judges who are preserved by the constitution from accountability can radically alter the constitution and place in peril the most vulnerable section of our society" (quoted in Gallagher, p. 92). However, this criticism was unusual, for despite the fact that the government of the day appoints judges and attaches great importance when doing so to the political links of potential appointees, the courts are widely seen as "above" politics and no government has attributed political motives to a judge who has delivered a decision that it did not like.

Ireland is sometimes seen as possessing only weak judicial review, but the reality is that judicial review is very significant there; for example, the Irish courts have proved much readier to identify unenunciated rights than their American counterparts (Beytagh, 1992). As in Germany, the courts in Ireland can exercise power not merely by striking down legislation but also by imposing their own interpretation on it. The courts approach each statute with the "presumption of constitutionality"; that is, "if a statutory provision is open to differing constructions, one constitutional, the other not, the court must opt for the former" (Casey, pp. 290–93). Although this might seem to strengthen the position of parliament—it means that less of its legislation will be struck down than if there were no presumption of constitutionality—it can work to limit the power of parliament, because it may mean that the court chooses the narrowest of a number of meanings that an act could have and consequently reduces the scope of the act.

We have seen, then, that courts that have the power to strike down legislation can be significant political actors. Clearly, this can be frustrating for political parties and governments, amounting to a veto by a small number of unelected individuals on policies that might have had widespread support. However, there may be times when political actors welcome the intervention of the courts. Some of those politicians who complain that the courts have prevented them from fulfilling election pledges may be secretly relieved not to have to try to implement policies in which they never really believed, or may be thankful to be able to pass political hot potatoes to the courts for resolution.

Weak Judicial Review

We now turn to those countries where the courts have no power to strike down legislation on the ground of incompatibility with the constitution. This has been the case in Britain, where the absence of a formal codified constitution leads to a degree of vagueness as to what the constitution stipulates in any given situation, so the question of unconstitutionality simply has not arisen—although the incorporation into British law of the European Convention on Human Rights in the year 2000 may prove a significant development in this area. The courts, of course, play a role in interpreting the laws, but they cannot strike down a law. The conventional view is that "English judges have acquired a reputation second to none in the free world for subservience to the government and the executive" (Waldron, pp. 126–27). However, it does not follow, as is sometimes assumed, that the courts are irrelevant in deciding what governments can and cannot do, and in fact judges in Britain are proving increasingly troublesome for governments. "English courts are increasingly willing to tell the government officials, at both national and local levels, that their action is wrong" (Kritzer, p. 156; see also Gordon; Johnson, 1998). They have the power to prevent ministers from exercising power beyond their legal authority (*ultra vires*), although parliament may then change the laws to confer the desired power on the minister. The courts have been particularly active in preventing government efforts to tighten restrictions on the number of refugees and asylum seekers admitted to Britain (Sterett, pp. 435–38). A senior judge, speaking in 1995, declared that judicial review as such had not existed in Britain before 1977 but had been developed subsequently by the courts (Griffith, 1997, p. 326). Nowadays, government departments have to expend considerable time in working out how to avoid court review of their actions (Kritzer, pp. 156–63).

Some feel that the courts should have more power still. In the 1990s, a reformist group of legal academics and others drafted a written constitution for the United Kingdom, under which a supreme court would have the power to declare acts of parliament unconstitutional (Institute for Public Policy Research). However, on the left of the British political spectrum there has always been a reluctance to give the judiciary more power. Even though the courts have become increasingly willing to check governments of all persuasions, as we have seen, left-wing critics have often seen the judiciary as fundamentally conservative. The British judiciary has been accused of upholding "the fears and prejudices of the middle and upper classes," of broadly sharing the values of the Conservative Party, and of demonstrating and applying these values in cases involving race relations, trade unions, government secrecy, police powers, and other social issues (Griffith, 1997, pp. 290–343; see also Griffith, 1993). On every major issue to come before the courts in the last thirty years, says Griffith, "the judges have supported the conventional, established and settled interests" (Griffith, 1997, pp. 340–41), although not all writers on the British courts would necessarily accept this analysis.

The absence of provision for the courts to strike down laws also applies to a number of other countries. The courts of the Netherlands are expressly prohibited by Article 120 of the constitution from considering the constitutionality of laws, and until the 1960s there was little pressure for the introduction of judicial review. However, the courts can declare government measures to be *ultra vires* and can annul acts of parliament that contravene European treaties to which the Netherlands is a party. Perhaps due to a declining respect for politicians and an increased respect for the courts, the courts have become more assertive and have sometimes exercised a self-conferred de facto right of judicial review. The question of explicitly enshrining judicial review in the constitution has been discussed in recent years, partly in response to trends in other European countries (Scheltma, pp. 206–7; Andeweg and Irwin, p. 235; ten Kate and van Koppen, pp. 148–49; van Koppen, pp. 83, 91). In Switzerland the highest court—the Federal Tribunal—can strike down legislation passed by the cantons, but not that passed by the federal parliament. In Belgium, judicial review can be exercised only regarding laws concerning the balance of power between different levels of government (Brewer-Carías, pp. 261–62).

Judicial review is not a strong feature of political life in the Scandinavian countries; only in Norway does it have long roots, and even there it has never assumed great significance. In Sweden the unimportance of judicial review has its roots in political culture rather than in the constitution, for judicial review is provided for in the constitution in terms more explicit than those in the American constitution. Swedish opinion has traditionally been hostile to judicial review because of the feeling that since power emanates from the people, the decisions made by the parliament elected by the people (the Riksdag) should not be open to challenge. Moreover, Swedish politics is not

BOX 2–2

THE COURTS AND POLITICS

France

Although judicial review as such does not exist, partly because of a fear of "government by judges," a quasi-judicial body, the Constitutional Council, can consider the constitutionality of legislation after it has been passed by parliament and before it is signed into law by the president. Appointment to the Council takes place very much on political grounds. In the first half of the 1980s, the Council, then dominated by right-wing appointees, made a number of rulings restricting the Socialist government's freedom of action, but when the right-wing parties won power in 1986, and again in 1993, the Council continued its activist approach and caused even more annoyance to the right than it had to the Socialists.

Germany

The Federal Constitutional Court, whose members are appointed on a cross-party basis, exerts a significant impact on policymaking. It has made major political decisions, curbing the extent to which the abortion laws could be liberalized in both 1975 and 1993, and banning two political parties in the 1950s. The nonpartisan and serious manner in which it approaches its work has given it considerable national prestige, and parliament invariably defers to its judgments; indeed, parliament is sometimes criticized for being too ready to anticipate its reactions and restricting itself for fear of falling foul of the court.

Italy

The postwar Italian judiciary has been highly politicized, with factions of judges linked to the major political parties. Judges and magistrates can become well-known nationally through taking the initiative in tackling what they identify as problems, and although some see them as all too often motivated by a desire for publicity, the role of judges in the fight against organized crime and the corruption of Italian politics in the mid-1990s earned them respect. The Italian Constitutional Court has also been highly regarded, and over the years it has generally worked to enhance the civil liberties of citizens, for example by declaring repressive legislation dating from the fascist era to be invalid.

Netherlands

There is no tradition of judicial review in the Netherlands, with Article 120 of the Dutch constitution declaring that the courts cannot review the constitutionality of acts of parliament. The courts, then, have generally had relatively little impact on politics, although they are coming to play an increasing role by interpreting the words of laws when parliament passes rather vague legislation and by reserving the right to annul government measures that go beyond what legislation permits.

Spain

The Spanish Constitutional Court has the power to exercise abstract review of a law if requested to do so by a group of fifty deputies or fifty senators. After the Socialist party won power in 1982, the court was used by the right-wing opposition as a means of slowing the pace of radical legislation, but its decisions are not widely seen as politically motivated. Eight of its twelve members are appointed by the parliament by consensus among the parties, with two appointed by the government and two by the body representing Spanish judges.

Sweden

The Swedish constitution provides for judicial review, but there is no tradition of the courts declaring laws to be unconstitutional, with the left-wing parties in particular being suspicious of the idea of allowing the courts to overrule the democratically elected parliament. However, a judicial body does give advisory opinions on the constitutionality of proposed legislation, and its advice carries considerable weight. Judges are rigorously nonpartisan, and in some ways see themselves as administrators with closer links to the state bureaucracy than to lawyers in private practice.

United Kingdom

Because there is no document called "The British Constitution," the possibility of legislation's being declared unconstitutional does not exist. The judges do, however, have the right to declare the behavior of public authorities to go beyond those authorities' allotted powers, and their decisions in some such cases have brought them into the field of political controversy. Critics have accused the British judiciary of being implicitly sympathetic to the views of the Conservative Party and of not showing sufficient concern for civil rights.

legalistic; Swedes turn instinctively to the political process rather than to the courts to bring about change, and there are few lawyers in the Riksdag (Board, 1991, pp. 180–81, 185; Stjernquist). Judicial review has been permitted only since a constitutional amendment in 1979, but no court declared any law unconstitutional until the early 1990s, and even this decision was overturned by the Court of Appeal (Holmström, p. 160). However, this may underestimate the role of the courts in this area, for there is provision for a body called the Lågradet (Law Council), which is composed of judges from the Supreme Court and the Supreme Administrative Court, to give its advice on proposed legislation. Its opinion as to whether the legislation appears to be in conflict with the constitution is given "considerable weight" by the government and parliament (Board, 1988, p. 183). Indeed, government departments when preparing legislation go to some lengths to anticipate the Law Council's views and to ensure that legislation conforms with these (Holmström, p. 159). In Finland, too, the apparent insignificance of judicial review is slightly misleading, for the president has the power to refuse to ratify bills passed by parliament, and is unlikely to ratify any bill that the Supreme Court has found to be in conflict with the constitution (Brewer-Carías, pp. 172–73; Katz, p. 283).

THE APPOINTMENT OF JUDGES

When judges have significant power to constrain political actors, the question of who appoints judges takes on particular significance. The potential for interaction between the judiciary, the executive, and the legislature is seen clearly in this area. Although, as we would expect, practice varies from country to country, the appointment of judges is politically controlled in most countries. We will look first at appointments to constitutional courts, and then at the appointment of "ordinary" judges.

Constitutional Courts

Members of constitutional courts are appointed mainly by political authorities, but the spirit in which this power of appointment is exercised varies. In France the right to appoint members of the Constitutional Council is seen as a perk of office and is monopolized by the party or parties that control the levers of power. The Constitutional Council contains nine members, each of whom serves a nine-year term. The President of France, the president of the lower house of parliament (the National Assembly), and the president of the Senate each appoint one member every three years. There are no formal legal or other qualifications for membership of the Council, and "the single most important criterion for appointment to the Council is political affiliation," with 59 percent of those appointed between 1958 and 1988 being former government ministers or parliamentary deputies (Stone, 1992, p. 50). For example, in 1986, with his Socialist Party about to lose power at parliamentary elections, President Mitterrand appointed his Minister for Justice to the presidency of the Council. However, Bell says that despite a widespread impression of political patronage, most appointments have been justified on grounds of merit, and generally "quality has prevailed over political allegiance" (Bell, p. 37).Those appointed are usually politicians "in the twilight of their careers," so the average age of Council members in the 1980s was 74, though in the 1990s it dropped to 64 (Stone, 1992, p. 53; Bell, p. 54). Because the turnover of members of the Council can be slower than the turnover of governments, a new government is liable to be faced with a council dominated by appointees of its political opponents.

In Germany, Austria, Italy, and Spain, parliament also makes some or all of the appointments to the constitutional court, but the somewhat less confrontational nature of politics in these countries means that the court is not a political battleground in the same way that the Constitutional Council is in France. In Germany, half of the sixteen members of the Federal Constitutional Court are appointed by the Bundestag (the federal parliament) and the other half by the Bundesrat (which represents the governments of the Länder). The parties play the main role in deciding whom to appoint, and care is taken to balance the list of nominees among the various parties in broad proportion to their strengths in parliament (Holland, 1988, p. 93; Kommers, 1997, pp. 21–22). In addition, the various Länder are also quite proportionally represented. In Italy, similarly, the main parties operate a formula that ensures that each receives its proportionate share of appointments. In Austria, seven of the thirteen voting members of the constitutional court are nominated by the Socialist Party, and the other six are nominated by the People's Party (Müller, p. 116). In Spain, four of the twelve members of the Constitutional Tribunal are appointed by the Congress of Deputies and four by the Senate, with a requirement in each case that a three-fifths majority is needed to approve the nominees, which ensures that cross-party consensus is needed (Brewer-Carías, p. 227). In each of these four countries, unlike France, members of the constitutional courts must possess strong legal qualifications; usually they must meet the requirements needed to become a judge.

The Court System

In most countries, the government of the day has a major role in deciding on the appointment and promotion of judges, and judges can be removed from office by a majority vote in parliament. Indeed, Mary Volcansek (1992, p. 5) speaks of "a tendency toward greater politicization in the judicial appointment process" in Europe, and the interaction between the courts and politics in appointments, and other areas, is illustrated for a variety of countries by Sturgess and Chubb (pp. 122–51). However, this of itself does not necessarily lead to a politically biased judiciary. Even if governments do use their role in the appointment and promotion process to favor men and women of their own outlook, they are realistic enough to know that judges cannot be kept on a political leash. In some countries, notably in Scandinavia, the political culture militates strongly against any attempt to politicize the judiciary: in Sweden, for example, there is "a long and deeply engrained tradition of an independent judiciary, insulated from the pressures and vicissitudes of partisan party politics" (Board, 1988, p. 186). In Ireland, as we have seen, the Supreme Court is the final arbiter on constitutional matters, as in the USA, and appointment to this body is entirely in the hands of the government of the day, although judges need to have demonstrable legal expertise. It is accepted that all governments favor barristers of their own political persuasion when making judicial appointments, though, equally, it is generally felt that once judges are appointed, they sever their political connections and behave without regard to their former allegiance.

Moreover, the option of dismissing a judge who has given decisions inconvenient to the government of the day, although legally possible, is usually politically unthinkable, as it would be regarded as unjustified interference with the judicial process by the public in most, if not all, European countries. For example, although the two houses of parliament in Britain (the House of Commons and the House of Lords) can dismiss a judge, no judges have been dismissed since early in the nineteenth century.

In Britain, party patronage in judicial appointments is felt to have died out by the end of the Second World War (Drewry, p. 15). In France, though, Shapiro suggests that "judges who wish to succeed professionally are likely to give the regime the kinds of decisions it wants even though the politicians apply no direct pressure" (Shapiro, p. 156). Belgian courts have been described as "eager to reflect in their decisions mainstream opinion or contemporary legislative policy" (Verougstraete, p. 106), perhaps partly because prior to 1991 appointments to the judiciary were made mainly on a political basis. Courts in Greece are also widely believed, rightly or wrongly, to take account of the wishes of the government of the day when reaching decisions in cases with political overtones.

Perhaps the most overtly politicized judges are to be found in Italy—ironically, the country where judges have perhaps a higher degree of formal independence from government than anywhere else. There are four political factions or currents (*correnti*) in the judiciary—two on the left and two on the right—which in the 1980s were associated with the main Italian parties, and even though some of the parties to which they were linked have disappeared, the *correnti* continue to thrive (Guarnieri, p. 163). These factions play a decisive role in promotions within the judiciary. Judges and magistrates belonging to the left wing current bestow on themselves the power of judicial review, and without referring the matter to the only body qualified to judge (namely the Constitutional Court), refrain from applying legal norms that they claim to be in conflict with the constitution (Di Federico and Guarnieri, pp. 175–77). All the Italian parties attempt to build up a pool of sympathetic judges by offering inducements, such as seats in parliament or well-paid positions on commissions, and the partisan ties and loyalties of investigating magistrates are "perceived as motivating or thwarting criminal investigations" (Volcansek, 1991, p. 127). In an attempt to "extract a more benevolent attitude" from the judiciary, Italian governments have readily met the demands of magistrates, who as a result have become the highest-paid members of the state sector and are automatically promoted to the top of their scale regardless of performance (Guarnieri, pp. 159–60; Di Federico and Guarnieri, p. 179). Magistrates may have their own political goals to achieve as well as, or rather than, purely financial ones. The term "assault judges" has been coined for judges and magistrates who use their positions to "tackle what they see as problems, which may be a person, an institution or a condition" (Volcansek, 1991, p. 126) and as a result often receive widespread publicity. In the mid-1990s the unearthing of the massive Tangentopoli (Bribesville) scandal, which entailed numerous links between politicians and organized crime, was initiated by magistrates from Milan, who achieved nationwide prominence. The crisis in the political system that resulted left the judges even stronger than before and with even fewer constraints on their activities (Guarnieri).

In the 1990s, there were signs that the Spanish judiciary was starting to develop along similar lines, with the emergence of politically aligned associations among the judges and magistrates, the readiness of some members of the judiciary to seek to rectify what they saw as shortcomings in the political system, and an increasing backlog of cases due to a certain lack of efficiency in the judicial system (Heywood, pp. 117–20; Newton, p. 303).

JUDGES AND LAWMAKING

Under all legal systems, judges apply the law, but under some legal systems judges can also make the law. When looking at the role of the courts in making law in various countries, it is useful to adopt the conventional distinction between two general types of legal systems: the common law tradition and the civil law tradition. As we will see, this distinction is less clear-cut in reality than it is in theory, but it is still useful for understanding the different approaches to the role of the courts across Europe. Common law systems are confined to Britain and English-speaking former British colonies. Within Europe, only Britain and Ireland are classifiable as common law countries. Outside Europe, examples of common law countries are most of the United States and Canada, as well as Australia and New Zealand. Most European countries belong instead to the civil law tradition, which originated within a continental tradition of "Roman" law that has now been transformed into a comprehensive system of legal codes. Codified legal systems of one form or another prevail in all European states other than Britain and Ireland; more generally, this group includes many former continental European colonies, including Louisiana, much of Latin America, and parts of Canada.

The fundamental difference between the two is that common law systems rely less on "laws," seen as acts of parliament, and more on "the law," seen as the accumulated weight of precedent set by the decisions, definitions, and interpretations made by judges. Central to the common law tradition is the principle of *stare decisis* (let the decision stand): in other words, a judge considers himself or herself bound by judgments in previous essentially similar cases. Many key legal principles and rules are thus established not in statutes made by the legislature but in judgments made by the judiciary. In a British, Irish, or American court, a precedent, if it applies to the case in question, *is* the law. Judges do not merely apply in a mechanistic way the laws made by parliament; they actually play a part in making the laws, by pronouncing judgments that will be drawn on by other judges when interpreting the law. The common law approach is to resolve specific disputes in a "pragmatic and improvisatory way," and statutes, particularly in England, are passed partly to build on or classify existing case law (de Cruz, p. 105).

The essential feature of a codified legal system, in contrast, is that the ultimate foundation of the law is a comprehensive and authoritative legal code. Upon this foundation is built a superstructure of statutes enacted by the legislature. Every legal decision, in principle, can be deduced from the legal code and subsequent enacted statutes. No reference need be made to any existing body of case law. The code, when it is introduced, wipes the legal slate clean and starts afresh. The first and most influential of the modern legal codes is the Napoleonic Code, the *Code Napoléon,* which emerged as a part of the new order after the French Revolution. The five basic codes upon which all of French law still rests are the Civil Code (1804), the Code of Civil Procedure (1806), the Code of Commerce (1808), the Code of Criminal Procedure (1811) and the Penal Code (1811). Subsequent legislation has built extensively on these, although changes have often been incorporated as amendments into the original codes. The influence of the *Code Napoléon* can be clearly seen in the legal systems of Belgium, Luxembourg, the Netherlands, Italy, Spain, and Portugal. The second major source of codified European law is the German Civil Code of 1900. Besides Germany, the five Scandinavian countries—Norway, Sweden, Denmark, Finland, and Iceland—are usually identified, for historical and cultural reasons, with this tradition. Differences between the German and French traditions are minor compared with the difference between all codified continental traditions on the one hand and the Anglo-American system of common law on the other.

In civil law countries, then, judges do not in any sense "make" law; they merely apply the law made by parliaments. Judges in France are expressly forbidden by the Civil Code from going beyond the case at hand to lay down general rules amounting to a regulation. Judges are mere legal technicians, whose decisions could in theory be made equally well by a computer into which the appropriate rules and the facts of the specific case had been fed. Because of this, judges typically have a lower standing (often significantly lower than that of law professors) than their counterparts in common law countries, where judges are usually appointed from the ranks of senior lawyers. In civil law countries, law students usually have to choose before the end of their studies whether to become private lawyers, prosecutors, or judges (Holland, 1991, p. 8), and accordingly judges are sometimes seen as having the attitudes of bureaucrats to a much greater degree than common law judges, who acquire the outlook of the law profession in their country rather than that of permanent civil servants. In Sweden, for example, judges "tend to see themselves as administrators"; both careers are in the bureaucracy, and there is some interchangeability between judges and administrators (Board, 1991, p. 185).

The role of the judiciary (and of parliament) can be expected to vary between civil law and common law countries. In civil law countries, the judiciary is (at least in theory) much less important than parliament: it merely applies the law made by the legislators. Moreover, in France and in many other continental European systems, parliamentary debates, committee reports, and other public pronouncements that are related to the passing of the legislation—the *travaux préparatoires* (preparatory works), as they are usually called—may be used as sources of a legal opinion as to what parliament had in mind when it passed a law. This is typically ruled out in a common law system such as that of Britain, in which the sum total of the work of the legislature is the text of the laws that it enacts. In common law countries, therefore, the potential for conflict between legislature and judiciary can be expected to be greater, because when judges can "make" law, the law that they make might not coincide with the preferences of legislators.

Having outlined this clear distinction between the civil law tradition and the common law tradition, one must say that there is general agreement that the lines between the two are rapidly becoming blurred. In the words of Peter de Cruz, "recent trends have indicated that the common law and civil law systems have been coming closer together in their use of cases and statutes" (de Cruz, p. 36). In Britain and Ireland, law is increasingly based on statute: the volume of legislation has expanded, and in cases where precedent and statute point to different decisions, judges are obliged to give priority to statute. Moreover, it is not unknown for the courts in Britain to consult parliamentary debates to clarify the meaning of particular pieces of legislation (Oliver). In civil law countries, precedent is of increasing significance. Indeed, it is arguable that it always was important, and that its absence from judges' written decisions gives a misleading impression. Martin Shapiro observes that the French legal code, for example, does not really consist of detailed rules that provide the answer to every case; rather, it consists of principles that the judges must interpret. When doing this, the judge "is acknowledging the body of legal doctrine built up around the bare words of the code by previous cases"—in other words, is following precedent (Shapiro, pp. 134–35). Although *stare decisis* is not officially recognized, hundreds of volumes of case reports are published, and lawyers in France and in other civil law countries cite precedents in their arguments in court just as British or American lawyers do (Shapiro, p. 147; de Cruz, p. 67). In Italy, judges are expected to take account of decisions in previous cases, and "it seems doubtful that judicial precedents are de facto less binding in the Italian judicial process than in countries where judges are formally bound by judicial precedents" (Di Federico and Guarnieri, p. 175). Similarly, in Sweden judges "have always deferred somewhat to precedent, and in recent years the tendency appears to be growing" (Board, 1988, p. 185). In the Netherlands, too, since 1919 the courts have increasingly become interpreters of the law rather than mere appliers of it, partly because parliament has been inclined to include in statutes "vague norms" that leave considerable discretion to the judges. In areas such as euthanasia and abortion, the Supreme Court has in effect produced case law where parliament was unable to pass detailed legislation (ten Kate and van Koppen, pp. 146–47; Andeweg and Irwin, pp. 235–37; van Koppen, pp. 84–85).

Judges, then, can to some extent make law in both common law and civil law countries, and as such they can be important actors in the process of policymaking. When they are required to make decisions in cases in which political parties or pressure groups have an interest, they are, whether they like it or not, part of the political process. Although judges might like to maintain that they merely hand down impartial decisions based on the application of relevant laws or precedents, it is unrealistic to imagine that the political and personal viewpoints of the judges themselves play no part in determining the decisions they make. As Benjamin Cardozo, member of the U.S. Supreme Court from 1932 to 1938, put it, "The great tides and currents which engulf the rest of men do not turn aside in their course and pass the judges idly by" (quoted in Abraham, p. 357).

All of this goes to show that the judiciary can have a significant role in politics when it comes to applying and interpreting laws. In common law countries, judges can play a part in "making" the laws by delivering judgments that then become precedents to be drawn on by subsequent judges. Even in civil law countries, judges can—indeed, must—exercise more discretion than some accounts acknowledge in their portrayals of judges in civil law jurisdictions as mere appliers of unambiguous statutes and codes. In most countries—Italy is the most notable exception—the judiciary is not explicitly politicized, and judges are generally seen as "nonpolitical" or "above politics." Still, realists accept that the personal and political views of judges will have some bearing on the judgments they deliver, in both common and civil law jurisdictions.

CONCLUSION

The courts in many European countries have increasingly found themselves compelled, or presented with the opportunity, to make decisions on the legality or constitutionality of the actions of political authorities. Pressure groups and individuals perceiving a threat to their rights or interests have turned with growing frequency to the courts for redress. Dedicated constitutional courts such as those in Germany and Austria must be counted among the political actors of those countries, in the sense that they have the power to constrain and even direct government and parliament, as must the Constitutional Council in France and the Supreme Court of Ireland. Even in countries where courts cannot or do not strike down legislation as unconstitutional, such as Britain, the Netherlands, and Sweden, close examination reveals that the judiciary is by no means as passive and irrelevant to decision making as some have assumed.

For many, this is a welcome development. As we shall see in Chapter 4, parliaments don't usually seem to be able to impose a meaningful check on governments, because they are dominated by the same political parties that are in government. Government ministers in most European countries are not kept awake at nights wondering whether or not parliament will approve a bill they have drawn up, but many ministers clearly do worry about whether the courts will approve their plans, and, indeed, they go to some lengths to ensure that their schemes will meet with the approval of the judicial authorities. Supporters of the power of the courts to block proposals emanating from government and parliament argue that there are rights so fundamental that not even a majority can ride roughshod over them, and the courts and the constitution provide a necessary check on the exercise of power by governments. A more pragmatic defence is that the judiciary prevents government policy in certain areas from drifting too far from the middle of the road; this was especially apparent in France from the early 1980s to the mid-1990s, where governments of both left and right had their wings clipped by the Constitutional Council.

Opponents of the growing power of the judiciary make the point that it contradicts the very notion of representative government. Judicial review, for its critics, entails giving power to a handful of unelected, unaccountable, and unrepresentative individuals to override the wishes of those who were elected by the people and upon whom the people will be able to pass judgment at the next election. Nor are such critics placated by the claim that judicial review prevents governments from enacting extremist policies; they argue that in practice, the backgrounds and values of the judiciary mean that the political impact of the courts' interventions is decidedly favorable to the conservative side of the spectrum.

Quite clearly, arguments about the wisdom of judicial review, which have been animatedly discussed in the United States for the last two centuries, will never be definitively resolved. Systematic data on the opinions of the European public on the issue of judicial power are lacking, though we may note that observers from a range of countries do not detect any popular resentment at the growing influence of the courts, and indeed in some countries the judicial authorities are more highly regarded than parliaments or political parties, the archetypal actors of representative government. What is certain is that the impact of the judiciary on politics in Europe has been growing steadily in recent years, and no account of European governance can neglect the role of courts and constitutions.

REFERENCES

Abraham, Henry J.: *The Judicial Process: An Introductory Analysis of the Courts of the United States, England and France,* 7th ed., Oxford University Press, New York and Oxford, 1998.

Andeweg, Rudy B., and Galen A. Irwin: *Dutch Government and Politics,* Macmillan, Basingstoke, 1993.

Barreiro, Belén: "Judicial Review and Political Empowerment: Abortion in Spain," *West European Politics,* vol. 21, no. 4, 1998, pp. 147–62.

Bell, John: *French Constitutional Law,* Clarendon Press, Oxford, 1992.

Bellamy, Richard (ed.): *Constitutionalism, Democracy and Sovereignty: American and European Perspectives,* Avebury, Aldershot, 1996.

Benz, Arthur: "A Forum of Constitutional Deliberation? A Critical Analysis of the Joint Constitutional Commission," in Klaus H. Goetz and Peter J. Cullen (eds.), *Constitutional Policy in Unified Germany,* Frank Cass, London, 1995, pp. 99–117.

Beytagh, Francis X.: "Individual Rights, Judicial Review, and Written Constitutions," in James O'Reilly (ed.), *Human Rights and Constitutional Law: Essays in Honour of Brian Walsh,* Round Hall Press, Blackrock, Co. Dublin, 1992, pp. 147–62.

Board, Joseph B.: "The Courts in Sweden," in Jerold L. Waltman and Kenneth M. Holland (eds.), *The Political Role of Law Courts in Modern Democracies,* Macmillan, Basingstoke, 1988, pp. 181–98.

Board, Joseph B.: "Judicial Activism in Sweden," in Kenneth M. Holland (ed.), *Judicial Activism in Comparative Perspective,* Macmillan, Basingstoke, 1991, pp. 175–88.

Bogdanor, Vernon: "Conclusion," in Vernon Bogdanor (ed.), *Constitutions in Democratic Politics,* Gower, Aldershot; 1988, pp. 380–86.

Brewer-Carías, Allan R.: *Judicial Review in Comparative Law,* Cambridge University Press, Cambridge and New York, 1989.

Carcassonne, Guy: "The Constraints on Constitutional Change in France," in Joachim Jens Hesse and Nevil Johnson (eds.), *Constitutional Policy and Change in Europe,* Oxford University Press, Oxford and New York, 1995, pp. 152–77.

Casey, James: *Constitutional Law in Ireland,* 2d ed., Sweet and Maxwell, London, 1992.

Currie, David P.: *The Constitution of the Federal Republic of Germany,* University of Chicago Press, Chicago and London, 1994.

de Cruz, Peter: *Comparative Law in a Changing World,* Cavendish, London, 1995.

de Franciscis, Maria Elisabetta, and Rosella Zannini: "Judicial Policy-Making in Italy," in Mary L. Volcansek (ed.), *Judicial Politics and Policy-Making in Western Europe,* Frank Cass, London, 1992, pp. 68–79.

Di Federico, Giuseppe, and Carlo Guarnieri: "The Courts in Italy," in Jerold L. Waltman and Kenneth M. Holland (eds.), *The Political Role of Law Courts in Modern Democracies,* Macmillan, Basingstoke, 1988, pp. 153–80.

Drewry, Gavin: "Judicial Politics in Britain: Patrolling the Boundaries," in Mary L. Volcansek (ed.), *Judicial Politics and Policy-Making in Western Europe,* Frank Cass, London, 1992, pp. 9–28.

Finer, S. E., Vernon Bogdanor, and Bernard Rudden (eds.): *Comparing Constitutions,* Clarendon Press, Oxford, 1995.

Fusaro, Carlo: "The Politics of Constitutional Reform in Italy: a Framework for Analysis," *South European Society and Politics,* vol. 3, no. 2, 1998, pp. 45–74.

Gallagher, Michael: "The Constitution," in John Coakley and Michael Gallagher (eds.), *Politics in the Republic of Ireland,* 3d ed., Routledge, London, 1999, pp. 71–98.

Gordon, Richard: *Judicial Review: Law and Procedure,* Sweet and Maxwell, London, 1996.

Griffith, John: *Judicial Politics Since 1920: A Chronicle,* Blackwell, Oxford, 1993.

Griffith, J. A. G.: *The Politics of the Judiciary,* 5th ed., Fontana, London, 1997.

Guarnieri, Carlo: "The Judiciary in the Italian Political Crisis," *West European Politics,* vol. 20, no. 1, 1997, pp. 157–75.

Heywood, Paul: *The Government and Politics of Spain,* Macmillan, Basingstoke, 1995.

Holland, Kenneth M.: "The Courts in the Federal Republic of Germany," in Jerold L. Waltman and Kenneth M. Holland (eds.), *The Political Role of Law Courts in Modern Democracies,* Macmillan, Basingstoke, 1988, pp. 83–107.

Holland, Kenneth M.: "Introduction," in Kenneth M. Holland (ed.), *Judicial Activism in Comparative Perspective,* Macmillan, Basingstoke, 1991, pp. 1–11.

Holmes, Stephen: "Pre-Commitment and the Paradox of Democracy," in Jon Elster and Rune Slagstad (eds.), *Constitutionalism and Democracy,* Cambridge University Press, Cambridge, 1988, pp. 195–240.

Holmström, Barry: "The Judicialization of Politics in Sweden," *International Political Science Review,* vol. 15, no. 2, 1994, pp. 153–64.

Institute for Public Policy Research: *A Written Constitution for the United Kingdom,* Mansell, London, 1995.

Johnson, Nevil: "Constitutionalism in Europe since 1945: Reconstruction and Reappraisal," in Douglas Greenberg, Stanley N. Katz, Melanie Beth Oliviero and Steven C. Wheatley (eds.), *Constitutionalism and Democracy: Transitions in the Contemporary World,* Oxford University Press, New York and Oxford, 1993, pp. 26–45.

Johnson, Nevil: "The Federal Constitutional Court: Facing up to the Strains of Law and Politics in the New Germany," in Klaus H. Goetz and Peter J. Cullen (eds.), *Constitutional Policy in Unified Germany,* Frank Cass, London, 1995, pp. 131–48.

Johnson, Nevil: "The Judicial Dimension in British Politics," *West European Politics,* vol. 21, no. 1, 1998, pp. 148–66.

Katz, Alan N.: "Scandinavia," in Alan N. Katz (ed.), *Legal Traditions and Systems: An International Handbook,* Greenwood, Westport, 1986, pp. 273–88.

Kommers, Donald P.: "The Federal Constitutional Court in the German Political System," *Comparative Political Studies,* vol. 26, no. 4, 1994, pp. 470–91.

Kommers, Donald P.: *The Constitutional Jurisprudence of the Federal Republic of Germany,* 2d ed. Duke University Press, Durham, N.C., and London, 1997.

Kritzer, Herbert M.: "Courts, Justice, and Politics in England," in Herbert Jacob et al., *Courts, Law, and Politics in Comparative Perspective,* Yale University Press, New Haven and London, 1996, pp. 81–176.

Lancaster, Thomas D.: "The Government of Spain," in Michael Curtis (ed.), *Western European Government and Politics,* Longman, New York, 1997, pp. 282–340.

Landfried, Christine: "The Judicialization of Politics in Germany," *International Political Science Review,* vol. 15, no. 2, 1994, pp. 113–24.

Morel, Laurence: "France: Towards a Less Controversial Use of the Referendum?", in Michael Gallagher and Pier Vincenzo Uleri (eds.), *The Referendum Experience in Europe,* Macmillan, Basingstoke, 1996, pp. 66–85.

Müller, Wolfgang C.: "Austrian Governmental Institutions: Do They Matter?", in Kurt Richard Luther and Wolfgang C. Müller (eds.), *Politics in Austria: Still a Case of Consociationalism?* Frank Cass, London, 1992, pp. 99–131.

Murphy, Walter: "Constitutions, Constitutionalism, and Democracy," in Douglas Greenberg, Stanley N. Katz, Melanie Beth Oliviero and Steven C. Wheatley (eds.), *Constitutionalism and Democracy: Transitions in the Contemporary World,* Oxford University Press, New York and Oxford, 1993, pp. 3–25.

Newton, Michael T.: *Institutions of Modern Spain: a Political and Economic Guide,* Cambridge University Press, Cambridge, 1997.

Norton, Philip: *The Constitution in Flux,* Martin Robertson, Oxford, 1982.

Oliver, Dawn: "Pepper v. Hart: A Suitable Case for Reference to Hansard?" *Public Law,* Spring 1993, pp. 5–13.

Preuss, Ulrich K.: "The Political Meaning of Constitutionalism," in Richard K. Bellamy (ed.), *Constitutionalism, Democracy and Sovereignty: American and European Perspectives,* Avebury, Aldershot, 1996, pp. 11–27.

Provine, Doris Marie: "Courts in the Political Process in France," in Herbert Jacob et al., *Courts, Law, and Politics in Comparative Perspective,* Yale University Press, New Haven and London, 1996, pp. 177–248.

Sartori, Giovanni: "Constitutionalism: a Preliminary Discussion," *American Political Science Review,* vol. 56, no. 4, 1962, pp. 853–64.

Scheltma, Michiel: "Constitutional Development in the Netherlands: Towards a Weaker Parliament and Stronger Courts," in Joachim Jens Hesse and Nevil Johnson (eds.), *Constitutional Policy and Change in Europe,* Oxford University Press, Oxford and New York, 1995, pp. 200–13.

Shapiro, Martin: *Courts: A Comparative and Political Analysis,* University of Chicago Press, Chicago and London, 1981.

Shapiro, Martin, and Alec Stone: "The New Constitutional Politics of Europe," *Comparative Political Studies,* vol. 26, no. 4, 1994, pp. 397–420.

Sterett, Susan: "Judicial Review in Britain," *Comparative Political Studies,* vol. 26, no. 4, 1994, pp. 421–42.

Stjernquist, Nils: "Judicial Review and the Rule of Law: Comparing the United States and Sweden," *Policy Studies Journal,* vol. 19, no. 1, 1990, pp. 106–15.

Stone, Alec: *The Birth of Judicial Politics in France: The Constitutional Council in Comparative Perspective,* Oxford University Press, New York and Oxford, 1992.

Stone, Alec: "Constitutional Politics and Malaise in France," in John T. S. Keeler and Martin A. Schain (eds.), *Chirac's Challenge: Liberalization, Europeanization, and Malaise in France,* Macmillan, Basingstoke, 1996, pp. 53–83.

Sturgess, Garry, and Philip Chubb: *Judging the World: Law and Politics in the World's Leading Courts,* Butterworths, Sydney, 1988.

Suksi, Markku: *Bringing in the People: A Comparison of the Constitutional Forms and Practices of the Referendum,* Martinus Nijhoff, Dordrecht, 1993.

Tate, C. Neal, and Torbjörn Vallinder (eds.): *The Global Expansion of Judicial Power,* New York University Press, New York, 1995.

ten Kate, Jan, and Peter J. van Koppen: "Judicialization of Politics in the Netherlands:

Towards a Form of Judicial Review," *International Political Science Review,* vol. 15, no. 2, 1994, pp. 143–51.

van Koppen, Peter J.: "Judicial Policy-Making in the Netherlands: The Case-by-Case Method," in Mary L. Volcansek (ed.), *Judicial Politics and Policy-Making in Western Europe,* Frank Cass, London, 1992, pp. 80–92.

Verougstraete, Ivan: "Judicial Politics in Belgium," in Mary L. Volcansek (ed.), *Judicial Politics and Policy-Making in Western Europe,* Frank Cass, London, 1992, pp. 93–108.

Volcansek, Mary L.: "Judicial Review in Italy: a Reflection of the United States?", *Policy Studies Journal,* vol. 19, no. 1, 1990, pp. 127–39.

Volcansek, Mary L: "Judicial Activism in Italy," in Kenneth M. Holland (ed.), *Judicial Activism in Comparative Perspective,* Macmillan, Basingstoke, 1991, pp. 117–32.

Volcansek, Mary L: "Judges, Courts and Policy-Making in Western Europe," in Mary L. Volcansek (ed.), *Judicial Politics and Policy-Making in Western Europe,* Frank Cass, London, 1992, pp. 1–8.

Volcansek, Mary L.: "Political Power and Judicial Review in Italy," *Comparative Political Studies,* vol. 26, no. 4, 1994, pp. 492–509.

Waldron, Jeremy: *The Law,* Routledge, London and New York, 1990.

3

THE EXECUTIVE

THE HEAD OF STATE

The most distinctive features of European parliamentary democracies have to do with the political executive, the "government" that actually runs each country. By far the most important of these features is that the executive in general, and the chief executive in particular, are not elected directly. Instead, they are chosen, indirectly, from the legislature. Related to this is the fact that the head of state is not in most cases the chief executive (France is the exception). Rather, he or she is a figure who is intended to be "above" day-to-day politics, someone who is more of a figurehead, albeit one with a number of significant symbolic, procedural, and diplomatic roles.

European countries do not tend to have a clear-cut formal separation of powers between legislature and executive as in the United States. In European parliamentary democracies, however, there is nearly always a very clear separation of powers between the political executive and the constitutional head of state. This is a historical product of the evolution of many European states from traditional autocratic monarchies into the democracies that exist today. Many modern European states, indeed, are still headed by monarchs: the list of "constitutional monarchies" embraces Belgium, Britain, Denmark, the Netherlands, Norway, Spain, and Sweden, while Luxembourg's head of state is a grand duke (see Table 3-1). Furthermore, Europe's republics have tended to evolve a role for the president, as head of state, that is very much like that of a constitutional monarch. This role is typically that of a mature public figure above the mundane, albeit vital, details of day-to-day politics, fulfilling instead the elevated functions required of any head of state in a constitutional democracy.

These functions are symbolic (as a personal embodiment of the nation for all to see and for some to love and respect); procedural (presiding over major state

TABLE 3-1   HEADS OF STATE IN WESTERN EUROPE, 2000

	Constitutional status of head of state	Head of State (January 2000)	When came to office	How came to office
Austria	President	Thomas Klestil	1992	Direct election
Belgium	Monarch	King Albert III	1993	Heredity
Denmark	Monarch	Queen Margrethe II	1972	Heredity
Finland	President	Tarja Halonen	2000	Direct election
France	President	Jacques Chirac	1995	Direct election
Germany	President	Johannes Rau	1999	Election by legislature
Greece	President	Kostis Stephanopoulos	1995	Election by legislature
Iceland	President	Ólafur Ragnar Grímsson	1996	Direct election
Ireland	President	Mary McAleese	1997	Direct election
Italy	President	Carlo Azeglio Ciampi	1999	Election by legislature
Luxembourg	Grand Duke	Grand Duke Jean	1964	Heredity
Malta	President	Guido de Marco	1999	Election by legislature
Netherlands	Monarch	Queen Beatrix	1980	Heredity
Norway	Monarch	King Harald	1991	Heredity
Portugal	President	Jorge Sampaio	1996	Direct election
Spain	Monarch	King Juan Carlos	1975	Heredity*
Sweden	Monarch	King Carl XVI Gustaf	1973	Heredity
Switzerland	President	Adolf Olgi	2000	Election by legislature
United Kingdom	Monarch	Queen Elizabeth II	1952	Heredity

*Spain was a republic from 1931 to 1975. Juan Carlos, grandson of the king ousted in 1931, was nominated by the dictator General Franco to succeed him as head of state, and took over this position when Franco died in 1975.

occasions such as the opening of parliament, providing the final ratification of laws, and so on); or diplomatic (the most important of these being greeting other heads of state and visiting dignitaries). The only real European exception to this model is France, which has a much less clear-cut separation of powers between parliament and the presidency and, in consequence, a much more "politicized" presidency, along U.S. lines.

"Semi-Presidentialism" in France

The president of France has the formal power to appoint the prime minister and chair cabinet meetings; he or she can also dismiss the prime minister and dissolve parliament. Even so, France does not have a full-fledged presidential system like that of the United States, because the constitution clips the president's wings in a number of ways. In consequence, what operates in France is a blend of the parliamentary system practiced in most other western European states and American-style presidentialism. These arrangements have formed the basis for a model of a "semi-presidential" system, which was of considerable interest to the constitution-builders of the newly democratizing states of eastern Europe. (For a discussion of the concept of semi-presidentialism, Elgie 1999a).

For a long time after the introduction of France's new constitution in 1958, the president's party had a majority of seats in the National Assembly, and the president's preeminence was not challenged. This meant that it was not easy to tell whether the French president could exercise real power in the face of determined opposition. It was unclear whether what appeared to be the considerable power of the president was at least in part a product of having the same party typically in control of both the legislature and the presidency. Since 1986, however, there have been several periods during which the positions of president and prime minister have been controlled by different parties, and we have learned quite a bit more about the relationship between the two offices.

Between 1986 and 1988, and between 1993 and 1995, the socialist President François Mitterrand was confronted by a legislature controlled by the parties of the right. In 1986, Mitterrand chose the right-wing leader Jacques Chirac as prime minister—he had little choice, as any other appointee would have been voted down by the assembly—and there was an uneasy two-year period of "cohabitation" during which each leader felt constrained by the powers of the other. This came to an end when Mitterrand defeated Chirac in the 1988 presidential election; Mitterrand immediately dissolved the assembly, and the socialists won enough seats at the ensuing elections to be able to form a government with the aid of some centrist members of parliament.

The term of office of the French president is quite long, at seven years. Thus, Mitterrand was still in office when the situation was repeated in 1993: the right won a sweeping victory in legislative elections and came to dominate the assembly. Mitterrand was once more forced to appoint a right-wing prime minister, this time Edouard Balladur, and to begin another period of cohabitation. This time the cohabitation proved

French President Francois Mitterrand (right) and Prime Minsiter Jacques Chirac during their uneasy political "cohabitation." © Orban/Corbis/Sygma

President Mitterrand and Prime Minister Balladur, however, found cohabitation more congenial, despite their different political backgrounds. © Denange Francis/Liaison Agency

to be more harmonious, perhaps because Mitterrand, now an old man at the end of his political career, did not see Balladur as a rival. It may also have been because Balladur himself, who had ambitions to run as a candidate in the 1995 presidential elections but knew he would not be contesting the presidency with Mitterrand, adopted a less confrontational attitude. This period ended when, after a period of infighting among the Gaullists, it was Jacques Chirac, not Edouard Balladur, who won the presidential election for the Gaullists. Chirac appointed another Gaullist, Alain Juppé, as prime minister and both offices were once again, briefly, in the hands of the same party.

Having turned his face against calling a general election after winning the presidency, Chirac was forced to call one on less favorable terms in 1997. The elections were won by the left, and on 2 June 1997, Chirac appointed the Socialist leader Lionel Jospin to the position of prime minister. Jospin immediately formed a coalition administration that included both the Communists and the Greens. Once more, there was a radical divergence between partisan control of the presidency and that of the prime ministership. Once more, the power of a French president was seen to wane very considerably when he was confronted by a prime minister of a different party. (For a discussion of relations between President and government in France, see Elgie 1999b).

Thus the power of a French president is the product of a complex interaction between formal constitutional provisions and practical party politics. Formal powers seem to place the office of president in a class of its own in Europe. Practical politics show us that these formal powers only really begin to bite when both presidency and prime ministership are in the hands of the same party. While a general election that mandates a prime minister from a different party can constrain the French president in many important ways, in no other Western European country does the president have so important a position. European heads of state are not entirely without power, however. In particular, presidents who have been elected directly by the people potentially have at least moral authority behind them if they choose to intervene in the political process.

Directly Elected Presidents

Directly elected presidents can be found in six countries. Besides France, these are Finland, Austria, Iceland, Ireland, and Portugal. Of these, Finland has in the past come closest to being "semi-presidential" in nature. The Finnish constitution gives the president a central role in foreign policy, and the special circumstances of Finland's long land border with the former Soviet Union made this power a very important one throughout the Cold War. The long-serving President Kekkonen did more than anyone else to establish harmonious relations with Finland's powerful and potentially dangerous neighbor. The Finnish president was then also able to wield considerable influence in domestic policy. Even then, the initiative in policymaking lay with the government. Following the disintegration of the former Soviet Union and the end of the Cold War, a series of constitutional reforms in the 1990s significantly cut back the powers of the Finnish president. A two-term (twelve-year) limit was put on the tenure of any president. And the president's independent powers to dismiss a government that had not been defeated in the legislature, to dissolve parliament and to call new elections were removed. The result is a Finnish presidency that now has more or less the same, rather weak, powers as those found elsewhere in western Europe. (For a discussion of the powers of the Finnish president, see Arter, 1999).

In Austria, Iceland, Ireland, and Portugal, the president exercises certain responsibilities in specified circumstances but in practice does not get involved in day-to-day politics. In Ireland, for example, the political role of the president is extensively and explicitly curtailed by the constitution. The Irish president is not permitted to leave the state "save with the consent of the government" (Article 12.9). Any "message or address" to the nation "on any matter of national or public importance" must receive the approval of the government (Article 13.7). With a very few specific exceptions, any other power of the president can be exercised "only on the advice of the Government" (Article 13.9). Even so, the Irish president does have two important powers that could be politically important in certain circumstances.

The first is the power to refer bills passed by the legislature to the Supreme Court in order to test their constitutionality, a power that has been used on twelve occasions, some of them controversial. (This was discussed in Chapter 2.) The second is the power to refuse a dissolution of the legislature so as to allow new elections, once the prime minister has lost a vote of confidence. This power has never formally been used in Ireland; dissolutions have always been granted when asked for.

Nonetheless, the very existence of this explicit provision is an important constraint on the freedom of Irish prime ministers to call elections whenever they feel like it. Indeed, in November 1994 Mary Robinson, then Irish president, was deemed unlikely to grant a dissolution that many politicians wanted, following the collapse of the incumbent government coalition. As a result, for the first time in the history of the state, a new government was formed without an intervening election. This example illustrates very clearly that formal constitutional powers, including those of the president, do not actually have to be used in order to have a significant impact on events. The simple fact that they *might* be used can be very important in itself.

Indirectly Elected Presidents

In the thirteen other republics, the president is elected indirectly, usually by members of parliament. In none of these countries is the political role of the president particularly prominent. Despite this, it is unwise to write off any president, even one with apparently only formal powers and no history of political intervention. This is clearly demonstrated in the early 1990s by the actions of the Italian president during a time of turmoil in the Italian party system which was racked by a succession of massive financial scandals. In the face of these scandals and of the consequent collapse in the legitimacy and credibility of most of the established parties, President Cossiga abruptly ended a period of relative silence. He began to make regular and influential interventions in public debates, speaking directly to the nation on television for more than a hundred hours in 1991. With considerable public support, and using a series of what he described as "pickaxe blows" (*picconate*), he supported electoral and other institutional reforms, urged early elections, influenced the government formation process, and generally made his presence felt. (See Bardi for a description of this period.)

In a sense what we see here is the other side of the French coin. The French president is undeniably strong, but is much stronger when formal constitutional powers are reinforced by a favorable political situation. Other presidents, such as those in Italy or Ireland, are undeniably weak, but may become stronger in the event of a failure of the mainstream political system. It is obviously unwise, therefore, to write off the potential political power of any European president in times of crisis, even if it is easy to underestimate that power when things are running smoothly. (For a comprehensive and very useful discussion of the role of presidents in modern political systems, see Shugart and Carey.)

Monarchs

Those European countries that do not have presidents still have monarchs as heads of state. Many European monarchies are very ancient institutions, and monarchs might be thought of as anachronisms in the twenty-first century. They still can have an important role to play, however, although this is typically even farther removed from the cut and thrust of party politics than the role played by presidents. In the past some monarchs have succumbed to the temptation to intervene politically, using their power and position to favor some parties over others. This has usually caused widespread resentment and has rebounded on those who have tried it. It was the main factor behind referendums leading to the abolition of the monarchies in Greece and Italy, and the Belgian monarchy survived only narrowly in a vote in 1950. Royal houses that have remained aloof from partisan politics have managed to survive, and given the often high degree of public cynicism toward politicians, a king or a queen may command more respect than an elected leader.

The outstanding example of a monarchy playing an important role in society comes from Britain, where the queen sits at the apex of the social system and is even the head

Pomp and ceremony as Queen Elizabeth II presides over the state opening of the United Kingdom Parliament. © British Information Services

The former Duchess of York is one of a generation of British "royals" who enjoyed a more worldly and informal public persona than their predecessors. © AP/Wide World Photos

of the established church, the Church of England. Over a century ago, the constitutional authority Walter Bagehot identified the monarchy as a powerful force for preserving the status quo, commenting that the British working classes would never rebel against the established order because to do so would be to rebel against the queen, to whom they were intensely loyal. For much of the modern era, the British monarchy was so popular that the chance of any drastic change in its role seemed very slim. Modern media and changing attitudes have recently subjected the British royal family to intense, uncontrolled, and increasingly less respectful publicity, however. This publicity has focused not just on the glory and magnificence of the royal family in all its works and pomps, as it did to a large extent in the past, but also on the divorces, marital infidelities, and other forms of worldly behavior that have tended to portray members of the royal family as being pretty much the same as anyone else. For a monarchy that has traditionally based its popular appeal on being utterly different from everyone else, this has been a traumatic change, and little attempt has been made as yet to adjust to it. Some commentators now argue that the role of the British monarchy has been fundamentally diminished as a result.

No other European monarchy wraps itself in as much pomp and ceremony as the British royal family, but a monarch's very existence as a symbol of the nation can be important. King Baudouin of Belgium used to describe himself as "the only Belgian," a reference to the fact that virtually all others in the linguistically divided country think of themselves first and foremost as either Flemish (if they speak the Flemish language) or Walloon (if they speak French). The monarchy is one of the few symbols with which both language groups can identify.

In Spain, the monarchy exercised a vital political role in the years after the death of the dictator Franco in 1975. King Juan Carlos, designated as successor to the dictator General Franco, was expected to perpetuate the old authoritarian system. In fact, he quickly dismantled the Franco dictatorship and set up Spain's return to democracy. His intervention was also decisive in thwarting an attempted military coup in 1981. In successfully standing up to the leaders of the coup and ordering troops back to bar-

An attempted coup d'état in action: Spanish soldiers seize temporary control of the parliament building. This coup failed, and King Juan Carlos played a crucial role in protecting Spain's transition to democracy. © Hulton-Deutsch Collection/Corbis

racks, Juan Carlos played a major and widely respected role in protecting the Spanish transition to democracy. While the Spanish monarch does also have formal powers to designate a prime minister, who then takes office subject to a majority vote in the legislature, these powers have not been significant in practice, given election results that have usually been decisive. However, the combination of moral authority and formal powers means that the Spanish monarch retains considerable potential to play an important political role in the event of serious failure in the mainstream political process. (See Heywood, Chapter 4, for a discussion of the Spanish monarchy and its relations with the legislature and executive.)

In other countries, monarchies have deliberately shed themselves of the mystique often assumed to attach itself to royalty; members of the Swedish or Dutch royal families are as likely to be seen out and about shopping as observed dressed in the regalia of office. As the Dutch queen, not to mention Prince Philip, husband of the British queen, have found out, making the sorts of comments that are normally reserved for politicians can lead to considerable public disapproval. The political role of heads of state in constitutional monarchies is thus for the most part passive. Even so, as we saw with the case of Spain, the potential is always there for a more active role in extreme political circumstances.

Overall, then, modern Europe's monarchs and presidents cannot be dismissed as mere ciphers. Apart from the explicit powers that some of them have in the area of government formation, which we discuss later in this chapter, they can play a significant part in legitimizing the entire political system. However, it is true to say that they generally keep out of the risky business of day-to-day politics, so that real executive power in today's European states is typically in the hands of the executive branch of government rather than those of the head of state. At the top of this political executive sits the prime minister.

THE PRIME MINISTER

The political boss of most European countries, clearly, is not the titular head of state but a political chief executive. This position goes under many titles in different European languages but is almost always referred to in English translations as "prime minister"—although Austrian and German chief executives are always called chancellors.

A European prime minister is typically not only the chief executive but also the head of one of the main legislative parties, often the largest. The combination of these roles can create a position of very considerable power—far greater than that of a U.S. president. This is especially true in countries with a tradition of single-party majority governments, such as Britain or Greece. In these countries, the only real threat to prime ministerial power comes from inside the governing party itself, and such threats usually can be dealt with. (This is not always the case, however, as Margaret Thatcher learned to her cost when, in 1990, she was forced out of the position of British prime minister by internal power politics within her own party.) Even in more typical European coalition systems, it is usually the case that the prime minister has gained office by virtue of having a powerful bargaining position in the legislature, and therefore operates from a position of strength.

Margaret Thatcher was one of the most powerful prime ministers in postwar Europe . . .
© Dylan Martinez/Reuters/Archive Photos

. . . yet fell dramatically from grace as the result of internal politics within the Conservative Party. © Jacob Sutton/Liaison Agency

All of this means that while the formal powers of the prime minister are typically laid down in the constitution, the real power of almost all European prime ministers flows from practical politics as much as explicit rules. Perhaps the most important aspect of the power of a prime minister is the fact that he or she is the person approved by the legislature as the political head of the government. As we will see, this means that the choice of a new prime minister is the first and most important task of the new legislature after an election has been held. If the election result means that the incumbent prime minister can remain in office, then, for all practical purposes, he or she has "won" the election—even if the election resulted in the loss of large numbers of popular votes for the prime minister's party. If the election result means that the incumbent prime minister cannot remain in office—the ability to do which is tested in ways that we will discuss shortly—then the prime minister has in effect "lost" the election. Given the very tight discipline of most European political parties, this means that the prime minister's party will leave government and that a new party leader will become prime minister. Changes in prime minister are thus the most obvious and dramatic changes that can result from typical European elections. The practical political effect of this is that prime ministers and potential prime ministers have an utterly central role in the entire process of party competition.

A second important facet of the power of a typical European prime minister arises from the rather modest role of the head of state, which we have just discussed. In almost every European country with the exception of France and the possible past exception of Finland, the prime minister is also the country's premier political figure, the most important embodiment of the government in both domestic and international affairs. Both in popular political imagination and in that of the international media, a strong prime minister personifies the government of the country. The most obvious manifestations of this can be seen in the "summit conferences" that punctuate international diplomacy. Many other government members and senior civil servants are of course active in these, but the images that get into the media are of prime ministers shaking hands outside grand rooms, striking their most distinguished poses and reading out weighty joint communiques.

A third formal role that gives a prime minister massive practical political power arises from his or her combined position as both "first among equals" in the cabinet and head of a major political party. A prime minister typically has the formal power to hire and fire cabinet ministers. As we will see in Chapter 12, this power is very much constrained by the need to come to practical political terms with the leaders of other parties. The prime minister may have the formal authority both to appoint and to dismiss cabinet ministers from other political parties, but may well not have the practical political ability to do so. Even in coalition cabinets, however, the prime minister typically has immense power over ministers from his or her own party. This means that he or she is a very important gatekeeper, has great control over the political careers of party colleagues, and decides the distribution of the most coveted set of prizes in the political game. Obviously, this is a situation almost guaranteed to ensure widespread obedience, even if not genuine and heartfelt loyalty, from party colleagues.

A fourth element in the power of the prime minister is derived from the incredible complexity and specialization of the tasks involved in administering any modern state. It might be thought that this weakens the role of the prime minister—how can anyone be in control of all of this, or even know a fraction of what is actually happening? Of course, there is much that goes on that the prime minister does not know about, but the important thing is that he or she sits at the very center of the entire process. Whereas other members of the cabinet are given specific tasks, the prime minister's job is to coordinate these tasks and set the agenda for action. The prime minister thus has access to information about every branch of government, unlike any other politician, however senior, and this information is obviously a tremendous source of power. As guardian of the government's agenda, furthermore, the prime minister can play a large part in deciding which proposals are discussed by the government, in what order, and which of them are buried. Political scientists are paying increasing attention to the great—if often unobservable—power wielded by those who set the political agenda (Rosenthal).

There are several other sources of prime ministerial power, but it should be more than apparent by now that a typical European prime minister is a very powerful person in his or her own country. Nonetheless, it is also the case that a prime minister is by no means a dictator. This is because an unwanted prime minister can be disposed of, sometimes ignominiously and at very short notice, by one of three basic methods.

The first requires an election. An unpopular prime minister can be voted out of office if his or her party loses so many seats at an election that it is no longer possible to win the nomination of the legislature. The important point here is that it is possible in almost every European country, if the prime minister loses support in the legislature for one reason or another, for his or her opponents to force an early election and hence

BOX 3-1

EXECUTIVES AND HEADS OF STATE

France

France has an unusual executive structure in the European context, having a president who is powerful and directly elected. Executive power is vested jointly in the president and the cabinet (Council of Ministers). Typically, the president asks a senior legislator in his own party to head a cabinet, which may be a single-party administration or a coalition. When a president of a different party comes into office, he or she can dissolve the legislature once in any twelve-month period. The assumption behind this is that his or her party, having just won the presidential election, will win the subsequent legislative election and then be able to form a government. On three occasions since 1986, however, French presidents have been forced to "cohabit" with prime ministers from a different party. In these situations, the power of the French president is significantly undermined.

Germany

The powers of the German head of state, the federal president, are among the weakest in Europe. After a general election the president nominates a prime minister, the federal chancellor, but almost all other actions of the president must be countersigned by the chancellor. As a consequence, the role of president is largely ceremonial, although, as with the British monarch, the head of state could in theory refuse to call elections when asked to do so by the chief executive. This has never actually happened in either country. The ability of the legislature to remove the executive is constrained by the need for a constructive vote of no confidence, which requires that the legislature can bring down a government only if it can also agree on a replacement. Such a vote has been proposed only twice (in 1972 and 1982) and has succeeded only once (in 1982).

Italy

The Italian president is indirectly elected by an electoral college comprising both houses of the legislature and fifty-eight representatives of regional parliaments. He has some practical political power, arising from the right to dissolve the legislature and the fact that he remains in office for seven years. Given the chaotic state of the scandal-racked Italian party system during the 1990s, the stability provided by the presidency did much to enhance the role of the office and Presidents Cossiga and Scalfaro were significant political figures. In government formation, the president may nominate any legislator as prime minister, takes account of deals between parties when doing this, and does not necessarily nominate a party leader. Changes to the Italian electoral system during the 1990s, however, have encouraged the formation of pre-electoral coalitions—necessary to win first-past-the-post elections in multiparty systems. This has had the effect that the voters via election result, rather than the president, have chosen the incoming prime minister.

Netherlands

The Dutch constitution makes no reference whatsoever to parliamentary government, vesting all executive authority in the monarch, who appoints ministers and dismisses them at will (Art. 86.2). In practice the Netherlands has developed a parliamentary government system, although the queen still plays quite an active role in government formation. After an election or a government resignation, the queen consults all party leaders, then typically appoints an elder statesperson as *informateur* to identify the person best placed politically to lead government formation negotiations. These negotiations can be very lengthy, involving the agreement of an extensive, detailed, and technical government program, a process that can take up to six months. Once a prime minister–designate has agreed on a coalition deal with other parties, the queen appoints cabinet ministers on his or her advice, although there is a strong tradition that individual parties have control over who fills their portfolios.

Spain

Under Article 97 of the 1978 constitution, executive authority is vested in a cabinet led by a prime minister. The king proposes a candidate for the office of prime minister, and the candidate is elected by an absolute majority of the legislature. Typically, however, the results of elections in Spain have been decisive enough to give the king no practical role in government formation. The active role taken by the king in the transition to democracy has given the office high prestige. However, as it happens, Spanish election results have for the most part been sufficiently clear-cut to accord the king little effective room for discretion in the government formation process.

Sweden

The Swedish monarchy has very little real power and since 1975 has been removed entirely from the government-formation process. Instead, the speaker (chair) of the legislature nominates the prime minister, having consulted the leaders of each legislative party. If not more than half of the legislature votes against the proposal, it is approved, a procedure that allows the formation of governments that do not have the publicly expressed support of a majority of the legislature. The procedure in a vote of no confidence is similar. A new election must be held after four unsuccessful attempts to approve a prime minister. Once approved, the prime minister appoints other cabinet members, who are not subject to legislative approval.

United Kingdom

The United Kingdom is the only state in Western Europe without a codified constitution, so government formation is governed by custom and precedent rather than by written rules. The electoral system ensures that one-party government is virtually endemic, so that in practice the monarch asks the leader of the party with a plurality of seats in the House of Commons to form a government, even when (as in 1951 and February 1974) another party has won more votes. The leader of the largest party typically nominates a cabinet of senior party legislators, which requires no formal investiture vote in the House of Commons. Because the party almost invariably has a legislative majority, the only possibility of defeat arises from splits in the government party.

force the prime minister out of office. In order for this to happen, the prime minister must have alienated at least some former supporters. If the original majority in favor of the prime minister is transformed into a majority against, this must mean that some of his or her original supporters have joined the ranks of the opponents who voted the prime minister out of office. When this happens, an election can result and the prime minister's fate is then in the hands of the voters.

The second method of getting rid of an unwanted prime minister does not require an election, but does require a change in the coalition of legislators that originally put the prime minister into office. Politicians controlling the votes of a majority of legislators may get together and decide to replace the incumbent prime minister. They can do this by using a vote in the legislature if the prime minister does not do the decent thing and resign first. In quite a few European countries—Belgium, Finland, France, and Italy are examples—it is common for the prime minister to be changed as a result of legislative politics, without an intervening election. Although Italy is best known for this phenomenon, five governments formed and fell in Belgium between April 1979 and November 1981, without an intervening election. Similarly, three different prime ministers headed French governments, again without an intervening election, between July 1988 and March 1993.

The third way of dismissing a prime minister comes from within his or her own party. We have already noted that a prime minister is typically, though not inevitably, the leader of a major political party. This means that his or her practical political position can be destroyed quickly and effectively if he or she loses the party leadership. We will look in Chapter 10 at the internal politics of European political parties. For now, what is important is that parties can and do get rid of their leaders on a periodic basis, whether or not formal procedures are in place to do this. Losing the party leadership makes no official change in the status of the prime minister as prime minister: the seal of office given by the head of state cannot formally be taken away by any decision of a political party. Nonetheless, the position of a prime minister who has been stripped of the party leadership is always seen as untenable, forcing the person concerned to resign from office.

What is in some ways remarkable about this process is that the prime minister of the country, the most powerful political figure in the land, can be changed on the basis of the decisions of a small number of people inside a particular political party. In 1990, for example, a few hundred members of the British Conservative parliamentary party removed Margaret Thatcher, one of postwar Europe's best-known, longest-serving, and most powerful prime ministers, and replaced her with John Major. None of the 60 million or so other members of the British public was involved in this process, although it is fair to say that her increasing unpopularity in opinion polls was an important factor in her fall. Many of the members of parliament who helped force her out of office were motivated by a fear that Thatcher's unpopularity could cost them their seats at the following election.

Thus, although most European prime ministers are powerful chief executives while they remain in office, their positions can be snatched from them suddenly and sometimes quite brutally. Moreover, although some of the powers of, and constraints on, the prime minister are spelled out in the formal rules of the game, the effective position of most European prime ministers at the very heart of the political system depends, to a large extent, on their being able to hold their own in the cut and thrust of practical politics.

THE CABINET

If the prime minister is the political chief executive in a typical European parliamentary democracy, the political executive as a whole—the country's board of directors—is the cabinet. For most practical political purposes, we can think of the prime minister and the cabinet between them as being the "government" of the country. The cabinet comprises a set of ministers, and each minister plays two vital political roles. One is as the head of a government department; the other is as member of the cabinet itself, which at least in theory makes most of the important political decisions.

The first role of a cabinet minister is to be the political head of one of the major departments of state. These departments can vary dramatically in size, both between and within countries. In Sweden, for example, the core civil service is very small, since so much policy implementation and administration is decentralized. Thus it has been estimated that fewer than three thousand civil servants are directly involved in the policy process in Sweden (Larsson). This contrasts with the huge size of a number of government departments in Britain, for example. Whatever the size of the department concerned, however, its administration of government is made politically accountable by virtue of the fact that each government department is under the jurisdiction of a cabinet minister. This minister is directly responsible to the cabinet as a whole for the affairs of his or her department, as well as being responsible for this to the legislature, and thus, via the legislature, to the electorate. If there are any problems in the department, the theory is that the buck stops with the minister, whether the minister knew about the problems or not. Indeed, a minister may even be forced to resign in response to a problem or scandal of which he or she had no knowledge. It is this accountability that gives the minister an incentive to ensure that the department is run properly. It must be said that in practice, however, there is an increasing reluctance on the part of ministers to resign in response to departmental problems over which they did not, and in practice could not, have any real knowledge. The real-world position is that ministers tend to be forced out of office over major policy catastrophes or scandals for which they bear at least indirect responsibility, and otherwise are given a hard time politically, but rarely sacked, when something bad happens on their departmental watch.

The second key role for a cabinet minister is as a member of the government, which is legally viewed in each European parliamentary democracy as a collective entity. What this means is that members of the cabinet sink or swim together, bound by a doctrine of "collective cabinet responsibility." This doctrine means that even though ministers may debate issues very intensely in cabinet meetings, once a cabinet decision has been taken, it becomes cabinet policy. Every cabinet member is then bound not only to observe the decision but also to defend it in public, even if he or she violently opposed it in private. If a minister cannot stand over a cabinet decision in this way, then he or she must resign or face dismissal; this type of situation is in practice one of the main sources of ministerial resignations.

In Greece, for example, collective cabinet responsibility is enshrined in a formal set of cabinet bylaws. Every cabinet decision must be signed by a majority of cabinet ministers, and even though individual ministers can record their dissent, they cannot state this dissent in public once a collective decision has been made. Failure to observe this rule can lead to dismissal. A minister is obliged to sign all decisions relating to his or her own ministry, or face dismissal (Koutsoukis). While the Greek case involves a very explicit set of rules, the informal rules of the cabinet game are much the same in most European parliamentary democracies.

Regardless of the formal or informal rules, one of the hard facts of political life is that members of a cabinet do pretty much sink or swim together. Sometimes an individual minister may be thrown to the sharks as punishment for a major but self-contained blunder, but for the most part when a cabinet runs into trouble it runs collectively into trouble. It is this, more than any written rules or cabinet procedure guidelines, that in practice forces collective responsibility upon the cabinet. (For reviews of the role of the cabinet in a number of European countries, see Blondel; Blondel and Muller-Rommel; Laver and Shepsle.)

This second role for cabinet ministers, as a member of the body responsible for making most key political decisions on behalf of the government, sharply distinguishes cabinet ministers in parliamentary democracies from those in presidential systems such as that of the United States. In presidential systems, the role of a cabinet minister is far more clear-cut: it is to look after a particular policy area and typically be the political head of a government department. Responsibility for the overall political strategy of the government lies elsewhere, typically with the president and his or her staff.

The twin roles of a minister, as individually accountable head of a government department and as member of a collectively responsible cabinet, interact in a potent manner, given the vast volume and complexity of the business that any government must conduct. In Sweden, for example, it is estimated that the cabinet makes about twenty thousand collective decisions every year. Not surprisingly, most of these are waved through, by the hundreds, in formal weekly half-hour cabinet meetings (Larsson). The "real" business tends to be discussed in far more informal settings, including daily lunches that all ministers who are in Stockholm tend to eat together. While the details may differ, this sheer weight of business can be found in most modern European cabinet systems. The bottom line is that there is a huge volume of formal business to be nodded through, accompanied by a much smaller number of urgent, complex policy problems and initiatives.

This vast volume of business means that the only effective way in which a fully developed and implementable policy proposal can be put to the government is that it be developed within one or more government departments. The cabinet does not and cannot simply sit around in a meeting and make policy in a vacuum. Real-world policy making on complex issues involves the cabinet's accepting, rejecting, or amending specific and detailed policy proposals that are presented to it, based on extensive and often very technical documentation. Only the government department with responsibility for the policy area in question has the resources and expertise to generate such a proposal. Thus, only the minister in charge of the relevant department is in a position to present the policy proposal at cabinet, giving him or her a privileged position in the policy area in question.

An important consequence of this is that cabinet decisions on many matters are organized on departmental lines. There is in effect an intense division of labor in cabinet decision making, with each cabinet minister being responsible for bringing forward policy proposals in his or her area of jurisdiction. Conversely, cabinet ministers are poorly placed to make a substantial contribution to the formation of policy in areas over which they have no jurisdiction. The minister of foreign affairs does not have access to the departmental resources and expertise to develop detailed proposals on education policy, for example. The minister for education does not have the resources to develop detailed proposals on housing policy.

All of this combines to underwrite a norm that in the Dutch case, for example, is described as the "tacit rule of nonintervention," according to which it is frowned on for ministers to intervene in debates that are not directly relevant to their own portfolios. In part, this arises out of an understanding that as a minister it is not wise to give a hard time to a cabinet colleague whose future support might be critical for one of your own pet projects. In part, it also arises from a situation in which Dutch ministers do not have large teams of political advisers, and therefore tend to be briefed for cabinet meetings by their own civil servants. These may not know much, or may not be inclined to tell the minister much, about the affairs of other departments (Andeweg and Bakema).

This situation in Holland is fairly typical of other cabinet systems. The huge pressure of work creates a de facto division of labor that gives a cabinet minister a near monopoly on policy initiation in his or her area of departmental jurisdiction. Cabinet decisions may appear to be made collectively, both constitutionally and on the face of things. However, the practical policy decision that a cabinet typically has to make is between keeping the status quo and moving to some specific alternative policy that has been developed by the minister and department with responsibility for the issue in question. The result is that the effective choice of policy outcomes by the cabinet is very much structured along departmental lines. Although all ministers do take collective *responsibility* for every cabinet decision, each minister does not, and indeed cannot, have equal input into the *formulation* of every decision that is taken. In this sense, cabinet ministers inevitably put themselves into one another's hands.

THE MAKING AND BREAKING OF GOVERNMENTS

Parliamentary Democracy and Legislative Majorities

The fundamental principle of European parliamentary democracy, as we have seen, is that the executive is responsible to the legislature. The key constitutional devices by which this requirement is tested are legislative votes of investiture and confidence in the government. A government cannot form if it does not have the support of a majority of legislators. This support may be demonstrated by a legislative vote of investiture, in which a particular government is proposed and voted on and takes office if it wins majority support. Such support may be implicit rather than explicit if legislators abstain rather than vote against a prospective government, when a vote against it would defeat the proposal.

The practice of parliamentary government does not depend on the existence of a formal legislative investiture procedure, however. Even if no investiture vote is needed before a government can take office, the executive in a parliamentary government system must have the implicit support of a legislative majority. From the first moment it presents itself to the legislature, any government must be able to survive a possible challenge to its viability.

The procedural device that provides the legislature with the opportunity to challenge the viability of a government is the "vote of no confidence." The opposition may propose a motion of no confidence in the incumbent government. If this vote is carried, the government is deemed to have lost the confidence of the legislature and, under almost any European constitution, must resign. Motions of no confidence thus allow the legislature to replace the executive whenever a majority of legislators choose to do so. Alternatively, a government that is under pressure may propose a "vote of confidence" in itself or may convert an opposition motion of no confidence into a motion of confidence. If the confidence motion is defeated, then the government also must resign. In a number of European constitutions, the main legislative vote on the government's annual budget is also treated formally as a vote of confidence. For obvious reasons, the main budget vote informally has this status everywhere.

Table 3-2 lists a range of factors that have to do with the birth and death of governments and shows that it is almost always the rule that a government defeated in a confidence vote must resign. Switzerland is the only real exception to this process: Swiss governments, once formed, do not have to face legislative confidence votes. For this reason alone, Switzerland is typically not seen as a "parliamentary government" system. Even where there is not an explicit constitutional provision for this—the main examples are

TABLE 3-2   CONSTITUTIONAL FACTORS IN GOVERNMENT LIFE CYCLES

Country	Does head of state play active role in government formation?	Is formal investiture vote needed?	Must government resign if it loses confidence vote?	Can government dissolve legislature?	Can legislature dissolve legislature?	Maximum time between elections
Austria	No	No	Yes	Yes	Yes	4 years
Belgium	No	Yes	Yes	Yes	No	4 years
Denmark	No	No	Yes	Yes	No	4 years
Finland	Yes	No	No*	No	No	4 years
France	Yes	No	Yes†	Yes‡	No	5 years
Germany	No	No	Yes§	Yes	No	4 years
Greece	No	Yes	Yes	Yes	No	4 years
Iceland	No	No	Yes	Yes	No	4 years
Ireland	No	Yes	Yes	Yes	No	5 years
Italy	Yes	Yes	Yes	Yes	No	5 years
Luxembourg	No	No	Yes	Yes	No	5 years
Malta	No	No	Yes	Yes	No	5 years
Netherlands	Yes	No	Yes	Yes	No	4 years
Norway	No	No	Yes	No	No	4 years
Portugal	Yes	Yes	Yes	Yes	No	4 years
Spain	Yes	Yes	Yes**	Yes	No	4 years
Sweden	No	Yes	Yes†	Yes	No	3 years
Switzerland	No	Yes	No	No	No	4 years
United Kingdom	No	No	No	Yes	No	5 years

Source: Laver and Schofield, 1990.
*President "may" accept resignation in the event of a no-confidence vote.
‡Absolute majority if legislature required to pass no-confidence vote.
‡After one year.
§No-confidence vote must designate new federal chancellor.
**Motion of no confidence in prime minister must specify successor.

Britain and Finland—there is nonetheless a very strong presumption that a government will in fact resign if defeated in a confidence vote. The requirement that executives that have lost the confidence of the legislature must resign is thus the most basic rule of parliamentary government—fundamental in building and maintaining a government in modern Europe. If a government cannot win parliamentary confidence votes, then there is no point in its forming. If it cannot keep winning them, it cannot remain in office.

A major consequence of the fact that confidence votes determine the life and death of governments in parliamentary government systems, as we have seen, is that European executives do not have fixed terms of office, but are liable to be replaced at any time by the legislature. Thus, although individual European legislators are not particularly powerful people when it comes to passing laws and influencing specific policies, they do collectively have the power to make and break governments. (We discuss the role of legislators in modern Europe more extensively in Chapter 4.)

The fact that control over the life and death of governments is exercised through the legislative procedure of the confidence/no-confidence vote has far-reaching consequences for the degree of control that the people, via their public representatives, have over what governments actually do. While the legislature may seem to have sweeping powers to make and break governments, these powers may often in practical terms be as useful as the power to use a sledgehammer to crack a nut. In effect, the main form of legislative control over the entire executive is to throw the executive out at will. But many small transgressions by the executive may not be sufficient to warrant such extraordinary measures, and may thus go unpunished. This situation can be exploited by a canny executive, which can use its power to bring matters to a head by threatening a vote of confidence in order to force an uppity opposition to back down over many minor matters. In this way, an incumbent executive in a parliamentary democracy can get far more of its own way than the formal constitutional position might suggest. (For a fascinating elaboration of this situation in the case of France, see Huber.)

Even though the vote of confidence is a standard across nearly all European systems, most other constitutional rules of the game associated with the birth and death of governments vary considerably from place to place. These, too, are summarized in Table 3-2, and the overall process of building and maintaining a government is illustrated by the flowchart in Figure 3-1, taken from Laver and Schofield (1998: 63). Figure 3-1 shows clearly that two general factors are important in the process of building and maintaining coalition cabinets in Western Europe. The first has to do with the fact that no matter where you are and no matter how chaotic things might seem to be, there is always an incumbent government. The second has to do with the fact that some mechanism must be found for vesting the government formally with constitutional authority, a task usually performed by some ceremonial officer of state.

Heads of State and *Formateurs*

All governments derive their fundamental legitimacy (to put things in a rather grandiose way) and their legal recognition under the constitution (to look at the nuts and bolts of the matter) from somewhere. Thus, there is always something "above" a government, typically the constitution. In Europe there is always a person, typically the head of state, who has the job of "investing" each new government with its formal constitutional authority. As we saw, a European head of state may be a relatively powerful figure, as in France, or a much more purely ceremonial figure, as in Germany. Even if the head of state has very little power, however, one job he or she must always do is participate in the formal transfer of authority from one administration to another.

This naturally raises the question of which particular government the head of state should transfer governing authority to. In other words, where do new governments actually come from? Governments do not just emerge from thin air or appear under gooseberry bushes; they are formed by particular members of the political elite as a result of a very explicit and highly charged political process. Furthermore, while the vote of every legislator may in theory be needed to determine who is entitled to a seat at the

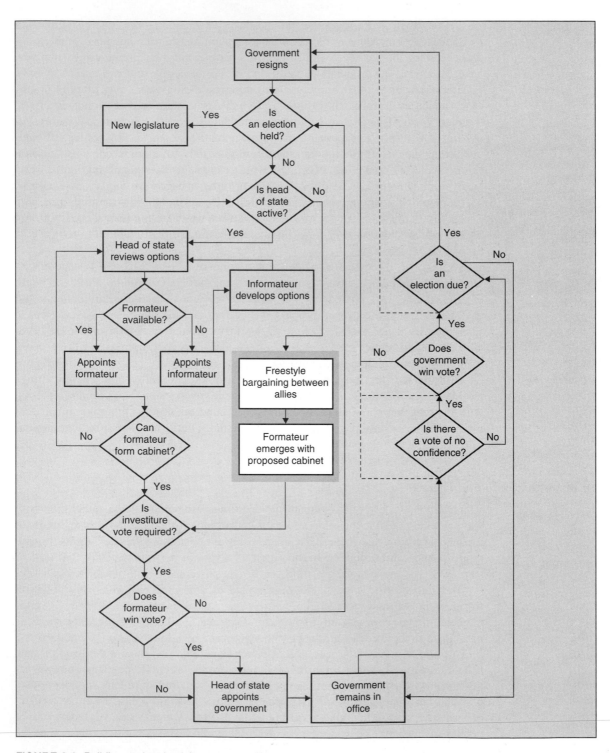

FIGURE 3-1 Building and maintaining a government.

cabinet table, the tight discipline of most European political parties means that in practice the actual business of forming a government is done by a small group of senior politicians. This group typically comprises the party leaders, in consultation with potential cabinet ministers. In general, therefore, we can think of the building of a government as something that is thrashed out between party leaders and presided over by the head of state.

Table 3-2 and Figure 3-1 show that European countries can be divided into those in which the head of state plays an active role in government formation and those in which he or she has a purely formal "swearing in" function, doing little more than passing on the seals of office and shaking the hand of the incoming prime minister. Where the head of state does play an active role, this typically involves choosing a particular senior politician to initiate the process of forming a government, effectively designating this person as a potential prime minister. This designated government builder is referred to by political scientists, adopting the usage of a number of European countries, as a *formateur.*

In some countries, Greece for example, it is formally laid down that in the event that no single party has a legislative majority, the head of state should first designate the leader of the largest party as *formateur.* If this person fails to form a government, then the head of state must then ask the leader of the second-largest party to be *formateur,* and so on. This procedure has the interesting consequence that the process of government formation is very sensitive to election results, giving all parties a real incentive to fight elections hard in order to become the largest. This runs counter to the conventional wisdom about coalition government, which is that coalition weakens the link between voters and governments. Where this rule is rigidly applied, of course, the role of the head of state in government formation could equally well, though less congenially, be filled by a machine that identified the largest party.

In other countries, Britain and Ireland for example, the strong implicit convention is that the initiative lies with the outgoing government. Even if the government has lost support in the election that has just been held, the outgoing prime minister is still given a chance to form another administration–to be the first *formateur*—before some rival is put in the driving seat. This may often be no more than a formality; a badly beaten prime minister typically concedes defeat on election night. Nonetheless, outgoing prime minister Edward Heath held onto office in Britain for a few days after losing the February 1974 election, before conceding that he could not form a government. Similarly, in Ireland in 1989, outgoing prime minister Charles Haughey spent some days trying to form a minority government before accepting the need for a coalition. In each case, the outgoing prime minister had a clear "first mover" advantage in the government formation process.

In other European countries, the head of state plays a far more active role in building governments, using real discretion and judgment in selecting a *formateur.* In the Netherlands and Finland, for example, playing a part in the process of forming a government has traditionally been one of the main jobs of the head of state. Of course, even in countries where the constitution provides that the head of state should behave like a machine, a particularly intractable political stalemate may force a president or monarch to use discretion to break a deadlock. A further device may be deployed in such circumstances in order to insulate the head of state from partisan politics. This involves the nomination of an *informateur,* usually an elderly senior politician or non-partisan public figure assumed to have no personal political ambition. Such a person may arrange formal round-table meetings between party leaders or move among politicians in an altogether more informal manner. His or her job is to investigate the range of politically feasible coalitions and identify people for the head of state to designate as coalition builders, or *formateurs.*

This system is an important part of the government formation process in the Netherlands, for example. The process begins after an election, when the queen consults senior politicians to get a sense of which governments are feasible and which individuals would be suitable *informateurs.* On the basis of these discussions, she appoints an *informateur,* who investigates practical combinations of parties that might both command a legislative majority and be able, in general terms, to agree on policy. Once the *informateur* has identified the most plausible possibility, and the *formateur* best placed to bring this about, the *formateur* is appointed and given the job of actually putting together a government. If this is successfully completed to the mutual satisfaction of all of those involved in the proposed government, and if these parties self-evidently command a legislative majority, then the *informateur* publicly announces his or her success and the queen installs the new government, without a formal legislative investiture vote. Thus the Dutch queen plays quite a significant part in the government formation process. Given this, the *informateur* system is designed to insulate her from explicit involvement in any associated political controversies, and to avoid the spectacle of the head of state trailing in person from party leader to party leader, trying to do the deal that puts together a government.

Choosing Cabinet Ministers

Once the *formateur* has been officially chosen, the next item of business is to choose a cabinet. If no single party has a legislative majority, then the system of parliamentary government implies that the cabinet must be acceptable to a majority of the legislature if it is to gain and retain office. Thus, the composition of the cabinet must be settled before the government first presents itself to the legislature. The identity of the cabinet ministers chosen is one of the major factors that legislators take into account when deciding whether to support the government, either explicitly in an investiture vote or implicitly by not attempting to remove it with a vote of no confidence. The group of cabinet ministers, taken as a whole, must be acceptable to the legislature and hence, indirectly, to the electorate.

The head of state invariably appoints to the cabinet any politician who has been nominated by the prime minister for a particular portfolio and accepted (explicitly or tacitly) by the legislature. Making nominations for cabinet appointments is thus one of the most important practical sources of prime ministerial power in Europe, particularly as European cabinet nominees are not subjected to the intense process of individual scrutiny and investigation faced by their U.S. counterparts. In single-party majority cabinets, the power of the prime minister to choose cabinet ministers is limited only by the internal politics of the governing party. In coalition cabinets, however, what almost invariably happens in practice is that each party leader nominates particular ministers to the subset of portfolios that have been allocated to his or her party during government formation negotiations. The prime minister and other party leaders may veto the occasional particularly controversial nomination by another party leader, but in effect the power to choose cabinet ministers for "their" portfolios rests with the leaders of each government party.

Because of its impact on real policy outputs, therefore, the overall distribution of cabinet portfolios to senior politicians is a vital part of the process of building a government and is something that party groups take very seriously when deciding whether or not to support a proposed new cabinet. Once a particular set of cabinet ministers has been installed in office, then control over many aspects of public policy passes to them. The legislature can reassert control only with considerable difficulty and typically only on the basis of cataclysmic threats to bring the entire government tumbling down.

Since being a cabinet minister is such a difficult and important job—one of the most vital in the country—we might expect that there would be only a limited set of particularly able politicians who are up to it. It is here that the twin roles of the cabinet minister, that of being political head of a government department and that of representing a party in the government, may well come into conflict. Politically, cabinet ministers may be chosen either for their loyalty to the party or for their ability to represent varying strands of opinion in it. The vagaries of internal party politics may well dictate that a party leader feels compelled to include some internal party opponents in the cabinet. Other leaders may choose to banish such opponents to the wilderness and reward only loyal colleagues. Whatever political considerations are taken into account, there will be a limited set of senior party politicians that the leader wishes to appoint to cabinet positions. At this point in determining who these people are, the leader will probably not yet have considered their ability to run a major government department.

It is clear that no party leader has an incentive to put a complete idiot in charge of a government department, as this is likely to have repercussions for the government as a whole. The person nominated must be someone judged to be at least capable of holding down the job without major scandal or disgrace. But it must be said that a party leader's room for maneuver in making cabinet nominations will already be seriously limited by the politics of the situation before administrative ability is taken into account. The process of choosing cabinet ministers, therefore, is by no means guaranteed to pick the team of people best able, in administrative terms, to run the major departments of state. This, of course, puts a premium on the administrative skills of the permanent civil service, a matter to which we will be returning in some detail in Chapter 6.

Typically, cabinet ministers will also be parliamentarians, although this varies considerably between European states. Indeed, in some countries a minister must resign from the legislature on being appointed to the cabinet; France, Norway, and the Netherlands are examples of this. At one extreme is a small group of countries—notably Britain and Ireland—in which cabinet ministers are almost always members of parliament. At the other extreme is a group of countries in which only between one-half and about two-thirds of cabinet ministers are past or present parliamentarians; Austria, the Netherlands, France, Finland, Norway, and Sweden are in this category. Other European countries can be found somewhere between these poles (de Winter). When cabinet ministers are not members of parliament, by far the most likely alternative occupation is civil servant. In the Netherlands, Sweden, Finland, Norway, and France, about one-quarter of all cabinet ministers are former civil servants. Elsewhere the proportion is much smaller (Thiebault).

Clearly, employing a senior civil servant as cabinet minister increases the chances of having someone who knows how to run a government department; the main factor taken into consideration in nominating a civil servant to the cabinet is thus his or her political persuasion. As we will see in Chapter 6 when we discuss the role of the bureaucracy in modern Europe, maintaining an overt political profile is acceptable in some European civil services, such as that in France, but it is more or less taboo in others, such as that of the United Kingdom. When cabinet ministers are drawn from the ranks of the civil service, however, it will obviously be necessary for those making the appointment to have a pretty good idea about the political orientations of those they are appointing. Thus, the practice of making such appointments encourages senior civil servants with designs on a cabinet seat to establish some sort of political profile and in this way politicize the civil service.

Whatever their background, however, the bottom line is that once they have been appointed to the cabinet, ministers are senior politicians charged simultaneously with running a government department, participating in the collective governance of the country, and representing the views of a particular political party in decision making at the highest level. It is this very politicization of the cabinet that ties the government to the party system and hence to the country as a whole. If a country were run by a powerful cabinet with no ties to the party system, it would in effect be a bureaucratic dictatorship.

Investiture

Once an agreement to form a new government has been forged and a cabinet has been chosen, attention shifts to the mechanics of installing it. These vary considerably across Europe, as Table 3-2 shows. In some countries—Belgium and Italy, for example—it is necessary for a proposed incoming government to submit to an explicit formal legislative investiture vote before it can take office. In other countries—Denmark and Finland, for example—there is no formal investiture vote, though the incoming government is obviously exposed to the possibility of defeat as soon as it confronts the legislature. Governments in these countries face an "implicit" investiture vote as soon as they assume office.

This distinction is important, as Kaare Strom has demonstrated, because the absence of a strict legislative investiture test makes it easier to form minority governments, in which the government parties themselves do not have a legislative majority but must instead rely on "outside" support from other legislative parties (Strom). Once a government has been installed, particular issues leave a minority government open to challenge; a particular piece of legislation or a particular policy may rouse the anger of sections of the opposition. As we will see, however, one strategy for minority governments, if they are not forced to face the test of putting together an overall majority on investiture, is to skip, on an issue-by-issue basis, from one legislative majority to another, with each majority made up of different parties. In such cases—Denmark is usually cited as the classic example—the government's "majority" may comprise one set of parties for one issue and quite a different set for a different issue.

In countries with a formal investiture requirement, however, this is not possible. The incoming government must present the legislature with a general policy program and a set of nominations for all cabinet positions. It must put together majority support in the legislature for the entire package and cannot rely on different majorities on different issues, because a single investiture vote must pass judgment on all of these important matters taken together.

Defeat and Resignation

Once a government has been installed in office in a typical European parliamentary democracy, it is free to govern until it is defeated in a vote of confidence or no confidence, or until an election is called. Once an election has been called, or once a government has been defeated in a confidence vote, the incumbent government remains in office to run the country as a "caretaker" administration.

In this regard it is important to remember that even if there sometimes seem to be periods when a country is "between" governments after one government has fallen and before a new government has formed, there is always a legal government, every minute of every day. This is because, to put it bluntly, somebody must always be available to sign the checks, and somebody must always have a finger on the trigger. Thus, when a government resigns, it does not actually stop being the government. Rather, resignation amounts to a declaration on the part of the incumbent government that it will step down and go quietly the moment an alternative administration takes over the seals of office. In the meantime, the outgoing government remains in office. If putting together an alternative government proves to be a problem, then a "caretaker" administration such as this can stay in power for quite some time, a situation that is not uncommon in Belgium and the Netherlands, where negotiating a new government can take weeks or even months. Conventionally, a caretaker government does not attempt to exploit its position by implementing any controversial new policy measures. But it does remain the legal government; its cabinet ministers remain the legal heads of government departments, with the power to set policy, to make patronage appointments, and so on.

Once a government has taken office, therefore, it remains in power until it can no longer win crucial votes in the legislature, and even after this it remains as a caretaker administration until it can be replaced by some viable alternative. The loss of parliamentary support by an incumbent government typically is brought about by the return of a new legislature after an election that was "lost" by the government, or by a change in the system of alliances in an existing legislature. The system of alliances in the existing legislature obviously changes if one of the government parties resigns and joins the opposition. It also changes if one or more of the parties that are not in the government, but whose support was essential for the government's ability to win crucial legislative votes, withdraw that support.

Faced with such a situation, the government often will resign rather than playing things out to the bitter end. Although shocks and scandals do sometimes fall out of a clear blue sky to destroy individual political careers or even whole governments, high-level politics in every country is a hothouse, in which everyone knows an awful lot about what everyone else is likely to do in particular circumstances. Prime ministers thus usually know when their government is going to be defeated, and often want to avoid any political damage caused by an explicit and bloody defeat. They may well leave office on their own terms before being defeated, by resigning on some pretext or another; indeed, this is probably the most common way in which a "beaten" government is forced from office in Europe. On the other hand, there may be circumstances—although these in practice tend to be rather rare—in which a prime minister sees an advantage in forcing opponents to show their hand in public on some issue and will therefore force the opposition actually to play things out according to the formal rules of the game.

There are obviously no hard and fast rules about this, but the important point to remember is that even when we do not observe governments being defeated in *actual* confidence votes, the need to win *potential* confidence votes is the fundamental criterion of the viability of any government. Once a government cannot win confidence votes, it can be defeated at will by the opposition. Whatever the precise circumstances of the government's demise, its political death warrant has been signed, whether or not an actual confidence vote takes place.

PUTTING IT ALL TOGETHER

The institutional theory of parliamentary government concentrates the political accountability of the entire governmental process on one key institution, the legislative vote of confidence in the executive. Parliamentary government can be said to be representative government because the legislature is held to represent the population as a whole (a matter to which we return in Chapter 11) and because the government is responsible to, and can be dismissed by, the legislature (Chapter 12). The administration of government is conducted by a civil service, overseen by ministerial masters who are themselves responsible to the cabinet and thus to the legislature.

In theory, of course, the legislature itself can legislate: it can pass laws that implement policy decisions. But control by the government over both the legislative agenda and the civil service—vital in the planning and drafting of effective legislation—greatly undermines the practical political effect of this theoretical legislative role. What a legislature can do in theory, and what legislatures regularly do do in practice, is to eject the government from office—either in an explicit confidence vote or in the threat to defeat the government in one if need be. This sweeping power can be used only in important political circumstances, giving incumbent governments considerable latitude to get their own way, even against the wishes of the majority, on many minor matters.

Nonetheless, one of the core principles of modern European parliamentary democracy is that a government must be able to survive in the legislature. This, when all is really said and done, is what makes modern European politics democratic.

REFERENCES

Andeweg, Rudy, and Wilma Bakema: "The Netherlands: Ministers and Cabinet Policy," in Michael Laver and K. A. Shepsle (eds.): *Cabinet Ministers and Parliamentary Government,* Cambridge University Press, New York, 1994, pp. 56–72.

Arter, David: "Finland," in Robert Elgie (ed.), *Semi-Presidentialism in Europe,* Oxford University Press, Oxford, 1999, pp. 48–66.

Bagehot, Walter: *The English Constitution,* Fontana, London, 1993 [first published 1867].

Bardi, Luciano: "Italy," *European Journal of Political Research,* vol. 22, 1993, pp. 449–460.

Blondel, Jean: "Cabinet Government and Cabinet Ministers," in Blondel and Thiebault (eds.), *The Profession of Government Minister in Western Europe,* Macmillan, London, 1991.

Blondel, Jean, and F. Muller-Rommel (eds.): *Cabinets in Western Europe,* Macmillan, London, 1988.

Elgie, Robert: "The Politics of Semi-Presidentialism," in Robert Elgie (ed.), *Semi-Presidentialism in Europe,* Oxford University Press, Oxford, 1999a, pp. 1–21.

Elgie, Robert: "France," in Robert Elgie (ed.), *Semi-Presidentialism in Europe,* Oxford University Press, Oxford 1999b, pp. 67–85.

Heywood, Paul: *The Government and Politics of Spain,* Macmillan, London, 1995.

Huber, John: *Rationalizing Parliament: Legislative Institutions and Party Politics in France.* Cambridge University Press, Cambridge, 1996.

Koutsoukis, Kleomenis: "Cabinet Decision-Making in the Hellenic Republic, 1974–1992," in Michael Laver and K. A. Shepsle (eds.), *Cabinet Ministers and Parliamentary Government,* Cambridge University Press, New York, 1994, pp. 270–82.

Larsson, Torbjörn: "Cabinet Ministers and Parliamentary Government in Sweden," in Michael Laver and K. A. Shepsle (eds.), *Cabinet Ministers and Parliamentary Government,* Cambridge University Press, New York, 1994, pp. 169–86.

Laver, Michael, and Norman Schofield: *Multiparty Government: The Politics of Coalition in Europe,* University of Michigan Press, Ann Arbor, 1998.

Laver, Michael, and K. A. Shepsle (eds.): *Cabinet Ministers and Parliamentary Government,* Cambridge University Press, New York, 1994.

Rosenthal, Howard: "The Setter Model," in James M. Enelow and Melvin J. Hinich, eds., *Advances in the Spatial Theory of Voting,* Cambridge University Press, Cambridge, 1990, pp. 199–235.

Shugart, M. S., and J. M. Carey: *Presidents and Assemblies: Constitutional Design and Electoral Dynamics,* Cambridge University Press, New York, 1992.

Strom, K: *Minority Government and Majority Rule,* Cambridge University Press, Cambridge, 1990.

Thiebault, J.-L.: "The Social Background of Western European Cabinet Ministers," in Blondel and Thiebault (eds.), 1991.

de Winter, L.: "Parliamentary and Party Pathways to the Cabinet," in Blondel and Thiebault (eds.), *The Profession of Government Minister in Western Europe*, Macmillan, London, 1991.

4

PARLIAMENTS

With only a few exceptions, European states are run according to the principles of parliamentary government, a set of institutions and behavior patterns that gives a particularly important role to political parties. Put simply, the decisive body in running the country is the government, but the government is answerable to, and can be dismissed from office by, the parliament elected by the voters at general elections. In classical liberal democratic theory, the government merely does the bidding of parliament: parliament makes the laws and lays down the policies, and the government dutifully carries them out. In reality, this was never really the way things worked, and it certainly does not sum up the relationship between governments and parliaments today. In fact, many have suggested that the wheel has turned full circle and that now governments make all the decisions and parliaments merely rubber-stamp these.

There are many reasons why the initiative lies with governments rather than with parliaments. The most important one concerns the central role played in European politics by cohesive, disciplined political parties that can ensure that all of their members in parliament vote the same way on all important issues. Before we examine the power of parliaments, though, we need to clarify just what we mean by "parliament," which should not be looked upon either as a unitary actor or as a body that has an essentially competitive relationship with the government. Rather than ask about the extent to which parliament controls or is controlled by government, we need to examine the role of parliaments in a number of areas, including sustaining the government, lawmaking, and scrutiny of the government. After this, we consider in depth the crucial role played by political parties in determining the place of parliaments in European political systems, and then assess the significance of the representation that is provided to Europeans by the constituency role of members of parliament. Finally, given that a number of states have a second chamber, often termed an "upper house," as well as a directly elected first chamber, often termed the "lower house," we consider whether it makes a difference whether parliaments have one chamber or two.

PARLIAMENTS AND GOVERNMENTS

The question most frequently asked about parliaments is this: how much power do they have *vis-à-vis* governments? But even though this question is very common, it is arguable that in most of modern Europe, it is simply "the wrong question," or, at best, "more confusing than it is illuminating" (Andeweg and Nijzink, p. 152). When, as in virtually every European country except Switzerland, the government is elected by parliament and can be ousted from office by it, it makes little sense to envisage parliament and government as two distinct bodies vying for power. In a presidential system, when president and parliament are elected independently of each other, such a perspective does make sense, just as it used to in European countries in centuries past when the monarch appointed a government without having to consult parliament. In the parliamentary systems of government that characterize modern Europe, however, it is more realistic to see parliament as wielding power *through* the government that it has elected than to see it as seeking to *check* a government that has come into being independently of it. This is especially applicable when, as is the case in many countries, many or most members of the government are also members of parliament. In such cases the government might be seen as a committee of parliament, one to which parliament has delegated certain specialized duties—in this case, governmental duties.

The reason why the "governments versus parliaments" framework is not particularly helpful for analyzing European parliaments is that both of these institutions, like nearly every other aspect of political life, are dominated by political parties, and these parties are powerful and generally well disciplined. As early as 1867, the British political journalist Walter Bagehot wrote of the House of Commons that "party is inherent in it, is bone of its bone, and breath of its breath" (Bagehot, p. 160). The behavior of both members of parliament (MPs) and ministers is likely to be conditioned more by their membership in a party than by their belonging to either parliament or government (Andeweg and Nijzink, p. 152). Virtually all parliamentarians in Europe belong to some political party or other, and their party expects them to support the party line on all important issues when it comes to voting in parliament. If the party is in government, this means that its parliamentarians are expected to support the government on all issues. If the parties making up the government command between them a majority of seats in parliament, they can realistically expect all their proposals to be approved by parliament.

For the most part, then, when we talk about "parliament" or "the legislature," we are not really talking either about a monolithic body or about the interaction of a large number of independent legislators; in practice, we are talking about the interaction of a small number of political parties. The organization of parliament's work is usually built around the various party "groups." We can take Germany as a fairly typical example. Here, the groups are termed *Fraktionen,* and the Bundestag has been described as a *Fraktionenparlament*—in other words, a parliament dominated by the party groups. The *Fraktionen* dominate the life of the Bundestag. The leaders of the *Fraktionen* form a "Council of Elders," which prestructures all debates, allocating speaking time in such a way that there is hardly any scope for spontaneous action by individual MPs. Each *Fraktion* decides which member goes onto which committee, and can recall members from a committee (Schüttemeyer, pp. 35–39). Although the dominance of the *Fraktionen* and their leaders in Germany is perhaps more marked than such dominance in many other countries, this is only a matter of degree; everywhere, MPs are very strongly oriented to their party groups, and it is the norm for the overwhelming majority of a party's MPs to vote with the party group in parliament. Parliaments all over Europe are dominated by party blocs; every parliament is to a greater or lesser degree a *Fraktionenparlament,* even if it is only in Germany that this specific term is used.

In this context, any constraints imposed by parliament on government come not from a monolithic body called "parliament," but from one of three possible sources. One source may be rules, which are not easy to change, that allow the opposition to block or defeat government plans. This is especially likely at times of minority government, and though minority government is sometimes seen as exceptional, examination of the record shows that nearly 30 percent of postwar European governments have fallen into this category (see Table 12-2). There might, alternatively, be rules requiring certain legislative or other measures to achieve the support in parliament of a qualified majority, perhaps three-fifths or two-thirds; this means that such measures need the support of at least some of the opposition parties. A second kind of constraint could be cultural; in some countries there may be political cultural considerations that inhibit the government from railroading its proposals through in the face of strong objections from the opposition, even if the formal rules allow the government to do this. The third is that the government may receive only conditional support from its own MPs, who may refuse to support it in some circumstances.

Writing over twenty years ago, Anthony King suggested that parliaments could be better analyzed not in terms of relations between "parliament" and "government" but in terms of a number of "modes" in which key players might interact (King). This typology has been refined by Andeweg and Nijzink, who identify (i) an inter-party mode, in which relations between different actors in parliament and government are determined primarily by their respective party affiliations; (ii) a cross-party mode, in which ministers and MPs combine to interact on the basis of cross-party interests; (iii) a non-party mode, in which government and parliament interact without regard to party (Andeweg and Nijzink, pp. 153–54). The third, non-party, mode corresponds to the "traditional" model that sees government and parliament as two separate bodies and seeks to assess the relative power of each, but in reality, given the centrality of parties to European politics, it is the inter-party mode that characterizes most of the behavior of ministers and members of parliament. However, we can expect to find a degree of variation across Western Europe, brought about by different institutional rules, contingent circumstances, and political cultures.

In discussing this, we can draw on Arend Lijphart's distinction between two categories of democratic regime. The first is the Westminster-type "majoritarian" model; the United Kingdom provides the clearest European example, with Greece, France, and Malta also displaying many of the characteristics of political systems in this category (Lijphart, p. 248). In the archetypal majoritarian system, the government of the day has an assured majority among members of parliament and can rely on getting all of its legislation through virtually unscathed, provided it does not embark on a course of action so far removed from traditional party policy (or so unpopular in the country at large) as to alienate a significant number of its own followers. In such a case, it would be likely to make concessions to its dissidents. The majority party or coalition is prepared, if necessary, to railroad all of its legislation through, regardless of the feelings of the opposition. Effective constraints from any quarter of parliament are so low that the situation is virtually one of "cabinet dictatorship." Moreover, the opposition sees its role as one of criticizing the government rather than trying to influence it. The second of Lijphart's categories is the consensus model; the clearest European example here is Switzerland, with Germany, the Netherlands, and Austria also in this category. As the name suggests, the emphasis here is on finding a broad consensus in parliament if possible, rather than on merely imposing the will of the parliamentary majority. In countries in this category, as in Belgium, cabinets "tend to have a genuine 'give-and-take' relationship with parliament" (Lijphart, p. 36).

Our expectation, then, would be to find that in Lijphart's majoritarian-model countries, virtually all relationships between governments and parliaments take place in the inter-party mode, with MPs and ministers having a strong party orientation that transcends any sense of "parliament" or "government" as institutions. In contrast, in consensus-model countries, we would expect to encounter somewhat greater recourse to the cross-party or non-party mode. With this in mind, we shall examine the record of European parliaments with respect to a number of roles in which they interact with governments.

THE ROLES OF PARLIAMENTS

Later in the chapter, we shall look in detail at the "upper houses" of parliaments that exist in a number of countries. However, in virtually every one of these countries, and in almost every respect, the lower house is the more significant. In most of our discussion, then, we shall concentrate on the activities and impact of the lower house. This house can have a role to play in three areas. The first concerns the creation, sustaining, and possible termination of governments; the second is legislating; the third involves scrutinizing the behavior of governments. We will examine the significance of European parliaments on each of these dimensions.

Appointing and Dismissing Governments

As we saw in Chapter 3, the government in most European countries is responsible to the legislature—typically, to the lower house. It often needs the approval of parliament to take office in the first place, and in nearly all countries parliament can force the resignation of the government by passing a motion of no confidence in it (for full details, see Table 3-2). This in itself shows that the familiar contrast between the "powerful" U.S. Congress and the "weak" parliaments of Europe is simplistic. Whatever else it can do, Congress cannot dismiss the administration, but even the humblest European parliament (with the sole exception of the Swiss parliament) has the power to turn the country's government out of office. If a parliament does pass such a motion of no confidence in the government, the latter usually has two options: either to resign and allow parliament to elect a new government, or to dissolve parliament and call a general election. One exception to this is Norway, where the life of a parliament is fixed at four years and "premature" general elections are not allowed. In addition, three countries—Belgium, Germany, and Spain—employ the "constructive vote of no confidence," which means that parliament may dismiss a government only if it simultaneously specifies a new prime minister in whom it has confidence.

It is true that European parliaments rarely use this power. For example, even in Finland and Italy, where the turnover of governments has been extensive, government defeats in confidence motions have been rare; in Finland there have been only four since 1918, and no Italian government had ever lost such a vote until Romano Prodi's centre-left coalition lost a confidence motion by one vote in October 1998. However, parliaments use this power so rarely because usually they do not need to use it; when a government knows that it has lost the confidence of parliament and that it faces certain defeat there, it will often bow to the inevitable and resign anyway. What is important is not how often parliament has used the power, but the fact that it possesses it in the first place. Because governments know that they can be dismissed from office by parliament at any time, they must be sensitive to the feelings of the key actors in parliament—which is to say, their own MPs and, if the government controls only a minority of seats, the opposition. Moreover, because most European countries use proportional representation electoral systems, which rarely give "artificial" parliamentary majorities to parties that win less than a majority of votes, most European governments depend for their existence on legislative coalitions composed of more than one party. This means that if the legislative coalition backing the government should collapse for any reason, an executive can fall quite suddenly, without necessarily losing an actual confidence vote in parliament. Thus it is quite common in some countries—Finland and Italy are the classic examples—to see changes in government between elections as a result of developments in legislative politics, changes on which the electorate is not asked to pass judgment. This power of parliaments, of course, is balanced by the constitutional authority of governments in most European countries to dissolve the legislature and force an election whenever they choose, as we saw earlier (see Table 3-2 for details). We need to bear in mind, though, that in most countries governments do not really have a completely free hand as to when they call elections. (We discuss this further in Chapter 11.)

Parliaments and Lawmaking

Parliaments, then, usually have the power to throw governments out of office, but this is rather a drastic measure. For the most part, those members of parliament whose attitude to the government is not simply one of uncritical support might prefer to share the task of lawmaking with governments, rather than simply leave this role entirely to government with the sanction of dismissing the government if it does not perform in a satisfactory manner. However, European governments are not always keen to allow MPs a real role in making laws. As we have seen, the very high levels of party discipline in parliament mean that if a government controls a majority of seats, it will usually expect to be able to rely on party discipline to push its program through the legislature. In addition, the government controls the civil service, a key element in planning and implementing legislation.

This marks one of the key differences between parliamentary and presidential systems of governments. The point is spelled out by Richard Rose: in liberal democracies, the American president is "the only government leader likely to have more than half his proposals rejected. A government with a parliamentary system is virtually certain of having at least two-thirds of all government proposals enacted as law" (Rose, p. 69). Moreover, not only do government proposals generally get adopted by European parliaments; the other side of the coin is that, in most countries, proposals not initiated by the government are usually unsuccessful. Members of parliament in Europe simply do not see themselves as American-style "legislators" with the role of initiating and piloting through pieces of legislation. Although most parliaments contain provision for a bill to be proposed by a deputy[1] or a group of deputies (termed a "private member's bill" in the United Kingdom and some other countries), such a bill, unless it is trivial in content, rarely becomes law unless the government decides not to oppose it (Mattson and Strøm, pp. 478–79). In terms of the standard categorizations of legislatures, European parliaments are "reactive" rather than "active," in that they possess modest rather than strong policy-making powers (Mezey, p. 36). A common theme in studies of European politics has been the "decline of parliaments," which have everywhere, according to some perceptions, lost to the grasping hands of governments the power they supposedly possessed late in the nineteenth century. By the middle of the twentieth century, it was generally agreed that governments acted while parliaments just talked.

Having said this, the amount of variation around Europe is such that we cannot dismiss all European parliaments as mere rubber stamps. As we would expect from our earlier discussion, the variation here is related to Lijphart's distinction between majoritarian and consensus systems of governments. Three institutional features of parliaments reflect this distinction and affect the significance of parliament's role in law-making. The first is that in parliaments in "majoritarian" systems, the government tends to control the parliamentary agenda, whereas in "consensual" systems this is decided either by consensus among the party groups, or by the president of parliament after consultation with the party groups (Döring). The second is that in consensual parliaments the most important work is done in committees, whereas in parliaments in majoritarian systems the floor of the chamber is the main arena. The third is that in parliaments in consensual systems, bills typically go to committees before they are debated by the full parliament, which increases the likelihood that they will be amended by cross-party consensus, whereas in majoritarian systems it is more common for bills to go to committees only after they have been approved by the whole house, by which stage the issues may have become highly politicized.

---

[1]Members of parliament have many different titles across Europe. In this chapter, we use the terms "deputy," "member of parliament," "MP," and "parliamentarian" interchangeably.

Although it may seem an unimportant feature, one indicator of the nature of parliament is often to be found in the seating arrangements in the chamber (these are illustrated in Andeweg and Nijzink, p. 158). In some parliaments, government ministers and their opposition counterparts face each other across the chamber, each with their own backbench supporters ranged behind them.[2] This format might seem almost designed to engender a confrontational attitude between government and opposition and to lead to an "inter-party" mode of behavior, and indeed, the parliaments that are organized in this way (namely those of Britain and Ireland) operate in just this way. At the other end of the scale, some governments (in Iceland, Switzerland, Italy, Austria, Portugal, Finland, Greece, and the Netherlands) sit together facing the entire chamber of MPs, an arrangement that may be more likely to lead to some kind of collective consciousness on the part of MPs that they constitute a body that is genuinely separate from government. Members of parliament are usually seated by party, but in Norway and Sweden they are grouped by constituency, while in Iceland places are allocated by lot.

Parliaments and Lawmaking in Majoritarian Countries   As examples of government-dominated parliaments, we can look briefly at the parliaments in Greece, Spain, Britain, France, and Ireland. The Greek parliament (the Vouli) takes the majoritarian model to perhaps its furthest extreme, showing, notwithstanding the previous paragraph, that seating arrangements do not always determine the spirit in which parliaments operate. The two main parties, New Democracy and PASOK, are bitter rivals, even though there are far fewer genuine policy differences between them than there were in the past. Almost all Greek governments are single-party majority governments, and the opposition in parliament has been powerless, with government taking no account of its views. Oppositions (both of PASOK and of New Democracy) have responded by being as obstructive as they could be within the rules of parliament, with their approach generally taking the form of "endless lists of speakers who make repetitive speeches which add nothing to what has already been said" (Alivizatos, p. 145). Parliament operates according to "a model of spectacular confrontation," and the chamber is merely a forum for "vague, repetitive and usually outdated monologues" (Alivizatos, pp. 144, 147). Virtually every bill passed by the Vouli is a government bill. Committees exist, but they are all chaired by government party members and have a majority of government supporters. Another southern European parliament, Spain's Cortes, is also government dominated, and has what has been described as a "docile" attitude to the government (Heywood, p. 100). In like manner, the relatively unstudied Portuguese parliament does not pose much of an obstacle to governments (at least when the government has a majority); most of the bills that it passes are private members' bills, but for the most part these are very small in scope, perhaps proposing to redesignate a town as a city, and they are comparable to the *leggine* (little laws) for which the Italian parliament has been notorious, as we shall see below (Leston-Bandeira, pp. 147–50). Portuguese members of parliament lack the resources to scrutinize government behavior closely even if they wished to; for example, the typical MP has to share an office with four other MPs.

---

[2]In this chapter, we use the term "backbencher" to denote any MP who does not hold a government position and who is not a leading opposition MP.

In the United Kingdom, the main nongovernment party, unlike nongovernment parties elsewhere in Europe, receives a special status—that of "Her Majesty's Opposition"—but, ironically, it has less influence than nongovernment parties in most other countries. Governments routinely command overall majorities in the House of Commons, and the opposition is reduced to making speeches against the government's proposals not in the hope of bringing about a change in its plans, but as part of an attempt to persuade the electorate that the opposition has alternative and better policies. For opposition members of parliament, speaking in the chamber, though ostensibly a contribution to the policy-making process, is no more fruitful than "heckling a steamroller," in the words of Labour MP Austin Mitchell. Critics see the Commons as a place of theatre rather than a serious working body, with debates dominated not by those with most expertise but by MPs who possess "meretricious rhetorical skills" (Kingdom, pp. 384–85). The Commons has developed a reasonably comprehensive system of committees since the early 1980s, but these play a role in overseeing the behavior of government rather than in actually making laws or policies. Even though speeches by MPs have scarcely any effect on legislation, the House of Commons spends quite a lot of its time on debates—mainly, some believe, as part of a strategy by the party leaderships to keep their restive MPs out of mischief and concentrated instead on the main party battle (Budge et al., p. 421).

In Ireland, virtually all legislation consists of government bills; a private member's bill passed in 1989 was the first in over forty years. As in Britain, parliament has been strengthening its committee system in recent years, and major reforms in the 1990s greatly expanded the scope of committees both in examining legislation and in scrutinizing the work of governments, although the real power still lies firmly with the government (Gallagher). In Ireland, as in Britain, the government has virtually complete

The British House of Commons is often seen as a place of theatre rather than a serious working parliament. Government ministers and opposition leaders face each other across the chamber in a confrontational manner and try to score political points off each other; these MPs are termed "frontbenchers", and the rank-and-file MPs who sit behind them and support them are "backbenchers". © Hulton-Deutsch Collection/Corbis

The Swedish parliament, the Riksdag, in session. Members sit grouped by geographical constituency, not by party, in complete contrast to the seating arrangements in the House of Commons, which encourage an "us versus them" mentality among British MPs. Government ministers in Sweden sit together in a separate section on the lefthand side of the parliament. © Toni Sica/Liaison Agency

control of the parliamentary agenda (Döring, p. 225). Another similarity between Ireland and Britain is that more than anywhere else in Europe, government and parliament are almost entirely "fused"—that is, all or almost all government ministers are simultaneously members of parliament, and in such cases any idea of a clear distinction between government and parliament seems especially artificial. It is worth noting, indeed, that all over western Europe, most ministers, even if they are not current MPs, were MPs at some stage (Andeweg and Nijzink, p. 160).

In France, the National Assembly is not effective at calling the government to account, though it does have slightly more initiative than its British counterpart in lawmaking. There is more likelihood of private members' bills being accepted by the government, and on a number of occasions governments have modified their own bills in response to the feeling of parliament. However, such modifications are likely to occur only if there is hostility among government supporters as well as among opposition deputies, as governments under the Fifth Republic constitution have many weapons at their disposal for brushing aside a recalcitrant opposition (Keeler; Safran, pp. 234–38).

Parliaments and Lawmaking in Consensus Countries   Turning to more consensual systems, we will look at the examples provided by Germany, Austria, the Netherlands, Scandinavia, and Italy. In Germany, the highly developed committee system in the

Bundestag is the main focus of parliamentarians' working week. Bundestag committees concentrate on technical details of bills rather than on general principles, which are more likely to be the subject of partisan debate, with the government prevailing. As long as the opposition does not obstruct the passage of bills, the government of the day is usually prepared to be flexible on the details, and there is a good deal of negotiation and compromise between government and opposition. The result is that on average, over half of all bills are amended in committee, with the great majority of routine legislation then being passed unanimously by the full parliament. As a rule, the opposition does not criticize government proposals full-bloodedly; in return, the government allows the opposition almost to "cogovern"—though relations usually become more confrontational as an election approaches (Schüttemeyer, pp. 42–44). The consensual nature of dealings between the *Fraktionen* in the Bundestag—that is, the frequent adoption of the "cross-party" mode—compared with the confrontational style of the British House of Commons, where the "inter-party" mode dominates, was made clear by the way in which the two parliaments dealt with the Maastricht Treaty in the early 1990s (Maor).

The Austrian parliament, the Nationalrat, is a significant institution in its own right. Its committees are sometimes charged with devising legislation in a particular area, with the full parliament virtually certain to accept their recommendations. Increasingly, the Austrian government merely outlines the main principle of proposed legislation and leaves it to parliament to work out the details. In addition, government backbenchers are more likely than in the past to reopen discussion on bills that the government had hoped were finalized and to be incorporated as "experts" in cabinet-level negotiations (Müller, p. 105).

In the Netherlands, too, committees of the lower house (the Tweede Kamer, or Second Chamber) play an important role in considering legislation. Although governments aim to ensure that their legislative proposals pass through parliament without too much trouble, parliament can set its own agenda and timetable, and is not dominated by government to the same extent as legislatures in more "majoritarian" systems. A significant proportion of bills passed do so with amendments agreed between government ministers and the Second Chamber (Gladdish, pp. 109–11). The MPs of a party that is represented in parliament do not necessarily feel bound to back every decision of the cabinet, and in the mid-1990s a government proposal concerning the route that a new road should take was defeated by parliament because some MPs of the liberal VVD party, which was part of the government, did not back it (Laver). While this case is exceptional, it demonstrates the relative separation of government and parliament in the Netherlands, which is markedly greater than in "fused" systems such as Germany or Britain. In the Netherlands, as in France, Norway, Portugal, and Sweden, government ministers cannot simultaneously be members of parliament, although in practice most Dutch ministers are former MPs.

Scandinavian parliaments are generally thought of as relatively powerful, as "working parliaments" rather than debating societies (Arter, pp. 200–44; Damgaard, 1994; Petersson, pp. 77–114). Scandinavian political culture emphasizes modesty and conscientious work rather than theatrical self-advertisement, and most Scandinavian MPs are oriented towards detailed consideration of the small print of legislation in committe work rather than towards making dramatic speeches in the parliament chamber (Arter, p. 215). A group of members of, say, the Finnish Eduskunta working their way line by line through a bill regulating the water supply may make for less exciting television viewing than a British opposition MP delivering a withering rhetorical attack on the government in the chamber of the House of Commons, accompanied by a chorus of supporting or dissenting voices with a bewigged Speaker in the chair trying to keep order, but there is no doubt about which makes more impact on the shape of legislation.

Denmark's parliament, the Folketing, is a significant institution. Some of its committees have real power: the Finance Committee handles the budget and can grant expenditures at any time on behalf of the whole parliament, and the Market Relations Committee oversees matters relating to the European Union, with the government needing to get authorization from it before taking a stand. Opposition parties, then, do not have to oppose the government all the time; they can actually make or influence policies (Damgaard, 1992, pp. 39–41, 48). Minority government is quite common in Denmark, and at such times the Folketing can be especially powerful. This was particularly marked in the 1980s: between 1982 and 1988, Denmark was ruled by a minority four-party coalition (the "four-leaf clover"), and this government often found itself having to implement bills emanating from the opposition. On over one hundred occasions, the Folketing passed bills, resolutions, and motions against the wishes of the government, but the government chose to stay in office "even if it had to implement policies with which it strongly disagreed" (Damgaard, 1992, p. 32). In Norway, Finland, and Iceland, too, committees play an active role in the legislative process, while in both Iceland and Sweden MPs have such input by serving on government commissions, which are very important in formulating policies (Arter, pp. 157, 227). In the Scandinavian countries, as in Italy and the Netherlands, the government has relatively little power to determine parliament's agenda (Döring, p. 225).

If the Greek parliament is at one end of the scale, being totally dominated by government, then the Italian parliament, the Chamber of Deputies, is close to the other end. Until 1988 there was provision for secret ballots, and since nearly all votes were secret, party leaders were unable to ensure discipline. Before 1990, the government's agenda-setting power was exceptionally weak: the agenda was set entirely by agreement among the leaders of the various party groups. In that year the rules were changed so that the government now has at least some input into the agenda. Committees, again in contrast to the general European pattern, have explicit lawmaking powers: they can give final approval to some legislation without having to refer it to the full parliament, and they scrutinize all other legislation. Until the late 1980s, most laws were so-called "little laws" (*leggine*), whose scope in many cases was minimal, and they were passed by committees rather than by the full parliament. It was a common diagnosis that the Italian parliament passed too many *leggine* and not enough substantive laws, although some disputed this analysis (Kreppel). Since the late 1980s, though, the percentage of bills that is approved in committee has declined dramatically (Della Sala, p. 91). The unusual power of the Italian parliament relative to government has not done much for its status in the eyes of the public, however. Its image in the past has been that of an ineffective, fractious legislature, whose members spent their time passing *leggine* to placate constituency interests while dragging their feet over more important decisions, which in practice are more likely to be made by agreement among the various political parties than by discussion in parliament. Consequently, when the entire Italian political system was enveloped by crisis in the first half of the 1990s, the demand was for greater system effectiveness, and the ability of parliament to block government plans seemed to be part of the problem rather than part of the solution.

Parliaments and Oversight of Government

Only some parliaments, then, play a part in influencing or making the laws, but all parliaments see themselves as having the role of overseeing the work of government. This function of scrutiny or oversight is, not surprisingly, carried out with different degrees of effectiveness across Europe. Parliaments have a number of methods of carrying out this role. Needless to say, opposition MPs are far more likely to want to scrutinize the government by means of parliamentary mechanisms than are government MPs.

Nearly all European parliaments have, as part of their weekly routine, some kind of "question time" (Wiberg, 1995). This gives members of parliament the right to submit questions in writing to ministers, and these questions must be answered within a fixed time, varying from three days in some parliaments to a month in others. In some countries there is a "question time" every day during which some questions are answered verbally by ministers; in other countries "question time" takes place less frequently. In every country, there are also questions that are answered in writing rather than in the chamber of parliament. Parliamentary questions allow members of parliament to extract information from the government. In many countries, however, they are used in practice more to try to embarrass the government by asking awkward questions than to find anything out, as the questioner already has a good idea what the answer is. In response, ministers often aim to produce answers that, although not untruthful, give away as little as possible. The pattern right across Europe is of an often dramatic increase in the number of questions that MPs are asking. A study of parliamentary questions in the Nordic countries found a very consistent increase in the number of questions asked over time, with most questions coming from opposition deputies. This rise was attributed to the growth of the public sector and an increase in education levels among deputies (Wiberg, 1994). Much the same pattern has been noted for many other countries. To give just two examples, between the mid-1960s and the mid-1990s, the number of questions asked per annum rose in France from 5,500 to 12,700; in Ireland, it grew from 4,300 to 16,000 (Safran, p. 243; Gallagher, p. 192). This upsurge in activity is usually seen as evidence that parliaments are wielding their oversight powers more effectively, or, at least, that opposition MPs are making more noise than they used to.

A similar but somewhat weightier weapon that most parliaments can employ is the interpellation, which differs from a simple question in that the reply from the minister can be debated by parliament if a sufficient proportion of deputies request this. There are far fewer interpellations than questions, but the number of interpellations too is increasing in parliaments that make provision for them.

The most effective method through which parliaments keep an eye on the behavior of governments is by means of a system of committees set up to monitor government departments: one committee oversees the performance of the Minister for Agriculture,

BOX 4-1

THE POWER OF PARLIAMENT

France

The constitution of the Fifth French Republic marked a reaction against the experience of the Fourth Republic (1946–58), in which parliament was thought to have too much power to thwart governments without being able to achieve anything very effectively itself. In consequence, the National Assembly is ineffective when it comes to overseeing the actions of the government or the president. The constitution specifies the areas in which parliament can legislate and allows the government to act by decree in all other areas, and it also contains many other devices to guarantee the dominance of the government over parliament. Some governments allow the National Assembly some degree of influence when it comes to discussing and amending bills, but if there is a confrontation the government holds all the cards. Deputies are seen by their constituents as emissaries from their districts to central government and have large casework loads.

Germany

The lower house of the German parliament, the Bundestag, is well organized, and its members (MdBs) have better resources to assist them in their work than parliamentarians elsewhere in Europe. The main emphasis of its work is not in grand debates on general principles of legislation in plenary session but in detailed scrutiny of legislation in committees, where there tends to be a good deal of cooperation between government and opposition parties. The work of each MdB is closely overseen by the parliamentary group (*Fraktion*), leaving little scope for spontaneous parliamentary action by individual MdBs.

Italy

The Italian parliament, the Camera dei Deputati, is less dominated by the government than most European parliaments. It can set its own agenda, and it assumes that it has a right to be consulted by the government before the government introduces legislative proposals. Its committees are powerful and can actually pass laws without reference to the full parliament. Much of its legislative output over the years, though, has consisted of "little laws" of benefit only to microsectional interests, which deputies have promoted in order to win favor with their constituents. When the Italian political system entered a state of crisis in the 1990s, the ability of parliament to block government action was widely seen as part of the problem, and steps have been taken to make it easier for the executive to govern effectively.

Netherlands

The lower house, the Tweede Kamer (Second Chamber), is by no means a rubber stamp for government. It can set its own agenda and timetable, and it plays an influential role in amending bills. Because government members cannot, under the constitution, simultaneously be members of parliament, there is, at least psychologically, a greater separation between executive and legislature than is the case in most other European countries, where government ministers are usually also members of parliament. Parliamentary activity has increased greatly since the 1960s, although opinions are divided as to whether parliament is any stronger as a result.

Spain

The Spanish parliament was suppressed during the Franco dictatorship (1939–75) and since being reinstated by the new democratic regime its pattern of operation has been evolving. Under the majority Socialist government of 1982–93 it had a marginal position, with the prime minister, Felipe Gonzáles, rarely taking the trouble to visit it even to inform it of the government's activities, let alone to be questioned. Although minority government over the following seven years potentially enhanced the role of parliament, in practice key decisions are still taken elsewhere, and the Cortes is not seen as one of Europe's more significant parliaments.

Sweden

The Riksdag differs from most parliaments in that members are arranged in the chamber according to the constituency that they represent, not the party to which they belong. For example, the twelve MPs for the northerly Västerbotten county occupy the adjacent seats 329–340 in the 349-member Riksdag. Not surprisingly, this can lead to "log-rolling" between MPs from the same region of the country on issues of regional concern, although for the most part MPs act strongly along party rather than regional lines. Deputies can play an effective part in the policy-making process, partly through the role they play on the commissions of inquiry that are set up to consider how problems should be tackled. Although politics in Sweden has in some ways become more conflictual, with the emergence of two clear-cut alternative governments, in parliamentary committees there is still a tendency to negotiate and to seek consensus.

United Kingdom

Ironically, although those who refer to a "golden age" of parliaments usually have in mind the House of Commons at some times during the nineteenth century, today's British parliament is among the weakest of European parliaments. A combination of single-party majority governments and a party system based on conflict between the two main parties leaves the parliamentary opposition with very little influence on legislation or on policy in general. The British tradition places great emphasis on plenary sessions in the main debating chamber—perfor-

mance in debates is important, for instance, in deciding which MPs should be promoted to leadership positions—even though there are few signs that those outside "Westminster World" follow parliamentary debates with much interest or that debates have any effect on government policies. Committees, the main forum for the work of most modern parliaments, have traditionally had a much less significant role in the House of Commons, although since the early 1980s they have been increasingly effective in scrutinizing the work of government.

another that of the Minister for Education, and so on. Such committees usually have the power to call the relevant government minister before them to defend his or her performance in office, and civil servants can be asked to make available to the committee the information on which ministers have based their decisions. Every parliament makes use of such committees to some extent, although, as usual, practice varies from case to case. Scrutiny of government by committees can be quite effective in Germany, Britain, and Denmark, for example, but it is not a strong feature of parliament in Sweden, Greece, France, or Italy. When committees become significant, interest groups seek to "colonize" them, so there is a tendency for the agriculture committee to be dominated by farmers and the education committee by teachers, for example, with each committee seeking extra resources for the special interests that dominate it. This pattern has been noted in a variety of countries, including Germany and Belgium (Saalfeld, 1999, pp. 57–61; de Winter, 1999, pp. 95–97). In such cases, even in majoritarian-model countries, MPs are prepared to operate in "cross-party" mode.

PARLIAMENTS AND PARTIES

All relations between governments and members of parliament, as we have seen, take place within a context dominated by political parties. Greater power for "parliament" therefore would really mean more power not for a unitary body called "parliament" but for the *Fraktionen* (the parliamentary party groups), or for specific actors within them. If the government controls only a minority of seats, then "more power for parliament" is in practice likely to mean "more power for the opposition." During periods of majority government, the main constraints are imposed not by the opposition but by the backbench MPs of the governing party or parties, and it is particularly difficult to tell how much influence these members wield. If government MPs are unhappy about a government proposal, this is rarely expressed in votes against the measure on the floor of parliament; instead, the matter will be raised behind closed doors at meetings of the *Fraktion,* and if backbench reservations are strong enough, the minister may have little choice but to amend or withdraw the proposal. What goes on at

these meetings, though, is unknown both to the public and to all but the most assiduous researchers.

In the context of party domination of parliament, it is notoriously difficult to try to
measure the power of any parliament. If a parliament approves every government proposal without making any amendments, we cannot be sure whether this indicates a
supine parliament or whether the government, obeying the law of anticipated reactions,
is taking care not to make any proposals without first making sure that parliament will
approve them. Consequently, studies of European parliaments do not usually indulge
in "roll-call analysis" as a means of gauging a given parliament's strength. One study
that did take the trouble to work out precise figures found that only 0.08 percent of individual votes cast in the Danish Folketing between 1990 and 1996 broke with the party
position (Skjaeveland, pp. 125–26). Clearly, when parliamentary members of any given
party vote together 99.92 percent of the time, it is obvious that the actors are the parliamentary party blocs, not individual parliamentarians. Indeed, in both the Netherlands
and Portugal the official proceedings normally record the votes of parliamentary parties rather than of individual MPs (Andeweg and Nijzink, p. 172). In Chapter 10 we
shall look in greater detail at the internal politics of political parties, but we can see
even at a cursory glance that the leaders of these parties are far more important people, politically, than the typical rank-and-file members of parliament.

The high degree of solid party voting among parliamentarians might suggest that
members of parliament are mere "dumb sheep" or "lobby fodder" who must tamely
vote in whatever manner the party leaders direct. This would underestimate the role of
parliamentarians. Although it is true that unpleasant punishments await those deputies
who are disloyal to the party, as we discuss farther on, the relationship between parties and individual members of parliament is not based entirely on the imposition of
discipline. For one thing, members of parliament belonging to the same party have a
natural sense of identity; their instincts are always to vote with their party out of a
sense of loyalty and common purpose, and for the most part they are glad to keep in
line and do not need to be threatened. Discipline within the parliamentary parties in
the Netherlands, for example, comes from group cohesion rather than from fear of punishment for stepping out of line (Gladdish, p. 113). Moreover, decision making within
each parliamentary party may be fairly democratic, so even those members who dislike a particular decision will go along with it if it represents a majority view. If a majority of a government party's backbenchers dislike a government proposal, the minister may be forced to withdraw it. For that reason, the success of virtually all government
legislation in European parliaments may represent the outcome of a bargaining process
with government backbenchers, rather than indicating backbench irrelevance. Governments will not proceed with legislation that their backbenchers have already indicated
they will not support. In Germany, it is common for the chairperson of each government *Fraktion* to attend cabinet meetings to ensure that government proposals are acceptable to the *Fraktion* (Schüttemeyer, p. 39). In Britain, too, while government backbenchers cannot succeed in having wholesale changes made to proposed legislation,
they may be able to persuade ministers to accept amendments if they approach the minister privately (Brand).

However, even if governments in some countries have to work a little harder than they used to for the backing of their parliamentarians, the picture is still one of very strong party solidarity in parliament. The existence of large and disciplined voting blocs is central to the practice of European parliamentary democracy. The coherence of European parties when compared, for example, with their U.S. counterparts depends on two basic and related behavioral phenomena. The first is that voters tend to vote for parties rather than for individual candidates. The second is that individual parliamentarians think of themselves first and foremost as members of their party's parliamentary group rather than as individual members. We will return to political parties several times in our subsequent discussions. However, we must explore these particular points now in order to be able to provide a comprehensive picture of European parliamentary democracy.

Voters Vote for Parties

When most Europeans vote in parliamentary elections, they are voting primarily for parties rather than for persons. Even in those few countries where the myth that voters choose people rather than parties is still cherished, prominent and colorful individuals who eschew parties and fight elections as independents usually come to a sticky end—often at the hands of faceless opponents wielding nothing but a party label. Most European parliamentarians have got where they are by being candidates of political parties rather than by being particularly outstanding individuals in their own right.

European voters tend to vote for parties rather than people in legislative elections precisely because when they vote, they feel that they are helping to choose a government. Because it is the government that has the initiative in shaping public policy, voters' main concern is with which party or parties will control the government rather than with the personal qualities of individual candidates. They therefore have strong incentives to look for a clear-cut choice between alternative governments, or, at the very least, between party blocs powerful enough to change the complexion of governments during the process of coalition bargaining. Except in very finely balanced situations, a legislator who is not a member of a political party is not likely to have much of an impact on government formation and maintenance, the single most important job of European legislatures.

The primacy of parties over individual candidates in Europe is made explicit in some countries where the electoral system is such that voters simply choose a party ticket without being able to express a view on specific candidates, something that we discuss in detail in Chapter 11. Even in countries where voters do have an opportunity to vote for individual candidates, the fact that it is parties rather than individual candidates who are ultimately important in European elections means that European legislators get a far smaller "personal vote" (that is, the vote won by a candidate because of his or her perceived merits rather than because of the party he or she represents) than their American counterparts. This is a direct consequence of the system of parliamentary government, and it has a number of political effects. Three are of direct relevance here.

First, because the size of a politician's personal vote is so much smaller in Europe than it is in the United States, the fate of European candidates is determined much more by national political forces than it is by what particular people have done for particular local constituencies. European politicians who want to advance their careers face incentives to concentrate on national politics rather than on the provision of goodies for their local constituents.

A second, related, matter is that incumbent candidates have much less of a built-in advantage in Europe than they do in the United States. In the United States, the incumbent is the one who brings home the bacon, thereby building a personal vote that provides a strong insulation from winds of political change at the national level. Many local incumbents in the United States are able to survive what appear to be national landslides against their party, resulting in an average reelection rate of incumbents of over 90 percent in House elections since the war. In Europe, in contrast, being an incumbent gives little inherent advantage when it comes to the next election. In Britain, for example, individual MPs can do far less for their constituents than their American equivalents can. As Cox puts it, "the mainstays of the U.S. Congressman's particularistic usefulness to his constituents"—civil service patronage and "local improvement" bills securing public expenditure on rivers and harbors, railways, roads, dams, canals, and so on—were all largely shut off from the influence of the backbench MP from the middle of the nineteenth century onwards (Cox, pp. 133–34). Because the personal vote is so much smaller in Europe, when the political tide turns against a particular party its candidates tend to lose their seats, no matter who they are or what they have done for their constituencies. It is true that under some list systems of proportional representation, parties can protect their senior politicians by placing them high on party lists (see Chapter 11) and that under other electoral systems, which pit candidates of the same party against each other, there is such a thing as a personal vote for individuals within the party fold. Even so, prominent politicians can disappear abruptly from parliament simply because their party is doing badly.

The third, and probably the most important, consequence of the fact that European voters vote for parties rather than for people is that party labels are very valuable commodities in Europe. This makes party legislators unwilling to do anything—such as voting against the party line in parliament—that might cost them the label at the next election, for if they are not picked as party candidates in the next election (a subject to which we return in Chapter 10), their political careers may well be over. And this, of course, is one of the main reasons European legislative parties are so highly disciplined. The battlefields of European politics are littered with the corpses of those who have defied the party line.

Parliamentarians and Party Discipline

As we have pointed out, parliamentarians usually follow the party line in parliament mainly because this is what their instincts tell them to do, not because they are being threatened with dire sanctions if they do not do so. If their instincts should happen to tell them to vote against the party line on some issue, however, they quickly discover that a range of punishments awaits those who stray from the fold. To put it another way, there are powerful incentives to vote the party line, whatever an MP's private policy preferences. We have already seen that one such incentive is fear of losing the party label at the next election, given that voters choose parties rather than people because it is parties rather than individual MPs that can influence the shape of governments. Party leaders have power over rank-and-file members of parliament because the latter know that if they become habitually disloyal to the party line in parliament, the candidate selectors (usually a group of local party activists) may well deny them access to the party label at the next election, and thereby cast all but the most resilient out into the political wilderness. The extreme case here is perhaps Ireland, where in July 1993 the parliamentary group of the country's largest party, Fianna Fáil, decided that in future any deputy who voted against the party line on any issue (or even abstained) would automatically be expelled from the parliamentary party. In Britain, the parliamentary parties have what are termed "whips" (the term refers to the "whipping in" of foxhounds in hunting, and as such is revealing of the strength of tradition in the House of Commons) whose job it is to ensure that all MPs follow the party line in votes. The whips control access to some of the perks of being a parliamentarian, such as attractive committee assignments, trips abroad, and so on, and every MP knows that such benefits will go to loyal MPs rather than to rebels. If need be, the whips will ensure the expulsion from the parliamentary group of persistent mavericks (Budge et al., p. 424).

A second source of power for party oligarchs is that if they are not already senior government members, then they are the people who will be senior government members when the party next gets into government. This means that European party leaders are the gatekeepers to political office; they can use this position to reward those who are loyal to the party and punish those who are not. In Britain's House of Commons, the most closely studied European parliament, there is clear evidence that the increase in party cohesion in parliamentary voting around the end of the nineteenth century was strongly linked to an increase in the number of MPs seeking ministerial posts and concluding that the best way of gaining preferment was to remain loyal at all times to the party leadership, and this in turn led to voters developing a strong party rather than personal orientation at elections (Cox, pp. 75–79). This now applies to virtually every European parliament. Thus, party discipline is made much stronger by the system of parliamentary government. Because the legislature is the main recruiting ground for members of the executive in most countries, those who aspire to executive office must behave themselves in the legislature. If they do not, they will displease those with the power to promote them.

PARLIAMENTARIANS AND CONSTITUENCY REPRESENTATION

The formal role of parliaments in the process of representation is clear enough, and to a greater or lesser degree may be stated in a country's constitution: the people elect their representatives, and these representatives, answerable to the people at the next election, sustain, monitor, and can ultimately oust the government. For many Europeans, though, a more tangible form of representation provided by their MPs receives little or no constitutional recognition. This takes the form of constituency representation, whereby an MP promotes and defends the interests of his or her geographical constituency, of particular sectors within that constituency, or of individual constituents. Whether an ordinary European feels "represented" by his or her MP may depend less on the views that the MP expresses in the chamber of parliament or in a committee than on whether the MP will take up a matter of personal concern to them and help secure some redress of a grievance. Because this kind of behavior is not constitutionally prescribed, there is sometimes a tendency to neglect it. It is possible to read some works on certain European parliaments without realizing that for many MPs, much more time is spent dealing with constituency work than on the formally assigned tasks of an MP, such as taking part in debates or sitting on committees.

In real life, constituency work does loom very large in the lives of many, probably most, MPs around Europe. For example, research in France produced a diary of a typical rural French MP (reproduced in Safran, pp. 223–24), which describes the MP arriving in Paris on Tuesday morning and returning to his or her constituency on Thursday evening. Friday, Saturday, Sunday, and Monday are all spent in local political activity, and even while the deputy is in Paris, some of his or her time is spent in following up constituency business. In Britain, the typical backbencher spends most of each weekend on constituency work, as well as about three hours of each day on which parliament is sitting (Norton and Wood, p. 48); there has been a huge increase in the volume of constituency work since 1970. In both Belgium and Ireland, members of parliament are likely to be buttonholed by their constituents at virtually any time of the day. In Belgium, "when MPs participate in local social life, they return home with their pockets full of beercards on which they have noted down the requests of people they met at these social gatherings," while in Ireland an MP is not safe from being approached by a constituent with a problem even when relaxing in the pub on a Sunday evening (de Winter, 1997, pp. 141–42; Gallagher and Komito, p. 207). In Scandinavian countries, too, MPs tend to be strongly locally oriented (Heidar). In small countries, links between citizens and MPs can be especially close: in Malta MPs are very active constituency workers, while in Iceland, over half of the voting population claims to know an MP personally (Arter, p. 211). In contrast, there are some countries, such as Germany and the Netherlands, where performance of constituency duties is only a relatively minor role for MPs.

The causes and consequences of this kind of representation are a matter of some dispute. When trying to explain variations in the amount of constituency work carried out by parliamentarians in different countries, many writers identify the electoral system as important. Under certain electoral systems, as we shall discuss in more detail in Chapter 11, candidates within a party are competing with each other, as well as with candidates of other parties, and thus have a strong incentive to try to build up a personal vote. Some electoral systems provide individual MPs with a much greater incentive to cultivate a personal vote than others do (Carey and Shugart). This might help to explain why MPs operating under these electoral systems, as in Ireland and Malta, do a great deal of constituency work, while those in countries where there is little or no incentive to cultivate a personal vote, such as Germany, do relatively little. On the other hand, weighing against this argument is the fact that MPs in Britain and Belgium are not provided with any electoral incentive to undertake constituency work and yet are assiduous constituency workers. One explanation for this is that in both countries

MPs derive psychological gratification from doing constituency work, which, moreover, they believe is one of their duties as MPs (Norris, p. 47). In addition, in Belgium particularly, MPs fear that they will fall out of favor with their party's candidate selectors unless they maintain a high local profile (de Winter, 1997, p. 142).

The consequences of constituency work for the political representation of Europeans are mixed. On the one hand, immersion in constituency duties, whether it is casework for individual constituents or activity on behalf of the constituency as a whole, may distract MPs from their purely parliamentary roles, leaving them with less time to play a part in formulating legislation and scrutinizing government activity. On the other hand, it keeps MPs in touch with people who live ordinary lives and provides a form of representation that to many people is more meaningful than the representation of opinion. In that way it builds support for the political system as a whole, as well as reducing the alienation of those who would otherwise have no ready conduit to the state and transmitting values and information in both directions between the state and individual citizens.

EUROPEAN PARLIAMENTS: ONE CHAMBER OR TWO?

The question of whether there should be one or two legislative chambers is one of the most venerable when it comes to parliamentary design. The main arguments in favour of "bicameralism"—that is, having two chambers—are that a second chamber can act as a check on the possibility of an overbearing majority in the lower house, and that it may be able to discuss policy proposals in a more reflective manner than the highly politicized lower house, drawing on non-party technical expertise. The main argument against bicameralism is summed up in the frequently-quoted comment of the Abbé Sièyes, more than two hundred years ago, to the effect that "if the second chamber agrees with the first it is superfluous, and if it does not, it is pernicious."

Since upper houses are rarely in a position to block governments or lower houses, second chambers in Europe are often seen as unimportant. Tsebelis and Money, however, argue that bicameralism can make a significant difference to a country's politics. They maintain that its impact is inherently conservative, as its effect is to protect the status quo, and they argue that the relationship between the two houses is determined not only by the formal rules about how much power each has, but also by how much bargaining power each house possesses in some particular conflict. For example, if the upper house has the power to delay legislation for a year, as Britain's House of Lords does, then at times when an election is less than a year away the upper house will have greater power. The lower house will then have to decide whether to press ahead with its preferred measure, knowing that it might well end up with nothing, or reach a compromise in order to get at least part of its proposals passed into law before the election. Of course, the upper house, knowing of the "impatience" of the lower house in this situation, will be tempted to drive a particularly hard bargain. Lijphart, too, identifies "strong bicameralism" as a key feature of his model of "consensus democracy." The conditions of strong bicameralism are, first, that the upper house is not elected on the same basis as the lower house and, second, that it has real power (Lijphart, p. 39). In western Europe, he judges, only the Swiss and German systems amount to strong bicameralism (Lijphart, p. 212).

TABLE 4-1   SECOND CHAMBERS OF PARLIAMENT IN WESTERN EUROPE

Country	Name of second chamber	Size of second chamber	Comments
Austria	Bundesrat	64	Elected by state parliaments
Belgium	Senate	71	40 directly elected; 21 indirectly elected; 10 co-opted
Denmark	—	—	Upper house abolished in 1953
Finland	—	—	Large parliamentary committee acts as quasi–second chamber
France	Senate	321	Elected mainly by local councillors
Germany	Bundesrat	69	Composed of members of state governments, or their designated substitutes
Greece	—	—	
Iceland	—	—	
Ireland	Senate	60	43 indirectly elected; 11 appointed by prime minister; 6 elected by university graduates
Italy	Senate	326	315 are directly elected
Luxembourg	—	—	21-member Council of State plays the same role as a second chamber
Malta	—	—	
Netherlands	First Chamber	75	Indirectly elected
Norway	—	—	Directly elected parliament divides into two chambers
Portugal	—	—	Large parliamentary committee acts as quasi–second chamber
Spain	Senate	257	208 directly elected; the other 49 indirectly elected
Sweden	—	—	Upper house abolished in 1970
Switzerland	Council of States	46	Nearly all directly elected
United Kingdom	House of Lords	670	Mainly appointed for life by government of the day, plus some remaining hereditary peers

Sources: Inter-Parliamentary Union web site (www.ipu.org), and parliamentary web sites (to which the IPU site provides links); Tsebelis and Money, pp. 48–52.

In this light, the impact of bicameralism depends primarily on the composition and the powers of a second chamber, if one exists. As Table 4-1 shows, the position varies around western Europe, with ten of the nineteen states having a second chamber. The two factors that seem to have the strongest influence on whether a state is bicameral are size and centralization; the nine states without a second chamber are all small, unitary states. Of the ten states with an upper house, only two are both small and unitary (Ireland and the Netherlands); the rest are either federal (Austria, Belgium, Switzerland), large (France, Italy, Spain, the United Kingdom), or both (Germany).

The most common route to the upper house is indirect election or appointment by local or provincial councils. The First Chamber in the Netherlands is elected by members of the twelve provincial councils; members of Austria's Bundesrat are appointed by the state parliaments; and forty-three of the sixty members of Ireland's Seanad are elected by local councillors, with eleven appointed by the prime minister and the other six elected by university graduates. French senators are elected for nine-year terms by an electorate consisting mainly of local councillors, with a third of them standing down every three years; since the composition of the electorate is biased in favor of rural areas, the right-wing parties enjoy an almost permanent majority in the Senate. In Germany, the Bundesrat (also known as the Federal Council) consists of the prime ministers and certain other members of the Land governments, and although these individuals often appoint substitutes to attend meetings, the substitutes are of course people of their own political complexion. In all of these cases, it can happen that the local or regional bodies that elect or appoint members of the upper house are dominated by the parties that are out of power at the national level, and so the upper house can act as a significant check on the government. In Germany, indeed, this has usually been the case since 1969 (Saalfeld, 1998, p. 49). Prior to the 1998 election, for example, the left-wing opposition had controlled a majority in the Bundesrat and had been able to wring concessions on a number of issues from the centre-right federal government. The 1998 election brought to power an SPD–Green coalition, which for a while enjoyed a majority in both houses. In 1999, however, this government suffered a series of defeats in German Land elections and, as a result, faced an opposition majority in the Bundesrat. However, since the priorities of, say, a CDU Land government and the CDU's national leadership do not always coincide, opposition members in the Bundesrat are sometimes more willing to cooperate with the government than their counterparts in the lower house would wish.

There may seem to be only a weak argument for a directly elected second chamber that is not designed to provide a different kind of political representation from that in the first chamber. In four countries, however, direct election plays a significant role. This is most obvious in Italy, where all but a handful of senators are elected by the people at the same time that the lower chamber is elected, and the second chamber does little more than replicate or obstruct the first. In Belgium, Spain, and Switzerland, most members of the upper house are directly elected; in these cases, the role of the upper house is to protect regional or cantonal interests.

The most distinctive upper house is Britain's House of Lords, where for many centuries the majority of members held their positions simply by inheriting them. Even though many hereditary peers rarely or never attended parliament, their existence was widely seen by left-wing and liberal forces in Britain as an anomaly in the democratic era, and the Labour government elected in 1997 developed plans to reform the Lords fundamentally, so that the hereditary component in the Lords would first be drastically reduced and then be eliminated altogether. The first part of this scheme was implemented in 1999; in the short term, until a more fundamental reform could be devised, the number of hereditary peers with voting rights was reduced to 92. Of the remaining members, 26 were bishops (including two archbishops) and the other 552 were "life peers," that is, individuals appointed for life by the government of the day. Many critics of the House of Lords argued, therefore, that even these plans did not bring about a second chamber that was particularly representative.

Also distinctive is Luxembourg's Council of State (which is not technically a second chamber, although it plays the same role), whose twenty-one members, once appointed, hold office until the age of 72. They are nominally appointed by the head of state, the grand duke, although in practice the nominations are controlled by the three major parties.

Parliaments in the other eight Western European countries—Denmark, Finland, Greece, Iceland, Malta, Norway, Portugal, and Sweden—have only one chamber. In some of these countries, there are devices that go some way toward creating a second chamber. For example, after each election Norway's parliament, the Storting, divides into two chambers, although about 80 percent of its work is done by the two chambers sitting together in plenary session (Rommetvedt, p. 80). In both Finland and Portugal, the parliament contains one large committee (besides a number of regular committees) that serves as a kind of "mini-parliament" or "internal second chamber" (Anckar, p. 188; Braga da Cruz and Lobo Antunes, p. 166).

Whether upper houses matter depends largely upon how much power they have. Constitutional rules usually prescribe that disputes between the two houses must be resolved by means of a navette (shuttle), whereby bills on which the two chambers disagree pass back and forward between them until some conflict resolution mechanism comes into play. This might be, for example, a stipulation that the lower house prevails after the measure has shuttled back and forth a certain number of times; or provision for a committee composed of members of both houses to meet and attempt to resolve the deadlock (see Tsebelis and Money, pp. 54–70). Almost invariably, the upper house has less power than the lower house; the only exception is in Italy, where the Senate has exactly the same powers as the Chamber of Deputies, so that every bill must pass both houses to become law and the cabinet is answerable to both houses equally.

Typically, the upper house is able only to delay legislation passed by the lower house, but sometimes it can veto certain types of legislation (for example, legislation changing the constitution). In Germany, the Bundesrat has a veto over legislation that affects the power of the states (the Länder); in addition, if it defeats a bill on any other subject by a two-thirds majority, only a two-thirds majority in the lower house (the Bundestag) can overrule it. In addition, since a 1992 amendment to the constitution, the Bundesrat has had a strong voice in the formulation of the line that German ministers are to take within the Council of the European Union (which we discuss in Chapter 5). Originally it was expected that only a small proportion of legislation would require the consent of the Bundesrat, but in practice most legislation has turned out to fall into this category (Saalfeld, 1998, pp. 49–50).

In Britain, the House of Lords, which in the nineteenth century could veto bills, has had its power reduced in successive reforms, so by the start of the twenty-first century it could only delay bills by a year. It is not completely irrelevant, though, since by defeating a government bill when an election is less than a year away it effectively kills the bill. The preponderance of hereditary peers before the reforms in November 1999 meant that the House of Lords was instinctively more sympathetic to Conservative governments than to Labour governments, though during the long period of Conservative rule from 1979 to 1997 it did occasionally sink government measures, such as a 1986 bill to allow Sunday trading and a 1997 attempt to increase police powers (Budge et al., p. 420). The Irish upper house, Seanad Éireann, can do no more than delay bills for ninety days. The French Senate has even less power than the already weak French lower house: it can refuse to pass bills coming from the lower house, and has sometimes been obstructive to government plans as a result, but if it pushes its obstruction too far, the government can and does exercise its own power to call upon the lower house to deliver a decisive vote on the bill (Safran, pp. 230–34). Even less significant is the Spanish Senate, which "is widely seen as a useless body" (Heywood, p. 100).

THE SIGNIFICANCE OF PARLIAMENTS: AN ASSESSMENT

In most discussions of parliaments in Europe, as we have noted, the phrase "decline of parliaments" crops up somewhere along the line. It sums up a feeling, which seems to have been around since the early years of the twentieth century, that parliaments are not what they were. Once upon a time, so the feeling goes, they really ran countries and swept governments into and out of office as they pleased, whereas nowadays they have been reduced to mere rubber stamps, glumly approving whatever proposals governments place before them. Needless to say, both of these images are exaggerated. The "golden age" of parliaments never really existed, certainly as far as most countries are concerned. And today's parliaments, though perhaps lacking in excitement, can do useful work in improving legislation through detailed examination in committees.

Certainly, it is clear that parliaments, considered as institutions, do not play an active role in the decision-making process. In many countries, members of parliament suffer from a sense of irrelevance, certainly as far as plenary sessions are concerned. There is genuine uncertainty as to whether anyone is listening when a deputy speaks, as chambers are virtually empty and newspapers, television, and radio devote very little time or space to reporting the speeches that parliamentarians make. In Denmark, there is even a joke that an MP wishing to keep something secret should announce it in the Folketing, because then it is certain that nobody will hear it. The reasons for this are not difficult to identify. The whole business of making policy is now so complex that governments spend a lot of time consulting with experts in the civil service and with the major interest groups involved, such as business interests, trade unions, and farmers' groups (see Chapters 6 and 14). If a package can be put together that satisfies all these groups, the government will be reluctant to allow parliament to tinker with it. Moreover, the procedural devices that parliaments have at their disposal are often less effective than questioning by journalists in the mass media when it comes to getting straight answers from government members; in many cases, the media has become the main means by which governments are forced to give an account of themselves to the general public.

On the other hand, some factors are working in favor of parliaments. For one thing, members of parliament are becoming more professional. In a number of countries, there has been a decline in the number of MPs who combine this role with another job; the trend is toward parliaments of full-time professional politicians. Moreover, parliaments are becoming better resourced, although in no country, not even Germany, do they have anything like the personal staffs that American congress members enjoy.

Parliaments are becoming more active, according to most quantifiable indicators; MPs are asking more questions, initiating more interpellations, and, it seems, spending more time in committees. Most important of all, the government remains the government only for as long as it retains the confidence of parliament. It is true that right across Europe, parliament very rarely votes a government out of office, but this should not obscure the importance of this relationship. Governments are well aware that parliament does have this ultimate power, and so they act with this consideration always in their minds, ensuring in particular that their own MPs do not become disaffected.

We have seen that the relevance of parliaments varies from country to country, but this variation is not random. We can detect a clear pattern. In particular, as we would expect, the inter-party mode of behaviour dominates in those countries characterised by Lijphart as "majoritarian." Relations between members of parliament and government ministers, or among MPs, are determined by their respective party affiliations; there is at all times a keen sense that the government and MPs of the government party or parties are on the government "side," while the rest are on the opposition "side." If government MPs amount to a majority, governments need only retain the loyalty of their own backbenchers to ensure that all their proposals are approved by parliament. This model applies to such countries as the United Kingdom, Greece, France, Malta, and Ireland. In "consensus" systems, while the inter-party mode is still the most common, cross-party or non-party modes are also manifested. MPs of different parties may combine on some issues, and there may be a sense across party lines of "parliament" as a body that can and should scrutinize government, and perhaps formulate policies with or without the full agreement of government. This model fits such countries as Switzerland, the Netherlands, Belgium, Germany, and Austria.

Any overall assessment of parliaments, however, simply cannot ignore the central role of political parties. The power of a parliament at any given time will depend to a great extent on the balance of power between parties and on the distribution of power within the government parties. It is difficult to overestimate the importance of party discipline in setting the whole tone of politics in a typical European country. The system of parliamentary government would not work without it, because the party oligarchs who constitute the political executive would never know when they would be able to retain the support of the legislature. Governments would thus be liable to fall unpredictably and would have no guarantee of being able to implement their legislative programs. This scenario reads very much like a description of the political chaos that beset the European system in which party discipline was at its lowest: the French Fourth Republic (1946–58). Here, discipline was almost as weak as it typically is in the United States, and the result in a parliamentary government system was chronic political instability. Effective government was impossible, and the outcome was not, in any real sense, more power in decision making for parliament, but, rather, political chaos and the discrediting of the political class generally. This situation was brought to an end in 1958, with the establishment of the Fifth Republic and the creation of a strong, separately elected executive president. The dismal history of the Fourth Republic illustrates the fact that parliamentary government cannot exist without party discipline.

Above all, it explains why political parties feature so prominently in our account of representative government in modern Europe.

REFERENCES

Alivizatos, Nikos: "The Difficulties of 'Rationalization' in a Polarized Political System: the Greek Chamber of Deputies," in Ulrike Liebert and Maurizio Cotta (eds.), *Parliament and Democratic Consolidation in Southern Europe: Greece, Italy, Portugal, Spain and Turkey,* Pinter, London, 1990, pp. 131–53.

Anckar, Dag: "Finland: Dualism and Consensual Rule," in Erik Damgaard (ed.), *Parliamentary Change in the Nordic Countries,* Scandinavian University Press, Oslo, 1992, pp. 151–90.

Andeweg, Rudy B., and Lia Nijzink: "Beyond the Two-Body Image: Relations Between Ministers and MPs," in Herbert Döring (ed.), *Parliaments and Majority Rule in Western Europe,* Campus Verlag and St Martin's Press, Frankfurt and New York, 1995, pp. 152–78.

Arter, David: *Scandinavian Politics Today,* Manchester University Press, Manchester and New York, 1999.

Bagehot, Walter: *The English Constitution,* Fontana, London, 1993 [first published 1867].

Braga da Cruz, Manuel, and Miguel Lobo Antunes: "Revolutionary Transition and Problems of Parliamentary Institutionalization: The Case of the Portuguese National Assembly," in Ulrike Liebert and Maurizio Cotta (eds.), *Parliament and Democratic Consolidation in Southern Europe: Greece, Italy, Portugal, Spain and Turkey,* Pinter, London, 1990, pp. 154–83.

Brand, Jack: *British Parliamentary Parties: Policy and Power,* Clarendon, Oxford, 1992.

Budge, Ian, Ivor Crewe, David McKay, and Ken Newton: *The New British Politics,* Addison Wesley Longman, Harlow, 1998.

Carey, John M., and Matthew Soberg Shugart: "Incentives to Cultivate a Personal Vote: A Rank Ordering of Electoral Formulas," *Electoral Studies,* vol. 14, no. 4, 1995, pp. 417–39.

Cox, Gary W.: *The Efficient Secret: The Cabinet and the Development of Political Parties in Victorian England,* Cambridge University Press, Cambridge, 1987.

Damgaard, Erik: "Denmark: Experiments in Parliamentary Government," in Erik Damgaard (ed.), *Parliamentary Change in the Nordic Countries,* Scandinavian University Press, Oslo, 1992, pp. 19–49.

Damgaard, Erik: "The Strong Parliaments of Scandinavia: Continuity and Change of Scandinavian Parliaments," in Gary W. Copeland and Samuel C. Patterson (eds.), *Parliaments in the Modern World: Changing Institutions,* University of Michigan Press, Ann Arbor, 1994, pp. 85–103.

Della Sala, Vincent: "The Italian Parliament: Chambers in a Crumbling House?", in Philip Norton (ed.), *Parliaments and Governments in Western Europe,* Frank Cass, London, 1998, pp. 73–96.

Döring, Herbert: "Time as a Scarce Resource: Government Control of the Agenda," in Herbert Döring (ed.), *Parliaments and Majority Rule in Western Europe,* Campus Verlag and St Martin's Press, Frankfurt and New York, 1995, pp. 223–46.

Gallagher, Michael: "Parliament," in John Coakley and Michael Gallagher (eds.), *Politics in the Republic of Ireland,* 3d ed., Routledge, London, 1999, pp. 177–205.

Gallagher, Michael and Lee Komito: "The Constituency Role of TDs," in John Coakley and Michael Gallagher (eds.), *Politics in the Republic of Ireland,* 3d ed., Routledge, London, 1999, pp. 206–31.

Gladdish, Ken: *Governing from the Centre: Politics and Policy-Making in the Netherlands,* C. Hurst, London, 1991.

Heidar, Knut: "Roles, Structure and Behaviour: Norwegian Parliamentarians in the Nineties," in Wolfgang C. Müller and Thomas Saalfeld (eds.), *Members of Parliament in Western Europe: Roles and Behaviour,* Frank Cass, London, 1997, pp. 91–109.

Heywood, Paul: *The Government and Politics of Spain,* Macmillan, Basingstoke, 1995.

Keeler, John T. S.: "Executive Power and Policy-Making Patterns in France: Gauging the Impact of Fifth Republic Institutions," *West European Politics,* vol. 16, no. 4, 1993, pp. 518–44.

King, Anthony: "Modes of Executive-Legislative Relations: Great Britain, France, and West Germany," *Legislative Studies Quarterly,* vol. 1, no. 1, 1976, pp. 11–34.

Kingdom, John: *Government and Politics in Britain: An Introduction,* 2d ed., Polity Press, Cambridge, 1999.

Kreppel, Amie: "The Impact of Parties in Government on Legislative Output in Italy," *European Journal of Political Research,* vol. 31, no. 3, 1997, pp. 327–50.

Laver, Michael: "Divided Parties, Divided Government," *Legislative Studies Quarterly,* vol. 24, no. 1, 1999, pp. 5–29.

Leston-Bandeira, Cristina: "Relationship Between Parliament and Government in Portugal: An Expression of the Maturation of the Political System," in Philip Norton (ed.), *Parliaments and Governments in Western Europe,* Frank Cass, London, 1998, pp. 142–66.

Lijphart, Arend: *Patterns of Democracy: Government Forms and Performance in Thirty-Six Countries,* Yale University Press, New Haven and London, 1999.

Maor, Moshe: "Government and Opposition in the Bundestag and House of Commons in the Run-Up to Maastricht," *West European Politics,* vol. 21, no. 3, 1998, pp. 187–207.

Mattson, Ingvar, and Kaare Strøm: "Parliamentary Committees," in Herbert Döring (ed.), *Parliaments and Majority Rule in Western Europe,* Campus Verlag and St Martin's Press, Frankfurt and New York, 1995, pp. 249–307.

Mezey, Michael L.: *Comparative Legislatures,* Duke University Press, Durham, N.C. 1979.

Müller, Wolfgang C.: "Austrian Governmental Institutions: Do They Matter?" in Kurt Richard Luther and Wolfgang C. Müller (eds.), *Politics in Austria: Still a Case of Consociationalism?* Frank Cass, London, 1992, pp. 99–131.

Norris, Pippa: "The Puzzle of Constituency Service," *Journal of Legislative Studies,* vol. 3, no. 2, 1997, pp. 29–49.

Norton, Philip, and David M. Wood: *Back from Westminster: British Members of Parliament and their Constituents,* University of Kentucky Press, Lexington, 1993.

Petersson, Olof: *The Government and Politics of the Nordic Countries,* Publica, Stockholm, 1994.

Rommetvedt, Hilmar: "Norway: From Consensual Majority Parliamentarianism to Dissensual Minority Parliamentarianism," in Erik Damgaard (ed.), *Parliamentary Change in the Nordic Countries,* Scandinavian University Press, Oslo, 1992, pp. 51–97.

Rose, Richard: *Understanding Big Government: The Programme Approach,* Sage, London and Beverley Hills, 1984.

Saalfeld, Thomas: "The German Bundestag: Influence and Accountability in a Complex Environment," in Philip Norton (ed.), *Parliaments and Governments in Western Europe,* Frank Cass, London, 1998, pp. 44–72.

Saalfeld, Thomas: "Germany: Bundestag and Interest Groups in a 'Party Democracy'," in Philip Norton (ed.), *Parliaments and Pressure Groups in Western Europe,* Frank Cass, London, 1999, pp. 43–66.

Safran, William: *The French Polity,* 5th ed., Longman, New York and Harlow, 1998.

Schüttemeyer, Suzanne S.: "Hierarchy and Efficiency in the Bundestag: The German Answer for Institutionalizing Parliament," in Gary W. Copeland and Samuel C. Patterson (eds.), *Parliaments in the Modern World: Changing Institutions,* University of Michigan Press, Ann Arbor, 1994, pp. 29–58.

Skjaeveland, Asbjørn: "A Danish Party Cohesion Cycle," *Scandinavian Political Studies,* vol. 22, no. 2, 1999, pp. 121–36.

Tsebelis, George, and Jeanette Money: *Bicameralism,* Cambridge University Press, Cambridge, 1997.

Wiberg, Matti (ed.): *Parliamentary Control in the Nordic Countries: Forms of Questioning and Behavioural Trends,* Finnish Political Science Association, Helsinki, 1994.

Wiberg, Matti: "Parliamentary Questioning: Control by Communication?", in Herbert Döring (ed.), *Parliaments and Majority Rule in Western Europe,* Campus Verlag and St Martin's Press, Frankfurt and New York, 1995, pp. 179–222.

de Winter, Lieven: "Intra- and Extra-Parliamentary Role Attitudes and Behaviour of Belgian MPs," in Wolfgang C. Müller and Thomas Saalfeld (eds.), *Members of Parliament in Western Europe: Roles and Behaviour,* Frank Cass, London, 1997, pp. 128–54.

de Winter, Lieven: "Belgium: Insider Pressure Groups in an Outsider Parliament," in Philip Norton (ed.), *Parliaments and Pressure Groups in Western Europe,* Frank Cass, London, 1999, pp. 88–109.

5

THE EUROPEAN UNION
AND REPRESENTATIVE
GOVERNMENT

In the previous chapters of this book and in Chapters 7 to 15, we focus primarily on the politics of representation in the individual countries of Europe, identifying general patterns and broad trends as well as interesting variations and idiosyncrasies. In this chapter and the next, we turn our attention to other levels of government. In Chapter 6, we examine subnational government, looking at the division of powers within countries between central, regional, and local governments. In this chapter, we look at supra-national government, as we consider a new development, quite different from anything that has ever taken place in any other part of the world, that in recent years has made European politics even more intriguing than before. We are referring to the moves toward a pooling of sovereignty among many European states, expressed most tangibly in their membership in the European Union (the EU). Although some would like the EU to reach the point where it facilitates close and smooth cooperation between the governments of the member countries and then to stop, others hope that the Union is going down a road that will inevitably end in a federal Europe. In this chapter, we assess the significance of the emergence of the EU as a major factor in politics in contemporary Europe.

First of all, we will outline the evolution of the European Union since the dream of European unity began to be taken seriously in the 1940s. We will then look at how the EU works and consider whether it has made national governments less important political actors. As in the other chapters of this book, we shall examine the process whereby interests are turned into policies, which entails asking who plays what role in the decision-making process and to whom the various actors are accountable. Finally, we will attempt to assess the direction of the Union and the chances that a United States of Europe will one day parallel the United States of America.

Before we begin, we had better clear up one matter of terminology that may confuse, namely, the distinction between the European Community (EC) and the European Union. The EC consists of three separate "communities," as we shall see in the next section, and has been evolving since the 1950s as an entity with political institutions each of which has defined powers and responsibilities. The European Union, on the other hand, came into existence in November 1993. It is envisaged metaphorically as a kind of building (a temple, in the eyes of enthusiasts) resting on three "pillars." One of these pillars is the EC; the other two are cooperation on foreign and security policy, and cooperation on judicial and home affairs. The EU, then, is a new body, not just another name for the EC or a revamped EC. However, for the sake of simplicity we shall refer to the body under discussion as the EU throughout, even though, strictly speaking, the EU did not come into existence until 1993.

THE DEVELOPMENT OF EUROPEAN UNITY

Given the record of war between European countries during the first half of the twentieth century and for many centuries before that, the prospect of a united continent might not have seemed bright in the 1940s. However, the very ruthlessness and destructiveness of modern warfare were factors that led to a conviction among the postwar political elites in a number of countries that such conflict must never again take place on European soil. The causes of World War II were, of course, many and varied, but two of the more obvious were unbridled and sometimes rabid nationalism (manifesting itself both in xenophobia and in the persecution of internal minorities) and the diktat imposed on the vanquished Germany after World War I. However understandable the latter might have been from the viewpoint of the victorious allies, it served merely to fuel German resentment and was eventually seen to have contained the seeds of the Second World War (1939–45). For this reason, once World War II was over, the politicians of the wartime allies looked for ways to integrate Germany into the postwar European framework rather than ostracize it; they also looked for structures that would promote cooperation rather than rivalry between the countries of Western Europe. The emergence of the "iron curtain" dividing Europe, following the imposition of communist regimes in the Stalinist mold on the reluctant populations of Eastern and Central European states, heightened a belief in the West that adherence to common democratic political values was something worth preserving.

Despite all of this, the road toward even a partial undermining of the traditional fetish of absolute national sovereignty was long and rocky (for details, see Dinan, pp. 9–201). The first tangible step along the road to what some hoped might one day become a federal Europe was taken in April 1951 with the signing of the Treaty of Paris, which established the European Coal and Steel Community (ECSC). The treaty came into effect in July 1952. Many countries were invited to take part in the creation of this new body, but in the end only six did so: France, Germany, Italy, and the three Benelux countries (Belgium, the Netherlands, and Luxembourg). By joining the ECSC, member states ceded some of their sovereignty to a supranational body. The institutions of the ECSC corresponded broadly to those of today's European Union. The ECSC had a quasi-government (known as the High Authority) whose nine members (appointed by the member states) were obliged to make decisions in the interest of the ECSC as a whole, not in the interest of the member state from which they came. The High Authority made decisions regarding investment and production levels of coal and steel and had the power to impose fines on governments if they disobeyed its decisions. There was also a quasi-parliament called an Assembly, with little real power, whose members were appointed by national parliaments, and there was a Council of Ministers, containing ministers from national governments, which could in some circumstances amend or reject the decisions of the High Authority. In addition, there was a Court of Justice, which could arbitrate between the institutions if there were complaints that the High Authority was exceeding its powers. The presence of these supranational bodies was enough to dissuade Britain from joining, and Britain's economic significance at that time was such that a number of smaller countries (particularly Ireland and the Scandinavian countries) felt that their fortunes depended on the British market and also remained aloof.

The European Coal and Steel Community worked very satisfactorily from the viewpoint of the member states, and this led to a discussion of the idea of extending the range of policy areas in which countries might agree to combine in similar organizations. In the summer of 1955, the foreign ministers of the six countries met in Messina, Sicily, and decided to work toward the establishment of a customs union that would involve the creation of a common, or single, market embracing all the countries. They invited Britain to join them in this enterprise, but the invitation was declined. The British, while keen on the idea of turning Western Europe into a free trade area, were still suspicious of any supranational political authority with the right to constrain their own government, and they remained unconvinced that their destiny lay primarily with the rest of Europe. The ideas of the six ECSC countries were fleshed out over the next two years, and in March 1957 two Treaties of Rome were signed.

Each of these two treaties established a new community. The more important and wide-ranging in scope was the Treaty of the European Economic Community (EEC), which laid down policy aims and guidelines concerning the establishment of a common market and the creation of a common policy in areas such as agriculture and transportation. The other treaty was the Euratom Treaty, which dealt with atomic energy and covered matters such as the pooling of resources and research.

As a result, the six countries involved were now members of three different communities: the ECSC, the EEC, and Euratom. Each of the two new communities had a set of institutions based on those of the ECSC: a quasi-government (now termed a Commission rather than a High Authority), a quasi-parliament (the Assembly), a Council of Ministers, and a Court of Justice. Sensibly, it was decided that only one Assembly and one Court of Justice were needed to serve all three communities. However, the Commission/High Authority and the Council of Ministers continued to exist in triplicate until the mid-1960s, when the 1965 Merger Treaty, which came into effect in 1967, merged the three sets of institutions into one. Technically, there are still three communities, but after 1967 the body to which the member states belong was generally known as the "European Community" before the European Union was established in 1993. The three founding treaties, together with subsequent treaties and acts amending the original treaties, make up what is in effect the Union's written constitution.

TABLE 5-1   MEMBER COUNTRIES OF THE EUROPEAN UNION

Country	Date of joining the EU
Belgium	1958
France	1958
Germany	1958
Italy	1958
Luxembourg	1958
Netherlands	1958
Denmark	1973
Ireland	1973
United Kingdom	1973
Greece	1981
Portugal	1986
Spain	1986
Austria	1995
Finland	1995
Sweden	1995

Note: The first six countries were all founding members of the EEC and of Euratom in 1958 and were all already members of the ECSC. The remaining countries joined all three communities upon their respective accessions. The European Union itself came into existence in November 1993.

Since 1958, the European Union (EU), as we shall henceforth call it, has grown to fifteen countries (see Table 5-1). The first enlargement did not take place until 1973. The British government, having remained aloof from the EU when it was being established, changed its mind dramatically in the early 1960s. Britain now came round to the view that Europe was likely to be far more significant in its future foreign and trade relations than either the United States or the Commonwealth. Consequently, the Conservative government announced in 1961 that Britain would apply for EU membership, and several of the countries dependent on the British market, such as Denmark and Ireland, followed suit. However, Britain found that the EU door was no longer open. Although five of the EU countries would have welcomed British membership, the French president, Charles de Gaulle, responded with an emphatic negative. Because each EU member state has veto power regarding the question of admitting new members, this put an end for the time being to the prospect of Britain's joining, and the other applicants decided not to press their bids for membership. The same thing happened in 1967: there was a bid by Britain and those countries heavily dependent on its market, followed by a veto of the British application by de Gaulle and a drawing back by the other applicants. It was only after de Gaulle's retirement from French politics in 1969 that enlargement could be seriously contemplated. Four countries opened negotiations with the EU in 1970 and signed a Treaty of Accession in 1972. Three of them—Britain, Denmark, and Ireland—joined the EU the following year. The fourth, Norway, did not; the issue generated a deep division in Norwegian society, culminating in a referendum in which the people voted by a narrow majority against EU entry (Wyller).

Following this, the next three new members were all southern European countries with a history of authoritarian government. Greece was under military rule from 1967 to 1974, and when civilian rule and democratic elections were restored, the new government was quick to ask to be admitted to the EU, using the argument that EU membership would help consolidate its still fragile democracy and strengthen its economy. Negotiations took a long time to complete, but Greece eventually became the tenth EU member in 1981. Portugal and Spain had both experienced long periods of dictatorship, under Salazar and Franco, respectively, before democracy was inaugurated (in Portugal) or restored (in Spain) in the mid-1970s. In these cases, too, the new governments were keen to have their countries incorporated into the EU, both to bolster the political system and to reap economic benefits. Again negotiations were protracted, and it was not until 1986 that Spain and Portugal joined. In the 1990s, three countries that had maintained a policy of neutrality during the Cold War—Austria, Finland, and Sweden—joined. In contrast to the 1980s entrants, these three were all wealthy countries, and in each there was a substantial number of people, both before and after EU entry, who were fundamentally opposed to EU membership.

Enlargement has affected the nature of the EU considerably. The original six members were close to one another geographically and, with the exception of southern Italy, had very similar levels of wealth and economic development. Two languages (French and German) were enough for virtually all informal transactions between members of the political elite. Even if it did not always operate entirely harmoniously, the EU in its original form was much more of a cozy club than its expanded version proved to be. With fifteen members, it has become a much less homogeneous organization. Geographically, it embraces two offshore islands, Britain and Ireland, as well as one country, Greece, that does not share a border with another member state. The range of languages and cultures is much broader than was the case before 1973, and the new southern European members, in particular Greece and Portugal, are far less wealthy than the original six. The process of making decisions is more complex and often more protracted than was the case when there were only six member states, and if the Union still consisted of only these six, it is likely that the process of European integration would have advanced much farther than it actually has.

The original treaties have been supplemented by other major treaties. The Single European Act of 1987 reformed the Union's decision-making process and signalled a commitment to create a single market with no trade barriers between member states, as well as bringing about changes in the internal decision-making procedures that reduced the ability of individual member states to block proposals that they did not like. In December 1991, in the Dutch city of Maastricht, the Treaty on European Union was agreed (it was formally signed two months later and finally came into operation in November 1993), creating the EU and marking a qualified success for those who hoped to see the eventual emergence of a federal Europe. The Amsterdam Treaty of 1997, though an anti-climax in some ways given the effort that had gone into it, brought about some streamlining of EU decision making and enhanced the position of the European Parliament.

Supporters of the Maastricht Treaty celebrate in France after the referendum there In September 1992 produced a narrow majority in favour of ratifying the treaty. © Macon/Rea/SABA Press Photos

HOW THE EUROPEAN UNION WORKS

It is often said that because the EU is a unique body, its system of government cannot be compared with that of individual countries. However, as Hix (p. 2) observes, the questions that we would ask when trying to ascertain how domestic politics worked in any country can also be asked about the EU, and the methods that we might use to tackle these can also be applied to the EU. In Chapter 4 we outlined two models of democracy identified by Lijphart, which he terms the "Westminster model" and the "consensus model." He cites the European Union as an archetypal example of the latter, because of the way in which, as we shall see in the course of this chapter, power is diffused among a number of institutions, with none being dominant (Lijphart, pp. 42–47). The EU has four main institutions: the Commission, the European Parliament, the Council, and the Court of Justice. Outlining the powers of these institutions is made especially complicated by the fact that the power of each varies somewhat from "pillar" to "pillar"; as a broad generalization, we can say that the Commission in particular has more power in policy areas that come under the first pillar, that is, the European Community, while the national governments, acting through the Council, are relatively more powerful over issues arising under the other two pillars, that is, cooperation on foreign and security policy, and cooperation on judicial and home affairs. Consequently, there is sometimes argument about which pillar a particular matter properly belongs with, since this will affect the ability of the national governments to block a Commission proposal.

The Commission is the body that initiates most proposals for legislation. Its proposals go to the Council of the European Union, made up of ministers from the governments of the fifteen member states, which immediately forwards them to European Parliament. The Parliament considers them and sends them back to the Council, together with its recommendations. The fate of the proposals then depends on whether the Parliament and the Council are in agreement, and, if not, on which precise set of rules is invoked to resolve their disagreement, because different sets of proposals fall under different sets of rules. The most powerful institution within the EU is the European Council, which consists of the heads of government of the member states. Questions of the applicability or interpretation of EU law are decided by the Court of Justice.

We now look in more detail at the role played by each of these institutions (for accounts of how the EU works, see Dinan; Hix; Nugent; Wallace and Wallace). We follow the flow of policies through the EC's decision-making process, from Commission to Parliament to Council. We need to bear in mind that the Council, though only third in this sequence, may in reality be more important than either the Commission or the Parliament because it may have the power to alter or reject proposals backed by the other two bodies. However, whereas once this was true of virtually every kind of proposal, increasingly the Parliament stands on an approximately equal footing with the Council in determining the fate of proposals. In addition, the European Council has become the most powerful body of all and has emerged as the place where the really important decisions are now made within the Union, and so we examine its role in some detail.

The Commission

The Commission looks, at least at first sight, like the "government" of the EU. In reality, it is more of a hybrid between a government and a civil service, as the Council also has a governmental role. The Commission, which is headed by a president, consists of twenty members, each with a specific policy jurisdiction (or "portfolio"). Each of the largest five countries (Britain, France, Germany, Italy, and Spain) has two commissioners, and the remaining ten countries have one apiece. Until the mid-1990s, the governments of the member states agreed among themselves who should be the president of the Commission, and then each government appointed its own commissioner(s). The Maastricht and Amsterdam treaties greatly enhanced the role of the European Parliament in the appointment process. The procedure now begins with the governments nominating, by agreement among themselves, a person as president; the Parliament can approve or reject this nominee. If it approves him or her, then the governments, in consultation with the president, nominate their commissioners. Thus in 1999 the incoming president, Romano Prodi, was consulted by the fifteen governments about the suitability of potential nominees, and the president's say in this matter is now comparable to the power of many prime ministers within European countries to select government ministers. Once a full twenty-member team of commissioners has been put together, the entire proposed Commission requires the approval of the Parliament before it can take office.

The Commission president can make a big difference to the development of the EU: he or she is a significant actor, with the right to attend all meetings of the most powerful body in the EU, the European Council, which we discuss later. Under the former French finance minister Jacques Delors (president from 1985 to 1994), some major steps were taken towards integration. His successor Jacques Santer (1995 to 1999) was not the first choice of most heads of government, and, with the added disadvantage of coming from the EU's smallest country, Luxembourg, was relatively ineffective. Romano Prodi, his successor, started with the advantage of being a political heavy-weight, as a former Italian prime minister. Prodi was able to be more assertive than his predecessors about the composition of his Commission, strengthened by the additional powers conferred upon the president by the Amsterdam Treaty of 1997. In addition, he secured from each commissioner upon appointment an undertaking that should he ask them to resign, they would do so, whereas previous presidents were unable to dismiss individual commissioners whose behavior was tarnishing the entire Commission. The president is not quite the "prime minister of Europe," a phrase used by Walter Hallstein, who was Commission president in the 1960s, but he is at least coming to look more like a prime minister of the EU.

The Commission has a five-year term in office and is based in the "European quarter" in the eastern part of Brussels, the capital of Belgium. Most commissioners are former senior politicians in their home countries (MacMullen). The members of any one Commission are likely to have different party backgrounds, reflecting the compositions of the governments that appoint them. For example, the Commission appointed in 1999 consisted mainly of left-wing politicians, since at that time most governments in EU member states were controlled by left-of-center parties, while in the European Parliament elected in 1999 the center-right parties held the upper hand. Commissioners also vary in ability; some are chosen as the people who seem likely to be able to achieve most, either for the country or for the EU as a whole, but the appointment of others results from political deals done between parties in the member states, while in some cases the appointment of a commissioner is used to get rid of a politician "who cannot be tolerated at home for one reason or another, inflated self-importance and lack of scruples being two of them" (Peterson, p. 562).

Once the commissioners have been appointed, the president and the other nineteen commissioners together decide which commissioner should be given which portfolio, with the president having the decisive voice. Member governments often lobby vigorously to get "their" commissioner assigned to a significant position, but such lobbying is likely to be less effective in the future, given the enhanced position of the president. The portfolios, which correspond to ministries in domestic government, include economic and financial affairs, agriculture, external economic affairs, industrial affairs, social affairs and employment, environment, regional policy, and so on. Each commissioner-designate appears before a European Parliament committee to be questioned, and finally the Commission must receive a vote of approval from the European Parliament before it can enter office.

Although commissioners are nominated on national lines, they are emphatically not in the Commission to represent national interests—at least in theory. Upon taking office, each commissioner has to take an oath to the effect that he or she will serve the overall interest of the EU and will not take instructions from a national government or from any other body. After all, another Union institution, the Council, exists expressly to safeguard national interests, as we will see. Despite this, it is tacitly accepted that commissioners do not suddenly slough off their national identities the moment they are appointed and become transformed into Euromen or Eurowomen. A commissioner speaking at the weekly Commission meeting may well draw on knowledge of his or her own country to make a point, in a way that sometimes comes close to special pleading for that country. And because every commissioner ultimately depends on a government back home for reappointment, he or she is unlikely to want to alienate that government. This is not to say that any commissioner acts as a government puppet, but undoubtedly governments do expect "their" commissioner to give them advance warning of impending developments and generally advise them as to how to maximize benefits for the country. In addition, a commissioner from, say, Finland might well receive representations from Finnish interest groups, which are likely to see him or her as "the Finnish commissioner."

The Commission has two main powers. First, it has the primary responsibility for initiating legislation, and it sends a steady stream of proposals and recommendations into the EU's policy-making process, though it usually tests the water first to ensure that its proposals have a realistic chance of being accepted by the other institutions, especially the Council. As a result, the Commission spends a lot of its time consulting the fifteen governments and the major interest groups about its ideas, thereby ensuring that the proposals it feeds into the decision-making process are likely to make headway. In addition, the Council as a whole, national governments individually, and the Parliament all attempt to use the Commission to push matters forward in areas that are important to them. Although it is true that only the Commission can actually initiate most legislation, in practice the commission is often more of a mediator and broker between various interests than a real independent initiator.

The Commission's second power is that it is responsible for trying to ensure that others in the Union are doing what they are supposed to be doing. When EU legislation is passed, this generally imposes obligations on the fifteen national governments and/or parliaments to take action, either by introducing domestic legislation or by implementing a policy. If this is to mean anything, then clearly someone has to check that these obligations are being fulfilled, and the Commission has this role. However, the Commission is grossly understaffed, with only about twenty thousand employees, and is unable to monitor Union-wide policy implementation in anything like a comprehensive fashion, so it tends to concentrate on potential major breaches, such as failure to comply with directives concerned with the free movement of goods. If it discovers a case where a national government has apparently failed to meet its obligations, it informs the government of its view and waits a reasonable time, usually a couple of months, for a response. If the government in question is uncooperative, the Commission can refer the case to the Court of Justice, although this step has to be taken in only a small minority of cases. Partly because of the Commission's limited resources, implementation of Union law is becoming a significant problem, as we shall see later in the chapter.

The Commission, then, plays a vital role in providing an overall Union viewpoint on important matters, however attenuated or diluted this may sometimes appear, and in negotiating with and mediating between the other actors in the decision-making process. In addition, the Commission represents the Union externally in important ways: it negotiates trade issues with other international actors, and its president attends the gatherings of the heads of government of the wealthiest seven nations in the world, known as "G7." However, the Commission is a far cry from the engine of European integration that some would like it to be. It contains a mix of both nationalities and political views; a typical Commission contains commissioners from most of the main political tendencies in the EU, apart from the extremes of the left and right. In the past, the fact that it is appointed in a piecemeal fashion by fifteen different governments of varying political persuasions has sometimes led to its having no overall goal or program of the sort that national governments usually adopt, and Commissions have sometimes seemed to lack a sense of purpose. However, a powerful and dynamic president may be able to avoid this problem by ensuring that the incoming Commission sets out a clear program and works to achieve it.

The European Parliament

If the Commission is a quasi-government, then the European Parliament (EP) can reasonably be described as a quasi-parliament. Although it has styled itself the "European Parliament" ever since the early 1960s, it was only in 1986 that the Council of Ministers finally agreed to change its formal name from "European Parliamentary Assembly" to "European Parliament." It has three main powers, which concern appointment and dismissal of the Commission, legislation, and the budget.

The power of the Parliament in the appointment of the Commission has existed only since 1993. After each five-yearly EP election, the parliament is consulted on the appointment of the next Commission president, and then the new Commission as a whole must be approved by a vote in the EP before it takes office. The EP can also dismiss a Commission, if a motion to censure the Commission is passed by a two-thirds majority and those voting for the motion amount to more than half of the total number of Members of the European Parliament (MEPs). Most fundamental conflicts within the EU tend to see the EP and the Commission ranged on the same side, in favor of greater European integration, with the Council on the other, defending the position of the national governments, and so the EP is unlikely to reach a position of complete disgruntlement with the Commission very often. Events in 1999, however, following

The controversial EU commissioner Edith Cresson, with other commissioners, awaits the result of the censure motion against the Commission in the European Parliament in January 1999. The Commission narrowly survived this vote, but following further allegations of mismanagement and corruption, many of them centering on areas for which Edith Cresson was responsible, the entire Commission resigned two months later. © AFP Worldwide

evidence that there was mismanagement and corruption within the Commission bureaucracy for which commissioners were not taking appropriate responsibility, showed that this EP power has real substance. In January of that year a motion to dismiss the Commission was defeated by a margin of only 293 to 232 votes, and two months later, as EP dissatisfaction with the Commission continued to rise, the Commission preempted further steps against it by resigning en masse. However, it remains true that the EP has no real weapons to use against the Council, which is where the greatest power still lies.

The EP's role in the legislative process, the second area where it plays a part, is limited but expanding. Its precise position in the legislative process varies according to the type of legislation under discussion, with its role in most areas covered by either "co-decision," where it has the power to reject legislation; "cooperation," where the Council has to take its views seriously; or "consultation," where it is consulted by the Council but the Council need not take its views on board (for details see Hix, pp. 64–65, 366–75). In a few particularly important areas, the "assent procedure" comes into play; here, a specified step cannot be taken by the EU without the EP's express approval. Steps of this type include the admission of new member states; all major international agreements, including association agreements between the EU and other countries; the adoption of a uniform electoral system for EP elections; and regulation of the role of the European Central Bank. Successive treaties have been increasing the EP's powers in the legislative process.

Finally, the EP has a significant role in deciding the EU's budget (for the budgetary procedure see Laffan and Shackleton; Nugent, pp. 389–412). The EP is kept informed as the budget is being drafted, and the final outcome represents the result of negotiations between the EP and the Council on the basis of the Commission's proposals. At the final stage, the EP is entitled to make some changes in certain areas of spending. If these changes satisfy it, the president of the Parliament signs the budget into law. If the EP is still not satisfied—in other words, if it would like to make changes greater than those it is allowed to make under the terms of the treaties—then it can reject the entire budget. In order to do this, it needs a two-thirds majority, provided that those voting for rejection constitute a majority of all MEPs. Although this happened several times in the 1980s, since then the EU has committed itself to more medium-term financial planning, so that the parameters of the budget are broadly settled well in advance of the detailed preparation, and the scope for disagreement between the various EU institutions is much smaller than it was in the past.

Having outlined the Parliament's powers, we turn now to its composition and operation. The Parliament contains 626 members, who come from the member states in approximate proportion to their population, although the smaller states are generously overrepresented in per capita terms (see Table 5-2). Direct elections to the EP have taken place at five-yearly intervals every June since 1979. The elections take place in all countries within a few days of each other; the different dates reflect different national traditions as to the day of the week (usually Thursday or Sunday) on which elections are held. No results are released from the early-voting countries until voting is completed in every country. Although the EEC Treaty speaks of a uniform electoral system being used for European Parliament elections, this can happen only when all

TABLE 5-2 SEATS IN THE EUROPEAN PARLIAMENT AT THE 1999 ELECTION

Country	Population	Seats	Population per MEP	Seats entitlement if seats were strictly proportionate to population
Germany	82,061,000	99	828,899	138
United Kingdom	59,009,000	87	678,264	99
France	58,608,000	87	673,655	98
Italy	56,868,000	87	653,655	95
Spain	39,323,000	64	614,421	66
Netherlands	15,609,000	31	503,516	26
Greece	10,498,000	25	419,920	18
Belgium	10,181,000	25	407,240	17
Portugal	9,550,000	25	382,000	16
Sweden	8,848,000	22	402,182	15
Austria	8,072,000	21	384,381	13
Denmark	5,284,000	16	330,250	9
Finland	5,140,000	16	321,250	9
Ireland	3,661,000	15	244,067	6
Luxembourg	424,000	6	70,667	1
Total	373,136,000	626	596,064	626

member governments acting in the Council agree on one and the EP itself approves it. Every country uses some variant of proportional representation (PR) to elect its MEPs, though not necessarily the same one that it uses in domestic elections.

Elections to the European Parliament are, in some senses, rather curious affairs. They are impressive in their own way, as the people of fifteen countries, with a total electorate of nearly 290 million, turn out at about the same time to elect a genuinely transnational body, the only one of its kind in the world. But they are a far cry from being the EU equivalent of general elections at the national level. In general elections, the question of the composition of the next government is uppermost in voters' minds, even if, as we will see in Chapter 12, government formation is sometimes a complex process not directly brought about by the preferences expressed by voters. But in European Parliament elections, it is often hard to say exactly what is at stake. No government is accountable to the EP, and, as we have seen, the EP still has rather limited powers. Many voters undoubtedly conclude that in fact nothing much is at stake, and so only a minority actually turn out to vote (see Table 5-3). Turnout is usually lowest in Britain, where only about a quarter of the electorate turned out in 1999. Overall turnout is declining steadily at EP elections, to levels well below the comparable figures for domestic general elections (Blondel et al.). If EP elections are intended to provide democratic legitimacy for the EU's decision-making process, they must be adjudged a failure. For the most part, the parties that fight EP elections are the same ones

TABLE 5-3 RESULTS OF EUROPEAN PARLIAMENT ELECTIONS, JUNE 1999

	Austria	Belgm	Denmk	Finlnd	France	Germny	Greece	Irelnd	Italy	Luxmbg	NethInd	Portgl	Spain	Swedn	UK	Total
Seats	21	25	16	16	87	99	25	15	87	6	31	25	64	22	87	626
Electorate, millions	5.8	7.3	4.0	4.1	40.1	60.8	8.9	2.9	49.3	0.2	11.9	8.7	33.8	6.7	44.4	289.1
Votes, millions	2.9	6.7	2.0	1.2	18.8	27.4	6.7	1.4	34.9	0.2	3.6	3.5	21.3	2.6	10.7	144.0
Turnout, %	49.4	91.0	50.4	30.1	46.8	45.2	75.3	50.2	70.8	87.3	30.0	40.0	63.0	38.8	24.0	49.8
MEPs in each group:																
EPP	7	6	1	5	21	53	9	5	34	2	9	9	28	7	37	233
Socialist	7	5	3	3	22	33	9	1	17	2	6	12	24	6	30	180
Liberals	—	5	6	5	—	—	—	1	8	1	8	—	3	4	10	51
Greens	2	7	—	2	9	7	—	2	2	1	4	—	4	2	6	48
United Left	—	—	1	1	11	6	7	—	6	—	1	2	4	3	—	42
Europe of Nations	—	—	1	—	12	—	—	6	9	—	—	2	—	—	—	30
TGI	—	2	—	—	5	—	—	—	11	—	—	—	—	—	—	18
EDD	—	—	4	—	6	—	—	—	—	—	3	—	—	—	3	16
Independents	5	—	—	—	1	—	—	—	—	—	—	—	1	—	1	8

Note: The EPP is the European People's Party (Christian Democrats). The Green group includes MEPs from nationalist parties in a number of countries. The Europe of Nations group is dominated by parties opposed to further European integration. The TGI (Technical Group of Independents) is a tactical alliance between groups of different outlooks who register as a group to benefit from group privileges. The EDD is the "Europe of Democracies and Diversities" group, who are opposed to further European integration and in some cases opposed to the EU per se. Turnout figures are based on total votes, including invalid votes, except for the United Kingdom, where they are based on valid votes only.

that dominate national politics, though in some countries there are slightly different party systems at the two levels (Hix and Lord). In Denmark anti-EU parties that do not contest national elections fare well at EP elections, and in France six seats were won in 1999 by a movement created to defend the interests of "rural traditions" such as hunting and fishing.

This lack of clarity about the real purpose of European Parliament elections arises partly because, despite the theory, they are not fought on the basis of European issues. Indeed, few could say if pressed just what "European issues" really are. It is true that there are pan-EU political groups that correspond quite closely to the party families that we discuss in Chapter 8, the most important of which are the Socialists and the European People's Party (representing Christian Democratic parties), but these are little more than very loose umbrella bodies linking national parties, and the manifestos that they issue at EP elections are very bland and completely indistinguishable from each other (Irwin). EP elections are fought on the ground in each country by national parties rather than by these transnational groups, and the parties stress national issues when campaigning. Although they may be criticized for this "parochial" behavior, the parties are inclined to argue that there is no other way of generating any interest at all among the electorate. The consequence is that the performance of the current national government tends to become the main EP election issue in each individual state. When the EP election falls midway in the domestic electoral cycle, it is seen by voters, the media, and the political parties alike as a midterm test of the national government's popularity, although voters are not necessarily simply passing judgment on their government's record (van der Eijk and Franklin).

Once the elections have been held, the MEPs sit in the Parliament's chambers in Strasbourg and Brussels according to their political group, not according to the country they represent. The EP operates very much along party lines, like national parliaments throughout Europe. In the Parliament elected in 1999, a loss of seats by the Socialists gave the two main centre-right groups, the EPP (Christian Democrats) and the Liberals, a dominant position. These groups reached an agreement on filling the prestigious position of EP president: for the first half of the parliament's term the office would go to Nicole Fontaine, a French EPP member, and in January 2002 she would be succeeded by Pat Cox, an Irish MEP from the Liberal group. The MEPs from each national party maintain a separate existence within the EP groups (thus, for example, there is a British Labour group, a French Socialist group, and so on, within the Socialist group, each with its own internal structure). Voting within each of the political groups is fairly solid, even if less so than in most European national parliaments (Hix and Lord, pp. 134–36). A group may punish mavericks by not giving them places on delegations or committees, or in extreme cases by fining them, though generally EP groups prefer to let national groups impose discipline on their own members. If a national group chooses to go its own way in a vote, there is nothing the EP group as a whole can do (Jacobs et al., p. 92). Research conducted in 1996 showed that notwithstanding this group solidarity, for most MEPs the most important focus of representation was their own country rather than "Europe as a whole"; MEPs from every country except Germany felt this (Wessels, p. 216).

The EP does most of its work through committees, of which there are approximately twenty at any one time, corresponding to the main areas of EU activity. Seats on the committees are shared out among the political groups in proportion to their size; within each political group, posts are distributed among the various countries represented within the group. Besides holding committee meetings, the Parliament meets in week-long plenary sessions twelve times a year, at which it considers reports from the committees and votes on declarations or proposed amendments to legislation. As in most national parliaments, attendance in the chamber during plenary sessions tends to be low.

The EP, as we have seen, does not have most of the powers that belong, at least in theory, to domestic parliaments in Europe. It cannot dismiss or appoint the Council of ministers, which plays an important governmental role, and it cannot initiate or promulgate legislation. One mark of the EP's weakness is its lack of control over its location. With both the Commission and the Council offices based in Brussels, it would seem natural for the Parliament also to be there, and most MEPs would prefer this. Instead, its operations are scattered around three countries. Although it holds its committee meetings in Brussels, which is the seat of most of the real action in the Union, it holds its plenary sessions in Strasbourg, in northeastern France, while most of its administrative staff are based in Luxembourg. Decisions on its location are in the hands of the Council, representing the national governments, and neither the French nor the Luxembourg government has been prepared to give up the prestige and such financial benefits as may arise from having the Parliament meet in its territory. Consequently, truckloads of documents are constantly on the road between Brussels, Luxembourg, and Strasbourg, at a considerable cost in terms of time and money.

The EP has always faced problems in its ceaseless campaign to gain more power. It may well be that the Parliament stands fairly low in public esteem, given the low turnout at EP elections and the way these are dominated by domestic rather than European political issues. This weakens any claim by the EP to represent the views of the European public on European issues. The regular proceedings of the EP receive little media coverage in the member states, and when the EP does get into the news, it is quite likely to be for all the wrong reasons: allegations about MEPs engaging in "creative accountancy" over their expenses surface from time to time, for example. Members of the EP are often exasperated by this approach by the media, complaining that the serious work they do in EP committees goes virtually unreported, while the most minor misdemeanors, real or alleged, are blown up out of all proportion. But although they have a fair point, it remains a fact that the EP has been unable to mobilize European public opinion in its perennial quest to gain greater powers. Although in principle EU citizens want the EP to have more power, both the level of information they possess and their degree of trust are quite low, and there is little tangible sign of public demand for a more central role for the EP (Wessels and Diedrichs, p. 147).

Yet, notwithstanding all this, the EP is unquestionably growing in power and significance within the EU's decision-making process. Every reform of the EU's institutions brings some increases in the EP's powers, albeit sometimes only marginal ones. Moreover, the EP is a relatively new institution; MEPs are still learning how to use their existing responsibilities to maximum advantage, and it is possible that they will in the future be able to use the powers they have, especially those in the areas of the budget or the appointment and dismissal of the Commission, in such a manner as to get their way in other matters. The EP thus has the potential to become a major actor in the Union's decision-making process, precisely because of the separation of its role from that of the executive. The EP, like the U.S. Congress but unlike parliaments in most European countries, is able to vote against individual items of legislation without thereby risking bringing down a government. Moreover, its members see the job of an MEP as a worthwhile one in itself, and this attitude would apply even more if the EP were given extended powers (Katz and Wessels, p. 236). In contrast to some national parliaments, the EP is not, and is unlikely to become, a mere stepping-stone on the way to a position in a European government. It is thus likely that MEPs in a more powerful EP will take their parliamentary role more seriously than do many deputies in national parliaments in Europe. Unconstrained by any incentive to be loyal to the executive so as not to jeopardize their promotion prospects—a factor that partly explains the solid party bloc voting among government backbenchers that we witness in national European parliaments, as we saw in Chapter 4—MEPs may in future become more significant players within the EU's policy-making process.

The Council of the European Union

So far, the Council has been mentioned quite frequently in this chapter, and we have noted that it has considerable power, but its precise nature has not been spelled out. The Council of the European Union represents the governments of the fifteen member states of the EU. Although there is in principle only one Council, in practice there are many; to put it another way, the Council meets in many guises. This is so because each national seat on the Council is filled not by the same person every time but by the national minister with responsibility for the policy area that is to be discussed. Thus, if a forthcoming meeting of the Council is going to discuss EU transport policy, each government sends its transport minister (or at least a very senior civil servant from the transport ministry) to the meeting; if farm prices are to be discussed, it sends its agriculture minister; and so on. The Council meets in one form or another about eighty to one hundred times a year, with the foreign and agriculture ministers meeting most often, perhaps once a month, and the other ministers meeting less frequently.

At any given time, one of the member states holds what is termed the Council presidency, and meetings of the Council are chaired by the minister from this country. The presidency rotates among the member states in a fixed order designed to ensure something close to alternation between large and small states, with each country having the office for six months. The period of each country's presidency is too short to make this a very significant role. It is generally reckoned that the "lead-in" period for a new policy is about eighteen months, so it is clear that the country holding the presidency cannot bring any new initiative to fruition; the most it can do is speed up or slow-pedal some of those projects already on the books. In recent years, there has been more coordination between adjacent presidencies in an attempt to avoid the situation where a new presidency might try to reverse the priorities of the preceding one.

When the Commission sends a proposal over to the Council, the Council forwards a copy to the Parliament and also begins extensive scrutiny of the proposal itself. The

Council has a large and complex network of around one thousand specialist committees and subcommittees, staffed mainly by senior national civil servants (Hix, pp. 41–44). This process, known as "comitology," is the first stage at which representatives of the national governments have a chance to assess the proposal. Not surprisingly, quite a few proposals are killed off at this stage if the committee finds it impossible to reach an agreement and explicitly rejects or simply shelves the proposal. The best the Commission can hope for is not unanimous approval from the committee, which is unrealistic to expect, but an agreement to pass the proposal on to the next stage of the decision-making process, subject to some or all of the member states entering specific reservations about it.

From the specialist committee, the proposal goes to a body called COREPER, the Committee of Permanent Representatives, which consists of the heads of the permanent delegations maintained in Brussels by each country. These senior diplomats and their staff iron out as many as possible of the problems identified by the specialist committee, and before Council meetings they brief the ministers about areas where agreement has and has not been reached. All proposals pass from COREPER to a meeting of the Council itself. The Council, unlike the Commission, has no permanent presence in Brussels; indeed, it has no permanent physical existence at all. When a Council meeting is to take place, the relevant ministers fly in from the respective national capitals, and they usually go home again a day or two later. Although both the Commission and the EP maintain information offices for the public in many cities across the Union (and, indeed, outside it), the Council has none. Far from being open and transparent, it has been described as "that most opaque of EU institutions" (Hayes-Renshaw and Wallace, p. 275).

When the ministers do gather in Brussels, they are likely to be faced with a number of proposals that have come through the Union's policy-making process, and perhaps with other decisions as well. In areas where COREPER has reached an agreement, the Council needs merely to give formal ratification to the proposal or decision. If COREPER has proved unable to sort out the problems, the ministers themselves will try to break the deadlock, with horse trading that may cross policy areas. For example, the Spanish transport minister might agree to support a point being made by his or her Austrian counterpart on the understanding that later in the year, when the Fisheries Council is meeting, Austria will back Spain's case for a larger fish quota. The kind of wheeling and dealing that goes on at Council meetings makes it easy to understand why the Council would prefer to relegate the European Parliament to the periphery of decision making, rather than risk having complicated deals unravelled by the EP's insistence on some point. However, as we have seen, the EP can no longer be swept aside as easily as it could in the past, and on more and more issues Council members must now bear in mind the EP's preferences when making deals among themselves. Every important piece of legislation must be approved by the Council, it is true, but increasingly the approval of the EP is required as well.

The manner of Council decision making can be important in bolstering its power. The treaties provide several ways for the Council to make decisions: by unanimity, by qualified majority, and by simple majority (the last of these is hardly ever used). Unanimity is needed when the Council wants to amend a Commission proposal against the wishes of the Commission, and on major constitutional questions, but successive

TABLE 5-4 VOTES PER COUNTRY IN THE COUNCIL OF THE EUROPEAN UNION WHEN DECISIONS ARE MADE BY QUALIFIED MAJORITY

Country	Population	Council Votes	Population per Council Vote	Council votes entitlement if votes were strictly proportionate to population
Germany	82,061,000	10	8,206,100	19
United Kingdom	59,009,000	10	5,900,900	14
France	58,608,000	10	5,860,800	14
Italy	56,868,000	10	5,686,800	13
Spain	39,323,000	8	4,915,375	9
Netherlands	15,609,000	5	3,121,800	4
Greece	10,498,000	5	2,099,600	3
Belgium	10,181,000	5	2,036,200	2
Portugal	9,550,000	5	1,910,000	2
Sweden	8,848,000	4	2,212,000	2
Austria	8,072,000	4	2,018,000	2
Denmark	5,284,000	3	1,761,333	1
Finland	5,140,000	3	1,713,333	1
Ireland	3,661,000	3	1,220,333	1
Luxembourg	424,000	2	212,000	0
Total	373,136,000	87	4,288,919	87

Note: A majority requires 62 votes, and a blocking minority requires 26.

treaties have greatly reduced the number of other situations in which it is required, and qualified majority voting is now the most common method of decision making. When a decision is reached by qualified majority, each minister wields a number of votes corresponding approximately to his or her country's population, though, as with the allocation of EP seats, the small countries are generously overrepresented (see Table 5-4). The total number of votes among the fifteen ministers is 87, and 62 (71 percent) of these are needed for a majority. It can be seen from the table that at least eight countries are needed to produce a qualified majority, and at least three to produce the 26 votes that make up a blocking minority.

In the past, the Council preferred to operate on the basis of unanimity so as not to overrule any state that had a strong objection to any proposal. This was codified in the so-called Luxembourg Agreement of 1966, which for the next twenty years was interpreted as allowing any state to veto any proposal by claiming that its "vital national interests" were at stake. The result was a very slow-moving decision-making process, until the use of qualified majority voting was extended by successive treaties from the mid-1980s onwards. Nowadays, many decisions are made on the basis of qualified majority voting, and some observers speculate that the national veto has fallen into such disuse that in effect it no longer exists. However, it is true that the Council still prefers to operate on the basis of consensus, and that if a country, or a group of countries, has strong objections to a proposal that has majority support, the majority will try to find a way of accommodating the objections, or will even postpone the decision indefinitely, rather than railroad the proposal through (Hayes-Renshaw and Wallace, p. 275). This "culture of consensus" springs largely from a feeling that, in the long run, imposing policies upon countries that intensely dislike them would not be good for the EU's legitimacy or for the successful implementation of its policies.

The European Council

The European Council (not to be confused with the Council of the European Union) was created formally in 1974, and its first meeting was held in Dublin in March 1975. It consists of the heads of government of the fifteen member states (the fifteen foreign ministers, the president of the Commission, and another commissioner also attend European Council meetings). It meets at least twice every year, that is, at least once in each of the two countries that hold the presidency of the Council of the European Union during each year, and these summit meetings attract extensive press coverage. All the major steps forward taken by the EU have been initiated either by the European Council or by the Commission, and at the very least they have needed the backing of the European Council to get going.

The Maastricht Treaty of 1992 gave its central role explicit mention, stating that the "European Council shall provide the Union with the necessary impetus for its development and shall define the general political guidelines thereof," and this position was confirmed and strengthened by the Amsterdam Treaty. Even so, the authority of the European Council is essentially political rather than legal. Its lack of legal powers is more realistically seen as a lack of constraints; its relationship with the rest of the Union's decision-making structure is that of a free-floating agency, able to intervene in any area at any time.

Some advocates of closer European integration regret the central position of the European Council when it comes to major decisions. It seems to confirm the position of the member states and their governments, rather than the Union institutions (the Commission and the Parliament), as the central actors in the EU, and gives the impression that the EU is still more of an intergovernmental organization than a supranational one. On the other hand, it could be argued that the EU would be far less relevant to the member states were it not for the direct interest and involvement of the heads of government in shaping its affairs, and, moreover, that if EU initiatives and policies are to make fundamental progress, they need behind them the weight that only the heads of government can supply.

The centrality of the European Council, and the important role of the Council of the European Union, raise fundamental questions about democratic accountability within the EU. The Commission is accountable to Parliament (which approved its appointment and can dismiss it), and the Parliament is accountable to the European public through the direct elections held every five years. But to whom are the Council of the EU and the European Council accountable? The short answer is: to no one. It is true that all the heads of government attending a European Council meeting, as well

The heads of government of the EU member states pose for the traditional "family photo" at the Helsinki meeting of the European Council in December 1999. At these meetings, the most important business is done well away from the cameras. © Christian Vioujard/Liaison Agency

as all the ministers attending a Council meeting, are individually accountable to their own parliaments for what they have or have not done at the meeting—though how effective parliaments are in enforcing this accountability is another question. But neither the Council of the EU nor the European Council as an institution is in any way answerable or accountable to anyone at all, either in theory or in practice. The move away from unanimity to qualified majority voting as the basis for decision making has compounded this: whereas when decisions required unanimity, each minister could be asked by his or her national parliament why he or she did not veto a proposal, under qualified majority voting no single minister has this power. The lack of accountability of important decision makers has led to much talk of a "democratic deficit" within the EU, and given that the Union will admit only democracies to membership, some have asked ironically whether the EU itself would be eligible for EU membership if it had to apply (for a discussion of these issues, see Andersen and Eliassen; Craig; Weiler).

The Court of Justice

The Court of Justice is based in Luxembourg and consists of fifteen judges, one from each member state. It interprets and applies EU law and the Union's constitution (in other words, the treaties). Its decisions are binding on all member states, and this marks one of the main differences between the EU and other international organizations. Although a state may refuse to accept a judgment made by another international court (such as the International Court of Justice at The Hague or the European Court of

Human Rights at Strasbourg), those states belonging to the EU cannot pick and choose among the judgments of the Court of Justice. Its decisions override those of domestic courts, and it is accepted throughout the Union that EU law overrides domestic law, even though this is not explicitly stated in the treaties (for a discussion of the relationship between the two, see Alter). The Court of Justice is in effect the final court of appeal in the EU; there is no higher authority. In giving its judgments, the Court has not confined itself to the treaties (which are concerned mainly with economic matters); it has also looked for inspiration to the constitutions of the member states and to the European Convention on Human Rights. It has taken a creative rather than a positivist approach to its role—that is, it has supplied interpretations to fill gaps in the Union's legislation and has cited its own case law rather than feeling confined strictly to the letter of the treaties (Shapiro, 1992).

Domestic courts frequently refer cases to the Court if a question of the interpretation of Union law is involved. In addition, one government or the Commission may take another government before the Court for failing to meet its obligations; such cases (which in practice are almost invariably brought by the Commission rather than by another government) often concern a state's alleged discrimination against imports from other EU countries. As a result of such cases, the Court has stated, to give a few examples, that it is not permissible for a member state to fund advertising campaigns designed to promote domestic products; to discriminate against workers—with regard to employment, pay, or other conditions of work or employment—on the basis of nationality; or to conduct excessive checking or inspection of imported goods. The growing recourse to the Court has created problems by greatly increasing its workload. In 1989 a "Court of First Instance" was introduced to share the load and speed up the process of justice, though it still takes about two years on average from the lodgement of a case with the court for a decision to emerge.

Even though the Court possesses political antennae, "taking care in its judgmental policy not to push the willingness of the Member States over the limit" (Hunnings, p. 132), implementation of its judgments has become a cause of some concern. The Court of Justice, unlike domestic courts, has no police force or army to enforce its judgments. Until November 1993, when the Maastricht Treaty came into operation, it did not possess any formal sanctions for use against those who do not obey its decisions. Since that date, it has been able to impose fines on member states for such disobedience or for failing to implement Union laws. It has seen this power as a sanction of last resort, but, as it notes sadly, "there are times when the penalty procedures . . . seem to offer the only possibility of inducing a Member State to come into line." As of the end of 1998, there had been fourteen cases in which these penalties were imposed; in one case, Italy was incurring fines at the rate of 185,850 euros per day for failing to comply with a judgment on urban water treatment (Commission of the European Communities, pp. 5, 11–12). The Court must rely on the law enforcement agencies of the member states and, hence, ultimately on their governments to enforce compliance. In general, it is true, "the declaratory judgment is its own sanction," and states usually seek to avoid judgments against them (Freestone and Davidson, p. 152). However, this does not always apply, and the Court sometimes experiences great difficulty in trying to secure implementation of its judgments.

In such cases, it is confronted not by explicit refusal to comply with a Court judgment but by delaying tactics: states receiving an adverse judgment from the Court sometimes respond by saying that they will need time to consider the full implications of the verdict, a process that in some cases has apparently required several years. Moreover, certain governments seem to be little put out by receiving judgments against them. Table 5-5, which shows the position in 1998, reveals that there is significant national variation. The Scandinavian countries and Britain—ironically, some of the most Eurosceptic countries—have the best record of compliance, and southern European countries the worst. Greece, which had been a member for only eighteen years, had been the subject of nearly eight times as many actions as Denmark, which had been a member for twenty-six years. In some of the cases where the state had not complied with a judgment, the original judgment had been delivered in the 1980s! Generally speaking, the national governments concerned do not take such an indulgent attitude to the enforcement of judgments given by their own domestic courts, although it is probably true to say that the degrees of rigor with which domestic laws and EU laws are enforced in each country are strongly correlated.

TABLE 5-5   ACTIONS OF THE EUROPEAN COURT OF JUSTICE WITH RESPECT TO THE MEMBER STATES

	Actions for failure to fulfill obligations		Judgments with which state has not yet complied as of 31 December 1998
	1998	1953–98	
Austria	4	5	0
Belgium	22	225	15
Denmark	1	21	0
Finland	1	1	0
France	22	185	10
Germany	5	122	5
Greece	17	160	12
Ireland	10	84	3
Italy	12	355	11
Luxembourg	8	86	4
Netherlands	3	59	1
Portugal	5	41	5
Spain	6	60	12
Sweden	1	1	0
United Kingdom	1	41	4
Total	118	1446	82

Sources: Court of Justice of the European Communities, *Annual Report 1998: Synopsis of the Work of the Court of Justice and the Court of First Instance of the European Communities,* Court of Justice of the European Communities, Luxembourg, 1999, p. 106; Commission of the European Communities, *Sixteenth Annual Report on Monitoring the Application of Community Law (1998),* Office for Official Publications of the European Communities, Luxembourg, 1999, pp. 230–40.

WHAT DOES THE EUROPEAN UNION DO?

As time has passed, the range of policy areas in which the EU shows an interest has steadily increased. In recent years the emphasis has been on establishing a single market and a single currency across the Union. In addition, in an attempt to give the EU a human face and to moderate some of the effects of giving market forces fairly free rein, members of the Union have set about creating a "People's Europe" or a "Social Europe." In terms of where the EU's money is spent, the main policy area remains agriculture.

Single Market and Single Currency

For many years a prominent concern of the Union was the completion of the single internal market. The Union has long been colloquially known in Britain as the "Common Market," and although it is much more than this, the aim of creating a common European market certainly features strongly in the EEC Treaty of 1957. A common market would mean that goods and services could be marketed and sold with equal ease all across the Union; there would be no barriers to trade within the Union. Only in the second half of the 1980s was real political will put behind the achievement of this by the Commission, with the target of completing the single market by the end of 1992. Even if in the event the target was not fully reached, the progress was impressive, and most of the remaining barriers to trade have subsequently been removed, although some still exist. For example, one state may ban imports from another on what the Commission believes to be spurious health grounds, or one government may give state aid to a company in its own country in such a way as to give that company an unfair advantage against other EU competitors.

Beyond the single market lies the possibility of a single economy. Economic and monetary union (EMU) is another long-standing goal of European integrationists, and after approximately twenty years of groundwork that produced few tangible results, a decisive step was taken in the late 1990s with the establishment of a common European currency, termed the euro. The European Council agreed that the currency of all the member states whose economies met a number of "convergence criteria" would be able to join the scheme as from 1 January 1999; the criteria were designed to rule out countries whose burden of debt, current budget deficit, inflation rate and/or interest rates were too high. In the mid-1990s it seemed that very few states would be able to meet these terms, but drastic changes of financial policy in certain countries, and a degree of fudging in some cases, meant that by the deadline only one country, Greece, unambiguously failed to meet the criteria. In addition, three countries that could have qualified (Denmark, Sweden, and the United Kingdom) took political decisions not to enter the single currency, which left the currencies of the other eleven countries locked together at what were described as "irrevocable fixed rates." For example, there are 6.55957 French francs to the euro and 1.95583 German marks to the euro, and these rates are not subject to fluctuation in the same way as that of the euro against the dollar.

Under the scheme for EMU, these old notes and coins would continue to circulate for a further three years. During this period, those moving among these eleven countries

The common EU currency, the euro, was launched in 1999, and although the banknotes themselves were not due to circulate until 2002, their design was finalized several years in advance. The launch of the euro was seen as a triumph by proponents of closer European integration, but the new currency disappointed its supporters in its first year of life by losing value steadily against other currencies such as the US dollar and the pound sterling.
© SIPA Press

could expect to find prices increasingly quoted not just in the local currency but also in euros. For example, a newspaper purchaser travelling from Ireland to Portugal could find, in the first country, the *Irish Times* on sale at "£0.85—1.08 euros," and in the second, *A Bola* on sale at "120 escudos—0.60 euros," enabling easy comparison of prices. In the first half of 2002, the old notes and coins were set to be phased out and replaced by euro-denominated banknotes and coins. The long-term future of the common currency was by no means assured. The economies of the participating countries are diverse, with a range of economic cycles, and it remains to be seen whether governments that breach the terms of EMU by running large budget deficits will be reined in as provided in the scheme for EMU. If all countries obey the rules, certain key economic levers—control over interest rates, public spending, and some taxes—will be outside the control of national governments.

A People's Europe

There are nowadays very few policy spheres in which the EU is not concerned, at least to some degree. The EU has the aim, even if this is not precisely expressed in any of the treaties, of bringing about an equality of civil and social rights, of living and working conditions, of opportunities, and of income across the Union; this is sometimes characterized as building a "Social Europe" or a "People's Europe." To this end it has tended to get involved in virtually all policy areas, even including some not enumerated in the founding treaties. It has issued legal instruments covering such diverse subjects as the size and grading of eggs, the purity of tap water to which citizens are entitled, the length of time truck drivers can drive without a break, the safety and cleanliness of the sea at bathing beaches, the extent to which countries can reserve their coastal waters for the exclusive use of their own fishing fleets, equal pay for men and women, the rights of consumers, and aid for the Third World.

In addition, the Union has the aim of reducing the significant disparities in wealth that exist within its boundaries; this is known in the characteristically opaque Euro-jargon as "cohesion policy." Ever since the three southern European countries joined in the 1980s, there have been large wealth differences among regions, and some feared that the moves toward a single market might be of most benefit to a "golden triangle" covering the southeastern part of England, parts of France, northern Italy, and most of Germany, with the rest of the Union becoming ever more peripheral. Table 5-6 shows the degree of variation between the member states, with GDP per capita in

TABLE 5-6   GROSS DOMESTIC PRODUCT OF EU MEMBER STATES, AND CONTRIBUTIONS TO AND RECEIPTS FROM THE 1998 BUDGET

	Gross domestic product in 1998 per capita, $	Share of 1998 EU budget revenues contributed, %	Share of 1998 EU budget expend-iture received, %	Net gain/loss as % of EU budget	Net gain/loss per capita, euros
Luxembourg	38,616	0.3	0.1	−0.2	−315
Denmark	32,934	2.1	2.1	0	−36
Austria	26,210	2.5	1.8	−0.7	−102
Germany	26,056	25.1	14.3	−10.8	−128
Sweden	25,852	2.9	1.8	−1.1	−127
Finland	24,484	1.4	1.3	−0.1	−44
Belgium	24,432	3.8	2.4	−1.4	−140
France	24,398	16.5	16.6	+0.1	−3
Netherlands	24,107	6.2	2.9	−3.3	−195
United Kingdom	23,006	15.2	9.6	−5.6	−96
Ireland	22,287	1.2	4.4	+3.2	+583
Italy	20,323	12.9	11.9	−1.0	−37
Spain	14,129	7.0	17.2	+10.2	+165
Greece	11,366	1.6	8.2	+6.6	+435
Portugal	10,574	1.3	5.5	+4.2	+296
Total/Average EU	22,285	100.0	100.0	0	−29

Note: Countries are ranked in order of per capita gross domestic product.

Sources: Gross Domestic Product as Table 1.2. EU budget 1998 from Official Journal of the European Communities, C349, vol. 42, Dec. 3, 1999, *Court of Auditors: Annual Report Concerning the Financial Year 1998,* Office for Official Publications of the European Communities, Luxembourg, p. 13, and Annex 1, p. xv. Figures for expenditure refer to where the sums were spent, not payments to the member states, and exclude a "miscellaneous" category of spending that amounted to 7.2 percent of expenditure.

Luxembourg over three times the corresponding figures for Greece and Portugal. The table shows that the budget has some redistributive effect, in that four of the five poorest countries receive more from the EU budget than they give to it. The difference between the German inflows and outflows is so great that Germany is sometimes described as the "paymaster" of the Union, and with its increased financial burden following German unification there was growing unhappiness there with the scale of its contribution (Laffan, pp. 54–56). To try to even out the fruits of economic growth, the EU has set up a number of "structural" funds, the most important of which are known as the Regional Development Fund and the Social Fund, to attempt to promote development in the less wealthy parts of the Union, particularly Greece, Portugal, Spain, Ireland, and southern Italy (Allen). Under these headings, the Union funds schemes to give job training to the unemployed throughout the EU and to combat unemployment in the peripheral regions. The size of these funds increased greatly in the 1990s, and, at least partly in consequence, wealth per capita in Ireland, and to a lesser extent Greece, Portugal, and Spain, made notable strides towards the EU average.

As to the substance of EU policies, it would be difficult to categorize these unequivocally as either basically left-wing or basically right-wing; indeed, the EU comes under attack from both the left and the right. Some of its decisions, such as its insistence on deregulation of industries such as telecommunications, tend to promote private enterprise and free trade. However, it also adopts a very interventionist approach to agriculture and is active in defending the social rights of groups in society that suffer discrimination of one sort or another, such as women, migrant workers, and workers in general. Its policies to promote gender equality (Mazey) have had particular impact in countries where women have not traditionally experienced equality. In Spain, for example, membership of the EU has been judged "substantially beneficial as far as matters of equal treatment are concerned," and in Ireland the need to implement EU directives has been one of the main spurs for successive governments to introduce gender equality legislation (González Jorge and Almarcha Barbado, p. 154; Galligan, pp. 310–11). The growing steps towards a single EU economy will make it difficult for any country to pursue policies that drift very far to the right or the left of the consensus, a consensus sometimes termed the "European social market" or "neo-liberalism meets the social market" (Hix, pp. 238–40). This may be a concern for some governments; on the other hand, the claim that "the EU made us do it" (or "the EU stopped us doing it") can be a useful excuse for a government secretly relieved at the chance to wriggle out of unwise election promises (Smith).

In order to make the EU clearly and directly relevant to its citizens and to justify the claim that a "People's Europe" is being constructed, the Union has attempted to create symbols with which Europeans can identify. The EU has its own flag, consisting of twelve gold stars arranged in a circle on a blue background, which can be seen flying from many public buildings across the Union alongside the appropriate national flag; it also has its own anthem (the prelude to Beethoven's "Ode to Joy"). The passports of all EU countries are now issued in a uniform size and color, and holders of a passport of any EU country do not have to pass through customs when they visit another EU country, or, when crossing an internal EU frontier, even pass through a border control.

BOX 5-1

THE EUROPEAN UNION

France

France was one of the six original members of the EEC in 1958. Under General de Gaulle, the French president from 1958 to 1969, France opposed the admission of Britain, but de Gaulle's attitude toward the EU was not too different from that displayed by certain British governments after 1973. De Gaulle was in favor of the economic benefits that the Union brought but was very suspicious of any steps that might dilute the traditional sovereignty of the state. Since his departure from office, France has been more willing to contemplate closer integration among the member states, but despite the rhetoric of some of its leading politicians, it is not generally seen as being at the forefront of the integrationists. France joined the single currency in the late 1990s, though its left-wing government expressed concern that the thinking behind monetary union attached more importance to fiscal rectitude than to combating unemployment. France has consistently been a strong defender of the Common Agricultural Policy, from which its inefficient agriculture sector benefits greatly.

Germany

For Germany, one of the six founders, membership in the EU offered the prospect both of economic gains and of political rehabilitation after World War II. As the member state with the largest economy in the Union, Germany has picked up the largest share of the bill for funding the EU. In the past, most Germans have been willing to see this as a price worth paying, even in pure economic terms, for securing access to the huge EU market for their efficient industries, but in recent years there have been signs of a feeling that their country is asked to shoulder an unfairly large proportion of the contributions to the EU's budget. When the single currency was established in 1999, concern was expressed in Germany that too many countries, including some that had not shown convincingly that they were capable of adhering to disciplined economic policies, were being admitted to the scheme.

Italy

Italy was one of the founders of the EU, which has brought significant economic benefits to the country, although its wealth is concentrated heavily in the northern half of the country. The southern half of the country and the two main islands, Sicily and Sardinia, are among the poorest regions of the EU, and they also tend to feature prominently in accounts of fraud within the EU. Italy has a less-than-glorious record when it comes to implementing Union law and complying with judgments of the Court of Justice. Despite its size, Italy has generally been content to allow other countries, particularly France and Germany, to take the lead in shaping the future direction of the Union. Among both politicians and the public, enthusiasm for moves toward a federal Europe is high. When the single currency scheme was launched in the late 1990s, it was widely assumed that Italy would be unable to meet the conditions for entry, but several years of atypically austere budgets enabled the country to (just) meet the entry terms.

Netherlands

The Netherlands was one of the founding members of the EU, but as a small country it has accepted that its impact on decisions will be relatively marginal. Attitudes toward the EU in general, as well as specific attitudes toward closer integration, are broadly favorable, even though the Netherlands is a significant net contributor to the EU budget. Unlike the governments of some other small countries, which fear that a supranational EU government would lead to their interests being overlooked in favor of the larger countries, Dutch governments believe that such supranational bodies, by making decisions in the broader European interest, are more likely to benefit them than a purely intergovernmental arrangement would.

Spain

Soon after the first democratic election in forty years was held in 1977, Spain applied for membership in the EU, and after a protracted period of negotiations, it joined on January 1, 1986. The potential economic benefits of membership were a powerful incentive, but just as important were the political implications. Under the long rule of the dictator Franco, Spain had been isolated from Western European political thought and developments, and joining the EU was an ideal opportunity to join the mainstream rather than remain on the fringe. In addition, it was felt that the risk of a military coup by far-rightists attempting to restore a quasi-Francoist dictatorship would be greatly reduced if the country were part of (and were benefiting economically from its membership in) a community committed to the preservation of liberal democratic values. Spain is one of the more integrationist of the member states and favors an expansion of the role of the European Parliament. It is also the largest net beneficiary from the EU budget.

Sweden

Sweden has a long-standing policy of neutrality, which kept it out of World War II. This led to its refusal for many years to consider joining the European Union. Until the late 1980s, the communist bloc regarded the EU as an antisocialist organization and refused to have any dealings with it. In the context of this perception of the Union, it was felt in Sweden that joining the EU would be incompatible with the country's neutrality. The ending of the Cold War and of the old bipolar world order, however, led to a rapid reassessment of Sweden's attitude. The country became a member of the EU in 1995, following a referendum in which 52 percent of the voters supported membership. Enthusiasm soon cooled, though, and by the start of the new century Sweden was seen as one of the least satisfied members of the EU, along with Denmark, Finland, and the United Kingdom.

United Kingdom

Britain stood aloof from the moves toward European in-

tegration in the late 1940s and the 1950s. By the time it had changed its mind, in the early 1960s, the previously welcoming climate had grown chillier, and it had to wait until 1973 to gain admittance. Once Britain was inside the EU, its former ambivalence reasserted itself. Successive governments resisted attempts to promote closer integration of the member states, and Britain was sometimes accused of having, psychologically at least, one foot inside the EU and one still outside it. One writer, Stephen George, in his book *The Awkward Partner,* describes Britain as "still awkward after all this time." Under Margaret Thatcher and John Major, its minimalist attitude toward such aspects of European integration as a common currency and guaranteed protection for the rights of workers across the Union irritated many other members in the 1980s and 1990s, but after the change of government in 1997, when Tony Blair's Labour party entered power, Britain's rhetoric changed greatly, albeit without any great change in policy. The question of relationships with Europe is a major and contentious issue in British politics; it divides each of the two main parties,

Agriculture

In the past, agriculture has not only accounted for the bulk of the EU's budget but also been one of the areas in which it has been hardest to find agreement. In recent years, though, it has slipped down the political agenda, yet, through the Common Agricultural Policy (CAP), it still consumes most of the Union's expenditure. Although the proportion of the Union's labor force working in agriculture has fallen from over 25 percent in the late 1950s to less than 7 percent, the share of Union spending going to agriculture has consistently been far in excess of this. Having exceeded 60 percent in nearly all budgets of the 1970s and 1980s, it fell to around 50 percent in the 1990s; it is not projected to fall below this in the foreseeable future.

The CAP is intended to establish a single, or common, market in agricultural products so that they cost the same anywhere within the EU, and to guarantee agricultural incomes. The setting of prices in most sectors is not left to the market. Instead, agricultural prices are very highly regulated, with the Council fixing prices for nearly all products—prices that are invariably higher (often several times higher) than world market prices. In order to protect EU farmers from competition from lower-cost producers elsewhere, levies are imposed on imports coming into the Union. Because prices are fixed above world levels, production quotas must be set, and the Commission undertakes to buy up, at a guaranteed and high "intervention" price, what farmers are unable to sell on the open market. The results of the CAP are highly satisfactory for most EU farmers (especially large farmers, who have benefited most from its operation) but less so for consumers, who have to pay higher food prices than they otherwise would. They are also unsatisfactory for other major food exporters (such as the United States and Australia), whose produce is at a disadvantage when competing with heavily subsidized EU farm exports, and for producers in developing markets, who are compelled to compete with surplus EU produce dumped on the market at very low prices. In recent years, partly in response to such criticisms, the emphasis of agricultural policy has moved from price support to income support.

Despite successive reforms that have curbed the worst of the excesses for which the CAP became notorious in the 1980s—the surpluses that were termed the beef and butter mountain and the wine lake, which were stored in warehouses for years on end before being either fed to animals or simply destroyed—the CAP remains a very expensive feature of the EU's operations. In addition, the sheer size of the agriculture budget and the convoluted nature of the schemes established by the CAP provide plenty of opportunity for fraud. Further reform of the CAP, in order to reduce the payments given to farmers so as to free up funds to benefit EU citizens generally, is widely agreed to be desirable, but in every country, and at the EU level, farmers' interest groups are powerful and governments of all political complexions are reluctant to alienate such a well-organized lobby, as we discuss further in Chapter 14. The outcome is that "consumers can be certain of one thing: in defiance of basic economic principles, food prices will remain high in the EU even though supply far exceeds demand" (Dinan, p. 350).

Some 4,000 German farmers demonstrated in March 1999 against Commission proposals that would have reduced subsidies to farmers, proposals that the demonstrators maintained would amount to a "war against farmers." Predictably, when the European Council met in Berlin to make its decision on the proposals, the package was watered down as a number of leaders, especially French President Jacques Chirac, responded to pressure from the powerful farmers' lobbies.
© AFP Worldwide

THE EUROPEAN UNION: INTERGOVERNMENTAL OR SUPRANATIONAL ORGANIZATION?

The EU contains elements of two kinds of polity. One is the intergovernmental organization, in which the governments of sovereign member states cooperate without giving up the ultimate right to make their own decisions. The second is the supranational body, in which the ultimate power rests with the common institutions and the national governments have room to maneuver only within the framework of policy decided at the collective level. Developments such as the increasing power of the European Parliament and the introduction of a common currency suggest that the EU may be moving in the direction of a supranational organization, but at the same time, the EU still seems to bear some of the characteristics of an intergovernmental organization. We can see the continuing relevance of the intergovernmental model when we examine two of its aspects: the implementation of policy, and the financing of the EU.

How fully EU legislation is implemented across the EU is unknown, in the absence of detailed study. It is generally accepted, though, that implementation is far from uniform or perfect. In the words of Martin Shapiro (1999, p. 29),

> Implementation, as we all know, is in the hands of the administrations of the Member States. As to that implementation, there is a basic rule: Don't ask, don't tell. . . . Everyone knows it would be a miracle if all Member State administrations were implementing most EU regulations, let alone directives, in approximately the same way.[1]

There is widespread concern that at least some member states make only token efforts to secure the enforcement of EU decisions about which they happen not to feel strongly or which they had never really supported in the first place (see Peters). Should such states wish to do this, they have many strategies short of outright disobedience, such as lack of implementation; lack of enforcement; lack of application; evasion; non-compliance by the legislature, executive, or judiciary; and benign non-compliance (Snyder, p. 56). Of course, the Commission, which is responsible for implementing EU law, tries its best to spot and deal with all of these strategies.

Even if a state is willing to implement the legislation, this might prove time-consuming or complicated. For one thing, EU legislation is full of impenetrable jargon and acronyms, so the EU has had to produce a thesaurus of this jargon, known as "Eurovoc," which runs to five volumes (Burns, p. 438). Civil servants attempting to implement legislation sometimes find themselves unable, due to its vagueness or ambiguity, to understand what obligation it imposes or what action it requires, and the Commission is seen as prone to supply unsatisfactory or tardy answers to questions seeking clarification (Bekkers et al., pp. 467–68). The structure of national administration may not be conducive to the implementation of EU policy. In the Netherlands, some items of legislation require action from more than one government

---

[1]Regulations and directives are different kinds of EU legislation. Regulations, once adopted at the EU level, are immediately binding in every country without needing approval at the national level. Directives bind the member states to take appropriate steps, within a specified period, to achieve a stipulated end, but allow each member state to choose the methods of achieving this end.

department, and different departments are accustomed to using different methods of issuing regulations, leading to deadlock or confusion. Matters might be improved if one department were in charge of overall coordination, but in fact three different departments are competing for this role, and none possesses the authority to impose itself (Bekkers et al., pp. 474–75).

The relatively low level of finances controlled by the Union institutions as opposed to the national governments also suggests intergovernmentalism. There is a ceiling on the size of the EU's budget relative to the total GNP of the member states for each year; this ceiling stands at 1.27 percent, illustrating the way in which the resources available to the EU institutions are dwarfed by those controlled by national governments. This is partly because some responsibilities usually shouldered by the central government in a federal state, such as defense, are handled at the national level within the EU. However, small as the figure of 1.27 percent is, it represents a steady upward trend since 1973, when the EU budget was only 0.5 percent of member states' GNPs. The 1999 budget stood at 97 billion euros, which represented 1.11 percent of the combined GNP of the member states and 2.5 percent of their total public expenditure. This figure of 97 billion euros amounted to about 260 euros per person (at prevailing exchange rates in mid-2000, around $243, or £162).

The Union is financed on the basis of what are termed "own resources." This means that it does not receive a block grant from the fifteen governments, which would give it an overtly subordinate and dependent position; instead, it has a statutory right to the revenue derived from the flow of money into and around the Union. The EU has two main sources of "own resources" revenue: it receives 1.0 percent of what national governments collect from the main indirect tax in the Union—the Value Added Tax (VAT)—and it also keeps the duties collected from trade with countries outside the EU. In addition, a direct levy is imposed on member states in proportion to their gross national products (GNPs); this source of revenue, which has a progressive effect on wealth distribution, has been growing in significance since it was introduced in the late 1980s, and has now become the largest revenue source (Nugent, pp. 393–96).

Trying to decide whether the EU is essentially supranational or essentially intergovernmental raises what Brigid Laffan (p. 264) refers to as "one of the great dilemmas when analysing the Union—should we see strength or weakness?" Focusing on the difficulties of uniform implementation of legislation and the small proportion of resources controlled at the EU level emphasizes how far the EU has still to go before being considered a truly supranational body. On the other hand, it is clearly more than a merely intergovernmental body, and has moved closer to being a genuinely supranational polity than any before it. We shall now consider whether it will move farther in this direction in the future.

THE FUTURE OF THE EUROPEAN UNION

Ever since the first of the three Communities, the ECSC, was founded in the early 1950s, there have been some who have hoped, and others who have feared, that the existing Union framework would become the vehicle for a process generally termed "European integration," ending in the creation of a federal Western European (or even all-European) state, similar in its political structure to the United States of America. The feasibility of this idea has ebbed and flowed over the years, but at the start of the new century, following the integrationist measures brought about by the Maastricht and Amsterdam treaties and with the common currency in place, the auguries for a move in the direction of a federal Europe looked brighter than they had perhaps ever been. Certainly, if full European monetary union, covering all the member states, is achieved, it could be argued that it would be illogical, inconsistent, and undemocratic not to have EU-wide political institutions to monitor economic decisions made at the EU level.

There is some variation among the member states on the question of giving more power to the Union institutions (in other words, the Commission and the Parliament) and taking power away from the national governments (in other words, the Council). Of course, there are also nuances of opinion within each country, and there may be differences between verbal positions and the action a government takes when it comes to the crunch. Even so, a certain degree of generalization is possible. Some countries are traditionally *communautaire;* in the forefront of the integrationists can be found Belgium, Italy, the Netherlands, Germany, and Spain. Others are notoriously recalcitrant when it comes to European integration. The countries that generally lead the resistance to moves toward greater unity are Britain, Denmark, and Sweden, but several other states—Austria, Finland, and probably France—would not be far behind them, even though they are usually content to let others take the lead.

The moves toward European integration that have taken place over the past fifty years have been instigated almost entirely by political elites rather than by the European public. This is not to say that ordinary Europeans are opposed to European integration, but it would be wrong to pretend that there is great enthusiasm for more than the most visible manifestations, such as the ability to cross borders without the need for a passport. The most important decisions have been taken by governments and ratified by parliaments; in seven of the present fifteen member states, the people have never been consulted directly. The other eight countries have held sixteen referendums between them (see Table 5-7). Of these referendums, three—those held in France and the United Kingdom—can only doubtfully be seen as involving genuine consultation. Both French referendums were primarily exercises in domestic battles, their aim being to boost the fortunes of the government party and to sow discord among the opposition parties (Morel). Britain, unlike the other two countries that joined the EU in 1973, did not hold a referendum before entry, but the Labour Party, which was in opposition when Britain joined, returned to office in 1974, and the following year, after a somewhat cosmetic "renegotiation" of the terms of British entry, held a referendum on whether Britain should remain in the EU.

Both Denmark and Ireland have constitutions that have made referendums compulsory on each step toward integration, given the implications that this has for national sovereignty. The Irish public has consistently given strong support but Danish voters have been more lukewarm, and in June 1992 they surprised the EU establishment by voting against ratification of the Maastricht treaty. After initial uncertainty right across the EU as to how to respond to this vote, the European Council, meeting in Edinburgh in December 1992, agreed that the Danes could opt out of certain provisions of the Treaty (in particular, Denmark would not have to participate in the common European

TABLE 5-7   REFERENDUMS ON EUROPEAN INTEGRATION, 1970–99

	Country	Issue	Yes %
23.4.72	France	Allow enlargement of EC	68.3
10.5.72	Ireland	Join EC	83.1
25.9.72	Norway	Join EC	46.5
2.10.72	Denmark	Join EC	63.3
5.6.75	United Kingdom	Remain within EC	67.2
27.2.86	Denmark	Ratify Single European Act	56.2
26.5.87	Ireland	Ratify Single European Act	69.9
18.6.89	Italy	Mandate for Italian MEPs	88.1
2.6.92	Denmark	Ratify Maastricht Treaty	49.3
18.6.92	Ireland	Ratify Maastricht Treaty	69.1
20.9.92	France	Ratify Maastricht Treaty	51.0
6.12.92	Switzerland	Join European Economic Area	49.7
18.5.93	Denmark	Ratify Maastricht Treaty as modified by Edinburgh Agreement	56.7
12.6.94	Austria	Join EU	66.6
16.10.94	Finland	Join EU	56.9
13.11.94	Sweden	Join EU	52.2
28.11.94	Norway	Join EU	47.8
22.5.98	Ireland	Ratify Amsterdam Treaty	61.7
28.5.98	Denmark	Ratify Amsterdam Treaty	55.1

Source: Gallagher and Uleri (1996); *European Journal of Political Research* data yearbooks.

currency and would not take part in decisions relating to defense matters). The revised package was put to the Danes in May 1993 and was approved by a 57–43 margin (Svensson). In 1998 both the Danes and the Irish endorsed the Amsterdam Treaty. Although referendums were held in 1994 in Austria, Finland, and Sweden on joining the EU, none of these countries held a referendum on Amsterdam, and it seems that only in Denmark and Ireland can the voters expect to be consulted automatically on future integrationist steps.

Surveys conducted across the EU in 1999 give an insight into the views of the public (see Table 5-8). Those in Italy and the Netherlands are Euro-enthusiasts on every measure, and the Irish, Belgians, and Luxembourgers are usually at or near the top of the table. Euroskepticism is strongest in Sweden and the United Kingdom, with the Finns and Austrians also generally near the bottom on the enthusiasm scale. These figures come from just one poll, but the pattern is very consistent over the series of Eurobarometer polls, which are conducted every six months. The last column in Table 5-8 shows widespread support for allowing policies in a number of areas to be made at the EU rather than the national level. In Italy, respondents would prefer this for all eighteen policy areas about which the question was asked (of course, cynics might attribute this to Italians' lack of faith in their own governments rather than to

TABLE 5-8   ATTITUDES TOWARD THE EU AMONG CITIZENS OF THE MEMBER STATES, 1999, (%)

	Is country's membership of EU good or bad?		Has country benefited from EU membership?		In favor of single currency?		Average level of support for joint EU decision making
	Good	Bad	Yes	No	Yes	No	
Ireland	78	3	86	3	71	12	47
Luxembourg	77	3	65	15	85	9	51
Netherlands	73	5	67	19	71	23	61
Italy	62	5	51	19	84	9	66
Portugal	59	4	71	11	59	23	49
Spain	55	4	48	21	70	15	53
Greece	54	11	67	18	65	21	47
Denmark	51	23	62	23	44	48	39
Belgium	47	8	44	32	76	17	61
France	47	14	44	27	68	26	54
Finland	45	19	43	40	58	37	35
Germany	44	11	35	39	57	33	51
Austria	36	23	37	40	53	30	47
Sweden	34	33	21	55	39	47	34
United Kingdom	31	23	31	37	28	55	39
Whole EU	49	12	44	29	61	28	52

Source: Eurobarometer, no. 51, pp. B26, B28, B42, B53.
Notes: The questions asked were as follows:
1. "Generally speaking, do you think that [our country's] membership is a good thing, a bad thing, neither good nor bad?"
2. "Taking everything into consideration, would you say that [our country] has on balance benefited or not from being a member of the European Union?"
3. "What is your opinion on the following statement? Please tell me whether you are for or against it. 'There has to be one single currency, the euro, replacing the [national currency] and all other national currencies of the Member States of the European Union.'"
4. "Some people believe that certain areas of policy should be decided by the [nationality] government, while other areas of policy should be decided jointly within the European Union. Which of the following areas of policy do you think should be decided by the [nationality] government, and which should be decided jointly within the European Union?" Eighteen different policy areas were then listed, and the table shows the average level of support in each country for EU as opposed to national-level decision making.

any admiration for the EU per se); Italy was followed by Belgium, where EU-level decision making was preferred for fourteen of the policies, and by France and the Netherlands, where it was preferred for thirteen policies. At the other end of the scale, in Sweden respondents preferred to allow EU-level decision making in only four of the eighteen areas, and Sweden was followed by Finland (five areas), Denmark (six areas) and the UK (seven areas). The policy areas where EU-level decision making was most popular were foreign policy towards countries outside the EU, the fight against drugs, and humanitarian aid; those where respondents were most likely to feel that policy making should be at the national level were education, health and social welfare, and rules concerning the media.

The EU faces the looming challenge of enlargement, with at least thirteen further countries having applied to join. These are ten former communist countries—five of these, namely the Czech Republic, Estonia, Hungary, Poland, and Slovenia, head the queue, with Bulgaria, Latvia, Lithuania, Romania, and Slovakia one stage farther behind—along with three others, Cyprus, Malta, and Turkey. Switzerland (where in a December 1992 referendum the people narrowly voted against joining the "European Economic Area," a free trade area including all the EU member states and a number of non-EU members), Iceland and Norway are the only countries that at this stage seem unlikely to want to join the European Union. Enlargement creates its own momentum; the more countries join, the greater will be the disadvantages for those few still left out, and the greater their incentive to get on the bandwagon.

The existing EU members have decidedly mixed feelings about the possible admission of the postcommunist countries. On the one hand, their rundown economies and industries and, in many cases, their lack of a sustained tradition of liberal democracy do not make them the most attractive of prospective partners. The CAP and the structural funds could not survive in their present form if they had to meet the demands of ten or thirteen new and poorer members. On the other hand, it would be in the economic and security interests of the present EU member states if the former communist countries became stable, prosperous democracies. Moreover, the EU has always been sensitive to accusations that it is a "rich man's club" and, just as it admitted Greece and Portugal, despite their relative lack of development, when they emerged from periods of dictatorship, so it feels obliged to listen sympathetically to pleas from Eastern Europe that democracy may not survive there unless the EU allows the countries of the region to join.

Enlargement to some degree seems inevitable, and this is likely to slow the pace of integration, as the range of interests and traditions coming under the Union umbrella will increase still further. One practical impediment to the achievement of close union between even the existing fifteen states is the language difficulty. There are at present eleven "official" languages in the EU: Danish, Dutch, English, Finnish, French, German, Greek, Italian, Portuguese, Spanish, and Swedish. Any of these can be used in any Union forum, thus creating the need for a sizeable army of translators to be present whenever Union business takes place. In informal discussions, either English or French tends to be used, as there are few politicians or officials who are not reasonably fluent in at least one of those languages. Language is often a badge of identity, and so the profusion of languages imposes a limit to the closeness of identity that can be expected to develop.

Enlargement also will pose major questions for some of the institutional arrangements within the EU. The Amsterdam Treaty tackled one of these issues by deciding that the size of the EP must not exceed 700 members, no matter how many new countries join, which will entail existing member states taking a cut in their allocation of seats. Still, other problems remain. It is generally acknowledged that the Commission is already too large, with twenty members, and a thirty-member Commission would make even less sense. However, any proposal to compel the smaller countries to take turns in nominating commissioners would provoke a very hostile reaction from these countries. The larger countries might be willing to make concessions on Commission places in exchange for a reweighting of Council votes so that these reflect population size more closely (see Table 5-4). Similarly, the question arises of whether each country will still have its turn in holding the Council presidency for six months, or whether the smaller countries will have to accept a back seat. Enlargement, then, contains the risk of introducing tensions between the larger and smaller countries or gradually clogging up the decision-making machinery.

REPRESENTATIVE GOVERNMENT IN THE EUROPEAN UNION

The decision-making process within the European Union is so complicated that very few ordinary Europeans have more than a minimal grasp of it or could say with certainty just who should be held responsible for the policies that emerge. Not only do the EU's political structures make it impossible to "throw the rascals out" if voters do not like the outputs of policy, but it is virtually impossible for disgruntled voters even to identify the rascals who should be thrown out. Responsibility for some EU policy that does not work out well on the ground could be the fault mainly of government ministers acting in the Council, of one or more commissioners, of MEPs, or of some official working outside political control—or, in the complex polity that the Union is, quite probably some combination of these. Responsibility is diffuse, and it is particularly difficult to bring decision makers to account when no one seems to know exactly who the decision makers are. Voters are never presented with alternative programs for the future direction of the EU, or even with alternative sets of decision makers to choose between. The EU may or may not provide good government—and it is fair to say, as Table 5-8 showed, that most Europeans are not too dissatisfied with its performance—but it cannot be said to amount to particularly representative government.

How could the EU's policy-making process be made more responsive and accountable to ordinary citizens? One idea is to provide for more referendums across the EU to allow the voters a direct voice on major decisions. One objection to this is the claim that when EU referendums take place, voters are more likely to express their views on the government of the day than on the EU issue at stake. Upon closer examination, though, this claim hardly stands up (Gallagher, pp. 239–40). A stronger objection is that it is questionable whether there is really a European "demos" to make such decisions (see the essays in Auer and Flauss, especially that by Bryde). Moreover, whereas the introduction of EP elections in 1979 could be presented as simply the extension to EU level of practice at the national level, the same rationale could not be offered for the introduction of EU-wide referendums, given the national variation in the use of the referendum (see Chapter 11). A second idea entails introducing direct elections for the president of the Commission, to allow Europeans to choose their chief executive just as Americans do. One such scheme would require candidates to be nominated by a set number of national MPs or MEPs, and then to compete for "presidential mandates" across the EU, with a run-off between the top two candidates if no one won an overall majority on the first round—the same system as that used for the election of French presidents (Laver et al.). However, this would be a radical step: the national governments would lose a significant element of the control that they possess at present, and the impact of a directly-elected president on the functioning of the EU's political system would be unpredictable, so this idea is unlikely to be adopted in the foreseeable future.

To defend itself against charges that it is keen to accrete as much power to itself as possible, the Commission stresses that the EU should operate according to the principle of "subsidiarity"—that is, that decisions should be made by the smallest body that is capable of taking them. Thus, the EU should not make decisions or try to run business that national governments are perfectly capable of looking after. This approach is very much to the liking of the more anti-integrationist governments, which are reluctant to let more power than is absolutely necessary drift upward to the EU. The principle of subsidiarity does not mean, of course, that power should necessarily rest with national governments; if applied fully, it also means that within each country as much power as possible is devolved downward, to provincial, regional, or local governments. In practice, the extent to which subsidiarity is genuinely applied as the basis of decision making, as manifested in the distribution of power between national and subnational governments, varies widely from country to country around Europe, as we shall see in the next chapter.

REFERENCES

Allen, David: "Cohesion and Structural Adjustment," in Helen Wallace and William Wallace (eds.), *Policy-Making in the European Union,* 3d ed., Oxford University Press, Oxford, 1996, pp. 209–33.

Alter, Karen J.: "The Making of a Supranational Rule of Law: The Battle for Supremacy," in Ronald Tiersky (ed.), *Europe Today: National Politics, European Integration, and European Security,* Rowman and Littlefield, Lanham, MD, 1999, pp. 305–36.

Andersen, Svein S. and Kjell A. Eliassen (eds.): *The European Union: How Democratic is it?,* Sage, London, 1996.

Auer, Andreas and Jean-François Flauss (eds.): *Le Référendum Européen,* Bruylant, Brussels, 1997.

Bekkers, V. J. J. M., A. J. C. de Moor-Van Vught, and W. Voermans: "Going Dutch: Problems and Policies Concerning the Implementation of EU Legislation in the Netherlands," in Paul Craig and Carol Harlow (eds.), *Lawmaking in the European Union,* Kluwer Law International, London, 1998, pp. 454–78.

Blondel, Jean, Richard Sinnott, and Palle Svensson: *People and Parliament in the European Union: Participation, Democracy and Legitimacy,* Clarendon Press, Oxford, 1998.

Bryde, Brun-Otto: "Le Peuple Européen and the European People," in Andreas Auer and Jean-François Flauss (eds.), *Le Référendum Européen,* Bruylant, Brussels, 1997, pp. 251–74.

Burns, Tom: "Better Lawmaking? An Evaluation of Lawmaking in the European Community," in Paul Craig and Carol Harlow (eds.), *Lawmaking in the European Union,* Kluwer Law International, London, 1998, pp. 435–53.

Commission of the European Communities: *Sixteenth Annual Report on Monitoring the Application of Community Law (1998),* Office for Official Publications of the European Communities, Luxembourg, 1999.

Craig, P. P.: "Democracy and Rulemaking within the EC: an Empirical and Normative Assessment," in Paul Craig and Carol Harlow (eds.), *Lawmaking in the European Union,* Kluwer Law International, London, 1998, pp. 33–64.

Dinan, Desmond: *Ever Closer Union: An Introduction to European Integration,* 2d ed., Macmillan, Basingstoke, 1999.

Freestone, D. A. C., and J. S. Davidson: *The Institutional Framework of the European Communities,* Croom Helm, London and New York, 1988.

Gallagher, Michael: "Conclusion," in Michael Gallagher and Pier Vincenzo Uleri (eds.), *The Referendum Experience in Europe,* Basingstoke, Macmillan, 1996, pp. 226–52.

Gallagher, Michael, and Pier Vincenzo Uleri (eds.): *The Referendum Experience in Europe,* Basingstoke, Macmillan, 1996.

Galligan, Yvonne: "Women in Politics," in John Coakley and Michael Gallagher (eds.), *Politics in the Republic of Ireland,* 3d ed., Routledge, London, 1999, pp. 294–319.

George, Stephen: *An Awkward Partner: Britain in the European Community,* 3d ed., Oxford University Press, Oxford, 1998.

González Jorge, Celia, and Amparo Almarcha Barbado: "Equal Treatment of Women," in Amparo Almarcha Barbado (ed.), *Spain and EU Membership Evaluated,* Pinter, London and St. Martin's Press, New York, 1993, pp. 146–56.

Hayes-Renshaw, Fiona, and Helen Wallace: *The Council of Ministers,* Macmillan, Basingstoke, 1997.

Hix, Simon: *The Political System of the European Union,* Macmillan, Basingstoke, 1999.

Hix, Simon and Christopher Lord: *Political Parties in the European Union,* Macmillan, Basingstoke, 1997.

Hunnings, Neville March: *The European Courts,* Cartermill, London, 1996.

Irwin, Galen: "Second-Order or Third-Rate? Issues in the Campaign for the Elections for the European Parliament 1994," *Electoral Studies,* vol. 14, no. 2, 1995, pp. 183–99.

Jacobs, Francis, Richard Corbett, and Michael Shackleton: *The European Parliament,* 3d ed., Cartermill, London, 1995.

Katz, Richard S. and Bernhard Wessels: "Parliaments and Democracy in Europe in the Era of the Euro," in Richard S. Katz and Bernhard Wessels (eds.), *The European Parliaments, the National Parliaments, and European Integration,* Oxford University Press, Oxford, 1999, pp. 231–47.

Laffan, Brigid: *The Finances of the European Union,* Macmillan, Basingstoke, 1997.

Laffan, Brigid and Michael Shackleton: "The Budget," in Helen Wallace and William Wallace (eds.), *Policy-Making in the European Union,* 3d ed., Oxford University Press, Oxford, 1996, pp. 71–96.

Laver, Michael, Michael Gallagher, Michael Marsh, Robert Singh, and Ben Tonra: *Electing the President of the European Commission,* Trinity Blue Papers in Public Policy 1, Department of Political Science, University of Dublin, Dublin, 1995.

Lijphart, Arend: *Patterns of Democracy: Government Forms and Performance in Thirty-Six Countries,* Yale University Press, New Haven and London, 1999.

MacMullen, Andrew: "European Commissioners 1952–1995: National Routes to a European Elite," in Neill Nugent (ed.), *At the Heart of the Union: Studies of the European Commission,* Macmillan, Basingstoke, 1997, pp. 27–48.

Mazey, Sonia: "The Development of EU Equality Policies: Bureaucratic Expansion on Behalf of Women?", *Public Administration,* vol. 73, 1995, pp. 591–609.

Morel, Laurence: "France: Towards a Less Controversial Use of the Referendum?", in Michael Gallagher and Pier Vincenzo Uleri (eds.), *The Referendum Experience in Europe,* Basingstoke, Macmillan, 1996, pp. 66–85.

Nugent, Neill: *The Government and Politics of the European Community,* 4th ed., Macmillan, Basingstoke, 1999.

Peters, B. Guy: "The Commission and Implementation in the European Union: Is There an Implementation Deficit and Why?", in Neill Nugent (ed.), *At the Heart of the Union: Studies of the European Commission,* Macmillan, Basingstoke, 1997, pp. 187–202.

Peterson, John: "The European Union: Pooled Sovereignty, Divided Accountability," *Political Studies,* vol. 45, no. 3, 1997, pp. 559–78.

Shapiro, Martin: "The European Court of Justice," in Alberta M. Sbragia (ed.), *Euro-Politics: Institutions and Policymaking in the "New" European Community,* The Brookings Institution, Washington, D.C., 1992, pp. 123–56.

Shapiro, Martin: "Implementation, Decisions and Rules," in J. A. E. Vervaele, G. Betlem, R. de Lange and A. G. Veldman (eds.), *Compliance and Enforcement of European Community Law,* Kluwer Law International, The Hague, 1999, pp. 27–34.

Smith, Mitchell P.: "The Commission Made Me Do It: The European Commission as a Strategic Asset in Domestic Politics," in Neill Nugent (ed.), *At the Heart of the Union: Studies of the European Commission,* Macmillan, Basingstoke, 1997, pp. 167–86.

Snyder, Francis: "The Effectiveness of European Community Law: Institutions, Processes, Tools and Techniques," in Terence Daintith (ed.), *Implementing EC Law in the United Kingdom: Structures for Indirect Rule,* John Wiley, Chichester, 1995, pp. 49–87.

Svensson, Palle: "Denmark: the Referendum as Minority Protection," in Michael Gallagher and Pier Vincenzo Uleri (eds.), *The Referendum Experience in Europe,* Basingstoke, Macmillan, 1996, pp. 33–51.

van der Eijk, Cees and Mark Franklin (eds.): *Choosing Europe? The European Electorate and National Politics in the Face of Union,* University of Michigan Press, Ann Arbor, 1996.

Wallace, Helen and William Wallace (eds.): *Policy-Making in the European Union,* 3d ed., Oxford University Press, Oxford, 1996.

Weiler, J. J. H.: "European Models: Polity, People and System," in Paul Craig and Carol Harlow (eds.), *Lawmaking in the European Union,* Kluwer Law International, London, 1998, pp. 3–32.

Wessels, Bernhard: "Whom to Represent? Role Orientations of Legislators in Europe," in Hermann Schmitt and Jacques Thomassen (eds.), *Political Representation and Legitimacy in the European Union,* Oxford University Press, Oxford, 1999, pp. 209–34.

Wessels, Wolfgang and Udo Diedrichs: "The European Parliament and EU Legitimacy," in Thomas Banchoff and Mitchell P. Smith (eds.), *Legitimacy and the European Union: The Contested Polity,* Routledge, London and New York, 1999, pp. 134–52.

Wyller, Thomas: "Norway: Six Exceptions to the Rule," in Michael Gallagher and Pier Vincenzo Uleri (eds.), *The Referendum Experience in Europe,* Basingstoke, Macmillan, 1996, pp. 139–52.

6

LEVELS OF GOVERNANCE

Elections, political parties, and parliaments are the first things in most people's minds when they think about representative government in modern Europe. However, most of the key public decisions that affect what happens in the real world deal with a wide range of matters that are certainly political but lie outside the realm of legislative politics. At a grand international level, they may concern decisions such as how friendly the government should be to an important trading partner involved in gross violations of human rights. Difficult trade-offs might have to be made, for example, between imposing economic sanctions and protecting the jobs of workers employed by major exporters. At a national level, public decision making may have to do with important aspects of macroeconomic policy, such as level of pay and staffing in major parts of the public sector (like the health, education, or police services). At a regional level, it can be concerned with matters such as major investments in public transport or other aspects of the communications infrastructure. At a local level, public decisions may involve important aspects of land use planning and zoning—making trade-offs, for example, between the need for more new housing in a particular area and the protection of recreational open space for those who already live there. At the level of the individual citizen, important decisions on the practical implementation of policy must be made about matters such as whether particular individuals are deemed eligible for given health or welfare benefits, or how much income tax they do actually pay, given what the law says they should pay.

A large part of the business of running a country, of real-life governance, is about administering the machinery of state. It is about making practical policy decisions that give expression to the general principles that might have been contested and eventually settled in the arenas of representative politics. This means that a large part of how representative government really works on the ground has to do with the relationship between politics and public administration. As we saw when looking at the role of the executive in Chapter 3, the formal link between politics and public administration in European representative democracies is provided by the twin roles of a government minister as both member of the political executive, the cabinet, and head of a major administrative department. This focuses our attention on the interaction between politics and public administration at the national level, and in particular the interaction between senior politicians and senior civil servants.

Another important aspect of real-life governance concerns *where* each public decision is made—in particular, whether key decisions are made at the local, regional, or national level. The jurisdiction of any government is never all-embracing. Even in the most totalitarian of societies, "the government" does not tell people how many times to chew their food, when to breathe, or what to dream about. In these respects, at least, we are each of us self-governing principalities, and there is no such thing as an absolutely unitary state. As we move from the level of the individual decision maker to the level of the national government (and beyond this to supranational institutions), we find a large number of different places in which decisions are made. These range from the family, to the street, to the neighborhood, to the district, to the town, to the county, to the region, to the province, and on to the nation-state. This reflects a reality in which different decisions bear in different ways on different geographical groups of individuals, who therefore have different interests in affecting the outcome. Thus, a decision about whether or not the national government builds a new bridge in some particular place has vastly different consequences for different people, depending on where they live. The lives of people who live right beside the bridge may be ruined by its noise and disruption. People who live in the region but not in the immediate locality of the bridge may find the bridge saves them hours each week behind the wheel of an automobile and reduces the risk of their being involved in a fatal accident. Those who live elsewhere in the country but too far away ever to use the bridge may be forced to pay for part of it with their taxes while getting, as they see it, no benefits from it. The extent to which the interests of these different constituencies of individuals are represented in the eventual outcome is affected crucially by whether the ultimate decision is made at the local, regional, or national level.

The themes that we have touched upon here raise huge questions, each of which could occupy a lifetime's research or a fat book in its own right. Here, we focus on some of the key issues, since if we are interested in representative government it is important to have some sense of how and where the outputs of representative decision making are implemented. We look first at the relationship between politicians and the civil service at national level, before moving on to consider the different geographic levels at which decisions might be made.

POLITICIANS AND THE CIVIL SERVICE

A typical modern European government, as we have seen, comprises a cabinet chaired by a prime minister and composed of a set of ministers who are usually senior party politicians. Most ministers are not only members of the cabinet as a collective entity, but also individually responsible as the political heads of important government departments. Looking at the relationship between minister and department from the top down, the doctrine of individual ministerial responsibility means that it is the minister's job to make sure that his or her department actually does implement government policy. This is a particularly important job when government policy changes. The minister must ensure that the department does not just blithely go on with its day-to-day routine, doing things exactly as it has always done them. If this job is not done, then "official" government policy may change at the level of the cabinet, but nothing may really change on the ground.

Looking at the relationship between minister and department from the bottom up, the doctrine of individual ministerial responsibility means that the "buck stops" with the minister for administrative mistakes and misjudgments in his or her department. The theory is certainly that the minister must resign, or at least offer to resign, in the face of serious civil service blunders, even when he or she had no personal dealings with the matter. Indeed, the convention that a minister may have to resign in such circumstances is what gives all ministers an incentive to police their departments with vigilance. In practice, however, as noted in Chapter 3, not all ministers do offer to resign as a result of blunders in their departments in which they had no close "hands-on" involvement. Indeed, recent examples of this happening are actually quite hard to come by, and the tendency for politicians to unload the blame for such problems onto civil servants appears to be growing. (See Woodhouse, 1994, for a more detailed discussion of this matter.)

The extent to which a European cabinet minister is really able to police the bureaucracy in his or her particular area of jurisdiction has long been a topic of heated debate. The formal position —typically promoted by the civil service itself— is that the civil service is no more than a loyal and efficient administrative apparatus, a neutral policy-implementation machine that merely puts into practice decisions made elsewhere, provides information to facilitate future decisions, and has no opinions about any of this. According to this ideal, policing the bureaucracy is simply a technical administrative problem of designing the appropriate monitoring systems, because the interests of politicians and bureaucrats will never conflict. Of course, a complicated modern world may need a complicated bureaucracy to administer it, so even this is not a trivial problem. Essentially, however, it remains the technical problem of designing a system that works, rather than the political problem of controlling a complex system of decision makers, all with their own private agendas.

In practice, few people, even civil servants, regard the civil service as an automatic implementation machine. This raises the vital issue of political, as opposed to purely administrative, control of the state bureaucracy. Here we focus on two important factors that affect the political relationship between ministers and senior bureaucrats. The first concerns the political culture of the civil service itself—in particular, the way in which this derives from patterns of recruitment and training. The second concerns the extent to which ministers can select their senior civil service advisors and thereby feel more confident in political terms that they are being advised by people who are not pursuing conflicting policy objectives.

Civil Service Culture

Considering first the culture of the national civil service, we find that, as with legal systems, European bureaucracies can rather easily be divided into two broad types. Once more we will see that although these broad differences are helpful in giving us a way to think about things, the differences are often much smaller in practice than they might seem at first sight. On the one hand, there is a style of civil service in the British mold. Supporters would describe this as "generalist"; opponents, as "dilettante." This type of bureaucracy is characterized by a heavy reliance on civil servants who succeed or fail on the basis of their general administrative and managerial skills, as opposed to any particular areas of technical expertise. This type of administrative system tends to reproduce itself on the basis of a very heavy emphasis on peer group pressure and socialization into a particular decision-making culture, as opposed to technical training in particular skills.

The archetypal case of a generalist civil service can be found in Britain. The generalist style was also inherited by the Irish civil service, and strong tendencies in this direction can also be seen in Italy, Spain, and Portugal. Britain, however, is by far the most influential example of this type of bureaucracy. The image, and to some extent the reality, is of a civil service staffed at senior levels by classics scholars from prestigious private secondary schools and universities. Although various commissions of inquiry into the British civil service have commented on this situation and recommended policies designed to end it, the pace of change clearly remains very slow (Hennessy). Perhaps most important, there are still separate career tracks for those— be they statisticians engineers, or scientists—who are recruited on the basis of specific technical expertise and for those who are recruited as generalist administrators. Those attempting to make the transition from (more junior) specialist to (more senior) generalist still face many obstacles. Those recruited as fast-track general administrators, imbued with the culture that this tends to imply, still have a clear head start over their more technocratic rivals.

The main European alternative to the generalist civil service culture epitomized by Britain is usually seen as having a far more technocratic ethos, characterized by a much greater reliance on specialists and technical training, either in administrative skills or in specialized roles such as economist, engineer, or lawyer. The French civil service, for example, is divided into a series of administrative "corps," known as the *Grand Corps de l'Etat,* membership in which is absolutely essential for a successful career in the civil service. These corps recruit, train, and socialize members on the basis of what is effectively an alternative higher education system outside the university sector. They have a series of dedicated schools, in particular the *Ecole Polytechnique,* which specializes in technical education, that replace a university undergraduate degree and recruit students on the basis of an intensely competitive examination. A specialized administrative education is given by the *Ecole Nationale d'Administration* (ENA), which recruits students who have an undergraduate degree, once more on the basis of a very competitive examination that candidates spend a long time preparing for. Despite periodic attempts to liberalize this process and open up other methods of entry, almost all entrants to the senior civil service in France follow one of these routes.

Although it might seem as if this pattern of civil service education in France ought to produce an administrative elite with a high degree of technical expertise, French civil servants may find themselves doing jobs that bear little concrete relationship to their technical training. As with most forms of education almost everywhere, however, what is of primary importance is the process by which students are socialized into a particular culture. The most relevant aspect of this in the present context is the technocratic approach to problem solving by administrative elites, rather than any specific area of expertise, which in all civil services (in common with most other careers) is most effectively learned on the job.

The German civil service is also generally felt to have a technocratic ethos, though the emphasis in this case is on legal training, and a very high proportion of German civil servants have a legal background. Recruitment to the senior civil service takes place after undergraduate university education. It is intensely competitive and based on a general state examination consisting largely of law and political science—making these subjects preferred choices for undergraduates hoping to enter the civil service. In common with France, however, and unlike Britain, Germany has a civil service whose recruitment and socialization process is education oriented and subject focused; this generates in German civil servants a self-image of the technocratic public administrator.

The reasons for the emergence of a generalist civil service in Britain, in contrast to the systems observed almost everywhere else in continental Europe, are of course many and varied. Page argues convincingly that a very important reason has to do with military exigencies. As an island not successfully invaded since 1066, Britain traditionally depended for its survival as a state on its navy, always thought of as the "senior service." Behind the effective shield of the British Navy, Page argues, the construction of an efficient land-based system of administration was never a necessity, and more traditional, feudal administrative cultures were able to survive, even prosper. The lack of any realistic threat of the invasion of U.S. territory can also be used to explain why there has never been a need for a tightly organized and technocratic bureaucracy in the United States.

In stark contrast, the history of continental Europe is a history of military struggles between land-based empires that have been largely determined by the efficiency and effectiveness of armies. The administrative culture that derives from this can be traced back to the Romans, and many of today's continental European bureaucracies have a culture that was already very well developed in both Prussia and Napoleonic France. Whether we are talking about Frederick the Great, Bismarck, or Napoleon Bonaparte, we are talking about autocrats in formal control of a large area of land under constant threat of attack from rivals. The ability to build an administrative machine capable of establishing and maintaining that control as a military reality on the ground was what set these men apart from their less successful rivals. The bureaucracies that emerged to do this job, Page argues, were tightly structured along military lines, developing a technocratic culture that can be seen to this day.

Although much is made of such differences by those whose primary intellectual concern is with the internal workings of the bureaucracy, their impact on the interface between the partisan political system and the civil service may not be so great as some suggest. It is more or less the received wisdom these days, both among more traditional institutional theorists in the tradition of Wildavsky, for example, and among economic modelers in the tradition of Niskanen, that all bureaucracies can be seen as groups of people concerned to advance their own interests, typically by increasing the size of their agencies and maximizing their budgets. A more recent variation of this position has been put forward by Dunleavy, who argues that civil servants are interested not so much in maximizing budgets as in making their jobs more congenial. This results in what he calls "bureau shaping" by public administrators. Thus civil servants in the department of finance may advise against wholesale tax reform, for example, not because of any impact this might have on the size of their empire but because such reform may promise to upset a well-oiled administrative system, and even threaten established intradepartmental power structures. This results in a general tendency, other things being equal, for bureaucracies to resist political change that runs counter to bureaucratic interests.

Such tendencies are likely to affect all civil services, regardless of their administrative cultures. To the extent that they do, arguments about the different civil service cultures that prevail in different European states may tend to exaggerate the practical differences we will find on the ground. This view also suggests that control of the bureaucracy is a political as well as a technical administrative problem, the matter to which we now turn.

The Politicization of Senior Bureaucrats

The need for political as well as administrative control of the bureaucracy explains why the issue of the politicization of parts of the senior civil service is such an important matter. Even if the civil service were nothing more than a well-oiled and unfeeling machine to which politicians could issue orders that would be carried out to the letter, ministers would still need to be able to rely upon people who shared their own political viewpoints for help with developing new policy proposals. If the civil service does indeed have an agenda of its own, furthermore, then ministers are likely to want to have in key positions people they can trust politically, to make sure that what politicians decide is fact carried out when policy implementation passes down the line. The more complex and technical policy areas become, the less transparent is the implementation process, and the greater the need for ministers to have policy specialists from their own political camps, either in the senior echelons of their departments or at least with an overview of them.

Despite these pressures, nowhere in Europe do we find the highly politicized system of appointments to the senior civil service that exists in the United States. When a U.S. president changes, so does a high proportion of the most senior bureaucrats in the main departments of state. A large group of lawyers, academics, and other professionals known to be sympathetic to the president's views are brought in, typically from outside the government system as a whole, to take over the levers of power. A vestige of a "spoils" system designed to reward those who helped the president get elected, this system is now used far more to ensure that the president can take effective political control of the senior bureaucracy.

At the opposite extreme to this are Britain and Ireland, where official civil service culture is strenuously nonpartisan. When a new minister takes office and walks into his or her department for the first time, this is very much a voyage into the unknown. He or she will be greeted by the civil service head of the department, most likely a total stranger who has been in the same department for thirty years or more and knows every nook and cranny of it. All of the papers of the former minister typically will have been removed, and the new minister will have to familiarize himself or herself with the new job on the basis of briefings by senior civil servants. If the political "master" and civil "servants" do not get along, there is not much to be done about it; this is the hand that the minister has been dealt, and the minister must play it. If a new minister is particularly powerful it may be possible to get the department head moved, but even then there will be a very limited choice of candidates from which to pick a successor.

On the other side of this coin, most senior British and Irish civil servants take a positive pride in being able to serve different political masters and have been thoroughly socialized over a long career into the need to do their very best for the minister of the day. Even though they are not prohibited from voting, many do not vote in practice, not wishing to register a partisan preference, even privately. A very striking example of this could be seen in late 1999, with the formation of the cabinet to take over a range of executive functions in Northern Ireland (explained on page 154). Martin McGuinness, a high-profile Sinn Féin politician who had been central to many aspects of the conflict between the unionist and nationalist communities in Northern Ireland, was appointed as the new Northern Ireland Minister of Education—one of the big-budget departments in the new administration. No matter how surprised senior civil servants

Well-known republican activist Martin McGuinness, following his appointment as Northern Ireland Minister of Education in 1999, meets the head of his civil service department for the first time. © United Kingdom PA Photos Limited

might have been at the identity of their controversial new ministerial boss, top bureaucrats took care to be photographed smiling and greeting him warmly as he arrived for his first day of work. This, indeed, was one of the enduring public images of the dramatic installation of a new executive in Northern Ireland.

In general, while they typically pride themselves on being nonpartisan, it is not the case that senior civil servants are indifferent to who their political masters might be. But if they do have a preference for one minister over another, this is usually based not upon policies but rather on the desire to have a strong political boss rather than a weak one. What senior civil servants most like tends to be a really powerful minister, a "big beast of the jungle," in the words of Tony King, who can fight and win the department's case in cabinet and who will not be forced into embarrassing public climbdowns. (For a lengthy but outstanding treatment of the British civil service in these terms, see Hennessy.)

Even in Britain, however, recent trends are towards the creation of a new political cadre within the senior civil service. When Labour Party leader Harold Wilson first became British prime minister in 1964, after a long period of Conservative rule, he feared that the civil service would not cooperate in a series of major policy changes that he wished to implement. He therefore appointed a number of "outsiders" with well-known Labour credentials to specially created positions as personal advisors to minister. For the most part, the career civil servants resented what they saw as interlopers and were able in a passive but effective manner to freeze them out of the decision-making process. Margaret Thatcher distrusted the senior civil service as much as Harold Wilson had and also appointed her own personal advisors from outside the government system, fearing that public servants might well not cooperate in the massive cutbacks of the public service that she wished to implement. When Labour returned to power under Tony Blair in 1997, political advisors to key ministers continued to be very important players in the policy-making process. For many ministers, key advisors came to be seen as gatekeepers in the system. Many of these were policy specialists with solid Labour credentials. Thus, in addition to providing technical advice, they were able to be the eyes, ears, and sometimes even voice of the minister in the policy process. The net result was a system in which the policy-making role of the senior civil service was "supplemented," at the very least, by a more politicized cadre of ministerial advisors.

A similar device was used by the Irish Labour Party when it went into a coalition government in 1993. Labour ministers appointed "outside" policy activists with Labour sympathies to newly created positions of "programme managers," each of whom had a roving brief to advise the minister and coordinate policy within his or her department. These people operated within the civil service, but were not part of the administrative system and had an unambiguously political brief. Versions of this practice have continued since then in Ireland under various coalition governments, with one of the most important architects of the Northern Ireland peace process being a key political advisor to the Prime Minister of the Fianna Fáil–Progressive Democrat coalition that formed in 1997. The system thus appears to have become entrenched, with civil servants divided on its merits. Some dislike the politicization that it brings to the senior civil service. Others regard the job of senior civil servant as one that very often has an inevitable political dimension, and prefer a system in which "political" advice to their minister is given by someone with an explicitly political brief. In this sense, they see the burgeoning system of political advisors as protecting the core civil service from politicization. (For a discussion of the programme manager system in Ireland, see O'Halpin.)

On continental Europe, there is a higher level of politicization of the senior civil service in countries such as Belgium, France, and Germany. In France, this has been quite explicitly institutionalized into a system of ministerial *cabinets,* teams of trusted ministerial advisors. The head of the team, the *directeur de cabinet,* may indeed be endowed with the authority of the minister. (The term *cabinet* when used in this context is always pronounced as a French word, as if spelled "cabinay," to distinguish it from the cabinet of ministers, with a "t," that forms the government.)

These *cabinets* are teams of about twenty to thirty policy professionals on whom the ministers can rely for two important forms of support that might well otherwise be missing. The first is to ensure that ministerial policies are actually carried out on the ground; members of the *cabinet* in effect are the minister's eyes and ears within the department. The second is to advise the minister on developments outside the department that are likely to have a bearing on the minister's departmental responsibilities. As we have noted, in the very complex environment in which any modern cabinet minister must work, ministers are for the most part forced to concentrate on their own departmental briefs. A department's career civil servants also may be preoccupied with rather specific departmental responsibilities. As a result, there is a danger that developments outside the department may catch the minister by surprise, because a real-world policy problem is likely to have an impact on a range of government departments, even if one department has ultimate responsibility for dealing with it. The *cabinet* will keep track of events outside the minister's department, reporting on external developments that the minister needs to be aware of and acting as a point of contact with other government departments.

Although in theory the *cabinet* system gives French ministers the opportunity of appointing outside policy advisors to guard against being railroaded by the civil service, in practice the vast majority of members of a typical ministerial *cabinet* are civil servants. As we saw in Chapter 3 when discussing the executive, however, many French ministers are themselves former civil servants, and the political affiliations of French civil servants are often more explicit than elsewhere in Europe. This makes it easier for an incoming minister to select a team of civil servants for the *cabinet* who can be relied on to share his or her general political approach.

The system of French ministerial *cabinets* also can be found in Belgium, where there is also a substantial turnover in the minister's senior civil service team when political power changes hands. It cannot be found in quite such an explicit and institutionalized form in any other European country, although the trend is running strongly in the direction of having more people involved as part of a personal team of advisors tied to a particular minister.

In the Netherlands, for example, ministers seek advice from a wide range of policy professionals, commissioning studies and policy reviews that are conducted outside the career civil service, by people whose political affiliations are often quite explicit. This is in the context of a system under which only the very top positions in a government department are open to any political input in the nomination process, while those appointed in this way stay in their posts after the minister leaves office. This may well lead ministers to feel that the political loyalties of senior civil servants differ from their own. In recent years there have been several incidents in which the loyalty of senior civil servants has been discussed, leading to a revival of interest in the doctrine of ministerial responsibility (*Ministeriele Verantwoordelijkheid*).

In part, of course, the trend towards more explicitly political ministerial *cabinets* is probably no more than an explicit recognition in an increasingly technocratic world of something that has always been there. This is the need for ministers to have access to expert advice that they feel comes from an ideologically sympathetic perspective, and which is based outside the civil service department of which they are the political head.

Conclusion: The Increasing Accountability of Public Servants?

Overall, there can be no doubt that regardless of its culture and style, public administration is political, and that public bureaucrats are in many senses politicians in their own right. Senior civil servants make important decisions about policy implementation, albeit under the auspices of political bosses, that have important implications for the allocation of resources among different social actors—something that is of the very essence of politics. They are also responsible for much of the preliminary work that goes into the development of new policy initiatives—and thus leave their fingerprints all over the making of public policy in many subtle ways. The interaction between the senior civil service and the political executive is thus a vital one to understand for all who are interested not only in the implementation, but also in the shaping and making of important public policy decisions.

At the purely administrative level, furthermore, increasing skepticism about the management style associated with the traditional "big government" public sector has led to a growing influence of the ideas of "new public management." These stress the need for a clear sense of mission in each public sector department, the need for a strategic plan for how to realize this vision, the need for a "client-centered" approach to service delivery, and the need for the public sector to be held clearly accountable for any failure to deliver. Although only in the very early stages of implementation, these managerial developments, combined with a situation in which *cabinet* ministers seem less and less inclined to "take the rap" for everything in their jurisdiction, are likely to make the public accountability of senior civil servants a matter of increasing concern.

LEVELS OF GOVERNANCE

Despite their similarities in many other respects, modern European states vary considerably in the levels at which certain key decisions are made. Traditionally, for example, Britain and Ireland have been highly centralized, with most important decisions being made at the national level. Other countries, especially Switzerland but also Germany and Austria, for example, have traditionally been far more decentralized. Taking European countries as a whole, however, there appears to be a strong tendency during recent decades towards greater decentralization: the shifting of important decisions on policy making and policy implementation to a more local or regional arena. This has been evident even in countries such as Britain and France, noted for much of their recent history as having very centralized decision-making regimes (Batley; Stoker). In countries that already have well-established institutions for local decision making—for example, Sweden and Denmark—yet more powers are being handed over to local authorities.

There are two different, though related, features of the decentralization of decision making in modern Europe. The first has to do with the distinction between "federal" and "unitary" states (although, as we will see, this distinction is becoming blurred by the increasing powers of the regional tier of government in a number of European countries). The second has to do with the system of local government. It is possible for unitary states, as we shall see, to have strong systems of local government. And it is also possible for federal states to have weak local government systems.

FEDERAL GOVERNMENT IN MODERN EUROPE

Although most people feel that they know one when they see one, it is actually quite difficult to produce an abstract definition of a federal state. In the European context this is complicated by the fact that the main examples of federal states—Switzerland, Germany, Austria and, since 1993, Belgium—are not only very diverse institutionally, but also differ in striking respects from non-European federal states such as the United States, Canada, and Australia. It is further complicated by the fact that countries such as Spain and Britain, once bastions of centralized governance, have moved strikingly towards the establishment of strong regional administrations and assemblies with substantial powers. In doing so they now look far more "federal" than they once did.

This is not, however, the place to luxuriate in the theoretical nuances of various definitions of federation, confederation, and federalism (see Burgess 1993; Elazar, 1997; P. King). We merely pause to note that most authors agree that "federation" implies an irrevocable entrenchment of some level of regional (state) government within the national decision-making process, with significant powers that are protected by the constitution.

In the remainder of this section, we explore federal government in modern Europe in a more empirical manner. We leave to one side the post-1993 Belgian case, which is an attempt at a constitutional solution to the country's longstanding problem of incorporating deeply entrenched language communities into national governance, rather than an exemplar of federalism European-style. It involves a unique and complex interaction between three geographical units—Brussels, Flanders, and Wallonia—and three language communities: Flemish, French, and German. To further complicate matters, Brussels, the "bilingual" capital of Belgium, in practice has a huge majority of French speakers, yet is geographically located within Flemish-speaking Flanders. (See Fitzmaurice for a discussion of post-1993 Belgian federalism.) In what follows, therefore, we outline the territorial distribution of decision making in Switzerland and Germany, which almost all observers take to be federal states, whatever definition they use.

(The remaining major example of federalism in Europe, Austria, can be seen as being much closer to Germany than to Switzerland.)

Federal Government in Switzerland

There is some difference between the romantic image and the practical reality of federal government in Switzerland. The romantic image dates the Swiss confederation back to 1291 and portrays it as a loose union of ancient provinces, called cantons, that arouse intense loyalties among their citizens and only grudgingly cede very limited powers to the Swiss central government. The reality of the modern Swiss state is that it is governed according to a federal constitution that dates from 1875 and that was framed on the basis of European observations of, among other things, the experience of federalism in the United States. Nonetheless, twenty-five of the twenty-six cantons that form the constituent parts of the union are indeed very old, although Jura was formed from a part of Berne in 1980. Earlier Swiss federations had united three of these cantons (from 1315 to 1515), thirteen of them (from 1515 to 1798), and all twenty-five (from 1815 to 1875). (For a discussion of the evolution of the Swiss federation, see Hughes.) As Hughes points out, none of these cantons was ever really a fully autonomous state as we would now understand the term—another parallel with the constituent states of what is now the United States. Furthermore, when we actually look at what the cantons have the power to do, this turns out to be quite limited, on a par with the power of typical local authorities in many European countries.

What underpins Swiss federalism has as much to do with the social structure as with the constitution. In the first place, a canton does evoke strong feelings of traditional loyalty among many of its citizens, to the extent that the canton is often their primary focus of political affiliation, as opposed to the Swiss state itself. Probably more important than historical loyalties are two potent sources of ethnic division in Switzerland. These are language—the population is divided between French, German, and Italian speakers; and religion—the population is divided between Protestants and Roman Catholics. Although these two cleavages cut across one another taking the country as a whole, so that not all members of the same language group have the same religion, and vice versa, language and religious frontiers nonetheless do follow the borders of cantons rather closely.

Almost all cantons comprise an overwhelming majority of one or the other language group, for example, and are strictly unilingual. The different language groups keep very much to themselves at the local level, and only at the federal level does social and political life become bilingual or even trilingual. Because language defines the communication structure of any society, the distribution of language groups in Switzerland is almost bound to impede any process of centralization.

Religious groups are also sorted between cantons in a very structured manner. Individual cantons are either mostly Protestant or mostly Roman Catholic, a relic of the historical role of the cantons in assimilating or resisting the Reformation. Because organized religion provides almost as powerful a cultural network as language, this geographical pattern of religious affiliation also serves to establish the canton as a focus of social and political life. (See Linder, pp. 1–37, for a discussion of the political impact of religious and linguistic diversity in Switzerland.)

Despite these obvious sources of individual loyalty to the canton, there is more or less general agreement that the trend in Switzerland has been towards greater centralization. The list of functions formally allocated to the federal government is long and growing longer; local councils in "unitary" systems such as Sweden and Denmark typically have more functions than Swiss cantons. (Linder, pp. 40–44, sets out the relative powers of the federation and the cantons in Switzerland.) Furthermore, the end of the Cold War and the possible entry of Switzerland into the European Union, challenging a traditional position of neutrality, may well focus political attention more on the Swiss federal government.

Nonetheless, the cantons do have substantial powers and are responsible for the administration of much of the welfare state, overall policy for which is set at the federal level. They have power to set local taxes, including income taxes, and above all their autonomy is deeply entrenched in the constitution. One very important manifestation of this autonomy is Article 3 of the federal constitution, which vests all future powers in the cantons. New powers can be given to the federal authority only if this is agreed to by the cantons and by the people in a referendum. This clearly limits the growth of federal government. The result is that the share of both taxes and spending under the control of the federal government in Switzerland is much lower, for example, than that controlled by the federal government in the United States, and very much lower than in unitary government systems such as the Netherlands or Spain (Linder, p. 43). The power of central government in Switzerland is further weakened by the longstanding custom that the presidency of the Swiss Federation rotates between senior politicians on an annual basis, resulting in a situation that means the vast majority of Swiss citizens do not know who their president is. In general, the particular character of Swiss federalism means that the visibility of Swiss national politicians is lower than that of national politicians in most other modern European states.

A second important manifestation of the constitutional entrenchment of the autonomy of the canton can be seen in the relationship between the two chambers of the Swiss legislature. As in most federal systems, the lower house (the National Council) is elected on a one-person-one-vote basis to represent the population as a whole, and the upper house (the Council of States) is designed to represent the interest of the constituent states of the federation, the cantons. The Council of States thus has two representatives from every full canton. The cantons themselves determine how these representatives are selected, although they are now for the most part directly elected, often by majority rule. If both upper and lower houses do not pass legislation, then it cannot be passed; there is no provision for one house to overturn the vote of the other by special majority. This means that the autonomy of the cantons vis-à-vis the central government is entrenched somewhat more deeply than that of the constituent parts of the German federal state, to which we now turn.

Federal Government in Germany

The historical and cultural context of the German federal state is quite different. The current German constitution, or Basic Law, was effectively framed for what was then West Germany by the victorious Western Allies in 1949. It was a quite explicit piece of constitutional engineering, using a federal structure to prevent the emergence of the type of powerful centralized state seen in Bismarck's Prussia and Hitler's Third Reich. Indeed, so concerned were the Allies to decentralize the German state that the implementation of an extensive system of local government was already well under way by the end of 1945. Although some of the constituent states (Länder) of West Germany—Bavaria, for example—had long historical traditions, many were formed from scratch from the areas that the three Western occupying powers, Britain, France, and the United States, happened to control. There was a huge variation in the sizes of the states. Some, such as Bremen, are no more than moderate-size cities; others, especially North-Rhine Westphalia, are bigger than many European countries.

Not surprisingly given this context, the German federal arrangements set out in the Basic Law borrowed heavily from U.S. experience. Furthermore, given the fears of the Allies at the time, the federal structure is given an "eternal guarantee" in Articles 20 and 79 of the Basic Law: abolishing the federal system in Germany would in effect require a revolution that overthrew the constitution as a whole. (We should note, however, the experience of countries such as France in 1958 and Ireland in 1937, both of which introduced completely new constitutions on the basis of the consent of a majority of the population. These and a number of other examples show that constitutional guarantees such as this, however "eternal" they might purport to be, are never really absolute.) The reunification of Germany in October 1990 resulted in the assimilation of 16 million people living in five Länder from the former East Germany. In addition, with the unification of Berlin, this city became a Land in its own right, so there are sixteen Länder in the united Germany. Subsequent plans to merge the Länder of Berlin and Brandenburg were agreed to by the respective governments in 1995, but were rejected by the voters in a referendum in 1996. The post-unification system of Länder, therefore, seems likely to persist. Obviously, some adjustments were necessary, but the essential structure of the West German federal state, as laid down in the Basic Law, remained the constitutional basis of the new Germany. (For a recent discussion of post-unification federalism in Germany, see Bräuninger and König.)

The division of responsibilities between the Länder and the German federal government (the Bund) gives a list of designated powers to either the central government or the Länder, with the powers of the Länder having been strengthened somewhat in 1994. In addition, there are quite a large number of "concurrent" areas in which both the federal government and the Länder may pass laws, although federal law takes precedence over Land law in concurrent areas. The federal government deals with matters such as defense, foreign trade, and major instruments of macroeconomic policy. Powers explicitly reserved to the Länder include control over education and the mass media, but Article 30 of the Basic Law permits Länder to legislate on any matter that is not explicitly stated to be the preserve of the federal government.

Politically, the Länder are represented at the federal level in the upper house of the federal parliament, the Bundesrat. As we saw in Chapter 4, Land members of the Bundesrat are not elected directly (in contrast, for example, to members of the U.S. Senate). Rather, they are delegations from the Land governments, the number of delegates being related, though by no means proportional, to the population of the Land in question. Thus, the Bundesrat is sometimes referred to as a "conclave of states." Each delega-

The German Bundesrat moved to Berlin following reunification. © AP/Wide World Photos

tion—the members of which are typically members of the Land cabinet—votes as a bloc under the instructions of the Land government. The Bundesrat has considerable powers to block the passage of bills passed by the lower house, the Bundestag, all of which must be submitted to it. If a bill is defeated in the Bundesrat by an ordinary majority, then this veto can be overturned by the lower house with an ordinary majority. If a bill is defeated with a two-thirds majority, then a two-thirds majority in the Bundestag is needed to overturn the veto. And if a bill affects the constitutional position of the Länder or the balance of taxes between the federal government and the Länder (this includes a lot of bills), then the Bundesrat has an absolute veto.

When the two houses are controlled by different party groupings, this division of powers leads to potential confrontation and the clear possibility of legislative gridlock, so that the presence of the Länder is definitely felt in federal politics. The two houses, furthermore, can quite easily have different patterns of political control, because Land elections do not take place at the same time as federal elections and voting patterns at the Land level may differ from those at the federal level. Recent research by Bräuninger and König has, however, shown that in many actual policy areas, the power of the federal government to set the agenda may well give it more power in practice than formal rules might otherwise indicate.

The legal balance of power between the federal and the Land governments is adjudicated by a Federal Constitutional Court (FCC), discussed in Chapter 2. The economic balance of power—so vital in practical politics, whatever the legal position—is guaranteed by the fact that the Länder have significant sources of tax revenue from both indirect taxes and a guaranteed proportion of federal income tax revenues. This means that the federal government has not traditionally been able to use the power of the purse strings to bring Länder governments to heel, though this situation changed somewhat with the addition of the far poorer eastern Länder to the German federation.

The extent to which the Länder come into open conflict with the federal government and the extent to which each Land pursues policies without regard to what goes on elsewhere are mediated by a very extensive system of ad hoc committees. These are designed both to resolve potential conflicts before these become explicit and to coordinate the activities of different Länder, creating a coherent development of public policy across the Länder as a whole.

Overall, therefore, German federalism is underwritten by an explicit and powerful constitutional structure, and appears to operate effectively despite the fact that many of the Länder are not places to which citizens have strong traditional affiliations. Furthermore, with the exception of staunchly Roman Catholic Bavaria, Länder boundaries do not closely follow those of ethnic, religious, or language groups. Essentially, German federalism is a political and constitutional, rather than a cultural, phenomenon.

One implication of this is that German federalism may change as the political environment changes. As Burgess and Gress have pointed out, both reunification and membership in the European Union (EU) may have fundamental implications for German federalism, both of them producing centralist tendencies. Reunification, as we have seen, has added five Länder from the former East Germany, all much poorer than those of the former West Germany. The policy of bringing public and personal services in these new Länder toward the standard enjoyed by those in the west generates a need for huge cash transfers, from western Länder through the federal government to the eastern Länder. This clearly increases the role of the federal government.

The European Union may undermine the role of the German Länder in different ways, since EU institutions are more clearly tailored to the workings of unitary states. As Europe takes over powers from its member states, some of these are transferred from the Länder to the EU by virtue of German membership in the EU and without the formal consent of the Länder. In compensation for these transfers of sovereignty, European states have gained representation in the EU decision-making system, especially the EU Council of Ministers. But power over EU decision making is in large part wielded by the federal government in the case of Germany. The net effect is to weaken the power of the Länder and to strengthen the power of the federal government (Burgess and Gress, pp. 169–76).

Both reunification and European integration have generated lively debates between the Länder and the federal authorities in Germany. The fact that they have indicates that the federal ideal is now deeply rooted in the German political system. And the fact that this can be achieved in the relatively short period of time since the introduction of the new Basic Law in 1949 suggests that, notwithstanding some spectacular failures around the world, constitutional engineering can sometimes fulfill its basic objectives.

THE GROWING IMPORTANCE OF REGIONAL GOVERNMENT

Regional Government in Spain

Despite the powerfully centralist system of governance in Spain, imposed under the dictatorship of General Franco that ended with Franco's death in 1975, many Spanish regions have powerful local traditions and have long demanded autonomy. The province of Catalonia has been at the forefront of these, even receiving limited autonomy between 1913 and 1923 before the imposition of military governments, first under General Primo de Rivera and then under General Franco, that were deeply committed to turning Spain into a strong unitary state. When the Spanish constitution was rewritten at the end of the Franco era, the relative power of regional and central governments was a major bone of contention between left and right. The left wanted Spain to be a federal state; the right was utterly opposed to this. The result was a compromise. The new constitution recognized a series of "autonomous communities," and some communities with strong historical traditions were granted more autonomy than others.

There are seventeen autonomous communities, in effect regional governments, in Spain. Each of these has many of the political and administrative trappings of a mini-state, with a legislature, an executive, and a president, as well as a civil service and a high court. Certain important powers are reserved by the constitution to the national government: for example, defense, foreign policy, macroeconomic policy, and certain major aspects of the social welfare system. Regional powers, which must be exercised in a way that does not conflict with the national constitution, include important areas such as education and health care. The ability of the regions to raise taxes independently, obviously crucial to the possibility of taking truly autonomous decisions on many aspects of public policy, depends upon the national government's ceding specific powers of taxation to specific autonomous communities. The reality, for nearly all communities, is that most of the important powers of taxation have been retained by the national government. This means that their main source of funds is grants from the central state. A few communities, such as the Basque Country and Navarra, have powers to collect a wide range of taxes locally and pass a large share of this on to central government—but in practice they must set these taxes at the same rate as those for the rest of the country.

Despite their relatively limited powers to vary national tax rates, some of the autonomous communities have maintained a strongly independent local line on many nonfinancial aspects of public policy. Perhaps the most striking of these is Catalonia, with a distinctive language, a long history, and Barcelona, one of Europe's major cities, as its capital. The "government" of Catalonia presents itself in many ways as being on a par with the national government, and in 1992, the year of the Barcelona Olympics, the Catalan president created the position of Foreign Minister. Furthermore, the Catalan rather than the Spanish national anthem has been played on state visits abroad by the Catalan president. While Catalonia is ahead of the others in presenting itself as having potent features of an independent state, several other of Spain's autonomous communities do have foreign relations departments, mostly used to promote regional interests within the EU.

Overall, there can be no doubt that the evolution of regional government in post-Franco Spain challenges the traditional neat separation of countries into those that have a federal system of governance and those that are unitary states. Formally, Spain remains a unitary state, with any power at the disposal of the regions being ceded by the central government. The constraints on central government in taking back these powers—as has indeed previously happened in Spain—depend more upon practical politics than upon the letter of the constitution. Despite its formal unitary status, however,

The Catalan and Spanish flags fly side by side over the Catalan parliament. © Richard Pasley/ Liaison Agency

the practical political autonomy of a regional state such as Catalonia is probably far greater than that of a typical Land or canton in "federal" Germany or Switzerland. (For a discussion of the system of government in post-Franco Spain, see Heywood.)

The "Devolution" of Power in the United Kingdom

The very name "United Kingdom of Great Britain and Northern Ireland" hints strongly at the regional diversity underlying a union of what can be seen as four separate units. Great Britain comprises the countries of England, Wales, and Scotland, while how, precisely, to describe Northern Ireland is in itself an intensely political matter. Each of these units has very strong regional traditions.

While the English conquest of Wales dates from 1282, there remains a strong Welsh nationalist movement, and the Welsh language—utterly different from English—remains in widespread everyday use. English unity with Scotland came much later, with the succession of a Scottish king to the English throne in 1603, consolidated by an Act of Union in 1707. Many Scottish institutions—the legal and educational systems, for example—have remained quite distinct from those in England and Wales. While Scots Gaelic is very much less current than Welsh as an everyday language, Scottish national identity has remained very strong. This has formed the basis for a very successful and effective Scottish nationalist movement that was given a huge boost by the discovery of major offshore oil reserves in Scottish waters; this allowed a plausible case to be made that Scotland could be financially self-sufficient. After a long and troubled history of relations between Britain and Ireland, the current province of Northern Ireland came into being with British withdrawal in 1921 from the twenty-six counties of what was later to become the Republic of Ireland. The remaining six counties of Northern Ireland remained under the control of the British State, and the United Kingdom of Great Britain and Northern Ireland (UK) came into being.

The postwar emergence of strong nationalist movements in Wales and Scotland—together with continuing sectarian strife between "unionist" and "nationalist" communities in Northern Ireland—kept the issue of regional governance very firmly on the UK political agenda from the late 1960s on. Although there were a number of unsuccessful attempts to find a constitutional settlement for Northern Ireland, little was done about the constitutional position of Wales and Scotland during the long period of Conservative government that ran from 1979 to 1997. Immediately on taking office in 1997, however, Labour Prime Minister Tony Blair announced referendums on the creation of regional parliaments for Scotland and Wales—in the case of Scotland, with an executive that would have certain tax-varying powers. These were held in September 1997 and resulted in the subsequent creation and election (using a proportional mixed-member electoral system that was in itself a great innovation for Britain) of Scottish and Welsh regional assemblies. The first elections to the new Scottish Parliament and Welsh *Senedd* took place in May 1999, and powers were devolved to these taking effect on 1 July 1999.

The powers devolved to Scotland are considerably more than those devolved to Wales. There is a separate Scottish cabinet—the Scottish Executive—with its own first minister filling a role that could almost be described as that of "the Prime Minister of Scotland." Because of the strong element of proportional representation in the new electoral system that was used, the result of the first election was the formation of a coalition executive combining Labour and the Liberal Democrats—another first for Britain. Very significantly, the Scottish Parliament, based in Edinburgh, has the right to vary the rate of income tax levied in Scotland (by up to three pence in the pound).

The new Scottish parliament meeting in Edinburgh in 1999. © AP/World Wide Photos

It also has powers over education, health, environment, economic development, local government, transport, sports, and agriculture, among other things. Powers reserved to the British Parliament in Westminster include defense, foreign policy, large-scale economic management, and the social security system. Powers devolved to Wales are rather fewer. There is no Welsh executive, there is no right to vary income tax, and fewer functions can be performed locally, leading some to decry the Welsh Assembly as no more than a talking shop. (For a discussion of regional government in Britain, see Kingdom, 1999).

As part of the Northern Ireland Peace process, the "Good Friday Agreement" and consequent legislation created a new provincial assembly for Northern Ireland. This is based in Belfast, with substantial powers to be devolved to a Northern Ireland Executive with a cabinet and a First and Deputy First Minister, consequent upon the successful implementation of all aspects of the agreement. The rights of both nationalist and unionist communities are protected by a complicated system of qualified majorities needed to pass resolutions in the Assembly, and a requirement that both parties be represented in the "power-sharing" Executive in strict proportion to their representation in the Assembly. Elections to the Assembly were held in 1998. After much delay resulting from protracted negotiations over the "decommissioning" of IRA weapons, power was devolved to the Northern Ireland Assembly and Executive in December 1999. However, following unionist pressure over the lack of progress on the decommissioning issue, the British government suspended the Northern Ireland Executive in late January 2000, even though this had been in operation for no more than a few weeks. De facto "direct rule" over Northern Ireland was thereby restored to Westminster for a short period, before being returned to Belfast again in June 2000. (For a discussion of Northern Ireland politics leading up to the peace process, see McGarry and O'Leary, 1997.)

In the short space of two years, therefore, very significant steps were taken to shift power in the United Kingdom away from London and towards regional capitals. The term used to describe this is "devolution": the granting of power from the center to some local region. The constitutional implication of "devolved" as opposed to "federal" government is that what has been given away could in theory be taken back by another new government with a huge parliamentary majority. This did indeed happen when the British government reimposed direct rule on Northern Ireland in 1972 in response to the intense communal violence in the province, setting aside a regional assembly at Stormont that had wielded considerable local power without intervention from Westminster over a fifty-year period. Furthermore, the difference between devolved and federal government is highlighted in the clearest possible way by events in Northern Ireland in January 2000. That which the British government had "given" to Northern Ireland, it could also take away by rushing legislation through the Westminster parliament in a matter of hours, motivated by the political exigencies of the month. However pressing those political exigencies might have been, such action would have been utterly unthinkable in a federal system.

Notwithstanding the Northern Ireland experience, the practical politics of abolishing the Scottish and Welsh Assemblies and the Scottish Executive, now that these have been created, might make this a very unattractive prospect in the short to medium term. Indeed there is nothing to prevent the Scottish Executive from organizing a referendum on the total independence of Scotland from the United Kingdom, and thereby provoking a serious constitutional crisis. It will, therefore, take a long time before these arrangements can be seen as sufficiently entrenched to be regarded as an irrevocable move toward a British variant of strong regional government that comes quite close to federalism; the changes are very significant nonethless.

LOCAL GOVERNMENT

Many of the services that governments provide, such as health care and education, are delivered to the "end user" at a local level—in schools, hospitals, and the like. Much of the regulatory activity of government, such as land use planning or pollution control, operates on the ground at the local level. It is thus inevitable in practice that at least some of the machinery for delivering public policy outputs will be "decentralized" in the sense that it is located at the local level near the end user. Whatever the political system, local government, in the sense of local public administration, is inevitable in the real world.

There are also sound theoretical and philosophical reasons for a decentralization of decision making. Aside from the argument about practical efficiency that we have just discussed, there is the argument that a division of powers helps to avoid a single monolithic state machine. There is also the argument that increasing the possibilities for ordinary citizens to get involved in the state's everyday workings enhances the legitimacy of the political system.

It is no accident that strongly authoritarian regimes, such as Franco's Spain or Salazar's Portugal, have relied upon highly centralized structures of governance. It is simply very difficult to run an authoritarian regime if power is highly decentralized. Having an entrenched decentralized system of governance, therefore, provides a check on the excessive accumulation of power in the hands of a tiny elite. From the perspective of the ordinary citizen, furthermore, the probability of having any real impact on decision making declines as the decision-making unit gets larger and more remote. A highly centralized state offers little possibility for the ordinary citizen to make any impact, either real or imaginary, and may result in citizens' coming to feel powerless and alienated. This in turn may undermine the popular legitimacy of the state. A more decentralized regime may well offer more opportunities for citizen participation, and hence encourage more of a sense that the regime is legitimate and worthy of popular loyalty.

Notwithstanding these general arguments, which apply to all countries, the precise form that local government takes, together with the extent to which it is locally politically accountable, varies considerably from country to country in modern Europe, although all modern European countries have some form of elected local government.

The key variables are these: the structure of the system of local government, together with the size and number of local government units; the policy areas in which local government has real power; the financial basis of the local government system; and the relative powers of local and national governments in the event of a conflict. Despite the diversity of European local government systems, we can develop some generalizations about these key variables.

The Structure of Local Government

Almost every European country has more than one level of local government; most have two levels, some have three. The most basic unit of local government in nearly every European country—often called a commune or municipality—is typically small and ancient in its origins. However, nearly all of these did undergo major reorganization at some stage during the nineteenth century, when the foundations for most modern European systems of local government were laid. Both of these facts are seen in Spence's description of Italy; notes that "it is not uncommon for historians to trace the development of the commune as an almost unbroken process beginning in the twelfth century and continuing into the present day" (Spence, p. 74). He goes on to argue, however, that the present system of communes in Italy was imposed by Napoleon as recently as 1802, and that the overall structure of local government can be dated to Italian unification in 1861. Similarly, although the English system of parishes and boroughs is very old indeed, the current system of local government can be traced more directly back to a series of major reforms beginning in 1835, and the parish no longer has any political significance. In Ireland, the division of the country into the counties that remain today as the basic local administrative units began with the Norman conquest and was more or less complete by the end of the seventeenth century (Coakley). France's communes, not surprisingly, can also be traced to the Napoleonic era. The Swedish system of local government established in 1863 created municipalities based upon administrative units that were already several hundred years old (Wallin). In Denmark, the communes were created in 1841 to take over many of the functions formerly fulfilled by parishes. German local government also has a long tradition, as shown by the extensive set of rights enjoyed by its medieval cities. This tradition was broken under Hitler's strongly centralist Third Reich, however, and the current system of municipalities (*Gemeinde*) derives from the arrangements put in place by the Allies in the immediate aftermath of World War II.

In almost every European country there is at least one additional tier of local government between the basic unit of the commune or municipality and the national government. (For an overview of European local government structures, see Norton.) These are typically described as provinces or counties, and there are obviously far fewer of them. There are nineteen in Norway, for example; fourteen in Denmark; and twelve in the Netherlands. In some countries, especially those with very large numbers of communes or municipalities, the number of provincial areas is larger. There are over ninety departments in France and over ninety provinces in Italy, for example. In these cases, there is then an additional, regional level at the top of the local government pyramid and below the national government. (There are seventeen regions in Spain and fifteen in Italy.) In countries such as Spain and Britain, as we have seen, the power of regional governments is now such that they have resulted in a system of governance that lies somewhere between traditional "federal" and "unitary" models. In others, such as the Netherlands, the powers of the regions are somewhat weaker.

Overall, therefore, we note that many European states, one way or another, have a system of local government that starts with the commune or municipality and ends with a set of regional or provincial administrations that number somewhere between twelve and twenty-five. Typically, although there is obviously a reducing number of units at each "higher" level of local government, the relationship between levels is not strictly hierarchical in the sense of one level reporting to, and needing sanction from, the next level. Rather, there tends to be a division of labor between levels of local government that is defined either in the constitution or in the national legislation that underpins the local government system. (An exception to this rule is Germany, where the system of municipal government is effectively under the jurisdiction of the regional Länder governments.) Indeed, it is sometimes the case that "lower" levels of local government are considerably "more important" than "higher" ones, if we define importance in terms of the range and significance of the public functions for which they have responsibility. Middle-level agencies are often responsible for strategic planning and coordination, whereas lower-level agencies actually produce and deliver services on the ground. In general, this leads us to the crux of the issue when evaluating any level of local government, which has to do with the significance of the role it fulfills, and the degree of autonomy it has in fulfilling it.

The Functions, Finances, and Autonomy of Local Government

Although discussions of the functions, finances, and autonomy of local government might seem to raise quite different issues, they are in practice so intimately interrelated as to be inseparable, because, as we have noted, a very wide range of government policy outputs must be delivered at a local level. The central government may, of course, set up locally based agencies, responsible directly to the central bureaucracy, to administer these policies. This was traditionally the preferred solution in Italy, where, before a series of reforms in the mid-1970s, it was estimated that there were about sixty thousand such agencies (Spence). More commonly, however, the central government mandates local government to administer particular policy areas on its behalf. In these cases, it is vital to know the extent to which the local government bureaucracy is forced to implement a national policy slavishly and the extent to which local government agencies are free to modify national policies on their own initiative.

Although the range of public services administered locally is actually rather similar in many European countries, the level of local autonomy varies quite considerably. Because it is usually safe to assume that real political power follows the purse strings, the level of de facto autonomy of particular local governments depends to a crucial extent on their ability to raise and spend money independently of the national government. Intimately related to this matter is the extent to which local people have a real input into local government decision making. Traditionally such input was seen in terms of conventional voting in local elections. Recently, however, and in the wake of worries about popular alienation from public decision making at all levels, local government agencies in a number of countries have set up a number of interesting experiments in innovative ways to involve local people in local decision making.

It would be an immense task, quite beyond the scope of our purposes here, to run through all of the powers of the different levels of local government in each European country. (Much of this information can be found in Norton.) There are, however, some general patterns. Almost all local councils, even those with relatively fewer powers, play an important role in land use planning and environmental control: the zoning of development, the processing of individual applications for new development, the issuing of certain licenses and permits, and the monitoring of noxious land uses. Most also have the duty of providing a range of services to local property: fire protection, garbage collection, public utilities, and possibly also police. (There is, however, considerable variation in the organization of European police forces—several are organized nationally.) Other important aspects of the local infrastructure that are often the responsibility of local councils are local public transport and the local road system, as well as one or more of three important aspects of the welfare state: the school system, personal health care and social services, and public housing.

Even though almost no European local council is responsible for every one of these functions, many councils oversee a number of them. Even in "centralist" France, it typically falls to local communes to build and maintain local roads, schools, libraries, and tourist offices; to dispose of refuse; and to take care of other aspects of minor local infrastructure. In Italy, this list must be expanded to include local government provision of health care, personal social services, housing, land use planning, pollution control, and local public transport. In Scandinavia, at the other end of the scale, most aspects of a comprehensive welfare state are supplied on the ground by the local government system. In Sweden in the late 1980s, for example, 32 percent of the entire workforce was employed by the public sector, 7 percent by the national government, 15 percent by municipal governments, and 10 percent by regional governments (Wallin, p. 99). The vast bulk of the day-to-day activity of the Swedish welfare state, therefore, was conducted within the local government system. The pattern is similar in other Scandinavian countries, with the list of functions of the Danish communes, for example, being far longer than those provided by many national governments.

To what extent is the activity of local councils "mere" policy implementation at the behest of the national government, a role that could in many ways be performed just as well by a local branch of the central bureaucracy? Here we need to look at both the formal legal position and the power of the purse. But in doing so, we must always remember that in all European countries it is almost undoubtedly true that the powers of local government are, or can be, constrained in important ways at the national level.

From a constitutional point of view, an interesting illustration of this can be found in the "free commune" or "deregulated local government" experiments that have been tried in a number of Scandinavian countries (for descriptions of these, see Gustafsson; Lodden; Rose). These experiments started in Sweden but quickly extended to Denmark, Norway, and Finland. They allowed certain municipalities to be designated as free communes. These were then allowed to make proposals that would allow them to opt out of national laws in certain specified policy areas that did not affect individual rights, health, and well-being in order to be able to develop more effective local arrangements. Areas specifically indicated included land use planning, the organization of local administration, fees and service charges (in Norway), and education (in Denmark). The first thing that is striking about this, of course, is that such a policy was needed in the first place. This in itself indicates that despite the size of Scandinavian local government systems, on most matters local councils were implementing national policies rather than deviating from these on the basis of local initiative. The most important thing to note, however, is that the entire experiment was orchestrated by the central

The difference that local land-use planning can make: a tranquil canalscape in Amsterdam . . .
© Alessandra Quaranta/Black Star

. . . and a depressing housing environment in the former East Germany. © Rainer
Unkel/SABA Press Photos

government in each country. Only certain municipalities were approved by the central governments for these experiments. And all proposals for local initiatives had to be approved by the national government before they could come into effect; by no means were all of them approved (Rose).

The key feature of the Scandinavian free commune experiments, shared by every other European system of local government, is that change could take place only with the approval of the national authorities. In this sense, the constitutions of European unitary states put the boot very firmly on the national, rather than the local, government foot. Unlike federal arrangements that are typically deeply entrenched in the constitution, making them impossible to be changed by the government of the day, the precise system of local government is more typically determined by legislation. This makes it easier to reform the local government system and also acts as an important constraint on the ability of local councils to defy the national government in any systematic manner.

Very clear examples of the cavalier treatment of the local government system by national governments can be seen in both Britain and Ireland, neither of which has traditionally provided any constitutional protection whatsoever for local government. One round of British local government reorganization in 1974, for example, casually swept away counties that had been in existence for many centuries, creating new areas that people had never heard of before. In 1985, the powerful, Labour-controlled Greater London Council, which had become a thorn in the side of Margaret Thatcher's Conservative government, was simply abolished, and its powers redistributed between unelected authorities and smaller local councils. The change of government from Conservative to Labour in 1997 heralded equally dramatic changes in the opposite direction. In addition to the creation, discussed above, of new regional assemblies and administrations for Scotland, Wales, and Northern Ireland, the Labour government under Tony Blair engaged in some radical new thinking in relation to local government. This involved a clear preference for creating stronger local executives; a first step towards this was the creation of the very high-profile position of elected mayor of London, for which the first elections were held in May 2000. Taken together with other local government reforms, this was a development that promised to give considerable extra power to the London region. The lack of any entrenched constitutional position for local government in Britain, however, taken together with a long tradition of centralist government, means that recent reforms must be seen as a "devolution" of power from central or local government. Functions that are devolved by central government can also be taken back again.

In Ireland, the system of domestic rates (local property taxes), which was a vital part of the revenue base of local councils, was abolished by the central government, without even the need for legislation, in 1978. Irish governments have traditionally had little compunction in postponing scheduled local council elections when these were forecast to prove politically embarrassing. Only in 1999 was a constitutional amendment passed that specifically referred to the local government system and mandated the holding of local elections every five years. The desire to attract European Union regional funding also prompted attempts in 1999 to establish a new tier of regional government in Ireland. Local government in Ireland remains weak and ineffective and attempts to restructure its finances have so far proved unsuccessful. There is a clear recognition that local government reform is on the agenda in Ireland: the Irish government announced in December 1999, for example, that a system of directly elected local mayors would be put in place by 2004. Nonetheless, there remains an inherently "top-down" approach to local governance. This means that the debate tends to be conducted in terms of which particular powers could safely be devolved to local authorities without threat to the unitary system, rather than in terms of which functions can be fulfilled only by national governments.

It is, of course, inconceivable that the national government could behave in ways such as these toward states in a federal system, in which intergovernmental relations are embedded in the constitution. In a very real sense, therefore, local governments in almost every European country ultimately can do only what they are allowed to do by their central government. Powers that are given can be, and sometimes have been, taken away.

Despite this ultimate constitutional reality, there is a very wide variation between countries in the level of autonomy that local councils are allowed by central government, and nowhere is this more evident than in the system of local government funding. Everywhere in Europe, there are three basic sources of local government financing. These are local taxes on property, business, or income; local service charges; and transfers from higher levels of government. One of the best measures of differences between countries in the degree of local autonomy has to do with how much freedom local councils have to raise money from these various sources as they please, and then spend this money as they see fit.

At one extreme, we find Denmark, where the commune is the main tax-gathering agency for the state as a whole, remitting the appropriate funds to the central government. The communes are the government agencies that collect the information on which the tax and welfare system is based. Danish communes finance their very extensive activities on the basis of local income taxes, the rates of which can be set locally by the commune and vary from about 13 percent to about 32 percent. In addition, both counties and communes may raise a local land value tax, the level of which the communes also have freedom to determine. There are also transfers of funds from the central government in the form of block grants, which can be used to compensate for the unequal revenue-gathering abilities of different communes in a country in which the same welfare system applies to all. Overall, even though much of the expenditure by Danish communes is on the administration of a welfare state effectively determined at national level, the high level of local discretion in revenue raising does provide considerable scope for local policy making.

At the opposite extreme we find countries such as Ireland and Italy, in which local councils have very little scope for independent revenue raising. In Ireland, as we have seen, one of the main sources of local revenue was domestic property taxes and rates, abolished at a stroke in 1978. These revenues were replaced by a block grant from the central government that puts it overwhelmingly in control of the local government system. A rather similar situation arose in Italy in 1982, when fiscal reforms "effectively denied the communes the power to finance their services through local taxation, by abolishing a number of taxes on housing, families, goods, services, and businesses.

These changes robbed the communes of something in the region of 92 percent of their income. . . . The result of the transfer of financial responsibility from the periphery to the centre was that Italy had one of the largest systems of transfer finances in the western world" (Spence, p. 85). Since then, against a background of massive local authority indebtedness, the Italian central government has played an ever more dominant role in local government finances.

Britain, too, has seen major central government attacks on the financial independence of local government. As a result of a series of reforms during the 1980s, local councils were first prohibited from setting rates for local property taxes at will, while both spending and revenue raising had to comply with strict central government guidelines. Councillors who defied the central government were threatened with the suspension of the council and its replacement with a government-appointed commissioner, and even with imprisonment. Subsequently, domestic rates were abolished and replaced with a local "poll tax," so called because every adult on the electoral register was liable to pay a fixed charge. This innovation proved massively unpopular, provoking widespread violent demonstrations and contributing in no small way to Margaret Thatcher's downfall. After her departure, the poll tax was replaced with a "council tax," a modified system of the old property tax, but one that remains firmly under the control of the central government. (For a discussion of local government financing in Britain, see Kingdom, 1993, 1999.)

Poll tax riots: the reform of British local government finance turns ugly. © AP/Wide World Photos

Most other European countries fall somewhere between these extremes. In the Netherlands, for example, less than 10 percent of local expenditure is raised locally; the remainder comes from central government grants, many of them already earmarked for particular projects and programs. Similarly, as we have seen, most of the high-profile regional governments in Spain, including the Catalan government, derive up to 80 percent of their income from central government grants.

In France and Belgium, in contrast, a far higher proportion of local spending is funded from local taxes, especially on land, property, and businesses (Hunt and Chandler). Germany cleaves more closely to the Scandinavian pattern, with the funding to local government coming from income taxes, business, and property taxes. In the German case, however, the local councils receive a fixed proportion, currently 15 percent, of all national income tax raised in their local area. Local taxes on business are also shared on a rigid basis with higher levels of government, with municipal councils retaining 60 percent and passing the remainder on to regional and federal government.

Popular Participation In Local Decisions

Central government control over the local purse strings is obviously one key indicator of the autonomy of local decision making in modern Europe. Another is the nature and extent of popular participation in local decisions. One distinctive approach to local participation can be found in Switzerland. Here, local participation can take the form of "direct" rather than representative democracy, with many local referendums and even a tradition of *Landsgemeinde* (popular assemblies held in the open) for making deci-

The open public assembly in Appenzell, an example of a traditional form of local participation in Switzerland, was abolished in 1997. © AP/Wide World Photos

sions in several small cantons. Rates of participation in local referendums are often very low, however, and since 1997, a number of cantons have abolished the system of *Landsgemeinde.* The largest open assembly in Switzerland (to which women had been admitted only since 1991) was abolished in Appenzell in September 1997 and similar abolitions have occurred, or are being considered, elsewhere.

In most of modern Europe, the traditional method of involving citizens in local decision making has been through a system of elections to local councils—in effect, viewing local politics as a microcosm of politics at the national level. There are very wide variations in levels of participation in local government elections across Europe, with the highest levels to be found in Scandinavia, Luxembourg, Belgium, and Italy, and the lowest in Britain, Greece, Portugal, and the Netherlands (Hoffmann-Martinot et al.). The general trend across Europe, however, has been for turnout in local elections to decline. Combined with what appear to be steady declines in turnout at national elections, and relatively low levels of turnout at European parliament elections, this has led to a concern that European voters may be getting increasingly alienated from politics.

This concern on the part of political elites at declining levels of popular participation in traditional models of representation in local decision making has been accompanied by an increased interest at the grassroots level in alternative forms of political expression. As we will see in Chapter 14, a wide range of formal and informal social groups in what we can generally think of as civil society can all play a part in the process of making decisions. Popular participation in such groups, which may deal with either single "pet" issues or matters of more general concern, can be an important way of bringing people into the decision-making process.

This combination of an elite concern at declining turnout in local elections with an increasing popular awareness of alternative forms of participation has resulted in an increasing interest in experimental methods of involving ordinary people in public decision making, especially at the local level. A common theme in these experiments has been a desire to make decision making more interactive and "deliberative." These approaches set out to go beyond the mere aggregation of individual preferences that is typical of institutions such as elections and referendums. Reasoned discussion, dialogue, and debate at the local level are intended to allow a range of options to be developed, examined, challenged, and evaluated. Proponents claim the following benefits of this approach: an improvement in citizen awareness and information; an increased sense of local involvement; a general willingness of citizens to take account of the views of others; and an increase in the level of popular acceptance of the decisions that are eventually taken. (See Elster, 1998 and Fishkin, 1997 for a discussion of the ideas of deliberative democracy.)

At a practical level, recent experiments in places such as Denmark and the Netherlands have attempted to put these ideas into practice. In the county of Funen in Denmark, for example, a series of decisions about the future of county hospitals was made on the basis of local deliberative techniques. In particular, a traditional survey of one thousand individuals was supplemented with a day-long "deliberative hearing" of the issue by seventy-five representative local citizens. Experts were brought in and interrogated, policy makers made presentations, and the eventual policy emerged

BOX 6-1

REGIONAL AND LOCAL GOVERNMENT

France

The basic units of local government in France are communes (of which there are thousands), departments (of which there are ninety-six), and regions (of which there are twenty-two). Communes are very old units of local government that may be cities the size of Marseilles or tiny villages. In practice they fulfill a range of different functions, depending on their size; large communes may have an extensive set of functions. Departments are local administrative units of the central state. At the head of each department is a prefect, a civil servant appointed by the Ministry of the Interior. Before local government reforms of 1982, prefects were very powerful, and their power remains considerable. Regions are a recent innovation, dating from 1964. Each region is headed by a regional prefect, typically one of the departmental prefects in the region. Regions do not have significant powers; the most important units of local government remain communes and departments.

Germany

Germany is a federal state in which sixteen local state governments (Länder) have extensive powers entrenched in the constitution. The interests of the Länder are further protected by their control of the upper house of the legislature, the Bundesrat. Local government, the basic units of which are about nine thousand municipalities (Gemeinden), derives its authority from the Länder. The municipalities have a very wide range of powers and can act in all policy areas not specifically allocated to the Länder or the federal government. Between the municipalities and the Länder are counties (Kries), which have a general coordinating role. Overall, however, the Länder and the municipalities are the key to the German local government system.

Italy

Italy has a three-tier local government system: regions, provinces, and communes. Of these, the provinces have the smallest contemporary role, and the regions in theory have considerable power. In practice, the constitutional court has tended to favor the national government in disputes with the regions, however. Local communes have significant powers, although all levels of local government in Italy are hampered by a centralized system of financing and an extensive role for local field agencies of the central government. A general climate favoring institutional reform in the wake of a series of high-profile corruption scandals led to the introduction of elected mayors in major cities in the early 1990s.

Netherlands

Local government in the Netherlands is based on a system of provinces and municipalities, with lower tiers being subject to the control of higher tiers and the national government. The local administrative head is a burgomaster, appointed by the central government, although there are proposals to replace this position with that of an elected mayor. Almost all of the funding for local government in the Netherlands comes in the form of grants from the central government, most of them earmarked for specific purposes. In consequence, the local government system in the Netherlands does not have a high degree of formal autonomy, although recent experiments in local democracy suggest a desire to increase practical public participation in local decision making.

Spain

One of the most striking responses to the ending of a long period of centralized authoritarian rule in Spain was the setting up of a comprehensive system of local and regional authorities, with considerable local autonomy. The major innovation was the introduction of the seventeen autonomous regions, each with its own legislature and executive headed by a regional president elected by the legislature. Below the level of region are fifty provinces and about eight thousand municipalities, each with its own elected councils. There is some overlap between the powers of different tiers of local government that causes certain procedures to be rather cumbersome. Although much of the financing of local and regional government comes from the central government, certain regional governments have used their constitutional powers to establish a very independent line. This makes Spain one of the European countries characterized by a high degree of regional autonomy, yet falling short of a constitutionally federal system.

Sweden

The Swedish local government system comprises 284 municipalities and twenty-three county councils. Although Sweden is unambiguously a unitary state, a large part of the extensive Swedish welfare system is administered by agencies of local government. Furthermore, there has been a strong tendency toward decentralization in recent years; almost all of the growth of the Swedish welfare

Continued . . .

Continued . . .

state has been at local level. A very important feature of this system is that local services are financed by local taxes, mostly on income, and that local authorities are free to set whatever level of tax they find necessary.

United Kingdom

The local government system in Britain has long been a political bone of contention, with local authorities challenging national governments' attempts to impose central policies, and national governments responding by taking functions away from local authorities and reducing their power to set local taxes. Local government in Britain is entirely under the control of the national government, can be reformed with ordinary legislation, and has no constitutional protection. The main local authorities are county councils, which retain considerable powers in matters such as policing, housing, transportation, and education. Nonetheless, the ability of these councils to adopt independent policies is reduced by the relatively high degree of central government control over local government finances. The recent introduction of Scottish, Welsh, and Northern Ireland regional assemblies, the Scottish with tax-varying power, and of an elected mayor for London, do represent a significant move towards decentralization in Britain, however.

as a result of intense interactive discussion among what might be thought of as a "citizens' jury." Similarly, in the Netherlands, the local community of Zeewolde, with fifteen thousand inhabitants, developed a new policy on public safety out of a series of local seminars, debates, and surveys, and a photo competition, that directly involved about two hundred citizens in the policy-making process. Also in the Netherlands, the city of Enschede, with about 150,000 inhabitants, delegated responsibility for the redesign of a public square to a working group that comprised delegates of interest groups and a sample of directly involved citizens. They organized debates, public excursions to other cities, and a survey to involve citizens in the eventual decision that emerged.

Many of these experiments are at a very early stage, yet they are obviously very significant for the entire concept of representative democracy, especially at the local level. In the face of declining levels of turnout in elections to traditional representative institutions, they at least hint that the way forward may not necessarily be found in attempts to force turnout up again. Rather, they suggest that the answer may be to find new ways for ordinary people to participate in the key public decisions that affect them.

CONCLUSIONS: FEDERAL GOVERNMENT, LOCAL POLITICS, AND DECENTRALIZATION

The European variations we find in patterns of local governance tell us as much about national political cultures as about anything else. In Germany and Scandinavia, we see a strong decentralizing ethos. This is reflected both in the large scale of the operations of local or state governments and in their substantial sources of revenue. Elsewhere in Europe, especially in countries with a long-standing imperial tradition that favors a strong centralized state, local government tends to be significantly weaker, in terms of both what it can do and how it chooses to do it. Governments in such countries seem much less willing to allow local governments to develop alternative power bases that might ultimately challenge their authority.

TABLE 6-1   FISCAL DECENTRALIZATION AND STRUCTURE OF GOVERNANCE IN EUROPE

	Strong local government	Weak local government
Federal	Germany (31%)* Switzerland (40%)	Austria (22%)
Unitary	Denmark (30%) Finland (24%) Norway (20%) Sweden (32%)	Belgium (5%) Britain (9%) France (9%) Greece (4%) Iceland (n.a.) Ireland (4%) Italy (3%) Luxembourg (n.a.) Malta (n.a.) Netherlands (10%) Portugal (4%) Spain (9%)

Sources: Lijphart, 1999; Castles, 1999.
*In parentheses is a country's share of regional and local taxes as a percentage of total tax revenue

A federal constitution and a strong local government system both provide significant ways of decentralizing power. Taken together with the share of public taxation raised at a local or regional level, they provide a convenient scheme for classifying European states in terms of the decentralization of their structures of governance. Table 6-1 combines recent work by Lijphart and by Castles on these matters. Lijphart (p. 189) classifies governance structures into those that are federal or unitary, and into those that are centralized or decentralized, in the sense of having weak or strong local government systems. Castles (p. 34) constructs a measure of "fiscal decentralization" based on the proportion of total tax revenue that is raised at the subnational level. Table 6-1 puts these two measures together, reclassifying as "unitary" pre-1993 Belgium, the Netherlands, and Spain—which Lijphart for cultural reasons had classified as "semi-federal."

The figures show quite clearly that *either* a federal constitution *or* a strongly local government system is associated with a high level of tax decentralization. In contrast, the level of tax decentralization is much lower in unitary states with weak local government systems. The high levels of tax decentralization in the Scandinavian countries show that the structure of local government can go a long way towards shifting important aspects of politics away from the center. The Austrian case shows that a federal constitution can have the same effect in a country with an otherwise weak local government system.

Overall, however, it is the effective impact of the local citizenry on local decisions that must be taken as the most potent indicator of real decentralization, which is why recent experiments in alternative modes of local participation should be watched with such interest.

REFERENCES

Batley, R.: "Comparisons and Lessons," in R. Batley and G. Stoker (eds.), *Local Government in Europe: Trends and Developments,* Macmillan, London, 1991, pp. 1–20.

Bräuninger, Thomas and Thomas König.: "The Checks and Balances of Party Federalism: German Federal Government in a Divided Legislature," *European Journal of Political Research,* vol. 36, 1999, pp. 207–34.

Burgess, Michael: "Federalism and Federation: A Reappraisal," in M. Burgess and A.-G. Gagnon (eds.), *Comparative Federalism and Federation: Competing Traditions and Future Directions,* Harvester Wheatsheaf, Hemel Hampstead, 1993, pp. 3–14.

Burgess, Michael and F. Gress: "The Quest for a Federal Future: German Unity and European Union," in M. Burgess and A.-G. Gagnon (eds.), *Comparative Federalism and Federation: Competing Traditions and Future Directions,* Harvester Wheatsheaf, Hemel Hampstead, 1993, pp. 168–86.

Castles, Francis: "Decentralisation and the post-war political economy," *European Journal of Political Research,* vol. 36, 1999, pp. 27–53.

Coakley, J.: "The Foundations of Statehood," in J. Coakley and M. Gallagher (eds.), *Politics in the Republic of Ireland,* 3d ed., Routledge, London, 1999.

Dunleavy, P.: *Democracy, Bureaucracy and Public Choice: Economic Explanations in Political Science,* Harvester Wheatsheaf, Hemel Hampstead, 1991.

Elazar, Daniel: "Contrasting Unitary and Federal Systems," *International Political Science Review,* vol. 18, 1997, pp. 237–51.

Elster, Jon (ed.): *Deliberative Democracy,* Cambridge University Press, Cambridge, 1998.

Fishkin, James: *The Voice of the People,* Yale University Press, New Haven, 1997.

Fitzmaurice, John: *The Politics of Belgium: A Unique Federalism,* Westview, Boulder, Co. 1996.

Gustafsson, A.: "The Changing Local Government and Politics of Sweden," in R. Batley and G. Stoker (eds.), *Local Government in Europe: Trends and Developments,* Macmillan, London, 1991, pp. 170–89.

Hennessy, P.: *Whitehall,* Secker and Warburg, London, 1989.

Heywood, Paul: *The Government and Politics of Spain,* Macmillan, London, 1995.

Hoffmann-Martinot, Vincent, Colin Rallings, and Michael Thrasher: "Comparing Local Electoral Turnout in Britain and France: More Similarities than Differences?" *European Journal of Political Research,* vol. 30, 1996, pp. 241–57.

Hughes, C.: "Cantonalism: Federation and Confederacy in the Golden Epoch of Switzerland," in M. Burgess and A.-G. Gagnon (eds.), *Comparative Federalism and Federation: Competing Traditions and Future Directions,* Harvester Wheatsheaf, Hemel Hampstead, 1993, pp. 154–67.

Hunt, M. C. and J. A. Chandler: "France," in J. A. Chandler (ed.), *Local Government in Liberal Democracies,* Routledge, London, 1993, pp. 53–72.

King, A.: "Ministerial Autonomy in Britain," in M. Laver and K. A. Shepsle (eds.), *Cabinet Ministers and Parliamentary Government,* Cambridge University Press, New York, 1994.

King, P.: *Federalism and Federation,* Croom Helm, London, 1982.

Kingdom, J.: "England and Wales," in J. A. Chandler, (ed.), *Local Government in Liberal Democracies,* Routledge, London, 1993, pp. 7–27.

Kingdom, J.: *Government and Politics in Britain: An Introduction,* 2d ed., Polity Press, London, 1999.

Lijphart, Arend: *Patterns of Democracy: Government Forms and Performance in Thirty-Six Countries,* Yale University Press, New Haven, 1999.

Linder, W.: *Swiss Democracy: Possible Solutions to Conflict in Multicultural Societies,* Macmillan, London, 1994.

Lodden, P.: "The 'Free Local Government' Experiment in Norway," in R. Batley and G. Stoker (eds.), *Local Government in Europe: Trends and Developments,* Macmillan, London, 1991, pp. 198–209.

McGarry, John and Brendan O'Leary: *Explaining Northern Ireland: Broken Images,* Blackwell, Oxford, 1997.

Niskanen, W.: *Bureaucracy and Representative Government,* Aldine-Atherton, Chicago, 1971.

Norton, A.: *The International Handbook of Local and Regional Government Status, Structure and Resources in Advanced Democracies,* Edward Elgar, Cheltenham, 1991.

O'Halpin, Eunan: "Partnership Programme Managers in the Reynolds/Spring Coalition," *Irish Political Studies,* vol. 12, 1997, pp. 78–91.

Page, E. C.: *Political Authority and Bureaucratic Power: A Comparative Analysis,* 2d ed., Harvester Wheatsheaf, Hemel Hampstead, 1992.

Rose, L. E.: "Nordic Free-Commune Experiments: Increased Local Autonomy or Continued Central Control?" in D. S. King and J. Pierre (eds.), *Challenges to Local Government,* Sage, London, 1990, pp. 212–41.

Spence, R. E.: "Italy," in J. A. Chandler (ed.), *Local Government in Liberal Democracies,* Routledge, London, 1993, pp. 73–98.

Stoker, G.: "Introduction: Trends in European Local Government," in R. Batley and G. Stoker (eds.), *Local Government in Europe: Trends and Developments,* Macmillan, London, 1991, pp. 1–20.

Wallin, G.: "Towards the Integrated and Fragmented State: The Mixed Role of Local Government," in J.-E. Lane (ed.), *Understanding the Swedish Model,* Frank Cass, London, 1991, pp. 96–121.

Wildavsky, A.: *The Politics of the Budgetary Process,* Little, Brown, 1964.

Woodhouse, Diana: *Ministers and Parliaments: Accountability in Theory and Practice,* Clarendon Press, Oxford, 1994.

7

PATTERNS IN PARTY POLITICS AND PARTY SYSTEMS

This book is about the politics of representation in modern Europe. Much of it, in some way or other, is about party politics. In this chapter we therefore look at the political parties that lay claim to representing the interests of European voters. Most of these parties can be classified as belonging to one of a small number of party "families": the Christian democratic family, for example, or the social democratic family, or liberal family, and so on. We consider in detail these party families in the following chapter. In this chapter we explore the way in which the character of political competition in any given country is conditioned by a particular constellation of competing parties that together make up a national party system. We also report the results of recent elections in these countries.[1] As we will see, although every country has a distinctive blend of party families, and hence a distinctive party system, there are also striking similarities between party systems in different countries. As a general introduction to the key themes that we will be discussing, therefore, we look in this chapter at the party systems of seven Western European countries.

The countries that we have chosen and to which we return systematically at points throughout the text have not been selected at random; together they capture key variations in the core themes that we discuss. They include all the "big" countries (Britain, France, Germany, Italy, and Spain), as well as two of the most interesting smaller democracies (the Netherlands and Sweden). They include very old democracies (Britain and France), as well as a relatively new democracy (Spain); party systems dominated by two large parties (Britain and, to a lesser extent, Germany); and systems with many parties (Italy and the Netherlands). They include systems long dominated by socialist

---

[1]The sources used for these results are Mackie and Rose (1991, 1997), the *Political Data Yearbook,* and, for the most recent results, various national and international websites.

parties (Spain and Sweden), by Christian democratic parties (Germany and Italy), and by conservative parties (Britain). They include systems in which elections are conducted under a plurality voting system—Britain and France—as well as those that employ different forms of proportional representation (PR): Germany, Italy, the Netherlands, Spain, and Sweden. Finally, they include systems that invariably produce single-party governments (such as Britain), those that invariably produce coalition governments (Germany, Italy, and the Netherlands), and those that alternate between single-party and coalition governments (Sweden).

As we argued in the Preface, we in no sense claim that the countries we have selected are "typical"; it should already be clear that there is no such thing as a typical Western European country. We have chosen the seven party systems described below because, among them, they include most of the types of variation that we must use if we are to be able to describe the complex mosaic of Western European party systems. Later, in Chapter 15, we will look at the emerging party systems in postcommunist Europe.

SEVEN WESTERN EUROPEAN PARTY SYSTEMS

Party Politics in the United Kingdom

The British party system is often seen as one of the simplest and most clear-cut in Western Europe. Two large and more or less evenly matched parties confront each other. On one side is the Labour party, a social democratic party that initially mobilized in order to promote and defend the interests of the working class. The party has always enjoyed a close relationship with the trade union movement and has traditionally seen itself as the political wing of a wider labor movement. Despite this, Labour governments have sometimes found themselves in bitter confrontation with the trade unions over attempts to impose national income policies, notably during the long 1978–79 "winter of discontent" that led to Labour's defeat in the 1979 general election and ushered in the era of Conservative governments, led by Margaret Thatcher until 1990 and then by John Major until 1997.

The Conservative party is Labour's main opponent. Like all traditional Conservative parties in Western Europe, the major aims of the Conservatives in the United Kingdom are to defend the rights of private property, to encourage market forces, and to resist the encroachment of the state into spheres of (especially economic) activity they see as properly the realm of unregulated private individuals. For most of its history, the party has also defended the traditional moral order, even if this has meant state involvement in regulating personal morality. The Conservatives have also been advocates of tough law-and-order policies and nationalist foreign policy stances based on a strong military profile. This has often led the party to advocate high levels of public spending on policing and national defense, and more recently it has helped push the party into a more Euroskeptic stance. In contrast to the support for Labour, the Conservatives' strongest support comes from middle-class voters and the most privileged sectors of British society.

As Table 7-1 shows, the Conservatives won a majority of seats in the UK parliament following the elections of 1983, 1987, and 1992, thanks in part to a disproportional

TABLE 7-1 ELECTIONS IN THE UNITED KINGDOM SINCE 1983

Party	1983		1987		1992		1997	
	% Votes	N Seats	% Votes	N Seats	% Votes	N Seats	% Votes	N Seats
Conservatives	42.4	397	42.0	376	41.9	336	30.7	165
Labour	27.6	209	30.7	229	34.9	271	43.3	419
Liberals*	13.7	17	12.8	17	17.8	20	16.8	46
Social Democrats*	11.6	6	9.7	5	–	–	–	–
Scottish Nationalists	1.1	2	1.4	3	1.9	3	2.0	6
Welsh Nationalists	0.4	2	0.4	3	0.5	4	0.5	4
Irish Nationalists	0.8	2	0.8	4	0.7	4	1.1	5
Irish Unionists	1.4	15	1.2	13	1.2	13	1.4	13
Referendum party	–	–	–	–	–	–	2.6	–
Others	0.8	–	1.1	–	1.1	–	1.6	1
All	100.0	650	100.0	650	100.0	651	100.0	659

Party Composition of Government in the 1990s:

    1979–97: Conservative single-party government

    1997–   : Labour single-party government

*The Social Democrats and the Liberals formed an electoral pact—the Alliance—in 1979 and 1983; the two parties subsequently merged under the name Liberal Democrats.

Source: The sources used for these results and all others reported in this chapter are Mackie and Rose (1991, 1997), the *Political Data Yearbook,* and, for the most recent results, various national and international websites.

first-past-the-post electoral system (see Chapter 11). In fact, this extended period of Conservative rule began in 1979, when Margaret Thatcher won her first election victory. The period from 1979 to 1997 marked an unprecedented period of single-party dominance in British politics, and, following Sartori's classification, actually transformed the United Kingdom from a two-party system into a "predominant party system," that is, a system in which a single party manages to win a majority across four consecutive legislative periods (King; Sartori, pp. 192–201). During this period, the Conservatives sought to weaken the power of the trade unions, to reduce the size of the state sector, and to sell off many public enterprises to the private sector (see Chapter 13). Throughout the same period Labour offered more or less consistent opposition to this program, resisting attacks on public spending, opposing encroachments on trade union rights, and defending existing levels of public provision of a range of goods and services.

The opposition between these starkly contrasted partisan views was clearly of major importance to the people of Britain. Which view was to prevail had fundamental implications for the basic concerns of almost every individual citizen. This important ideological decision was also sharply defined for voters, as only these two major parties had a realistic chance of winning an overall legislative majority. Voters were therefore in effect choosing between two alternative governments with clearly distinctive policy profiles. In the United Kingdom, the party that wins an election with a working majority has every opportunity to implement its policy program. In 1979, for example, the Conservatives held an overall majority of forty-three seats in the 635-seat House of Commons; in 1983, when reelected, they enjoyed a majority of 144 seats in the newly enlarged 650-seat House; in 1987, they enjoyed a majority of 102 seats. Given such clear majorities, the Conservative governments of the 1980s had little fear of defeat and hence experienced few real difficulties in pushing through their strongly partisan program. In 1992, however, they were reduced to a majority of just twenty-one seats over all the other parties taken together, and thereafter they were obliged to move a little more cautiously. In 1993 their problems were also exacerbated by internal divisions over the Maastricht Treaty and over the move toward European Union (EU; see Chapter 5), when a small group of Conservative members of Parliament (MPs) who opposed the treaty consistently voted against their own government. In May 1993, at the time of the crucial parliamentary vote over Maastricht, the government was therefore obliged to rely on the votes of the Ulster Unionists in order to get its proposals through Westminster. By the time the 1997 election was held, defections from the Conservative party in Westminster and a series of bruising by-election defeats had destroyed the party's overall majority, and it ended the parliamentary term as a minority government.

This image of clear-cut confrontation between two sharply distinguished parties, each hoping to form a majority government on its own, is, of course, something of a simplification. There are, for example, several small regionally based nationalist—and anti-nationalist—parties. There is the Scottish National party, as well as a Welsh nationalist party (Plaid Cymru). In Northern Ireland, which remains an integral part of the United Kingdom, there are two parties that advocate breaking away from the United Kingdom and favor eventual unity with the Irish Republic: the Social Democratic and Labour party (SDLP) and Sinn Fein, the latter being also strongly supportive of the Irish Republican Army (IRA). There are also two unionist parties that fight to preserve Northern Ireland as part of the United Kingdom: the Ulster Unionist party and the Democratic Unionist party. But despite often winning substantial support in their own local areas and taking some seats in the House of Commons, these parties hardly impinge at all on the British party system taken as a whole. In 1997, for example, the total number of seats won by regional parties in the House of Commons was only twenty-eight, fewer than 7 percent of the Labour total!

Of greater potential importance as a deviation from pure two-party politics in Britain is the presence of a "center" party or parties. Represented in the main by the long-established Liberal Party, this center group traditionally promoted policies that fell between the more radical alternatives of Labour and the Conservatives, and it wins some support from both major social classes. The center received a major electoral boost in the early 1980s when the Social Democratic Party, a moderate faction of the Labour party, split off as a result of what it saw as the unwelcome growth of the Labour left. Together, the Liberals and Social Democrats formed an alliance of the center and posed perhaps the greatest postwar challenge to the dominance of two-party politics, which itself was particularly polarized during the 1980s. In 1987 the center alliance won almost 23 percent of the vote, just 8 percent less than Labour. Indeed, in the southern part of England, this alliance actually displaced Labour as the major challenger to the Conservatives.

However, even this development had little real impact. Despite the electoral popularity of the Liberal–Social Democratic alliance, the bias against third parties in the British simple-plurality voting system (see Chapter 11) left the two allied parties with only seventeen out of 650 seats for their 23 percent of the vote. When the chips were down, the alliance did little to disturb the traditional British two-party system—at least at the parliamentary level. Thereafter, the majority of members of the SDP joined the Liberals in a new, but still electorally weak Liberal Democrat party, that won almost 18 percent of the vote in 1992 and almost 17 percent in 1997. On this last occasion, however, the electoral swing away from the Conservatives was so great that the Liberals were able to enjoy a tactical advantage, and although their overall share of the vote fell slightly, they managed to win a record forty-six seats, more than double those achieved in 1992.

The biggest change in 1997 was of course the overwhelming victory of Labour under its new leader, Tony Blair. Before the 1997 election, Labour had languished in opposition for eighteen years, and had chosen initially to challenge the increasingly right-wing government of Margaret Thatcher by adopting quite a marked left-wing program. This strategy, to say the least, had proved unsuccessful. Indeed, by moving to the left, Labour had alienated many of its more moderate leaders and voters, some of whom then shifted across to the new SDP. Following its 1987 defeat, however, Labour slowly began to reorganize and adapt, initially under Neil Kinnock, and later under John Smith and then Tony Blair. By the time Blair had cemented his control over the party, the move towards the moderate center of the political spectrum had become unstoppable.

Blair discarded many of the older left-wing policies and campaigning styles, and partly modeling himself on the U.S. Democratic party under Bill Clinton, made a determined effort to appeal to middle-class voters and to promote centrist policies. "New" Labour, as he insisted on referring to his party, was different from "old" Labour. A number of the existing social democratic commitments were maintained, but these were to be recast as "traditional values in a modern setting." Part of the change involved the removal of the famous "Clause IV" from the party constitution, a clause which had committed the party—in principle, if not in practice—to wholesale public ownership. New Labour was not going to advocate old-style socialism. Nor was it to convert completely to the neoliberalism of the Conservative party, although it did insist it was pro-business and it accepted a large number of the Thatcherite reforms enacted by previous Conservative governments. Instead, New Labour was to advocate the so-called "Third Way," an approach to policy making and to governance that owed much to the ideas then being advanced by Blair's intellectual guru, the sociologist Anthony Giddens, Director of the London School of Economics (Blair; Giddens; Marquand).

Although Labour's additional electoral gains in 1997 amounted to less than 10 percent, the translation of its higher vote total through the simple-plurality electoral system provided the party with a record majority in Westminster. Moreover, it also left the Conservatives with their smallest share of seats ever. In parliamentary terms, this was a major landslide, and the Conservatives were left without a single parliamentary seat in either Scotland or Wales.

Since achieving office in 1997, Labour has embarked on a massive program of reform, not only in the social and economic sphere, but also in constitutional terms. In less than three years, for example, devolved government has been introduced in Scotland and Wales, the House of Lords has been reformed through the abolition of voting rights for hereditary peers; a system for the direct election of the city mayor has been introduced for London, with a similar system soon to follow for other major cities; and a commission has been established to consider changes in the electoral system for Westminster with a view to achieving greater proportionality.

As the opposition to this active and ambitious Labour government, the Conservative party finds itself more and more isolated, and in an effort to carve out a more distinctive profile it has turned increasingly to emphasizing its stance in defense of British independence in Europe. Being significantly more skeptical towards European integration than Labour, and also more skeptical than most mainstream center-right parties across Europe, the Conservatives have increasingly taken on the image of a nationalist party. And since their defeat in 1997 has left them without any seats in Westminster from districts in either Scotland or Wales, this image is also one of a specifically English nationalist party. Although it is still too early to say with any certainty, it seems that the end of the 1990s have witnessed a fundamental transformation in British politics and in the party system. (On the traditional British party system, see Finer; for a more recent assessment, see Webb).

Party Politics in Sweden

In Sweden, as in Britain, there is a major socialist party that initially mobilized in order to promote and defend the interests of the working class and forged strong links with the trade union movement. There is also a Swedish conservative party, now known as the Moderates, which sets out to defend the interests of the middle class and the more privileged sectors of the population. In this sense, Sweden is no different from Britain, with the representation of class interests taking the form of a partisan conflict between left and right. But it is here that the parallels end, for as Table 7-2 shows, the actual balance of forces on both the left and the right in Sweden differs sharply from that in the United Kingdom.

The Swedish Social Democrats have been much more successful than the British Labour party, holding governmental power in Sweden almost without interruption from the early 1930s through the mid-1970s. Indeed, the Social Democrats in Sweden have been the most successful socialist party in Western Europe and have used this success to establish one of Western Europe's strongest and most egalitarian welfare states.

The second point of contrast between Sweden and Britain is that despite their success, the Swedish Social Democrats have never monopolized the representation of the left. They have always been challenged by a small but persistent Communist party, now renamed the Left party, which usually wins about 5 percent of the popular vote, but which doubled its support in the election of 1998. The challenge posed to the Social Democrats by the Left party is nevertheless a reasonably amicable one, and the smaller party has often supported its larger rival in parliament, enabling the Social Democrats to take control of the government even when they do not command a majority of seats, as was the case from 1982 to 1991 and has been since 1994.

TABLE 7-2   ELECTIONS IN SWEDEN SINCE 1988

Party	1988		1991		1994		1998	
	% Votes	N Seats	% Votes	N Seats	% Votes	N Seats	% Votes	N Seats
Social Democrats	43.6	156	37.7	138	45.2	161	36.6	131
Left Party/ Communists	5.9	21	4.5	16	6.2	22	12.0	43
Ecology party	5.5	20	3.4	–	5.0	18	4.5	16
Liberal party	12.2	44	9.1	33	7.2	26	4.7	17
Center party	11.4	42	8.5	31	7.7	27	5.1	18
Christian Democrats	3.0	–	7.1	26	4.1	15	11.8	42
Moderate (Conservative)	18.3	66	21.9	80	22.4	80	22.7	82
New Democracy	–	–	6.7	25	1.2	–	–	–
Others	0.1	–	1.0	–	1.0	–	2.6	–
All	100.0	349	100.0	349	100.0	349	100.0	349

Party Composition of Government in the 1990s:

1982–91:	Social Democratic single-party government
1991–94:	Coalition of Moderates, Liberals, Center, & Christian Democrats
1994– :	Social Democratic single-party government

A third point of contrast with Britain is that unlike the British Conservatives, the Swedish Moderates fall very considerably short of monopolizing the nonsocialist opposition in parliament. On the contrary, the Swedish center and right are quite severely fragmented. In addition to the Moderates, there is a small Liberal party, which commanded some 10 percent of parliamentary seats during the 1980s and draws support primarily from middle-class voters who are reluctant to endorse the more conservative Moderates. Since 1988, however, support for this party has fallen back considerably. There is also a Center party, which initially grew as an agrarian party seeking to represent the interests of Swedish farmers and now draws support from across the social spectrum; it won around 12 percent of parliamentary seats in the 1980s, but it too has fallen back in the 1990s.

Part of the reason these two parties have fared less well in recent elections is the sporadic but quite substantial growth in support for the once-marginal Christian Democrats, which commanded almost 12 percent of the vote in 1998, and which formed part of the center-right coalition from 1991 to 1994. This is a largely Protestant party that campaigns in defense of traditional values against the rise of more permissive attitudes. The Moderates, which polled an average of just over 20 percent in the 1990s, have also grown, but unlike the British Conservatives, they still have to remain content with the idea that they are just one of a group of nonsocialist parties competing on the center right of the Swedish party system.

Although the Social Democrats were helped by this fragmentation on the center right, they have not had it all their own way. The three stronger parties of the center right cooperated to form a series of anti-socialist coalitions in the late 1970s and early 1980s, and from 1991 to 1994, together with the Christian Democrats, they returned once more to government.

The overall pattern of votes in Sweden has therefore tended to be quite finely balanced between the left and center-right blocs, a "two-bloc" competition that had a lot of similarities with the two-party competition that characterized British politics for much of the postwar period. That said, there are signs that this pattern might now be breaking down. The Ecology Party, which is reluctant to define itself in left-right terms, suddenly emerged to win more than 5 percent of the vote and twenty seats in 1988, although, by falling below the 4 percent threshold, it then lost its representation in parliament in 1991. Since then, it has come back again, winning eighteen seats in 1994 and sixteen in 1998. The 1991 election also witnessed the emergence of New Democracy, a protest party of the right, that mobilized on the basis of a popular dissatisfaction with politicians from the traditional parties and with traditional politics more generally. Although this party suffered severe internal conflicts and then failed to win reelection to parliament in 1994, its short-lived success does indicate that there may still be room for party growth on the far-right of the Swedish party spectrum. Indeed, far-right parties have recently enjoyed renewed electoral success in neighboring Denmark and Norway. In Denmark, two far-right parties polled a total of almost 10 percent of the votes in the 1998 general election, while in Norway in 1997 the far-right Progress party polled more than 15 percent of the vote. (For a classic account of the Swedish party system, as well as Scandinavian party politics in general, see Berglund and Lindstrom, as well as Einhorn and Logue; for a more contemporary assessment, see Arter.)

Party Politics in Germany

On the face of it, at least for most of the postwar period, the German party system has appeared very similar to that of Britain. Here, too, there are two main protagonists: the Social Democrats (SPD), the traditional party of the working class, and the Christian Democrats (CDU/CSU), the main representative of conservative interests. Lying strategically between these two parties, with a small but enduring presence, is a liberal party, the Free Democrats (FDP). Although the Free Democrats poll fewer votes than their British counterpart, they have always won quite a substantial representation in the Bundestag, the lower house of the German parliament, as the electoral system ensures that all parties polling 5 percent or more of the vote (or winning three seats in the single-member districts) are represented in proportion to their electoral support (see Chapter 11).

Despite superficial similarities between the British and German systems, however, there are also striking contrasts. In the first place, the relatively strong parliamentary presence of the Free Democrats has helped to ensure that neither of the two major parties has been able single-handedly to command a majority of seats in the Bundestag. In Germany, therefore, in contrast to Britain, coalition government has been the norm. Indeed, the last occasion on which a single party secured an overall majority in the Bundestag was in 1957, when the Christian Democrats, under their powerful and popular leader Konrad Adenauer, won just over 50 percent of the votes and 54 percent of the seats. Even then, however, a coalition government was formed, with the CDU being joined in government by the now-defunct German party, which then held seventeen seats in the Bundestag. Since then, the FDP has provided necessary coalition support for each of the major parties, and (with one exception during the "grand coalition" between the CDU and the SPD from 1966 to 1969) it served as junior partner in every government from 1961 to 1998. The FDP cooperated with the CDU from 1961 to 1966 and resumed support in 1982, and it cooperated with the SPD from 1969 through 1982.

In addition to its powerful governmental role, the FDP can be distinguished from the British Liberals in two other respects. First, it promotes an emphatically conservative liberalism. It emphasizes individual as opposed to collective rights and lays a greater emphasis than even the CDU on the need to roll back the state and maximize private freedoms. Second, the FDP's roots can be found in secular opposition to Catholic politics rather than in liberal opposition to secular conservatism. Despite its brokerage role in government formation, the FDP can therefore be seen as being substantially to the right of the British center parties, and more akin in many ways to the British Conservatives.

The second major point of contrast with Britain concerns the CDU. First, as its name implies, the CDU is not simply a conservative party; it is also a Christian party, a party that has traditionally placed substantial weight on the defense of religious values against the secularism of both the SPD and the FDP. Heir to the primarily Catholic Center Party of Weimar Germany, which was the major representative of the moderate right in the period prior to the mobilization of nazism, the postwar Christian Democrats have since broadened their support base through an explicit appeal to Protestant voters. This pan-Christian strategy was encouraged by the fact that a large proportion of the Protestant electorate in Germany resided in what was to become the German Democratic Republic (East Germany), thus undermining the potential for the emergence in West Germany of distinctively Protestant parties such as those that proved so crucial in Dutch politics (to be discussed later in this chapter). Second, the "Christian Democrats" are effectively two parties, the CDU proper and its permanent political ally, the Bavarian Christian Social Union (CSU). Unlike the CDU, the CSU is distinctively Catholic, and to the extent that it operates autonomously, is generally regarded as the most conservative party in Germany.

The third, albeit less marked, contrast with Britain is to be found in the character of the socialist party, the SPD. From its origins in the late nineteenth century as the most radical and powerful socialist party in Europe, when the SPD leadership included some of the foremost Marxist intellectuals in the international socialist movement, the party has developed into one of the most moderate and centrist social democratic organizations in Western Europe. The SPD was effectively excluded from office in the early years of postwar West Germany, and it suffered from the reaction against political extremism that flowed in the wake of both nazism and the communist takeover of East Germany. In 1959, in an effort to acquire a legitimate role in the new state, the party adopted what became known as the Bad Godesberg program, accepting the principle of the free-market economy and a commitment to the North Atlantic Treaty Organization (NATO), and effectively endorsing the policies then being pursued by the incumbent Christian Democratic government. This transformation was finally completed in 1966, when, as noted, the party joined in a grand coalition with the Christian Democrats. Since then, the degree of ideological conflict between the two major parties has often been quite insignificant, and the German party system was often regarded as among the most consensual in Western Europe (e.g., see Klingemann).

The traditional combination of alignments based on class (SPD versus CDU and FDP) and religion (CDU versus SPD and FDP) once led Pappi (pp. 12–14) to view the German party system as being characterized by a "triangular" rather than "unidimensional" pattern of competition. According to this view, various alliances can and do prove possible. Thus, the moderate socialism of the SPD and the residual Catholic emphases of the CDU could find common ground in a defense of the welfare state and of consensual rather than confrontational policy making. The SPD and FDP, in turn, could find common ground in rejecting the incorporation of Catholic values into public policy (on issues such as abortion and divorce, for example). And the CDU and FDP could find—and most often have found—common ground in their defense of the interests of private property and capital.

In the 1980s, two factors emerged that helped to undermine this particular, and often quite cozy, balance. In the first place, since 1983 a new, radical Green Party managed to win sufficient electoral support to push it past the 5 percent threshold imposed by the German electoral system and to help it gain strong representation in the Bundestag. This expansion of the number of parties in parliament offered the possibility that party competition could well develop into a confrontation between two rival blocs, with the SPD and the Greens confronting the CDU and the FDP. To be sure, it was always known that there would be much difficult negotiation and internal party conflict before the SPD and the Greens agreed on a common program for government. Nevertheless, the presence of the Greens did have the potential to destroy the pivotal role of the FDP in German politics and create a two-bloc pattern quite similar to that which characterizes party competition in Sweden, for example. This potential was finally to be realized in 1998.

The second, and incomparably the more important, recent development has been the collapse of East Germany and the unification of the two German states in 1990. Greater Germany then accommodated more than 12 million new voters who had yet to be socialized into stable partisan identities and whose political behavior could therefore prove quite volatile for some time to come (see also Chapter 15). In the first democratic elections in East Germany in March 1990, these new electors voted overwhelmingly for the Christian Democrats (which won 47 percent of the poll), with the Social Democrats winning just 22 percent and the reformed Communist Party winning 16 percent. The Christian Democratic successes were later confirmed in the first Bundestag elections of the newly unified state, which were held on December 2, 1990 (Table 7-3). These were the first all-German elections since Hitler seized power in 1933, and once again they left the coalition of the Christian Democrats and the liberal FDP with a clear overall majority, in which they held a total of 398 seats in the newly enlarged Bundestag, as against 264 seats for the combined opposition parties. Indeed, the FDP success was even more marked than that of the CDU, and the party then polled a substantially larger share of the vote in the eastern part of the country than in the west.

A number of other aspects of these crucial and unprecedented elections should also be underlined. In the first place, and as part of the transitional arrangements prior to

TABLE 7-3 ELECTIONS IN UNITED GERMANY SINCE 1990

Party	1990		1994		1998	
	% Votes	N Seats	% Votes	N Seats	% Votes	N Seats
Christian Democrats (CDU/CSU)	43.8	319	41.5	294	35.1	245
Social Democrats (SPD)	33.5	239	36.4	252	40.9	298
Free Democrats (FDP)	11.0	79	6.9	47	6.2	44
Greens*	5.1	8	7.3	49	6.7	47
Democratic Socialists (PDS)	2.4	17	4.4	30	5.1	35
Republicans	2.1	–	1.9	–	1.8	–
German Peoples' Union (DVU)	–	–	–	–	1.2	–
Others	2.1	–	1.6	–	3.0	–
All	100.0	662	100.0	672	100.0	669

Party Composition of Government in the 1990s:

1982–98: Coalition of Christian Democrats and Free Democrats

1998– : Coalition of Social Democrats and Greens

*Includes (West German) Greens and (East German) Alliance '90/Greens in 1990.

complete unification, the rule whereby parties require a national minimum of 5 percent of the vote in order to win representation in the Bundestag (see Chapter 11) was modified for the purposes of these first all-German elections. Rather than treating the threshold as applying to Germany as a whole, it was agreed that a party would need 5 percent in either the area that was formerly West Germany or the area that was formerly East Germany. Thus, although the former East German Communist Party, now reorganized as the Party of Democratic Socialism (PDS), won only 2.4 percent in terms of the nation as a whole, it won some 10 percent of the vote in the former East Germany, which was double the threshold and sufficient to win the party seventeen seats in 1990. The Greens, on the other hand, were weakened by this rule, failing to reach the threshold in the west (they polled only 4.7 percent) and continuing to be represented in the Bundestag only under the auspices of the Bundnis '90, the alliance of East German citizens' movements that included New Forum, the popular movement that had spearheaded the 1989 protests and revolution. The two groups formally merged in November 1992.

Second, despite the success of the incumbent coalition, the German party system after 1990 was to prove more fragmented than at any point in the previous thirty years. Five parties were represented in the Bundestag, ranging from the Greens/Bundnis '90 to the reformed East German Communist Party, the PDS. Political problems had also begun to accumulate in the new Germany. The government was having to cope with the arrival of unprecedented numbers of immigrants, refugees, and asylum seekers, as well as with a rising tide of xenophobia and racist violence. In 1992, for example, some four hundred thousand asylum seekers arrived in Germany, all looking for both jobs and housing. In the same year, seventeen people, including a number of non-Germans, were killed in extremist violence, and more than 2,200 persons were injured. Meanwhile, unemployment continued to remain particularly high in the former East German area, and voters there were increasingly disillusioned with the lack of economic and social progress, while in the western areas voters were also increasingly discontented about having to bear the burden of the economic costs of reconstruction and resettlement. Symptomatic of this discontent has been a small growth in support for extreme-right parties such as the Republicans and the German People's Union, which together polled some 3 percent of the vote in 1998. More in general, German commentators now regularly point toward the growth of what they call *Politikverdrossenheit,* or disillusion with politics, a syndrome that has also been increasingly noted in other advanced western democracies (Poguntke and Scarrow; Norris).

It was therefore not completely unexpected when an alternative Red-Green coalition of the SPD and the Green party under the leadership of Gerhard Schröder eventually defeated Helmut Kohl's long-standing CDU-FDP coalition in 1998. In fact, this was not only the first time that the Greens had become part of a coalition in Germany, but it was also the first time that an incumbent German government had been thrown out of office in its entirety, and a wholly new government installed in its place.

As in the United Kingdom, the change of government had been made easier by the increasingly moderate stance adopted by the SPD—although Schröder himself preferred to speak of the "new middle" rather than the "third way." Ironically, one of Schröder's first crises, which was prompted by the sudden resignation of the more left-wing SPD deputy leader Oskar Lafontaine, occurred precisely on the day when Schröder was intending to make a speech heralding the publication of a German translation of Giddens's *Third Way.*

The agreement between the SPD and the Greens had also been forged by necessity, of course: as in the UK, both parties had become increasingly frustrated by the long tenure in office of their center-right opponents. Nevertheless, relations between the two parties are not easy, and the new government proved not to be very popular with voters, going down to a series of defeats in local and Land elections in 1999. The pressure on the new government eased early in 2000, however, as the CDU was suddenly rocked by a series of financial scandals. The CDU leader and long-term Chancellor, Helmut Kohl, was forced to resign his chairmanship of the party after admitting that he had received illegal party donations, and the party image suffered badly as a result. Midway through its first term, and now facing an opposition which appeared to have lost much of its credibility, the new SPD-Green coalition looked set to cement its hold on office. That said, the internal problems of the coalition are such that nobody is completely ruling out the prospect of the return of a grand coalition between the CDU and the SPD. (On the traditional German party system, see Smith; for a more recent assessment, see Jeffery; Padgett.)

Party Politics in the Netherlands

Like politics in Sweden and unlike that in Britain and the former West Germany, Dutch politics is highly fragmented. Many parties compete for electoral and parliamentary support. Nor does the Netherlands have competition between two clearly distinguished

TABLE 7-4   ELECTIONS IN THE NETHERLANDS SINCE 1986

Party	1986		1989		1994		1998	
	% Votes	N Seats	% Votes	N Seats	% Votes	N Seats	% Votes	N Seats
Socialist party	–	–	–	–	1.3	2	3.5	5
Green Left*	3.2	3	4.1	6	3.5	5	7.3	11
Labor party (PvdA)	33.3	52	31.9	49	24.0	37	29.0	45
Democrats 66	6.1	9	7.9	12	15.5	24	9.0	14
Liberals (VVD)	17.4	27	14.6	22	19.9	31	24.7	38
Christian Democrats (CDA)	34.6	54	35.3	54	22.2	34	18.4	29
Reformed Political Union	1.0	1	1.2	2	1.3	2	1.3	2
Political Reformed party	1.7	3	1.9	3	1.7	2	1.8	3
Reformed Political Federation	0.9	1	1.0	1	1.8	3	2.0	3
Old People's Alliance	–	–	–	–	3.6	6	0.5	–
Union 55+	–	–	–	–	0.9	1	–	–
Center Democrats	0.4	–	0.9	1	2.5	3	0.6	–
Others	1.4	–	1.2	–	1.8	–	1.9	–
All	100.0	150	100.0	150	100.0	150	100.0	150

Party Composition of Government in the 1990s:

1989–94:   Coalition of Christian Democrats and Labor

1994– :   Coalition of Labor, Liberals and Democrats 66

*The Green Left is a merger of four different parties (the Communist party, the Pacifist Socialist party, the Radical Political party, and the Evangelical People's party), each of which last ran separate lists in 1986.

parties or blocs. Rather, three large parties, none in a position to win a working majority on its own, provide the major alternatives before voters. The various maneuverings of these parties create a shifting system of coalitions and alliances.

The first of these parties is a socialist party, the Labor Party (PvdA), which, until 1994, usually won a third of the vote, but which then fell back to just 24 percent, recovering to 29 percent in 1998. This is also more or less the share of parliamentary seats, since the Dutch electoral system is exceptionally proportional (see Table 7-4). Both programmatically and in terms of its electoral support, the party stands as the effective equivalent of the German, Swedish, and British social democratic parties. Indeed, it sometimes claims to be the true inventor of the "third way" or "new middle." The party based itself traditionally in the working class, and it promotes both the role of the welfare state and a more egalitarian distribution of social and economic resources. Given its relatively small size, however, it has little hope of forming a government of its own and is obliged to forge alliances with parties to its right.

Among these parties to Labor's rights is the Christian Democratic Appeal (CDA), which won more or less the same level of support as the Labour Party in the elections of 1986, 1989, and 1994. As its name implies, however, and like the major nonsocialist party in Germany, the Dutch CDA is not simply a conservative party. It also seeks to represent the views of Christian voters, both Protestant and Roman Catholic. Religious divisions, reflecting conflicts both between the different Christian denominations and between those who are generally proclerical and those who are anticlerical, have always been important in Dutch politics. For much of the postwar period, indeed, Protestant and Catholic voters were represented by two separate Protestant parties and one Catholic party. Since 1977, however, and partly as a result of the general weakening of religious ties and the decreasing political salience of interdenominational divisions, these three parties have united behind one pan-Christian party, the CDA. Over and above its defense of religious values, the CDA maintains a moderate conservative position in relation to social and economic policies, drawing electoral support from all major social classes. Most recently, however, it has entered into quite a serious—if possibly short-term—electoral decline. Indeed, between 1986 and 1998 its vote fell by almost half, and whereas it (or one of its denominational predecessors) played a pivotal and often dominant role in all postwar coalitions, it is now experiencing its second consecutive period in opposition.

The third major party in the Netherlands is the Liberal Party (VVD). This party has a much more distinctively middle-class electoral profile than the CDA, and usually won less than 20 percent of the vote. Most recently, however, it has been gaining support, and polled almost 25 percent in 1998. For a long time, the Liberals represented the main secular opposition to the Labor Party and proved far less willing than the CDA to compromise in the direction of Labor's social and economic concerns. At the same time, however, the VVD was also hostile to the representation of religious values in politics. In this respect it sometimes found common ground with the Labor Party in opposition to the CDA. Indeed, the Liberal Party first mobilized in Dutch politics primarily as middle-class opposition to the growing appeal of religious parties. (This links the Dutch Liberals to the German FDP and sets them apart from the British and Swedish Liberals, both of which originated as moderate middle-class alternatives to secular conservative opponents and both of which are still oriented toward more centrist policies.)

Thus, when it comes to class issues and an economic program emphasizing the need for a minimum of state intervention and a maximum reliance on market forces, the Dutch Liberals could always identify more strongly with the CDA than with Labor. In terms of the religious-secular divide, however, the Liberals found themselves on the same side as Labour. At the same time, because the CDA's conservative appeal is more moderate than that of the Liberals, the CDA sometimes sought alliances with Labor rather than with the other right-wing party.

The result, as might be expected, was—and still is—a shifting pattern of coalition government. In 1981, for example, the CDA formed a short-lived government coalition with Labor, a government that was displaced by a CDA-Liberal alliance in 1982. This government survived until 1989, when it was displaced by a CDA-Labor coalition. And this government, in turn, was replaced by a coalition of Labor, Liberals, and the small left-leaning liberal party, Democrats 66, in 1994—the so-called "purple coalition," the first Dutch government to exclude the Christian mainstream. At center stage in Dutch party politics, therefore, are three key actors that go in and out of government in a shifting series of alliances. This pattern is complicated by the presence of a number of smaller parties, on the left and on the right, and both secular and religious. These smaller left-wing parties include the increasingly important Green Left and the Socialist party, both of which have managed to attract some of Labor's more radical supporters. Whether either or both could grow sufficiently together with Labor to form a left coalition bloc, similar to that which succeeded in Germany in 1998, is still open to question. (On the Dutch party system, see Daalder; for a more contemporary assessment, see ten Napel; Andeweg.)

Party Politics in Italy

Reflecting on the nationalist revolution in early-twentieth-century Ireland, the poet W. B. Yeats once wrote that "all falls apart; the centre cannot hold." In contemporary Italy, where party politics is currently being reshaped to a degree unprecedented in any postwar European party system, the center also has been unable to hold, and the traditional system has fallen completely apart. The degree of change is such that it is still impossible to foresee what sort of alignment will emerge in the future, because it is as yet impossible to predict the future structure of Italian party politics, or, indeed, of the Italian political system as a whole.

At first sight, the traditional patterns of postwar party politics in Italy did not appear to differ very markedly from those in the other countries surveyed here. In Italy, as in each of the other countries, a left-right opposition lay at the heart of party competition, reflecting the confrontation between parties promoting working-class interests and those promoting the interests of better-off social groups. As in the UK and Sweden, the traditional left, represented in Italy by both a communist and a socialist party, usually won about 40 percent of the vote. And as in West Germany and the Netherlands, there was also a religious-secular divide, although in Italy proclerical forces are exclusively Catholic.

The distinguishing feature of the Italian party system was not so much the particular interests that were represented as the depth of the ideological divisions between the competing parties. The major party on the traditional left was the Italian Communist Party (PCI), which in early 1991, after much agonizing, and in reaction to the collapse of the communist regimes in Eastern and Central Europe, changed its name to the Democratic Party of the Left (Partito Democratico de Sinistra, or PDS), and even more recently to simply Democrats of the Left (DS). This was for a long time the strongest communist party in Western Europe, and averaged 29 percent of the votes during the 1980s. For most of the postwar era, the PCI retained the aura of a far-left opposition, and the strength of PCI support thus marked the Italian party system off from those of many other European democracies. At the opposite end of the left-right ideological spectrum in Italy was the neofascist Italian Social Movement (MSI), which usually polled about 6 percent of the vote.

Ranged between these extremes lay five more central parties. The biggest of these was the Christian Democratic Party (DC), which usually polled about 30 percent of the popular vote. Like the Dutch CDA, this party combined a moderately conservative economic appeal with the promotion of religious values.

Two other parties mobilized on the center right in Italy: the Liberals and the Republicans between them averaged about 7 percent of the vote. The tiny Liberal party was the more right-wing of the two and had an ideological position similar to that of its Dutch and German counterparts, while the Republicans reflected the more centrist politics characteristic of the liberal parties in both Sweden and the UK. Both were largely middle-class parties that endorsed many of the conservative economic appeals of the DC while rejecting its emphasis on religious values.

On the center left of the system sat the small Social Democratic party (PSDI), which usually polled about 4 percent of the vote. More influential on the left was the Socialist party (PSI), which usually polled about 12 percent of the vote and shared many of the concerns of the major social democratic parties in the United Kingdom, Sweden, the Netherlands, and West Germany.

The traditional Italian party system, therefore, comprised both a more fragmented and a more polarized set of alternatives than could be found in the other countries we have considered. As a consequence, it was impossible for a clear-cut left- or right-wing bloc to present itself to voters as a realistic governing option. On the left, the combined support of the PCI, PSI, and PSDI, together with that of the smaller radical parties, might have appeared sufficient to form a government coalition. Yet because of the perceived extremism of the PCI, this option seemed impossible to realize. There might also seem to have been a potential parliamentary majority on the right, but this option also proved impossible to realize given the far-right position of the MSI; suggestions by the Christian Democrats that they might deal with the MSI proved very unpopular with voters. The consequent exclusion of both ends of the political spectrum from government often left the remaining parties searching for a parliamentary majority through the creation of persistent—if unstable—governments of the center, in a pattern much like the one that prevailed in the French Fourth Republic (see later). The participants typically ranged from the socialists to the Christian democrats to the liberals, who combined into a five-party (*pentapartito*) or four-party coalition straddling the center left and the center right (Mershon).

As is clear from our phrasing, however, all this is now in the past tense, and the Italian party system is currently being reshaped to an extraordinary degree. Three factors are important here. In the first place, the end of the Cold War led to a decisive shift in which the new PDS abandoned the traditional communist character of the PCI and moved toward a more conventional social democratic position (the new party is now actually a member of the European Socialist Party federation). This has forced the other parties, and the voters, to accept that the PDS now has the potential to form part of a coalition government, and that, unlike the old PCI, it can no longer be excluded as a matter of principle. This in itself changes the terms of reference of traditional politics.

Secondly, an increasing discontent with the endemic corruption and clientelism that characterized Italian governments has fueled support for the Northern League (Lega Nord), which won almost 9 percent of the vote in 1992, and which also ended up as the biggest single party in parliament in 1994 (Table 7-5). The Northern League is a radical, right-wing, populist movement based mainly in the richer northern regions of Italy

TABLE 7-5   ELECTIONS IN ITALY SINCE 1987

Party	1987		1992		1994*		1996*	
	% Votes	N Seats	% Votes	N Seats	% PR Votes	N Seats	% PR Votes	N Seats
Greens	2.5	13	1.8	16	2.7	11	2.5	16
Communist party (PCI)[†]	26.6	177	–	–	–	–	–	–
Communist Refoundation	–	–	5.6	35	6.0	39	8.6	35
Democratic Party of the Left (PDS)	–	–	16.1	107	20.4	109	21.1	171
La Rete	–	–	1.9	12	1.9	6	–	–
Socialist party (PSI)/ Dini List[‡]	14.3	94	13.6	92	2.2	14	4.3	26
Social Democrats	3.0	17	2.7	16	–	–	–	–
Republicans	2.1	21	4.4	27	–	–	–	–
Liberal party	2.1	11	2.9	17	–	–	–	–
Democratic Alliance	–	–	–	–	1.2	18	–	–
Segni Pact	–	–	–	–	4.7	13	–	–
Christian Democrats (DC)[§]	34.3	234	29.7	206	–	–	–	–
Christian Democratic Center	–	–	–	–	–	29**	5.8	30
People's party/Prodi List	–	–	–	–	11.1	33	6.8	75
Forza Italia	–	–	–	–	21.0	99	20.6	123
Northern League	0.5	1	8.7	55	8.4	117	10.1	59
Social Movement (MSI)/ National Alliance	5.9	35	5.4	34	13.5	109	15.7	93
Radicals/Pannella List	2.6	13	1.2	7	3.5	6	1.9	–
Others	6.1	14	5.0	6	3.4	27	2.6	2
All	100.0	630	100.0	630	100.0	630	100.0	630

Party Composition of Government in the 1990s:

    1991–94:   Coalition of Christian Democrats, Socialists, Social Democrats and Liberals
    1994   :   Coalition of Forza Italia, National Alliance and Northern League
    1995–96:   Non-party government
    1996– :   "OliveTree Coalition," including Democratic party of the Left, People's Party,
                Greens, and Dini List (Italian Renewal)

*In 1994 and 1996, the % Votes refers only to the share of the vote in the PR districts, while the N Seats refers to the total number of seats won in both the PR and the single-member districts. Note also that the lists competing in the PR districts in 1994 and 1996 sometimes involved quite heterogeneous alliances of parties, and the overview provided in this table does not necessarily provide a wholly accurate party-by-party breakdown. For more complete details, see D'Alimonte (1998).

†The Communist party (PCI) split in 1991, with the majority of the party reorganizing as the social democratic Democratic Party of the Left (PDS), and with a minority maintaining a more orthodox communist position as Communist Refoundation (RC).

‡Although the Socialist party did not contest the 1996 election as an independent party, there was an official Socialist party list included in the list headed by Lamberto Dini.

§The Christian Democrats fell apart after 1992, and were succeeded by various smaller parties including the Christian Democratic Center (CCD) and the Popular party (PPI); in 1996 the PPI formed part of a list headed by Romano Prodi, which also included the former Segni Pact.

**All of the CCD seats in 1994 were won in the single-member districts.

that demands an end to the system whereby the taxes paid by its relatively prosperous supporters are used to fund welfare programs and public works in the poorer south and therefore help the government win support in the south. The party also advocates the creation of a federal structure in Italy, with three autonomous regions or "republics," including its own proposed Padania in the north. At the same time, in the south itself, a wave of anti-Mafia protests led to the formation of an anti-Mafia movement, La Rete, which won substantial local success and polled almost 2 percent in the 1992 and 1994 elections.

Third, and perhaps most important, support for the traditional governing parties, the Christian Democrats (DC) and the Socialists (PSI), was more or less completely undermined by the revelations of corruption and bribery uncovered by the so-called *mani pulite* (clean hands) investigation. This was an investigation by Italian magistrates that began in Milan in February 1992 and that has since spread to many other parts of the country. After little more than a year, at the end of March 1993, the investigation had led to accusations of bribe taking (*tangenti*) against more than 150 members of the Italian Parliament and against almost nine hundred local politicians. Those accused included many prominent figures in the DC and the PSI. Indeed, almost one-third of PSI MPs were by then under investigation, as were more than one-quarter of its party executives. The PSI leader, Bettino Craxi, fled to Tunisia.

The result was that the center of the old party system, in the form of the DC and PSI in particular, was effectively swept away. In fact, while the PSI more or less faded away, the DC broke up into disparate elements, including the more left-leaning Popolari (People's Party), on the one hand, and the more right-leaning Centro Cristiano Democratico (Christian Democratic Center), on the other.

In the 1994 general election, which was the first to be held under the new electoral system (see Chapter 11)—inaugurating the so-called "Second Republic"—and which witnessed the biggest shift in the political balance ever recorded in postwar Italy, the Northern League won just over 8 percent of the PR vote and 111 of the 475 single-member districts, to emerge as the biggest single party in the new parliament. The PDS came in a close second, with 20 percent of the PR vote and seventy-seven seats in the single-member districts (see Table 7-5). The neofascist MSI, now reconstituted as the National Alliance, was in third place, with 14 percent of the PR votes and eighty-six single-member districts. Perhaps the greatest surprise, however, was the strong showing of Forza Italia (literally: Go, Italy!), which had been formed just three months before the election by the media tycoon and owner of AC Milan soccer team, Silvio Berlusconi, and which won 21 percent of the PR vote and sixty-seven single-member districts.

Together with the Northern League and the National Alliance, Forza Italia had formed a joint right-wing electoral alliance (the Pole of Liberty) in opposition to the PDS, and this new alliance emerged from the election with a clear overall majority in the Chamber of Deputies, the lower house of parliament. The three parties later went on to form a government under the premiership of Berlusconi, which included in the cabinet five ministers drawn from the neofascist National Alliance/MSI. The left had also formed an electoral alliance (the Progressives) under the leadership of the PDS, which included remnants from the old PSI, as well as the more orthodox Communist Refoundation, the Greens, and other reformist movements, and this bloc of parties constituted the major opposition to the new right-wing government.

Berlusconi's government proved fragile, however, not least due to tensions between the Northern League and the National Alliance, and it was quickly replaced by a "technical" non-party government. Then in 1996 came the second major change of the Second Republic, when the so-called Olive Tree alliance, dominated by the PDS, but led by Romano Prodi, leader of the People's party, won a narrow overall majority. The new alliance also included the Greens, as well as new groupings that had emerged from the remnants of the old socialist and liberal center, and won grudging support from the Communist Refoundation. For the first time since 1947, former Communists had managed to win government. For the first time also, there was a complete alternation in government.

For now, at least, politics in Italy has taken the form of a bipolar confrontation of left and right. Should this persist, then the new party system will end up looking completely different from that which prevailed in the "First Republic" under Christian Democratic centrist domination. But the blocs of both left and right are still fragile coalitions, and they may not easily hold together. Since 1996, for example, the governing center-left coalition has been reconstructed three times under three different prime ministers, the most recent of these being the former socialist Giuliano Amato, who took over the leadership of the coalition in April 2000 following major gains by the right in regional elections. Moreover, there are also signs that a new independent center might emerge, building support from among the left of the right bloc and among the right of the left bloc, and basing itself primarily among the remnants of the old DC. Should that prove to be the case, then the old center-based system could yet assert itself once more. (On the traditional Italian party system, see Farneti. For a preliminary analysis of the new patterns of party politics, see D'Alimonte; Bartolini and D'Alimonte; Bull and Rhodes; Newell and Bull; Daniels.)

Party Politics in France

The current French constitution dates from 1958, which marked the beginning of the French Fifth Republic. Before this, France was governed under the constitution of the Fourth Republic, dating from 1945. During the Fourth Republic the French party system bore many similarities to that of postwar Italy. Politics on the left was dominated by a large pro-Moscow Communist Party (PCF), which polled an average of about 27 percent of the vote. There was also a steadily weakening Socialist Party, which averaged less than 19 percent of the vote. The center was occupied by The Radical Party, which won an average of 12 percent, and by the Catholic Popular Republican Movement (MRP), which polled over 25 percent in the 1940s but then fell back to just 12 percent in the 1950s. On the right, a conservative party persisted throughout the period, with around 13 percent of the vote. In the 1950s, however, the conservatives were marginalized by two rivals on the right, the Gaullists (winning 22 percent of the vote in 1951) and the far-right Poujadists (winning 12 percent in 1956), both reflecting opposition to the constitutional arrangements of the Fourth Republic. Faced with anti-constitutional opposition from both left and right, which proved both more extremist and more powerful than in Italy, the center was unable to hold and the result was chronic political instability.

Two key changes have occurred in the party system during the early years of the Fifth Republic (Bartolini, pp. 104–15). First was the emergence of a much more clearly defined bipolar pattern of competition, much like the two-bloc model in the Swedish case, in which the left, represented by the Socialist Party (PS) and the Communist Party, competed against the right, represented by the new Gaullist party (RPR) and the coalition of forces that organizes under the label Union for French Democracy (UDF). The emergence of this bipolar pattern was facilitated by the abandonment of the proportional electoral formula that had been used in the Fourth Republic and its replacement by a double-ballot majority system, which encourages competition between just two candidates in each constituency in the second round of voting (see Chapter 11). It was also encouraged by the introduction of a directly elected president in 1962, in a process that also involves just two candidates competing in the second round of voting (see Table 7-7).

The second change that occurred during the Fifth Republic was a shift in the balance of forces within both the left and the right. For a variety of reasons, both ideological and institutional (Bartolini), the PCF has been increasingly marginalized in recent years, and the left is now dominated by the Socialist party. Throughout the 1980s the PS, together with its electoral allies among the left radicals (MRG), commanded the largest share of the vote in France. The PCF has now fallen to just 10 percent of the poll and plays at most a supporting role for the PS. Indeed, in 1981, for the first time ever, the PS emerged with an overall majority of seats in the lower house of the French parliament, although it initially chose to govern in coalition with the PCF. Earlier that same year, with PS candidate François Mitterrand, the left had won the presidency for the first time ever.

There has also been a substantial shift in the balance of forces on the right, with the disappearance of the MRP and with the development of a more or less stable and evenly balanced alliance between the Gaullist RPR and the UDF. (The latter, like the early center-right electoral alliances in Spain (discussed later in this chapter), combines liberal, Christian, and conservative forces.) Party competition in the Fifth Republic, therefore, not only took the form of a much better defined confrontation between left and right, but was also (at least until recently) increasingly dominated by the more moderate of the forces within each bloc. The polarization of the Fourth Republic appeared a thing of the past.

This pattern may now be changing, however, especially on the right, where the UDF and RPR are being challenged by the extremist National Front. The National Front mobilizes a strongly racist and xenophobic political appeal and has clocked up some significant electoral successes in the southern parts of France in particular. The problem for the mainstream right is that future support for the National Front may be sufficient to prevent the UDF and RPR from achieving a majority in either the presidential or the parliamentary elections. Should they try to come to terms with the National Front, however, and should they attempt to forge a new and more broadly defined alliance on the right, they risk losing their more moderate voters—and some of their leaders—in the center. The problem is a major one for the mainstream right: in the 1997 parliamentary elections, the National Front polled almost 15 percent of the vote, although it obtained almost no seats by the double-ballot majority voting systems (Table 7-6). Further problems have also been precipitated by conflicts over Europe, with a strong Euroskeptic faction developing within the RPR in particular. This faction ran a separate list of candidates in the 1999 European Parliament elections and enjoyed considerable success.

The Socialists played the dominant role in French government for most of the 1980s. Mitterrand was reelected to the presidency for a second seven-year term of office in 1988,

TABLE 7-6   LEGISLATIVE ELECTIONS IN FRANCE SINCE 1988

Party	1988		1993		1997	
	% Votes*	N Seats	% Votes*	N Seats	% Votes*	N Seats
Greens	0.4	0	7.6	0	6.3	8
Communist party (PCF)	11.3	27	9.2	23	9.9	37
Socialist party (PS)[†]	37.6	280	18.5	60	25.5	246
Other left	0.4	0	3.6	10	5.3	29
Union for French Democracy (UDF)	18.5	129	19.1	213	14.7	109
Rally for the Republic (RPR)	19.2	128	20.4	247	16.8	139
Other right	2.9	12	5.0	24	4.7	8
National Front (NF)	9.6	1	12.4	0	14.9	1
Others	0.1	0	4.3	0	1.9	0
All	100.0	577	100.0	577	100.0	577

Party Composition of Government in the 1990s:

1989–93:	Coalition of Socialist party and Left Radicals
1993–97:	Coalition of Rally for the Republic and Union for French Democracy
1997– :	Coalition of Socialist party, Left Radicals, Communist party, Greens and other left.

*Voting percentages refer to first-ballot results only.
[†]includes Left Radicals

and the PS also maintained control of the Cabinet from 1981 to 1986, a control it regained from 1988 to 1993 and most recently again in 1997, under the prime ministership of Lionel Jospin. Initially elected on quite a radical program of social and economic reform, which included a commitment to the widespread nationalization of private-sector services, the PS has since become more centrist, and, as Machin (p. 68) has observed, has now developed a more "modernizing, moderate and managerial image."

Despite modernization of the PS, however, and perhaps even as a consequence of it, the party lost a great deal of its support in the 1993 election, falling to a level of less than 19 percent of the first ballot votes, its lowest share of the vote in twenty years, and winning just sixty parliamentary seats. The biggest gainers in 1993 were the two center-right parties, the UDF and RPR, which, despite a very modest increase in electoral support, almost doubled their parliamentary strength and went on to form a new conservative government. The National Front also picked up more support in 1993, as did the two ecology parties, Génération Ecologie (Ecology Generation) and Les Verts (the Greens), but none of these managed to win any seats. In France, as in Italy, and also to an extent in Germany and Sweden, the shift toward these new "protest" parties of the left and right is regarded as symptomatic of a more general disillusion with traditional politics and with the evidence of political corruption. One of the campaign strategies adopted by the National Front, for example, was a generalized attack on the

TABLE 7-7   PRESIDENTIAL ELECTIONS IN FRANCE SINCE 1988

Party	1988		1995	
	1st Round % Votes	2nd Round % Votes	1st Round % Votes	2nd Round % Votes
Greens	3.8	–	3.3	–
Communist party (PCF)	6.8	–	8.6	–
Socialist party (PS)	34.1	54.0*	23.3	47.4
Rally for the Republic (RPR)	19.9	46.0*	39.5[†]	52.6
Union for French Democracy (UDF)	16.5	–	–	–
National Front (NF)	14.4	–	15.0	–
Other left	4.5	–	5.6	–
Other right			4.7	–
Total	100.0	100.0	100.0	100.0

*The second ballot contestants were outgoing President François Mitterrand (PS), the eventual winner, and Jacques Chirac (RPR).

[†]The RPR (Gaullists) ran two candidates in the first ballot, Jacques Chirac and Eduard Balladur, and the figure of 39.5% refers to their combined vote. There was no UDF candidate in that first ballot. Chirac, who was the higher-polling Gaullist candidate and who came second to the eventual first-ballot leader, Lionel Jospin (PS), then went on to win the presidency in the second ballot.

"Gang of Four," the four traditional parties (PCF, PS, UDF, and RPR) that have dominated political life in Fifth Republic France.

Despite losing the 1995 Presidential election to the Gaullist Jacques Chirac (see Table 7-7), the Socialists came back to power in the parliamentary election two years later. Chirac had called this election in the hope of building on his own success and so further strengthening the center-right majority in parliament. In the event, the strategy backfired, and a new, more broadly based left-wing coalition was formed by the Socialists and the Communists, this time together with the Greens. On the left, it seems, it is easier to build and maintain new coalitions than on the right. (On long-term developments in the French party system, see Bartolini; Machin; on more contemporary developments, see Hanley; Appleton.)

Party Politics in Spain

Before the collapse of Communist rule in Eastern Europe in 1989 and 1990, Spain was one of Europe's youngest democracies. The elections held in Spain in 1977, two years after the death of the right-wing dictator General Franco, were the first since Franco had seized power after the defeat of the democratic Republican forces in the Civil War of 1936 to 1939. As in the early years of many other new democracies, the first period of Spanish democracy was characterized by the creation of many new parties and by great electoral volatility.

The early stages of the transition to democracy in Spain were dominated by the Union of the Democratic Center (UCD), a broad coalition of various center-right and center-left groups under the leadership of Adolfo Suarez, a former minister in Franco's cabinet and the first prime minister of democratic Spain. This coalition of forces, although electorally successful in 1977 and 1979, was also inherently very fragile and collapsed dramatically in 1982, when its share of the vote fell from 35 percent to less than 7 percent (Hopkin, 1999a). Suarez himself had resigned as prime minister and had abandoned the party in 1981, setting up a new party, the Social and Democratic Center, that eventually disappeared in the mid-1990s.

With the collapse of the UCD, the key role in the Spanish party system passed to the Socialist Party (PSOE), which polled almost half the votes in 1982 and almost 40 percent in 1989. With the help of the bias shown toward larger parties in the Spanish electoral system, this level of support guaranteed Socialist Party government in Spain from 1982 to 1996, although it lost its overall majority in 1993.

Socialist dominance in Spain was also facilitated by the fragmentation of the center-right opposition; indeed, even into its second decade of democracy, Spain's remained among the most fragmented of the European party systems. The largest single party on the right is currently the Peoples Party (PP), formerly known as the Peoples Alliance, which initially formed the dominant group within the sporadically cohesive Peoples Coalition, a federation of diverse parties that embraced liberal, Christian democratic, and conservative factions, and that grew to obtain almost 35 percent of the vote in 1993. Since then the PP has overtaken the PSOE, emerging as the single biggest party in 1996, and forming a single-party minority government, and then going on to win an absolute majority in 2000 (Table 7-8).

TABLE 7-8   ELECTIONS IN SPAIN SINCE 1986

Party	1986		1989		1993		1996		2000	
	% Votes	N Seats	% Votes	N Seats	% Votes	N Seats	% Votes	N Seats	% Votes	N Seats
United Left (IU)	4.6	7	9.1	17	9.6	18	10.5	21	5.5	8
Socialist party (PSOE)	44.3	184	39.6	176	38.7	159	37.6	141	34.1	125
Democratic & Social Center (CDS)	9.2	19	7.9	14	1.8	–	–	–	–	–
People's party (PP)	26.1	105	25.8	106	34.8	141	38.8	156	44.5	183
Convergence & Union (CiU)	5.0	18	5.0	18	5.0	17	4.6	16	4.2	15
Basque Nationalists (PNV)	1.4	6	1.2	5	1.2	5	1.3	5	1.5	7
Herri Batasuna (HB)	1.2	5	1.1	4	0.9	2	0.7	2	–	–
Others	8.2	6	10.3	10	8.0	8	6.5	9	10.2	12
All	100.0	350	100.0	350	100.0	350	100.0	350	100.0	350

Party Composition of Government since 1982:

    1982–96:   PSOE single-party government

    1996– :   PP single-party government.

Other forces on the center right include the Catalan Convergence and Union (CiU), a loose alliance of conservative, Christian, and liberal elements united in their support for greater regional autonomy for Catalonia. Though a relatively small party in Spanish terms—it polls only around 5 percent of the vote in Spain as a whole—the CiU has proved remarkably adept at bargaining with its larger opponents on behalf of Catalan interests. In return for important economic and political concessions, it supported the minority PSOE government from 1993 to 1996, and supported the minority PP government from 1996-2000.

Opposition to the left of the political spectrum is focused primarily in the Spanish Communist Party (PCE), which was one of the major parties in the ill-fated Second Spanish Republic (1931 to 1936) and which had also constituted one of the most powerful clandestine oppositions to Francoism during the period of the dictatorship. The PCE and its leader, Santiago Carrillo, were also at the forefront of the shift toward Eurocommunism in Western Europe in the late 1970s, when a number of leading communist parties sought to distance themselves from Moscow and attempted to forge a new, more consciously democratic strategy for reform (e.g., Lange and Vanicelli). But despite some early speculation that the PCE might emerge as the leading party of the left and thus occupy a position similar to that of the PCI in Italy, the party has, in fact, remained quite marginal. It was only through the recent formation of an electoral cartel, the United Left, with a number of other small parties of the left that the PCE could be seen as a serious political force, polling almost 11 percent of the vote in 1996, before falling back to less than 6 percent in 2000.

The fragmentation of the Spanish party system has also been compounded by the emergence of a plethora of regional political forces, far too many to be listed separately in Table 7-8. In addition to the Catalan coalition, parties representing the local interests of Andalusia, Galicia, Aragon, Valencia, and the Canary Islands have also won representation in the Cortes, the Spanish parliament. Regionalism is strongest in the Basque country in northern Spain, supporting two important parties, the Basque Nationalist party (PNV), a pro-independence conservative party; and Herri Batasuna (Popular Unity), a radical left-wing nationalist party that also endorses ETA, a Basque paramilitary organization engaging in an armed struggle against the Spanish state. Although ETA had declared a cease-fire in October 1998, they renewed their armed campaign at the end of 1999. The Basque region is one of the most distinctive and industrially prosperous in Spain, with a population of over two million and with its own language and culture. Two-thirds of Basque voters now support one or other of the Basque national parties, and the region has been plagued by a level of political dissension and violence almost comparable to that which until recently prevailed in Northern Ireland.

The overall picture is thus of a fragmented but increasingly structured party system in which conflicts between the left and the right overlay and intersect conflicts between the center and the periphery and between church and state. Indeed, it is sometimes difficult to conceive of Spain as having a single "party system" in the sense in which this concept applies to the more established Western European democracies. The parties themselves are, in the main, loosely organized coalitions of different interests and different leaders that, with the notable exceptions of the powerful Socialist Party, and more recently the People's party, have tended to drift in and out of relatively transitory electoral cartels. The recent growth in support for the PP may finally signal the beginnings of a more sharply defined bipolar pattern of competition, however, and may also yet lead to a regular process of alternation in government. One possibility is that the Spanish party system will develop along much the same lines as that in the United Kingdom, with a major party of the center left (PSOE) competing against a major party of the center right (PP), and with a number of smaller and especially regional parties jostling around the edge of this battle. A second possibility is that each of the major parties will attempt to forge enduring alliances with some of the smaller parties, pushing Spain toward a Swedish-style, two-bloc competition. (On the Spanish party system in general, see Hopkin, 1999a, 1999b; Linz and Montero.)

UNIFORMITY AND DIVERSITY

Each of the party systems that we have considered has at its core a basic confrontation between the left and the right, reflecting the polarization of class interests. Each also contains one or more parties that we might think of as being at the center. Beyond this, however, differences between systems appear to be more striking than similarities.

Thus, in Sweden and the United Kingdom, liberal parties are to be found between the left and the right, and they reflect a more moderate class alternative than that promoted by conservative parties. In the Netherlands and Germany, on the other hand, traditional liberalism has its roots in conservatism—and the liberal parties are mainly to be found on the right. In Sweden and the United Kingdom, class confrontations define the only major dimension in politics, although in Sweden the pattern is more complex, given the secondary role of agrarian and religious interests. In Italy, the Netherlands, and Germany, on the other hand, religion traditionally has provided a major dimension of party competition.

Differences also extend to the pattern of government formation. In France, Spain, Germany, Sweden, and the United Kingdom, the left can hope to govern alone. In the Netherlands the left has long been too weak, and in Italy, except perhaps now in the so-called "Second Republic," it has been too divided, to do so; in each case the left has been obliged to forge coalitions with parties on the center and right. Finally, although Germany, the Netherlands, Sweden, and Britain have strongly structured party systems, France and, to a lesser extent, Spain have systems that include loose and often fragmented alliances that lack the cohesion and discipline normally associated with European political parties. The shape of the new Italian party system is still too uncertain to define.

Given such diversity, to speak of a "typical" Western European party system is clearly unrealistic. Nonetheless, the countries in certain groups do seem quite similar to one another. The Swedish party system, for example, has been compared with the party systems in Denmark and Norway by observers who speak of a typical "Scandinavian" party system (Berglund and Lindstrom; Einhorn and Logue). The Netherlands has been compared with Belgium and Switzerland in an extensive literature that treats them as "consociational democracies" responding to very deep-seated social and ethnic cleavages (Lijphart; Luther and Deschouwer). The deep ideological divisions in the Italian party system before the 1990s have been compared with those in France between 1946 and 1958 and with those in Finland, as examples of "polarized pluralism" (Sartori). The southern European democracies of Greece, Spain, and Portugal have also been extensively compared in a literature that highlights the common problems experienced by parties in the consolidation of new democracies (Morlino), and it is now interesting to see in each of these three systems the possible development of a British-style two-party system. In short, although it may be far too simplistic to speak of European politics as a set of variations on a single theme, it is reasonable to think of European politics as reflecting variations on a limited set of themes.

One theme that recurs in almost all Western European countries concerns the role of the left-right dimension in structuring politics. The terms "left" and "right" have always been widely accepted as part of the common political currency of Western Europe. To be on the left has traditionally meant supporting a communist or socialist party claiming to represent the interests of the organized working class. Every Western European country, without exception, has such a party. This, more than anything else, is the common theme in the politics of representation in Western Europe, and it also, incidentally, marks off the Western European experience from that in the United States.

To be on the center and right has meant supporting those who stand against the communist or socialist parties. On the center right, however, there are few features common to all the Western European countries. In some countries, parties of the right have a distinctly religious basis; in others, they are secular. In some countries, parties of the right traditionally have included those reflecting rural or farming interests; in others, they include those representing a particular cultural or linguistic subculture. One of the most striking features of Western European party politics is thus that although the left has been reasonably homogeneous and has traditionally been represented by at most two parties, the right has been more fragmented, including religious, secular, agrarian, nationalist, and other parties under the same broad umbrella.

Describing the right and the left in terms of the class interests that were traditionally represented by particular parties is only part of the story. There is also clearly a separate ideological sense in which we can speak of such parties as having programs that are on the left or right of the political spectrum. The problem here is that although it is easy to identify parties that mobilized in defense of particular social interests, it is less easy to specify who is on the left or the right in purely ideological terms.

The problem is compounded by the actual behavior of parties. In the 1970s and early 1980s, for example, the major social democratic parties in Britain, Denmark, and the Netherlands experienced splits that led to more right-wing elements within these parties setting up alternative organizations: Democratic Socialists 7'0 in the Netherlands, the Center Democrats in Denmark, and the Social Democratic Party in the UK. In terms of traditional interest representation, all three of these new parties might be regarded as being on the left in that all derived from the historic political alignment forged by the working class. In ideological terms, however, these parties were far from being on the left, and often empathized with the traditional parties of the center right of their respective party systems.

A similar problem arises in relation to the traditional right. In Italy, for example, a split from the traditionally right-wing Liberal Party in the mid-1950s led to the formation of the Radical Party. Although it spurned alliances with the Socialist and

Communist parties, the Radical Party quickly developed ideologically into one of the most left-wing of Italian parties. A similar split occurred in the Dutch Liberal party in the mid-1960s. The new party that formed as a result, Democrats 66, clearly aligned itself on the ideological left. In all of these cases, the "sociological" or "organizational" alignment of the new parties ran counter to their developing "ideological" positions.

Yet another confusion is of more recent origin and concerns the mobilization of environmentalist, or "green," parties in Western Europe. This is a relatively new but increasingly relevant and pervasive phenomenon that has emerged from the organizational traditions of neither the left nor the right. Indeed, these parties are sometimes claimed to reflect a wholly "new" politics that, in terms of both social support and organizational form, represents a genuine challenge to traditional alignments. Increasingly, however, these new parties are seen as moving toward the ideological left of the political spectrum, particularly when they demand both radical economic change and new forms of social justice. In practice, these parties now often find themselves in alliances with social democratic parties. Here, too, therefore, organizational and social definitions of the left and the right fit uneasily with more strictly ideological criteria.

When a country has two or more parties on the traditional left—a socialist and a communist party, for example—we might expect them to act in concert in an attempt to realize shared goals. In practice, however, this is often not the case. In Italy, as we have seen, the Socialist Party traditionally cast its lot with the Christian Democratic Party and smaller parties of the right and refused to consider an alliance with its communist ideological neighbor. Even though the combined vote of the Italian left sometimes exceeded 40 percent, prior to the 1990s Italian voters were never offered the prospect of a left-wing coalition government. Relations between Communists and Socialists have also often been very strained in France. Here, however, an eventual alliance of the two parties did lead to an unprecedented left-wing victory in the presidential elections of 1981, a victory that was later repeated in the presidential elections of 1988 and in the parliamentary elections of 1989. Prior to this historic breakthrough, the French Socialists had often despaired of finding common ground with their communist neighbors and had opted instead to chase alliances on the center and right of the party system.

More recently—in Italy in 1996, in France in 1997, in Germany in 1998, and in Belgium in 1999—socialist parties have gained government office through alliances with the newer Green parties, and one of the more important consequences of the rise of Green parties in Europe has been to add sufficient strength to the broad bloc of the left to allow it to regain control of government after long periods of center-right dominance. Indeed, by the end of 1999, socialist parties—whether alone, or in alliance with Greens or parties of the center—were in government in all but three (Spain, Luxembourg, and Ireland) of the fifteen member states of the European Union. For the first time in postwar history, the major party of the left was in government in all four of the major Western European polities at the same time (France, Germany, Italy, and the UK).

Maintaining alliances on the right now proves more problematic, particularly since the recent rise of the extreme right. Many of the new far-right parties—such as the National Alliance and the Northern League in Italy, the National Front in

France, the Flemish Block in Belgium, or the Progress parties in Denmark and Norway—may share many concerns with their more moderate neighbors of the right. Their sheer extremism, however, often makes it difficult for them to form or sustain cooperative arrangements with these neighbors. In party systems that are ideologically polarized, indeed, it is usually easier for parties of the center right to find common ground with parties of the center-left than it is to find common ground with some of their fellow right-wing parties. This has certainly proved to be the case in Austria, for example, where the increasingly extremist positions adopted by the right-wing Freedom Party under the leadership of Jörg Haider served to isolate his party from coalition building in the 1990s, while at the same time strengthening his capacity to appeal to voters as an outsider seeking to challenge the control of the established parties. The isolation of the Freedom Party came to end in 2000, however, when, following its major success in the 1999 elections, it formed a new coalition government with the center-right People's Party. The inclusion of Haider's party in the New Austrian government provoked widespread protests both at home and abroad, with many of the other European Union members states threatening to sever their bilateral relations with Austria. Although these protests had little practical effect, they nevertheless served to underline the increasing concern felt throughout Europe about the possible inclusion of extreme right parties in government.

In almost all of the countries that have been surveyed here, as well as in many other European countries, there is evidence of a growing disillusion with politics, and there seems to be increasing room for the mobilization of protest movements and "anti-party"—or anti-establishment—parties. The sources of this protest are potentially legion. The persistence of economic problems certainly fuels dissatisfaction, as does the perceived growth in social inequalities. A rising tide of racism creates new tensions that are difficult to resolve. The integration of nation-states within the European Union (see Chapter 5) and the internationalization of economies appear to leave many voters wondering about what responsibilities, if any, still remain with their own national governments. As in the United States, there is also an increasing concern with political corruption and patronage and a growing sense that politicians are concerned only with looking after themselves. All of these factors help explain the increasing support for parties of the extreme right, on the one hand, and for "new politics" parties of the left, on the other. They also help explain the increasing appeal of flash parties, which suddenly emerge on the campaign trail and equally suddenly disappear. None of these parties falls within the traditional molds, and each challenges both the conventional left-right alignments and the conventional divisions within the left and within the right. As yet, of course, such anti-party parties account for only a very small share of the popular vote in European democracies, and in this sense the traditional patterns still continue to dominate political life. At the same time, however, there is little denying the sense of vulnerability now being felt by some of the most powerful European parties on both the left and the right.

Although the terms "left" and "right" might seem to provide a convenient shorthand for describing party politics in different countries using broadly similar terms, superficial similarities nevertheless can be deceptive. Moreover, as the new centrist policies of the "Third Way" or "New Middle" gain ever-widening support, the use of terms such as "left" and "right" becomes less meaningful. Given the range of variation that can be found in the different party systems of Western Europe, an alternative response might be to claim that as every country is different, we should simply look at the countries one at a time (accepting that, in reality, we will probably have time for only the big ones). Yet, as we have suggested, although each of the countries considered at the beginning of this chapter is clearly distinctive, each does represent something of a pattern, with elements that can be found elsewhere.

One of the most convenient ways of providing an overview of the combination of uniformity and diversity that characterizes the Western European party mosaic is to speak of "party families." Thus, even though there are differences between "Christian democratic parties" in different countries, there are also striking similarities that go far beyond mere name and religious affiliation. Such parties tend to be located on the center right of the system, to be flanked by both social democratic and other right-wing parties, to be commonly found at the heart of government coalitions, and so on. Accordingly, we move our discussion forward by looking in the next chapter at the main party "families" in Western Europe. Our intention in doing this is to highlight the point that although no two parties are exactly alike, the parties in particular groups do bear striking resemblances to one another.

REFERENCES

Andeweg, Rudy B.: "Parties, Pillars and the Politics of Accommodation: Weak or Weakening Linkages? The Case of Dutch Consociationalism," in Luther and Deschouwer, 1999, pp. 108–133.

Appleton, Andrew: "Parties Under Pressure: Challenges to 'Established' French Parties," *West European Politics*, vol. 18, no. 1, 1995, pp. 52–77.

Arter, David: "Sweden: A Mild Case of 'Electoral Instability Syndrome'?" in Broughton and Donovan, 1999, pp. 143–62.

Bartolini, Stefano: "Institutional Constraints and Party Competition in the French Party System," in Bartolini and Mair, 1984, pp. 103–27.

Bartolini, Stefano, and Roberto D'Alimonte: "Majoritarian Miracles and the Question of Party System Change," in D'Alimonte, 1999, pp. 151–69.

Bartolini, Stefano, and Peter Mair (eds.): *Party Politics in Contemporary Western Europe*, Cass, London, 1984.

Berglund, Sten, and Ulf Lindstrom: *The Scandinavian Party System(s)*, Studentlitteratur, Lund, 1978.

Blair, Tony: *The Third Way: New Politics for the New Century*, Fabian Society, London, 1998.

Broughton, David, and Mark Donovan (eds.): *Changing Party Systems in Western Europe*, Pinter, London, 1999.

Bull, Martin, and Martin Rhodes (eds.): *Crisis and Transition in Italian Politics*, Cass, London, 1997.

Daalder, Hans: "The Dutch Party System: From Segmentation to Polarization-And Then?" in Hans Daalder (ed.), *Party Systems in Denmark, Austria, Switzerland, the Netherlands, and Belgium*, Frances Pinter, London, 1987, pp. 193–284.

D'Alimonte, Roberto (ed.): *The Italian Elections of 1996: Competition and Transition*, special issue of the *European Journal of Political Research*, vol. 34, no. 1, 1998.

Daniels, Philip: "Italy: Rupture and Regeneration?" in Broughton and Donovan, 1999, pp. 71–95.

Einhorn, Eric S., and John Logue: "Continuity and Change in the Scandinavian Party Systems," in Wolinetz (ed.), 1988, pp. 159–202.

Farneti, Paolo: *The Italian Party System (1945-1980),* Frances Pinter, London, 1985.

Finer, S. E.: *The Changing British Party System, 1945–79,* American Enterprise Institute, Washington, D.C., 1980.

Giddens, Anthony: *The Third Way: The Renewal of Social Democracy,* Polity Press, Cambridge, England.

Hanley, David: "France: Living with Instability," in Broughton and Donovan, 1999, pp. 48–70.

Hopkin, Jonathan: *Party Formation and Democratic Transition in Spain: The Creation and Collapse of the Union of the Democratic Centre,* Macmillan, Basingstoke, 1999a.

Hopkin, Jonathan: "Spain: Political Parties in a Young Democracy," in Broughton and Donovan, 1999b, pp. 207–31.

Jeffery, Charlie: "Germany: From Hyperstability to Change?" in Broughton and Donovan, 1999, pp. 96–117.

King, Anthony: "The Implication of One-Party Government," in Anthony King et al., *Britain at the Polls 1992,* Chatham House, N.J., 1993, pp. 223–48.

Klingemann, Hans-Dieter: "Electoral Programmes in West Germany," in Ian Budge, David Robertson, and Derek Hearl (eds.), *Ideology, Strategy and Party Change,* Cambridge University Press, Cambridge, England, 1987, pp. 294–323.

Lange, Peter, and M. Vanicelli (eds.): *The Communist Parties of Italy, France and Spain,* Allen & Unwin, London, 1981.

Lijphart, Arend: *Democracy in Plural Societies,* Yale University Press, New Haven, 1977.

Linz, Juan J., and José Ramón Montero: *The Party Systems of Spain: Old Cleavages and New Challenges,* Working Paper 1999/138, Juan March Institute, Madrid, 1999.

Luther, Richard, and Kris Deschouwer (eds.): *Party Elites in Divided Societies: Political Parties in Consociational Democracy,* Routledge, London, 1999.

Machin, Howard: "Stages and Dynamics in the Evolution of the French Party System," in Mair and Smith, 1990, pp. 59–81.

Mackie, Thomas T., and Richard Rose: *The International Almanac of Electoral History,* 3d ed., Macmillan, Basingstoke, 1991.

Mackie, Thomas T., and Richard Rose: *A Decade of Election Results: Updating the International Almanac,* CSSP, Glasgow, 1997.

Mair, Peter, and Gordon Smith (eds.): *Understanding Party System Change in Western Europe,* Cass, London, 1990.

Marquand, David: "Progressive or Populist: The Blair Paradox," in David Marquand, *The Progressive Dilemma,* 2d ed., Phoenix Giant, London, 1999, pp. 225–46.

Mershon, Carol A.: "The Costs of Coalition: Coalition Theories and Italian Governments," *American Political Science Review,* vol. 90, no. 3, 1996, pp. 534–54.

Morlino, Leonardo: *Democracy Between Consolidation and Crisis: Parties, Groups, and Citizens in Southern Europe,* Oxford University Press, Oxford, 1998.

Napel, Hans-Martien ten: "The Netherlands: Resilience Amidst Change," in Broughton and Donovan, 1999, pp. 163–82.

Newell, James J., and Martin Bull: "Party Organisations and Alliances in Italy in the 1990s: A Revolution of Sorts," in Bull and Rhodes, 1997, pp. 81–109.

Norris, Pippa (ed.): *Critical Citizens: Global Support for Democratic Governance,* Oxford University Press, Oxford, 1999.

Padgett, Stephen (ed.): *Parties and Party Systems in the New Germany,* Dartmouth, Aldershot, 1993.

Pappi, Franz Urban: "The West German Party System," in Bartolini and Mair, 1984, pp. 7–26.

Poguntke, Thomas, and Susan Scarrow (eds.): *The Politics of Anti-Party Sentiment,* special issue of the *European Journal of Political Research,* vol. 29, no. 3, 1996.

Political Data Yearbook: annual publication of the *European Journal of Political Research,* 1992–.

Sartori, Giovanni: *Parties and Party Systems,* Cambridge University Press, Cambridge, England, 1976.

Smith, Gordon: *Democracy in West Germany: Parties and Politics in the Federal Republic,* 3d ed., Gower, Aldershot, 1986.

Webb, Paul: *The Modern British Party System,* Sage, London, 2000.

Wolinetz, Steven B. (ed.): *Parties and Party Systems in Liberal Democracies,* Routledge, London, 1988.

8

PARTY FAMILIES

As we argued in the preceding chapter, although no two political parties are quite the same, the parties in particular groups may share a considerable family resemblance. Three conventional characteristics can be used to define different party families in Western Europe (Mair and Mudde).

First, parties can be grouped according to some shared origin; parties that mobilized in similar historical circumstances or with the intention of representing similar interests can be treated as having a distinct family resemblance. On these grounds all socialist or social democratic parties, for example, can be considered as belonging to the same family, as can all agrarian parties. This might be termed the genetic approach.

The second sort of family resemblance is defined by the parties themselves, in terms of the ways they forge links across national frontiers. Such a link may take the form of a transnational federation, such as that established by various liberal parties. It also may take the form of joining institutionalized multinational political groups, such as those to be found in the European Parliament (see Chapter 5). Although this involves only the fifteen member states of the European Community (Austria, Belgium, Denmark, Finland, France, Germany, Greece, Ireland, Italy, Luxembourg, the Netherlands, Portugal, Spain, Sweden, and the United Kingdom), it nevertheless offers a clear guide to the extent of cross-national partisan collegiality in Western Europe (see Hix and Lord). In this case we are concerned with how parties act.

The final way party families can be identified has to do with the extent to which the policies pursued by one party in one country are similar to those pursued by another party in another country. There are some problems with this, because the "same" policy may mean quite different things in the practical politics of two different countries.

But to ignore professed policies altogether when looking for similarities between parties would clearly be to stick our heads in the sand. It matters what parties say.

Although no single one of these criteria—genetics, behavior, or discourse—provides a clear-cut classification, a judicious balance of the three suggests that we can think in terms of about nine main party families in Western Europe. In this chapter we present a brief description of each of these families. We also chart changes in their electoral strength over the past half-century of democratic development in Western Europe, and we contrast the changing patterns of support they enjoy in different countries.

Despite problems of definition, we have divided these different families of parties into two broad groups: families of the left, which include social democrats, communists, the new left, and the Green parties; and families of the center and right, which include Christian democrats, conservatives, liberals, agrarian or center parties, and the far right. For each family, where relevant, we include a table reporting average electoral support in each of the countries in the 1950s, 1960s, 1970s, 1980s, and 1990s. When presenting these comparative data we concentrate mainly on those countries that have had an uninterrupted history of democratic politics since the 1950s, with separate figures being provided for Greece, Portugal, and Spain. Later, in Chapter 15, we will also discuss the relevance of these broad family distinctions to the newly emerging postcommunist party systems.

After discussing the different party families, we consider in the rest of the chapter how different families fit together to make up different party systems. Although, as we have said, there is no single composite, or "typical," European party system, it is quite clearly the case that once we describe party systems in these broad terms, there are only a few types of party system that are different from one another in really important respects.

FAMILIES OF THE LEFT

There are four relevant party families to be found on the left-wing side of the political spectrum in Western European party systems. Social democratic parties are the strongest and most enduring of Western Europe's political families, not only on the left but also in European politics taken as a whole. Communist parties are a very clear-cut group, traditionally comprising those parties that began as pro-Soviet splits from social democratic parties in the wake of the Russian Revolution of 1917. The third and fourth families on the left are the "new left" and the Greens, which represent more varied collections of more recently formed parties, often grouped together under the general label "left-libertarian parties" (Kitschelt, 1988). All four families can be seen as representing the contemporary left in Western European politics; however, they clearly incorporate among them some huge variations in both ideology and interest representation.

The Social Democrats

Organized social democracy is one of the oldest surviving political forces in Western Europe. Even in the 1990s, the social democrats remain the single most important group in contemporary politics. The majority of the social democratic parties first entered electoral politics in the last quarter of the nineteenth century and were initially mobilized to represent the political interests of the growing working class, often acting in concert with the trade union movement. In some cases, as in the United Kingdom, a social democratic party was actually created by the trade unions in order to represent their interests in parliament. In other cases, as in the Netherlands, a political party was formed first in its own right and later established links with the trade unions (Bartolini; Sassoon).

As the franchise was extended to include more and more working-class voters, the social democratic parties grew in support. In the majority of European countries they gained their first experience of government in the years immediately following World War I. By the late 1940s the position of the social democrats in European politics was well established. It was largely as a result of their intervention that most Western European welfare states were expanded during the 1950s and 1960s (Flora).

As Table 8-1 shows, the strongest social democratic presence in contemporary Western Europe can be found in Austria, Denmark, Germany, Malta, Norway, Sweden,

TABLE 8-1   MEAN ELECTORAL SUPPORT FOR SOCIAL DEMOCRATIC PARTIES, 1950–2000.

	1950s	1960s	1970s	1980s	1990s
Austria	43.3	45.0	50.0	45.4	37.2
Belgium	35.9	31.0	26.6	28.0	23.8
Denmark	40.2	39.1	33.6	31.9	36.0
Finland	25.9	26.9	25.1	25.4	24.4
France	25.9	18.6	22.1	35.0	24.4
Germany	30.3	39.4	44.2	39.4	36.9
Iceland	19.5	15.0	14.8	17.1	20.3
Ireland	10.9	14.8	12.7	8.9	14.9
Italy	18.0	19.4	14.4	16.4	25.7
Luxembourg	37.1	35.0	35.4	32.3	24.8
Malta	54.9	38.5	51.2	49.0	48.1
Netherlands	30.7	25.8	31.9	31.0	26.5
Norway	47.5	45.4	38.8	37.4	36.0
Sweden	45.6	48.4	43.7	44.5	39.8
Switzerland	26.0	26.0	25.7	21.2	21.0
UK	46.3	46.1	39.1	29.2	38.9
Mean (N = 16)	**33.6**	**32.1**	**31.8**	**30.7**	**29.9**
Greece				43.5	43.8
Portugal				28.7	39.4
Spain				43.5	39.4
Mean (N = 19)				**31.9**	**31.6**

Note: Since Greece, Portugal, and Spain did not become fully democratic until the mid-1970s, decade averages are reported only for the 1980s and 1990s.

Source: For this and other tables in this chapter, see Chapter 7, note 1. The calculations involved here and in the tables in Chapter 9 are drawn from an ongoing project analyzing aggregate data on voters, parties, and governments in Western Europe from 1950 to 2000. For additional analyses, see Mair (1999a, 1999b, 2000).

and the UK, where in each case the average social democratic share of the vote was more than 35 percent during the 1990s. Social democracy has also proved a very powerful political force in Greece, Portugal, and Spain, where democracy was reestablished in the 1970s following periods of authoritarian rule, and where social democratic parties averaged around 40 percent of the vote in the 1990s.

In a second group of countries—Belgium, Finland, France, Italy (principally the former communist Democratic party of the Left), Luxembourg, and the Netherlands—the social democratic share of the vote averaged around 25 percent during the 1990s. In Iceland, Switzerland, and particularly Ireland, the social democrats are weaker. Social democrats have traditionally polled relatively poorly in Ireland, where the Labour party has long been the Cinderella of European social democracy. In the Irish election in 1992, however, there was an unprecedented if temporary surge of support for the party, which almost doubled its vote to more than 19 percent.

In general, as can be seen from Table 8-1, the electoral position of social democracy has declined slightly during the postwar period, from an average of almost 34 percent in the 1950s to just less than 30 percent in the 1990s. This decline was most marked in Belgium, Luxembourg, Norway, and the United Kingdom, although the really low point in the UK was reached in the 1980s, when support fell below 30 percent. But the steady electoral decline of social democracy is not pervasive. By comparison to the 1950s, social democrats in the 1990s polled a greater share of the vote in Germany, Ireland, and Italy. In addition, in Denmark, Iceland, and the UK, the social democratic vote in the 1990s was higher than that recorded in the 1980s, while in France it was precisely in the 1980s that the peak in support was recorded.

These data therefore offer a useful early lesson that it is difficult to generalize about patterns of party support across Western Europe as a whole. Not only do the aggregate electoral strengths of the parties differ considerably from one country to the next, but their patterns of development also vary—showing growth in some countries, decline in others, and more or less trendless fluctuations in yet others.

Now that European welfare states have been established for such a long period, it is easy to forget the radicalism that was once an integral part of social democracy in Western Europe. In many cases, the social democratic parties adopted an explicitly Marxist philosophy and ultimately envisaged the replacement of capitalism by a genuinely socialist order. During the period in which the franchise was being expanded to include the working class, social democratic parties sought the full extension of political rights and the introduction of social policies designed to protect the interests of workers and of the unemployed.

With time, however, the initial radical impulse of social democracy began to wane. As Michels argued, electoral imperatives implied more professional organizational techniques, and this did much to blunt the parties' political purism. A further push toward moderation occurred when the Russian Revolution of 1917 precipitated splits in the socialist movement. The consequent creation of communist parties drew away many of the more radical members from the social democratic parties. The moderation of the views of the social democratic parties was also, in part, a product of their very success. The experience of participating in government, particularly in the wake of World War II, increased pressures toward ideological compromise and firmly ensconced social democratic parties at the heart of the political order they initially had sought to overthrow. Finally, much of the early radicalism of the social democrats was dissipated as a result of the successful implementation of their short-term policies: full political rights were won, and welfare states grew quickly in most European countries.

As a consequence of all this, the social democrats came to settle for a political role based on managing a mixed economy. They steadily dropped what Kirchheimer described as their "ideological baggage" and extended their electoral appeal to the middle class, particularly the middle class working in the rapidly expanding state sector, thus becoming catchall parties. This drift towards moderation has become even more accentuated in the 1990s, as social democratic parties throughout Europe come to terms with the limits to state intervention set by the demands of the international global economy. Within the increasingly integrated European union area, of course, these limits are even more pronounced (Scharpf). But although some might perceive this to have frustrated social democratic appeals in the 1990s, it is quite remarkable to note the extent to which they have recorded recent successes, gaining access to government at the end of the 1990s in almost all Western European countries.

Despite their increased moderation, the policy emphases of contemporary social democratic parties retain a commitment to welfarism and egalitarianism, even though they now tend to place less emphasis on the need to control and regulate economic life. Social democratic party manifestos no longer present a direct ideological challenge to the capitalist order in Western Europe. What remains of their traditional radicalism has passed either to increasingly marginalized communist parties or to "new left" and Green parties that first came to prominence in the 1970s and 1980s. (On social democracy in general, see Cuperus and Kandel; Gillespie and Paterson; Kitschelt, 1994; Padgett and Paterson; Paterson and Thomas.)

The Communists

Significant communist parties could traditionally be found in fewer countries than their social democratic rivals, and, in the main, they have also proved substantially less successful at winning votes. Moreover, since the collapse of the Berlin Wall in 1989 and the breakdown of the communist regimes in Eastern Europe and in the former Soviet Union (see also Chapter 15), those communist parties that have remained in Western Europe have been engaged in a process of reform and have sometimes either dropped their ideological labels (as in Finland and Sweden) or effectively disappeared as independent forces (as in the Netherlands and Norway). Even before this, however, as can be seen from Table 8-2, communist parties commanded a substantial proportion of the vote only in Italy and, to a lesser extent, in Finland, France, and Iceland. Explicit communist parties were effectively nonexistent in Ireland, Malta and the United Kingdom, and have now become even more marginalized in Austria, Belgium, Denmark, Norway, and Switzerland. Although they have proved more serious contenders for votes in the new southern European democracies—Greece, Portugal, and Spain—there has recently been some slippage in their vote in these countries too, and success—as in Spain—has required the formation of electoral alliances with other left groupings. In general, across the whole postwar period, average electoral support for

TABLE 8-2   MEAN ELECTORAL SUPPORT FOR COMMUNIST PARTIES, 1950–2000

	1950s	1960s	1970s	1980s	1990s
Austria	4.3	1.7	1.2	0.7	0.4
Belgium	3.4	3.7	2.9	1.4	0.2
Denmark	4.5	1.0	3.0	0.9	–
Finland	22.1	21.6	17.6	13.9	10.7
France	23.9	21.4	21.0	12.4	12.6
Germany	1.1	–	–	–	4.0
Iceland	16.4	16.3	23.7	15.3	9.6
Ireland	–	–	–	–	–
Italy	22.7	26.1	30.7	28.3	6.7
Luxembourg	11.6	14.0	8.2	5.1	2.8
Malta	–	–	–	–	–
Netherlands	4.4	3.2	3.4	1.1	–
Norway	4.3	1.8	1.0	0.9	–
Sweden	4.2	4.2	5.1	5.6	7.6
Switzerland	2.7	2.6	2.4	0.9	1.1
UK	–	–	–	–	–
Mean (N = 16)	**7.9**	**7.3**	**7.5**	**5.4**	**3.5**
Greece				12.1	9.5
Portugal				16.0	9.7
Spain				6.1	9.9
Mean (N − 19)				**6.3**	**4.5**

Note: Since Greece, Portugal, and Spain did not become fully democratic until the mid-1970s, decade averages are reported only for the 1980s and 1990s.

communist parties fell from almost 8 percent in the 1950s to less than 4 percent in the 1990s, the most recent decline being partly accounted for by the split in the Italian Communist party (PCI), which leaves a relatively small party still in the communist camp (Communist Refoundation) in the 1990s and places a bigger party (the PDS) in the social democratic family.

Yet, even these relatively modest voting figures tend to exaggerate the importance of communist parties in those countries where they might appear on the face of things to have counted as a relevant political force. In Italy, for example, which traditionally hosted the strongest and most important of the Western European communist parties, the 1980s had already witnessed a major erosion of the distinctively communist element in both party ideology and party organization. In France, on the other hand, the distinctively communist identity of the French Communist party (PCF) has been jealously guarded at substantial electoral cost. The 1980s witnessed a major electoral decline of the PCF to the benefit of its more moderate and increasingly successful socialist rival. In Iceland, the People's Alliance (PA) has largely shied away from promoting a distinctive communist identity. It includes quite a substantial social democratic component, and in the 1999 election it took part in an electoral alliance with the Women's party and the social democrats. Finally, the communist party in Finland, the former Finnish People's Democratic Union (FPDL), banned prior to World War II, enjoyed a peculiar status owing to the country's close geographic and cultural links with the Soviet Union. Even here, however, the FPDL was an alliance that included a social democratic component. The strains in this eventually led to a split between more moderate and extreme elements in 1985. Both sides have now joined together again in the new and more moderate Left-Wing Alliance.

The European communist parties were almost all formed in the immediate wake of the Russian Revolution of 1917, espousing Leninist principles and advocating the revolutionary road to socialism. They thereby established themselves as a radical alternative to the parliamentarism of social democracy. These parties were formally aligned with and took their lead from the Soviet Communist Party. This leadership was organized initially through Comintern, the Communist (or Third) International, which lasted from 1919 to 1943. It was later organized through the less formal Cominform network, which lasted from 1947 to 1956. This alliance with Moscow, together with the evident radicalism of the communist parties, ensured that they were typically regarded as anti-system oppositions, and as such, they often polarized the party systems in which they operated.

Inevitably, they had little experience with government office, although, in the immediate wake of World War II, bolstered by the credibility that they had achieved as a result of their crucial role in the anti-fascist resistance, several communist parties were to enjoy brief periods as partners in the widely based coalition governments that sought to reestablish democratic politics in countries such as Austria, Belgium, Denmark, Finland, France, and Italy. Since then, communist parties have been involved in government only in Iceland, Finland, and, since the early 1980s, France. Beyond this, however, they have sometimes offered the parliamentary support necessary to sustain other parties in office while not formally joining the cabinet. In Italy, for example, the PCI acted to sustain the Christian Democrats in office in the late 1970s, while Communist Refoundation currently helps to keep the PDS-dominated Olive Tree alliance in government. In Sweden, the small but remarkably persistent Communist Party, now renamed the Left Party, has regularly provided the parliamentary support necessary to maintain the Social Democrats in office.

In part as a response to electoral decline or stagnation, in part as a means of ending their political isolation, many Western European communist parties began to distance themselves from Moscow during the postwar period. This shift heralded the emergence of "Eurocommunism" in the 1970s, in which the Italian, French, and Spanish parties, in particular, sought to elaborate a distinctive non-Soviet strategy for achieving political power. However, this strategy of legitimation did not reap the hoped-for political rewards, and the 1980s witnessed further electoral decline.

Partly as a result of the Eurocommunist strategy, the policy emphases of communist parties did not differ markedly by the mid-1980s from those of their social democratic rivals, and they also began to emphasize questions of welfare, social justice, and the need for democratic decision making. Where they do still differ from the social democrats is in their emphasis on state involvement in the economy and in their greater skepticism about the free market. They stress the need for a controlled economy as well as for more public ownership, and they are much more critical about the benefits of European integration. They are also much more explicit in their claim to represent the specific interests of the traditional working class and trade unions in contrast to the more catchall electoral appeal of social democracy. (For a useful assessment of the Western European communist parties in the immediate wake of the end of the Cold War, see Bull and Heywood).

The New Left

The third party family on the left is usually described as the "new" left. As can be seen from Table 8-3, patterns of popular support for the new left make it easier to understand the general decline of social democratic and communist voting. Through to the 1980s, the trend in support for the new left ran counter to that for the traditional left,

TABLE 8-3   MEAN ELECTORAL SUPPORT FOR NEW LEFT PARTIES, 1960–2000

	1960s	1970s	1980s	1990s
Austria	–	–	–	–
Belgium	–	–	–	–
Denmark	7.7	8.3	14.4	7.7
Finland	–	–	–	–
France	–	–	–	–
Germany	–	–	–	–
Iceland	–	–	7.8	7.4
Ireland	–	1.4	3.9	3.2
Italy	2.2	3.3	4.0	–
Luxembourg	–	–	–	–
Malta	–	–	–	–
Netherlands	3.0	4.0	2.6	2.4
Norway	4.0	6.9	6.8	8.4
Sweden	–	.	.	–
Switzerland	–	0.9	2.3	0.3
UK	–	–	–	–
Mean (N = 16)	**1.1**	**1.6**	**2.6**	**1.8**
Greece			–	–
Portugal			–	–
Spain			–	–
Mean (N = 19)			**2.2**	**1.5**

Note: Since Greece, Portugal and Spain did not become fully democratic until the mid-1970s, decade averages are reported only for the 1980s and 1990s.

rising from just 1 percent in the 1960s in Western Europe as a whole to almost 3 percent in the 1980s before falling back again—to the benefit of the Greens—in the 1990s. This suggests a reshuffling rather than a decline of the left.

The first new left parties emerged in the 1960s. These tended more toward an orthodox Marxist position, having often emerged as a result of divisions within the established communist parties. The later new left parties, on the other hand, tended to be stimulated by the wave of student radicalism of the late 1960s, and they have also been spurred on by the growing ecology movement. Indeed, it is often difficult to distinguish these new left parties from more orthodox Green parties (see below), and since the emergence of the latter, the two groups have frequently worked in concert. The Dutch Green Left, for example, is an alliance between Greens, new left parties, and the old Communist Party. (See also Kitschelt, 1988, who groups both types of parties under the label "left-libertarian.")

As Table 8-3 shows, new left parties have established themselves in only a scattering of the Western European polities, and even where they exist, they often remain quite marginal. It is only in Denmark in the 1980s, when two new left parties were competing, that the new left vote reached double digits. Even here, however, the average vote had dropped by half in the 1990s. Outside Denmark, new left support has proved notable only in Iceland (where it includes the Women's Alliance), and Norway. In this sense it may be regarded as a primarily Scandinavian phenomenon.

Not least as a result of their diverse origins, the policy emphases of new left parties reflect a wide-ranging set of concerns. On one hand, the new left parties echo traditional communist parties in their opposition to market forces and their concern for public ownership and a controlled economy. Again like traditional communist parties, and quite unlike their Green allies, they emphasize an explicit appeal to the traditional working class. And although they stress a commitment to the welfare state, social justice, and environmental protection, in common with all left parties, they also promote a more libertarian trend of freedom and democracy. Finally, they also tend to be more skeptical about European integration.

Green Parties

Radical left politics can be seen as having developed in four distinct phases. As we have seen, the first, most important, and most enduring of these phases was the emergence of social democratic parties in the late nineteenth century. The second phase involved the split in social democracy in the wake of the Russian Revolution and the consequent emergence of the communist alternative. Here, too, the new parties proved reasonably enduring, and, in certain limited instances, grew to a majority position on the left. The third phase was the mobilization of the new left in the 1960s and 1970s, a movement that managed to establish itself in mainstream politics in only a handful of countries, and in these largely at the expense of the traditional communist parties. Finally, in the late 1970s and 1980s came the fourth phase: the emergence of "Green," or ecology, parties. Green parties tend to poll only a small percentage of the total vote. Nevertheless, their recent growth and pervasiveness have generated substantial interest among students of the Western European party mosaic.

TABLE 8-4   MEAN ELECTORAL SUPPORT FOR GREEN PARTIES, 1980–2000

	1980s	1990s
Austria	4.1	6.6
Belgium	6.0	10.9
Denmark	0.7	2.2
Finland	2.7	7.0
France	0.9	8.4
Germany	5.1	6.4
Iceland	–	3.1
Ireland	0.4	2.1
Italy	1.3	2.7
Luxembourg	6.4	9.3
Malta	–	1.5
Netherlands	1.1	5.6
Norway	0.1	0.1
Sweden	2.9	4.3
Switzerland	5.0	6.3
UK	0.3	0.3
Mean (N = 16)	**2.3**	**4.8**
Greece	0.2	0.6
Portugal	–	0.3
Spain	–	1.0
Mean (N = 19)	**2.0**	**4.1**

Table 8-4 shows that by the 1990s, Green parties had gained a respectable level of electoral support in the vast majority of Western European countries. To be sure, the Green alternative remains essentially marginal by comparison to its larger rivals, and on the average accounted for little more than 2 percent of the vote in Western Europe in the 1980s and for less than 5 percent in the 1990s. But the Greens represent a new and growing phenomenon, and average figures mask the increase in Green support that has occurred in the most recent elections. They also mask substantial variations between countries. In Belgium, for example, average Green support exceeded 10 percent in the 1990s. In Austria, Finland, France, Germany, Luxembourg, and Switzerland, these parties polled an average of between 6 and 9 percent. The Netherlands also comes close to this level, although the Green alternative there is one that competes as part of an electoral coalition involving also the new left and the former Communist party.

In contrast, there is as yet no effective Green representation in Malta, Norway, or the United Kingdom. In the latter case, however, the British Green party did poll almost 15 percent of the vote in the 1989 British direct elections to the European Parliament. This was the largest national vote share ever won by a Green party, but

BOX 8-1

THE LEFT

France

The most notable development within the left in France has been the eclipse of the traditionally powerful and strongly pro-Soviet Communist Party (PCF) and the corresponding rise of the Socialists (PS) under François Mitterrand. The left as a whole was stronger in France in the 1980s than at any other period since the 1950s, but the PS, the dominant group within the left, fell back again in the 1990s. With more internal electoral flux on the left, the Greens finally began to make some headway, and in 1997 they entered government as part of a broad coalition with the Socialist party and the communists. Mitterrand, the Socialist candidate, won the presidential elections in 1981 and 1988, but the party's candidate in 1995, Lionel Jospin, was defeated.

Germany

It was in Germany that the Green movement initially mounted what appeared to be the most severe challenge to the traditional left in Western Europe. The Social Democrats (SPD) had long enjoyed an effective monopoly of the left, helped largely by the fears of extreme politics in the wake of nazism and by the long-term constitutional ban on the Communist Party. Now that monopoly has been broken by the successful mobilization of a Green vote, on the one hand, and by the unexpected success of the former East German communist party, on the other. Thanks to a new alliance with the Greens, however, the SPD found itself returning to government in 1998 for the first time in sixteen years.

Italy

Italy used to have the largest communist party in Western Europe (the PCI), which, since the collapse of the communist regimes in Eastern Europe and in the former Soviet Union, has split into a major social democratic party, now know as the Democratic Left, and a smaller and more traditional communist party, Communist Refoundation. The left was always divided in Italy, with the PCI persistently excluded from government and with the Socialists (PSI) and centrist Social Democrats (PSDI) forming an essential part of the five-party coalition that held government in Italy throughout the 1980s under the leadership of the Christian Democrats. The old Italian party system has now completely broken down, however, and the PSI has effectively disappeared. In 1996,

for the first time ever, a coalition led by the left won office in Italy. The coalition includes the Democratic Left, the Greens, and left-leaning elements of the old Christian Democrats. Whether these parties can stay together as a coherent bloc remains open to question.

The Netherlands

The Dutch left was often excluded from government, with the Christian Democrats (CDA) and Liberals (VVD) usually managing to win a majority of seats. In fact, between 1958 and 1989, when it finally managed to dislodge the Liberals and replace them as the partner of the CDA in government, the Labor Party (PvdA) had been in government on only three occasions, totaling less than seven years. Electoral support for the PvdA grew in the early 1990s before falling back again, but since 1994 the party has been in government as the major party in a center-left coalition. Two parties to the left of Labor, the Green Left and the Socialist party, increased their votes in the 1998 election.

Spain

The Socialist Party (PSOE) was for a long time the most successful of the parties in Spain, forming a single-party majority government following the elections of 1982, 1986, 1989, and 1993. In 1996 it was overtaken by the conservative People's party. The PSOE has also been one of the most moderate of Europe's socialist parties, a factor that did much to slow down the mobilization of a successful opposition on the center right. Despite its initial hopes following the transition to democracy, the Communist Party (PCE) has failed to make a major impact in politics and has now joined forces with other left-wing critics of the PSOE in a loose alliance called the United Left. Like Greece and Portugal, Spain has never really witnessed the emergence of a new left or Green party, but other left-wing forces are represented within the various nationalist and regionalist groups.

Sweden

Sweden, often seen as the model for radical social democracy, long maintained what was perhaps the most successful Social Democratic party (the SAP) in Western Europe. This party dominated government for more than forty years and built up and maintained the most advanced welfare state in Europe, as well as what is arguably the most regulated society. However, although successful in both electoral and policy terms—it held government continuously from 1932 until 1976—the SAP is by no means free from challenges on the left, including the more recently formed Ecology Party. The Communist Party, now known as the Left Party, which has also enjoyed a persistent if relatively small electoral following, tends to cooperate with rather than oppose its larger social democratic neighbor, and it currently supports the minority single-party SAP government that has now been in office since 1994.

United Kingdom

Although the Labour Party spent the entire 1980s in opposition, Britain is unique in the extent to which a single party has monopolized the left. Even though a number of leading communists gained prominence inside the trade union movement, the Communist Party has never been successful in elections, its high point being in 1945 when it won just over one hundred thousand votes and two MPs. Nor has any new left or Green party made any impact in recent Westminster elections. In 1997, following eighteen years in opposition, Labour swept back into power under the leadership of Tony Blair. Advocating what he calls the "Third Way," Blair's "New" Labour government has begun a massive program of social and constitutional reform.

given the British electoral system (see Chapter 11), it yielded not a single seat. (Conversely, with a lower share of the vote, the Scottish Green party did manage to win representation in the new devolved Scottish parliament in 1999.) Nor have Green parties made any significant impact in the new democracies of southern Europe, although Green members of parliament were elected in 1989 in Greece and as part of the broad United Democratic Coalition in 1987 in Portugal.

Even though a major electoral breakthrough has so far eluded Green parties in Europe, in other respects they are now beginning to achieve some political success, entering new government coalitions in Belgium, Finland, France, Germany, and Italy in the late 1990s. In Luxembourg, the Netherlands, and Switzerland, such success also might come in the near future. In the end, this may constitute the most important contribution of these new parties: providing the additional support necessary to allow the formation of center-left governments. Without the Greens, for example, it would have been impossible for any left-wing coalition to displace the center-right governments in France, Germany, or Italy during the latter half of the 1990s.

The policy emphases of Green parties, as might be expected, give pride of place to the need to protect the environment. This involves promoting policies that would curb economic growth and require substantial regulation of industrial and commercial activity. Green manifestos also emphasize the need for international peace and disarmament and urge an increase in the level of development aid provided for Third World countries. They emphasize social justice, particularly the need for equal treatment of women, as well as of ethnic and racial minorities. Green parties also stress participatory democracy and even attempt to structure their own organizations in such a way as to allow maximum grassroots involvement. Finally, and as with the other smaller parties of the left, they tend to question the value of further European integration. Bearing in mind the rapidly rising salience of the issues valued by the Green parties, we might also judge their success in terms of the extent to which these issues now rank so highly on the policy agendas of all political parties on the left. (On Green parties in general, see Müller-Rommel, 1989; Delwit and de Waele.)

FAMILIES OF THE CENTER AND RIGHT

The party families of the right are more heterogeneous than those of the left, and, as we shall see, they also show much more evidence of flux in their aggregate electoral support over time. These families include the Christian democrats, made up of parties that temper mainstream conservatism with a defense of religious values; conservative parties, distinguished from the Christian democrats by a more strident antisocialist rhetoric as well as by the absence of traditional links with organized religion; and liberal parties, a heterogeneous group that includes centrist parties such as the British Liberals and quite right-wing parties such as the Dutch Liberals. There is also a group of agrarian or center parties that originally mobilized in defense of farming interests in a variety of Western European countries. Finally, there is a family of extreme-right parties, characterized by the promotion of racist and xenophobic political appeals.

The Christian Democrats

For most of the postwar period, the Christian democratic family constituted the largest single group on the center right of Western European politics. This family has a base in most established Western European democracies, the main exceptions being Iceland, Malta, and the United Kingdom. It also has emerged as at least a marginally relevant political force in both Portugal and Spain.

The Christian democratic family contains a number of distinct strands. The first is primarily Roman Catholic in origin and includes Christian parties that began to mobilize in the last half of the nineteenth century and are now among the strongest in Western Europe. This strand is made up of Christian democratic parties in Austria, Belgium, Italy, Luxembourg, and Switzerland, although the Swiss party now also wins support from Protestant voters.

The second strand in Christian democracy comprises two parties that draw substantial support from both Catholics and Protestants. The German Christian Democratic Union (CDU) and its Bavarian sister party, the Christian Social Union (CSU), were both formed in 1945 in the period of immediate postwar reconstruction. They built on the legacy of the former Catholic Center party, one of the dominant parties in Germany before the Nazi regime. In 1945, however, in a deliberate effort to erode the divisions that had been so evident in the prewar period, the new CDU sought the support of both Catholics and Protestants. This cross-denominational appeal has become even more pronounced since German unification, since the eastern parts of Germany contained quite a high proportion of Protestant voters. The second biconfessional Christian democratic party is the Dutch Christian Democratic Appeal (CDA), which was originally divided into three separate parties, the Catholic People's party and two smaller but persistent Protestant parties, the Anti-Revolutionary party (ARP) and the Christian Historical Union (CHU). These formed a federation in 1975 and then fused into a single party in 1980. Both the CDU/CSU and the CDA, with their substantial Protestant components, can be differentiated from the essentially Catholic parties in the first strand of Christian democracy. In all other respects, however, not the least in their inheritance of a long tradition of confessional politics and in the strong bargaining positions they now enjoy in their respective party systems, these two strands of Christian democracy fill rather similar roles in party politics.

The third strand is largely Protestant and is of more recent origin: the parties involved often first contested elections only after World War II. It is also more marginal in electoral terms. It comprises the Christian Democrats of Denmark, Norway, and Sweden, together with the minor evangelical and reformed Protestant parties in the Netherlands and Switzerland. The Swedish party has enjoyed quite a strong surge of support in the 1990s, and took part in the Swedish center-right coalition government in the mid-1990s. The Christian People's party in Norway has also done particularly well in the 1990s, polling almost 14 percent of the vote in 1997 and going on to become the senior partner in the new minority center-right coalition that displaced the minority social democratic government after that election.

Over and above these cases of quite explicitly Christian parties, a Christian democratic element can also be identified in France and Ireland. The French case is the more interesting of the two, because a substantial Catholic party, the Popular Republican Movement, was among the most influential in the French Fourth Republic (1946 to 1958). With the shifting center-right alliances that have characterized French politics since 1958, however, the distinct Christian alternative has all but disappeared. Much of its more conservative support was eventually captured by the Gaullists, and the more moderate elements operate under the Center Social Democrat label within the loose alliance called the Union for French Democracy.

In Ireland, where the population is still more than 90 percent Catholic and rates of church attendance are by far the highest in Western Europe, there is no tradition of organized Christian democracy. In recent years, however, one of the leading parties of the center right, Fine Gael, has affiliated with the transnational federations of Christian democratic parties—the European People's party and the European Union of Christian Democrats—and the party is also affiliated with the Christian democratic People's group in the European Parliament in Strasbourg. Hence, although historically outside the Christian democratic tradition, Fine Gael has proved willing to adopt this transnational organizational identity.

As Table 8-5 shows, and notwithstanding the more recent successes of the smaller Protestant parties, Christian democracy as a whole has experienced quite a substantial erosion of electoral support towards the end of the postwar era, falling from an average of almost 21 percent in the 1950s to less than 15 percent in the 1990s. Among the most dramatic declines has been that experienced in the Netherlands, where the various Christian parties accounted for more than half the vote in the 1950s, as against less than a quarter in the 1990s. In 1994, the dominant Christian party, the CDA, recorded its worst-ever result, polling just over 18 percent of the vote. There has also been a marked decline in neighboring Belgium, where the Catholic parties (one Flemish and one Walloon) have lost almost half their support, and where they finally have also lost their presence in government.

In Italy, the Christian democratic vote has been drastically reduced, with the allegations of corruption destroying the party after 1992 and leaving behind a group of divided smaller parties that split between the alliances of left and right. In Austria, the People's party has lost around one-third of its support, principally to the benefit of the

TABLE 8-5   MEAN ELECTORAL SUPPORT FOR CHRISTIAN DEMOCRATIC PARTIES, 1950–2000

	1950s	1960s	1970s	1980s	1990s
Austria	43.8	46.9	43.2	42.2	28.7
Belgium	45.4	36.3	33.7	27.8	23.1
Denmark	–	–	3.9	2.4	2.2
Finland	–	0.6	2.9	2.8	3.4
France*	–	–	–	–	–
Germany	47.7	46.3	46.0	45.9	40.1
Iceland	–	–	–	–	0.2
Ireland[†]	28.1	33.4	32.8	33.9	26.3
Italy	41.3	38.6	38.5	33.6	17.8
Luxembourg	37.5	34.3	31.2	33.3	30.3
Malta	–	–	–	–	–
Netherlands	53.2	49.8	37.8	36.6	23.3
Norway	10.3	9.0	11.9	8.7	10.8
Sweden	–	1.1	1.6	2.4	7.7
Switzerland	24.2	24.4	23.2	22.2	18.8
UK	–	–	–	–	–
Mean (N = 16)	**20.7**	**20.1**	**19.1**	**18.3**	**14.5**
Greece				–	–
Portugal				6.9	7.3
Spain				2.2	–
Mean (N = 19)				**15.9**	**12.6**

Note: Since Greece, Portugal, and Spain did not become fully democratic until the mid-1970s, decade averages are reported only for the 1980s and 1990s.

*Since the mid-1970s, the Christian democrats in France, together with conservative and liberal forces, have contested elections as part of the UDF alliance; as such, their electoral support has been grouped together with that of the conservatives (see Table 8-6).

[†]For the purposes of this analysis, the Irish party Fine Gael is classified as Christian democratic.

far-right Freedom party. Indeed, in the most recent election in 1999, the Freedom party narrowly managed to outpoll the People's party. Elsewhere, particularly in Germany, Luxembourg, and Switzerland, the Christian vote has also fallen. What is striking, however, is that with the exception of the small Protestant Party in Sweden, no country has experienced a sustained increase in Christian democratic support over the postwar period. Taken together, the electoral record of Christian democracy in postwar western Europe reflects the most substantial change experienced by any of the nine party families.

The dominant strand in Western European Christian democracy was always represented by the Catholic parties in particular. Even in the case of the biconfessional parties, the Catholic heritage has been well to the fore. This particular heritage dates back to the nineteenth century, when Catholic mobilization took place in response to secularizing and anticlerical impulses from both conservatives and liberals (Kalyvas).

Since then, however, the issues that first generated these conflicts between church and state have been largely settled, and the parties themselves have developed into mainstream components of the center right. Their religious emphases surface only in response to the appearance on the political agenda of moral issues such as abortion, euthanasia, and divorce, on which the established Christian churches have strong views. The smaller Protestant parties share these positions but add a concern for reversing what they see as the general trend toward permissiveness and ungodliness. The Norwegian and Swedish parties, for example, have campaigned strongly against both alcohol use and pornography.

Christian parties can easily be distinguished from their conservative counterparts (discussed next) because their popular base, their social concerns, and their reluctance to promote policies that might lead to social conflict have always inclined them (the Catholic parties in particular) toward a more centrist, pro-welfare program. Indeed, the impetus behind the development of welfare states in postwar Europe derived almost as much from Catholic pressure as it did from social democracy. This was particularly true in countries such as Belgium, the Netherlands, and Italy, where social democracy has always remained relatively weak (Kersbergen; Wilensky). In short, Christian democratic parties have traditionally tended to be state-oriented parties, sharing common ground with the social democrats in their opposition to neoliberal, libertarian, and individualistic policies. Apart from some of the smaller Protestant parties, these Christian parties are also among the strongest advocates of European integration. (On Christian democracy, see Kalyvas; Caciagli et al.; Hanley; Kersbergen.)

The Conservatives

Across Western Europe in general, conservative parties have begun to poll an even bigger share of the votes than the Christian democrats. This is not so much due to their own success—they have risen only slightly from an average of just under 18 percent in the 1950s to just over 18 percent in the 1990s (Table 8-6)—but because their overall vote has held reasonably firmly, while that of the Christian democrats has come close to free-fall. Conservative parties also poll particularly well in Greece and Spain, where they constitute the principal opposition to the social democrats. What is most striking about the conservative vote is that even this high level of average support is depressed by the fact that conservative parties do not compete in a number of countries. Where they do exist, conservative parties often do very well, winning about 40 percent in the 1990s in France, Iceland, Ireland, and the UK. Indeed, in Malta, which is the purest version of two-party system to be found in Western Europe, the Nationalist party—which some would argue is more closely akin to a Christian democratic party—polled more than 50 percent of the vote in the 1990s.

As with liberal and Christian families, there are several strands within conservatism in Western Europe. One important strand includes what we might think of as "national" parties, which marry a conservative socioeconomic appeal with an emphasis on the pursuit of national interests. This strand includes the Independence party in Iceland, Fianna Fáil in Ireland, the French Gaullists, and the British Conservatives. All four parties, which also tend to be the most successful in the family, stress the importance of

TABLE 8-6   MEAN ELECTORAL SUPPORT FOR CONSERVATIVE PARTIES, 1950–2000

	1950s	1960s	1970s	1980s	1990s
Austria	–	–	–	–	–
Belgium	–	–	–	–	–
Denmark	18.4	21.3	10.5	19.5	13.3
Finland	14.2	14.2	19.6	22.9	19.5
France*	44.2	55.6	50.3	42.7	39.7
Germany	–	–	–	–	–
Iceland	41.3	39.5	36.8	38.4	38.8
Ireland	46.0	45.7	49.1	45.9	39.2
Italy	–	–	–	–	13.9
Luxembourg	–	–	–	–	–
Malta	35.9	52.7	48.3	50.9	50.5
Netherlands	–	–	–	–	–
Norway	18.7	20.2	20.9	28.1	15.7
Sweden	17.0	14.4	15.4	21.1	22.3
Switzerland	–	–	–	–	1.2
UK	47.6	42.7	41.0	42.2	36.3
Mean (N = 16)	**17.7**	**19.1**	**18.2**	**19.5**	**18.2**
Greece				41.8	44.0
Portugal				–	–
Spain				25.9	33.3
Mean (N = 19)				**20.0**	**19.4**

Note: Since Greece, Portugal, and Spain did not become fully democratic until the mid-1970s, decade averages are reported only for the 1980s and 1990s.

*Since the mid-1970s, the UDF alliance, which is treated here as a conservative party, has brought together under one umbrella Christian democrats, conservatives, and liberals.

national shibboleths, and all decry the "anti-national" character of sectional or class politics. The new Forza Italia party in Italy might also be considered to belong to this group. A second distinctive strand within European conservatism is made up of traditional conservative parties in Denmark, Finland, Norway, and Sweden. These are characterized by more moderate opposition to state intervention, married to a commitment to a consensual approach to policy making.

Although the conservatives are more clearly on the right than the Christian democrats, the two families can in many ways be viewed as functional equivalents. Both represent the major alternative to the appeal of social democracy, and, what is more telling, the two families rarely flourish within the same party system. Where secular conservatism is strong, Christian democracy tends to be weak or nonexistent (in the Scandinavian countries, Malta, the United Kingdom, Greece, and Spain). Where Christian democracy is strong, secular conservatism tends to be weak or nonexistent (in Austria, Belgium,

[handwritten margin note: Cons- CD as alternative forms of anti S.D.]

Germany, and the Netherlands). In Italy, it is precisely the conservative Forza Italia which is now attempting to take the place of the shattered Christian democrats.

The policy priorities of the conservative family are quite distinctive. Although the conservatives share some degree of commitment to welfarism with all other party families, this ranks lower in conservative party programs than in the programs of other parties on the right. Rather, conservative parties emphasize the need to support private enterprise and to encourage fiscal austerity. They also emphasize government efficiency, as well as law and order. Moreover, in many countries they also stress the importance of traditional national values, and they are sometimes quite ambiguous in their attitudes to European integration. (On conservative parties in general, see Girvin.)

The Liberals

Electoral support for liberal parties in Western Europe has increased in the postwar period and now stands at an average of just over 10 percent of the total vote in the 1990s (Table 8-7). The liberal presence is also pervasive. The small island states of Iceland and Malta are the only established European democracies that do not have a relevant liberal party, whereas liberal parties, broadly defined, have emerged in both Portugal and Spain. Ireland has also witnessed the emergence of a liberal party in the 1980s, the Progressive Democrats. This party polled more than 11 percent of the vote in its first electoral outing in 1987, and although its vote declined thereafter, the party did succeed in twice entering a government coalition with Fianna Fáil. The fact that Ireland did not have a liberal presence before the late 1980s suggests an intriguing but probably spurious relationship between small island polities, on the one hand—Iceland, Ireland, Malta—and a rejection of liberalism, on the other! Finally, although a strong liberal tradition exists in France, the present liberal tendency has been largely subsumed within the loose, wide-ranging alliance of the Union for French Democracy (UDF).

As Table 8-7 shows, despite the fact that the liberal parties are present in almost all European countries, there is substantial variation in liberal strength. During the 1990s, for example, the liberals won an average of more than 20 percent of the vote in Belgium, Luxembourg, the Netherlands, and Switzerland—all of which belong to the well-known group of consociational democracies (Lijphart; Luther and Deschouwer). The Dutch figure is truly striking, for although it now encompasses two parties, the left-leaning Democrats 66 and the more conservative Liberal party, there has been an almost fourfold growth: from just less than 10 percent in the 1950s to almost 35 percent in the 1990s. Liberals also poll reasonably well in the UK, averaging more than 17 percent in the 1990s.

Elsewhere, however, they are quite marginal in electoral terms, failing to come even close to double figures in all other countries where they compete. The exception is Portugal, where the Liberals have become the main opposition to the social democrats, and where they have risen to an average of almost 40 percent of the vote in the 1990s. Yet even in countries where liberal support falls below 10 percent, the parties concerned often exert a political influence far exceeding that suggested by their low legislative weight. Their position, which is sometimes close to the center of the party system,

TABLE 8-7   MEAN ELECTORAL SUPPORT FOR LIBERAL PARTIES, 1950–2000

	1950s	1960s	1970s	1980s	1990s
Austria*	8.4	6.2	5.6	7.4	5.0
Belgium	11.5	18.3	15.4	21.1	22.6
Denmark	8.1	9.3	8.3	5.6	4.0
Finland	7.1	9.7	5.4	0.9	1.7
France†	–	–	–	–	–
Germany	8.6	9.4	8.2	8.9	8.0
Iceland	–	–	–	–	1.8
Ireland	–	–	–	3.5	4.7
Italy	4.8	8.1	5.4	6.9	5.8
Luxembourg	12.6	13.6	21.8	17.5	20.7
Malta	–	–	–	–	–
Netherlands	9.9	12.8	19.7	25.5	34.6
Norway	9.8	9.5	5.8	3.4	4.1
Sweden	22.1	16.3	11.8	10.8	7.0
Switzerland	31.4	32.9	31.1	30.1	24.8
UK‡	5.1	9.9	14.7	23.9	17.3
Mean (N = 16)	**8.7**	**9.8**	**9.6**	**10.3**	**10.1**
Greece			–	–	–
Portugal				27.3	39.4
Spain				4.6	3.2
Mean (N = 19)				**10.4**	**10.8**

Note: Since Greece, Portugal, and Spain did not become fully democratic until the mid-1970s, decade averages are reported only for the 1980s and 1990s.

*The Austrian Freedom party is considered as a liberal party through to the end of the 1980s, and as an extreme-right party in the 1990s.

†Since the mid-1970s, the liberal forces in France, together with conservatives and Christian democrats, have contested elections as part of the UDF alliance; as such, their electoral support has been grouped together with that of the conservatives (see Table 8-6).

‡Includes Liberal-SDP Alliance in the 1980s.

allows them to take on a crucial role as junior partners in coalition governments of the center right as well as the center left (Keman). Indeed, liberal parties are governing parties *par excellence*—though ironically, in the United Kingdom, where the liberal vote has at times exceeded that in virtually every other European country, they have never won office in the postwar period.

Although the liberal political family is often seen as a "center" group in Western European politics, in practice these parties represent a diverse range of ideological concerns. Historically, liberal parties have been associated with the impulse to extend the franchise, to promote individual rights, and to resist clerical influences in political life. Prior to the emergence of social democracy, liberal parties thus constituted the first real opposition to conservatism and the right. Some of these concerns have survived and are more or less common to all European liberal parties: an emphasis on individual rights and a residual (though increasingly less relevant) anticlericalism. Over time, however, other liberal concerns have mutated, and two clear strands of European liberalism can now be identified.

Within the first strand, an emphasis on individual rights has led to a concern for fiscal rectitude and opposition to all but minimal state intervention in the economy. This right-wing strand of liberalism has been particularly important in Austria, where the Freedom party used to be regarded as the most rightist of European liberal parties, but is now better grouped with the extreme right (we discuss this later in this chapter). The right-wing strand is also important in Belgium, Germany, Italy, Luxembourg, the Netherlands, and Switzerland, and this is the position toward which the Progressive Democrats in Ireland have now gravitated. Thus, this brand of liberalism has tended to emerge in countries that are also characterized by strong Christian democratic parties and hence where the anticlerical component of liberalism was once important. Indeed, anticlericalism in these countries has two distinct forms, being represented on the left by socialist and/or communist parties and on the right by secular liberal parties.

The second strand of European liberalism reflects a more centrist, if not left-leaning, position in which a concern for individual rights and progressive politics has engendered an emphasis on social justice and egalitarianism. This is the strand that has tended to emerge in countries where the main right-wing group is a conservative party that has taken over the more anti-interventionist liberal tendency and where the anticlerical component in liberalism has proved less relevant. This strand is evident in Denmark, Norway, Sweden, and Britain, and is also represented by Democrats 66 in the Netherlands.

Those parties that reflect the more libertarian strand of liberalism have experienced greater electoral success in recent years, increasing their share of the vote in Belgium and the Netherlands in particular. In contrast, the more centrist welfare-oriented liberal parties, particularly those in Scandinavia, have tended towards a steady erosion of support over the postwar period. The exception is Britain, where two centrist parties, both left-leaning, experienced a major increase in support during the 1980s, largely at the expense of the Labour Party.

Above all, however, European liberal parties have demonstrated a strong appetite for participation in government, and the policies implied by the different ideological strands of liberalism have not been allowed to get in the way of this. In Belgium and Luxembourg, for example, governments have tended for a long time to alternate between coalitions of the center left (Christians and social democrats) and those of the center right (Christians and liberals). In Germany, on the other hand, notwithstanding their philosophy, the liberals have played the role of center parties in government-formation negotiations, switching support from time to time between social democrats and Christian democrats. In Scandinavia, yet another pattern is apparent: the dominance of the social democrats encourages liberals, as well as agrarian or center parties, to join forces with the other bourgeois parties to construct a "broad-right" anti-socialist coalition. In each case, however, the liberals are regular participants in the politics of government formation.

The presence of two major strands of liberal ideology and the diversity of liberal party strategies suggest that any overall depiction of liberal party policy concerns may be misleading. Although the left-leaning British, Norwegian, and Swedish liberals traditionally have placed a major emphasis on the need for a controlled economy, this emphasis has been largely absent from the programs of the Austrian, Dutch, and Italian liberals. In common with most other parties, however, all liberal parties share a commitment to welfarism, and in common with the left and the agrarian parties, they also stress the need for environmental protection.

What can also be taken as reasonably characteristic of all liberal parties is an emphasis on freedom, democracy, decentralization, and social justice, reflecting a continuing and pervasive concern for individual rights and freedoms, as well as a reluctance to tolerate more authoritarian styles of governing. In a curious way, therefore, liberal parties now reflect a set of political appeals that echoes elements of both the new left and the traditional right. This may well stem from the shared contemporary orientation of all three groups toward an essentially middle-class electoral constituency. (On liberal parties in general, see Kirchner.)

The Agrarian or Center Parties

As can be seen from Table 8-8, although agrarian parties do not exist at all in many Western European countries, where they do exist, they tend to be quite large. Agrarian parties have sometimes contested elections in both Ireland and the Netherlands, but they are essentially a Scandinavian phenomenon with a strong presence in Denmark, Finland, Iceland, Norway, and Sweden. Outside the Nordic area, an agrarian party persists only in Switzerland. Even so, the Swiss "agrarian" party is actually an alliance between a peasant party and two quite different parties and is only marginally compatible with other members of the agrarian political family. Outside Western Europe, in turn, agrarian parties now compete in elections in a number of postcommunist democracies (see Chapter 15).

As their name suggests, agrarian parties were primarily special-interest parties. They were initially mobilized in the late nineteenth and early twentieth centuries to represent the specific concerns of farmers and the agricultural sector. With the economic and demographic decline in this sector over time, agrarian parties have attempted to extend their appeal to middle-class urban voters. This shift was most clearly signaled by a change of name to Center Party in Finland, Norway, and Sweden (in 1965, 1959, and 1957, respectively). The strategy proved at least temporarily successful in Sweden, where support for the party grew to almost 22 percent of the vote in the 1970s. Most recently, agrarian parties also experienced a substantial increase in their levels of support in Denmark and Norway.

One result of this process of adaptation is a curious amalgam of agrarian party policy concerns. Despite their move away from a distinctively rural base, agrarian parties continue to stress the interests of agriculture and farmers and are the only party family to do so. Two other emphases also reflect their particular heritage: one on decentralization, which harks back to their essentially peripheral roots, and the other on environmental protection that, in its anti-industrial bias, is also characteristic of such parties. At the same time, however, agrarian parties also emphasize welfare provision, social justice, and the need for a controlled economy, which suggests a leftist orientation;

TABLE 8-8   MEAN ELECTORAL SUPPORT FOR AGRARIAN/CENTER PARTIES, 1950–2000

	1950s	1960s	1970s	1980s	1990s
Austria	–	–	–	–	–
Belgium	–	–	–	–	–
Denmark	22.9	20.0	15.1	11.4	21.0
Finland	23.6	23.7	24.1	25.2	24.6
France	–	–	–	–	–
Germany	–	–	–	–	–
Iceland	22.6	28.2	23.0	20.0	20.2
Ireland	2.8	0.5	–	–	–
Italy	–	–	–	–	–
Luxembourg	–	–	–	–	–
Malta	–	–	–	–	–
Netherlands	–	3.5	1.3	–	–
Norway	9.5	9.9	9.8	6.6	12.3
Sweden	11.0	14.2	21.8	12.2	7.0
Switzerland	12.1	11.2	10.8	11.1	16.5
UK	–	–	–	–	–
Mean (N = 16)	**6.6**	**6.9**	**6.7**	**5.4**	**6.4**
Greece				–	–
Portugal				–	–
Spain				–	–
Mean (N = 19)				**4.5**	**5.3**

Note: Since Greece, Portugal, and Spain did not become fully democratic until the mid-1970s, decade averages are reported only for the 1980s and 1990s.

and they favor both private enterprise and the maintenance of traditional moral values, which suggests quite a conservative impulse.

Although this mix of policy concerns allows agrarian parties to appeal to both the right and the left, their earlier positions in Scandinavian party systems suggested a quite close alignment with the social democrats. In both Norway and Sweden in the 1930s, for example, some of the most important welfare legislation was passed by social democratic governments supported by agrarian parties—a powerful if now old-fashioned version of a "red-green" alliance that helped lay the basis for the present advanced welfare states in these countries.

Nowadays, however, agrarian or center parties attempt to play the role of genuine center parties, bridging the gap between the social democrats and a fragmented bourgeois opposition. In this sense they can now be difficult to distinguish from more orthodox liberal parties (see above), especially when, as in Denmark, there is even a confusion in the names used by the parties (the name in English of the Danish Liberal party is the Social Liberals, whereas the agrarian/center party is known simply as the

Liberals). Indeed, the similarities among these groups are highlighted by the fact that the strongest agrarian parties have emerged in systems where liberalism is weak or nonexistent (the Scandinavian countries), whereas the strongest liberal parties tend to be found in countries where there is no agrarian presence (see also Steed and Humphreys).

In general, however, agrarian parties can be regarded as having drifted from the left toward the right over time. On the infrequent occasions when they win government office, they now tend to be the moderate allies of bourgeois coalition partners. (On the emergence of agrarian parties, see Elder and Gooderham; Urwin.)

The Extreme Right

The most striking development in the politics of the center right during recent decades has been the growth of parties of the extreme right. Indeed, whereas such parties were to be found only in Italy, France, and marginally in Germany in the 1950s, they now compete more or less seriously in Austria, Belgium, Denmark, France, Italy, Norway, and Switzerland. As yet, they have not begun to compete in Iceland, Ireland, Malta, or the United Kingdom, and they also are not present in Greece, Portugal, or Spain. Through small in European terms, they have tripled their vote in the last decades, rising from an average of just over 2 percent in the 1980s to more than 6 percent in the 1990s (Table 8-9), and outpolling the Greens.

The principal protagonists on the far right include the National Front in France, the National Alliance and the Northern League in Italy, National Action in Switzerland, the Freedom party in Austria, and the Flemish Block in Belgium. In addition, their ranks have been swelled by the Progress parties in Denmark and Norway. These parties began as tax-protest parties, but they have since settled down quite firmly on the far right of the political spectrum. Although the Republican Party and the German People's Union in Germany are not yet significantly relevant actors at the national level, a historical legacy and sporadic successes at the local level suggest that these might also not be discounted.

By and large, parties of the far right are small parties, although in Belgium and France they have proved sufficiently popular to have had a major impact on the direction and pattern of party competition at the national level, sometimes being in a position to deny a legislative majority to the parties of the center right. In early 2000 in Austria the far right FPÖ even managed to join government, serving as junior partner to the center-right People's Party. Moreover, in the wake of the collapse of the center in Italian politics, the former Italian Social Movement (MSI), which was reconstituted as the National Alliance, suddenly polled exceptionally well in the 1994 elections and later entered government with the Northern League and Forza Italia.

Extremely right-wing and often highly xenophobic, these parties are the heirs of the fascist and anti-system right-wing movements that rose to prominence in interwar Europe. They have sometimes taken up more contemporary issues, however, building a heterogeneous range of policy concerns that sometimes confounds easy understanding. The Swiss National Action, for example, now renamed the Swiss Democrats, places a high priority on environmental protection, an appeal that also figured highly in the

TABLE 8-9   MEAN ELECTORAL SUPPORT FOR EXTREME RIGHT PARTIES, 1950–2000

	1950s	1960s	1970s	1980s	1990s
Austria[*]	–	–	–	–	22.0
Belgium	–	–	–	1.5	9.7
Denmark	–	–	11.0	6.6	7.5
Finland	–	–	–	–	0.3
France	4.3	–	–	6.7	14.2
Germany	1.1	2.1	–	0.3	2.5
Iceland	–	–	–	–	–
Ireland	–	–	–	–	–
Italy	11.1	6.3	6.7	6.6	20.9
Luxembourg	–	–	–	1.2	1.2
Malta	–	–	–	–	–
Netherlands	–	–	–	0.6	1.8
Norway	–	–	3.5	7.1	10.8
Sweden	–	–	–	–	2.6
Switzerland	–	–	4.8	4.3	7.6
UK	–	–	–	–	–
Mean (N = 16)	**1.0**	**0.5**	**1.6**	**2.2**	**6.3**
Greece				–	–
Portugal				–	–
Spain				–	–
Mean (N = 19)				**1.8**	**5.3**

Note: Since Greece, Portugal, and Spain did not become fully democratic until the mid-1970s, decade averages are reported only for the 1980s and 1990s.
[*]The Austrian Freedom Party is classified as extreme right in the 1990s.

former MSI circles in Italy, as well as in other smaller parties on the extreme right (e.g., Ignazi, 1989; Mudde).

At their core, however, there are at least two appeals which characterize the new extreme right (Mudde; Betz; Taggart). First, almost without exception, they mobilize against immigration and against those policies which are seen to promote multiculturalism. These are nationalist and racist parties in the main, sometimes extremely so, and they have also served as a focus for the more strident opposition to European integration.

Second, as "outsider" parties, they mobilize against the political establishment and what they see as the self-serving character of the political class. In this they have been bolstered by the increased allegations of political corruption that are now current in many of the Western European polities (Heywood), as well as by the more generalized disillusion and indifference that tends to characterize many European voters. This latter protest is often self-sustaining. Because these parties are so extreme, there is a reluctance on the part of the established parties to consider them as suitable coalition allies. And as long as they remain excluded from processes of government formation, they

BOX 8-2

THE CENTER AND RIGHT

France

The 1980s and 1990s have witnessed increasing divisions and fluctuations within the French center and right. The traditional dominance of the Gaullists (RPR) was challenged by the growth in the more centrist liberal-Christian-conservative alliance of the UDF, led by Giscard d'Estaing. The problem for the Gaullists has been further compounded by the recent electoral successes of Jean Marie Le Pen's National Front, an extreme right-wing party that campaigns mainly on immigration issues. In 1981, for the first time in the history of the Fifth Republic, the center right lost the presidency to the socialist candidate, François Mitterrand. They lost again in 1988, but Jacques Chirac of the RPR regained the office in 1995. The center right has also been divided by conflicts over Europe, with an anti-European faction of the RPR winning significant support in the elections to the European Parliament in 1999.

Germany

The center right dominated governments in Germany during the 1980s and for much of the 1990s. In 1982, the small and quite conservative Liberal Party (FDP) withdrew from its thirteen-year coalition with the Social Democrats and joined forces with the Christian Democrats (CDU/CSU) under Helmut Kohl. This coalition survived in office until 1998, when it was displaced by an alliance of the SPD and the Greens. The CDU in particular suffered a loss of support because of popular discontent with the costs and difficulties that followed German unification. Although extreme-right parties have managed to win some electoral support in recent elections, they have not yet managed to break through the 5 percent electoral threshold.

Italy

The center right was the dominant political force in Italy throughout most of the postwar period, and the Christian Democrats (DC) played the dominant role in every government, being the party that provided the prime minister in all but a handful of the fifty postwar governments. Yet, although powerful, the DC remained dependent on the support of other small parties, including the two center parties, the Liberals and the Republicans, and in later years, the center-left Socialist party. In the wake of the corruption scandals and the collapse of the old party

system in the mid-1990s, the DC all but disappeared, and following the 1994 elections, a new government was formed by a right-wing alliance composed of the Northern League, the National Alliance (the successor to the neofascist MSI), and the newly formed conservative Forza Italia. Within less than a year, however, the alliance had fallen apart. The collapse of the DC led to the formation of a number of smaller successor parties, one of which, the Populari, joined forces with the former communists in Italy's first left-wing coalition government in 1996.

The Netherlands

The traditionally dominant Christian Democratic Appeal (CDA) actually is quite a young party, formally dating from 1980, when the Catholic People's Party (KVP) merged with two smaller Protestant parties (the ARP and the CHU). The CDA was in government continually until 1994, most often in coalition with the relatively conservative Liberal Party (VVD) and, after 1989, with the Labor Party (PvdA). In 1994, its support began to drop considerably, and it also fell from office for the first time. Compensating for the dramatic decline of the CDA on the center right has been the growth in support for the right-wing liberal party, the VVD. Since 1994, together with the smaller and more left-leaning liberal party, Democrats 66, the VVD has been part of the Labor-led "purple coalition." While parties of the extreme right have recently managed to win the occasional seat in parliament, their electoral support remains very limited.

Spain

Following the initial but short-lived success of the Union of the Democratic Center (UCD), the center right in Spain proved to be both weak and fragmented. More recently, the dominant force on the center right has been the conservative People's Party (PP), which emerged from a difficult history fraught with alliance and schism, and which brought together conservative, liberal, and Christian factions. In 1993, the PP recorded its first big success, polling almost 35 percent of the vote, less than 4 percent behind the PSOE, and in 1996 it overtook the PSOE to become the single biggest party. In 2000 it won an overall majority in parliament. Although extreme right-wing elements can be found in Spanish politics, such as the National Unity Movement, they have achieved no significant electoral support.

Sweden

The dominant party on the divided center right in Sweden is the relatively conservative Moderate Unity Party.

Like the other center-right parties in Sweden, it has rarely enjoyed government office, although it did join in government with two other center-right parties, the Center Party and the Liberal Party, from 1976 to 1978 and again from 1979 to 1981. In 1978–79 the Liberals alone remained as a minority government, and in 1981–82 they shared power with the Center Party, again as a minority. From 1991 to 1994 a new center-right coalition held office, this time incorporating the Christian Democrats, who recorded significant electoral gains in the 1990s. The 1990s also witnessed a sudden but very short-lived surge for the far-right New Democracy party.

United Kingdom

The center and the right are far from friendly toward each other in Britain. The Conservative Party held government from 1979 to 1997, for most of that time under the dynamic leadership of Margaret Thatcher. The result was that many supporters of the center parties found increasingly common ground with Labour in their opposition to Conservative policies. At the beginning of the 1980s it seemed that the center, in the form of the old Liberal Party and the newly formed Social Democratic Party, was going to become a major force in British politics. However, votes failed to be translated into parliamentary seats, given the electoral system, and the challenge fizzled out. The Social Democrats then disbanded their new party, and the majority of the members merged with the Liberals to form the new Liberal Democratic Party. Since losing office in the landslide election of 1997, the Conservatives have increasingly emphasized a Euroskeptic appeal. Meanwhile, the Liberals have begun to work closely with the new Labour government of Tony Blair.

can continue to assert a populist—and often popular—anti-establishment appeal. This is certainly a large part of the reason the Austrian Freedom party in particular has proved so successful in recent elections. Whether it will still be able to assert this appeal with any credibility now that it forms part of a coalition government remains open to question.

More generally, the relative success of these new parties can also be linked to the growth of Green and left-libertarian protest on the left of the political spectrum. Ignazi (1992), for example, has suggested that the rise of the extreme right in recent years may reflect the other side of the "new politics" divide, in which the growing support for new left and Green parties is now being counterbalanced by a shift toward a new right—the one side representing the interests of those who have found themselves benefiting from post-industrialism, the other representing the interests of those who are being left behind (see also Müller-Rommel, 1998). In both France and Austria, for example, it is striking to see the extent to which these new parties of the right have made inroads into some of the traditional working-class constituencies of the social democratic and communist left. (On the extreme right in general, see Betz; Betz and Immerfall; Mudde; Ignazi and Ysmal.)

OTHER PARTIES

Although most European countries are presented as being "nation-states," in which the boundaries of nation and state coincide, many incorporate important local minorities of distinct national, linguistic, and ethnic groups. These groups often are represented by parties that have their basis in local ethnic or regional identities, with demands that range from greater regional autonomy to full-fledged independence. These parties, while linked to one another by their strong regional or ethnic concerns, vary immensely in their other policy positions and in their general positioning on the left-right scale.

Regionalist parties can be found in one form or another in almost all Western European states. But despite what are often quite high levels of electoral support in local power bases, these parties are relevant at the national level in only a handful of countries. Belgium, given its deep ethnic and linguistic divisions, provides the most striking examples, including various Flemish (Dutch-speaking) and Walloon (French-speaking) regional parties. Indeed, given that even all the mainstream Belgian parties have separate Flemish and Walloon organizations, and given that the Walloon organizations do not compete for Flemish votes, and vice versa, it is now almost impossible to speak of a single Belgian party system at the electoral level.

Also of some significance are the Swedish People's Party, the political voice of the Swedish-speaking minority in Finland, and a regular participant in Finnish coalition governments; the extremely nationalist Sinn Fein Party, which offers political support to the Irish Republican Army and mobilizes both in the Irish Republic and, within the United Kingdom, in Northern Ireland; various Basque separatist parties in northern Spain, including Herri Batasuna, which supports the armed struggle of Basque paramilitary organizations; and, in the United Kingdom, the Scottish and Welsh nationalists, together with constitutional nationalists and unionists in Northern Ireland.

In general, the strongest support for these parties is to be found in Belgium, Spain, and the United Kingdom. Although these parties remain a tiny electoral minority within most of Western Europe, it is important to remember that these movements do command substantial support in their local areas. Roughly two Basque voters in three support Basque nationalist parties, for example. In Northern Ireland, virtually all of the vote is won by nationalist or regional (including unionist) parties. Indeed, none of the mainland British parties is even willing to nominate candidates for elections in the province, and when the British Conservative Party tested the waters in Northern Ireland in a by-election in 1990, it was utterly trounced by local parties. (On ethnic, nationalist, and regionalist parties in general, see Rokkan and Urwin; De Winter and Tursan.)

There are also additional parties that compete in European elections but that defy simple categorization in terms of party families. These include a number of small Danish parties, including the long-standing Justice Party. Pensioners' parties have recently emerged in Finland, Italy, Luxembourg, and the Netherlands. Europe's first "antigreen" party, the aptly named Automobile party, was founded in Switzerland in 1985. It is also important to note that independent candidates and loose, ill-defined alliances can from time to time be significant in a variety of countries—most notably in France, Ireland, and the United Kingdom, where electoral systems place few obstacles in the way of independent candidacies.

It is in Portugal and Spain, however, that "other" parties have been most important—at least in the early years of their democracies. As these new party systems emerged in the wake of the transition to democracy in the late 1970s, a number of temporary and shifting alliances appeared, often involving protagonists who shared little other than a desire to ensure the consolidation of democratic practices. These alliances were oriented toward particular domestic problems of democratic transition and consolidation, bearing little relationship to the interests and programs of parties in the established democracies. In Portugal, for example, a group known as the Democratic Alliance polled more than 48 percent of the vote in 1980 and then fell apart into various factions and units. Two elections later, in 1985, the Democratic Renewal Party was created; it won more than 18 percent of the vote before falling back to 5 percent in 1987. The number and size of these loose electoral alliances in the 1980s in Portugal and, to a lesser extent, in Spain, offered an ample indication of the difficulties involved in consolidating a new party system, a problem that has also proved very apparent in the newly emerging postcommunist party systems (see Chapter 15).

OVERVIEW: PARTY FAMILIES AND PARTY SYSTEMS

Despite the diversity to be found both between and within the nine main party families that we have identified, some clear patterns are also present. Thus, strong social democratic parties rarely coincide with strong communist parties; agrarian parties do not usually find themselves pitted against major liberal parties; conservatives and Christian democrats rarely meet head-on within the same national party system. Moreover, although the range of party families is extensive, a few key families lie at the heart of party politics in most countries. These are the social democrats, the liberals, the Christian democrats, and the conservatives, and among these the social democrats are by far the biggest single alternative.

What is also striking about these four families is their age. Most were well established by the turn of the century. Although it is now part of the conventional wisdom to refer to the transformation of Western European party systems, the deep historical roots of most of the key contestants in European party competition should not go unnoticed (we discuss persistence and change in contemporary European politics in the following chapter).

These general patterns of political division as they appeared in the 1990s are summarized in Table 8-10, which also presents the relative strength of party families in Greece, Portugal, and Spain. Taking all nineteen democracies together, we can easily see the key position of the leading party families. The socialists clearly emerge as the most powerful political family, polling an average of almost 32 percent of the vote. They are followed by the conservatives (17 percent), the Christian democrats (13 percent), and the liberals (11 percent). The next biggest families are the agrarian or center parties and the extreme right, both averaging more than 5 percent, followed by the communists with less than 5 percent, and the Greens with just over 4 percent. This picture is not substantially different when one looks only at the sixteen long-established democracies, although in this case the Greens do outpoll the communists.

But there is also a striking balance here. If we take the conservatives and Christian democrats together—especially since they rarely compete against one another—we can see that they polled almost 31 percent of the vote in 1990s in Western Europe as a whole. This figure is just marginally less than the share of the vote polled by the social democrats, the principal left alternative to both. Taking all of the families of the center and right together, we can account for just less than 51 percent of the vote, or just over 45 percent if we leave the far right to one side. Taking the four families of

TABLE 8-10   MEAN ELECTORAL SUPPORT FOR THE MAIN PARTY FAMILIES IN THE 1990s

	Communist	New left	Green	Social democrat	Agrarian/ center	Liberal	Christian	Conservative	Extreme right
Austria*	0.4	–	6.6	37.2	–	5.0	28.7	–	22.0
Belgium	0.2	–	10.9	23.8	–	22.6	23.1	–	9.7
Denmark	–	7.7	2.2	36.0	21.0	4.0	2.2	13.3	7.5
Finland	10.7	–	7.0	24.4	24.6	1.7	3.4	19.5	0.3
France[†]	12.6	–	8.4	24.4	–	–	–	39.7	14.2
Germany	4.0	–	6.4	36.9	–	8.0	40.1	–	2.5
Iceland[‡]	9.6	7.4	3.1	20.3	20.2	1.8	0.2	38.8	–
Ireland	–	3.2	2.1	14.9	–	4.7	26.3	39.2	–
Italy[§]	6.7	–	2.7	25.7	–	5.8	17.8	13.9	20.9
Luxembourg	2.8	–	9.3	24.8	–	20.7	30.3	–	1.2
Malta	–	–	1.5	48.1	–	–	–	50.5	–
Netherlands	–	2.4	5.6	26.5	–	34.6	23.3	–	1.8
Norway	–	8.4	0.1	36.0	12.3	4.1	10.8	15.7	10.8
Sweden	7.6	–	4.3	39.8	7.0	7.0	7.7	22.3	2.6
Switzerland	1.1	0.3	6.3	21.0	16.5	24.8	18.8	1.2	7.6
UK	–	–	0.3	38.9	–	17.3	–	36.3	–
Mean (N = 16)	**3.5**	**1.8**	**4.8**	**29.9**	**6.4**	**10.1**	**14.5**	**18.2**	**6.3**
Greece	9.5	–	0.6	43.8	–	–	–	44.0	–
Portugal	9.7	–	0.3	39.4	–	39.4	7.3	–	–
Spain	9.9	–	1.0	39.4	–	3.2	–	33.3	–
Mean (N = 19)	**4.5**	**1.5**	**4.1**	**31.6**	**5.3**	**10.8**	**12.6**	**16.7**	**5.3**

*The Freedom Party in the 1990s is classified as extreme right, with the only Austrian liberal party remaining being the Liberal Forum.

[†]Communist support includes "other extreme left"; Conservative support includes the UDF, an electoral coalition of conservative, liberal, and Christian forces.

[‡]Social democrats, new left, and former communists competed on a joint "Alliance" platform in 1999, and this has been included here under the social democrat heading.

[§]Italian figures from 1994 and 1996 refer only to the share of the vote for seats allocated under the PR quota; the former communist PDS is classified as a social democratic party, and Communist Refoundation as a communist party; the Christian democratic vote in the 1990s incorporates a variety of smaller parties in 1994 and 1996, including those allied with the center-right bloc as well as the left-oriented list headed by Romano Prodi in 1996.

the left together, on the other hand, we come to a total of just less than 42 percent. The center and right have the advantage overall, but the differences are not great.

In terms of governing, on the other hand, it is the left that appears to have the advantage—at least at the beginning of the new century. At the beginning of 2000, social democrats were the leading (or only) party in government and occupied the office of prime minister in eleven of the eighteen Western European democracies (non–prime ministerial Switzerland excluded), and were partners in a further two governments (Belgium and Switzerland). At the same time, however, even a cursory survey of these particular governments suggests that family differences now count for less than they used to. In Finland, for example, the broad-ranging coalition government includes social democrats, (former) communists, Greens, and conservatives! In Austria, Italy, and Switzerland, the coalitions comprise both social democrats and Christian democrats, while in the Netherlands the social democrats are allied with the very conservative Liberal party.

It should now be more than obvious that when we take the nineteen polities of Western Europe together, we face quite a complex picture. Nowhere is party politics so simply and clearly set as in the intriguing case of Malta, where a fully mobilized electorate (Hirczy) divides almost exactly evenly between a powerful Labor party, polling 48 percent of the vote in the 1990s, and an equally powerful conservative party, polling just over 50 percent in the 1990s. Beyond Malta, the picture is more varied. Precisely why it is more varied we shall see in the next chapter.

REFERENCES

Bartolini, Stefano: *The Class Cleavage,* Cambridge University Press, Cambridge, 2000.

Betz, Hans-Georg: *Radical Right-Wing Populism in Western Europe,* St. Martin's Press, New York.

Betz, Hans-Georg, and Stefan Immerfall (eds.): *The New Politics of the Right: Neo-Populist Parties and Movements in Established Democracies,* St. Martin's Press, New York, 1998.

Bull, Martin J., and Paul Heywood (eds.): *West European Communist Parties After the Revolutions of 1989,* Macmillan, Basingstoke, 1994.

Caciagli, Mario, et al.: *Christian Democracy in Europe,* Institut de Ciències Polítiques i Socials, Barcelona, 1992.

Cuperus, René, and Johannes Kandel: *European Social Democracy: Transformation in Progress,* Friedrich Ebert Stiftung/Wiardi Beckman Stichting, Amsterdam, 1998.

Delwit, Pascale, and Jean-Michel de Waele (eds.): *Les Partis Verts en Europe,* Editions Complexe, Brussels, 1999.

De Winter, Lieven, and Huri Tursan (eds.): *Regionalist Parties in Western Europe,* Routledge, London, 1998.

Elder, Neil, and R. Gooderham: "The Centre Parties of Norway and Sweden," *Government and Opposition,* vol. 13, no. 2, 1978, pp. 218–35.

Flora, Peter: "Introduction," in Peter Flora (ed.), *Growth to Limits: The West European Welfare States since World War II,* vol. 1: *Sweden, Norway, Finland, Denmark,* de Gruyter, Berlin, 1986, pp. v–xxxvi.

Gillespie, Richard, and William E. Paterson (eds.): *Rethinking Social Democracy in Western Europe,* Cass, London, 1993.

Girvin, Brian (ed.): *The Transformation of Contemporary Conservatism,* Sage, Beverly Hills, 1988.

Hanley, David (ed.): *The Christian Democratic Parties: A Comparative Perspective,* Pinter, London, 1994.

Heywood, Paul: "Political Corruption: Problems and Perspectives," *Political Studies,* vol. 45, no. 3, 1997, pp. 417–35.

Hirczy, Wolfgang: "Explaining Near-Universal Turnout: The Case of Malta," *European Journal of Political Research,* vol. 27, no. 2, 1995, pp. 255–72.

Hix, Simon, and Christopher Lord: *Political Parties in the European Union,* Macmillan, Basingstoke, 1997.

Ignazi, Piero: "La Cultura Politica del Movimento Sociale Italiano," *Rivista Italiana di Scienza Politica,* vol. 19, no. 3, 1989, pp. 431–66.

Ignazi, Piero: "The Silent Counter-Revolution: Hypotheses on the Emergence of Extreme-Right Parties in Europe," in Ignazi and Ysmal (eds.), 1992, pp. 3–34.

Ignazi, Piero, and Colette Ysmal (eds.): "Extreme Right-Wing Parties in Europe," Special issue of the *European Journal of Political Research,* vol. 22, no. 1, 1992.

Kalyvas, Stathis N.: *The Rise of Christian Democracy in Europe,* Cornell University Press, Ithaca, 1996.

Keman, Hans: "The Search for the Centre: Pivot Parties in West European Party Systems," *West European Politics,* vol. 17, no. 4, 1994, pp. 124–48.

Kersbergen, Kees van: *Social Capitalism,* Routledge, London, 1995.

Kirchheimer, Otto: "The Transformation of the West European Party Systems," in Joseph LaPalombara and Myron Weiner (eds.), *Political Parties and Political Development,* Princeton University Press, Princeton, 1966, pp. 177–200.

Kirchner, Emil J. (ed.): *Liberal Parties in Western Europe,* Cambridge University Press, Cambridge, England, 1988.

Kitschelt, Herbert P.: "Left-Libertarian Parties: Explaining Innovation in Competitive Party Systems," *World Politics,* vol. 40, no. 2, 1988, pp. 194–234.

Kitschelt, Herbert P.: *The Transformation of European Social Democracy,* Cambridge University Press, Cambridge, 1994.

Lijphart, Arend: *Democracy in Plural Societies,* Yale University Press, New Haven, 1977.

Luther, Richard, and Kris Deschouwer (eds.): *Party Elites in Divided Societies: Political Parties in Consociational Democracy,* Routledge, London, 1999.

Mair, Peter: "Evaluation des performances politiques des partis verts en Europe," in Delwit and de Waele, 1999, pp. 23–41, 1999a.

Mair, Peter: "New Political Parties in Long-Established Party Systems: How Successful Are They?", in Erik Beukel et al.(eds.), *Elites, Parties and Democracy: Festschrift for Mogens N. Pedersen,* Odense University Press, Odense, 1999b, pp. 207–24, 1999b.

Mair, Peter: "In the Aggregate: Mass Electoral Behaviour in Western Europe, 1950–2000," in Hans Keman (ed.), *Comparative Politics,* Sage, London, 2000, forthcoming.

Mair, Peter, and Cas Mudde: "The Party Family and Its Study," *Annual Review of Political Science,* vol. 1, 1998, pp. 211–29.

Michels, Robert: *Political Parties: A Sociological Study of the Oligarchical Tendencies of Modern Democracy,* The Free Press, New York, [1911], 1962.

Mudde, Cas: *The Ideology of the Extreme Right,* Manchester University Press, Manchester, 2000.

Müller-Rommel, Ferdinand (ed.): *New Politics in Western Europe: The Rise and Success of Green Parties,* Westview Press, Boulder, Colo., 1989.

Müller-Rommel, Ferdinand: "The New Challengers: Greens and Right-Wing Populist Parties in Western Europe," *European Review,* vol. 6, no. 2, 1998, pp. 191–202.

Padgett, Stephen, and William E. Paterson: *A History of Social Democracy in Postwar Europe,* Longman, London, 1991.

Paterson, William E., and Alastair H. Thomas (eds.): *Social Democratic Parties in Western Europe,* Croom Helm, London, 1977.

Rokkan, Stein, and Derek W. Urwin (eds.): *The Politics of Territorial Identity,* Sage, Beverly Hills, 1983.

Sassoon, Donald: *One Hundred Years of Socialism: the West European Left in the Twentieth Century,* Tauris, London, 1996.

Scharpf, Fritz: *Governing in Europe: Effective and Democratic?,* Oxford University Press, Oxford, 1999.

Steed, Michael, and Peter Humphreys: "Identifying Liberal Parties," in Kirchner (ed.), 1988.

Taggart, Paul: "New Populist Parties in Western Europe," *West European Politics,* vol. 18, no. 1, 1995, pp. 34–51.

Urwin, Derek W.: *From Ploughshare to Ballotbox: The Politics of Agrarian Defense in Europe,* Universitetsforlaget, Oslo, 1980.

Wilensky, Harold L.: "Leftism, Catholicism and Democratic Corporatism: The Role of Political Parties in Recent Welfare State Development," in Peter Flora and Arnold Heidenheimer (eds.), *The Development of Welfare States in Europe and America,* Transaction Books, London, 1981, pp. 345–82.

9

CLEAVAGE STRUCTURES AND ELECTORAL CHANGE

Enormous historical legacies underpin the appeals that political parties make to the citizens of the various European polities, and similar legacies help determine how citizens respond to those parties. Indeed, Seymour Martin Lipset and Stein Rokkan, in one of the most cogent and influential accounts of the development of modern Western European politics, begin their analysis with events that took place more than four centuries ago, at a time when the very idea of mass political parties, let alone that of mass democracy, was unheard of. Those events and subsequent developments over the succeeding centuries continue to provide the parameters of contemporary politics in Western Europe.

To take a very clear-cut example, we saw in the preceding chapter that one of the most important distinctions between European party systems concerns whether the major party of the center right is a Christian democratic or a conservative party. We also saw that when there is a major Christian party, it typically depends on a substantial Catholic vote. And the presence or absence of this Catholic vote derives, in turn, from a history of religious division that dates back to at least 1517, when Martin Luther pinned his ninety-five theses to the door of a church in Wittenberg, thus initiating the Protestant revolt against the church of Rome and marking the beginning of what we now know as the Reformation.

The ensuing clash between traditional Catholic Europe and reforming Protestant Europe constituted the first serious division in what had previously been a unifying Christian culture. What we now know as Western Europe was effectively fractured in two. We can mark the boundary between the two parts on a map of Europe by drawing a line between the Dutch city of Rotterdam in the northwest and the Italian city of Venice in the southeast. To the south and west of this line lie most of the countries that remained loyal to Rome and that remain predominantly Catholic today: France, Spain,

Belgium, Luxembourg, Italy, and Austria, as well as the southern part of the Netherlands and southern Germany. To the north and east of this line lies Protestant Europe: the Scandinavian countries in particular, as well as northern and eastern Germany and the northern part of the Netherlands. Britain was also to form part of the Protestant north, whereas Ireland remained mainly Catholic (see also Table 1-1).

In most but not all of the Catholic countries, as we have seen, the major party of the center right has been or still remains an essentially Catholic Christian Democratic party. In all of the Protestant countries, the major party of the center right is a conservative party. In the Netherlands, the continental fissure also split the polity, leading, as we have seen, to the early mobilization of both Catholic and Protestant Christian parties.

What is clear beyond any shadow of a doubt is that the religious history of the past four centuries still overhangs the development of party politics in contemporary Western Europe—as well as helping to set the long-standing division between west and east (Prodromou). Given this, it is hardly surprising that the broad outline of Western European party systems has proved so enduring.

In this chapter, therefore, we describe the traditional cleavage structures that have underpinned Western European politics and we explore how they might have changed in recent years. We also explore whether the changes which have occurred might be leading towards the realignment of party systems or towards dealignment. Later, in Chapter 15, we will also look at the potential basis for cleavage structures in post-communist Europe.

THE MEANING OF CLEAVAGE

Before we consider the actual substance of the divisions that underpin contemporary Western European politics, it is important to be clear about precisely what we mean by the notion of a cleavage, which implies much more than a mere division, more even than an outright conflict, between two sets of people. In the 1980s, for example, before the end of the Cold War, there was a sharp division in a number of countries between those who favored the continued deployment of nuclear missiles and those who favored nuclear disarmament. This division cut deep and often led to violent conflict, in the form of protests and street demonstrations. It was also pervasive, being an important item on the political agenda in countries as diverse as the United Kingdom, Italy, West Germany, and the Netherlands. But the nuclear missile issue, although acute, pervasive, divisive, and conflictual, did not constitute a fundamental cleavage in the sense identified by Lipset and Rokkan, for whom a cleavage has three quite specific connotations (Bartolini and Mair, pp. 212–49).

First, a cleavage involves a social division that separates people who can be distinguished from one another in terms of key social-structural characteristics such as occupation, status, religion, or ethnicity. Thus, a cleavage may separate workers from employers, or Catholics from Protestants, or, as in Belgium, those who speak French from those who speak Dutch. A cleavage cannot be defined at the political level alone (as with the division over nuclear disarmament, for example).

Second, the groups involved in the division must be conscious of their collective identity—as workers or employers, for example—and be willing to act on this basis.

This sense of collective identity is of crucial importance in the emergence and maintenance of cleavages. Without it, no "objective" social division will be transformed into a salient sociopolitical cleavage. For example, although the gender division between men and women remains one of the most significant social divisions in all western societies, it has never really generated the sense of collective gender identity that could turn gender into a salient basis for a major political division (Kaplan; Lovenduski). Despite widespread feminist mobilization, Iceland is still the only Western European country to have produced a distinct and important women's party.

Third, a cleavage must be expressed in organizational terms. This is typically achieved as a result of the activities of a trade union, a church, a political party, or some other organization that gives formal institutional expression to the interests of those on one side of the division. In Britain, for example, although an objective social reality of distinctive national groups has always existed in Scotland and Wales, and although there has also been a clear collective sense of national identity within these groups, Welsh and Scottish nationalist politics have only sporadically achieved organizational expression. Hence, the nationalist cleavage in Britain has often been dormant.

It is important to maintain an emphasis on each of the three components of a cleavage, because this helps us to understand how cleavages can persist or decay. A change in the cleavage structure of a society can occur as a result of changes in the social divisions that underpin cleavages, as a result of changes in the sense of collective identity that allows cleavages to be perceived by those involved, or as a result of changes in the organizational structure that gives political expression to cleavages. As we shall see, recent experiences in Western Europe suggest evidence of change in all three components.

THE TRADITIONAL CLEAVAGE STRUCTURES IN WESTERN EUROPE

In their seminal analysis of the political development of Western Europe, Lipset and Rokkan argued that the parameters that would go on to determine later political alignments resulted from the interaction of four major historic cleavages. The first of these was the cleavage that divided the dominant culture (in the center of the state and nation) from subject cultures (in the periphery). The second was the cleavage that divided church from state. The third was the cleavage dividing those involved in the primary economy (typically in the countryside) from those in the secondary economy (typically in the town). The fourth was the cleavage that divided employers from workers (Lipset and Rokkan, pp. 13–26, reprinted in shorter form in Mair, 1990, pp. 99–111; see also Rokkan, Chapter 3).

The Center-Periphery Cleavage

The first of the cleavages to which Lipset and Rokkan refer is that between the "subject culture" and the "dominant culture," now more commonly described as the cleavage between a country's sociopolitical "center" and its "periphery." This center-periphery cleavage derives from the era during which both the boundaries and the political authority of modern European states were being forged. When these modern states were being built, an inevitable clash emerged. On one side were those, typically at the center of the political system, who sought to standardize the laws, markets, and cultures that lay within state boundaries. On the other side were those, normally in the periphery of the new states, who sought to preserve their independence and autonomy.

The desire for autonomy was rooted in a variety of factors. In some cases linguistic or minority national groups resisted the encroachment of what they regarded as essentially foreign government. In other cases religious groups resisted the new codes, customs, and values imposed from the center. Either way, pockets of resistance to centralization persisted in many of the developing nation-states. In some cases this resistance led eventually to secession, as when southern Ireland left the United Kingdom. In some cases it led to the granting of substantial local autonomy within the largest state, as with the separate Dutch-speaking (Flemish) and French-speaking (Walloon) communities in Belgium. In some cases it ended with effective absorption, as with the Breton minority in northwest France. The most common outcome, however, of this conflict between nation builders and subject populations was a diffuse but persistent tension between the two. This created a center-periphery cleavage in many Western European countries that remains visible to this day. It manifests itself in patterns of political attitude and voting behavior, as well as in the persistence of small ethnic, linguistic, or other cultural minorities. The center-periphery cleavage is salient even among some of the "smaller" democracies in which the geographic, as opposed to the sociopolitical, distance between the center and the periphery is not very large.

The Church-State Cleavage

The process of state building also created a second cleavage, at once more sharply defined and more critical. This involved the conflict between state builders and the church, a conflict epitomized by the secular challenge posed by the French Revolution more than two hundred years ago. This was, and remains, a conflict about rights and privileges. It had to do with whether policies on crucial questions of public morality and, above all, education would be determined by the state or by the church.

The church-state cleavage developed in very different ways in Protestant and Catholic societies. The newly formed Protestant churches were essentially national churches that had largely become "agents of the state" (Lipset and Rokkan, p. 15). They thus had little incentive to challenge the policies of the state. Indeed, it was often only as a result of an alliance with the state that these churches had been able to establish themselves as legal entities. (This was not always the case. In the Netherlands, for example, the more fundamentalist Protestant adherents of the Dutch Reformed Church also opposed the secular ideas of the French Revolution in 1789, prompting the creation of the Anti-Revolutionary Party, a party that remained a significant independent electoral force until the end of the 1970s, when it merged with two other Christian parties into the CDA.)

In the case of the Catholic church, the potential for conflict with the state was enormous. First, the Catholic church saw itself as being "above" the state, owing its allegiance to a supranational religious organization based in the Vatican. Second, the

Catholic church persistently sought to insulate its adherents from secularizing tendencies, creating an autonomous cultural environment that proved resistant to state penetration. Thus, Catholics sought to maintain their own independent schools and rejected state provision of secular education. They also sought to ensure that state laws on issues of public morality, such as divorce and censorship, would reflect Catholic values. Conflict between church and state was thus almost inevitable. This was obviously true in those countries where Catholics constituted a substantial religious minority, as in the Netherlands and Germany. It was also true, however, in countries such as France and Italy. In both countries, although the population was nominally all Catholic, the French Revolution prompted a major secular impetus that found expression in the anticlericalism of the early Liberal and Radical parties. In the exceptional case of Ireland, where the vast majority of the population remained practicing Catholics, secularism failed to take root, and, until relatively recently, state policy actually enshrined the Catholic belief system.

Thus, the practical impact of the church-state cleavage was very unevenly distributed, proving a major source of political mobilization only in those countries with a substantial Catholic minority. In those countries, as we have seen, Christian democratic parties now constitute a powerful electoral force. In the Protestant north and east of Europe, on the other hand, an accommodation between church and state was reached without too much difficulty. No substantial religious cleavage emerged, and so room was left for the mobilization of alternative cleavages.

The Rural-Urban Cleavage

The third cleavage identified by Lipset and Rokkan concerns the conflict between the traditionally dominant rural interests and the new commercial and industrial classes of the cities. This conflict was already apparent in the medieval period but became particularly acute with the beginning of the industrial revolution. Although acute, however, the rural-urban cleavage was not always persistent. In Britain and Germany, in particular, but also in most of the rest of continental Western Europe, divisions between the two groups did not form an enduring partisan conflict. In Scandinavia, on the other hand, as well as in parts of Eastern Europe, urban interests proved much more dominant, and sustained rural opposition to the urban elites resulted in the creation of powerful agrarian parties that have persisted—in a modified form—into the beginning of the twenty-first century.

But although the rural-urban cleavage may now be largely dormant in relation to conflicts between traditional landed and urban interests, there is also a sense in which the cleavage may now be acquiring a new, "postindustrial" relevance. Two factors are involved here. First, like the United States, many European countries now face severe problems in balancing the interests of city and country, problems that often derive from the concentrations of urban poverty and racial tension in inner cities, the remedies for which are seen to demand increasing government intervention and expenditure. At the same time, many wealthier citizens flee inner cities in search of suburban and/or rural comforts, eroding the tax base of cities while continuing to take advantage of their services, and thus generating a new clash of interests between city and country. Second, at least within the countries of the European Union (see Chapter 5), a new and sometimes violent conflict has arisen as a result of the drive to free the movement of agricultural produce between countries while reducing subsidies to farmers. City folk clearly favor the cheaper food produced by both strategies, but farmers are increasingly discontented with the threatened slump in their standard of living.

Farmers now make up a very small proportion of the work force in most Western European countries, and so it is unlikely that they could generate and sustain major new agrarian political movements. But (in France, for example) there are often enough of them to tip the balance between the existing parties, and they can therefore pose a threat to their traditional representatives on the center right. They also form an important lobby group (see Chapter 14), and anyone who recalls the very bitter conflict between the United Kingdom and France over beef exports in the late 1990s will need no reminding of the political weight farmers can wield.

The Class Cleavage

By far the most important cleavage to emerge from the industrial revolution was the conflict between the owners of capital together with their allies among the established elites, on the one hand, and the newly emerging working class, on the other. The process of industrialization meant that throughout nineteenth-century Europe, workers became increasingly concentrated in an essentially urban factory system. This provided a social environment in which they began to develop organizations, both trade unions and political parties, that sought to improve their conditions of work and to enhance their life chances. The increasing concentration of production enabled the organizations of the emerging working class to compensate for their lack of economic resources by mobilizing large groups of workers in collective action.

However, although the class cleavage is present in all Western European countries, its organizational expression shows at least two contrasting patterns (Bartolini). In all countries during the industrial revolution, and in the majority of countries thereafter, the political demands of workers were expressed by a socialist party. In the wake of the Russian Revolution of 1917, as we have seen, more radical workers shifted toward a communist alternative, and in a small number of countries, support for such parties equaled and even surpassed support for the socialist parties. According to Lipset and Rokkan (pp. 21–23), much of the explanation for the relative success of communist parties lies in how bourgeois elites first responded to the workers' demands. Where they were more accommodating and pragmatic, as in Scandinavia and Britain, workers eschewed radical alternatives and became integrated into national politics. Where the bourgeois response was more repressive and the extension of political and social rights to the working class was resisted most adamantly—as in France, Germany, Italy, and Spain—workers adopted a more radical agenda, preparing the ground for the later acceptance of communist parties. Thus, even though class cleavage is characteristic of all the Western European democracies, the political expression of working-class interests has in some countries been divided between a socialist party and a communist party, though this political division between socialists and communists does not itself have the properties of a separate cleavage, as we have outlined them.

BOX 9-1

TRADITIONAL CLEAVAGE STRUCTURES

France

Three cross-cutting cleavages have been of major importance in postwar France: a class cleavage, separating the right from the left; a religious cleavage, separating the Gaullists, the National Front, and the Catholic groups within the UDF from the Socialists, the Communists, and the liberal and conservative elements within the UDF; and a center-periphery tension that pervades all parties and reflects the inevitable and persistent response to the domination of Paris. In recent years, a new divide has begun to open up between the extreme-right National Front and other parties of the left and center right. Although the broad left-right division has remained remarkably stable in France, the individual party and other organizations that mobilize on left and right have never been particularly strong.

Germany

For much of the postwar period, the class cleavage has been the dominant cleavage in Germany, cross-cut by a formerly much stronger church-state cleavage. Rural-urban tensions, which proved important in the nineteenth century, have now effectively disappeared. Since the re-unification of east and west in 1990, Germany has experienced the reemergence of a version of the center-periphery cleavage, with the interests of the relatively poorer east conflicting with those of the richer west. Germany was also seen as one of the first countries to reflect an important divide between the old and the new politics on the left, although it now seems that the new politics challenge is being increasingly absorbed within conventional left-right competition.

Italy

Much like France, postwar Italy also experienced the three separate but cross-cutting cleavages of class, religion, and center-periphery. Growing secularization undermined the salience of the religious divide and led Italy to adopt legislation permitting both divorce and abortion. In the 1990s, the dominant Christian Democrat party broke apart, and was replaced in part by the secular Forza Italia. The class cleavage has also waned, particularly since the split in the communist party and the formation of the more moderate Democratic Left. Center-periphery tensions, on the other hand, are acquiring a new and more powerful resonance. This is not only reflected in the growth of the Northern League, but also exacerbated by the persistent inequalities between the richer north and the poorer south.

The Netherlands

Cleavages of class and religion are also the dominant cleavages in Dutch politics, although increased secularization and a blurring of class boundaries have tended to erode the strongly "pillarized" subcultures on which the traditional cleavage structure in the Netherlands rested. Although there are few if any remaining center-periphery tensions in the Netherlands—the country is simply too small for these—local identities prove remarkably strong and continue to be sustained by the very uneven geographic distribution of the different religious groups.

Spain

Two cleavages clearly dominate Spanish politics: the class cleavage and the center-periphery cleavage. Although the strength of the Socialist Party might suggest that class is substantially more important, no other Western European country contains such a range or variety of regionalist and nationalist parties. At the same time, however, the class cleavage also operates within the regional party systems, with left-right divisions cutting across local solidarities. Despite a long tradition of church-state conflict, religion has had a surprisingly marginal impact on politics since the transition to democracy.

Sweden

The rural-urban cleavage has been particularly important in Swedish politics, as in Scandinavian politics more generally. Since the strongly rural Agrarian party changed its name to the Center party in 1957 and began to appeal to a wider section of the Swedish electorate, however, the relevance of this cleavage has clearly waned. A secondary religious cleavage is reflected in the small but growing electoral following of the Christian Democrats, a Protestant party that campaigns against permissiveness and alcohol consumption, but the dominant cleavage in Sweden is clearly the class cleavage.

United Kingdom

Britain has perhaps the simplest cleavage structure in Western Europe. Class was by far the dominant traditional cleavage, with the less significant religious and rural-urban divisions having waned in the nineteenth century. A small center-periphery cleavage does persist, however, reflecting the multinational character of the United Kingdom state and pitting Scottish, Welsh, and Irish nationalists against the English center. Most recently, at the end of 1999, hope finally began to emerge for a settlement to the bitter conflict resulting from the cleavage between nationalists and unionists in Northern Ireland.

The Interaction of Different Cleavages

History has left a complex mosaic of social and political divisions in Western Europe. The cleavage between workers and employers has found expression in each Western European country, but cleavages relating to center-periphery, rural-urban divisions, or church-state relations emerged in ways that were specific to particular countries. Thus, although the major similarities between Western European political systems derive from the class cleavage, the major differences between them can be explained to a large extent by the idiosyncratic development of other, often preindustrial, social cleavages.

One way to distinguish Western European countries is in terms of the interaction between the various cleavages that are present in the system. As the class cleavage emerged in Austria, for example, it overlapped the important church-state cleavage. This resulted in the Christian Democratic Party, which represents both "owners" and the church, and the Socialist Party, which represents both workers and anticlericals. The two key cleavages cut along the same lines.

In the United Kingdom, in contrast, a single social cleavage has come to dominate politics. Church-state tensions were largely resolved through the creation of a national church during the Reformation, and the rural-urban cleavage was resolved when the landed aristocracy and the emerging industrial capitalists made common cause during the nineteenth century. The most important center-periphery tensions largely evaporated in 1921, with the secession of southern Ireland from the United Kingdom, a radical break that also helped to solve lingering problems of church-state relations reflected in opposition between the overwhelmingly Catholic Ireland and largely Protestant Britain. Until the partial reemergence of Scottish and Welsh nationalism in the 1970s, therefore, nothing remained to interact with the class cleavage in Britain itself, and the result has been the emergence of two large political blocs that were distinguished from each other almost exclusively on the basis of their traditional class appeals.

In other cases, important cleavages cut across one another. In the Netherlands, as we have seen, the church-state cleavage first resulted in the creation of the three different forces, representing Catholics, Protestants, and anticlericals. When the class cleavage emerged, however, it cut across the church-state cleavage. This implied the formation of a new party, the Labor Party (PvdA), which opposed both the bourgeois religious parties and the bourgeois anticlerical Liberal Party. In France, too, the church-state cleavage cuts across the class cleavage. The Catholic Popular Republican Movement (MRP) opposed the secular socialists and the communists on the one hand and the secular bourgeois liberals and radicals on the other, finding reasonably common ground with the more religiously inclined conservative Gaullist movement. In terms of social and economic policy, however, the MRP looked left and found itself making common cause with the workers' parties against the liberals, radicals, and Gaullists.

Overall, therefore, what we might think of as the "cleavage structure" of a particular society has two distinct features. The first has to do with the particular cleavages that have survived historically as important lines of social and political division. The second has to do with the extent to which these important lines of division cut across one another. Thus, a religious cleavage and a class cleavage may both run along the same lines (if all workers are Catholic, for example, and all owners are Protestant), or may cut across one another (if whether or not someone is a Protestant or Catholic has no bearing on whether he or she is a worker). It is this pattern of interaction between cleavages that has underpinned the traditional structure of party competition in most Western European states.

THE PERSISTENCE OF CLEAVAGES AND THE FREEZING OF PARTY SYSTEMS

Following the path-breaking work of Lipset and Rokkan, it became common to speak of the "freezing" of Western European party systems at about the time of the 1920s as a result of the remarkable persistence of the cleavages that underpin party politics. Cleavages could persist for four main reasons. First, they could persist when the interests with which the cleavage was concerned remained relevant and the groups that were polarized retained a sense of collective identity. Second, major alternative political identities were likely to be mobilized only when substantial bodies of new votes were incorporated into mass politics, and no such large-scale incorporation has occurred since the granting of universal suffrage. Third, the rules of the game are such that they tended to favor the persistence of those parties that devised the rules in the first place. Fourth, parties could attempt to isolate their supporters from competitors and thereby "narrow" the electoral market. Let us look at these factors more closely.

Cleavages persist first because they concern people who are divided from one another on the basis of real and enduring issues. As long as workers continue to feel that they have a common interest that is distinct from the interest of employers, or farmers, for example, and as long as this remains relevant at the level of politics and government, the cleavage around which workers are aligned is likely to persist. Conversely, if the social distinctiveness of being a worker becomes blurred or if it is no longer seen to be relevant politically, the class cleavage might become dormant. (This is precisely the argument which is now cited to emphasize the changing character of contemporary Western European politics.)

Second, cleavages persist because European electorates are now fully mobilized (Lipset and Rokkan; Rokkan). This helps explain why the "freezing" of many European party systems is typically said to have occurred around the 1920s. Lipset and Rokkan argued that the political alignments forged when a group of voters is newly enfranchised prove strong and enduring. They thus emphasized the importance of the 1920s, the period when universal suffrage was generally introduced. This is not, of course, to suggest that the cleavages that were relevant in the 1920s will always remain salient. Rather, it implies that subsequent political realignments involve winning the support of voters who are already aligned in terms of a particular cleavage structure, a more difficult task than attracting new voters with no established alignments. Another way to think of this is to consider the period leading up to universal suffrage as having set the parties in motion. Thereafter, these selfsame parties will tend to hold on to their monopoly of representation.

The third explanation for the persistence of cleavages has to do with the laws that govern the conduct of elections. As we will see in Chapter 11, the first-past-the-post electoral system that operates in Britain (and the United States) is often said to favor the development of a two-party system. The proportional representation (PR) systems that operate in the majority of Western European states are more conducive to multi-party politics. It might be argued that by not penalizing minority parties, PR electoral systems help maintain minor cleavages. Conversely, first-past-the-post systems, by squeezing out small parties, may eliminate minor cleavages and allow the most salient cleavage to dominate the system as a whole.

As Lipset and Rokkan forcefully remind us, however, the rules of the game do not emerge out of thin air; rather, they are legislated by political parties. They will there-fore tend to protect established interests (Lipset and Rokkan, p. 30; see also Sartori, 1987). Similarly, in a separate analysis of electoral systems, Rokkan (pp. 147–68) argued that the adoption of PR *resulted from,* rather than *leading to,* multiparty politics. Proportional representation electoral systems were adopted in countries where there were distinct cultural or linguistic minorities. When the mass working class was enfranchised in countries where other cleavages were already present, the rules of the game were often modified to ensure the continued representation of the existing smaller parties. This, of course, facilitated the persistence of the cleavages along which they aligned.

A fourth factor that encourages the persistence of cleavages has to do with party organization (see Chapter 10). In a desire to insulate party supporters from the compet-ing appeals of their opponents, many European parties initially involved themselves in a host of social activities. They attempted to establish a presence in many different areas of their individual supporters' lives, organizing social clubs, welfare services, recreational facilities, and the like, thus offering adherents a range of services to sustain them "from the cradle to the grave." Although such behavior was mainly a characteristic of working-class socialist parties (the best account is in Roth), this process of "encapsulation" was also attempted by some of the Christian parties, notably the old Catholic People's party in the Netherlands (Bakvis) and the People's party in Austria (Diamant; see also Houska).

This process of integrating and encapsulating supporters thus characterized many of the new mass parties that challenged the most elitist traditional "cadre" parties in the era of popular enfranchisement (Duverger; Neumann; Katz and Mair). These mass par-ties thereby helped create and sustain specific political subcultures in which they hoped that party voters would express a more permanent sense of "belonging" rather than make a more instrumental, and changeable, policy-oriented voting decision. These mass parties attempted to corner the electoral market by building long-term voter at-tachments. To the extent that they succeeded, they stabilized cleavage structures and the party systems on which these were based.

The persistence of cleavages and party systems is underlined most clearly in Lipset and Rokkan's work, which has since become the benchmark for many subsequent analy-ses of Western European party systems. Writing from the perspective of the late 1960s, and noting that the last new cleavage that had emerged had been the class cleavage, solidified some forty years before, Lipset and Rokkan (p. 50) rounded off their analysis with the conclusion that "the party systems of the late 1960s reflect, with few but sig-nificant exceptions, the cleavage structures of the 1920s. . . . The party alternatives, and in remarkably many cases the party organizations, are older than the majorities of the national electorates." This was to become known as the "freezing hypothesis": the idea that party systems in Western Europe had "frozen" into place in the 1920s, with any subsequent changes proving either marginal or temporary (Mair, 2000b).

The freezing hypothesis offered an influential theoretical and historical explanation for the stability of European electoral behavior in the 1950s and 1960s. This was the period in which the potentially vulnerable new West German party system had begun to be stabilized by the success of Konrad Adenauer's Christian Democrats and by the abandonment of radical policies by the Social Democrats in 1959. It was the period in which the policies of the Labour Party in Britain had become almost indistinguishable from those of the centrist Conservative government in a process of convergence that became popularly known as "Butskellism," a neologism derived from the names of R. A. Butler, then Conservative treasury minister, and Hugh Gaitskell, then leader of the Labour Party. It was the period in which the polarized party system of Italy seemed set to stabilize under the center-right control of the Christian Democrats and in which the unstable French Fourth Republic had been replaced by the potentially more stable presidential system of the Fifth Republic. It was the period of unchanging social democratic hegemony in Scandinavia. In more general terms, it was a period described by some observers as one in which there was a "waning of opposition" (Kirchheimer, 1957, 1966) and an "end of ideology" (Bell).

This seemingly pervasive political consensus, together with the marked increase in mass prosperity that characterized Western Europe in the first postwar decades, clearly enhanced the prospects for democratic stability in the continent. It also seemed to be accounted for rather neatly by the processes of inertia suggested by Lipset and Rokkan. When Rose and Urwin set out to test the freezing hypothesis, they found that

> "whatever index of change is used . . . the picture is the same: the electoral strength of most parties in Western nations since the war has changed very little from election to election, from decade to decade, or within the lifespan of a generation . . . the first priority of social scientists concerned with the development of parties and party systems since 1945 is to explain the absence of change in a far from static period in political history" (Rose and Urwin, p. 295).

FROM PERSISTENCE TO CHANGE

Political scientists became convinced during the late 1960s that European party politics had settled down into a very stable pattern. However, while Lipset, Rokkan, and others were putting the finishing touches to their various analyses of persistence, the image of tranquillity began to be rudely shattered. Signs of change had actually been apparent in 1968, when student protests and violent street demonstrations raged throughout Western Europe and the United States. There were also signs of a challenge to the consensus within more mainstream politics, however.

The stability of Norwegian politics, for example, was fractured in the early 1970s as a referendum on Norway's entry into the then European Community reawakened the dormant center-periphery conflict and provoked major splits in the traditional parties. In the United Kingdom in 1974, nationalist parties from Scotland and Wales won a record share of the vote, while in Northern Ireland the political violence that had erupted in 1968 continued unabated, claiming almost five hundred lives in 1972 alone. In Belgium, the rise of Flemish and Walloon nationalist movements provoked major splits in all three traditional parties, and in the Netherlands, the major Catholic party and its two traditional Protestant opponents were forced into an electoral alliance in order to stave off their severe electoral losses. Meanwhile, in Italy in 1976, the Communist Party won its highest share ever of the vote and came within 5 percent of overtaking the ruling Christian Democrats. In France in 1974, a candidate supported by both the Socialists and the Communists came within 1 percent of finally snatching the presidency from the center right. In short, it now seemed to be the case that "a week is a long time in politics," as former British Labour leader Harold Wilson once observed. "Stability" was the catchword of the 1950s and the 1960s; "change" became the catchword of the 1970s.

Nowhere were the changes of the 1970s better illustrated than in Denmark, for a long time "one of the most dull countries to deal with for a student of voting behavior" (Pedersen, 1987). This image was utterly transformed by the election of December 1973. The number of parties winning representation in the Danish parliament (Folketing) suddenly doubled from five to ten. The combined vote share of the four parties that had traditionally dominated Danish politics—Social Democrats, Social Liberals, Liberals, and Conservatives—fell from 84 percent to just 58 percent. A new right-wing antitax party, the Progress Party, suddenly emerged as the second largest party. These dramatic changes occurred during a period of only twenty-seven months since the previous Danish election and are summarized in Table 9-1.

Table 9-1 shows big changes in the vote shares of the parties. The Progress Party gained almost 16 percent of the vote. Other gains were made by the Center Democrats (7.8), Communists (2.2), Christians (2.0), and Justice party (1.2). The Social Democrats lost 11.7 percent of the vote. Other losses were suffered by the Conservatives (-7.5), Liberals (-3.3), Social Liberals (-3.2), and Socialist People's party (-3.1). If we summarize these changes by reference to Pedersen's (1979, 1983) well-known index of aggregate electoral volatility, then we see that the level of aggregate (or total) electoral volatility in Denmark between 1971 and 1973 was 29.1 percent, a very high figure indeed.[1] During the 1960s, for example, volatility in Denmark averaged 8.7 percent. In the 1950s, it averaged just 5.5 percent (see Table 9-10 later in this chapter).

---

[1] Calculations of levels of aggregate volatility must be treated very carefully, however, as the figures may be artificially raised as a result of one-off party splits and mergers. In this Danish example, for instance, the Center Democrats were not a wholly new party but rather a split from the Social Democrats. A more realistic index of volatility would therefore measure change in 1973 by comparing the combined vote share of the divided parties (25.6% + 7.8% = 33.4%) with the previous vote share of the Social Democrats (37.3%) in order to produce a figure of 3.9% for the net party change and a figure of 21.2% for the election as a whole (see Bartolini and Mair, 1990, pp. 311–12). Subsequent calculations of levels of electoral volatility reported in this chapter follow this latter rule.

TABLE 9-1   DENMARK'S "EARTHQUAKE" ELECTION OF 1973

	1971 % Votes	N Seats	1973 % Votes	N Seats
Social Democrats	37.3	70	25.6	46
Conservatives	16.7	31	9.2	16
Liberals	15.6	30	12.3	22
Social Liberals	14.4	27	11.2	20
Socialist People's party	9.1	17	6.0	11
Christian People's party	2.0	–	4.0	7
Justice party	1.7	–	2.9	5
Left Socialists	1.6	–	1.5	–
Communists	1.4	–	3.6	6
Progress party	–	–	15.9	28
Center democrats	–	–	7.8	14
Others	0.2	–	–	–
Total	**100.0**	**175**	**100.0**	**175**

Source: Unless otherwise stated, the sources for all tables in Chapter 9 are as those indicated in Chapter 7, note 1.

The first comprehensive analysis of changing levels of electoral volatility in Western Europe came, appropriately enough, from a Danish researcher, Mogens Pedersen (1979, 1983), whose work had been partly stimulated by the extraordinary level of change in his own country. Pedersen documented the changes that were also evident in Norway and the Netherlands, and, to a lesser extent, in Switzerland, the United Kingdom, Finland, and Sweden. He concluded that there was a significant "unfreezing" of European party systems. A similar conclusion was reached by Maguire, who replicated and updated Rose and Urwin's analysis at the end of the 1970s. Just one decade later, using identical statistical measures to those of Rose and Urwin, Maguire found evidence of much greater instability and argued that Western European party systems "cannot now be regarded as inherently stable structures" (p. 92). Although the priority stated by Rose and Urwin at the end of the 1960s had been to explain stability, by the end of the 1970s, for Maguire, the priority had become to explain why many party systems seemed to be subject to sudden change (see also Crewe and Denver; Dalton et al.).

CHANGE IN EUROPEAN CLEAVAGE STRUCTURES
AND ELECTORAL BEHAVIOR

The argument that post-1970s party systems in Western Europe had entered a period of quite sudden and pervasive change is by now received wisdom, with much of this change being attributed to fall-out from the decline of traditional cleavages (e.g, Inglehart, 1984; Franklin et al.). Indeed, contrary to the conclusions reached by Lipset and Rokkan, most observers now prefer to speak of the *de*freezing of traditional political alignments and party systems.

As we have seen, and following from the way in which they can be defined, cleavages can be subject to erosion or change in three distinct ways. First, the strength of cleavages may be affected by changes in the social structure, such as the shifting or blurring of class and occupational boundaries, or changes in religious affiliation. Second, the strength of cleavages may be affected by changes in collective identities and behavior, as might occur when workers no longer felt a sense of collective identity as workers, or Catholics no longer acted in concert in support of particular political preferences. Third, the strength of cleavages may be affected by the organizational and ideological behavior of parties, such as follows from the downplaying by parties of their appeals to specific social or cultural constituencies.

For the purposes of this chapter, we now want to look briefly at the evidence of change in cleavage strength in the first two of these three factors. Later, in Chapters 10 and 13, we will be paying much closer attention to party organizational and programmatic change (see also Kirchheimer, 1966; Katz and Mair, 1995; Krouwel, 1999).

Changing Social Structure

In Western Europe in 1960, an average of some 34 percent of all employment in the three main sectors of the economy was within agriculture, with some 40 percent in manufacturing, and some 26 percent in the service sector. By 1995, these relative proportions had changed to 12, 31, and 56 percent respectively (calculated from Crouch, pp. 433, 439). Indeed, by 1997, the agricultural sector was contributing less than 4 percent to the average gross domestic product in Western Europe, as against more than 28 percent from industry, and 68 percent from services (Table 1-3). We hardly need reminding that changes such as these will have had profound implications for politics and political representation.

It is not only important here to recognize that the last half-century has seen a major sea-change in the way people earn their livings. This will already be all too familiar to even the most cursory observer. What is at least as important is to recognize that within the different sectors, technological changes and economic modernization have led to the erosion of many traditional social boundaries. As the population has become more educated and more prosperous, lifestyles have begun to converge, and previous lines of divisions between different sectors of the population have tended to become blurred. In 1960, for example, women constituted an average of just 31 percent of the Western European labor force; by 1990, this figure had risen to over 40 percent (Lane et al., p. 37). Yet another indicator of change can be seen in the decline in the numbers of people belonging to the traditional blue-collar working class. According to one recent set of figures, the proportion of manual workers in the labor force fell from an average of close to 50 percent in Western Europe in 1960 to just 40 percent in 1995, including a decline from almost 54 percent to 36 percent in the Netherlands, from 54 percent to 35 percent in Sweden, and from 61 percent to just 33 percent in the UK (Crouch, pp. 456–57). In other words, as Ambrosius and Hubbard (pp. 76, 78) put it, dating it to the 1960s in particular, postwar Western Europe had witnessed the crossing of a major "socio-historical watershed" (for a comprehensive recent overview, see Crouch).

Nor was it just the economic categories that were changing in the 1960s and after. Religious identities and practice were also subject to erosion as Western Europe in general drifted towards being a more secular society. One of the first comprehensive studies to tap into this change, the World Values survey of 1981–82, revealed some striking contrasts (Inglehart, 1990, p. 191). While some 83 percent of those surveyed in the oldest cohorts (aged 65 or more) in Western Europe proved willing to describe themselves as "a religious person," this was true of only 53 percent of those in the youngest cohorts (aged 15 to 24). Already by then, of course, religious practice had also fallen off considerably. In Italy in the twenty years between 1956 and 1976, for example, regular church attendance among Catholics had fallen from 69 percent to 37 percent (Amyot, p. 44). In West Germany in the late 1980s only 25 percent of the electorate regularly attended church—as against 40 percent in the 1950s. Among Catholics alone, regular church attendance had fallen from over 50 percent to just 30 percent in the same period (Dalton, 1990, p. 103). Even in Ireland, where Catholicism had long held a particularly powerful sway, figures indicated that weekly church attendance had fallen from 81 percent as recently as 1990, to just 67 percent four years later (Hardiman and Whelan, p. 72).

It is perhaps in the Netherlands that this widespread process of secularization has proved the most striking—and it is also in the Netherlands that it has been most tellingly documented (see Irwin and van Holsteyn). Religious identity and practice have always constituted a key component in Dutch culture, where the long-standing tolerance of religious differences had been fostered by the existence of quite a sharp—or "pillarized"—division between three main denominations: Catholic, Protestant, and Calvinist. In 1959 these three main denominations covered some 75 percent of the Dutch electorate (Table 9-2). Moreover, these religious affliations were more than simply nominal: in that same year, some 51 percent of the electorate regularly attended church services, including some 87 percent of Catholics and some 88 percent of Calvinists. The Netherlands in 1959 was clearly a religious country. Already by 1986, however, this picture had changed dramatically. Although nominal religious adherents still constituted a small majority of the electorate (some 52 percent), religious practice had declined substantially, with only 17 percent of the electorate still regularly attending

TABLE 9-2   DECLINE OF RELIGIOSITY IN THE NETHERLANDS

	1959			1986		
	% Adherents in electorate	% Regular church attenders among adherents	% Regular church attenders in electorate*	% Adherents in electorate	% Regular church attenders among adherents	% Regular church attenders in electorate*
Catholics	37	87	32	31	26	8
Dutch Reformed	28	36	10	15	33	5
Calvinist	10	88	9	6	65	4
Total	**75**	**n.a.**	**51**	**52**	**n.a.**	**17**

*Calculated on aggregate percentages.
Source: Irwin and van Holsteyn.

church, among whom were just 26 percent of Catholics. By 1986, in other words, the Netherlands had been effectively secularized.

Changing Voting Behavior

In addition to these dramatic changes in the social structure of many European countries, there is also evidence of a waning of the sense of identification between particular groups and political parties that formerly represented their interests. In other words, even among the diminished pool of workers or religious practitioners there is evidence to suggest that there has been a falling off in collective partisan preferences.

One of the clearest illustrations of this change comes from survey data reporting the broad ideological (left versus right) preferences of the traditional social classes. Should traditional cleavages still hold sway, then even though there might be fewer workers in contemporary societies, we might still expect that they would maintain a preference for left-wing parties. And even though there might be more middle-class voters in the electorate, these should nevertheless reflect a preference for parties of the center and right. A simple—if somewhat crude—method of detecting these differential class preferences is by means of the "Alford index," which measures the extent to which support for the left is greater among the working class than among the middle class (Alford). In Britain in 1951, for example (Heath et al., 1985, p. 30), the Alford index was a relatively high 41 percent, a figure that is calculated by subtracting the amount of Labour support among non-manual classes (22 percent) from that among manual workers (63 percent). The higher the value of the index, therefore, the more pronounced is class voting, in the sense that workers are more likely to be voting left, with other classes voting center and right.

As Table 9-3 shows, levels of class voting as measured by the Alford index have declined quite substantially across the postwar period. From an average of almost 37 percent prior to 1960, the index falls to just over 29 percent in the 1960s, to 24 percent in the 1970s, and to just 19 percent in the 1980s. In other words, levels of class voting as indicated by this simple measure have been cut by half. To be sure, this index is particularly crude, and there are problems with its comparability across countries, given different ways of categorizing social classes. In Sweden, for example, the decline in class voting during this same period proved much less pronounced when lower-status non-manual workers were classified as middle class rather than working class (Sainsbury, 1987). In Britain, the adoption of a seven-category classification ranging from the higher-status service class to the unskilled working class suggests that the decline in class voting has actually been much more muted than might appear from a simple two-category classification. In 1964, for example, the Conservatives enjoyed a lead over Labour of 47 percent among the higher service class; in 1992, the last election before the Labour landslide, this lead was 50 percent. Among the unskilled working class, Labour's lead over the Conservatives in 1964 was 40 percent; in 1992, Labour's lead was 32 percent. Among the skilled working class, on the other hand, Labour's lead had fallen from 45 percent to just 13 percent, while among the lower-status service class the Conservative lead had fallen from 41 percent to 29 percent. Indeed, by 1997, it was Labour that had the lead in this group (Evans et al., p. 90; see also Evans, 1999).

TABLE 9-3   THE DECLINE IN CLASS VOTING

	1945–60	1961–70	1971–80	1981–90
Austria	–	27.4	28.9	18.3
Belgium	–	25.4	17.9	16.4
Britain	37.3	38.3	24.3	23.4
Denmark	39.8	52.0	28.1	20.9
Finland	48.4	50.2	36.9	35.7
France	24.4	18.3	17.0	11.7
Germany	36.0	24.8	14.9	13.4
Ireland	–	14.1	8.7	7.3
Italy	26.6	14.5	17.8	13.1
Netherlands	14.0	14.7	21.8	15.5
Norway	52.5	32.0	33.8	20.5
Sweden	51.0	40.7	37.3	32.7
MEAN (N)	**36.7 (9)**	**29.4 (12)**	**24.0 (12)**	**19.1 (12)**

Note: Values are those of the Alford index, measuring the difference between the percentage of manual workers voting for left-wing political parties and the percentage of non-manual workers voting for these same parties; the higher the index, the stronger is class voting.
Source: Nieuwbeerta, p. 53.

Thus even though the core middle class and core working class might still tend to reflect traditional voting preferences, the leakage between intermediary classes, and the declining cohesiveness even within the core itself, suggest that voting behavior in general is now less predictable in such social-structural terms.

A similar pattern is obviously evident in the relationship between religion and partisan preferences, although the implications of this are less far-reaching, since religious divisions have been part of the political arena only in certain countries. We should not underestimate the importance of religion to traditional voting behavior, however, in that religious differences exert a much more pervasive impact than the presence of explicitly religious parties might indicate. Religious differences may have helped to determine party choice in situations where the parties concerned were all ostensibly secular.

In France, for example, the decline of the Catholic party (MRP) in the early 1960s did not imply the wholesale decline of religion as a force in voting behavior. According to a 1978 survey, for example, more than 50 percent of regular churchgoers supported parties of the center right, against just over 20 percent of those who never attended church. This contrast led to the conclusion that about 20 percent of the variation in partisan choice between supposedly "secular" parties was actually explained by patterns of church attendance (Lewis-Beck, pp. 438–39). Overall, survey results in the 1960s indicated that religious divisions, when they were salient, actually had a stronger impact on party choice than social class (Lijphart).

As the evidence of growing secularization would suggest, however, this picture is now quite different—even among that minority who still practice. In the Dutch case, for example, not only was the Catholic church larger and more actively involved in the daily lives of its adherents in the 1950s (see Bakvis), but the vast majority of practicing Catholics also supported the then Catholic People's party (KVP). Indeed, according to a 1956 survey, the KVP, which was then the second-largest party in the Netherlands, enjoyed the support of an astonishing 95 percent of practicing Catholics! By 1977, the last election that the KVP contested as an independent party, its support among practicing Catholics had fallen to 67 percent (Irwin and Holsteyn, p. 39). Since then, of course, the Dutch Catholics have not even had the option of voting for their own party, in that the KVP merged with its two Protestant rivals in 1980 to form the pan-Christian CDA.

The contraction of both the traditional working class and the churchgoing public in contemporary Western Europe, together with a declining political cohesion even among those who retain traditional social-structural identities, has inevitably undermined the potential role of traditional social cleavages. This has resulted in the erosion of two of the most important subcultures in modern Europe, creating conditions in which individual preferences may replace collective identification as a basis for party choice.

Other forces also appear to be pushing European electorates in this direction. Dalton (1988, pp. 18–24), for example, suggested that Europe in the 1980s was experiencing the emergence of a more politically sophisticated electorate. This new electorate was characterized by high levels of education and had access, particularly through television, to a huge amount of information about politics. Dalton argued that this led voters to relate to politics on an individual rather than a subcultural basis. This trend was also compounded by a shift toward the privatization of consumption—of housing, health care, education, car ownership, and so on—promoting individualistic and fragmented political responses that some suggested were likely to push patterns of partisan preference in Western Europe much closer to those in the United States.

More generally, following one of the most comprehensive attempts to address this problem from a comparative perspective, Mark Franklin and his colleagues concluded that there has been a fundamental weakening of the relationship between social structure, including both class and religion, and voting behavior. The main findings of these authors are summarized in Table 9-4 and show that whereas social structural variables (including class, religion, gender, region, trade union membership, church attendance, and so on) were able to explain an average of some 23 percent of the variance in left voting when the first mass surveys were undertaken in these countries, this figure had fallen to just 15 percent by the mid-1980s. Only in Italy did social structural factors explain a greater share of the variance in the more recent period. The decline was most pronounced in Denmark, where the figure fell from 23 percent to just 9 percent, and in Ireland, where it fell from 11 percent to less than 2 percent. The argument advanced by this study did not suggest, however, that these changes had been brought about by the emergence of new cleavages or even by a change in the traditional cleavage structures themselves. Rather, in much the same way Dalton had argued, they suggested that the traditional cleavages had simply become less relevant to partisanship as a result of what they defined as the growing "particularization," or individualization, of voting choice (Eijk et al.).

Let us try to knit these various strands together. A cleavage, it will be recalled, is sustained by three separate elements: a distinct social base, a sense of collective identity, and a clearly defined organizational expression. In its most extreme form, a cleavage is

TABLE 9-4   THE DECLINING IMPACT OF SOCIAL STRUCTURE ON LEFT VOTING, 1960s TO 1980s

	% Variance explained in earlier period (year)	% Variance explained in later period (year)	Difference (%)
Belgium	29.9 (1973)	13.1 (1984)	−16.8
Britain	20.6 (1964)	11.3 (1983)	−9.3
Denmark	23.0 (1971)	9.0 (1987)	−14.0
France	8.3 (1968)	7.7 (1981)	−0.6
Germany (West)	8.2 (1968)	7.8 (1986)	−0.4
Ireland	11.2 (1969)	1.6 (1987)	−9.6
Italy	24.4 (1968)	28.5 (1988)	+4.1
Netherlands	35.0 (1967)	20.0 (1986)	−15.0
Norway	42.0 (1969)	34.0 (1985)	−8.0
Sweden	29.0 (1964)	18.0 (1985)	−11.0
Mean	**23.2**	**15.1**	**−8.1**

Note: This table summarizes the amount of variance in electoral support for parties of the left that can be explained (at the individual level) by a combination of social-structural variables including class, religion, trade union membership, church attendance, and so on. The variables in the West German study include only trade union membership, occupation, and education.
   Source: Adapted from Franklin et al., pp. 92, 109, 154, 189, 229, 245, 266, and 313.

therefore sustained through the creation of distinctive subcultures within which voting is an expression of social identity rather than a reflection of instrumental choice. In short, voters belong. As Richard Rose once put it, at a time when this sense of belonging was particularly pronounced, "to speak of the majority of voters at a given election as choosing a party is nearly as misleading as speaking of a worshipper on a Sunday 'choosing' to go to an Anglican rather than a Baptist or a Catholic church" (Rose, p. 100).

There is now ample evidence to suggest that these traditional demarcation lines are being blurred in contemporary Western Europe. Class divisions are becoming less pronounced, and widespread secularization has reduced the impact of religious divisions. Even within what remains of the traditional social groups, behavior is tending to become less collective, and the traditional variations in political preference between groups are tending to wane. Finally, as we shall see in later chapters, in what seems to be a response to these changes, political parties have begun to loosen their bonds with specific groups of voters and have begun to appeal to the electorate at large. In short, the evidence suggests a consistent trend toward a much less structured electorate and toward the fragmentation and "particularization" of political preferences.

However, before going on to look at where these changes might be heading, we do need to introduce a couple of important caveats. First, although class and religion may now have less impact on voting behavior than was the case in the 1950s and 1960s, their impact has not disappeared entirely. In Britain, for example, as we have seen, the higher-status service class still continues to register a preference for the Conservatives, and both the skilled and the unskilled working class still tend to opt for Labour. In the increasingly secular Netherlands, a majority of the now-diminished set of religious practitioners still votes for the CDA.

Second, while class and religion may now offer fewer voting cues, other identities retain a powerful impact. The large majority of Basque voters in Spain still vote for Basque parties. An even larger majority of Catholics in Northern Ireland still vote for Irish nationalist parties. Almost all Swedish-speaking Finns—they are not very numerous—still support the Swedish People's party. In Belgium, virtually every Flemish voter supports a Flemish party, while virtually every French-speaking voter supports a Walloon party. Indeed, these sorts of identity might even be becoming more pronounced. In 1972—and again in 1994—the old center-periphery cleavage in Norway was suddenly reawakened by the prospect of Norwegian entry into the European Union. A similarly dormant north-south conflict was reawakened in Italy, thanks to the mobilization efforts of the Northern League. And while class politics may be waning in Britain, there is ample evidence to suggest that Scottish, Welsh, and—through the Conservatives' new appeals—even English nationalism is growing in importance.

CHANGE TOWARD WHAT?

In a wide-ranging early discussion of electoral change in advanced industrial democracies, Russell Dalton and his colleagues (Dalton et al.; Flanagan and Dalton) put forward two general models that seek both to explain the nature of the changes occurring in Western European politics and to predict their potential consequences. Their first explanation is based on the role of cleavages. It suggests that as traditional cleavages wane in importance and new cleavages emerge, voters go through a process of "realignment." Their second explanation concentrates on the declining role of political parties. It suggests that almost regardless of the new issues and concerns arising in postindustrial societies, political parties as such will become less and less relevant to the representation of interests. Citizens will turn increasingly toward interest groups and other social movements in order to press their demands, producing a widespread process of "dealignment." Although both explanations emphasize the declining political relevance of factors such as class and religion, the realignment thesis stresses the growth of postmaterialist—quality of life—concerns (Inglehart, 1984), whereas the dealignment thesis suggests that electorates will become ever more unstructured. We will now turn briefly to assessing each of these arguments.

Toward Realignment?

Despite Lipset and Rokkan's earlier emphasis on the "freezing" of party systems, it has been argued that the new issues that arise in postindustrial societies reflect the emergence of a wholly new cleavage, one that, like more traditional cleavages, is characterized by a social base, a collective identity, and an organizational expression (Alber). In the first place, this new politics is associated with a distinct social base within the new middle class, particularly among younger voters and those with a university education. Second, the values of the new politics are also distinctive, laying particular stress on environmental protection, feminism, and the extension of democratic and social rights—what

Inglehart (1990, 1997) refers to as "postmaterialism" or "postmodernism." Third, this new politics is increasingly and pervasively reflected in the emergence of a distinct organizational expression, most clearly represented in the rise of Green parties in most parts of Western Europe, as well as in the earlier "new left" parties, that are increasingly seen as part of the wider new politics constituency. It is in this sense that what has become known as postmaterialism can be seen to constitute a new cleavage, the mobilization of which implies a potential realignment of party politics (see also Inglehart, 1984).

There are two reasons to suggest that this scenario may be exaggerated, however. First, and most obviously, despite the evident resonance of some of the issues associated with the new politics, these parties remain an essentially marginal electoral force. As we saw in Chapter 8, Green parties polled an average of some 5 percent of the vote in Western Europe in the 1990s, as against less than 2 percent for the new left. These figures are not to be dismissed, and they also conceal quite a bit of variation across the different polities. Nonetheless, they fail to signify a dramatic sea-change in aggregate voting alignments.

The second reason it may be precipitate to speak of realignment is that despite their own initial claims, the appeals of parties associated with the new politics are not really so very different from those of more traditional parties. There is a sense in which they need not be seen to represent a new dimension in mass politics, cutting across the left and the right; rather, they can be regarded as a new variation within the left. During their initial formation, Green parties often deliberately avoided applying terms such as "left" or "right" to their own politics. As Jonathon Porritt, a leading member of the British Green Party, put it,

> "We profoundly disagree with the politics of the right and its underlying ideology of capitalism; we profoundly disagree with the politics of the left and its adherence, in varying degrees, to the ideology of communism. That leaves us little choice but to disagree, perhaps less profoundly, with the politics of the center and its ideological potpourri of socialized capitalism" (Porritt, 1984, p. 43).

More recently, however, the capacity to maintain this distinctive approach has been undermined. As Green parties have begun to win seats in local assemblies and national parliaments, they have been obliged to come to terms with mainstream politics, and like their long-established competitors, they find it difficult to stand aloof from day-to-day political bargaining. Even more important, in such situations the Green parties have become increasingly associated with other parties of the left.

Thus, in both Belgium and Germany, Green parties have forged local alliances with established left-wing parties, and both later joined coalition governments together with the social democrats. A similar process happened in France and Italy. In the Netherlands, the tiny Green Party actually joined with the Communist Party and two small new left parties to form an electoral cartel, the Green Left. Indeed, Porritt's own emphasis had changed by the late 1980s. No longer rejecting notions of left and right, he argued that a crucial issue was the extent to which "today's Green parties [should] identify themselves specifically as parties of the left" (Porritt, 1989, p. 8).

In sum, if postmaterialist concerns do signify a potential for change within Western European party systems, this is likely to be a limited realignment that changes some of the terms of reference of the left-wing divide while leaving its essential basis intact. Thus, one of the few studies to address these questions to the politics of gender, which has long been a major concern of postmaterialism, found that attitudes toward gender inequalities did not actually constitute part of any new cleavage but, rather, were strongly associated with and absorbed within the older "left-right" divide (Evans, 1993). This sort of change and adaptation is by no means novel. As we saw in Chapters 7 and 8, the terms of reference of the left-right divide have often been in flux, and it can even be argued that it is primarily because of this flux that the distinction itself has remained so relevant for so long, in that the terms "left" and "right" are capable of taking on new meanings for successive generations of voters and parties in European politics. As Smith puts it, "it is precisely the 'plasticity' of left and right which enables [parties] to combine coherence and flexibility, to absorb new issues and ward off challenges" (Smith, p. 159). Hence, adaptation could be seen on the left, when the initial monopoly of the social democratic parties was challenged fundamentally by the mobilization of communist parties in the wake of the Russian Revolution of 1917 and again by the new left parties of the late 1960s and 1970s. The Green challenge of the late 1980s and the 1990s, to the extent that this challenge is contained within the broad left, may simply be another step in a long and continuing process of adaptation.

On the right, despite overall long-term continuity, the political terms of reference have also changed continually, most recently through the quite dramatic decline of Christian democracy and the more limited growth of liberal parties. New politics at this end of the spectrum has also enjoyed greater success, with the rise of extreme right-wing parties in such countries as Austria, Belgium, Denmark, France, Italy, Norway, and Switzerland, and with their overall mean levels of support rising from less than 1 percent in the 1960s to more than 6 percent in the 1990s.

Taking left and right as a whole, however, the most remarkable feature of all is the sheer persistence across the postwar decades. To be sure, the individual countries have varied in terms of their own national records (see Chapter 8). In addition, as we have seen, there has also been some limited reshuffling at the European level both *within* the left and *within* the right. But for compelling evidence of overall persistence, we need look no further than the summaries in Tables 9-5 and 9-6, as derived from the various family tables in Chapter 8.

TABLE 9-5 THE PERSISTENCE OF THE LEFT, 1950–2000
(N countries = 16)

	1950s	1960s	1970s	1980s	1990s
Social Democrats	33.6	32.1	31.8	30.7	29.9
Communists	7.9	7.3	7.5	5.4	3.5
New Left	–	1.1	1.6	2.6	1.8
Greens	–	–	–	2.3	4.8
All Left	**41.5**	**40.5**	**40.9**	**41.0**	**40.0**

Note: Figures refer to mean aggregate electoral support per decade; see tables in Chapter 8.

TABLE 9-6   THE PERSISTENCE OF THE CENTER AND RIGHT, 1950–2000
(N countries = 16)

	1950s	1960s	1970s	1980s	1990s
Conservatives	17.7	19.1	18.2	19.5	18.2
Christian Democrats	20.7	20.1	19.1	18.3	14.5
Liberals	8.7	9.8	9.6	10.3	10.1
Agrarian/Center	6.6	6.9	6.7	5.4	6.4
Extreme Right	1.0	0.5	1.6	2.2	6.3
All Center & Right	**54.7**	**56.4**	**55.2**	**55.7**	**55.5**

Note: Figures refer to mean aggregate electoral support per decade; see tables in Chapter 8.

Table 9-5 summarizes changes in the mean levels of electoral support for the different families of the left across the past half-century. For the left as a whole, this has been almost invariant: 41.5 percent in the 1950s, as against 40.5 in the 1960s, 40.9 in the 1970s, 41 in the 1980s, and 40 in the 1990s. And this continuity has ensued despite what has virtually been a wholesale transformation in society, economy, and culture (Crouch). Of course, within the left, and among the individual families, variation can be seen. The social democrats have fallen by almost 4 percent across the last five decades, while the communists have fallen by more than 4 percent. This slack has been taken up by both the new left and the Greens, and in this sense the left as a whole appears to have become more modern—or postmodern—than was the case in the earlier postwar years. In other respects, however, this reshuffling has made little practical difference. Despite greater fragmentation, alliances between the different left parties are just as feasible now as during the 1950s and 1960s—perhaps even more so, since the more hard-line communists have been partially edged out by the more accommodating Greens and new left. The left may now be more varied than before. It is certainly not weaker.

Table 9-6 summarizes the parallel changes in the mean levels of support for the different families of the center and right. Here, too, it is the sheer persistence over time that is most striking. These families of the center and right together accounted for 54.7 percent of the European vote in the 1950s, rising to 56.4 percent in the 1960s, and then barely changing from 55.2 percent in the 1970s to 55.7 percent in the 1980s, and finally 55.5 percent in the 1990s. (Because of the presence of "other" parties—see Chapter 8 —the two sets of families do not sum up to exactly 100 percent.) In this group of families, however, reshuffling has been more pronounced. While the conservative and agrarian/center parties have remained more or less unchanged at the European level, Christian democratic parties have fallen by almost one-third. An increasingly secular Europe is clearly less hospitable to these latter parties. Part of this loss has been made up by liberal gains, but the bulk of it has been compensated for by the rise of the extreme right. This, in fact, is not only a worrying development in itself, but also serves to undermine the overall position of the right, in that many of these new extreme parties are not regarded as acceptable coalition allies. One result of their success might therefore be to weaken the strategic position of the right by pushing the parties of the center into closer alignment with the left.

In short, if realignment is taken to mean the replacement by an alternative divide of the fundamental division between the right and the left, then the evidence in favor of realignment is far from convincing. If it is taken to mean a significant shift in party fortunes *within* both the left and the right, on the other hand, then a limited realignment may well be taking place. Then again, this is not a particularly new phenomenon; we have seen reshuffling before.

If, on the other hand, as Ignazi suggests, there is something qualitatively different about the "new politics" of the left and of the Green parties, and if this is now being challenged by the mobilization of "new right" parties, then we could be witnessing the emergence of a new cleavage in European politics. It is clearly too soon to speak of such a radical departure, however, and it must be remembered that despite their success, the parties of the new right, like those of the new left and the Greens, still account for only a very small share of the popular votes. Taken together, electoral support for the extreme right, the Greens, and the new left totaled just less than 13 percent during the 1990s. Even when taken together, in other words, they were still being outpolled by the ailing Christian Democrats.

Toward Dealignment?

The argument that there has been a "dealignment" of Western European party systems rests on three types of evidence. First, a decline in the extent to which voters identify with political parties and prove willing to turn out to vote for them. Second, the emergence of new political parties and the growth in electoral support for such parties. Third, the general increase in levels of electoral volatility (for a more detailed discussion, see Mair, 2000a). As we shall see, evidence regarding all three factors suggests that the hold of traditional parties in Western Europe is indeed being undermined, but, as we shall also see, even this conclusion should not be overstated.

Party Identification and Voter Turnout   One of the clearest symptoms of the process of dealignment in Western Europe can be seen in the declining levels of party identification, the psychological attachment that is seen to tie individual voters to particular party alternatives. At first sight, the evidence of such decline seems quite convincing. Although comparing these kinds of data across different national systems is sometimes problematic (see later), the figures summarized in Table 9-7 clearly suggest an erosion in the sense of party attachment felt by individual voters. Thus while an average of some 35 percent of voters in the nine European countries covered by the Eurobarometer surveys felt themselves attached to their parties of preference in the 1970s, this had fallen to 28 percent in the 1980s, and then to 26 percent in the early 1990s. This trend was also confirmed by various national election studies that were regularly held in a small number of European countries, and that reported a decline in the proportion of those identifying "strongly" with their parties from 27 percent across six countries in the 1960s, to 25 percent in the 1970s, and, albeit among only four countries, to just 20 percent in the early 1990s (Schmitt and Holmberg, pp. 126, 128). These

TABLE 9-7   THE DECLINE OF PARTY IDENTIFICATION

	1970s % Party identifiers	1980s % Party identifiers	1990s (1990–92) % Party identifiers
Italy	46	38	30
France	37	19	17
Germany	31	32	27
Denmark	36	33	30
Netherlands	36	32	28
Britain	37	32	37
Luxembourg	28	23	20
Ireland	38	27	25
Belgium	28	20	21
Mean	**35**	**28**	**26**

Note: Data refer to the proportion of survey respondents reporting an attachment or a close attachment to a party.
Source: Eurobarometer, as derived from Schmitt and Holmberg, p. 126.

falls proved also reasonably consistent across countries, with the proportion of identifiers falling steadily in Italy, France, Denmark, the Netherlands, Luxembourg, and Ireland (Table 9-7), and with the proportion of strong identifiers surveyed by the more occasional national election studies falling steadily in Britain and Sweden. Although the sense of attachment to party had not been completely obliterated by the early 1990s, these figures suggest that it was clearly beginning to wane.

In practice, however, we must be careful not to read too much into such figures. In the first place, information on party identification is based on survey data, and the cross-national use of survey data is notoriously fraught with problems. Questions must be translated into different languages, and anyway the same questions tend to mean rather different things in different countries, often leading to contradictory results (Sinnott). In addition to these methodological problems, there have been conceptual problems in applying what is essentially a U.S. notion of party identification in the European context (Thomassen). For a range of institutional reasons (the voter registration process, the holding of primaries, the holding of separate presidential and parliamentary elections), U.S. voters may be able to distinguish between identifying with a party, on the one hand, and voting for that party, on the other. European voters, in contrast, often change their party identification at the same time that they change their vote. Thus, even though party identification can remain quite stable in the United States, notwithstanding some electoral volatility, it does not tend to have the same degree of independent stability in Europe.

A second reason to be cautious when interpreting data on the dealignment of party identification in Europe is that many European voters have tended to identify primarily with social groups and only indirectly with political parties. Sections of the Italian electorate, for example, may have identified with the Christian Democrats only to the extent that they also identified with the Catholic church, which was associated with the

DC. In the same way, sections of the British electorate may have identified with the Labour Party only to the extent that they had a working-class identification, which then translated into a sense of belonging to the Labour Party as the party of the working class. In other words, precisely because many European parties were traditionally cleavage-based, the primary loyalty of a voter may be to the class or social group that defines a cleavage rather than to the party that represents it.

Perhaps the most serious problem with applying the notion of party identification in the European context is that there is evidence that voters in more fragmented party systems can identify with more than one party at the same time (Eijk and Niemoeller). Voters on the left, for example, may identify with both a socialist party and a communist party, maintaining a stable sense of belonging to the left bloc as a whole, while shifting their preferences from one party to another according to the particular circumstances of a given election. Given the evidence we have seen of the aggregate persistence of left and right over time, as well as that of the reshuffling that has taken place within each of these blocs, this interpretation seems at least intuitively plausible.

Thus, despite the fact that the evidence of declining party identification in Western Europe seems quite strong, interpreting this evidence is quite difficult. Rather than showing that European party systems are becoming "dealigned," patterns in these data may be a product of applying an inappropriate concept to European multiparty parliamentary democracies.

The evidence is somewhat clearer with regard to trends in voting turnout. Participation levels in national elections in Western Europe have usually far exceeded the levels recorded in the United States, but ever since observers began debating the extent to which traditional parties and party systems were being transformed, there has been a general expectation that these high levels of electoral participation would begin to decline. As we shall see in Chapter 11, voting has actually been obligatory in a small number of European polities. Even beyond these polities, however, turnout has been very high. In Malta, for example, where turnout is not obligatory, virtually every able voter now turns out on election day. In Denmark, Germany, Iceland, Italy, Luxembourg, the Netherlands, Norway, and Sweden, turnout levels well in excess of 80 percent are not uncommon. It is really only in Switzerland, and then only since the 1970s (when women were first given the vote) that the exceptionally low level of turnout in national elections approximates that in the United States, although it should also be pointed out that even in other countries, levels of turnout in elections to the European Parliament (Chapter 5) now often fall below those recorded in the U.S.

Nor, perhaps surprisingly, was there much change in this pattern of high turnout at national elections—at least through to the 1980s and at least at the cross-national European level (Andeweg). In the 1950s, for example, turnout levels averaged 84 percent (Table 9-8). In the 1960s, the average was 85 percent, falling to just below 85 percent in the 1970s and to just under 83 percent in the 1980s. There was not much variation here.

In the 1990s, on the other hand, the picture began to look quite different. Among the sixteen long-established democracies, turnout averaged less than 79 percent in the 1990s, falling below the 80 percent mark for the first time in postwar history, and dropping by a full 4 percent with respect to the 1980s. More strikingly, all but five of these countries (Belgium, Denmark, Malta, Sweden, and the UK) recorded their own lowest

TABLE 9-8   MEAN LEVELS OF ELECTORAL PARTICIPATION, 1950–2000

	1950s	1960s	1970s	1980s	1990s
Austria	95.3	93.8	92.3	91.6	83.8
Belgium	93.1	91.3	92.9	93.9	92.5
Denmark	81.8	87.3	87.5	85.6	84.4
Finland*	76.5	85.0	81.1	78.7	70.8
France	80.0	76.6	82.3	71.9	68.9
Germany	86.8	87.1	90.9	87.1	79.7
Iceland	90.8	91.3	90.4	89.4	86.4
Ireland	74.3	74.2	76.5	72.9	67.2
Italy	93.6	92.9	92.6	89.0	85.5
Luxembourg	91.9	89.6	89.5	88.1	87.1
Malta	78.7	90.3	94.0	95.2	94.7
Netherlands[†]	95.4	95.0	83.5	83.5	76.0
Norway	78.8	82.8	81.6	83.1	77.1
Sweden	78.7	86.4	90.4	89.1	85.0
Switzerland[‡]	69.0	64.2	52.3	48.2	43.8
UK	79.1	76.6	75.1	74.1	75.4
Mean (N = 16)	**84.0**	**85.3**	**84.6**	**82.6**	**78.6**
Greece				83.5	81.6
Portugal				78.0	64.3
Spain				73.5	77.6
Mean (N = 19)				**81.9**	**78.0**

Note: Since Greece, Portugal, and Spain did not become fully democratic until the mid-1970s, decade averages are reported only for the 1980s and 1990s.

*From 1975 onwards, Finnish citizens residing abroad were given the right to vote, but the figures reported here refer only the turnout among Finnish residents.

[†]From 1971 onwards (that is, including all 1970s elections), it was no longer obligatory for Dutch voters to attend at the ballot box.

[‡]Women in Switzerland were given the vote in federal elections for the first time in 1971.

decade average in the 1990s, while, with the exception of the UK, all recorded a lower turnout in the 1990s than in the 1980s. This is a marked change, and it suggests that European voters may be becoming more disengaged from the conventional political process. Such evidence would clearly serve the dealignment thesis.

Support for New Political Parties   The second obvious symptom of partisan dealignment is a trend toward increasing electoral support for new political parties. As political responses to the parties have become more individualized and as the links between parties and voters have become more attenuated, the space for the creation of new parties has increased. In some cases, as with the environmental or Green parties, new parties reflect the emergence of new issues. In other cases, however, new parties are simply the result of splits in old parties. In Britain, Denmark, and the Netherlands

TABLE 9-9   MEAN AGGREGATE SUPPORT FOR NEW POLITICAL PARTIES, 1960–2000

	1960s	1970s	1980s	1990s
Austria	1.7	0.1	4.1	11.5
Belgium	2.8	11.4	12.9	23.7
Denmark	8.7	26.9	30.7	24.9
Finland	1.6	8.2	13.7	22.3
France	16.3	29.1	27.1	41.7
Germany	4.3	0.5	7.5	13.9
Iceland	2.4	4.7	19.3	21.6
Ireland	0.3	1.4	7.9	10.0
Italy*	9.5	3.3	7.1	66.8
Luxembourg	3.1	12.0	11.5	22.4
Malta	13.1	0	0.1	1.5
Netherlands	2.3	26.6	44.5	45.9
Norway	3.9	13.6	15.1	19.7
Sweden	1.1	1.6	4.5	14.5
Switzerland	0.4	5.3	12.2	14.9
UK	0	0.8	11.6	2.3
Mean (N = 16)	**4.4**	**9.1**	**14.4**	**22.4**

Note: New parties are here defined as those which first began to contest elections no earlier than 1960.
*Calculated on basis of PR votes only in elections of 1994 and 1996.

in the 1970s and 1980s, for example, key figures abandoned mainstream socialist parties and formed new parties of the center left. In Belgium, the politicization of the linguistic divide in the 1970s led not only to the creation of new parties but also to splits in each of the main traditional parties.

In fact, as can be seen from Table 9-9, aggregate electoral support for new parties has risen steadily over the past forty years. The operational definition of new parties that we are using here is a very simple one: recalling that Lipset and Rokkan spoke in the late 1960s of the fact that the many of the parties then contesting elections "were older than the national electorates," we can make a very simple distinction between so-called "old" parties, being those that first began contesting elections prior to the 1960s; and "new" parties, being those that first began to contest elections from 1960 onwards. Indeed, these latter have proved thick on the ground: of the almost three hundred separate parties that have contested at least one election in the long-established democracies since 1960, some 60 percent have been formed since that date. To put it another way, only some 40 percent of parties contesting elections during these past four decades were formed prior to 1960 (Mair, 1999).

Given these large numbers, and given that the later the period the more likely it is that the numbers will have accumulated, it is not then very surprising to see their aggregate support building up. During the 1960s, when only some thirty of these new parties had already been formed, their total vote averaged just over 4 percent (Table 9-9). This grew in the 1970s, to just over 9 percent, and then to more than 14 percent in the 1980s. In the 1990s, the new-party share totaled more than 22 percent, thereby accounting for almost one in four votes then being cast in national elections in Europe.

In some of the countries involved, this growth has clearly been substantially above this average. In the newly made Italian party system, where new parties accounted for the vast majority of votes cast in 1996, their average share across the three elections of the 1990s was a massive 67 percent. In the Netherlands, where the CDA also counts as a new party, their share averaged almost 46 percent. In France, where party longevity is the exception, they averaged almost 42 percent. Indeed, it is really only Malta and the United Kingdom that have proved significantly inhospitable to new parties, notwithstanding the flurry of success enjoyed by the SPD in Westminster elections in the 1980s.

Taking these figures at face value, we might be inclined to read them as signifying a fundamental transformation in party alignments in Western Europe. The fact that the old parties formed before the 1960s have accounted for fewer than half those contesting elections over the past forty years, and the fact that the new parties formed since 1960 pulled in close to a quarter of the vote in Western Europe during the 1990s, must surely signal a major change.

But what sort of change is this? As we have already seen (Tables 9-5 and 9-6), most of the traditional party families are managing to hold their own in aggregate electoral terms. Indeed, the only old family that has really been shaken has been the Christian Democrats. We have also seen that the really new families—the new left and Greens, on the one hand, and the new extreme right, on the other—have not proved great vote winners to date, at least not across Western Europe as a whole. Moreover, some of the most successful "new" politics parties of the extreme right—including the Freedom party in Austria and the National Alliance (ex-MSI) in Italy—are themselves quite old parties, albeit now dressed in new ideological costumes.

What this therefore seems to suggest is that many of the votes going to new parties are actually going to new organizational alternatives that operate within recognizable— if not wholly traditional—parameters. This is not exactly the old politics: after all, newly-formed organizations are unlikely to present themselves as wholly belonging to the past. But nor is it necessarily the new politics. At best, it may be old politics in a new form. Hence it is not to surprising to find that the most successful of these new formations over the past forty years include parties such as the Dutch CDA, Forza Italia and the Democratic Left in Italy, the UDF in France, and the Left-Wing Alliance in Finland (Mair, 1999). To be sure, these are all new parties. But their politics will be familiar to even the most old-fashioned observer of Western European politics.

Here again, then, we seem to see evidence that speaks more of dealignment than of realignment. Loyalties to traditional parties are certainly ebbing. Otherwise, even these familiar-sounding new parties would never have enjoyed any real success. But while voters may well be willing to consider new alternatives, especially in the 1990s, and in this sense may be regarded as increasingly dealigned, they seem unwilling to transfer across to a wholly new politics.

Electoral Volatility   The third collection of evidence in favor of the dealignment thesis involves increased aggregate electoral volatility (Pedersen, 1979, 1983) which,

CHANGE TOWARD WHAT? **263**

precisely because it measure levels of flux from one election to the next, offers a very useful summary indicator of short-term changes in party support.

When the trend towards increased electoral volatility was first noted in certain countries in the 1970s, it was not in fact then seen to apply to Western Europe as a whole. Pedersen's own evidence from the 1970s, for example, pointed to an actual decline in volatility in France and West Germany and, albeit less marked, in Italy. In each of these countries, the party system was restructured in the early postwar years, following the reestablishment of the democratic process, and each party system was soon to be stabilized by a strong center-right party. In many other Western European countries, however, the 1970s did witness an erosion of the "steady-state" politics of the 1950s and 1960s, and since then the expectation has been that this sense of flux would eventually pass on to even the more stable polities.

Even by the 1980s, however, these expectations had not been borne out. Indeed, in Western Europe as a whole (Table 9-10), the 1980s witnessed a marginal decline in

TABLE 9-10   MEAN AGGREGATE ELECTORAL VOLATILITY, 1950–2000

	1950s	1960s	1970s	1980s	1990s
Austria	4.1	3.3	2.7	5.5	9.4
Belgium	7.6	10.2	5.3	10.0	10.8
Denmark	5.5	8.7	15.5	9.7	12.4
Finland	4.4	7.0	7.9	8.7	11.0
France	22.3	11.5	8.8	13.4	15.4
Germany	15.2	8.4	5.0	6.3	9.0
Iceland	9.2	4.3	12.2	11.6	13.7
Ireland	10.3	7.0	5.7	8.1	11.7
Italy*	9.7	8.2	9.9	8.6	22.9
Luxembourg	10.8	8.8	12.5	14.8	6.2
Malta	9.2	14.4	4.6	1.4	3.6
Netherlands	5.1	7.9	12.3	8.3	19.1
Norway	3.4	5.3	15.3	10.7	15.9
Sweden	4.8	4.0	6.3	7.6	13.8
Switzerland	2.5	3.5	6.0	6.4	8.0
UK	4.3	5.2	8.3	3.3	9.3
Mean (N = 16)	**8.0**	**7.4**	**8.6**	**8.4**	**12.0**
Greece				11.3	5.5
Portugal				15.0	11.9
Spain				14.2	8.8
Mean (N = 19)				**9.2**	**11.5**

Note: The values refer to levels of aggregate electoral volatility, measured as the sum of the percentage vote gains of all the winning parties (or the sum of the percentage vote losses of all the losing parties) from one election to the next. See Pedersen (1979, 1983).

*Calculated on basis of PR votes only in 1994 and 1996.

BOX 9-2

TRENDS IN ELECTORAL VOLATILITY

France

Largely owing to its relatively unstructured party system and to shifting patterns of alliance and schism between the different political leaders, France has always had one of the most volatile electorates in Western Europe. As the party system began to consolidate under the Fifth Republic, however, volatility tended to decline, falling below 10 percent for the first time in the 1970s. In the 1980s, volatility began to increase once again, and the elections of the 1990s proved more volatile than any since the 1950s.

Germany

Germany was traditionally characterized by an extremely volatile electorate, particularly during the interwar and early postwar years. During the 1960s, however, as the West German party system became consolidated, volatility tended to decline. Although the emergence of the Greens led to a more unsettled situation in the 1980s, the level of volatility has nevertheless not grown substantially. The highest level recorded in recent elections was a net shift of just over 11 percent in the very exceptional unification elections of 1990. Since the 1950s, however, mean volatility per decade has always remained below 10 percent.

Italy

Despite immensely unstable governments, Italy was for a long time characterized by a surprisingly stable pattern of electoral alignments, with volatility levels remaining below 10 percent in each of the decades from the 1950s to the 1980s. In the 1990s, on the other hand, with the complete remaking of the party system, volatility has risen to record levels. In 1994, for example, the first election of the so-called "Second Republic," volatility exceeded 36 percent, a level that had scarcely been seen in Western Europe in the twentieth century. Even in 1996, when things had begun to settle down, albeit perhaps only temporarily, volatility still exceeded 18 percent, more than double the postwar Western European average.

The Netherlands

The Netherlands, along with Denmark and Norway, was one of the classic examples of increasing electoral volatility during the late 1960s and the 1970s. Thereafter volatility tended to decline, and the party system stabi-

lized around the new patterns that began to emerge in the 1960s. In the election of 1989, for example, the net shift in votes was a little over 5 percent, less than half the levels recorded in the early 1970s. This all changed again in the 1990s, however, and volatility reached a record high of almost 22 percent in the election of 1994. This big jump in volatility reflected the sharp decline in support for both the Christian Democrats and Labor. Four years later, in 1998, things had still not settled down, with volatility reaching almost 17 percent, well above the levels recorded in the 1950s, 1960s, 1970s, and 1980s.

Spain

While Spain, like many other new party systems, appeared to have a relatively unstable electorate during its first elections, the high mean levels of volatility nevertheless disguise a pattern that is actually quite difficult to characterize. Although mean volatility in the 1980s was over 14 percent, almost double that in the same period in the "older" party systems of Western Europe, this high figure derives entirely from the very exceptional election of 1982, when support for the Union of the Democratic Center fell from 35 percent to less than 7 percent, and when the vote for the Socialist party rose from 31 percent to 47 percent. Overall volatility in that election reached a remarkably high level of over 36 percent, the same as that recorded in Italy in 1994. In the previous and subsequent elections, however, average volatility was much lower, and in the 1990s Spain's position relative to the older Western European systems had been reversed: it recorded a level of volatility which was only some two-thirds of that in the long-established democracies.

Sweden

Having gone through a prolonged period of electoral stability, Sweden, like its Scandinavian neighbors, experienced an upsurge in electoral volatility in the late 1960s and the 1970s. In Sweden, however, the change was not as marked as those that occurred in Denmark and Norway, and prior to the 1990s the net shift of votes never exceeded 10 percent. Volatility levels have proved consistently high during the 1990s, however, averaging out at close to 14 percent; this is well above the Danish figure, although still below that of Norway. For Sweden, this marks an important change in traditional patterns.

United Kingdom

Notwithstanding the temporary and radical electoral flux created by the growth of the third-party vote in the 1970s, as well as the threat posed by the alliance parties in the

1980s, electoral volatility has always proved relatively muted in postwar British elections. The most volatile postwar election was that in February 1974, when both the Scottish and Welsh Nationalists, as well as the Liberals, experienced a major surge in their fortunes, and when the overall electoral support won by the Conservatives and Labour fell to a postwar low. The level of volatility in that election was almost 15 percent. In 1997, with the Labour landslide, volatility rose sharply again to more than 13 percent.

volatility, a decline that was particularly marked in Denmark, the Netherlands, Norway, and the United Kingdom. Moreover, what could also be seen by the 1980s was that the level of aggregate vote shifts between the main class blocs on the left and right was much lower than the volatility within these class blocs (Bartolini and Mair, 1990; Mair, 1997, pp. 76–90). In other words, at least as far as the class cleavage is concerned, a very great proportion of electoral instability proved to be the result of switching votes between friends rather than between enemies, a trend that is also compatible with the notion that European voters may identify with more than one party at the same time.

But although this bloc volatility continues to remain relatively low, it is striking to note that elections in the 1990s now reveal that aggregate volatility as a whole has increased quite suddenly and quite markedly (Table 9-10), averaging some 12 percent among the long-established European democracies. The 1990s marked the first postwar decade in which the mean level of volatility across Western Europe as a whole pushed above 10 percent, marking an increase of almost half as much again relative to the 1980s. The growth in volatility in the 1990s has also proved remarkably consistent, with almost three-quarters of the individual countries registering their own peak postwar levels. The exceptions to this pattern include Denmark, where the really big electoral earthquakes hit in the 1970s, as well as France and Germany, which experienced considerable volatility in the wake of immediate postwar reconstruction. Luxembourg and Malta also peaked during earlier decades. Remarkably, however, it was only in Luxembourg that volatility in the 1990s proved lower than that in the 1980s. Here again, then, as we have seen with regard to levels of turnout and support for new parties, the 1990s seem quite different. Here again, we may be witnessing the first real signs of dealignment.

EVALUATING CHANGE AND STABILITY

Studies of Western European politics that set out to chart and explain change often conclude with the observation that change is neither so extensive nor so pervasive as was first imagined. "Even if change is widespread," concludes one account, "it is important not to overstate its extent. Although few party systems have been as constant as they once appeared to be, all exhibit substantial elements of continuity" (Wolinetz, p. 296). Taking all the evidence presented in this chapter together, we can see that contemporary Western European politics is characterized at least as much by continuity as by change.

To be sure, the image of transformation is seductive; but the shock of the new can blind us to the persistence of the old.

The continuities can be easily summarized. The overall balance between the broad left bloc and the broad center-right bloc is remarkably constant. There is also a very low level of aggregate vote redistribution across the class-cleavage boundary. The principal political protagonists, most notably the social democrats and the conservatives, have proved very resilient. New parties, despite their pervasiveness and their electoral success, do not seem to have challenged the core of traditional alignments.

The changes are also evident, particularly in the 1990s. There is a growing individualization of political preferences and a weakening of collective identities. There is a decline in the distinctiveness of the social bases of party support. There have been changes in the terms of reference of the division between the left and the right. The balance of support for parties within each bloc has changed in certain cases. And a "postmaterialist" or "new politics" dimension has emerged, albeit without substantial electoral weight, in many of the more established Western European democracies. Above all, one of the most important party families, the Christian Democrats, has experienced a major decline in its aggregate electoral support. In addition, and perhaps most important of all, not only are voters proving less willing to participate, but evidence of increased volatility suggests that even those who do turn out to vote are now more willing to shift their individual party preferences.

The overall picture, then, seems to be one of "peripheral" change, with the "core" of the party systems remaining intact (Smith), and with the voters who continue to opt for these parties proving increasingly disengaged. European voters are less tied to parties than before and have shown themselves more willing to shift their preferences from one party to another. But they do so cautiously. On the left, voters may shift from a communist party to a socialist party, or from a socialist party to a new left or Green party, but they tend to remain on the left. Votes on the right may shift from a Christian party to a secular party, or from a liberal party to a more conservative party, but they tend in like manner to stay on the right. Ties to individual parties may have weakened, but ties to the broader identities of the left and the right appear to have been maintained. In this important sense, the notion that European party systems are "frozen" should not be dismissed too easily.

It must be emphasized, moreover, that the long-term stabilization of Western European party systems is not simply a function of the ties that bind distinct social groups (Catholics, workers, farmers, and so on) to parties or to blocs of parties. To be sure, social structure has certainly proved to be an important stabilizing element, especially in systems with strong social cleavages or subcultures, such as Italy, the Netherlands, and Sweden. But if social structure were the only freezing agent, then we would already have witnessed much greater change in electoral alignments in the 1970s and 1980s than we actually have. The fact is that many of the old traditional party families in Europe remain alive and kicking despite the widespread weakening of religious and class identities, and despite the long-term process of individualization. More specifically, if social structure were all that mattered, then we would have witnessed much more continuous change in a party system such as that in Ireland, where partisanship has long been characterized by a remarkable absence of social roots (Marsh), and yet where, at least until recently, the party system proved to be one of the most stable in Western Europe. In other words, to suggest that social structure alone is the freezing agent is to suggest that a frozen party system can exist only in a country in which there is also a frozen society, and this is patently implausible.

Party systems are in fact frozen by a variety of factors, of which social structure is just one of the more important (Bartolini and Mair, 1990; Sartori, 1990; Mair, 1997, pp. 199–223). They are also frozen by the constraints imposed by institutional structures such as the electoral system (see Chapter 11) and by the organizational efforts of the parties themselves (see Chapter 10). Most important, party systems are also frozen by the constraints imposed by the structure of party competition. In Italy, for example, the basis for a wholesale change in electoral preferences in the 1990s was laid partly by the "legitimation" of the PDS, which undermined the terms of reference by which Italian party competition had been structured since the late 1940s. Italian voters, as well as the Italian parties themselves, had long been constrained by the belief that there was no alternative to Christian Democratic government. And once such an alternative finally did emerge through the transformation of the unacceptable PCI into the highly acceptable PDS, this particular anchor was cut loose and voters began to shift in relatively great numbers.

Up to now, however, the sort of dramatic changes that have recently had an impact on the Italian party system remain exceptional, and whether similar ruptures will yet come to affect other Western European party systems is still unknown. It still remains to be seen, for example, whether the innovative red-green coalition that took office in Germany in 1998 will lead to a sea-change in how Germans understand the dynamics of their party system. It still remains to be seen whether the incorporation of the Greens into French government will signal a new pattern of government formation and party competition. Finally, and perhaps most important of all, it also still remains to be seen whether voters in the future will become even more disengaged, and whether aggregate voting outcomes will begin to reflect a more random distribution of preferences, leading to the possible erosion of long-familiar structures.

REFERENCES

Alber, Jens: "Modernization, Changing Cleavage Structures and the Rise of the Green Party in West Germany," in Ferdinand Müller-Rommel (ed.), *New Politics in Western Europe: The Rise and Success of the Green Parties and Alternative Lists,* Westview Press, Boulder, Colo., 1989.

Alford, Robert R.: *Party and Society: The Anglo-American Democracies,* Rand McNally, Chicago, 1963.

Ambrosius, Gerold, and William H. Hubbard: *A Social and Economic History of Twentieth-Century Europe,* Harvard University Press, Cambridge, Mass., 1989.

Amyot, G. Grant: "Italy: The Long Twilight of the DC Regime," in Wolinetz, 1988, pp. 12–30.

Andeweg, Rudy B.: "Elite-Mass Linkages in Europe: Legitimacy Crisis or Party Crisis?", in Jack Hayward (ed.), *Elitism, Populism, and European Politics,* Clarendon Press, Oxford, 1996, pp. 143–63.

Bakvis, Herman: *Catholic Power in the Netherlands,* McGill-Queens University Press, Kingston and Montreal, 1981.

Bartolini, Stefano: *The Class Cleavage,* Cambridge University Press, Cambridge, 2000.

Bartolini, Stefano, and Peter Mair: *Identity, Competition, and Electoral Availability: The Stabilization of European Electorates,* 1885–1985, Cambridge University Press, Cambridge, England, 1990.

Bell, Daniel: *The End of Ideology,* The Free Press, New York, 1960.

Crewe, Ivor, and David Denver (eds.): *Electoral Change in Western Democracies: Patterns and Sources of Electoral Volatility,* Croom Helm, London, 1985.

Crouch, Colin: *Social Change in Western Europe,* Oxford University Press, Oxford, 1999.

Dalton, Russell J.: *Citizen Politics in Western Democracies: Public Opinion and Political Parties in the United States, Great Britain, West Germany, and France,* Chatham House, Chatham, N.J., 1988.

Dalton, Russell J.: "The German Voter," in Gordon Smith, William E. Paterson, and Peter H. Merkl (eds.), *Developments in West German Politics,* Macmillan, London, 1990, pp. 99–121.

Dalton, Russell J., Scott C. Flanagan, and Paul Allen Beck (eds.): *Electoral Change in Advanced Industrial Democracies: Realignment or Dealignment?* Princeton University Press, Princeton, 1984.

Diamant, Alfred: "The Group Basis of Austrian Politics," *Journal of Central European Affairs,* vol. 18, no. 2, 1958, pp. 134–55.

Duverger, Maurice: *Political Parties,* Methuen, London, 1954.

Eijk, Cees van der, and B. Niemoeller: *Electoral Change in the Netherlands,* C. T. Press, Amsterdam, 1983.

Eijk, Cees van der, Mark Franklin, Tom Mackie and Henry Valen: "Cleavages, Conflict Resolution, and Democracy," in Franklin et al., 1992, pp. 406–31.

Evans, Geoffrey: "Is Gender on the 'New Agenda'?", *European Journal of Political Research,* vol. 24, no. 2, 1993, pp. 135–58.

Evans, Geoffrey (ed.): *The End of Class Politics? Class Voting in Comparative Context,* Oxford University Press, Oxford, 1999.

Evans, Geoffrey, Anthony Heath, and Clive Payne: "Class: Labour as a Catch-All Party?", in Geoffrey Evans and Pippa Norris (eds.), *Critical Elections: British Parties and Voters in Long-Term Perspective,* Sage, London, 1999, pp. 87–101.

Flanagan, Scott C., and Russell J. Dalton: "Parties under Stress: Realignment and Dealignment in Advanced Industrial Societies," *West European Politics,* vol. 7, no. 1, 1984, pp. 7–23.

Franklin, Mark, Tom Mackie, Henry Valen, (eds.).: *Electoral Change: Responses to Evolving Social and Attitudinal Structures in Western Countries,* Cambridge University Press, Cambridge, 1992.

Hardiman, Niamh, and Christopher Whelan: "Changing Values," in William Crotty and David E. Schmitt (eds.), *Ireland and the Politics of Change,* Longman, New York, 1998, pp. 66–85.

Heath, Anthony, Roger Jowell, and John Curtice: *How Britain Votes,* Pergamon, Oxford, 1985.

Houska, Joseph J.: *Influencing Mass Political Behavior: Elites and Political Subcultures in the Netherlands and Austria,* Institute of International Affairs, University of California at Berkeley, 1985.

Ignazi, Piero: "The Silent Counter-Revolution: Hypotheses on the Emergence of Extreme-Right Parties in Europe," *European Journal of Political Research,* vol. 22, no. 1, 1992, pp. 3–34.

Inglehart, Ronald: "The Changing Structure of Political Cleavages in Western Society," in Dalton et al., 1984, pp. 25–69.

Inglehart, Ronald: *Culture Shift in Advanced Industrial Society,* Princeton University Press, Princeton, 1990.

Inglehart, Ronald: *Modernization and Postmodernization: Cultural, Economic, and Political Change in 43 Societies,* Princeton University Press, Princeton, 1997.

Irwin, Galen A., and J. J. M. van Holsteyn: "Decline of the Structured Model of Electoral Competition," *West European Politics,* vol. 12, no. 1, 1989, pp. 21–41.

Kaplan, Gisela: *Contemporary West European Feminism,* Allen & Unwin/UCL Press, London, 1992.

Katz, Richard S., and Peter Mair: "Changing Models of Party Organization and Party Democracy: The Emergence of the Cartel Party," *Party Politics,* vol. 1, no. 1, 1995, pp. 5–28.

Kirchheimer, Otto: "The Waning of Opposition in Parliamentary Regimes," *Social Research,* vol. 24, no. 2, 1957, pp. 127–56.

Kirchheimer, Otto: "The Transformation of Western European Party Systems," in Joseph LaPalombara and Myron Weiner (eds.), *Political Parties and Political Development,* Princeton University Press, Princeton, 1966, pp. 177–200.

Krouwel, André: *The Development of the Catch-All Party in Western Europe, 1960–1990: A Study in Arrested Development,* Unpublished Ph.D. Thesis, Free University, Amsterdam, 1999.

Lane, Jan-Erik, David McKay, and Kenneth Newton: *Political Data Handbook OECD Countries,* 2d ed., Oxford University Press, Oxford, 1997.

Lewis-Beck, Michael: "France: The Stalled Electorate," in Dalton et al., 1984, pp. 425–48.

Lijphart, Arend: "Religious vs. Linguistic vs. Class Voting," *American Political Science Review,* vol. 73, no. 2, 1979, pp. 442–58.

Lipset, S. M, and Stein Rokkan: "Cleavage Structures, Party Systems and Voter Alignments: An Introduction," in S. M. Lipset and Stein Rokkan (eds.), *Party Systems and Voter Alignments,* The Free Press, New York, 1967, pp. 1–64.

Lovenduski, Joni: *Women and European Politics: Contemporary Feminism and Public Policy,* Wheatsheaf, Brighton, 1986.

Maguire, Maria: "Is There Still Persistence? Electoral Change in Western Europe, 1948–1979," in Hans Daalder and Peter Mair (eds.), *Western European Party Systems: Continuity and Change,* Sage, London, 1983, pp. 67–94.

Mair, Peter (ed.): *The West European Party System,* Oxford University Press, Oxford, 1990.

Mair, Peter: *Party System Change: Approaches and Interpretations,* Clarendon Press, Oxford, 1997.

Mair, Peter: "New Political Parties in Long-Established Party Systems: How Successful Are They?", in Erik Beukel Kurt Klaudi Klausen and Poul Erik Mouritzen. (eds.), *Elites, Parties and Democracy: Festschrift for Mogens N. Pedersen,* Odense University Press, Odense, 1999, pp. 207–24.

Mair, Peter: "In the Aggregate: Mass Electoral Behaviour in Western Europe, 1950–2000," in Hans Keman (ed.), *Comparative Politics,* Sage, London, 2000a, forthcoming.

Mair, Peter: "The Freezing Hypothesis: an Evaluation," in Lauri Karvonen and Stein Kuhnle (eds.), *Party Systems and Voter Alignments: Looking Back, Looking Forward,* Routledge, London, 2000b, forthcoming.

Marsh, Michael: "Ireland," in Franklin et al., 1992, pp. 219–37.

Neumann, Sigmund: "Toward a Comparative Study of Political Parties," in Sigmund Neumann (ed.), *Modern Political Parties,* University of Chicago Press, Chicago, 1956, pp. 395–421.

Nieuwbeerta, Paul: *The Democratic Class Struggle in Twenty Countries, 1945/1990,* Thesis Publishers, Amsterdam, 1995.

Pedersen, Mogens N.: "The Dynamics of European Party Systems: Changing Patterns of Electoral Volatility," *European Journal of Political Research,* vol. 7, no. 1, 1979, pp. 1–26.

Pedersen, Mogens N.: "Changing Patterns of Electoral Volatility: Explorations in Explanations," in Hans Daalder and Peter Mair (eds.), *Western European Party Systems: Continuity and Change,* Sage, London, 1983, pp. 29–66.

Pedersen, Mogens N.: "The Danish 'Working Multiparty System': Breakdown or Adaptation?", in Hans Daalder (ed.), *Party Systems in Denmark, Austria, Switzerland, the Netherlands and Belgium,* Frances Pinter, London, 1987, pp. 1–60.

Porritt, Jonathon: *Seeing Green: The Politics of Ecology Explained,* Blackwell, Oxford, 1984.

Porritt, Jonathon: "Foreword," in Sara Parkin, *Green Parties: An International Guide,* Heretic Books, London, 1989, pp. 7–9.

Prodromou, Elizabeth H.: "Paradigms, Power, and Identity: Rediscovering Orthodoxy and Regionalizing Europe," *European Journal of Political Research,* vol. 30, no. 2, 1996, pp. 125–54.

Rokkan, Stein: *Citizens, Elections, Parties,* Universitetsforlaget, Oslo, 1970.

Rose, Richard: *The Problem of Party Government,* Macmillan, London, 1974.

Rose, Richard, and Derek Urwin: "Persistence and Change in Western Party Systems since 1945," *Political Studies,* vol. 18, no. 3, 1970, pp. 287–319.

Roth, Günther: *The Social Democrats in Imperial Germany: A Study in Working-Class Isolation and National Integration,* Bedminster Press, Totowa, N.J., 1963.

Sainsbury, Diane: "Class Voting and Left Voting in Scandinavia," *European Journal of Political Research,* vol. 15, no. 5, 1987, pp. 507–26.

Sartori, Giovanni: "The Influence of Electoral Laws: Faulty Laws or Faulty Method?," in Bernard Grofman and Arend Lijphart (eds.), *Electoral Laws and Their Political Consequences,* Agathon Press, New York, 1987, pp. 43–68.

Sartori, Giovanni: "The Sociology of Parties: A Critical Review," in Mair, 1990, pp. 150–82.

Schmitt, Hermann, and Sören Holmberg: "Political Parties in Decline?", in Hans-Dieter Klingemann and Dieter Fuchs (eds.), *Citizens and the State,* Oxford University Press, Oxford, 1995, pp. 95–133.

Sinnott, Richard: "Party Attachment in Europe: Methodological Critique and Substantive Implications," *British Journal of Political Science,* vol. 28, no. 4, 1998, pp. 627–50.

Smith, Gordon: "Core Persistence: System Change and the 'People's Party,'" *West European Politics,* vol. 12, no. 4, 1989, pp. 157–68.

Thomassen, J. J. A.: "Party Identification as a Cross-Cultural Concept: Its Meaning in the Netherlands," in Ian Budge, Ivor Crewe, and Dennis Farlie (eds.), *Party Identification and Beyond,* Wiley, London, 1976, pp. 63–80.

Wolinetz, Steven B. (ed.): *Parties and Party Systems in Liberal Democracies,* Routledge, London, 1988.

10

INSIDE EUROPEAN POLITICAL PARTIES

As earlier chapters in this book have made clear, political parties play a vital role in European politics. In many parts of the world, parties can be peripheral or transient bodies: they may be built around a single leader and cease to exist when this leader disappears from the scene, as has occurred in some Third World countries. They may play a secondary role in what are essentially candidate-centered politics, as in the United States. In Europe, however, parties really matter. We have seen in earlier chapters that some European parties have a long history, having survived world wars and fundamental changes of regime. We saw in Chapter 4 that the institutions of European parliamentary democracy mean that it is party, rather than candidate, that Europeans vote for at election time. On the whole, government in Europe is party government, although other organizations, such as interest groups, sometimes appear to challenge this, as we shall see in Chapter 14. Consequently, the internal affairs of parties, although they are regarded by many Europeans as mundane and uninteresting, may make a significant difference to the politics of a country, by determining the nature of both the politicians and the policy packages that voters can choose between at elections. In this chapter, therefore, we move inside parties and ask what sort of bodies they are. We consider how well they are organized; how they make decisions; where they get their resources; how they are adjusting to important social changes, such as the increasing role of the mass media in politics; and how political parties make their distinctive contribution to the politics of representation in Europe.

WHAT DO PARTIES DO?

Political parties are present in, and indeed at the core of, politics in all west European countries. Even though many Europeans are cynical about parties and their motives, European politics would scarcely operate without them. They perform a number of functions that are crucial to the operation of modern political systems. Among these functions, we shall pick out four that are particularly important.

First, political parties structure the political world. As we have seen in earlier chapters and will also see in Chapter 12, parties are the key actors in the operation of governments and parliaments. If there were no parties—in other words, if every member of parliament were an independent with no institutionalized links with other members—the result would be something close to chaos. The only west European country that has come anywhere close to this situation in living memory was Fourth Republic France prior to 1958, when the parliamentary groups were numerous and internally incohesive, rendering stable government and cohesive policy making, except to the extent that the civil service filled the breach, impossible. Parties also structure the political world for many voters, who see politics in terms of the fortunes of parties as much as the fate of issues, especially at election times. Most individual voters don't have time to work out their views on every political issue, and many tend to follow their party's judgment on matters about which they have not thought deeply.

Second, parties recruit and socialize the political elite. To become a member of parliament in Europe, it is virtually essential that an individual first be selected by a political party as an election candidate. Likewise, someone who wants to become a government minister in almost any European country usually must be a senior member of a political party. Thus, gaining access to political power requires being accepted by a party, and usually being a leading figure in it. Parties also socialize the political elite; most government ministers have spent a number of years as party members, working with other party members and learning to see the political world from the party's perspective. In doing this, they become accustomed to working with others and learn about teamwork, about the need to coordinate their activities with other figures in the party and, most important, about the constraints that party discipline imposes on them. The control that European parties possess over elite recruitment and socialization marks one major difference between most of Europe on the one hand, and the USA and certain other presidential systems on the other. In the latter, the country's political leader often does not emerge from within the party organization, and in some cases complete political outsiders, such as Alberto Fujimori in Peru, can come through and win political power. This means that the political direction of such systems is inclined to be inherently less stable, whereas in Western Europe, where political parties control the channels of elite recruitment and socialization, the behavior of political leaders is usually more predictable, for better or worse.

Third, parties provide linkage between rulers and ruled, between civil society and the state. They constitute the main mechanism by which voters are linked to the political world, providing a flow of information in both directions. As we shall see later, many people have doubts as to whether parties are performing their linkage role effectively any longer.

Fourth, parties aggregate interests. Unlike interest groups, which we look at in Chapter 14, they put forward and try to implement packages of proposals, not just policies in one area of government. At election time, most parties put forward manifestos containing policies on many different issues, and thereby stand ready to give direction to government.

Party control of government, whether by one party or by a coalition of parties, should mean some more or less coherent program that the government aims to follow, rather than a situation in which disparate individual ministers each pursue their own ideas.

BASIC PARTY ORGANIZATION

Party organizations differ in detail around Europe, but the basic organizational elements are very similar. Members of a party belong to a local unit based on a geographic area, usually known as the *branch*. Ideally, the party will aim to establish branches all over the country in order to maintain a presence on the ground and to mobilize potential voters. The branches usually have a role—sometimes a decisive role—in selecting election candidates, and they are entitled to send delegates to the party's *annual conference,* which in many parties is nominally the supreme decision-making body. Delegates at the annual conference usually elect most members of the party's *national executive,* which runs the party organization between conferences, adjudicating on internal disputes. This works in conjunction with the party's *head office,* staffed by the party's own employees, who constitute a permanent party bureaucracy. The other main element in the party is the *parliamentary group* or *caucus,* comprising the party's elected deputies.

In the case of some parties, this basic picture is complicated by the presence of other bodies. A few parties, such as the French Socialists, are highly factionalized. Such parties contain a number of clearly defined groups, often quite institutionalized, with a continuous existence over time; the various factions jostle for power and position within the party. Other parties have had interest groups affiliated to them in the past; examples include the Labour parties in Britain, Norway and Sweden, though in each case the links have become much weaker in recent years. In federal countries, the party organizations in the various states may have considerable freedom of action. This is especially true of the German Christian Democrats and the Austrian People's Party (the latter also has interest groups, in the form of farmers', workers', and business leagues, attached to it).

Each party constitution usually gives the impression that the party is a smoothly functioning organization in which important decisions are reached through a fairly democratic process. The reality, as might be expected, is often rather different. Although some parties do operate reasonably peacefully (though not necessarily very democratically), others are wracked by constant internal tension. One very common source of conflict concerns the ideological "purity" of party policy. The battle lines are often drawn between party activists, for whom it may be of prime importance that the party adhere to the ideals that led them to join it in the first place, and party legislators, who may well wish to trim ideological sails in order to get into office. Internal conflict along these lines was very prominent, for example, in the British Labour Party during most of the 1980s.

PARTY MEMBERSHIP

Who Becomes a Party Member?

Belonging to a party is slightly more formal in Europe than in some other parts of the world, involving more than just expressing an inclination toward the party in question. Typically, to become a party member one has to pay a small annual membership fee and indicate (by signing some kind of pledge) that one accepts the basic principles of the party. Members are also expected, at least in theory, to attend regular local branch meetings.

Not surprisingly, most people who vote for a party do not go to the trouble and expense of actually joining it. Party members make up only a minority of party supporters as a whole. Just how large or small this minority is varies a lot, both from country to country and from party to party within countries. Indeed, it can be difficult to pin down exactly how many people really do belong to parties. Outsiders are often surprised to discover that some parties are simply not sufficiently centralized for anyone in a party to know how many members it has. In Switzerland, the most decentralized country in Europe, for example, party headquarters may have little knowledge of the party's position in the various cantons around the country. Similarly, most of the Green parties that began to emerge as a significant political force in the 1980s have, on principle, shunned the formal organizational structure of the established parties. Other parties may have a good idea of their membership but may be reluctant to disclose the information publicly.

Even when we do manage to get membership figures for a particular party, we sometimes need to treat these skeptically. Parties have an obvious incentive to claim more members than they really have, in the hope of increasing their legitimacy. In addition, the figures passed on to the head office by the local organizational units around the country may not be reliable; the number of delegates each branch can send to the annual conference may depend on how many members it has, so the larger it claims to be, the more delegates it can send. Local members may even pay membership dues for "ghost" members, creating "paper" branches, either in order to boost local representation in national bodies or to boost their own position in local intra-party competition, over candidate selection, for example. Another problem is the relatively subjective definition of membership in some cases. There may be people in some parties who invariably help the party campaign during elections but who never actually join and thus are not formally considered members. Other parties might still count as members people who, in fact, drifted away years ago but never explicitly resigned.

Still, when all the qualifications are made, we can come up with at least some reasonably hard facts on party membership in individual countries. The pattern for each country is summed up in Table 10-1. It can be seen that in most countries, only a small fraction of those who vote for a party are sufficiently committed to join it, and, as we shall see, only a minority of this minority can be considered active in the party. There are only five countries where a tenth or more of electors join a party: Iceland, Austria, Malta, Finland, and Luxembourg. The way in which the parties in Austria saturate society is well documented: about a fifth of all Austrians belong to a political party, and the parties permeate many aspects of ordinary life by providing social outlets together with a patronage system so extensive that even the most menial public-sector job can be hard to obtain unless one belongs to the party in whose gift it lies. An even higher proportion of Maltese electors are members of a party: the two main parties, the Maltese Labour Party (MLP) and the Partit Nazzjonalista or Nationalist Party (PN) have a social club in virtually every town of any size, which is the center of social life for many members, and they have a range of ancillary organizations. For example, the PN has separate associations for workers, the self-employed, pensioners, women, and young

TABLE 10-1 PARTY MEMBERSHIP AS A PERCENTAGE OF THE ELECTORATE

	Percentage of electorate that belongs to a political party	Trends in membership in recent decades
Austria	19	Decline from 28% in 1980
Belgium	7	Slight decline in past twenty years
Denmark	5	Decline from over 20% in the 1960s
Finland	11	Decline from 16% in 1980
France	2	Little change
Germany	3	Little change since 1960s
Greece	7	Figure has doubled since late 1970s
Iceland	17	No information
Ireland	4	Slight decline in past twenty years
Italy	4	Decline from 10% in 1980
Luxembourg	10	No information
Malta	30	Dramatic increase in early 1980s, stability since then
Netherlands	2	Now around half of the 1980 figure
Norway	7	Now around half of the 1980 figure
Portugal	5	Modest increase since 1980
Spain	3	Modest increase since 1980
Sweden	7	Slight decline in past twenty years
Switzerland	6	No information
United Kingdom	2	Now about a third of 1950s figures
Average	8	—

Source: For fifteen of the nineteen countries, data relate to 1995–98 and are from Mair and van Biezen, p. 12. For Iceland, the figure relates to 1987 (Hardarson, p. 145). For Luxembourg, the figure relates to the late 1980s (Jacobs, pp. 235–47). For Malta, data are from party web sites (www.mlp.org.mt/structur.htm, sites.waldonet.net.mt/alternattiva/frames.htm), and information supplied by the PN. For Sweden, the figure relates to 1997 (Widfeldt, 1999, p. 116).

people; it runs its own travel agency; and it has a section called "Team Sports PN" that organizes tournaments for members and supporters in various sporting activities, such as football, athletics, and snooker (information from the party's web site at www.pn.org.mt).

It is generally accepted that membership figures are declining right across Western Europe. From a survey of membership data in sixteen Western European countries between 1980 and the late 1990s, Mair and van Biezen found that the trend was downwards everywhere except in Greece, Portugal, and Spain, each of which had had authoritarian regimes prior to the mid-1970s. The mean percentage of the electorate that belonged to a party in these sixteen countries was 8.2 percent in 1980, but only 5.8 percent in the late 1990s (Mair and van Biezen, p. 12). Moreover, even the 1980 figures represent a decline from earlier decades. We can illustrate the decline by considering a few specific examples. In Denmark, over a fifth of all registered voters were party members in the early 1960s, but by 1995 only a twentieth belonged to a party. In Britain, individual membership in the Labour party fell from a peak of just over a million in 1952 to around three hundred thousand in the early 1990s, and Conservative membership dropped from around two million in the 1960s to three-quarters of a million in the early 1990s and to less than half this by 1998 (Seyd and Whiteley, p. 16; Whiteley, Seyd, and Richardson, pp. 22–25).

We can explain the decline in membership rolls by considering the reasons why people might join a party in the first place. It was suggested in the 1960s by Clark and Wilson that there are three main motives that might lead someone to join a party (see Ware, 1996, pp. 68–78; Clark and Wilson). One is *material,* the desire to gain some tangible reward, such as a public office or a public resource controlled by the party. This has been important in a few European countries, such as Austria, Belgium, and Italy; in Spain, too, "holders and seekers of public office make up a large proportion" of party membership (Colomer, p. 180). Even so, it is generally a minor factor, and is under attack in those countries where "the party card" is still an asset when it comes to being given a public sector job. The second motive is *solidary,* referring to the desire for social contact and a sense of comradeship; with the rise of a wide range of leisure opportunities and the decline in cohesiveness among subcultures and communities, this is also of declining importance. The third is *purposive*—in other words, directed towards a specific end; it refers to a desire to advance certain policy goals. This, too, is under challenge: the attraction of joining a party in order to promote a particular issue is weakened by the rise of social movements, single-issue pressure groups, and community action groups, which provide other, perhaps more satisfying, ways of participating. In Denmark, for example, the decline in party membership over the past few decades has been accompanied by an upsurge in political activities outside parties, with the educated middle class the most inclined to take part in these non-party political movements (Togeby, pp. 5–8).

To find out whether party members are socially representative of party voters, we would need a wealth of data that we simply do not possess. The fullest attempt to explore this question was made by Anders Widfeldt, who based his analysis upon large surveys of the public across Europe in 1988 and 1989. These surveys inquired about party membership, enabling Widfeldt to compare members of a party with other supporters of the party. He found that women were less likely to be members than men were: in thirty-four of the thirty-seven parties for which there were data, there was a lower proportion of women among party members than among other party supporters (Widfeldt, 1995, p. 147). Likewise, young people were underrepresented among party members while the middle-aged were overrepresented, and working-class people were underrepresented as members in virtually every party compared with their strength as party supporters (Widfeldt, 1995, pp. 154–57). He concludes, "the members of political parties in Western Europe are, on the whole, not socially representative of party supporters. Party members tend to be disproportionately male, middle-aged and middle-class" (Widfeldt, 1995, p. 165). There was no consistent pattern as to which parties had memberships that were closest to being a social cross-section of party supporters; in some countries, this was true of right-wing parties, while in other countries left-wing parties had this position.

BOX 10-1

MEMBERSHIP OF POLITICAL PARTIES

France

Reliable figures on party membership in France are hard to come by, but all reliable estimates concur on figures that represent a low proportion of voters. The Gaullists (RPR) have long been seen as having a relatively high number of members, but in the late 1990s the party's 150,000 members represented only 3.5 percent of those who voted for it at the 1997 parliamentary elections. The second main right-wing party, the UDF, is a conglomeration of a number of smaller groups and parties, which together do not have as many members as the RPR. The Socialist Party also has fewer members than the RPR, and less than 2 percent of its voters are party members. According to its own claims, the Communist Party has more members than the RPR and the Socialists combined, but given its record of electoral decline over the last two decades, few analysts are entirely convinced by the party's official figures. Members in all parties, with the occasional exception of the Socialists, have a reputation for being deferential toward their leaders.

Germany

Party membership in postwar Germany has fluctuated somewhat, but has been consistently low by general Western European standards. The Social Democrats (SPD) had the largest number of members prior to the 1990s, but by the end of that decade they had been overtaken by the combined strength of the two parties in the main right-wing bloc, the CDU and the CSU. The CDU in particular traditionally attached low priority to the recruitment of members, but after losing office in 1969 it set about strengthening its organization so as to challenge the dominance of the SPD on the ground. Its membership more than doubled during its thirteen-year period in opposition; in government from 1982 to 1998 membership fell slightly, but not to the same extent as SPD membership. The FDP has far fewer members, and the Greens are smaller still. Following the reunification of Germany in 1990, all the parties sought to extend their membership in the former East Germany, but only the Free Democrats were particularly successful in this.

Italy

The party with the most members in postwar Italy was the Communist party (PCI), which in the early 1990s was reborn as the PDS (Democratic Party of the Left), with far fewer members than the PCI. In the late 1980s two of the government parties, the Christian Democrats (DC) and the Socialists (PSI), had over two million members between them, but these parties both disintegrated as a result of the scandals that convulsed Italian politics in the early 1990s, and the evidence suggests that most of their members drifted away from politics. The only party to show membership (as well as electoral) growth in recent years has been the far-right Alleanza Nazionale (AN). Particularly notable has been the rise of Forza Italia, founded by the media tycoon Silvio Berlusconi, which has been described as a "virtual party," with no real organizational structure and a very small membership base, yet it was able to poll over 20 percent of the votes at elections and play a leading role in government from 1994 to 1995.

Netherlands

Over the last forty years, the membership of the Dutch parties has declined from a level that was never particularly high by general European standards. The drop has been most pronounced among the religious parties (now combined in the CDA); membership fell from about half a million in 1950 to fewer than ninety thousand in the late 1990s. The membership of the Socialist PvdA halved from the early 1980s to the late 1990s. In most parties, the activity of sections such as youth movements and women's groups has declined.

Spain

The Spanish parties had exceptionally small memberships in the years after the return to democracy in the late 1970s, but, unlike most European parties, they have been gaining rather than losing members since then. The right-wing AP doubled its membership during the 1990s, and the Socialists (PSOE) also showed a steady increase. Even so, overall membership levels remain low. The legacy of dictatorship is sometimes suggested as an explanation for the phenomenon, as it led to a political culture that did not encourage active participation in politics.

Sweden

Sweden has been displaying the familiar pattern of a decline in party membership in recent years, although the number of members has fallen less dramatically than in many countries. The largest party, the Social Democrats, used to have "indirect members" who were deemed to be party members because of their membership in trade

Continued . . .

Continued . . .

unions affiliated with the party, but this practice was ended in 1990. Taking this into account, the largest decrease in membership has occurred in the liberal People's Party (FP), with the number of individual members of the Social Democrats holding up relatively well by comparison. At the end of the 1990s, nearly half of Swedish party members belonged to the Social Democrats.

United Kingdom

Party membership in Britain has declined markedly since the 1950s, even allowing for the patchy data available on membership. Research in the early 1990s discovered that the average Conservative member was aged sixty-two; these members have a reputation for being more right-wing than Conservative MPs and are noted for their consistent calls at annual conferences for the restoration of capital punishment. The party had an estimated two to three million members in the 1950s and 1960s, but this had declined to only a third of a million by the end of the 1990s. Labour's figures followed a bell curve during the twentieth century. Up to the mid-1940s the party had on average around a third of a million members each year, but then membership rose to a peak of over a million in the early 1950s. The pattern since then has been one of steady decline, back again to around a third of a million in the late 1990s. The membership of all the other British parties is small.

These broad findings tally with information on some specific parties that have been studied in greater detail, such as the main British parties. Looking at the Labour party, Seyd and Whiteley found that only 26 percent of members, compared with 57 percent of party voters, were working class, and women made up only 39 percent of members, compared with 52 percent of party voters (Seyd and Whiteley, p. 39). In some ways, the British Conservative party membership was more representative than Labour's membership; for example, women achieved near-parity with men among members, comprising 49 percent of members compared with 55 percent of voters. The Conservative membership was least representative with regard to age: 67 percent of the members were over fifty-five, compared with only 35 percent of Conservative voters. To the horror of Conservative head office, which had hitherto not possessed detailed information on the composition of its membership, the researchers discovered that the average Conservative member was aged sixty-two (Whiteley, Seyd, and Richardson, p. 50).

The Activities of Party Members

What do party members do? In virtually all parties nowadays, members tend to be most active at election time, playing an important role in campaigning at the grassroots level. They may not be particularly successful when it comes to trying to persuade the floating voters to come off the fence, let alone trying to convert the supporters of other parties. But, in most countries, they have a part to play in mobilizing the faithful, by putting up posters, looking after party stalls and handing out leaflets in public places, and even, in a few countries such as Britain and Ireland, going from house to house and knocking on doors to rekindle dormant loyalties and to show that the party has a local presence. Between elections, undoubtedly, many party branches are not especially active. The more committed members attend branch meetings regularly, to discuss ways of expanding the organization at the local level or to decide their stance on issues due to arise at the next annual conference.

In most parties, only a small proportion of members, perhaps 10 percent in many cases, can really be considered activists, that is, regular attenders at local branch meetings and participants in the party's internal affairs (Svåsand et al., pp. 109–110). Many members do not attend any branch meetings at all. Surveys in Britain found that 36 percent of Labour members and 68 percent of Conservative members reported having attended no party meetings in the previous year (Seyd and Whiteley, p. 89; Whiteley, Seyd, and Richardson, p. 68). A similar pattern emerges from virtually every country for which some information exists. The general impression is that party organizations are merely "ticking over" except during election campaigns.

It was not always like this. As we mentioned in the preceding chapter, belonging to a party in the early years of the century could mean living within what was virtually a separate subculture in society. This was especially true of left-wing parties with a mass membership, such as the German SPD. Belonging to the SPD was almost a way of life. The party had its own newspaper, which members bought, read, and discussed with one another, and its branch offices all over Germany were centers of social activity for members, running stamp-collecting clubs and sports teams, organizing outings, and so on. It ran its own health service, paid for by members through a health insurance scheme, and sought to look after members and their families from the cradle to the grave. In 1906 it founded a training school in Berlin for the political education of members, grooming the most committed to take up places in the ranks of its full-time employees. Given that many members worked in factories alongside fellow party members and belonged to trade unions associated with the party, they were virtually cocooned from contact with the rest of German society.

But even in the heyday of mass parties, in the first half of the twentieth century, few European parties managed to achieve this degree of penetration of their members' lives. Not only has the number of party members generally diminished, as we have seen, but the commitment of those members may well have waned—though we should not imagine that a few decades ago party members behaved very differently, since the available evidence suggests that levels of activism among members were low throughout the twentieth century (Scarrow, pp. 181–94).

Certainly, some of the reasons people might once have joined parties now have much less force. The modern welfare state has taken over many of the functions that party insurance schemes once performed. A rise in living standards, a huge increase in leisure outlets, and the advent of television have all combined to reduce the appeal of spending evenings playing table tennis in the local party hall. The Austrian parties maintained a hold over their members for longer than most other parties, organizing a range of activities such as rambling, music, stamp collecting, sports, and gymnastics, but even their grip on their members' lives is waning; for example, in the early 1960s about 35 percent of the population read a party newspaper, but by the late 1980s this figure had dropped to just 7 percent (Plasser et al., p. 23). Fewer people were living in a party-dominated subculture, and the Maltese parties are now virtually unique in Europe in their capacity to structure their members' leisure activities to a significant extent. Television has undermined much of the rationale for party newspapers, so few European parties nowadays run their own papers, and when they do, these often run at a loss. The dedicated party activist, spending much of his or her free time debating and propagating the party's policy and ideology, is becoming a creature of the past, maybe indeed of a mythical and nonexistent past.

All of this does not mean that ordinary members no longer play a role within European parties. On the contrary, they are important in giving these parties a character quite distinct from that of their American counterparts. The role of European party members in certain key areas gives parties a reasonable degree of coherence, as we see when we look at power within parties.

POWER WITHIN PARTIES

Who controls European parties? Who wields power within them? In reality, there is no one answer to this question. It is just not the case that all power lies in one place and every other part of the party is powerless. Usually, the internal affairs of parties are characterized by a continuous process of accommodation and mutual adjustment. When it comes to the crunch, most party members at every level would rather keep the party together as an effective body than precipitate a destructive split—although, of course, sometimes internal differences are so great that a split does take place and a new party is formed, a development that is more common in new party systems than in established ones. More commonly, there is a constant process of give and take, and the party remains together precisely because a balance of power is respected and no one element tries to achieve complete control. The various elements in the party organization—the leader, deputies, rank-and-file members, and so on—may jostle for position, but there is rarely open warfare of the sort that in the United States is prone to break out at primaries. After all, they all belong to the same party and can be assumed to have a broadly similar political outlook. They are bound to disagree on details, but the leader and parliamentarians usually have some freedom of maneuver provided that they stay within the broad parameters of what is acceptable to the membership.

There are several important areas of activity in which conflict can arise within a party, and at which we might look in order to try to identify the most powerful actors within the party. Three, in particular, have the potential to be key battle sites. The first is the writing of the party's manifesto, the set of policies upon which it fights elections. The second is the election of the party leader, and the third is the selection of the party's parliamentary candidates. We shall examine each of these in turn.

The Party Manifesto and Program

Two of the party's policy documents are especially significant: the party manifesto, the formal declaration in which a party tells the voters what it will aim to do if it gets into government, and the party program, the statement of the party's aims and aspirations, which is generally updated every few years. Party members often differ among themselves as to what should be put in these documents, partly because not all members have exactly the same policy preferences, and partly because some members are more concerned than others with winning votes as opposed to maintaining ideological purity. Arguments about the party's policies often surface at annual conferences, where tension is sometimes apparent between parliamentarians and rank-and-file members.

The rank and file, especially in radical parties, is inclined to suspect the deputies of being seduced by the clublike atmosphere of parliament, of forgetting their roots, and of being willing to betray the party's principles in order to get into the comfortable seats of power. The deputies, in turn, may view some members as being unworldly zealots, who are unaware that compromises and bargaining are necessary in order to achieve at least part of what the party stands for, and are obsessed with policies that have no hope of ever being acceptable to the wider electorate.

Although some party activists may feel like fighting over every semicolon in the party's manifesto and program, in the belief that they are taking part in a battle for the party's soul, others conclude, as indeed do most political scientists, that this is probably not the most important arena of intra-party conflict. Parties feel that they have to have a manifesto, to show that they are to be taken seriously—and they would certainly be criticized if they didn't have one. However, there is no real expectation that many people will read it; realistically, everyone, including the party, knows perfectly well that most voters don't bother to read manifestos. At most, the party hopes that some of the main, or at least most vote-catching, ideas will be highlighted by the media. And although a manifesto is in theory a commitment by the party to do certain things if it gets into government, in practice few voters are so naive as to believe that a party, once in government, feels bound to do everything mentioned in its manifesto and to do nothing that is not mentioned there. Parties always have good excuses for not fulfilling their manifesto pledges; they will be able to point to some unexpected development that threw their plans off course, for example, such as a worldwide economic downturn. As we shall see in Chapter 13, even academics who have spent a lot of time on the question find it difficult to reach firm conclusions about the extent to which parties actually do what they promised to do.

Many election manifestos are drawn up by groups close to the party leadership, with little real membership involvement. If manifestos and policy programs come to be drawn up in such a way that the leadership is not keen on the result, then these documents are likely simply to gather dust from the moment they are published. The party's ministers in government, while always trying to keep the party onside, are unlikely to feel bound by the details of a manifesto that they can dismiss as the dreams of some fresh-faced enthusiasts in their twenties who have no experience of the real world. Examples abound of parties, especially left-wing parties, for which membership participation in drawing up supposedly key documents has meant very little. The French Socialist Party spent two years drawing up a campaign document for the presidential and parliamentary elections of 1988, but when the elections came around the leading figures in the party simply refused to use it (Gaffney, p. 74). The Austrian Socialists engaged in a lot of policy discussions from the late 1970s to the early 1990s, but these debates went on "in complete separation from the government's policies," and the real aim of the exercise was to allow neo-Marxism within the party to "wear itself out ideologically" (Müller, pp. 186–87). The Spanish Socialists engaged in a massive exercise from 1987 to 1990 to draw up a new program, involving 950,000 people and 14,900 debates, but once it was adopted little more was heard of it (Gillespie, 1993, pp. 93–94). Similarly, in Sweden the Social Democrats spent several years coming up with a party program in 1990, only for an economic downturn to make it largely irrelevant. However, the exercise was seen as not entirely wasted, since it served to enhance unity and integration within the party (Sainsbury, p. 57). In other words, the drawing up of manifestos and programs, while it might serve some useful functions for parties, can hardly be said to provide meaningful participation opportunities for members. Most members are well aware of this, and do not believe that even if they have a major input into the manifesto, they will really be determining the behavior of their party ministers in a future government.

Election of the Party Leader

A second important area of potential conflict is the election of the party leader. The leader of any organization can be expected to be more powerful than other members, and leaders of political parties are especially important because during election campaigns, the focus of the media is often upon the party leaders. In the case of some parties it may be hard to say who exactly the leader is: some parties have a party chairperson, a party president, and a parliamentary leader, with different people holding these positions and no clear designation of one as "the" leader. For some of these parties, such as the Norwegian center-right Høyre, it is conventional to see the real leader as the person who would become prime minister if the party came to hold that position in a future government (Heidar, p. 133). The same is true in Belgium and the Netherlands. Even this, though, is not an acid test: in both France and Italy prime ministers in the past have not necessarily been the most important persons in their parties.

Among parties for which we can clearly identify the leader, there is considerable variation in selection patterns (Scarrow et al.). In many parties—for example, in Denmark, Ireland, and the Netherlands—the parliamentary group (i.e., the party's deputies) plays the major or sole role. In many other parties, notably in Austria, Finland, Germany, Norway, and Sweden, a party congress or convention picks the leader. A model that is becoming more common is one that allows a direct vote among the entire membership, which is practiced in some or all parties in Belgium, France, and Britain. The motive for this may be to encourage new members by giving members a meaningful role, or, to take a more cynical view, to bypass the supposedly more "extreme" party activists, something that we discuss more fully later. In any case, if the leader does not have the confidence of the party's parliamentarians, his or her job will be very difficult, so even in those parties where the electorate is much wider than the parliamentary group, the deputies may play a key gatekeeper role. For example, to run for the office of Labour leader in Britain, it is necessary to be nominated by 12.5 percent of Labour MPs. Whatever method is chosen, leaders seem to be becoming less secure in their tenure of office than their predecessors were (Marsh, p. 231).

Selection of the Parliamentary Candidates

A third area that we might study in order to try to find out who really controls a political party is candidate selection. The selection of the individuals who are entitled to use the party's label when they stand for election plays a crucial role in the political recruitment process. Only the people selected as candidates can become members of parliament, and in virtually every country, most or all government ministers are present or former members of parliament. After the 1997 election in the United Kingdom, for example, 584 of the 659 MPs elected represented either the Conservative Party or the Labour Party. Each of these parties nominated 641 candidates, one in each mainland British constituency. The people who selected these 1,282 Conservative and Labour candidates, therefore, exercised an enormous power over who could and who could not get into the House of Commons and, beyond that, into government. Moreover, many seats in Britain are known to be "safe seats" for one or the other party, and in these cases selecting the candidate is tantamount to picking the member of parliament. In some other countries, too, the candidate selectors can reasonably be seen as choosing MPs. For example, in a number of European countries, as we shall see in the next chapter, the electoral system presents voters with a number of party lists, each list containing the names of candidates in a fixed order that the voters cannot alter. If a party wins, say, five seats in a particular district, these seats go to the top five names on the list, and it is the candidate selectors who determine which individuals are chosen to occupy these positions.

In 1997 Tony Blair became prime minister of Britain, swept into office with a huge majority on a powerful wave of personal popularity. However, in order to attain this

Tony Blair as the Labour candidate in the Beaconsfield by-election in 1982, along with the then Labour leader Michael Foot. Blair lost the by-election, which was in a safe Conservative seat, but the favourable impression he had made on Foot proved useful when it came to securing his selection as the Labour candidate in the safe Labour seat of Sedgefield the following year.
© United Kingdom PA Photos Limited

position, Blair had had first to become a Labour MP, and in order to achieve this, he had to be selected as a Labour candidate somewhere in a seat that his party had a chance of winning. By far the most difficult hurdle that he had to overcome was the last-mentioned. In the early 1980s he sought selection as the Labour candidate in a number of constituencies but he was picked in only one, the solidly Conservative constituency of Beaconsfield. He was unsuccessful in a number of attempts to be selected in constituencies where Labour had a realistic chance of winning the seat. Finally, shortly before the 1983 election, he sought to be selected as the party's candidate in the safe Labour seat of Sedgefield in the northeast of England, a constituency with which he had had no previous connection. He had first of all to persuade the skeptical members of a Labour branch in the constituency to nominate him for inclusion on the panel from which the short list would be picked. The branch did this, but all seemed lost when he was omitted from the short list of six that was drawn up by the handful of people who comprised the constituency executive committee. However, one of the members of the branch that had nominated him had become so impressed by Blair that he persuaded the committee at a late stage to add Blair to the short list. The 119 members entitled to make the decision then met all seven people seeking the nomination, after which they picked Blair as the Labour candidate; he duly won the seat at the election (Rentoul, pp. 91–137). If he had not managed to secure selection as a Labour candidate by a small number of people in one of the proverbial smoke-filled rooms, either in Sedgefield or in another constituency that was winnable for Labour, his political career would never have gotten off the ground.

Aspiring politicians who do not meet with the approval of these powerful gate-keepers, the major parties' candidate selectors, find that their political career is dead in the water. Candidate selection is thus a crucial step in the political recruitment process. For this reason, it is also a key area of internal party activity. If one section of a party, such as the party leader or the national executive, has control over the selection process, then this section can almost be said to control the party. Candidate selection is thus a vital matter in every individual European political party; it is also important—indeed, it is one of the key factors—in making European political parties very different from American parties.

European parties, unlike their American counterparts, control their own candidate selection—albeit, as we shall see, with considerable variation as to who exactly within the party can be said to occupy this controlling position. The only European country to employ American-style open primaries, in which anyone who wishes can participate, is Iceland, where primaries have been used since 1914 and have become common since the early 1970s. At the 1983 election, it was found that 29 percent of voters had taken part in a primary at that election, and 46 percent had participated in a primary at some time in their lives. Although, not surprisingly, party members and strong party identifiers are the most likely to take part, some nonmembers do so as well; in 1987, 57 percent of party members and 11 percent of nonmembers reported having taken part in primaries to select candidates at that year's election (Hardarson, pp. 156–65).

In every other country in Europe, the power to choose candidates is kept within the party. Perhaps surprisingly, given the importance of candidate selection in affecting the composition of parliament, the process is regulated by law in only a few countries. In

Finland, parties are legally obliged to open up the process of candidate selection to a direct vote of all their members, while in both Germany and Norway the law ensures that candidates are selected by local party organizations, with the parties' national executives having no power to overturn the decisions reached locally. In every other country, parties are in effect treated as private bodies and can make whatever arrangements they wish when they pick parliamentary candidates.

The farthest that any party outside Iceland goes down the road toward opening up its selection process to all and sundry is to adopt "party primaries," allowing each of its paid-up members a direct say in the choice of parliamentary candidates. This method of choosing candidates, though still employed by only a minority of parties, is becoming more common (Scarrow et al.). It is a method employed in Austria, Britain (by Labour and some of the smaller parties), Finland (where, as we have seen, it is obligatory under law), Ireland (by the second-largest party, Fine Gael), and the Netherlands (by D66). In addition, in some other countries, such as Belgium, Denmark, and Germany, there is provision for party primaries, though in practice other methods of candidate selection are sometimes employed.

More commonly, candidate selection involves interplay between the local and central party organizations, with the balance varying from case to case. Often, the key decisions are taken locally, with national actors sometimes attempting to influence the process. In many parties, the candidates are picked locally by the convention system: party members in each constituency choose delegates to attend a local nominating convention, also known as a selection conference, which picks the candidates. In most of these cases, the party's national executive has the power—though this is very rarely used—to veto the names chosen locally, and perhaps to add new ones. If the national organization is taking a particular interest in a local selection process—for example, out of concern to ensure that a particular individual is, or is not, selected—it is more likely to try to influence the key local members privately in advance through persuasion than to resort to its veto power after the event. In some parties, the choice is made by a local party committee, with the convention only giving formal ratification to the committee's choice.

In other parties, the balance is different, in that the ultimate decisions are taken nationally, with local organizations trying to influence the outcome. In the main right-wing parties in France, small groups set up by the national executives arrange many of the candidacies. In Europe's now-declining communist parties, too, the national executive is usually decisive, given the centralized nature of these parties. The British Conservative Party offers an interesting example of the interplay between central and local bodies. The party's head office plays an important role in screening aspirants for candidacies. It vets all these aspirants, weeding out many of them for one reason or another, and draws up a list of about eight hundred names of suitable people who are not already MPs. When a local party organization comes to make a selection for its own constituency, it picks about twenty-five people from this list for interview. These are whittled down progressively to just two or three, and the entire local membership then makes the final choice from these (Norris and Lovenduski, 1995, pp. 34–52). This degree of centralization is possible because in Britain, unlike every other country, it is not particularly important that an individual has roots in or connections with a constituency in which he or she hopes to be selected as a candidate.

The nature of the candidate selection process is determined partly by the electoral system. If a country is divided into single-member constituencies, there is, obviously, only one candidate to be selected in each, whereas in proportional representation (PR) systems based on multimember constituencies, several candidates are picked. The evidence from many countries, as we discuss in greater detail in the next chapter, is that under PR the selectors then aim to "balance the ticket," ensuring that both men and women are represented, along with individuals who will appeal to different sectoral or geographical interests within the constituency (Gallagher).

Does it matter who selects the candidates? It could matter if different actors within the party had different values and priorities, in which case whoever gained control of candidate selection could ensure that only those people holding certain political views were picked as candidates and, hence, had a chance of becoming parliamentarians. Alternatively, variations in this essentially private process might have a discernible impact upon public policy, if these variations led to differences in the proportions of women, young people, and ethnic minorities in parliament.

When we try to identify the values that selectors impart to the candidate selection process, we find that selectors everywhere tend to appreciate certain characteristics in aspiring candidates: having local roots is always welcomed (even in Britain, though it is by no means essential there), as is possessing a solid record as a party member. Sometimes, though, parties are willing to offer a candidacy to nonmembers who have proven appeal in the hope of thereby boosting the party's votes. For example, in Finland beauty queens and sports people with no party record are sometimes selected (Helander, pp. 64–65). Another universal pattern is that incumbent MPs are only rarely deselected; that is, they are nearly always picked to run again.

Most candidates in most parties are of higher socioeconomic status than the voters for the same parties, but this is not necessarily due to bias on the selectors' part. British candidate selectors are sometimes accused of favoring wealthy, upper-class men when making their choices, though an investigation of the selection process at the 1992 election concluded that the backgrounds of successful seekers after a nomination were not very different from those of unsuccessful ones, and so, apart from some possible discrimination against women by Labour selectors, there was little evidence of bias on the part of selectors (Norris and Lovenduski, 1997). In the Netherlands, a feeling that ordinary members overvalued long and faithful party service led to changes in candidate selection in several parties in the 1990s, with the national party organizations gaining more power and declaring their aim of ensuring the selection of more women and young people (Leijenaar and Niemöller, pp. 119–25). Beyond this, how far the selectors' own views impinge upon the nature of the candidates they select is a rather underresearched question. In some cases, there are suspicions that the members deliberately pass over aspiring candidates whose views are not the same as their own. In the 1980s, there was a widespread perception that members of the British Labour Party were left-wing "extremists" and that they were picking candidates of a similar persuasion, which might make the party unelectable. However, a study of British Labour Party activists found that although they saw themselves as farther to the left than Labour voters, they deliberately selected Labour candidates whose views were more moderate than their own so as not to damage the party's electoral chances (Bochel and Denver, p. 60).

BOX 10-2

SELECTION OF PARLIAMENTARY CANDIDATES

France

Parties in France tend to be dominated by a small number of prominent individuals, and this manifests itself in the candidate selection process. The two main right-wing parties, the RPR and UDF, usually fight elections in tandem, so they come to an arrangement as to which of them should contest each constituency. The central authorities of the parties, especially the national executives, play a decisive role in this and are also important in picking the candidates, though they need to be sensitive to the views of local notables. Communist Party candidates are chosen by the national executive. Local members have rather more say in the Socialist Party, although here, too, some central involvement is necessitated by the factionalized nature of the party; the factions are required to come to some overall arrangement on sharing the candidacies in order to preserve party unity. As in most countries, local roots are very important; most parliamentary deputies are simultaneously councillors (usually mayors) of their towns or villages, and resentment is created when candidates are "parachuted" by the central party authorities into constituencies with which they have no links.

Germany

Candidate selection is regulated by law, which ensures that the central authorities of the parties have very little power. Selection is carried out by local conventions consisting of delegates from party branches within the constituency. Once these local bodies have made their choice, the central bodies cannot enforce changes. There is very little variation between the parties. Although the German electoral system provides two routes to parliament (see Chapter 11), the parties do not look for different qualities in the candidates they nominate for the list seats and for the constituency seats; indeed, there is considerable overlap between the two sets of candidates.

Italy

The electoral system adopted in the mid-1990s, which is based primarily on single-member constituencies, has led to negotiations and deals among parties of the left and of the right as to which among a number of allied parties should present a candidate in each specific constituency. These deals are especially complicated on the left, because the center left is more fragmented than the center right. Once the allied parties have decided which one will contest which seat, candidate selection itself is a relatively oligarchic process. Candidate selection in the PDS (the former communists) is similar to that in the old PCI, with national leaders having the choice of the safest seats and the provincial and regional organizations making selections that require approval at national level. In the main right-wing party, Forza Italia, the dominance of the leader Silvio Berlusconi is reflected in the way candidates are picked, and, similarly, within the Lega Nord the leader, Umberto Bossi, retains considerable power over candidate selection, as over other matters of internal party life. In the Alleanza Nazionale, candidate selection is mainly under the control of the leadership group around the party leader, Gianfranco Fini.

Netherlands

There is some variation among the Dutch parties. The largest two, the CDA and the PvdA, took some power away from party members in the 1990s, with the central party organization exercising greater influence with the aim of selecting more women and young candidates than had been picked by the members, who had tended to place a high value on service to the party organization. In the liberal VVD, the national executive was already the most important actor; this party has been affected less than the CDA and PvdA by demands for democratization since the 1970s. A fourth party, Democrats '66, in contrast, places heavy stress on internal democracy and gives a postal vote in the candidate selection process to every paid-up member.

Spain

Because Spanish parties are leader dominated and have few members, it is not surprising to find that candidate selection is largely controlled by the leadership group. Although the leadership usually considers it wise to pay some regard to the feelings of the local party organization when settling on its lists around the country, it nonetheless retains a fairly free hand in deciding who should carry the party flag. Local activists occasionally show their displeasure with the centrally made selections by running dissident lists in the election, but these rarely achieve any success.

Sweden

As is the case in the other Scandinavian countries, central government and the central party authorities are less powerful in Sweden than across most of Western Europe. Local government is important, and, similarly, the

Continued . . .

Continued . . .

local party branches do not welcome or indeed expect any attempt on the part of party headquarters to dictate to them. Candidate selection in all the Swedish parties is carried out at the constituency level by conventions composed of delegates from the party branches in the constituency, and is firmly under the control of the local party organization. This even includes the Left Party, which deviates from the usual communist pattern of central control—a strong testimony to the Swedish concern for local autonomy.

United Kingdom

Candidate selection in Britain used to be dominated by local party activists, but in recent years there has been a movement toward giving ordinary members a direct voice. In the 1990s Labour adopted a "one member one vote" system, known by the acronym OMOV, allowing each member a direct vote in the selection process. This method is also employed by Britain's third party, the Liberal Democrats. The Conservative Party combines centralization and membership involvement. It maintains a list of about eight hundred centrally approved aspirant candidates, who have to go through a rigorous screening procedure, and constituency organizations are expected to draw up a shortlist from these names, with ordinary members making the final choice from this shortlist. Candidate selection in Britain is unusual in that, whereas parliamentarians in virtually every other country have roots in the constituency they hope to represent, selectors in Britain often pick someone with no previous connection with the constituency.

It may, indeed, not matter greatly exactly *who* within the party chooses the candidates, but it does matter a lot that it is *someone* within the party, and not the voters at large, who chooses them. Even if different actors within the party have different priorities and views on some issues, they all belong to the same party and are thus likely to have a broadly similar political outlook. Epstein (pp. 219, 225) points out that it is not necessary for the leadership to pick all the candidates directly, because the results of locally controlled selection are usually perfectly acceptable to it. Local party activists, just like the national leadership, want deputies who are loyal to the party line as defined nationally. For political parties, keeping candidate selection firmly under their own control has two great advantages. First, it helps retain the loyalty of ordinary party members. Deciding who will be allowed to use the party's name and resources in the election campaign is often the only real power members have, so allowing them to do this increases the party leaders' ability to retain a substantial body of cooperative members. Second, it enables the parties to behave as cohesive and disciplined bodies in parliament and in political negotiations with other parties. A European party organization controls access to its label at elections and can withhold it from parliamentarians who are not sufficiently loyal to the party line. Their American counterparts, lacking this power, cannot do this. The threats and blandishments of interest groups, political action committees (PACs), and constituents at large may all have to be taken seriously by American Congress members, but in Europe individual MPs must put the party first, last, and always. Defying the party line in parliament may lead to deselection at the next election, and they will have little chance of reelection without the party label. Outside the party there is no salvation, or at least no political career prospect.

For parliamentarians, this has the advantage of protecting them from the risk of being picked off one by one and from the threat of being targeted at the next election by powerful and well-funded single-issue interest groups. Whatever an interest group might threaten to do to a deputy who doesn't vote as it wants, it is nothing compared with what the party will do if the deputy doesn't vote as *it* wants. At the same time, the prospect of being deselected by the candidate selectors is a remote one for deputies who are loyal to the party. Most European parties have adopted a style of organization that keeps deputies on a fairly long leash held by the ordinary members but does not go so far as to make them mere poodles of unelected activists. Clearly, one could argue either in favor of the European model of strong and disciplined parliamentary parties, or in favor of the American pattern of greater independence of the individual Congress member. Regardless of which has more advantages, it is beyond dispute that disciplined and cohesive political parties are central to European parliamentary democracy, and that party control of candidate selection is essential to this. American-style direct primaries are incompatible with strong political parties (Ranney), and, in the last analysis, all the differences that are to be found within Europe are probably less significant than the differences between European and American candidate selection practices.

Sources of Party Finance

Because European parties do so much more as party organizations than U.S. parties, they need more resources. This is not to suggest that there is more money available in European politics than there is in the United States—almost certainly, the reverse is true. But in the United States most political funds are raised and spent by candidates rather than parties, whereas in Europe parties are much more central in raising and spending money, as in everything else.

European parties need money for two main reasons. First, they need it to run their organizations: to pay their head office staff and their telephone, postage, and other bills; to hold annual conferences and other meetings; and in some cases to support research institutions linked to the party. Second, they need cash to fight election campaigns, and this has become the main item of expenditure for nearly all parties. In the past, parties in most European countries were not allowed to buy television advertising space, though this is now possible in a growing number of countries (including Austria, Germany, Italy, the Netherlands, and Sweden). Even where this is still illegal, parties find plenty of other ways to spend money at election time: on newspaper and poster advertising; perhaps on a helicopter to whisk the party leader around the country on the campaign trail; on fax machines and mobile phones to keep candidates in touch with party headquarters; and on balloons, buttons, and general razzmatazz.

Parties get their money from a variety of sources (general overviews are given in Katz, pp. 124–32; Linton). Dues paid by members play a role, but nowadays they rarely produce more than a quarter of a party's income; the Netherlands, where membership dues comprise about half of party revenues, is a notable exception here (Koole, 1997). A second source of income exists when a party requests, or insists, that its parliamentary deputies and government ministers pay a proportion, perhaps as much as 10 percent, of their official salary into party coffers. Third, parties may engage in fund-raising activities, such as the garden fetes and church hall bazaars for which the British Conservatives are famous. Some parties publish their own newspapers, but these days, as mentioned, they are more often a drain on a party's coffers than a contributor to them.

interest groups and state-funding as regulation response .

Besides these three sources arising "internally," that is, from the party's own activities, there are also two important "external" sources of money. First, major interest groups back political parties whose policies they think will help them. In particular, business gives money to right-wing parties, and trade unions give money to left-wing parties. Second, in the great majority of European countries the state gives public money to political parties. Moreover, in almost every country there are benefits in kind, including free party broadcasts and mailings during election campaigns, as well as grants to the parliamentary groups to enable them to pay for secretarial and research assistance.

These two external sources of funding, contributions from interest groups and from the state, are linked, because concern about the consequences of parties becoming financially dependent on interest groups is one of the factors that has brought about the rise of state financing. Obviously, neither business corporations nor trade unions give money to parties simply out of bigheartedness. At the very least, they hope to help their chosen party get into government and implement policies broadly sympathetic to their own needs. Some sponsors may have more tangible benefits in mind. A business or a wealthy individual may give money to a party in the hope (or even on condition) that once in government, it will give the donor special access to decision makers, or even that the party's ministers will make a specific decision, perhaps on a tax liability or a request for land-use planning permission, that will repay the investment several times over. This is particularly likely to happen when, as is the case in many countries, there are no laws, or at most ineffective laws, compelling parties to disclose their financial sources.

The first European country to introduce state funding of its parties was West Germany in 1959. The German scheme has subsequently been expanded and altered several times and now involves huge sums of money. Parties winning more than 0.5 percent of the vote in an election receive 5 deutsche marks for every vote. This adds up to a lot of money, as around 50 million votes are cast at post-unification German elections. The result is that the German parties are awash with funds, and even after covering the costs of exceptionally large party bureaucracies and research institutes, they have enough left over to help like-minded parties in the poorer Mediterranean countries. In Germany's case, the past history of dictatorship may create a heightened willingness to spend a lot of money on preserving the institutions of liberal democracy. Other countries have rather more modest schemes, although the principle is the same: parties receive money in approximate proportion to their electoral strength. In some countries all the money is paid by the national government to the parties' national headquarters, while in others, especially in Scandinavia, a significant part of the cash flows from local government to the parties' local organizations. With expenditure rising constantly and most other sources of revenue proving erratic or unreliable, state-supplied income now looms large in the finances of parties in countries that have public funding schemes. In many countries that have state funding, this source of party income exceeds all other sources combined (Mair, pp. 141–42).

The pros and cons of taxpayer donation of money to political parties have been debated in many European countries. One argument, as we have seen, is that it frees parties from having to dance to the tune of wealthy financial backers and thus reduces

Former German Chancellor Helmut Kohl being confronted by journalists in 2000 over his admission that while in power he had received large financial donations for his party, the CDU, but had failed to declare these, in violation of the law. Kohl denied that government policy had ever been affected by a donation while he was in power, but refused to disclose the identity of the donors. © AP/Wide World Photos

corruption in politics generally. It may well have this effect overall, but it certainly does not eliminate the "sleaze factor" entirely, as periodic scandals demonstrate. In Italy, for example, an extensive scheme of state funding of parties did not prevent a number of parties engaging in corruption on a massive scale, in the "Tangentopoli" affair of the 1990s that we outlined in Chapters 2 and 7. In France, too, despite the introduction of state funding for parties in 1990, it seems to be tacitly accepted that local party organizations will fund themselves partly by siphoning off resources from the town or city councils that they control (Knapp and de Galès, pp. 283, 287–88). And in Germany, where, as we have seen, the parties receive lavish funding from the state, evidence emerges from time to time of the parties soliciting and receiving undeclared money from private sources. In late 1999 the former CDU Chancellor, Helmut Kohl, admitted that while in government he had received large donations on behalf of his party from business interests, though he refused to disclose the identity of the donors. Defenders of state financing maintain that there would be even more of this kind of thing if parties were entirely dependent on private sources (Mendilow, p. 112).

Another argument in favor of state financing is that not all parties can find wealthy interest groups that are keen to give them money. Generally speaking, right-wing parties receive large donations from business, and left-wing parties receive much smaller sums from trade unions. Center parties may get some money from business or, like the British Liberal Democrats, may not receive money from anyone. Parties whose policies appeal to no wealthy interest group—Green parties, for example—may receive only small sums from members and sympathetic individuals. State financing, besides coming without strings attached, is awarded according to a predetermined formula and thus seems to make competition "fairer." On the other hand, this line of argument can be used to rationalize a situation in which the parties already in parliament form a tacit "cartel," using their control of the state to vote themselves public money in a manner that reinforces their position by placing parties outside the cartel at a disadvantage (Katz and Mair, 1995, pp. 15–16).

Although some people claim that political parties are private bodies and as such have no right to expect money from the public purse, others point out that they fulfill a public function: they are essential to the workings of a democracy and therefore need to be sustained. Furthermore, the role of government has expanded greatly since the nineteenth century, and government is controlled by a ruling party or parties. Unless parties have the money to explore and expand policy options and to conduct research into the feasibility of their ideas, the country as a whole could suffer from the inadequately thought-out policies they promote.

The flow of money into a party is likely both to reflect and to reinforce the balance of power within the party. For donors other than the state, there is little point in giving money to people or groups within a party who have no power; it makes sense, obviously, for them to give money to those who wield the power and who can make the policy decisions that the donors wish to see. By doing this, of course, they further strengthen those to whom they give money. In Britain, it has been argued that both business donations to the Conservative central party organization and trade union donations to the Labour equivalent have reinforced the centralizing tendency within these parties (Fisher, p. 191). The pattern in Europe generally since the 1960s has been one of a dramatic increase in the amount of money going to central party bodies, both to the parliamentary party and to head office (Katz and Mair, 1992; Farrell and Webb).

Although every European party would no doubt like more money to finance its activities, most parties with reasonable levels of electoral support have sufficient resources to get their message across at elections. Individual party candidates fight elections on a national party platform and thus do not need much money to mount personal campaigns. The need for a personal campaign arises only when a preferential electoral system pits two or more candidates of the same party against each other (see Chapter 11). But even in these cases, a candidate who spends lavishly on a personal campaign rather than fighting as part of the party's team might well incur disapproval, perhaps from voters as well as from party members. Consequently, candidates are not beholden to interest groups and do not need the equivalent of America's PACs to bankroll their campaigns. Once again, we see in Europe the dominance of party over candidate, in marked contrast to the situation in the United States.

THE FUTURE OF EUROPEAN PARTIES

Even in the nineteenth century, it was recognized that European and American parties were different from one another. Writers from one continent were prone to praise the parties they knew and lament that those living on the other side of the Atlantic were not so fortunate; or, alternatively, they tended to see merit in the transatlantic model and express the hope that their own parties would change in that direction. Some writers, such as the Russian émigré Moisei Ostrogorski, lambasted both types of parties for different but apparently equally grave shortcomings. More recently, scholars have identified a number of phases through which parties as organizations have seemed to pass. Some have gone so far as to foresee the demise of European parties as distinct organizations, but others argue that while the organizational form of parties may be changing, European parties will remain strong organizations in certain respects and will continue to differ significantly from their American counterparts.

The Disappearance of European Parties?

There have been many attempts to assess changing patterns of European party organizations. In the 1950s the French writer Maurice Duverger maintained that the "mass party," with a large number of fee-paying members, a sizeable permanent bureaucracy in the head office, and a clear policy program, was the "new" or "modern" form of party, and foresaw a convergence towards this model (Duverger, p. 427). In contrast, Leon D. Epstein, writing in the 1960s, believed that mass parties belonged only to particular places and periods. He identified a number of "counter-organizational tendencies"—such as the increasing use of the mass media, especially television, during election campaigns, which reduced the need for thousands of ordinary party members to go out spreading the word in order to get the message across—that, he argued, would increasingly undermine the rationale for the existence of large-scale mass political parties (Epstein, pp. 233–60). In a similar vein, Otto Kirchheimer argued that changes in European society were bringing about changes in the type of party likely to flourish. Class lines were becoming less sharp, and the growth of the welfare state and the mixed economy had cut the ground from under the feet of old-style anti-system socialist parties, which had been dedicated to a radical transformation of society, with members living within a virtual subculture. The type of party best suited to current conditions was what Kirchheimer called "the postwar catch-all party," which tried to win votes from nearly all sections of society and would concentrate on general, bland issues such as better health and education services.

From this point of view, a party does not really need a large number of committed members. In the 1980s, Gunnar Sjöblom took this line of thought one step further and argued that members might actually be a handicap to a party, or at least to its parliamentarians. He suggested that various changes in society, such as increased mobility and the growing role of the mass media in conveying political messages, were leading to greater volatility among voters. People were suffering from "information overload"; they were confused by a never-ending stream of reports about proposals, decisions, and speculation, and were increasingly likely to vote on the basis of "political paraphernalia": trivial factors such as the style or appearance of the party leader (Sjöblom, p. 385). In this situation, members with a strong commitment to certain principles were a definite liability to the vote-hungry parliamentarians, who wanted the party to be able to change tack rapidly to take advantage of the shifting winds of public opinion. Party members trying to drum up support by faithfully plugging a traditional message were even seen as likely to have a counterproductive effect. Consequently, argued Sjöblom (p. 395), "it may be to the advantage of a party to have few and/or passive members."

Indeed, the deputy leader of the Spanish Socialist Party said in the 1980s that he would sooner have ten minutes of television broadcasting time than ten thousand members (Gillespie, 1989, p. 366). In most parties, the planning of election campaigns is carried out by "strategists" (often people who are not even party members) associated with and answerable to the party leader, rather than by any of the party bodies. Increasingly, many party elites rely on such professional advisors for policy formulation generally, thus minimizing the influence of ordinary members.

This argument seems to become even more persuasive when we think about the types of people who might make up the bulk of party members. We pointed out earlier that the factors that motivate people to join a party might be categorized as material, solidary, or purposive, and although each of these motives seems to be losing power, it may be that the first two have lost more of their force than the last. If this is the case, those joining for the third reason will form an increasing proportion of members, their ideological commitment no longer diluted by the more pragmatic members who joined for less explicitly political purposes. Even in the days before these trends got under way, there was already a plausible argument, backed up with evidence, to the effect that party members tend to be more "extreme" in their views than either voters or deputies (May). For example, in Sweden members of the main left-wing party hold views farther to the left than that party's voters, and members of the main right-wing party hold views that are farther to the right than that party's voters (Widfeldt, 1999, p. 263). This line of argument was expressed colorfully in the 1930s by an observer of the British Labour Party, who claimed that its local constituency organizations were "frequently unrepresentative groups of nonentities dominated by fanatics and cranks and extremists" (quoted in McKenzie, p. 194). Even if this is regarded as something of an exaggeration, it is quite plausible that members impose programmatic "costs" upon the party leadership by demanding that the party adopt certain policy stances as the price of their continued loyalty, and it may be that the policies they demand are ones that the voters as a whole do not find attractive (Strøm). Members, then, might saddle the party with vote-losing policies, in which case parliamentarians might prefer to dispense with members and instead communicate with the public entirely through the mass media.

Alternatively, rather than be dominated by unrealistic policy zealots, party organizations may come to attract only people who are interested in precisely that: party organization. Ware (1992, p. 79) quotes from a study of British Conservative members that concluded that "what all activists were interested in was not politics but organization." The Dutch PvdA engaged in some soul-searching in the late 1980s and early 1990s and concluded that the party suffered from a "meeting culture"; it demanded such high levels of participation that hardly anyone could reach them, so the organization had become "introverted" and obsessed with organizational questions (Wolinetz). In 1993 the second-largest party in Ireland, Fine Gael, established a commission to examine itself in the wake of some disappointing election results, and this too concluded that most activists were "essentially organization-oriented," which meant that the organization was inward-looking and of little value when it came to spreading the party's word locally. Party meetings, it said, were "tedious and uninteresting," and the party could not expect people to give up their time for "fruitless meetings or other pointless activity" (Fine Gael, pp. 39, 67, 40). In this scenario, members might not be a liability to the office-seeking leaders, but nor would they be much of an asset.

The Survival of European Parties

All of the above might suggest that European parties are on the road to becoming "modern cadre parties" or "head without a body" parties, with deputies in parliament but hardly any real presence on the ground. But this is, in fact, an unlikely scenario. Despite the unappealing picture sometimes painted of European party members, they are not in most cases quite the fanatical ideologues some accounts would lead one to believe. In all probability, most of them are ordinary sober citizens who join a party for a mixture of motives and whose attachment to certain general political principles is accompanied by a desire to see their party do well in elections. For example, as we saw earlier, Labour party activists in Britain when selecting candidates were found to subordinate their own personal views to the imperative of maximizing the party's electoral chances. A later study of Labour members found that Labour voters and members had similar attitudes on most issues; the only real exceptions concerned unilateral nuclear disarmament and increasing state control of industry, on which members were well to the left of Labour voters (Seyd and Whiteley, pp. 52–55).

Some studies have analyzed data that cast doubt upon the validity of May's argument that party activists are likely to hold more extremist opinions than MPs or voters. A detailed survey in Norway concluded that the pattern of attitudes varied from issue to issue, with MPs more likely than party members to hold the most "extreme" views (Narud and Skare). Research in Britain also concluded that members tended to be more centrist than MPs (Norris). In many parties, activists tend to be deferential toward the party leadership and prepared to go along with whatever it wants or does, provided, as we said, that it remains within the broad parameters of what is acceptable. To the extent that May's "law" is true, party leaders may be able to avoid its damaging effects by the seemingly paradoxical tactic of empowering individual members, especially those who do not attend branch meetings: if members are invited to decide issues of policy as atomized individuals, for example by means of a postal ballot in which members are able to vote without discussing the matter with other party members, the troublesome party activist layer of the party can be bypassed or marginalized (Mair, pp. 149–50). This trend is becoming more common across Western Europe, facilitated by the increasing use of centralized registers of party members held on computers.

Besides, even if they look at the matter in entirely self-interested terms, parliamentarians are aware that members have their uses. No matter how hi-tech election campaigns become, members demonstrating an active local party presence are still of benefit to the candidates. Even though television is the main political arena during election campaigns, it is an addition to rather than a replacement for the work done by the local organization. And although this local organization may not do a great deal between elections, there is a need to keep some kind of network in place during that period so that there is something to be activated at elections; if the local organization is allowed to atrophy, it will become very difficult to revive the party's unpaid workforce (Ware, 1992, p. 89).

Susan Scarrow (pp. 42–45) points out that, in theory at least, there are a number of other benefits that having members brings to a party. They bring legitimacy benefits, by fostering the impression, accurate or otherwise, that party leaders are at the apex of a principled movement rather than being merely a self-interested clique answerable to no one. For example, even in an era when election campaigns appear to be fought through the mass media, German voters still expect their parties to be visible locally as well; media strategies designed to market party elites need "validation" on the local level (Boll and Poguntke, p. 140). Members may also act as "ambassadors to the community," perhaps influencing the views of their friends and neighbors; a study of Labour members in a British constituency found that they were a visible and articulate local manifestation of the party (Martin and Cowley). In addition, members provide a source both of linkage with the wider electorate and of new ideas, as well as providing a recruitment pool from which party candidates and leaders can be drawn. Scarrow shows that in practice the main parties in Britain and Germany do try to recruit and keep members, despite the arguments of some academics who doubt the point of having members at all. If party membership is falling in Europe, this is happening because fewer people are interested in becoming members, not because parties are losing interest in having members.

Thus to talk about the "decline of party" in Europe is simplistic and misleading. It may be that parties' links with civil society are weakening, and that what could be termed "the party on the ground" is declining. Parties may be "withdrawing" from society, yet in other ways they are very active. Those faces of the party that could be termed "the party in public office," that is, the party organization in government and in parliament, and "the party in central office," that is, the headquarters and central organs of the party, may not be declining. Indeed, there is plenty of evidence that these aspects of many European parties are becoming stronger (Mair, pp. 120–54). Katz and Mair (1995) argue that earlier forms of party organization, such as the cadre, mass, and catch-all models, are being challenged or supplanted by what they term the "cartel party," in which the parties collude with each other in various ways, especially in the use of state resources to fund themselves, to such an extent that the parties virtually become part of the state rather than actors that link civil society with the state (for a critique of the cartel party model, see Koole, 1996).

European parties, then, are adapting rather than declining or disappearing. They continue to be vital organs of representation in European politics, and, despite suggestions that their members' views and backgrounds are likely to be unrepresentative of voters, we have seen that in many ways the political values and social profile of party members are not such as to distort profoundly the process of representative government. European parties will continue to be fundamentally different from American ones for as long as they retain control over the selection of their candidates, and there is no prospect of their relinquishing that prerogative. Elections in Europe will continue to center on parties rather than candidates. Electors will continue to vote for parties; seats in parliaments will continue to be divided among parties. The link between votes and seats is forged by electoral systems, and it is to this subject that we now turn.

REFERENCES

Bochel, John, and David Denver: "Candidate Selection in the Labour Party: What the Selectors Seek", *British Journal of Political Science,* vol. 13, no. 1, 1983, pp. 45–69.

Boll, Bernhard, and Thomas Poguntke: "Germany: The 1990 All-German Election Campaign", in Shaun Bowler and David M. Farrell (eds.), *Electoral Strategies and Political Marketing,* Macmillan, Basingstoke, 1992, pp. 121–43.

Clark, Peter B., and James Q. Wilson: "Incentive Systems: A Theory of Organizations", *Administrative Science Quarterly,* vol. 6, 1961, pp. 129–66.

Colomer, Josep M.: "Spain and Portugal: Rule by Party Leadership", in Josep M. Colomer (ed.), *Political Institutions in Europe,* Routledge, London, 1996, pp. 170–210.

Duverger, Maurice: *Political Parties,* 3d ed., Methuen, London, 1964.

Epstein, Leon D.: *Political Parties in Western Democracies,* rev. ed., Transaction Books, New Brunswick, N.J., 1980.

Farrell, David M. and Paul Webb: "Political Parties as Campaign Organizations", in Russell Dalton and Martin Wattenberg (eds.), *Parties Without Partisans,* Oxford University Press, Oxford, 2000, chapter 6.

Fine Gael: *Report of the Commission on Renewal of Fine Gael,* Fine Gael, Dublin, 1993.

Fisher, Justin: "The Institutional Funding of British Political Parties", in David Broughton, David M. Farrell, David Denver and Colin Rallings (eds.), *British Elections and Parties Yearbook 1994,* Frank Cass, London, 1995, pp. 181–96.

Gaffney, John: "The Emergence of a Presidential Party: The Socialist Party", in Alistair Cole (ed.), *French Political Parties in Transition,* Dartmouth, Aldershot, 1990, pp. 61–90.

Gallagher, Michael: "Conclusion", in Michael Gallagher and Michael Marsh (eds.), *Candidate Selection in Comparative Perspective: The Secret Garden of Politics,* Sage, London and Newbury Park, 1988, pp. 236–83.

Gillespie, Richard: *The Spanish Socialist Party: A History of Factionalism,* Clarendon, Oxford, 1989.

Gillespie, Richard: " 'Programa 2000': The Appearance and Reality of Socialist Renewal in Spain", *West European Politics,* vol. 16, no. 1, 1993, pp. 78–96.

Hardarson, Ólafur Th.: *Parties and Voters in Iceland: A Study of the 1983 and 1987 Althingi Elections,* Social Science Research Institute, University of Iceland, Reykjavík, 1995.

Heidar, Knut: "A 'New' Party Leadership?", in Kaare Strøm and Lars Svåsand (eds.), *Challenges to Political Parties: The Case of Norway,* University of Michigan Press, Ann Arbor, 1997, pp. 125–47.

Helander, Voitto: "Finland", in Pippa Norris (ed.), *Passages to Power: Legislative Recruitment in Advanced Democracies,* Cambridge University Press, Cambridge, 1997, pp. 56–75.

Jacobs, Francis (ed.): *Western European Political Parties: A Comprehensive Guide,* Longman, Harlow, 1989.

Katz, Richard S.: "Party Organizations and Finance", in Lawrence LeDuc, Richard G. Niemi and Pippa Norris (eds.), *Comparing Democracies: Elections and Voting in Global Perspective,* Sage, Thousand Oaks, 1996, pp. 107–33.

Katz, Richard S. and Peter Mair (eds.): *Party Organizations: a Data Handbook,* Sage, London and Newbury Park, 1992.

Katz, Richard S. and Peter Mair: "Changing Models of Party Organization and Party Democracy: The Emergence of the Cartel Party", *Party Politics,* vol. 1, no. 1, 1995, pp. 5–28.

Kirchheimer, Otto: "The Transformation of the Western European Party System", in Joseph La Palombara and Myron Weiner (eds.), *Political Parties and Political Development,* Princeton University Press, Princeton, 1966, pp. 177–200.

Knapp, Andrew and Patrick de Galès: "Top-Down to Bottom-Up? Centre–Periphery Relations and Power Structures in France's Gaullist Party", *West European Politics,* vol. 16, no. 3, 1993, pp. 271–94.

Koole, Ruud: "Cadre, Catch-all or Cartel? A Comment on the Notion of the Cartel Party", *Party Politics,* vol. 2, no. 4, 1996, pp. 507–23.

Koole, Ruud: "Party Finance Between Members and the State: The Dutch Case in Comparative and Historical Perspective", paper presented at the 17th World Congress of the International Political Science Association, Seoul, 17–21 August, 1997.

Leijenaar, Monique and Kees Niemöller: "The Netherlands", in Pippa Norris (ed.), *Passages to Power: Legislative Recruitment in Advanced Democracies,* Cambridge University Press, Cambridge, 1997, pp. 114–36.

Linton, Martin: *Money and Votes,* Institute for Public Policy Research, London, 1994.

Mair, Peter: *Party System Change: Approaches and Interpretations,* Clarendon Press, Oxford, 1997.

Mair, Peter and Ingrid van Biezen: "Trends in Enrolment in Political Parties in European Polities, with Particular Reference to Youth Enrolment", paper presented to the conference on Youth and Democracy, International IDEA, Stockholm, 17–19 June, 1999.

Marsh, Michael: "Introduction: Selecting the Party Leader", *European Journal of Political Research,* vol. 24, no. 3, 1993, pp. 229–31.

Martin, Alan and Philip Cowley: "Ambassadors in the Community? Labour Party Members in Society", *Politics,* vol. 19, no. 2, 1999, pp. 89–96.

May, John D.: "Opinion Structure of Political Parties: The Special Law of Curvilinear Disparity", *Political Studies,* vol. 21, no. 2, 1973, pp. 135–51.

McKenzie, Robert: "Power in the Labour Party: The Issue of 'Intra-Party Democracy'", in Dennis Kavanagh (ed.), *The Politics of the Labour Party,* George Allen and Unwin, London, 1982, pp. 191–201.

Mendilow, Jonathan: "Public Party Funding and Party Transformation in Multiparty Systems", *Comparative Political Studies,* vol. 25, no. 1, 1992, pp. 90–117.

Müller, Wolfgang C.: "The Catch-All Party Thesis and the Austrian Social Democrats", *German Politics,* vol. 1, no. 2, 1992, pp. 181–99.

Narud, Hanne Marthe and Audun Skare: "Are Party Activists the Party Extremists? The Structure of Opinion in Political Parties", *Scandinavian Political Studies,* vol. 22, no. 1, 1999, pp. 45–65.

Norris, Pippa: "May's Law of Curvilinear Disparity Revisited: Leaders, Officers, Members and Voters in British Political Parties", *Party Politics,* vol. 1, no. 1, 1995, pp. 29–47.

Norris, Pippa and Joni Lovenduski: *Political Recruitment: Gender, Race and Class in the British Parliament,* Cambridge University Press, Cambridge, 1995.

Norris, Pippa and Joni Lovenduski: "United Kingdom", in Pippa Norris (ed.), *Passages to Power: Legislative Recruitment in Advanced Democracies,* Cambridge University Press, Cambridge, 1997, pp. 158–86.

Plasser, Fritz, Peter A. Ulram, and Alfred Grausgruber: "The Decline of 'Lager Mentality' and the New Model of Electoral Competition in Austria", in Kurt Richard Luther and

Wolfgang C. Müller (eds.), *Politics in Austria: Still a Case of Consociationalism?* Frank Cass, London, 1992, pp. 16–44.

Ranney, Austin: *Curing the Mischiefs of Faction: Party Reform in America,* University of California Press, Berkeley and London, 1975.

Rentoul, John: *Tony Blair,* Little, Brown, London, 1995.

Sainsbury, Diane: "The Swedish Social Democrats and the Legacy of Continuous Reform: Asset or Dilemma?", *West European Politics,* vol. 16, no. 1, 1993, pp. 39–61.

Scarrow, Susan: *Parties and their Members: Organizing for Victory in Britain and Germany,* Oxford University Press, Oxford, 1996.

Scarrow, Susan, Paul Webb and David M. Farrell: "From Social Integration to Electoral Contestation: The Changing Distribution of Political Power within Political Parties", in Russell Dalton and Martin Wattenberg (eds.), *Parties Without Partisans,* Oxford University Press, Oxford, 2000, chapter 10.

Seyd, Patrick, and Paul Whiteley: *Labour's Grass Roots: The Politics of Party Membership,* Clarendon, Oxford, 1992.

Sjöblom, Gunnar: "Political Change and Political Accountability: A Propositional Inventory of Causes and Effects", in Hans Daalder and Peter Mair (eds.), *Western Europe Party Systems,* Sage, London, 1983, pp. 369–403.

Strøm, Kaare: "A Behavioral Theory of Competitive Political Parties", *American Journal of Political Science,* vol. 34, no. 2, 1990, pp. 565–98.

Svåsand, Lars, Kaare Strøm and Bjørn Erik Rasch: "Change and Adaptation in Party Organization", in Kaare Strøm and Lars Svåsand (eds.), *Challenges to Political Parties: The Case of Norway,* University of Michigan Press, Ann Arbor, 1997, pp. 91–123.

Togeby, Lise: "The Nature of Declining Party Membership in Denmark: Causes and Consequences", *Scandinavian Political Studies,* vol. 15, no. 1, 1992, pp. 1–19.

Ware, Alan: "Activist–Leader Relations and the Structure of Political Parties: 'Exchange Models' and Vote-Seeking Behaviour in Parties", *British Journal of Political Science,* vol. 22, no. 1, 1992, pp. 71–92.

Ware, Alan: *Political Parties and Party Systems,* Oxford University Press, Oxford, 1996.

Whiteley, Paul, Patrick Seyd, and Jeremy Richardson: *True Blues: the Politics of Conservative Party Membership,* Oxford University Press, Oxford, 1994.

Widfeldt, Anders: "Party Membership and Party Representativeness", in Hans-Dieter Klingemann and Dieter Fuchs (eds.), *Citizens and the State,* Oxford University Press, Oxford, 1995, pp. 134–182.

Widfeldt, Anders: *Linking Parties with People? Party Membership in Sweden 1960–1997,* Ashgate, Aldershot, 1999.

Wolinetz, Steven B.: "Reconstructing Dutch Social Democracy", *West European Politics,* vol. 16, no. 1, 1993, pp. 97–111.

11

ELECTIONS, ELECTORAL SYSTEMS, AND REFERENDUMS

Elections are central to representative government in Europe. Their significance is both practical and symbolic. In practical terms, they play a large role in determining who becomes part of the political elite. In addition, they have a major bearing on the formation of governments, although, given the frequent complexity of government formation in modern Europe, their impact in this respect may be only indirect (see Chapter 12). As we saw in the previous chapter, elections have become the focal point of activity for most European parties.

Elections are also important symbolically in most competitive party systems, legitimizing a country's political system in the eyes of its citizens. They offer a means of participating in politics at relatively low cost to the individual, in terms of time, money, and mental effort. For most people, indeed, voting in elections is their only active participation in the political process. Elections also give citizens the feeling that they are exercising choices on who should represent them in the national parliament and on who should form the next government, even though the vote of any individual elector is highly unlikely to have much impact on either matter.

Elections themselves consist everywhere of citizens casting votes for candidates and/or political parties, but there is considerable variation across Europe in the precise set of electoral laws that determines how the votes that are cast are transformed into seats in the legislature in each country. In this chapter, we consider the variations in electoral systems in some detail, because these variations can have a significant bearing on some of the major differences in party politics across Europe. A country's electoral system can affect the nature of its party system, the sociodemographic composition of its parliament, the accuracy with which voters' preferences are reflected in the composition of the legislature, and the likelihood that governments will be formed by a coalition of parties rather than by just a single party.

Elections decide which parties and which candidates hold seats in parliaments, but they do not necessarily reflect a judgment on issues. At general elections, a lot of issues may be mixed up together, and even if a particular party highlights one issue especially, the degree of support for that party cannot necessarily be interpreted as the voters' verdict on that issue. In a number of European countries, therefore, the device of the referendum is employed precisely to obtain the voters' decision on a specific issue. To some, this is a welcome development, as it provides for greater direct participation in the decision-making process; to others, it raises the fear that existing political institutions such as parliaments, governments, and political parties will be weakened. Therefore we shall end the chapter by assessing the role of referendums in modern European politics, and asking whether use of the referendum amounts to "direct democracy" and as such constitutes a challenge to representative government.

Before looking in detail at the nature and impact of electoral systems and the effects of referendums, we briefly outline some central aspects of the legal framework regulating elections in Europe—specifically, the nature of the electorate and the timing of elections.

ELECTIONS IN EUROPE

Who Votes?

Elections in all European states are now held under a universal adult franchise. In most countries, universal male suffrage had been won by the time of World War I and female suffrage by World War II, although women did not receive the vote until immediately after World War II in Belgium, France, Greece, and Italy, and not until the 1970s in Switzerland. Changing legal definitions of adulthood have brought down the voting age in many countries, characteristically to eighteen, although in a few countries it remains at nineteen or twenty. Most countries restrict voting rights to their own citizens, but the United Kingdom and Ireland allow each other's resident citizens to vote in their elections. Certain categories of citizens are disfranchised in many countries, including people serving prison sentences and those confined to mental institutions. Generally speaking, the qualifications needed to be an election candidate are the same as those for being a voter (for details, see Katz, 1997, pp. 246–61).

In European countries it is the responsibility of the state to ensure that the electoral register—the list of eligible voters—contains the names of all those entitled to vote, so the register is far more accurate than in the United States, for example, where the onus is on individuals to register themselves as voters. The proportion of the voting-age population that turns out to vote tends to be higher in Europe than in the United States, in most countries reaching between 70 and 85 percent. The exceptions are Switzerland, where turnout has fallen steadily since the war to below 50 percent, and, at the other end of the scale, Italy, along with some countries where voting is or has been compulsory (Belgium, the Netherlands, Luxembourg, and Austria). In all of these countries, turnout at many elections since the war has approached or even exceeded 90 percent. Since the late 1970s, though, turnout has been decreasing at elections all across Europe (see Table 9-8).

When Do People Vote?

In most countries, the law or constitution prescribes a maximum period between elections, but not a minimum; this maximum is four years in most Western European countries and five years in the rest (see Table 3-2). In Norway, Sweden, and Switzerland, in contrast, parliaments have a fixed life span of four years. Within these rules, the timing of parliamentary elections is usually, on paper at least, at the discretion of the government of the day. To be precise, governments, or sometimes specifically the prime minister, typically have the power to recommend a dissolution of parliament to a head of state who almost invariably takes this advice. In France, it is the president who has the right to call parliamentary elections at any time (though not more than once a year), even against the wishes of the government, which may be of a different political complexion. This happened when, immediately after being reelected in 1988, Socialist President Mitterrand dissolved the parliament without the approval of the right-wing government. French presidential elections are held at fixed seven-year intervals, though a move to a five-year presidential term has been discussed.

Since most governments, on paper, have complete freedom of action as to exactly when within this time span they call an election, we could expect that governments would choose to dissolve legislatures at times when they expected to do well in the subsequent election. This can undoubtedly make the timing of elections an important strategic variable—but in fact this really applies only to certain countries. In nine of the nineteen countries that we are considering, it is indeed accepted that the government may call an election pretty much whenever it wants; these countries are Austria, Denmark, France, Greece, Ireland, Italy, Malta, Spain, and the United Kingdom. In the other ten countries there is a more stable election cycle, fixed either by law, as in Norway and Sweden, or by practice and convention. For example, in Luxembourg it has become accepted that elections take place every five years, on the same day as elections to the European Parliament. In these ten countries a government that dissolved parliament early in the hope of gaining a partisan advantage would be seen as having "cut and run" and as having violated a political cultural norm. Conventions do not always carry the same force as law, so these established patterns can be disrupted by a major crisis or an unforeseen development, but in many European countries all the political actors have a pretty good idea several years in advance as to when the next election is coming round.

Parliamentary elections, of course, are merely one of a number of opportunities people have to vote in Europe. In all countries there are also elections for local councils (these are quite important in Scandinavia), and in several there are regional or provincial elections (for example, in Austria, France, Germany, Italy, Spain, and the United Kingdom), as we saw in Chapter 6. The member states of the European Union (EU) hold elections to choose members of the European Parliament; these elections, which we discussed in more detail in Chapter 5, take place every five years. In a few countries, as we noted in Chapter 3, the president is directly elected by the people; besides France, this occurs in Austria, Finland, Iceland, Ireland, and Portugal, as well as a number of postcommunist countries. In addition, as we shall see in the last section of this chapter, the referendum is employed in a number of European countries.

TYPES OF ELECTORAL SYSTEMS

In the rest of this chapter we concentrate on parliamentary elections, the most important political contests in every Western European country with the possible exception of France. In particular, we will concentrate on electoral systems, the mechanisms that turn the votes cast by people on election day into seats to be occupied by deputies in the parliament. The electoral system is what converts the choices of the voters into a legislature.

A wide variety of electoral systems is in use across Europe, and there is an equally wide selection of literature describing and tracing the history of these systems (see Carstairs; Farrell; Mackie and Rose). This variety reflects in part the different weights attached to different criteria in different countries. It also reflects the fact that the electoral law a country adopts is usually determined by the political elite of the day, some of whose motivations may well be partisan. In addition, electoral reformers have devised a plethora of systems and formulas, some of which have captured the imagination of politicians in various countries at various times. Having said this, we should note that it is not true that ruling parties constantly tinker with electoral systems for their own advantage; there have been very few major changes in electoral systems in Western Europe since 1945, and only in France and Greece has the electoral system been used as a political football (Cole and Campbell; Dimitras, 1994a).

For all this diversity, there are several systematic patterns in the profusion of electoral systems to be found in Western Europe (Lijphart 1994; Reynolds and Reilly; Taagepera and Shugart). One vital distinction is between proportional representation (PR) systems on the one hand and plurality, or majority, systems on the other. The former put more stress on the concept of proportionality, the numerical accuracy with which the votes cast for parties are translated into seats won in parliament. Under a PR system, if a party receives, say, 25 percent of the votes, it can expect to win close to 25 percent of the seats. If every party participating in an election were guaranteed exactly the same share of seats as of the votes it had won, we would describe that system as perfectly proportional, although this would not necessarily mean that the system was "perfect" in a normative sense. In practice, no electoral system can guarantee perfect proportionality, but PR systems attach greater priority to getting somewhere close to this goal. Plurality systems do not, of course, set out deliberately *not* to achieve high proportionality, but by prioritizing other criteria they accept a certain level of disproportionality as inevitable. An overview of Western European electoral systems in these terms is shown in Table 11-1.

PLURALITY SYSTEMS

Throughout the nineteenth century, elections in most countries were held under plurality systems, but a combination of factors led almost all countries to adopt some form of proportional representation in the twentieth century. At the moment, only two Western European countries do not use an electoral system that has at least an element of PR: these are the United Kingdom and France.

The electoral system used in the United Kingdom is the least complicated of all systems. It is the same as that employed for most elections in the United States, Canada,

TABLE 11-1   ELECTORAL SYSTEMS IN WESTERN EUROPE, 2000

	Basic category	Members of lower house	Number of constituencies (districts)	Significant changes since 1945*
Austria	PR (list)	183	43[†]	Introduction in 1992 of a third tier, increase from 9 to 43 districts, and minor expansion of effectiveness of preferential voting
Belgium	PR (list)	150	20[†]	None
Denmark	PR (list)	175	18[†]	Change of formula from DH to MSL in 1953
Finland	PR (list)	200	15	None
France	Non-PR (2-ballot)	577	577	Many (see text p. 308)
Germany	Additional member	656	329[†]	Minor changes in 1953 and 1956, 1984, and 1990
Greece	PR (list)	300	56[†]	Many changes, usually designed to benefit the government of the day
Iceland	PR (list)	63	9[†]	Minor change in 1987
Ireland	PR (STV)	166	41	None
Italy	Semi-PR/ additional member	630	476[†]	Abandonment in 1993 of previous highly proportional system
Luxembourg	PR (list)	60	4	No
Malta	PR (STV)	65	13	Winner in votes guaranteed majority of seats since 1987
Netherlands	PR (list)	150	1	Minor increase in effectiveness of preferential voting in 1998
Norway	PR (list)	165	20[†]	Change of formula from DH to MSL in 1953; addition of 8 national seats before 1989 election
Portugal	PR (list)	230	20	First democratic election in 1975
Spain	PR (list)	350	52	First democratic postwar election in 1977
Sweden	PR (list)	349	29[†]	Change of formula from DH to MSL in 1952; introduction of higher-tier seats in 1970; introduction of meaningful preference voting in 1998
Switzerland	PR (list)	200	26	None
United Kingdom	Non-PR (plurality)	659	659	None

*Abbreviations for electoral formulae: DH—d'Hondt; MSL—Modified Sainte-Laguë; STV—Single transferable vote.
[†]Country has "complex districting," i.e., higher-tier constituencies to iron out discrepancies arising from lower-level constituencies.
Source: Mackie and Rose; annual updates in the *Political Data Yearbook* of the *European Journal of Political Research.*

and India, for example. The country is divided into 659 areas, known as constituencies or districts, each of which returns one member of parliament (MP) to the House of Commons. Within each constituency, the candidate with the most votes, whether or not this is a majority over all others combined, wins the seat. The system is best named the single-member plurality (SMP) system, though it is often called "first past the post,"

TABLE 11-2   THE BRITISH ELECTORAL SYSTEM IN OPERATION, NORFOLK NORTH CONSTITUENCY, 1997 ELECTION

	Votes	% of votes
David Prior (Conservative)	21,456	36.5
N. Lamb (Liberal Democrat)	20,163	34.3
M. Cunningham (Labour)	14,736	25.1
J. Allen (Referendum Party)	2,458	4.2

Source: Rallings and Thrasher, p. 92.

in a rather dubious analogy with horse racing, or simply "the British system." Voters, on entering the polling station, are given a ballot paper listing all the candidates, and they write an X next to the name of the candidate they wish to vote for. An example of the operation of the system in a constituency in Norfolk, in East Anglia on the east coast of England, in the 1997 general election is shown in Table 11-2.

This system has the merit of simplicity, both for voters and for those who count the votes. It is also defended on the ground that as the MP, in this case David Prior, is the only representative for the constituency, responsibility for its interests lies unequivocally with him. This, it is claimed, helps forge a bond between the MP and the constituents that would be lost if several MPs were responsible for the same constituency. In terms of the national impact, as we discuss later, the system is praised for its tendency to produce single-party majority governments.

But the plurality system has its critics (many of their arguments can be found in Finer; see also Reeve and Ware). Three of the main points made against it are illustrated by the Norfolk North result. First, Prior was elected despite winning less than 40 percent of the total votes; in fact, 64 percent of the voters were not represented by a candidate of their favored party. It is probable that most Labour voters would have preferred the election of the Liberal Democrat candidate to the actual outcome, and so in a straight fight between the Conservative and the Liberal Democrat, the latter would have won. Therefore, the British system is criticized for not necessarily producing the MP who would be most representative of the voters' wishes and, worse, for producing results that are in some sense arbitrarily determined by the nomination of "vote-splitting" losing candidates.

Second, the Norfolk North contest presented Labour supporters in particular with a tactical choice: should they vote for the Labour candidate, or should they vote for the Liberal Democrat in order to keep the Conservative out? If they vote sincerely, in accordance with their true preferences, then this might have the effect of helping to bring about the election of the candidate they like least. Although no electoral system is completely "strategy-proof," the plurality system is almost guaranteed to force at least some voters to think strategically if there are more than two serious candidates.

Third, if the pattern of the Norfolk North result, with over 60 percent of the votes wasted on losing candidates, were repeated over the entire country, the House of Commons could be very unrepresentative of public opinion. In practice, the lack of "fairness" in individual constituencies tends to even itself out to some extent across the

TABLE 11-3   VOTES AND SEATS IN THE UNITED KINGDOM GENERAL
ELECTION OF 1997

	% of votes	% of seats
Labour	43.3	63.6
Conservatives	30.7	25.0
Liberal Democrats	16.8	7.0
Others	9.2	4.4
Total	100.0	100.0

Source: See source of Table 7-1.

country. Consequently, between 1945 and the 1970s, when nearly all the votes were won by the two main parties, Labour and the Conservatives, the national outcome in terms of seats was not grossly unrepresentative. But when a third party (the Liberals in 1974 and 1979, the alliance between the Liberal and the Social Democratic parties in 1983 and 1987, the Liberal Democrats in 1992 and 1997) began winning significant support, the national outcome fell much farther short of perfect proportionality, with the third party the main victim. This is illustrated by the result of the 1997 election (see Table 11-3). In this election, what appeared to be an overwhelming Labour win in parliament was in fact "manufactured" by the electoral system, as nearly three out of every five voters voted against Labour. The capriciousness of this electoral system was perhaps best illustrated by an election held outside Europe: the Progressive Conservatives in Canada, who had won a large majority of the seats on 43 percent of the votes in the 1988 election, found themselves reduced to just two seats in parliament after winning 16 percent of the votes in the October 1993 election.

Although the plurality electoral system may seem very firmly entrenched in the United Kingdom, it has come under increasing challenge in recent years. Indeed, the country now employs a variety of different electoral systems in different settings. When elections to the Scottish parliament and the Welsh assembly took place in 1999, these were held under a two-vote additional member system (we discuss this and other systems later in the chapter), comparable to that used in Germany. The 1998 elections to the Northern Ireland assembly, like all other elections in the province, were held under the single transferable vote, which is used in the Republic of Ireland. The European Parliament elections of 1999 to elect Britain's 84 MEPs took place using a closed-list system, like that used for parliamentary elections in Spain, with the country divided into eleven constituencies; the other three MEPs from the United Kingdom, those representing Northern Ireland, were elected under the single transferable vote. After its 1997 election victory, the incoming Labour government set up a commission, headed by the former minister Roy Jenkins, to examine the case for a new electoral system, with the idea of putting its recommendation to a referendum. The Jenkins commission reported in favor of a variant of the two-vote additional member system, but plans for a referendum were put on the back burner by the government (Dunleavy and Margetts).

One relatively modest modification that has been suggested by some British electoral reformers is the introduction of "preferential" voting rather than "X" voting. Voters would rank the candidates in order of preference by placing a number ("1," "2," etc.) next to each name. The counting process would no longer finish with the counting of the first preferences; instead, if no candidate had a majority, the lowest-placed candidate would be eliminated and his or her votes transferred to the other candidates, in accordance with the second preferences marked on them. So, in Norfolk North, the Referendum Party candidate, and then the Labour candidate, would be eliminated. Assuming that a majority of Labour voters gave their second preference to the Liberal Democrat candidate rather than to the Conservative, the Liberal Democrat would almost certainly be carried above the Conservative and would therefore win the seat. This electoral system is known as the *alternative vote,* or the single transferable vote in single-member constituencies. It is a majority system, as opposed to the British and French plurality systems, because the counting process continues until one candidate has a majority (50 percent plus 1) over all other remaining candidates.

No European country uses the alternative vote to elect its parliament (though it is employed in Australian elections), but a system that has some of the same properties is used in France. There, as in Britain, deputies are returned from single-member constituencies, but there is provision for two rounds of voting, on successive Sundays. If a candidate wins a majority of votes in the first round, he or she is elected; this happens on average in only about 5 percent of constituencies (Goldey, p. 552). Otherwise, it is followed by a second round of voting. Candidates who received the votes of fewer than 12.5 percent of those registered to vote (which on the basis of the 1997 election turnout equates to about 19 percent of the votes cast) in the first round are excluded, while the others are entitled to go on to compete in the second round. The candidate with the most votes (a simple plurality) in the second round wins the seat, even if he or she fails to achieve an overall majority. For this reason the French system is ultimately a plurality rather than a majority system, because a majority of votes, though of course sufficient, is not always necessary for election. (Presidential elections are held under the same system, except that only the top two candidates from the first round are allowed to proceed to the second, thus guaranteeing that the eventual winner will emerge with an absolute majority.)

This two-round double ballot system has some advantages over the British system, as it gives supporters of losing first-round candidates a chance to switch their second-round votes to one of the serious contenders. The first of the two rounds could also be used by the two main blocs as quasi-primaries, but the established right-wing parties, the RPR and the UDF, generally agree on a single right-wing candidate in each constituency before the first round, sharing the constituencies out between them. Thus, in 1997 there was just one candidate from the established right on the first ballot in 550 of the 555 mainland French constituencies (Goldey, p. 539). On the left, in contrast, the two main parties, the Socialists and the Communists, usually nominate a candidate each in every constituency for the first ballot, and the one with fewer votes then stands aside for the stronger on the second ballot. Over the years this has increasingly benefited the Socialists more than the Communists; the latter's first-ballot votes have steadily fallen, to the extent that many more Communist candidates stand aside for Socialists than vice versa, and, in addition, Communist voters switch to Socialist candidates on the second ballot more solidly than Socialist voters switch to Communist candidates.

In 1997, though, the Socialists came to preelection agreements both with minor parties and with the Communists (Goldey, p. 540).

But even if it does have the potential to give a slightly greater choice to the voters, the French system, like the British, does not overcome the problem, if such it is, of disproportional overall results. In 1968, for example, the Gaullists (now the RPR) won only 44 percent of the votes but 60 percent of the seats, and in 1981 the Socialists won 56 percent of the seats with just 38 percent of the votes. Most dramatically of all, in 1993, the two main right-wing parties (the RPR and UDF, the so-called brother enemies) won 80 percent of the seats with just 38 percent of the votes. Like the British system, the French two-ballot system assists the largest parties and penalizes smaller ones. In addition, it benefits parties close to the center, such as the RPR, the UDF, and the Socialists, and works against more extreme parties, such as the Communists (PCF) and the far-right Front National (FN). Such parties, even if their candidates make it into the second round, are very unlikely to win the run-off against the candidate of more centrist parties, and so they win a smaller share of the seats than of the votes. The PCF has some scope for deal-making with the Socialists, albeit on the Socialists' terms, and thus wins some seats, but the FN is generally treated as a pariah by the other parties, and usually ends up with few or no seats; in 1997, for example, it received 15 percent of the votes but won only one seat out of 577. For supporters of the double-ballot system, this pronounced penalization of "anti-system" parties is a definite merit (Sartori, p. 67).

In France, more than in any other country, the electoral system has been manipulated by ruling parties for their own benefit (for details, see Cole and Campbell). The two-round system was used for most of the period between 1831 and 1939, though other systems were often tried for short periods. After World War II, a PR system was used briefly, but in the early 1950s a new system was introduced, with the clear aim of discriminating against the Communist Party. The double ballot was brought back under de Gaulle in the late 1950s. The Socialists replaced it by PR for the 1986 election, partly to minimize their electoral losses, but the incoming right-wing administration promptly reintroduced the double-ballot system, under which subsequent parliamentary elections have been held.

PROPORTIONAL REPRESENTATION

Discontent with the anomalies produced by plurality or majority systems, combined inevitably with self-interested calculations by those parties that were faring, or seemed likely to fare, badly under such systems, led to discussion of electoral reform throughout Europe in the second half of the nineteenth century. By the end of World War II, nearly all countries had electoral systems based on PR. The key element in any PR electoral system is the multimember constituency. Seats are allocated to parties within each constituency in broad proportion to the votes each receives. Proportional representation systems cannot be based on single-member constituencies, because a single seat cannot be divided up proportionately, no matter what method is used to allocate it. As a general rule, indeed, the larger the district magnitude (i.e., the number of members returned from each constituency), the more proportional the national election result is likely to be. This, it should be stressed, applies only when a PR formula is used. If a plurality or majority formula is employed in multimember constituencies, as when American public representatives are elected from "at-large" districts, the result is highly disproportional, being even less considerate to minorities than a series of single-seat constituencies.

There are important variations among PR systems, but basically they can be categorized into list systems on the one hand and the single transferable vote (STV) system on the other. STV tends to be confined to the English-speaking world, and systems based on lists arc far more common in Europe as a whole.

List Systems

The basic principle of a list system is that each party presents a list of candidates in each constituency. Each list usually contains as many candidates as there arc seats to be filled in the constituency. The seats are then shared out among the partics in proportion to the votes they win, in accordance with a predetermined formula. Although PR is scarcely used at any level of elections in the United States, Americans were the first to think about ways of achieving proportional representation. They were interested not in the proportional allocation of seats to parties in accordance with the votes that each party receives, but in the proportional allocation to states of seats in the House of Representatives in accordance with the population of each state. Most of the PR methods used in Europe today were either used or discussed in the United States long before Europeans thought of them.

List systems differ from one another in a number of respects, and we discuss these in sequence. They include

1 the formulas used to award seats to parties within each constituency;

2 the matter of whether or not there is a second, higher, tier at which seats are awarded to override any imbalances that may arise at the constituency level;

3 the existence of thresholds, and

4 the degree of choice, if any, given to voters to express a preference for one or more specific candidates on the party list.

The picture is summarized in Table 11-4.

Electoral Formulas   Three different methods are used to decide how seats are shared out among parties. These are known as largest remainders, highest averages using the d'Hondt method, and highest averages using the modified Sainte-Laguë method. In the United States, largest remainders is known as the Hamilton method and d'Hondt as the Jefferson method; the latter was used for apportioning seats in the House of Representatives from 1790 to 1830. The "pure" Sainte-Laguë method is known in the United States as the Webster method; the modified version used in some Scandinavian countries has the effect of making it more difficult than under the pure version for small parties to win seats. We shall not elaborate the differences between these formulas in any detail (the mechanics are explained in Farrell, Chapter 4), because these differences are less important than the similarities. However, it should be noted that of these three

TABLE 11-4   FEATURES OF WESTERN EUROPEAN ELECTORAL SYSTEMS, 2000

	Constituency-level seat allocation formula*	Higher-tier seat allocation? (formula)	Threshold for participation in higher-tier seat share-out	Choice of candidate within party?
PR list systems				
Austria	LR	Yes (DH)	1 constituency seat or 4% of votes nationally	Yes, but largely ineffective
Belgium	LR	Yes (DH)	No	Yes, but largely ineffective
Denmark	MSL	Yes (LR)	2% of votes nationally needed for parliamentary representation	Yes
Finland	DH	No	—	Yes
Germany	Plurality	Yes (LR)	5% of votes or 3 constituency seats	No
Greece	DH	Yes (LR)	3% of votes nationally needed for parliamentary representation	Yes
Iceland	LR	Yes (DH)	5% of votes nationally	Yes, but largely ineffective
Italy	Plurality	Yes (LR)	4% of votes nationally	No
Luxembourg	DH	No	—	Yes
Netherlands	DH	No[†]	0.67% of votes nationally needed to qualify for seats	Yes, but largely ineffective
Norway	MSL	Yes (MSL)	4% of votes nationally	Yes, but largely ineffective
Portugal	DH	No	—	No
Spain	DH	No	—	No
Sweden	MSL	Yes (MSL)	4% of votes nationally or 12% in one constituency needed for parliamentary representation	Yes
Switzerland	DH	No	—	Yes
Other PR systems				
Ireland	STV	No	—	Yes
Malta	STV	Yes[‡]	See[‡] below	Yes
Non-PR systems				
France	2-ballot	No	—	No
United Kingdom	Plurality	No	—	No

*Formulae: DH—d'Hondt; LR—Largest remainders; MSL—Modified Sainte-Laguë; STV—Single transferable vote.
[†] There is only one (national) constituency.
[‡] In Malta, whichever of the two main parties wins a plurality of first-preference votes is awarded extra seats to give it a bare overall majority of seats, if it has not won an overall majority from the constituencies. This is the only situation in which there is any higher-tier allocation.

methods, largest remainders is the most generous in its treatment of small parties; modified Sainte-Laguë tilts the balance slightly toward larger parties; and the d'Hondt method favors large parties even more (Lijphart, 1994, pp. 96–97). All variants of PR are essentially similar in that they set out to award seats as "fairly" as possible to each party according to how many votes it won, although they are based on slightly different ideas as to exactly what is meant by the concept of "fairness" (Gallagher, 1991). They share a common attachment to the idea of proportionality, and in this they differ fundamentally from the plurality method, where other criteria take priority.

District Magnitude and Higher Tiers   The seat allocation method is just one factor determining how proportional the distribution of seats will be in relation to the way votes were cast. A second and often more important factor is district magnitude. If the average district magnitude is small, an election outcome is unlikely to be highly proportional, no matter what allocation formula is used. When France introduced PR for the 1986 election, the d'Hondt formula was used in constituencies that returned only six deputies on average, so although the outcome was much more proportional than the outcomes of elections held under France's usual single-member constituency system, it was less proportional than under most PR systems. In certain other countries, too, particularly Spain, this has an impact: Spain employs relatively small constituencies (district magnitude averages seven seats), and election results there sometimes deviate from perfect proportionality almost as much as results in countries using the British plurality system, with the major parties deriving a sizeable bonus.

One way of overcoming the problem is to use larger constituencies, averaging around twelve seats or more, as in Finland, Portugal, and Luxembourg. This is sometimes criticized on the grounds that the constituencies are made so large that voters might feel remote from their deputies. Another method is to have a second level of allocation at which disproportionalities arising at the constituency level can be ironed out (Taagepera and Shugart, pp. 126–33). In some countries, a certain proportion of seats is set aside at the start for this purpose: about 20 percent in Denmark, 20 percent in Iceland, 25 percent in Italy, 5 percent in Norway, 11 percent in Sweden, and 50 percent in Germany. These "higher-tier" seats are then awarded to the parties in the appropriate numbers to compensate them for any shortfall in the seats they won in the constituencies and thereby bring the overall distribution of seats as close to perfect proportionality as possible. In other countries (Austria, Belgium, Greece), the number of higher-tier seats is not fixed in advance, but the effect is just the same. What happens here is that each party's "wasted" votes from the constituencies—that is, the votes it has not used to earn seats—are pooled on a national or regional basis, and a distribution of the unallocated seats takes place in accordance with each party's unused vote totals. This ensures that very few of a party's votes are wasted.

The high number of national-level seats in Germany is needed because the formula used to allocate constituency seats is not a PR one at all: the country is divided into 328 single-member constituencies, where the seat is given to the candidate with the most votes, just as in Britain. As in Italy, each voter has two votes, one for the single-member constituency and a "second vote" for the national seats. The sharing out of the national seats is then carried out in such a way as to ensure that each party's total number of seats (constituency seats plus national seats) is proportional to its share of the second votes. This is often known as an "additional member" system, and in fact it has several different names, such as "mixed member proportional" or "personalized PR." It is also frequently categorized as a "mixed" system in which the list seats are distributed so as to "correct" the distortions created by the outcome in the single-member constituencies (Farrell, Chapter 5; Massicotte and Blais).

Whereas in Germany the electoral system is clearly a form of proportional representation, in Italy the combination of the relatively nonproportional plurality system to elect three-quarters of deputies and a PR system to elect the rest (in such a way as to make the overall result as proportional as possible) makes it hard to classify the electoral system neatly (see Katz, 1996, for a full account of this system). If the outcome in the constituency seats is not too disproportional, then the list seats will have the effect of making the overall result reasonably proportional. If, on the other hand, the constituency seats greatly overrepresent some parties and greatly underrepresent others, then the 155 list seats will simply prove too few to iron out the imbalances. Just how proportional the results of elections held under this system turn out to be will therefore vary from election to election—assuming the system is not changed again—depending on how the votes are cast in the 475 single-member constituencies.

At the first election held under this new system, in March 1994, the imbalances at the constituency level were quite substantial, with the right-wing alliance led by Silvio Berlusconi taking 63 percent of the 475 single-member seats; as a result, the list seats were insufficient to make the overall result particularly proportional. The right-wing alliance, with 43 percent of the PR votes, ended up with 58 percent of seats in parliament. At the second election, in 1996, the overall outcome was rather more proportional. Calculations of this are made difficult because it is hard to be precise about the exact number of votes received by each party. In the single-member constituencies, many deals were done among the parties within each bloc as to which party should run a candidate in which constituency. In addition, deals were done between these blocs and other parties concerning the trading of list votes for single-member constituency votes. In broad terms, though, it is clear that the victorious grouping in 1996 was not so overrepresented as the 1994 winners had been. In 1996 the center left (the Olive Tree bloc plus the communist RC), with 45 percent of the single-member constituency votes and 43 percent of the list votes, won 51 percent of the total number of seats (for the overall results of the election, see D'Alimonte and Bartolini, pp. 66–67; for the background and full analysis, see D'Alimonte). Discontent with the electoral system still exists, partly because of the profusion of parties that still exists in Italy, as we discuss later. Thus, in April 1999, there was a referendum on abolishing the second vote and the use of lists to fill a quarter of the seats. Although over 90 percent of the votes cast were in favor of this change, turnout fell fractionally short of the required 50 percent to make the result binding, and so the status quo survived. Another referendum on the same proposal in May 2000 met the same fate: this time 82 percent voted in favor of change, but turnout was only 32 percent and so the vote had no effect.

Thresholds   Even proportional representation electoral systems, despite their name, sometimes have features that give a built-in advantage to larger parties. This is due either to self-interest on the part of the larger parties, or to a disinterested concern that perfect proportionality could lead to a proliferation of small parties in parliament and thus to difficulty in forming a stable government, or to a combination of both factors. It is common, therefore, for electoral systems to employ a threshold that a party must overcome before it qualifies for seats. The best-known example is the German system, which allows only those parties that have either won at least 5 percent of the second votes, or won at least three constituency seats, to share in the national list allocation. It was very rare in pre-unification West Germany for any party other than the big two, the CDU/CSU and the SPD, to win even one constituency seat, but in 1994 the former communists, the PDS, qualified for list seats by this route due to their strength in east Berlin. In Sweden, parties must win 4 percent of the national vote to qualify for a share of the national allocation. In Austria, the threshold is low: a party need win only at least one seat in any of the forty-three regional electoral districts or win at least 4 percent of the votes nationwide in order to be awarded its share of higher-tier seats. The lowest barrier is in the Netherlands, where a party needs to reach a national vote threshold of a mere 0.67 percent to qualify for seats. It rarely happens that the threshold debars a Dutch party from receiving seats.

Thresholds are usually employed to limit the degree of proportionality achieved and could, if set too high, significantly distort the election outcome. This is precisely what has happened in Greece in many postwar elections. In the 1981 and 1985 elections, for example, participation in the higher-tier seat allocation was restricted to parties that had won at least 17 percent of the national vote. The consequence was to give a large benefit to big parties and to discriminate against smaller ones, and the outcome was thus likely to be as disproportional as that of a British election. This system was termed "reinforced PR," but in fact it was not proportionality but the parliamentary strength of the largest party that was reinforced (Dimitras, 1994a, p. 160). In 1985, the largest party, PASOK, won 54 percent of the seats with 46 percent of the votes, whereas the minor parties, with 13 percent of the votes between them, won only 4 percent of the seats. These discriminatory features were dropped before the first election of 1989, and the next three elections (two in 1989 and one in 1990) were held under a more conventional PR system. The system was then changed again so that only parties with at least 3 percent of the votes nationally could win any seats (Dimitras, 1994b).

Which Candidates Get the Seats Under List Systems?   So far, we have been discussing the ways in which the seats are divided up among the parties. Once this has been decided, a second question arises: which candidates on the party's list are awarded the seats that the party has won? This is dealt with in different ways. In some countries, the order of candidates drawn up by the party organization is a fixed ranking that the voters cannot alter. These systems are termed *nonpreferential*, with *closed* or *blocked* lists. In a second group of countries, in contrast, there is no default order; the voters alone decide which candidates are elected. These systems are termed *preferential*, with *open* or *unblocked* lists. Under such systems there is intra-party electoral competition, because candidates of the same party are competing against one another for personal votes. In between these two are cases where the party's ranking may stand as a default ordering but can be overturned if enough voters combine against it. These cases may in practice be either essentially preferential or essentially nonpreferential, depending on just what degree of coordination is needed among voters to overturn the ordering decided on by the party organization; in some countries it is very easy for voters to do this, and in others it is virtually impossible. The systems in operation are listed in Table 11-4 (for a more detailed analysis, see Marsh; Katz, 1986).

There are relatively few examples of PR list systems where the lists are completely closed. Countries in this category include Germany, Italy, Portugal, and Spain; the lists used on the one recent occasion when France used PR, in 1986, were also closed. In all of these cases, the order of candidates' names on the list is decided by the parties, and voters cannot alter it, so the candidate selectors, who draw up the party list, are in effect determining which of their party's candidates become members of parliament. In these countries, then, candidate selection plays an especially important role in the political recruitment process, as we saw in the previous chapter.

Countries in the second category, employing genuinely open lists where the voters determine which of a party's candidates are elected, include Finland, Luxembourg, and Switzerland. In Finland, the voters are all-powerful; they are obliged to express a preference for one specific candidate, and, within each party, those candidates receiving the most preferences win the seats (Kuusela). Election surveys in Finland show that over 40 percent of voters attach more importance to the choice of candidate than to the

Election officials empty a ballot box before counting the votes in Helsinki at the European Parliament elections in June 1999. © AFP Worldwide

choice of party. The impact on intra-party competition is clear from the fact that in the 1991 election campaign, 88 percent of election advertisements in the newspapers were for individual candidates and only 12 percent advertised a political party (Pesonen, pp. 116, 122). In Switzerland and Luxembourg, voters express as many preferences as there are seats in the constituency. They can cast a "list vote" for a party, which has the effect of giving one preference vote to each of the party's candidates, or they can cumulate two preference votes on one candidate. They can give their preferences to candidates on more than one party's list in an option known as *panachage,* which is confined to these two countries. One of the most fully studied of the preferential electoral systems was the one used in Italy until 1993. Within the Christian Democrats (DC) in particular, various factions and affiliated interest groups all tried to motivate voters to cast preference votes for their particular candidates. Politicians found guilty of corruption were inclined to blame the electoral system for forcing them into clientelistic "vote-buying" exercises of one sort or another, so the electoral system moved to the top of the "hit list" of Italy's political reformers and was fundamentally altered in 1993.

Turning to the third category, we find that in most cases the party candidate selectors draw up a list upon which the candidates appear in a particular order, and the voters have a greater or smaller degree of power to overturn this order. Usually, the voters can either cast a "list vote" endorsing the order drawn up by the party, or cast a "personal vote" for an individual candidate on the list; what varies is how likely these personal votes are to make any difference to the outcome. In Sweden and Denmark, personal votes can have an impact, and the lists in these countries are thus in effect open. In Sweden, since 1998 the election law has allowed candidates who receive preference votes from at least 8 percent of their party's voters to leapfrog candidates who were placed above them on the list but who receive fewer preference votes. At the 1998 election, about 40 percent of voters availed of the option of casting a personal vote, and an estimated sixteen of the 349 MPs owed their election to the personal votes they received (Arter, p. 299). The Danish system is similar, though the parties can choose how to present their lists; some forms give considerable choice to the voters, whereas others restrict it, and the degree of voter choice can vary from party to party as well as between and even within constituencies (Elklit).

In certain other countries, though, there are systems that in theory offer the opportunity for preferential voting for candidates but in practice are such that voters' preferences rarely overturn the ordering set by the parties. An example is the system used in Belgium: voters may cast either one preference vote for a candidate on the list or a "list vote," which is taken as an endorsement of the order in which the candidates appear on the list. The method of allocating a party's seats to its candidates means that concerted action on the part of voters is required to secure the election of a candidate not placed by the party in one of the favored positions, and this rarely happens. Although about half of Belgian voters cast personal rather than list votes, only a tiny proportion of seats (0.6 percent of the total since 1919) go to candidates who would not have been elected had the Belgian electoral system included no provision for preferential voting (De Winter, p. 21). In Norway, personal votes have never had any effect on the personnel elected (Petersson, p. 56).

BOX 11-1

ELECTORAL SYSTEMS

France

France does not use proportional representation to elect deputies to the National Assembly. Instead, it employs a two-round or "double-ballot" system. Metropolitan France is divided into 555 single-member constituencies (the overseas territories and departments return an additional twenty-two deputies to Paris). Within each constituency there can be two rounds of voting on successive Sundays. If a candidate wins an overall majority in the first round, he or she is elected as the deputy for the constituency, but this happens rarely. In the great majority of constituencies, no candidate wins a first-round majority, and the second round takes place a week later. Only those whose first-round votes exceeded 12.5 percent of the electorate are permitted to participate in the second round, unless the operation of this rule would leave fewer than two candidates entitled to take part, in which case the top two are both allowed through. In the second round, the candidate with the most votes, whether or not this amounts to a majority, wins the seat.

Germany

The German electoral system provides two routes to the lower house of parliament, the Bundestag. When voters enter the polling booth, they are faced with two ballot papers. One gives them a vote in the election of a member of parliament (MdB) for the local single-member constituency; half of the 656 members of parliament (the number is due to be reduced to 598 in 2002) are elected from single-member constituencies in exactly the same way as in the United Kingdom. The second ballot paper enables them to cast a list vote; the other half of the parliament is elected from party lists. The overall allocation of seats in the Bundestag is decided by these list votes. Each party is awarded as many list seats as it needs to ensure that its total number of seats (constituency seats and list seats combined) is proportional to the share of list votes it received. However, parties do not receive any list seats unless they have either won at least 5 percent of the list votes or won three constituency seats. If a party wins more constituency seats within any Land (province) than it is entitled to on the basis of its list votes, it is allowed to keep these extra seats, and the size of the Bundestag is expanded accordingly. In the October 1998 election there were thirteen of these ex-

tra seats (known as Überhangmandate), and the Bundestag therefore contained 669 members.

Italy

From the end of World War II until 1993, Italy had a very proportional type of PR system. Seats were awarded within large constituencies (average district magnitude was around thirty), with a higher tier to balance up the number of seats awarded to parties that had received less than their "fair share" in the constituencies. The system was a preferential form of PR; that is, voters for a party could indicate preferences for specific candidates on that party's list, thus generating competition for preference votes between candidates of the same party. The revolt against the political establishment in the mid-1990s focused (perhaps inappropriately) on the electoral system as a prime cause of the corruption of Italian politics, so in 1993 it was changed fundamentally. The new system was a compromise between those who wanted to adopt the British single-member plurality system and those who wanted to retain PR. Just over three-quarters of the deputies (475 out of 630) are elected from single-member constituencies. The remaining 155 seats are filled from national lists and awarded to parties that did not receive their proportional share of the constituency seats, provided they pass the qualifying threshold of 4 percent of the national vote. There is some pressure for a move to a purely plurality system, and referendum proposals intended to help achieve this in 1999 and 2000 failed only because turnout fell narrowly short of the 50 percent level required.

Netherlands

The Tweede Kamer (Second Chamber) contains 150 deputies, and when it comes to awarding seats to parties, the whole country is treated as one 150-member constituency. Each party presents a list of candidates, and the parties receive seats in proportion to their votes; the seat allocation formula used is the d'Hondt highest averages method. Parties receiving fewer than two-thirds of 1 percent of the total votes cast do not qualify for any seats; this is the lowest threshold, as a share of the national vote, employed by any country in Western Europe. Voters can cast a preference vote for a candidate on a party list, but in practice the casting of preference votes in the Netherlands has had very little impact on the composition of the parliament. Because there are no subnational constituencies, the system is sometimes criticized for being impersonal. In response, the government proposed in the mid-1990s a move to a system similar to that used in Germany, but the proposal was withdrawn following objections from small parties, who realized that such a system would reduce their chances of parliamentary representation.

Spain

The Congress of Deputies is elected from fifty-two constituencies, each of which, on average, returns only seven deputies, a relatively small figure for a PR electoral system. Within each constituency, the d'Hondt highest averages formula is employed; this tends to favor the large parties rather than the small ones. There is no higher-tier allocation to compensate parties for any underrepresentation in the constituencies. Voters have no choice of candidate; they simply cast a vote for one of the party lists that are offered.

Sweden

The Riksdag has 349 members and is elected by proportional representation based on two tiers. The lower tier consists of twenty-eight constituencies covering the country, which between them return 310 deputies. The remaining thirty-nine seats are held back for allocation at the second tier: they are distributed among the parties in such a way as to ensure that the total number of seats received by each party comes as close to its proportional share as possible. However, a threshold discriminates against small parties: those receiving fewer than 4 percent of the national votes are not awarded any of the thirty-nine higher-tier seats. There is provision for voters to indicate a preference for an individual candidate on a party list; until recently, the initial ranking order of the candidates on each party's list was in practice almost immune to alteration by the voters, but as from 1998 a rule change has meant that the preference votes that are cast can have a real impact on the outcome.

United Kingdom

The UK employs the single-member plurality system. The country is divided into 659 constituencies, each returning one Member of Parliament (MP) to the House of Commons. Within each constituency, the candidate winning the most votes, whether or not this amounts to a majority, becomes the MP. Other bodies within the UK are most commonly elected by forms of PR: either additional member systems (the institutions of devolution in Scotland and Wales), the single transferable vote (the Northern Ireland assembly), or a PR list system (the eighty-four members of the European Parliament elected from England, Scotland, and Wales).

In Austria, similarly, the type of preferential voting introduced in 1971 was so restrictive that over the next twenty years, only one candidate was elected by this route (Müller and Plasser, p. 25); a change to the electoral law in 1992 was designed to make preferential voting more effective at subsequent elections, but in fact only one candidate was elected out of list order in 1999 and none at all were in 1994 or 1995, so this change made little difference. The system in the Netherlands differs in some of the details, but the essential feature is the same: the party supplies a default order of candidates, and such a high degree of concerted action by voters has been needed to overturn it that the party's rank ordering has almost always stood. Only three candidates were elected due to preference votes between 1945 and 1994. Even this limited opportunity has been resented by the Dutch parties, which sometimes demand pledges from their candidates that if they are elected "out of order," owing to preference votes, at the expense of a candidate higher on the list, they will resign their seat in favor of the candidate whom the party organization had placed higher on the list. As in Austria, a recent change has liberalized the position slightly, and in 1998 two of the 150 MPs owed their election to the preference votes they received; this is still a very small percentage, but was seen as significant in the context of the record over the previous fifty years (Irwin, p. 274).

The Single Transferable Vote

The single transferable vote (STV) electoral system was devised in Britain in the middle of the nineteenth century, and enthusiasm for it has been largely confined to English-speaking countries. It is used to elect the parliaments of Ireland and Malta, and it was employed to elect Estonia's parliament at the 1990 election (for assessments of STV see Representation, 1996). In Ireland, the largest party, Fianna Fáil, has twice (in 1959 and 1968) attempted to have the system replaced by the British plurality system, mainly because it believed it would fare better under the latter, but on each occasion the electorate rejected the proposed change in a referendum. Like list systems, STV aims to give proportional representation to the shades of opinion within the constituency. Unlike them, it does not presuppose that those opinions are organized in terms of parties.

Voters cast a vote by ranking as many as they wish of the candidates, regardless of party, in order of their preference; they place a "1" next to the name of their favored candidate, a "2" next to the name of their second-favorite, and so on (for detailed explanations of how STV works, see Farrell, Chapter 6; Sinnott, pp. 104–13). The counting of votes revolves around the Droop quota. This is calculated as the smallest integer greater than $[v/(s + 1)]$, where v is the number of valid votes and s the number of seats in the constituency. The Droop quota is therefore one more than a quarter of the votes in a three-seat constituency, one more than a fifth in a four-seater, and so on. Any candidate who achieves the Droop quota is certain of election and does not need votes over and above this number; votes received by a candidate in excess of the Droop quota are termed surplus votes.

Any candidate whose total of first-preference votes equals or exceeds the Droop quota is declared elected. Unless it should happen that sufficient candidates are elected at this stage, the count then proceeds by distributing the surplus votes of the elected candidate(s), that is, the votes they possess over and above the quota. These votes are transferred to the other candidates, in proportion to the next preferences marked for them. If no candidate has a surplus, the candidate with the fewest votes is eliminated, and his or her votes are transferred to the other candidates, again in accordance with the next preferences marked. This process continues until all the seats have been filled.

What are the pros and cons of STV when compared with other PR systems? Its advocates make several points. First, it gives voters the opportunity to convey a lot of information about their preferences; they may rank all the candidates in order of choice, whereas under almost every other system they are limited to expressing a "Yes" verdict on one (or a few) and "No" on the rest. Second, when ranking candidates, voters are not constrained by party lines. Voters vote for candidates, not for parties, and STV works perfectly well—some say better—in nonpartisan elections. Some voters' preferences are not determined primarily by the candidates' party affiliations. These might be voters whose main concern is with an issue that cuts across party lines (such as abortion, European integration, or nuclear power, for example); or voters who want to affect the social composition of parliament, and thus wish to vote, say, for women or young candidates across party lines; or voters who want to elect a representative whose home base is in their own area of the constituency. Such voters can give their first-preference vote to, say, a pro-EU candidate from one party, and their second-preference to a pro-EU candidate from a different party. List systems do not offer this opportunity, and the apparent exceptions—those of Switzerland and Luxembourg, which offer *panachage*—are not really comparable.

This is because of the third argument in favor of STV, namely, that voters control the way their votes will be used. No vote can help a candidate unless it expresses a preference for him or her. This sets STV apart from all list systems, where a preference given to one candidate of a party might end up helping another candidate of the same party—a candidate whom, perhaps, the voter does not like. Under STV, voters can continue to give preferences after their first, knowing that a preference given to a candidate can never help that person against a candidate to whom the voter gave a higher preference. This is not the case under *panachage;* the voter giving a preference to a candidate of one party does not know which candidate of that party it will ultimately help, as it is added to the party's pool and could benefit any of its candidates.

Fourth, STV gives voters the opportunity to express an opinion as to the direction their party should take. If there is more than one tendency or faction within a party, voters can express higher preferences for candidates from the one they favor and affect the composition of the parliamentary group accordingly. STV shares this quality with preferential list systems and American primaries.

Under the single transferable vote electoral system, candidates have to appeal for personal support from the voters. The picture shows election banners for four candidates of the Nationalist Party in the Valletta constituency (district 1) in the Maltese election of 1996; in effect, these candidates were competing against each other as well as against candidates from the rival Maltese Labour Party. Guido de Marco and Austin Gatt were both elected, but Louis Cuschieri and Paul Borg Olivier were defeated. (Maltese election): Courtesy of John C Lane/ State Univ. of NY at Buffalo

Fifth, it ensures that voters can vote sincerely, knowing that even if their first-choice candidate is unpopular, the vote will not be wasted, as it can be transferred to another candidate in accordance with the second preference the voter has marked on the ballot paper.

But STV also has its critics, which explains why it has inspired so little enthusiasm on the European mainland. They make three points in particular. First, they are not impressed with the opportunity it gives voters to cross party lines. On the contrary, they feel that this might weaken the internal unity of parties and make them less cohesive. In elections, candidates of one party, rather than being able to concentrate on propagating party policies, must be alive to the possibility of attracting lower preferences from other parties' supporters. This might make the parties "fuzzy at the edges" as candidates adopt bland positions for fear of alienating any voter who might possibly give them a lower preference. Critics of STV argue that modern democratic politics, certainly in parliamentary systems, needs strong, cohesive parties to work properly, a subject that we discussed in Chapter 10, and that the idea of voting for candidates rather than parties, although all very well for other kinds of elections, is inappropriate for parliamentary elections. This argument is difficult to evaluate, because STV is used in too few countries for us to be able to tell whether it will tend to weaken parties. It must be said, though, that there is no evidence at all that parties in either Ireland or Malta are any less cohesive and disciplined than parties anywhere else. And even though Irish politics do tend to be relatively consensual, with few clear policy differences between the two main parties, Fianna Fáil and Fine Gael, the opposite is true in Malta, where the bitter rivalry between Labour and the Nationalists often spills over into violence.

The second criticism is that STV can realistically be used only in relatively small constituencies, thus raising the prospect of disproportionality (lack of complete correspondence between parties' shares of the votes and the seats). For example, STV is difficult to operate in constituencies larger than about ten seats, because the ballot paper could then contain thirty to forty names, and most voters' preferences will become meaningless after the first half-dozen or so. In both Ireland and Malta, the largest constituency size now used is five seats. Because votes are assumed to be cast for candidates rather than parties, it is impossible, without contradicting the principles on which STV is based, to have higher-tier seat allocation (without the use of a second vote as in Germany), although, as Table 11-4 explains, Malta does have such an allocation in reserve. In practice, though, the possibility of disproportionality does not seem to be a major problem, as election results in Ireland and Malta have been as proportional as those of other PR systems.

Third, it has been argued that STV facilitates the election of independent candidates, who may be able to wield undue power over a government that does not possess a secure majority. Independents, like center-party candidates, stand to benefit from an electoral system in which voters can rank order the options, because, precisely because they do not have a party label and thus do not alienate anyone, they may well be the second choice of many voters. Empirically, it is true that the election of independents is quite common in Ireland (six were elected in 1997 and five in 1992), whereas elsewhere in Western Europe independent members of parliament are virtually unknown. In times of minority government in Ireland, some independent deputies have been able to extract concessions from the government on local matters. Sinnott argues that STV thus makes possible circumstances in which "independents wield disproportionate power and create a potentially serious underlying threat to the stability of government" (Sinnott, p. 120). On the other hand, no independent has been elected to the parliament of Malta, the other country to use STV, since its independence in 1964.

WHY ELECTORAL SYSTEMS MATTER

The plethora of electoral systems used across Europe suggests that there is no simple answer to the question, "Which is the best electoral system?" But although there has been no trend toward a uniform electoral system, we have seen that the great majority of countries employ some version of PR. Only Britain and France use systems that do not embody the principle of PR. All the remaining Western European countries employ some type of PR: in fifteen countries a list system is used, and Ireland and Malta employ the single transferable vote. We have already reviewed the arguments about the relative merits of list systems and STV; we must now look at the wider question of the advantages and disadvantages of PR systems generally compared with plurality systems (for general discussions of electoral systems, see Cox; Katz, 1997; Lijphart, 1994; Grofman and Lijphart; Sartori, pp. 3–79).

There is a grossly simplistic portrait of the main consequences of these two types of electoral systems. It is said that plurality systems may produce disproportional results, with the largest two parties taking nearly all the seats in parliament, but that they also ensure stable majority governments. In contrast, it is said, PR systems lead to proportional outcomes, but this inevitably entails multiparty systems with parliamentary seats spread among a sizeable number of parties, which in turn produces a succession of unstable coalition governments. If these two pictures were accurate, assessing the merits of the two types of electoral systems would come down to the question of which criterion should have greater priority: "fair" representation of parties in parliament or strong, effective government. Needless to say, the actual situation with regard to these two factors is rather more complex than this. There are other criteria, too, that could be taken into account in an assessment of the merits of electoral systems. Do some systems give a better chance than others to women and minorities to win election to parliament? Are redistricting and gerrymandering greater problems under some systems than under others? The overall picture, based on the fifty-one elections held in the nineteen countries of Western Europe during the 1990s, is summarized in Table 11-5.

Proportionality

The proportionality of election results—the degree to which parties' shares of the seats correspond to their shares of the votes—does indeed tend to be significantly greater under PR than under plurality systems. Table 11-5 shows clearly that there was a large difference between the plurality systems of Britain and France, on the one hand, and all PR systems on the other hand, during the 1990s. Among PR systems, there is some variation. The most proportional outcomes occur in countries that use large district magnitudes (Austria, Denmark, the Netherlands, and Sweden), and also in Malta,

TABLE 11-5   ASPECTS OF ELECTORAL OUTCOMES IN WESTERN EUROPE IN THE 1990s

		Average figure for all 1990s elections				
	Number of elections during 1990s	Dispropor-tionality*	Effective number of parties (elective level)[†]	Effective number of parties (legislative level)[†]	Actual number of different parties in parliament[‡]	% women in parliament after most recent election
Austria	4	1.9	3.6	3.4	4.5	26.8
Belgium	3	3.2	9.8	8.5	11.7	23.3
Denmark	3	1.6	4.8	4.5	9.0	37.4
Finland	3	3.9	5.8	5.1	9.7	37.0
France	2	21.4	6.6	3.2	7.0	10.9
Germany	3	3.4	3.8	3.3	5.0	30.9
Greece	3	7.1	2.8	2.3	5.0	6.3
Iceland	3	2.1	4.0	3.7	5.3	34.9
Ireland	2	5.4	3.9	3.2	7.0	12.0
Italy	3	2.7[§]	6.6[§]	6.9	19.3	11.1
Luxembourg	2	4.2	4.7	4.1	5.5	16.7
Malta	3	1.6	2.1	2.0	2.0	9.2
Netherlands	2	1.6	5.4	5.1	10.5	36.0
Norway	2	3.9	4.9	4.2	8.0	36.4
Portugal	3	5.1	2.9	2.5	4.7	13.0
Spain	2	6.4	3.4	2.7	11.5	28.3
Sweden	3	2.1	4.3	4.0	7.0	42.7
Switzerland	3	3.6	6.7	5.8	15.7	23.0
United Kingdom	2	15.2	3.1	2.2	9.0	18.4
Average PR-list countries (N = 15)	2.8	3.5	4.9	4.4	8.8	26.9
Average PR-STV countries (N = 2)	2.5	3.5	3.0	2.6	4.5	10.6
Average plurality countries (N = 2)	2	18.3	4.9	2.7	8.0	14.6
Average all countries (N = 19)	2.7	5.1	4.7	4.0	8.3	23.9

*"Disproportionality" refers to vote–seat disproportionality as measured by the least squares index (Gallagher, 1991). The scale runs from 0 to 100, 0 representing full proportionality and 100 representing total disproportionality.

[†]"Effective number of parties" at elective level and at legislative level refers to the level of fragmentation in terms of votes and seats respectively (Laakso and Taagepera).

[‡]The "actual number of parties in parliament" excludes independent deputies.

[§]These figures for Italy refer to 1992 election only, given the difficulty of calculating vote figures for individual parties under the current Italian electoral system.

Sources: For election results, see source of Table 7-1. For women in parliaments, the website of the Inter-Parliamentary Union (www.ipu.org). All other figures are authors' calculations.

despite its small district magnitude of just five seats per constituency. The key factors in determining the level of proportionality are district magnitude and the level at which any threshold is set; the least proportional PR outcomes occur when thresholds and/or small district magnitudes assist the large parties and penalize small ones, as in Greece and Spain (Anckar). The 1990s pattern matches that found by Lijphart (1994, pp. 96–97) for the period from 1945 to 1990.

The Number of Parties

The formulation of the best-known causal relationship in the study of the effects of electoral systems is attributed to Maurice Duverger. It holds that the single-member plurality system favors a two-party system, the double-ballot majority system tends to produce multipartism tempered by alliances, and PR tends to lead to the formation of many independent parties (Duverger, p. 70). PR might be associated with a multiparty system either because it allows parties representing existing minorities to be viable, or, as Duverger sees it, because it artificially "multiplies parties in an otherwise dualistic world, while plurality . . . conforms to that natural dualism" (Taagepera and Shugart, p. 53). Under the French double-ballot system, many parties may contest the first round of voting, but there are strong incentives for parties to form alliances for the second-round contests. The British-style SMP system is associated with a two-party system because of both mechanical and psychological effects, as Duverger terms them. The mechanical effect is simply that smaller parties—in practice, all parties other than the top two—do not reap a proportional reward in seats for their share of the votes. Whereas under a PR system a party winning, say, 10 percent of the votes in every part of the country would end up with about 10 percent of the seats, under a SMP system such a party would probably win no seats, because it would not be the strongest party anywhere. The psychological effect comes about precisely because voters are aware of the mechanical effect: they know that if they cast their vote for a small party, this vote is likely to be wasted, and therefore the votes for such parties do not reflect their true level of support. We saw in the earlier discussion of the Norfolk North result in Britain in 1997 (Table 11-2) that the electoral system compelled any supporter there of Labour and the Referendum Party to decide whether to waste his or her vote on a candidate who was virtually certain to lose or to vote instead for one of the two candidates who had a real chance. In this example, Labour was the main party affected, but in most constituencies the Liberal Democrats are the third party and hence the main losers.

The precise meaning, status, and accuracy of Duverger's predictions have been the subject of an extensive literature (see, for example, Sartori, pp. 27–52; Taagepera and Shugart, pp. 142–55; Cox, pp. 13–33), and this is not the place to explore these issues fully. However, we can examine the evidence to see whether there are indeed fewer parties under non-PR than under PR systems. In order to do this, we need some satisfactory measure of the number of parties. Simply counting the number of parties is not sufficient; for example, in the British House of Commons around eight or ten different parties are usually represented, but Britain has never had anything like a genuine eight-party system. To deal with this, Laakso and Taagepera devised a measure that takes into account not only the number of different parties but also the relative size of each, which they call the "effective number" of parties. It is essentially a measure of fragmentation, registering the extent to which strength is concentrated or dispersed. The intuitive meaning to be put on an effective number of, say, 3.6 parties, is that there is the same degree of fragmentation as if there were 3.6 equal-sized parties (Laakso and Taagepera). One can calculate this number both at the elective level, by measuring the degree to which votes are dispersed among the parties, and at the legislative level, by measuring the degree to which seats are dispersed among the parties.

Table 11-5 shows that the pattern of party competition in Western Europe in the 1990s corresponded well to Duverger's predictions. In the two plurality countries, Britain and France, the reduction from the elective to the legislative level, brought about by the "mechanical" effect of the electoral system, is very marked. In Britain, something like a three-party system at the elective level is reduced to a two-party system in parliament. In France, the votes at elections are spread among many more parties than in Britain, but, partly due to the alliances and deals that Duverger predicts, parliamentary strength is far less fragmented than this. In PR systems, the fragmentation in parliament is only marginally less than that seen at the electoral level, as we would expect.

However, it is not invariably the case that PR is associated with multipartism. Certainly, this is true in some countries, most notably Belgium, where fragmentation has reached remarkable levels; at the June 1999 election, the strongest two parties received only 28 percent of the votes between them. In Finland, Italy, the Netherlands, and Switzerland, too, the effective number of parties in parliament exceeded five during the 1990s. Yet in many other PR countries (Austria, Germany, Greece, Ireland, Malta, Portugal, and Spain) parliamentary strength is little if at all more fragmented than in France, with its plurality system.

Two cases in particular show that the relationship between electoral systems and party systems is not a deterministic one. In Malta, the party system since independence has been the purest two-party system in Europe; since the start of the 1970s, the combined vote share of Labour and the Nationalists has averaged over 99 percent, neither party has fallen below 46 percent of the votes, and no other party has won a seat. This shows that while PR systems may well give parliamentary expression to a multiparty system if other factors, such as the number of political or social cleavages, cause voters to create one in the first place, PR does not by itself bring a multiparty system into being. Another interesting counterexample is Italy, where the change in the electoral system that was made in the mid-1990s, from a highly proportional version of PR to one in which three-quarters of the seats are filled by plurality contests in single-member constituencies, was expected to reduce the number of parties and present the voters with a clear choice between alternative governments. This was partially successful, in that, in 1996 especially, voters could identify a right-wing and a left-wing option for government, and the victory of the left produced the first complete change of government in postwar Italy. On the other hand, the effective number of parties in parliament actually rose, because the parties, as it has been put, chose to "proportionalize" the plurality element of the new system, doing deals that meant that small parties that were part of an alliance got a clear run in a few constituencies (Di Virgilio). This shows that a pre-existing party system can adapt to a new electoral system and will not necessarily be reshaped by it. As we saw in Chapter 7, both of the new blocs in Italy are fragile and internally incohesive, and it remains to be seen whether the current electoral system really will help to transform the party system in the long run.

Electoral systems, then, do play a major part, albeit not a deterministic one, in shaping party systems. If Britain and France adopted PR systems, seats in their parliaments would be much less concentrated in the hands of the two main parties. In France, the far-right FN would be a much more powerful presence in the National Assembly, and government formation might require alliances between the left and the mainstream right. In Britain, smaller parties such as the Liberal Democrats and the Greens would win both more votes and more seats, and single-party government might well become a thing of the past. The plurality electoral system may be all that keeps Britain (and, indeed, the United States) looking like a two-party system, and it is certainly the key to two-party domination of the legislature.

A plurality electoral system, with its tendency to produce competition between just two large parties, reflects the view that a majority should prevail over a minority. This in itself is an impeccable democratic principle. But it encounters problems in societies that are divided into a number of segments or interests and on issues where there are more than two positions. When there is no majority to represent, plurality systems tend to produce outcomes that favor inordinately the larger minorities and discriminate against the smaller ones. PR systems, in contrast, seek to reflect in parliaments the divergences that exist in society.

Coalition or Single-Party Government?

One argument against PR systems is that the very accuracy with which they reflect parties' electoral strengths in parliament creates problems when it comes to forming a government. It is extremely rare, under any type of electoral system, for one party to win a majority of the votes cast, so a single-party majority government is likely only if the largest party receives a bonus of seats that takes it over the magic 50 percent mark. Obviously, this is most likely to happen under a plurality system, where proportionality is lower and the largest party often wins a substantial bonus. For example, in Britain's 1997 election, Labour received only 43 percent of the votes, but won 63 percent of the seats, a bonus of 20 percent (in 1987 and 1992, the Conservatives' bonuses had been 16 and 10 percent respectively). Under a PR system, assuming that disproportionality is not introduced as a result of small district magnitudes, no party's seat bonus is very large. Consequently, a single-party majority government is possible only if one party actually wins a majority of votes (as has happened in Austria, Germany, Ireland, Malta, Portugal, and Sweden) or comes very close to it so that it needs only a small bonus to achieve a parliamentary majority (as has also happened in Austria, Ireland, Malta, and Sweden, as well as in Greece, Norway, and Spain). A survey of the record in twenty countries found that although single-party majority governments were formed after only 10 percent of elections held under PR, they emerged after 60 percent of those held under plurality or majority electoral systems, and another study, again of twenty countries, also found a strong relationship between non-PR systems and single-party government (Blais and Carty, p. 214; Woldendorp et al., p. 115).

Having said this, we must add that the relationship between electoral systems and government types is not entirely straightforward. It is true that in countries with the most fragmented party systems, such as Belgium, Finland, Iceland, Italy, Luxembourg, the Netherlands, and Switzerland, all or virtually all governments are coalitions. It is also true that Britain, owing to its non-PR electoral system, has not had a coalition government since 1945. However, the British electoral system has not always produced a stable majority government. Some British elections—the most recent being that of February 1974—produced no overall parliamentary majority for any party, and between 1976 and 1979 the minority Labour government was able to survive in office only because of the support of the Liberals, under the terms of an arrangement known as the "Lib–Lab pact." In France, too, the plurality system did not produce a majority government in either the 1988 or the 1997 elections, and indeed, if we think of the RPR and the UDF as separate parties, the Fifth Republic had only one single-party government (the Gaullist government formed after the 1968 election) until the Socialists formed such a government in the early 1980s. Likewise, in countries using PR systems, even though coalitions are far more common, there are still many cases of single-party government. The Austrian Socialist Party, Ireland's Fianna Fáil, the Norwegian Labor Party, the Swedish Social Democrats, and both Labour and the Nationalists in Malta have all had long spells in office alone, and other countries with PR have experienced single-party government for periods.

The Backgrounds of Parliamentarians

Proportional representation elections produce parliaments that differ from those produced by plurality elections. This is true not just as far as the representation of parties is concerned; it also applies to the profile of the individuals who sit on the parliamentary benches.

This is especially obvious when we look at the proportion of women in legislatures around the world. It has frequently been observed that there are more women in parliament in countries that use PR than in those where a plurality electoral system operates (Rule and Zimmerman). Table 11-5 confirms this pattern. The average for Britain and France, the two countries that do not use PR, is a mere 15 percent, compared with 25 percent for the other seventeen countries. (Representation of women in parliament in the East and Central European countries that we discuss in Chapter 15 is slightly lower than in Western Europe: the figures in January 2000 were 15.0 percent in the Czech Republic, 13.0 percent in Poland, 12.7 percent in the Slovak Republic, and 8.3 percent in Hungary.) In some countries, notably those in Scandinavia, along with the Netherlands and Germany, about a third or even more of parliamentarians are women. Of course, Scandinavian countries have a progressive attitude toward female participation in politics and in society generally (see the gender empowerment index in Table 1-1), but the broad tendency remains true even when we look at less progressive countries. Thus, Ireland, Italy, and Portugal, where the relatively traditional nature of society and the strength of Catholicism might suggest that women would find it hard to gain entry to the political elite, and Switzerland, where women were denied the vote until the 1970s, all had more women in their national parliaments than Britain until

A group of Swedish MPs, with approximately equal numbers of men and women, standing in front of the parliament building. In 2000, Sweden had a higher proportion of women among its MPs than any other European country. © AP/Wide World Photos

1997, when positive action by the Labour Party, which deliberately chose women candidates in a number of safe and marginal seats, led to a great increase in the number of female British MPs.

The explanation is to be found primarily in the multimember constituencies necessitated by PR. Under a single-member constituency system, the candidate selectors might well be reluctant to pick a woman as the party's sole candidate, using the excuse, genuine or otherwise, that they believe some voters will be less likely to vote for a woman than for a man. But when several candidates are to be chosen, it is positively advantageous for a ticket to include both men and women, for an all-male list of five or more candidates is likely to alienate some voters. It is noticeable that in Germany the proportion of women among the candidates elected from the lists has generally been considerably higher than the proportion among those elected from the single-member constituencies. The evidence as to whether, within the PR group, either STV, open-list systems, or closed-list systems give any special advantage to women is inconclusive. In closed-list systems, where the voters cannot alter the candidate selectors' rankings, the selectors could, if they wished, bring about gender equality in parliament by employing the "zipper" system of alternating women and men on the list: placing a woman first, a man second, a woman third, and so on. On the other hand, in countries where the selectors might wish to do this, it is quite likely that the voters too will believe in gender equality and will not use their preference votes specifically against women candidates. If this is the case, an open-list system, like STV, will neither assist nor damage women's electoral chances. Table 11-5 shows that of the six countries with most women, the top three (Sweden, Denmark, and Finland) all employ open-list systems, while in the next three (Norway, the Netherlands, and Iceland) the voters have little or no opportunity to alter the rankings of the candidate selectors. The empirical evidence therefore seems inconclusive, and Finnish data suggest that, at least when the political culture supports gender equality, open-list systems may be broadly neutral in their impact on the gender balance. Although men seem relatively reluctant to vote for a female candidate, women are keen to do so. In the 1991 Finnish election, 41 percent of all candidates were women, and though only 25 percent of men gave their vote to a female candidate, this was balanced by the 58 percent of women who voted for a female candidate (Pesonen, p. 117). The number of women elected in the two PR-STV countries is even lower than that in the plurality countries, but this may be due less to their use of STV and more to the fact that both countries, Ireland and Malta, are very Catholic; it is clear that, other things being equal, attitudes towards a political role for women are more favorable in Protestant countries.

There is less research on other underrepresented groups, but the same argument applies. Those who pick the party's candidate in a single-member constituency may be reluctant to take the risk of selecting a representative of an ethnic, religious, or linguistic minority, but candidate selectors in a multimember constituency will usually feel it wise to ensure that the ticket includes a cross section of the groups to which the party is hoping to appeal. Legislatures produced by PR elections thus tend to be more representative of the population that elects them, in terms of both the backgrounds of the parliamentarians and the relationship between votes won and seats received by political parties.

Redistricting and Gerrymandering

Elections to national or subnational legislatures in certain countries, especially the United States, seem to be inseparable from controversy over redistricting and gerrymandering. In the U.S., every new set of constituency boundaries drawn by the state legislature triggers a host of claims, and often court cases, arguing that the new districts are designed to reduce the representation of the minority party and/or an ethnic group. In contrast, European elections are virtually free from this kind of controversy.

The main reason for this is that districting—drawing constituency boundaries and allotting seats to each constituency—offers much less scope for gerrymandering or partisan bias under a PR electoral system. Gerrymandering is based on making sure that the opposition wastes as many votes as possible, but there are fewer wasted votes under a PR electoral system. Moreover, multimember constituencies mean that there are fewer boundaries to be drawn. In the extreme case, when the whole country is one big constituency, as in the Netherlands, there are no boundaries at all and thus no possibility of gerrymandering. In countries where district magnitude is large—such as Finland, where two hundred members of the Eduskunta are returned from just fifteen constituencies—it does not matter much how the country is divided up; the outcome within each constituency is bound to be reasonably proportional. The same applies in those countries that use higher-tier seat allocation (see Table 11-4), where any votes that had no effect (in other words, were wasted) at the constituency level can make

BOX 11-2

THE IMPACT OF ELECTORAL SYSTEMS

France

As in Britain, the electoral system, being based on single-member constituencies, greatly favors the large parties. Single-party majority government, though, is uncommon; only twice in the post-1958 Fifth Republic has one party won a majority of seats (the Gaullists in 1968 and the Socialists in 1981). The potential of single-member constituency systems to produce startling results was demonstrated by the March 1993 election, one of the most disproportional ever to have taken place in any country, when the right-wing parties won 460 of the 577 seats in parliament despite having attracted only 38 percent of votes in the first round of voting (which under a "pure" PR system would have earned them 221 seats). The main beneficiaries of the high disproportionality that is characteristically produced by the French system are the mainstream right-wing parties and, to a lesser extent, the Socialists. The main losers are small parties, together with the "extreme" parties: the communists on the left and the FN on the right.

Germany

Under the Weimar Republic established after World War I, Germany had highly proportional election results and very unstable governments. The electoral system adopted after World War II is often seen as having produced the best of both worlds: election results are still highly proportional, but there is no problem of government instability. The threshold that parties need to reach before qualifying for list seats has prevented the development of a situation where a multitude of small parties hold the balance of power. During the 1960s and 1970s only three parties (the SPD, the CDU/CSU, and the FDP) were represented in the West German Bundestag, before the Greens joined them in the 1980s. Although the Greens lost their representation in the 1990 all-German elections by falling below the threshold, they recovered their place at the 1994 and 1998 elections. A fifth party, the PDS (the former communists of East Germany) also managed to overcome the threshold at each of the elections of the 1990s.

Italy

Italy's pre-1993 electoral system guaranteed a high degree of proportionality, and a large number of minor parties usually gained representation. Voters' ability to indicate a preference for individual candidates on their chosen party's list generated considerable intra-party competition in and, indeed, between elections; this was especially pronounced within the Christian Democrats and reinforced the highly factionalized nature of that party. The new system adopted in 1993 was designed to have a very different impact. It is inherently less proportional than the previous system, with 75 percent of deputies being returned from single-member constituencies and only 25 percent being returned from lists, and the element of intra-party competition for preference votes from the electorate has been eliminated. The 1994 and 1996 elections held under this system were less proportional than previous Italian elections had been. Although the change had been expected to—and many had hoped it would—reduce the number of different parties in parliament, this number actually rose, because the major parties, rather than trying to use the majoritarian tendency of the plurality seats to crush smaller parties that were close to them on the political spectrum, preferred to do deals with them.

Netherlands

Because the Netherlands returns all its members of parliament in one nationwide constituency, proportionality is high, and the largest parties receive a negligible bonus of seats over and above their share of the votes. The absence of any subnational constituencies has led to some complaints that citizens do not have any local constituency representatives with whom they can identify and to whom they can take casework problems. There have been attempts over the years to try to counteract this by introducing provisions under which "personal votes," i.e., preference votes cast for individual candidates, would be more effective in determining which individual candidates are elected, and a change made before the 1998 election has made it slightly easier for these personal votes to have an impact.

Spain

Spain's electoral system is a version of PR, but it does not produce highly proportional outcomes. The main reason is the low number of members returned from the average constituency. In consequence, the largest parties receive a significant bonus from the electoral system, on occasions nearly as great as that received by the major parties in Britain and France. The largest party, the Socialist party, received a sizeable bonus during the 1980s, and regularly won an overall majority of seats, even though its share of the votes was consistently well

Continued . . .

Continued . . .

below 50 percent. In the 1993 election, too, the Socialists received a healthy bonus, which enabled them to retain power, but in 1996 it was the right-wing Popular Party that received the largest bonus and was able to form a minority government, and in 2000, with 44 percent of the votes, the Popular Party received an eight-point bonus and won 52 percent of the seats.

Sweden

The Swedish electoral system gives highly proportional results. Consequently, the largest party, the Social Democrats, rarely wins an overall majority of seats, even though its average share of the votes makes it one of Europe's strongest parties. By international standards, women are strongly represented in the Riksdag, and following its election of September 1998, Sweden had the highest proportion of women in parliament of any country in the world, with 149 women out of 349 MPs.

United Kingdom

The single-member constituency electoral system gives a large bonus of seats to the two largest parties, Labour and the Conservatives, which regularly win nearly all the seats in parliament even though smaller parties may take up to a third of the votes. An observer sitting in the gallery of the House of Commons would infer from the distribution of seats among the parties that Britain has an almost pure two-party system, but this impression is largely created by the electoral system. If Britain adopted a proportional electoral system, small parties, especially the Liberal Democrats, would win many more seats in the Commons, and the likelihood of single-party majority government, currently the norm, would be greatly reduced. Electoral reform is often discussed, but neither of the major parties, especially when it is in power, is keen on a move to proportional representation.

themselves felt at the higher level. In any case, in most European countries, no redistricting ever takes place. The constituency boundaries, like the boundaries of American states, are absolutely fixed over time, based usually on clusters of local administrative units such as counties. All that ever changes, in response to changes in population across the country, is the number of seats to be awarded to each constituency.

This leaves very few countries where redistricting can become a source of controversy: Britain and France, with single-member constituencies, and Ireland and Malta, which use PR (STV) in small constituencies regularly redrawn by the parliament. Even in these cases, some steps have been taken to take the subject out of the arena of partisan politics. In Ireland, an attempt in 1977 by the ruling coalition government to boost its chances of reelection by partisan redistricting backfired disastrously, and the government went down in world history as possibly the only one ever to implement a gerrymander that turned out to favor the opposition (Sinnott, pp. 114–15). After this debacle, the task of redistricting was handed over by all-party consensus to an independent commission. In Malta, the 1981 election gave the ruling Labour Party a majority of seats, even though the opposition Nationalists had won a majority of votes, mainly because the government had drawn the constituency boundaries to suit itself. To allay public discontent, a change was made to the electoral law so that if in the future a party won a majority of votes but only a minority of seats, it would be awarded as many extra seats as it needed to give it a majority. This provision had to be invoked at the next election, in 1987. The Nationalists, with 51 percent of the votes, won only thirty-one of the sixty-five seats, and Labour, with 49 percent, won thirty-four, so the Nationalists were awarded an extra four seats to give them a one-seat overall majority in an expanded sixty-nine-member chamber. In 1996, Labour won a majority of the votes but only a minority of the seats, so on that occasion it was the beneficiary of this provision.

Precise procedure, then, varies from country to country, but by a variety of methods the potential for redistricting to become a source of political controversy has been largely eliminated across the continent.

REFERENDUMS

Elections are archetypal institutions of representative democracy, but in a number of countries the people make certain decisions themselves, by means of the referendum. At a referendum, the people decide directly on some issue, rather than electing representatives to make decisions on their behalf. In the great majority of west European countries, a referendum can be triggered only by one of the institutions of representative government, such as the government, a parliamentary majority, a specified minority in parliament, or the president. In two countries, namely Italy and Switzerland, the people themselves can bring about a popular vote by means of provisions for the initiative (Uleri, 1996a, p. 12), without needing the endorsement of any other political actor.

The use of the referendum varies hugely across Western Europe. Between 1945 and 1995, around four hundred referendums took place in Western Europe—and one country, Switzerland, was responsible for three hundred of these (Gallagher, 1996, p. 231). Referendums are relatively common in Italy (forty cases during the same period), Ireland (seventeen) and Denmark (fourteen). In contrast, Germany and the Netherlands held no national referendums; Belgium, Finland, and the UK held one each; and Austria and Norway had two.

Most commonly, referendum issues are ones that cut across party lines, and given that party systems are usually based on the left-right spectrum, as we saw in Chapter 8, socioeconomic issues are not usually the subject of a referendum (Bogdanor, pp. 91–95). Instead, questions that concern national sovereignty or moral issues are often seen as particularly suitable for a direct vote by the people. In relation to sovereignty, seven countries have held referendums on membership in the European Union. Austria, Denmark, Finland, Ireland, and Sweden all held referendums before joining; the United Kingdom held one on withdrawal in 1975, two years after it had joined; and Norway held referendums on the subject in both 1972 and 1994, which on each occasion showed a majority against joining (see Table 5-7). In addition, both Denmark and Ireland hold referendums on every significant step of European integration, the rationale being the ceding of national sovereignty to a supranational institution. Iceland and Norway held referendums on independence—in each case there was near-unanimity in favor—and Belgium, Greece, and Italy have all held such votes on whether to opt for monarchy or a republic, only Belgium deciding in favour of monarchy.

Moral issues, too, have often featured as referendum topics. In Italy, after parliament had legalized divorce in 1970, opponents of this measure brought about a popular vote in 1974 to strike it down, and the people's decision to retain the divorce laws confirmed the liberalizing trend in Italian society. In Ireland, too, the legalization of divorce required the approval of the people in a referendum; in 1986 the vote was against change, but when a further referendum was held in 1995, there was a slim majority in favor, thus opening the door to the provision of divorce. Both Italy and Ireland have also held referendums on abortion.

A campaign rally, which attracted supporters of both sides of the argument, during Ireland's 1995 divorce referendum. The Catholic church made it clear that it thought the legalization of divorce would be bad for Irish society. The proposal to change the constitution to allow divorce was passed very narrowly, with 50.3 percent in favour. © United Kingdom PA Photos Limited

The impact of the referendum has, not surprisingly, been greatest in Switzerland, where fifty thousand people can, by signing a petition, launch an initiative and bring about a popular vote on any bill recently passed by parliament. Over the years only about 7 percent of bills have been challenged in this way; about half of these bills have been endorsed by the people and the other half have been rejected (Trechsel and Kriesi, p. 191). The impact on policy making is to incline those drawing up legislation to consult widely, in order to bring on board any group that might otherwise launch an initiative against the bill. In Italy, too, the use of the referendum has been very significant. Here, most popular votes have been "abrogative initiatives"—that is, they are launched by a petition signed by a prescribed number of voters, and they have the aim of repealing an existing law (Uleri, 1996b). In the early 1990s, two popular votes on aspects of the electoral system dealt hammer blows to the corrupt political establishment dominated by the Christian democrats (DC) and the socialists (PSI). The overwhelming support for both reforming measures was interpreted as an expression of popular disgust at the behavior of the ruling elite, which bowed to public pressure and left power, leading to a change in the electoral system used for elections to the lower house and to elections held three years ahead of schedule in March 1994. The rules in Italy require that for a law to be struck down by a referendum, there must be not only a majority of votes in favor of such a proposal but also a turnout of at least 50 percent. Consequently, if public opinion is known to be strongly supportive of some proposal, opponents are best advised not to vote at all in the hope of thereby invalidating the

BOX 11-3

THE REFERENDUM

France

France has a long history of referendums, going back to 1793. Most of its pre-1945 referendums were widely seen as dubiously democratic, being used by authoritarian rulers to legitimize their positions. More recently, the transition from the Third to the Fourth Republic was achieved by referendums in the mid-1940s, and in 1958 voters approved the inauguration of the Fifth Republic. In 1962, de Gaulle bypassed the old political elite by holding a referendum on the direct election of the president; the approval of the people for this measure had a major impact on the nature of the Fifth Republic. In 1969, a referendum brought about de Gaulle's downfall; he had tied his continuation in office to the success of an administrative reform proposal, and when the people rejected this measure, he resigned from office. From then to the end of the century, though, there were only three further referendums.

Germany

Two referendums were held under the Weimar Republic in the 1920s, and a further four took place under the Nazis in the 1930s. Needless to say, the last four were not in any way democratic exercises, and Hitler's use of the referendum may have brought the institution into disrepute in Germany. The postwar German constitution makes no mention of national referendums, and none has been held since 1938, although referendums occur at Land level.

Italy

Italy is second only to Switzerland in the number of popular votes that take place. Apart from Switzerland, it is the only country in Western Europe where the voters themselves can bring about a popular vote by means of the initiative, without needing the agreement of the government, parliament, or political parties. This allows pressure groups to place their own issues on the agenda, culminating in the slightly farcical exercise in June 1995 when voters found themselves called upon to vote on twelve different issues, some quite complex and obscure, on the same day. Some Italian referendums have been particularly important: in 1974 Italians voted to retain the laws permitting divorce, which the Catholic church and conservative groups had hoped would be struck down by the referendum, and in the early 1990s the votes to reform the electoral system constituted decisive blows against the corrupt and tottering political establishment.

Netherlands

The Netherlands is unique in Western Europe in never having held a national referendum. Despite this, or possibly because of it, the question of whether referendums support or damage democracy is debated more intensively in the Netherlands than virtually anywhere else. A number of referendums have been held at the local level on an experimental basis, and in the late 1990s there were moves to introduce legislation that would allow national referendums for the first time.

Spain

Spain has used the referendum institution sparingly. Two non-democratic referendums took place under the authoritarian Franco regime, and after his death in 1975 two further referendums authorized the transition to democratic politics, with a vote in favor of the political reform program in 1976 and approval of a new constitution in 1978. The only national referendum since then came in 1986, when the people voted narrowly in favor of Spain's remaining within NATO. In addition, a number of referendums have taken place at the regional level.

Sweden

Sweden held only five referendums during the twentieth century, on a rather eclectic range of subjects, including the prohibition of alcohol and even the side of the road on which motorists should drive. The most important referendum took place in 1994, when Swedes voted by a narrow margin in favor of their country's joining the European Union.

United Kingdom

Only one national referendum has taken place in the United Kingdom; that was in 1975, when by a two-to-one majority the people voted to remain within the European Community, which the UK had joined in 1973. However, the referendum has been used rather more within the component parts of the United Kingdom. In 1979 and 1997 there were referendums in Scotland and Wales on the devolution of powers; in each nation, the 1979 proposals did not receive enough support, but the 1997 proposals did, and they led to the creation of the Scottish parliament and the Welsh assembly that we discussed in Chapter 6. In addition, the package of proposals agreed to by political leaders in Northern Ireland in April 1998 (the Good Friday Agreement) was put to the people of the province a month later, and received endorsement by 71 percent to 29 percent.

result by preventing turnout's reaching the 50 percent threshold. This tactic was employed in the April 1999 and May 2000 referendums that we mentioned earlier, when proposals to change the electoral system were approved overwhelmingly by those who turned out to vote and yet were deemed not to have been approved by the people because turnout did not reach 50 percent. Supporters of change were especially disgruntled in 1999, when the officially recorded turnout was only slightly below 50 percent, because of their belief that the Italian electoral register contains the names of many people who have either died or emigrated, and so it is quite probable that turnout among Italians actually resident in Italy comfortably exceeded 50 percent in that year.

The referendum was employed less frequently in France in the 1980s and 1990s than in earlier decades, but on occasions it has been an important device. The character of the Fifth Republic was transformed by the referendum called by Charles de Gaulle in October 1962 on direct election of the president. De Gaulle had been made president in 1958 by the established parties, and by 1962 he had fulfilled the tasks they had hoped he would undertake. They may have planned to dispense with his services once his term ended, but de Gaulle outflanked them by his decision to call a referendum, despite a widespread opinion that constitutionally he did not have this power (Morel, pp. 73–74). The people voted by 62 percent to 38 percent in favor of the change, and this considerably enhanced the power and prestige of the president, at least when the president's party holds a parliamentary majority, as we saw in Chapter 3.

The referendum is an institution that might seem to be inherently in conflict with the system of "representative government" that this book is about. Indeed, some critics of the referendum argue against it precisely on the ground that it will weaken or undermine representative institutions. Perhaps, whenever a difficult issue arises, governments and parliaments will pass the buck to the people and propose holding a referendum rather than take the responsibility themselves. Or, in countries where the people can launch an initiative against a law passed by parliament, governments and parliaments may avoid taking tough but necessary decisions for fear that a popular vote will overturn these. Another risk is that people might vote for attractive ideas that can't really be implemented, or for expensive plans for which they are unwilling to pay (for example, by higher taxes), or for ideas that are at odds with the overall program of the government in such a way as to prevent the government from following any coherent policy.

Despite these fears, representative institutions have not been seriously challenged by the referendum. For one thing, as we have seen, in every country except Italy and Switzerland, elected representatives control access to the referendum, and therefore it is, as Butler and Ranney (p. 21) observe, "hard to believe that . . . the referendum seriously subverts representative democracy." In Switzerland representative institutions are by now well accustomed to operating in conjunction with the referendum. Only in Italy can the referendum be said to have had a destabilising effect; initiatives played a major role in bringing down the corrupt *partitocrazia* in the early 1990s, and could in theory make life difficult for more creditable political actors in the future. Political parties may also be seen as under threat from the referendum, because during referendum campaigns the running is often made by single-issue groups (or umbrella organizations covering a number of such groups), with parties, which may be internally divided on referendum issues, being sidelined. However, the referendum can in fact be a useful device for parties, acting as a "lightning rod," by removing awkward issues from the party political agenda (Bjørklund, pp. 248–49).

The idea of replacing representative government with some kind of "direct democracy" in which citizens would vote on virtually every issue is clearly completely unrealistic in a modern complex society. The sensible question to ask is thus not whether direct democracy is "better" than representative democracy. It is, rather, whether representative government and the referendum are inherently in conflict, or whether they can usefully complement each other. For the most part, the record in modern Europe suggests that the latter is the case.

CONCLUSION

Studies of electoral systems have come a long way over the past thirty years. Before then, some writers used to argue seriously that the adoption of PR in any country was virtually bound to lead to the collapse of democracy and the establishment of a dictatorship. Others claimed that PR was almost a guaranteed recipe for harmony, enlightened government, and a contented citizenry. Expectations of the difference that electoral systems can make are now much more realistic.

Even within this context, there is no doubt that electoral systems do matter. Proportional representation systems lead to parliaments that more closely reflect the distribution of votes than do plurality systems, and they are more likely to be associated with multiparty systems. They make gerrymandering more difficult and facilitate the entry of women and ethnic minorities to parliament. From a study of government performance in thirty-six countries, Arend Lijphart concludes that they can make a bigger difference than this; they can have an impact on many aspects of public policy. In countries that are close to the model of "consensus democracy," of which a PR electoral system is a key component, the record of government tends to be "kinder and gentler" when it comes to welfare spending, protection of the environment, use of harsh penal measures, and aid to developing countries, than it is in "majoritarian democracies," which use plurality or majority electoral systems. When it comes to macroeconomic performance and control of violence, too, consensus democracies have a slightly better record (Lijphart, 1999, pp. 258–300).

One of the areas in which electoral systems have their most visible consequences is government formation. PR formulas are much less likely than plurality or majority systems to manufacture single-party governments. Because it is very uncommon for a single party to win a majority of the votes cast, PR systems tend to be characterized by coalition government, the subject to which we now turn.

REFERENCES

Anckar, Carsten: "Determinants of Disproportionality and Wasted Votes," *Electoral Studies,* vol. 16, no. 4, 1997, pp. 501–15.

Arter, David: "The Swedish General Election of 20th September 1998: A Victory for Values over Policies?", *Electoral Studies,* vol. 18, no. 2, 1999, pp. 296–300.

Bjørklund, Tor: "The Demand for Referendum: When Does It Arise and When Does It Succeed?", *Scandinavian Political Studies,* new series, vol. 5, no. 3, 1982, pp. 237–59.

Blais, A., and R. K. Carty: "The Impact of Electoral Formulae on the Creation of Majority Governments," *Electoral Studies,* vol. 6, no. 3, 1987, pp. 209–18.

Bogdanor, Vernon: "Western Europe," in David Butler and Austin Ranney (eds.), *Referendums around the World: The Growing Use of Direct Democracy,* Macmillan and St Martin's Press, Basingstoke and New York, 1994, pp. 24–97.

Butler, David, and Austin Ranney: "Theory," in David Butler and Austin Ranney (eds.), *Referendums Around the World: The Growing Use of Direct Democracy,* Macmillan and St Martin's Press, Basingstoke and New York, 1994, pp. 11–23.

Carstairs, Andrew McLaren: *A Short History of Electoral Systems,* George Allen and Unwin, London, 1980.

Cole, Alistair, and Peter Campbell: *French Electoral Systems and Elections Since 1789,* Gower, Aldershot, 1989.

Cox, Gary W.: *Making Votes Count: Strategic Coordination in the World's Electoral Systems,* Cambridge University Press, Cambridge, 1997.

D'Alimonte, Roberto, (ed.): *The Italian Elections of 1996: Competition and Transition,* special issue of the *European Journal of Political Research,* vol. 34, no. 1, 1998, pp. 1–174.

D'Alimonte, Roberto, and Stefano Bartolini: "How to Lose a Majority: The Competition in Single-Member Districts," in D'Alimonte, 1998, pp. 63–103.

De Winter, Lieven: "Belgium: Democracy or Oligarchy?", in Michael Gallagher and Michael Marsh (eds.), *Candidate Selection in Comparative Perspective: The Secret Garden of Politics,* Sage, London, 1988, pp. 20–46.

Dimitras, Panayote Elias: "Electoral Systems in Greece," in Stuart Nagel (ed.), *Eastern Europe Development and Public Policy,* Basingstoke, Macmillan, 1994a, pp. 143–75.

Dimitras, Panayote Elias: "The Greek Parliamentary Election of October 1993," *Electoral Studies,* vol. 13, no. 3, 1994b, pp. 235–39.

Di Virgilio, Aldo: "Electoral Alliances: Party Identities and Coalition Games," in D'Alimonte, 1998, pp. 5–33.

Dunleavy, Patrick and Helen Margetts: "Mixed Electoral Systems in Britain and the Jenkins Commission on Electoral Reform," *British Journal of Politics and International Relations,* vol. 1, no. 1, 1999, pp.12–38.

Duverger, Maurice: "Duverger's Law: Forty Years Later," in Grofman and Lijphart, 1986, pp. 69–84.

Elklit, Jørgen: "Simpler than Its Reputation: The Electoral System in Denmark Since 1920", *Electoral Studies,* vol. 12, no. 1, 1993, pp. 41–57.

Farrell, David M.: *Electoral Systems: A Comparative Introduction,* Macmillan and St Martin's Press, New York and Basingstoke, 2000.

Finer, S. E. (ed.): *Adversary Politics and Electoral Reform,* Anthony Wigram, London, 1975.

Gallagher, Michael: "Proportionality, Disproportionality and Electoral Systems," *Electoral Studies,* vol. 10, no. 1, 1991, pp. 33–51.

Gallagher, Michael: "Conclusion," in Michael Gallagher and Pier Vincenzo Uleri (eds.), *The Referendum Experience in Europe,* Macmillan and St Martin's Press, Basingstoke and New York, 1996, pp. 226–52.

Goldey, D. B.: "The French General Election of 25 May–1 June 1997," *Electoral Studies,* vol. 17, no. 4, 1998, pp. 536–55.

Grofman, Bernard, and Arend Lijphart (eds.): *Electoral Laws and Their Political Consequences,* Agathon Press, New York, 1986.

Irwin, Galen A.: "The Dutch Parliamentary Election of 1998," *Electoral Studies,* vol. 18, no. 2, 1999, pp. 271–76.

Katz, Richard S.: "Intraparty Preference Voting," in Grofman and Lijphart, 1986, pp. 85–103.

Katz, Richard S.: "Electoral Reform and the Transformation of Party Politics in Italy," *Party Politics,* vol. 2, no. 1, 1996, pp. 31–53.

Katz, Richard S.: *Democracy and Elections,* Oxford University Press, New York and Oxford, 1997.

Kuusela, Kimmo: "The Finnish Electoral System: Basic Features and Developmental Tendencies," in Sami Borg and Risto Sänkiaho (eds.), *The Finnish Voter,* Finnish Political Science Association, Helsinki, 1995, pp. 23–44.

Laakso, Markku, and Rein Taagepera: "'Effective' Number of Parties: A Measure with Application to West Europe," *Comparative Political Studies,* vol. 12, no. 1, 1979, pp. 3–27.

Lijphart, Arend: *Electoral Systems and Party Systems: A Study of Twenty-Seven Democracies, 1945–1990,* Oxford University Press, Oxford and New York, 1994.

Lijphart, Arend: *Patterns of Democracy: Government Forms and Performance in Thirty-Six Countries,* Yale University Press, New Haven and London, 1999.

Mackie, Thomas T., and Richard Rose: *The International Almanac of Electoral History,* 3d ed., Macmillan, London, 1991.

Marsh, Michael: "The Voters Decide? Preferential Voting in European List Systems," *European Journal of Political Research,* vol. 13, no. 4, 1985, pp. 365–78.

Massicotte, Louis and André Blais: "Mixed Electoral Systems: A Conceptual and Empirical Survey," *Electoral Studies,* vol. 18, no. 3, 1999, pp. 341–66.

Morel, Laurence: "France: Towards a Less Controversial Use of the Referendum?", in Michael Gallagher and Pier Vincenzo Uleri (eds.), *The Referendum Experience in Europe,* Macmillan and St Martin's Press, Basingstoke and New York, 1996, pp. 66–85.

Müller, Wolfgang C., and Fritz Plasser: "Austria: The 1990 Campaign," in Shaun Bowler and David M. Farrell (eds.), *Electoral Strategies and Political Marketing,* Macmillan, Basingstoke, 1992, pp. 24–42.

Pesonen, Pertti: "The Voters' Choice of Candidate," in Sami Borg and Risto Sänkiaho (eds.), *The Finnish Voter,* Finnish Political Science Association, Helsinki, 1995, pp. 114–28.

Petersson, Olof: *The Government and Politics of the Nordic Countries,* Publica, Stockholm, 1994.

Rallings, Colin and Michael Thrasher: *Britain Votes 6: British Parliamentary Election Results 1997,* Ashgate, Aldershot, 1998.

Reeve, Andrew, and Alan Ware: *Electoral Systems: A Comparative and Theoretical Introduction,* Routledge, London and New York, 1992.

Representation: *The Single Transferable Vote,* special issue of *Representation*, vol. 34, no. 1, 1996, pp. 1–75.

Reynolds, Andrew, and Ben Reilly: *The International IDEA Handbook of Electoral System Design,* International Institute for Democracy and Electoral Assistance, Stockholm, 1997.

Rule, Wilma, and Joseph F. Zimmerman (eds.): *Electoral Systems in Comparative Perspective: Their Impact on Women and Minorities,* Greenwood Press, Westport CT, 1994.

Sartori, Giovanni: *Comparative Constitutional Engineering: An Inquiry into Structures, Incentives and Outcomes,* 2d ed., Basingstoke, Macmillan, 1997.

Sinnott, Richard: "The Electoral System," in John Coakley and Michael Gallagher (eds.), *Politics in the Republic of Ireland,* 3d ed., Routledge, London, 1999, pp. 99–126.

Taagepera, Rein, and Matthew Soberg Shugart: *Seats and Votes: The Effects and Determinants of Electoral Systems,* Yale University Press, New Haven and London, 1989.

Trechsel, Alexander H., and Hanspeter Kriesi: "Switzerland: The Referendum and Initiative as a Centrepiece of the Political System," in Michael Gallagher and Pier Vincenzo Uleri (eds.), *The Referendum Experience in Europe,* Macmillan and St Martin's Press, Basingstoke and New York, 1996, pp. 185–209.

Uleri, Pier Vincenzo: "Introduction," in Michael Gallagher and Pier Vincenzo Uleri (eds.), *The Referendum Experience in Europe,* Macmillan and St Martin's Press, Basingstoke and New York, 1996a, pp. 1–19.

Uleri, Pier Vincenzo: "Italy: Referendums and Initiatives from the Origins to the Crisis of a Democratic Regime," in Michael Gallagher and Pier Vincenzo Uleri (eds.), *The Referendum Experience in Europe,* Macmillan and St Martin's Press, Basingstoke and New York, 1996b, pp. 106–25.

Woldendorp, Jaap, Hans Keman, and Ian Budge: "Party Government in 20 Democracies," special issue of *European Journal of Political Research,* vol. 24, no. 1, 1993, pp. 1–119.

12

BUILDING AND MAINTAINING A GOVERNMENT

When the smoke has blown away after a typical election campaign, some parties will have won seats and votes and some will have lost them. But the real prize that is won or lost on these occasions, for most parties at least, is a place in the government. European voters, as we have seen, typically do not have the last word on this important matter. In most countries the membership of the government is decided, some time after the election is over, on the basis of bargaining between party leaders. This is the case because it is very unusual for a political party to get a majority of all votes cast—and proportional representation (PR) electoral systems create legislatures that reflect this pattern of electoral preference. Very, very few European political parties, therefore, ever win a majority of legislative seats. Almost all single-party "majority" governments are actually creations of an electoral system that gives legislative majorities to parties that win less than 50 percent of the votes. This means that governments formed by a single majority party are rare exceptions on the European scene, found in only a small number of countries.

In a broader sense, however, even single-party governments can also be seen as coalitions: coalitions of factions within the ruling party. These intra-party coalitions may be kept together, not as a result of any great affinity between those involved, but by little more than their mutual fear of electoral disaster. The best-known example of a single-party "coalition" of factions has been outside Europe, in Japan's Liberal Democratic Party (LDP). The LDP is split into very well-defined factions, but has governed Japan as a single-party administration for much of the postwar era. Japanese politics during this period has thus been as much about shifting coalitions within the LDP as about competition between different parties. Within Europe, the Italian Christian Democratic Party (DCI) was also divided into clearly defined factions before it broke up in the early 1990s, following a series of corruption scandals. Each DCI faction within the government was typically rewarded with a very precise share of the cabinet port-folios, almost as if it had been a distinct party in its own right (Mershon, 2001). Both of the main British parties, Labour and the Conservatives, have formed single-party governments marked by deep internal divisions. As in Japan, the factions have stayed together within the same party largely because of the way in which the electoral system would penalize them if they split. Because the first-past-the-post electoral system used in Britain typically punishes smaller parties and splinter groups so viciously, ex-plicit party splits can be very damaging; the fate of those who broke away from the British Labour Party to form the Social Democratic Party is a notorious example. One interpretation of the real political impact of the British electoral system, therefore, is that it forces big parties to stay together in one piece, however hair-raising the intra-party politics might be. This in turn means that most of the politics of coalition in Britain, and in other systems in which one-party government is the norm, takes place *within* parties rather than *between* them.

In a very real sense, therefore, coalition bargaining is fundamental to all political systems. In Britain (and indeed, in the United States), coalition bargaining takes place for the most part inside political parties as a result of the distorting effects of the plu-rality electoral system. In most continental European countries, election results are translated more or less proportionally into legislative seat distributions, and so coalition bargaining takes place both within and between political parties. Most governments are executive coalitions, in which more than one party is represented at the cabinet table. Most European single-party governments do not control legislative majorities; they must thus rely for their continued existence on legislative coalitions. In this case a group of parties supports the government in the legislature, even if only one party controls seats in the cabinet.

Once a government has formed in a coalition system, this is by no means the end of the story. The ability of a government to keep hold of the reins of power crucially depends on a continuous process of bargaining and negotiation between party leaders. The deals that were made to build the government in the first place can just as easily be unmade, bringing it tumbling down. At a certain point in time, various political vari-ables may come together to encourage politicians to create a particular government. If these variables change in unforeseen ways, then the same politicians may face differ-ent incentives and choose to destroy the government that they earlier created.

Thus, a coalition government can in theory be brought down at any moment by the defection of one or more of its legislative supporters. And those who oppose PR elec-toral systems typically do so, as we saw in the preceding chapter, on the grounds that "PR generates multiparty systems, which generate coalition governments, which are unstable." Many old saws have an element of truth in them, and this one is no excep-tion. As we will see, coalition governments do tend, on balance, not to last as long as single-party majority governments. At the same time, however, we should not forget that some of the most economically successful and politically stable governments in the postwar world have been the coalition administrations that have governed Germany, Switzerland, Luxembourg, and Austria for most of the period since 1945.

In the rest of this chapter, therefore, when we explore the making and breaking of governments in Western Europe, we will be considering mainly the workings of coalition government. We examine factors that affect the formation of European cabinets and the allocation of cabinet portfolios among parties. Because the specter of "unstable coalition government" is so often raised by opponents of PR, we also look at the durability of European governments, trying to understand why some governments last as long as is constitutionally possible while others form, fall, and re-form at a much faster pace.

GOVERNMENT FORMATION

As we have seen, the typical European election does not in any final sense settle the matter of who gets into government, although elections are often more decisive, even in a coalition system, than many people realize. Thus, if members of the incumbent government are reasonably happy with one another, if the election results are not too unfavorable for them, and especially if the government parties between them control a legislative majority, then the incumbent government may well decide to continue in office. No serious consideration may be given to a change of administration. The situation after the 1998 election in the Netherlands was a case in point. When the election was held, the incumbent government was a "purple" coalition that included the center-left Labour Party, a liberal centrist party in D66, and a center-right party, the VVD. This coalition had been formed after the previous election to keep the Christian Democrats out of government in Holland for the first time in the postwar era and, despite the occasional spat between the partners, had worked reasonably well. The coalition retained its majority at the election, although a few seats were reallocated within the coalition. To nobody's surprise, the same government continued in office.

Election results may also lead to predictable changes of coalition government. The Italian general election of 1996, for example, was fought between two rival electoral coalitions. The need to form coalitions of parties that fight elections as a cartel was brought about by a change in Italian electoral law, which, as we saw in Chapter 11, set out to reduce the number of parties in Italy by introducing a system of single-seat first-past-the-post elections for 75 percent of seats in the Italian legislature. The 1996 elections were largely fought out between a cartel of center-right parties, the *Polo della Libertà* (the Freedom Pole), and a center-left cartel, *l'Ulivio* (the Olive Tree). The *Polo* had won the previous election, in 1994, and had gone on to form the government. This had broken up after the defection of one of its members, and been replaced with a non-party government of experts. The parties of *l'Ulivio* fought the 1996 election on the basis of a common policy platform, and with an agreed candidate for prime minister. In effect, this electoral coalition offered itself to voters as a potential government. In collaboration with the refounded Italian Communist Party (RC), the *l'Ulivio* coalition won a majority of seats in the 1996 election, and went on to form the government. In this case, therefore, Italian voters had spoken, and had played a big part in changing the government, even in a coalition system with a large number of parties.

Thus, we should not get too bewitched by an image of the political future of most European states being settled by the wheeling and dealing of party leaders in smoke-filled rooms rather than by the electorate. Even in coalition systems, election results may in practice be politically decisive and the voters may have a direct say in government formation. They may confirm that an incumbent coalition will remain in office, or they may make it possible for a prearranged coalition in opposition to take over the reins of power.

Nonetheless, and this goes to the heart of the matter in most European parliamentary democracies in which one well-disciplined party does not control a majority of the legislature, the potential always exists for the government to be defeated, both immediately after an election and in the middle of its term of office. Therefore, even when an incumbent government remains in office apparently without incident, this is also the result of the politics of coalition. In a coalition system, political bedrock is that the government remains in office for as long as a majority of legislators prefer it to any realistic alternative. Thus, the way legislators feel about the precise composition of the government, the subject of the rest of this section, is an absolutely vital matter.

Before we can tell a sensible story about how European party leaders set out to bargain their way into government, therefore, and before we can discuss the factors that European legislators take into account when trying to decide which government to support, we must have at least some idea about what motivates politicians.

Office-Seeking Politicians?

As we have seen, each European government comprises a cabinet led by a prime minister. The prime minister is typically, though not invariably, the leader of one of the main political parties. Thus, in order to become a prime minister, it is almost always necessary to become a party leader first, a fact that gives much of the zest to the business of leadership selection in major European political parties. After the prime ministership, cabinet ministries are the most powerful political offices in the land. A seat at the cabinet table represents the pinnacle of a politician's career. Cabinet ministers are typically, though not invariably, senior party legislators, though who is or is not "senior" in a political party is a far less clear-cut matter than who is the party leader. Indeed, a party leader can turn a colleague into a senior politician by successfully imposing him or her as a cabinet minister.

The fact that the positions of prime minister and cabinet minister are such glittering political prizes provides one distinctive perspective on the making and breaking of governments. This is that politicians are mainly interested in the "intrinsic" rewards of office. To be a cabinet minister, after all, is to be a famous and powerful person. The desire for such fame and power—the "smell of the leather" (of the ministerial car)—may well be the most important motivation for many politicians even if few would ever admit this openly, or perhaps even to themselves.

Policy-Oriented Politicians?

Another important set of reasons for trying to get into government has to do with influencing public policy. If politicians want to make a difference in the way their country is run, one of the most effective ways they can do this is to get into the cabinet. This motivation, of course, is far more acceptable to the wider political world than naked political ambition, and is one that politicians are much more inclined to promote in public. Very few politicians, whatever their real hopes and fears, look for votes on the grounds that what they want to do if elected is make lots of money, get their picture in the newspaper every day, ride around in the back seat of a chauffeur-driven limousine, and have a large staff to boss around. Most European politicians, like their U.S. counterparts, campaign on the basis of promises about all the good that they can do for their country if the voters put them in a position of power. They usually claim that they don't want all of this power for its own sake, but rather in order to implement cherished and worthy policy objectives for the benefit of everyone.

The desire to consume the intrinsic rewards of office and the desire to have an impact on public policy, therefore, are different plausible motivations for the politicians involved in the making and breaking of governments. (For an extended discussion of this theme, see Müller and Strom.) As we will now see, however, different interpretations of government formation in modern Europe flow from these alternative assumptions about what drives politicians.

Office-Seeking Politicians and "Minimal Winning" Governments

Perhaps the best-known approach to the analysis of government formation in modern Europe is based on the assumption that politicians are driven above all else by the desire to enjoy the rewards of office for their own sake. This approach leads to predictions that the coalitions that form will be just enough to take the prize and no bigger—that "minimal winning" government coalitions are the most likely to be the European norm. Minimal winning governments carry no passengers; they include only parties whose legislative votes are essential for the government's majority.

The logic of this argument is straightforward. If being in government is valued in and of itself, then the set of cabinet positions is like a fixed set of trophies to be shared out by the winners of the government-formation game. Any government party whose votes are not essential to the government's legislative majority will be enjoying some of these trophies without having contributed any of the resources essential for their capture. Such "passengers" will therefore be excluded from the government by office-seeking politicians. This logic implies that government coalitions should comprise as few parties as possible, consistent with the need to win confidence votes in the legislature (Riker). The result is a minimal winning government. If a government does indeed include parties whose seats are not needed for its legislative majority, then it is called an "oversized" or "surplus majority" government. Both names, of course, suggest the rather curious—and, as we will see, unwarranted—implication that some governments can in some sense have "too much" support. Nonetheless, if a cabinet includes a party whose votes are not essential to keeping the government in office, then we do have to ask what else this party might be contributing. In this way, the notion of the minimal winning cabinet provides a useful basis from which to start thinking about the making and breaking of European governments. (For reviews of "office-driven" models of government formation, see Laver, 1998; Laver and Schofield.)

The "office-seeking" assumption also provides the basis for a number of "power indices," which measure the extent to which parties can exploit their position in the legislature during coalition bargaining. Two well-known power indices are the

"Shapley-Shubik" and "Banzhaf" indices, each named after their inventors. These indices are useful because they help to highlight the ways in which the distribution of bargaining power can sometimes differ quite starkly from the distribution of seats in the legislature.

One classic example of this occurs when there are two large parties that fall somewhat short of a majority, and the "balance of power" is held by a much smaller party. Imagine a legislature in which two parties win about 45 percent of the seats, and a smaller party wins about 10 percent. In this situation, the political facts of life, if politicians are concerned above all else to get into office, are that neither of the two larger parties can take power on its own, but that any two parties can take power together. In this sense, all three parties are in the same situation and have equal bargaining power despite their unequal size, giving the smaller party disproportionate power. This is actually quite similar to a situation that often arose in pre-unification Germany, with the much smaller Free Democrat Party holding the balance of power. This allowed the Free Democrats to be in most postwar German coalition cabinets, often with the more coveted cabinet portfolios, despite their small size. (The power index approach has recently been usefully extended to the balance of power between countries in the European Union Council of Ministers, and is useful in exploring the effect on this of different potential enlargements. Nurmi and Meskanen; Garret and Tsebelis; Holler and Widgren.)

Policy-Oriented Politicians and Ideologically Compact Governments

If the politicians who build governments want to leave their mark on public policy rather than merely to consume the fruits of office, then a different interpretation of government formation is called for. Public policy, after all, applies to everybody. It applies to those who are in government and those who are not, to voters and nonvoters alike. Above all, public policy cannot in any sense be "used up" at a faster rate if there are more parties in the government. Thus, abolishing the death sentence for convicted murderers is a policy that applies to all, whether they are in the government or outside it, murderers or not. If more people join the government, the policy is in no sense "diluted"; it is no better and no worse than it was before. Those who want no more than to see the death penalty abolished will be delighted when it goes, whether they are in or out of office at the time.

If politicians are driven by nothing but the desire to affect public policy when they set out to bargain their way into government, then the logic of the minimal winning coalition is eroded. If some other politician shares your policies, then there is no reason in the world, if all you are concerned with is policy, to keep this person out of office. In its pure form, this approach suggests that the only criterion that will be used in government formation is the ideological closeness of the coalition partners. The coalitions that form should contain parties whose policies are as compatible as possible. They will thus be ideologically "compact" in the sense that coalition members will tend to be closer together, rather than farther apart, in their ideological positions. In the extreme, if parties are concerned only with policy then this should lead to coalitions that are so compact that they comprise only a single party—even a very small one—with a very central policy position. If the other parties do not care at all about getting into office, then they may regard the policies of this very central government as being better than those of any other government that is likely to form. They may thus allow the central party to take power on its own and implement its policy program. As we will soon see, this logic underpins the formation of the so-called minority governments that have been quite common in postwar Europe.

Obviously, however, it is rather extreme to assume either that politicians are concerned only with feathering their own nests or that they are concerned only with the good of the country, whatever personal sacrifice is required. The truth is likely to be somewhere in between, and most current accounts of the politics of coalition in modern Europe are based on the assumption that politicians are concerned both with getting into office for its own sake and with having an impact on public policy. This leads to predictions that "minimal winning" coalitions will tend to form, because office motivations are important, but that these will be ideologically compact, because policy is also important. This leads in turn to the prediction that "minimal connected winning" coalitions will form; these are coalitions between parties that are adjacent to each other in policy terms, and that cannot lose a party off either "end" without losing their majority. Figures 12-1 to 12-3, later in this chapter will give examples of these.

Many authors now have constructed "policy-driven" models of government formation in modern Europe. These differ in a number of important respects, although most assume that there is more to policy-driven government formation than a single left-right dimension of public policy. For example, other policy dimensions that might well have a bearing upon government formation in particular countries include foreign policy, environmental policy, and the "liberal-conservative" dimension of social and moral policy on matters such as abortion or capital punishment. Some of these authors have constructed models that concentrate more or less exclusively on the policy positions of the political parties and their relative strengths in the electorate and/or legislature (Schofield, 1993, 1995; Grofman). Other authors have focused more upon institutional features of the government formation process. These features include the order in which parties are chosen to be *formateurs* (Baron; see also Chapter 3), the role of the vote of confidence procedure (Huber), or the need to allocate control of particular policy areas to particular cabinet ministers (Laver and Shepsle, 1996).

One common feature of all such models is that they highlight a strong tendency for the governments that form to adopt positions relatively close to the center of whatever policy dimensions are important. The net result is that the government formation process in a coalition system is likely to produce government policies that are less extreme than the policies of a number of the parties winning seats in the legislature. In this important sense, the politics of coalition appear to have a moderating effect on public policy outputs.

Minority Governments

So far, we have been implicitly assuming that the governments that form in modern European states are made up of parties that between them control a majority of seats in the legislature. This need by no means be the case, however. At first sight, the idea of a minority government—one that does not control a majority of seats in the legislature

—might seem to be at best a paradox and at worst downright undemocratic. When there is a minority government, after all, this means that there must also be a majority opposition in the legislature. This opposition could, in theory, throw the government out on its ear, but for some reason chooses not to do so. When there is a minority government, furthermore, an executive has taken office with no guarantee that it can stay there for any length of time, because it can be defeated at any moment at the pleasure of the opposition. Yet Kaare Strom has argued convincingly that minority government should be seen as a normal outcome of the process of democratic party competition in Europe, rather than as some sort of obstacle to it (Strom, 1990).

The main reasons minority governments are such a common outcome of party competition in modern Europe have to do with the role of party policy. After all, if politicians are motivated solely by the desire to get into office, then it is hard to see why they would choose to go into opposition when they have the legislative muscle to go into government. If politicians are concerned about policy, however, then there may well be circumstances in which policy objectives are better served from a place on the opposition benches than from a seat at the cabinet table. Parties may choose to stay in opposition, the better to fulfil their policy objectives.

Strom therefore looked at the influence over policy that can be wielded by the opposition, concentrating mainly on formal influence exercised through the legislative committee system (Strom, 1990). The influence of the opposition arises because it is actually rather rare for bottom-line decisions on important policy matters to be slugged out on the floor of the legislature. Many more political wars are waged in committees. Different European countries differ considerably, furthermore, in terms of the effectiveness of their committee systems and the policy influence that committees give the opposition. The more powerful the committee system and the greater the influence of the opposition, so the story goes, the lower is the incentive for opposition parties to get into the government, because they can be almost as effective outside it. And the lower the incentive to get into government, obviously, the greater is the likelihood of finding minority governments.

Strom tested this argument by looking at the size, scope, specialization, and power of the committee system in a number of European democracies. He found that the Norwegian committee system is the one that gives the opposition the most influence over policy. This is followed, according to Strom, by the committee systems of Iceland, Italy, Portugal, Sweden, and France. Strom suggested that the committee systems that afford the opposition the least influence over policy are in Britain and Ireland, followed by the Netherlands. Although we might well quibble with some of these individual categorizations, the general pattern is quite clear. The relatively high frequency of minority government in Scandinavia and Italy is consistent in these terms with the relatively high formal policy influence of the opposition, exercised through the committee system.

Laver and Hunt collected data that can be used to throw further light on the relationship between minority government and the political role of the opposition. A group of experts in the politics of each country was asked to rate that country in terms of the potential impact of the opposition on government policy. These figures are shown in Table 12-1, and the pattern is striking. The five countries scoring highest on opposition impact are once more the Scandinavian countries and Italy: the precise group with

TABLE 12-1 IMPACT OF OPPOSITION PARTIES ON
GOVERNMENT POLICY

Italy	7.1
Norway	6.8
Denmark	6.5
Sweden	5.2
Finland	4.9
Iceland	4.8
Portugal	4.3
Austria	4.1
Ireland	4.1
Luxembourg	4.0
Netherlands	3.6
Germany	3.5
France	3.4
Malta	3.3
Belgium	2.6
Greece	2.2
Spain	2.0
Britain	2.0

Note: Mean scores on a scale of 1 (low) to 9 (high).
Source: Laver and Hunt, Appendix B.

the highest frequency of minority governments. Although we can never be quite sure which is the chicken and which the egg, the accumulation of evidence lends strong support to the argument that if the opposition parties have a greater chance of having an impact on government policy, then opposition will be more attractive than would otherwise be the case, and the frequency of minority governments will increase.

A second interpretation of the ability of minority governments to stay in power—one that may be more appropriate outside Scandinavia—is based on policy divisions within the opposition (Laver and Shepsle, 1996). On this account, a minority government can survive and can even be quite stable simply because the opposition parties cannot agree on a replacement. Thus, governments can be politically "viable" with far less than a legislative majority. Although control over a legislative majority guarantees victory, this does not mean that failure to control a majority spells inevitable defeat. In particular, a party whose policies place it at the center of the political system may often find itself a member of every viable government. Laver and Shepsle call this a "strong" party; its strength derives from the fact that any government that excludes it is likely to be defeated in the legislature in favor of some government that includes it. And if a party cannot be excluded from government, then it obviously can credibly demand to be allowed to govern alone, even in a minority position. Thus, if some party is sufficiently central that it can split its political opponents in this way, it can form a viable minority government.

This logic may well underwrite a number of the minority governments formed in the past by the Christian Democrats in Italy and by the Social Democrats in Denmark. In each case, a substantial party with an ideological position toward the center of the ideological spectrum won less than a majority of seats, but faced a divided opposition. Some of the opposing parties were to the left of it; some, to the right. As a result of this ideological positioning of the parties, a coalition of opponents formed to evict the center party was not a very plausible possibility. Because it was very difficult to evict the "strong" center party from office, that party was in a very powerful bargaining position and could well have decided to go it alone. Even without a majority it could not be beaten. Indeed, the ability of a particular party to go it alone as a minority government, in the face of a divided opposition, is one of the acid tests of real bargaining power in the making and breaking of governments.

It should be quite clear from the foregoing discussion that minority government is very much a part of the political scenery in modern Europe. Any model of European politics that cannot give a convincing account of minority government, therefore, is seriously deficient. We should also note that each of the more plausible interpretations of minority government depends upon taking policy seriously. One possibility is that the opposition to a minority government is so divided over policy that it can provide no alternative. Another possibility is that the other parties accept a minority government because they expect to be able to fulfill policy objectives from a position on the opposition benches—by exploiting the committee system, for example. If voters are motivated by policy considerations, indeed, then a party may even *prefer* to stay on the opposition benches so that it can pick and choose the issues on which it makes a policy intervention. If it were in government, in contrast, then the same party would be forced to make heavily constrained policy decisions on many issues that were not of its own choosing, in this way alienating at least some of its supporters.

Either way, policy figures prominently in accounts of minority government. We might conclude from this that in those countries where minority government is common, policy must be an important factor in party competition. Policy also figures prominently in accounts of "surplus" majority government, the matter to which we now turn.

Surplus Majority Governments

Just as some cabinets may be able to survive with less than a parliamentary majority, others may include parties whose seats are not crucial to the government majority in the legislature. There may be several reasons for the formation of such "surplus majority" or "oversized" governments.

Immediately after World War II, for example, governments of "national unity" were formed in many European countries with the intention of involving all sections of society in the job of postwar reconstruction. These were typically surplus majority coalitions comprising all, or nearly all, major parties. Examples can be found in Austria, Belgium, Finland, France, Germany, Italy, Luxembourg, and the Netherlands. In most cases, and perhaps somewhat surprisingly in the circumstances, these arrangements tended to be short-lived. "Normal" party competition soon reestablished itself.

Government formation quickly came to involve some parties going into power and consigning others to the opposition.

There are still occasional and usually forlorn popular appeals, at times of major political or economic crisis, for governments of national unity. Although there may be public support for the idea that everyone should get together and pull the country out of trouble, politicians almost never respond to this. Grand coalitions are rare in modern Europe, and government formation is typically as much about who is left out of office as about who gets in.

Another reason we may find surplus majority governments has to do with the constitution. Countries have different requirements for constitutional amendments, but one requirement used by some countries involves winning a "qualified" majority vote in the legislature—that is, a majority of more than 50 percent of legislators, or two-thirds, or three-quarters, for example. In such circumstances, if constitutional reform is on the agenda, a cabinet may need a legislative majority of more than 50 percent to implement its policies. Additional parties may then be included in the government, whose seats are needed not to achieve a 50 percent majority, so as to achieve this higher threshold. In Belgium, for example, divisions between language communities have resulted in constitutional provisions that laws affecting relations between the communities require the assent of a majority in each language group and two-thirds of legislators overall. This in effect has meant that Belgian cabinets may sometimes need a two-thirds legislative majority in order to govern effectively. Such cabinets may superficially look "oversized," but they are in practice no larger than legally necessary in the circumstances.

There is another reason why a party whose votes are not essential for a government's majority may still be a vital member of the cabinet. Laver and Shepsle (1996) argue that a party may be essential for a stable government because its presence is required to send out certain signals about some aspect of government policy. For example, the seats of a party with a tough policy of cutting public spending may not be needed for a cabinet's majority. If this party is nonetheless in the cabinet, then public perceptions of the government as a whole may be that it is tough on public spending. If the party is excluded, then public perceptions may be that the government is softer on public spending. The party thereby contributes to the perceived policy profile of the government, rather than its parliamentary majority, and in this sense is not "surplus" to requirements at all.

Finally, Luebbert argued that a very clear strategic benefit can arise from carrying "passengers" in cabinet coalitions, especially for a dominant party. Once a government takes office, any party that is crucial to the government's majority can bring the entire executive tumbling down by withdrawing its support. Even very small parties have a potent threat with which to attempt to extract concessions from their cabinet colleagues, provided, that is, that their votes are critical to the government majority. In anticipation of this, a large party may choose to surround itself with a protective screen of weaker passengers so that no single other party is critical to the government majority. In this event, none of the weaker passengers can make serious demands once the government has formed, because every one of them is expendable (Luebbert, p. 79). To put it rather crudely, powerful parties might actually choose to carry passengers so that one or two can be tossed overboard without too much fuss if they start to get greedy.

Minimal Winning Government in Ireland

We will shortly be taking a comprehensive look at the types of government that form right across Western Europe, but the best way to get a feel for these types of government is to consider some specific examples. We begin with a minimal winning coalition.

The top part of Figure 12-1 provides some information about the situation in Ireland in early 1993. After the November 1992 general election, there were five parties with a part to play in the government formation process. There were also some one-person parties and independents that we ignore as serious players for the sake of simplicity. These parties are placed on a left-right policy dimension according to the extent to which they promoted raising taxes to increase public services, on the left, or cutting public services to cut taxes, on the right. (These data are taken from a collection of expert surveys of party positions in a wide range of countries, reported in Laver and Hunt and updated for this election by Laver, 1994). From left to right, the parties involved were Democratic Left (DL), the Labour Party (Lab), Fianna Fáil (FF), Fine Gael (FG), and the Progressive Democrats (PD). The number of seats won by each party (out of a total of 166) is also given.

The outgoing government was a minority Fianna Fáil caretaker administration formed after the acrimonious breakup in late 1992 of a bare majority coalition between Fianna Fáil and the Progressive Democrats. Fianna Fáil, however, lost badly in the election that followed, and, even forgetting the bad blood between them, an FF-PD coalition could no longer command a majority.

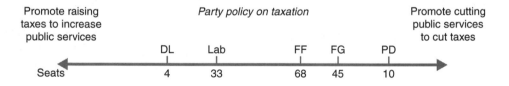

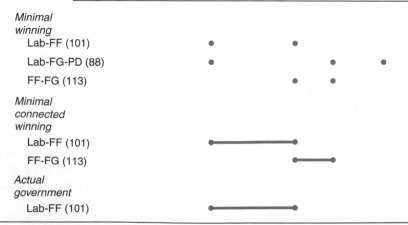

FIGURE 12-1   Coalition possibilities in Ireland, January 1993

During the election campaign, the Fine Gael party leader had proposed a "Rainbow Coalition" of Fianna Fáil's opponents, comprising Fine Gael, Labour, and the PDs. As Figure 12-1 shows, this commanded more than the 83 seats needed to win votes in the legislature, but it did include parties from almost all shades of the ideological rainbow. Fianna Fáil dubbed it the "Lethal Cocktail" in an attempt to knock some of the media shine off the idea of being governed by a "rainbow." Neither of the other two parties involved had agreed to the proposed rainbow during the election campaign. After the election results had been declared, it became clear that both Fianna Fáil and Fine Gael were the big losers, and that Labour was the big winner. A demoralized Fianna Fáil leader left government formation up to others, and there was intense media speculation about the rainbow coalition.

The possible coalition options during government formation in 1993 are given in the bottom part of Figure 12-1. First, the minimal winning coalitions are given. Obviously, any other party or parties could be added to each of these to create surplus majority coalitions. Minority governments would comprise less than the minimal winning coalitions, but minority governments still need to win votes of confidence; they thus need the explicit or implicit support of a majority coalition in the legislature, even if the cabinet partners themselves do not constitute a majority. Figure 12-1 shows that there were three possible minimal winning coalitions in Ireland in 1993. One was the Rainbow Coalition of Labour, FG, and PD. The other two were the Labour-FF and FF-FG coalitions.

One thing is immediately striking about this. Democratic Left was a member of no minimal winning coalition. Another way of putting this is that Democratic Left was essential to no legislative majority. In the indelicate language of coalition studies, Democrat Left was a "dummy" party—by implication, destined to watch government formation from the sidelines. A dummy party in a coalition system is the equivalent of the losing party in a two-party system, with no clear cut impact on the making and breaking of governments.

If party policy is important in government formation, as it usually is, then we need to consider the policy differences within various potential governments. Looking at the bottom part of Figure 12-1 again, we see that there were two minimal connected winning coalition cabinets, comprising only parties that were adjacent to each other on the left-right scale. These were the coalition between Fianna Fáil and Labour and that between Fianna Fáil and Fine Gael.

In order to go any further, we need one important piece of information about Irish politics. This is the fact that Fianna Fáil and Fine Gael are deeply hostile to each other, not as a result of economic policy but because they are political movements that sprang from the opposite sides of the Civil War that immediately followed the foundation of the new Irish state. For this and many other reasons, the two parties implacably refuse to go into government together. The bottom part of Figure 12-1 shows that this refusal has a dramatic impact on government formation in Ireland. Ruling out the FF-FG coalition, the only majority coalitions are Labour-FF, and Labour-FG-PD. Both require Labour to be in government, putting it very much in the driving seat in the government-formation process. As Figure 12-1 shows, the Labour-FF coalition was the most congenial for Labour in policy terms. What actually happened was that Labour

(a) June 30, 1989: Irish Prime Minister Charles Haughey resigns, (b) July 1, 1989: Fianna Fáil's Joe Walsh negotiates, (c) July 7, 1989: PD negotiators Pat Cox and Bobby Molloy, (d) July 13, 1989: PD leader Desmond O' Malley being appointed by President Hillery, (e) July 13, 1989: Fianna Fáil leader Charles Haughey being reappointed. © The Irish Times

leader Dick Spring, after abortive discussions with Fine Gael's John Bruton, eventually did reach a comprehensive and favorable coalition deal with Fianna Fáil. The result was a minimal connected winning coalition. The two parties were next to each other on the main policy scale, and the votes of both were vital for the government's legislative majority. (For a more extensive discussion of the formation of this government, see Farrell.)

Minority Government in Norway

As we have seen, although a government does need to win majority votes in the legislature if it is to govern effectively, the parties in the cabinet do not themselves need to command a majority and may instead form a minority administration. This is what happened after the September 1997 general election in Norway. Some information on the Norwegian party system after this election is given in the top part of Figure 12-2. Once more, party positions on a left-right dimension are given, taken from Laver and Hunt, together with legislative seat totals. Ranging from left to right, the parties are the Socialist Left (SL), Labour, the Liberals (Lib), the Christian Peoples' Party (CPP), the Center Party, the Conservatives (Con), and the Progress Party (Prog).

The traditional pattern of government formation in Norway has been an alternation in power between two "blocs" of the center right and the center left. Center-right governments have comprised a coalition of medium-sized and small parties, based around the Conservatives. Center-left Norwegian governments have typically been single-party

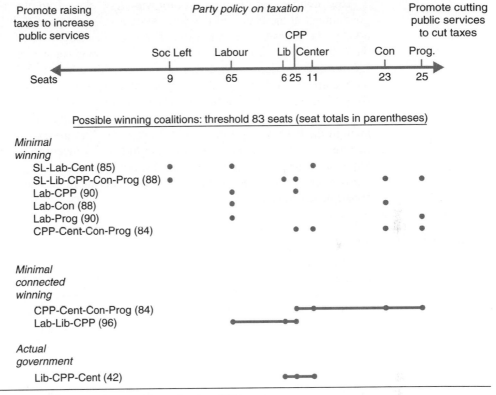

FIGURE 12-2   Coalition possibilities in Norway, October 1997

Labour administrations, often kept in office on the basis of "outside" support from other left-wing parties. The outgoing government in 1997 was a single-party minority administration controlled by the Labour Party. While the Norwegian economy was in good shape, it quickly became clear that the incumbent Labour Party was not doing well in the opinion polls. While the right as a whole remained divided over the controversial issue of EU membership, an issue that had dominated Norwegian politics in the 1990s, the three parties of the center—the Liberals, the Christian Peoples' Party, and the Center Party—announced their intention to form a government should Labour be defeated.

In the event, all left-wing parties lost votes and seats in the election, dropping to their lowest combined level of support since 1936 (Narud). The Labour government was thus forced to resign. It was replaced by the small center coalition proposed during the election campaign, a coalition that fell far short of a parliamentary majority and excluded the traditional anchor of right-wing governments in Norway, the Conservative party. Indeed, the administration that took over the government in October 1997 controlled only 42 of the 165 seats in the Norwegian legislature. Divisions within the right over the EU had thus broken the typical pattern of two-bloc politics in Norway.

This minority government conformed very closely to the pattern of a small government at the center of the party system that could continue in office because it divided the opposition. In order to defeat it, parties from both the right and the left of the minority government had to be able to agree upon some alternative. In effect, both Labour and the Conservatives had to find something that they both liked better than the incumbent minority government—a rather unlikely possibility. Since Norway has fixed-term parliaments, furthermore, with no provision for early dissolution, this removed any incentive the opposition parties might have had to bring down the government in the hope of cashing in on election gains. This means that they really did need to agree on some alternative if they were to have an incentive to bring down the government. In this case, therefore, the prospects for the incoming government were not too bad, despite its extreme minority status. (For more on the formation of this government, see Narud.)

Surplus Majority Government in Italy

Just as cabinets can sometimes be stable while controlling less than a majority of legislative seats, they may sometimes include more members than are strictly needed in order to control the legislature. This may be the case because the government needs a qualified majority of more than 50 percent for certain vital votes, as in Belgium, or there may be less tangible political considerations. Italy, for example, has a long tradition of "surplus majority" coalitions, one of which formed in May 1994. A simplified version of the Italian party system at this time is described in the top part of Figure 12-3. Party positions on a general left-right scale are listed at the top of the figure (taken from De Vries et al., supplemented by Ignazi). From left to right, the main parties were the Reformed Communists (RC); the Democratic Left (PDS); the Greens; the Democratic Alliance (AD); the Popular Party (PPI); Italian Renewal (RI); the Christian Democratic Center (CCD); the Democratic Union of the Center (UDC); the Northern League (LN); the National Alliance (AN), and Forza Italia (FI). A number of smaller parties have been omitted for the sake of clarity.

As we saw in Chapter 7, the Italian political system in the period leading up to the 1994 election had been thrown into convulsions by a range of corruption scandals that had undermined the traditional parties. Many formerly strong parties had declined dramatically or disappeared altogether, while many new parties had formed. In an attempt to produce a more stable party system, the electoral system had been reformed to one in which 75 percent of all seats were allocated in single-seat constituencies on a first-past-the-post basis, while the remaining 25 percent were allocated in regional constituencies using list-PR. The new system created very strong incentives for the formation of preelectoral coalitions of parties. This was the case because in order to avoid electoral disaster, "cartels" of parties needed to get together to decide which of them would fight which single-seat constituency. The PR element of the electoral system, however, which allocated seats to parties in a way that provided no incentive to form cartels, acted to preserve the identity of individual parties and held in check any pressure for wholesale mergers resulting in a small number of large parties.

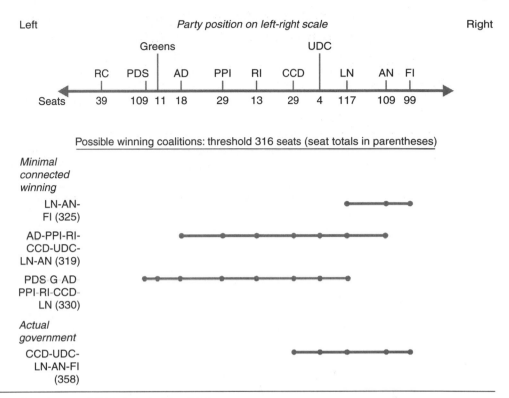

FIGURE 12-3 Coalition possibilities in Italy, May 1994

The result, for the 1994 election, was the formation of three "party cartels" to contest the single-seat constituencies. There was the "Freedom Pole" on the right, comprising the CCD and parties to the right of this in Figure 12-3. There was the centrist Pact for Italy, comprising the PPI and RI, and there was the Progressive Alliance, comprising AD and parties to the left of this in Figure 12-3. In the event, the election was won by the right-wing Freedom Pole, with media mogul and political newcomer Silvio Berlusconi, founder of the new party Forza Italia, as its candidate for prime minister.

The list of possible minimal winning coalitions in this eleven-party system is immense; its calculation is left to any reader with a spare afternoon to while away. However, there were only three possible minimal connected winning coalitions. Two of these involved a large number of parties, while the third involved the three large parties of the right. A government based on the Freedom Pole did in fact take office after twelve days of hard bargaining, with Berlusconi at its head. The government was remarkable in a number of ways. None of the main parties had been in government before, and the National Alliance was a party that could trace its traditions back to Italy's wartime fascists. Forza Italia was a brand-new, media-driven, party, while the Northern League was strongly driven by regionalist concerns. These three parties between them controlled a legislative majority, but despite this, the two smaller parties that had been part of the electoral cartel were also brought into government and awarded cabinet seats. Neither of these parties was needed to keep the government in office in terms of legislative seats, but both nonetheless formed part of this "surplus majority" administration.

There is a long tradition of surplus majority governments in Italy (see Table 12-2), so there is no reason to suppose that this one was a product of the new electoral system, though this does give added impetus towards surplus governments by encouraging the formation of large electoral cartels. Traditionally, the level of party discipline has been low and senior politicians may well have felt the need for some additional legislative cushion, over and above a bare majority, before agreeing to form a government. As we shall see when discussing Table 12-4, surplus majority governments, despite having additional legislative support, tend on average to last less long than those with bare majorities. This may be the case because those political circumstances that encourage a prospective government to take on surplus partners may well be more troubled, and thus unstable, than the norm.

As it happens, this particular surplus majority government did not last long. A number of serious divisions quickly opened up between the Northern League and Forza Italia. Among other things, these concerned the issues of federalism—a fundamental matter for the Northern League—as well as the fight against corruption and antitrust legislation (the latter very sensitive given Berlusconi's dominant position in the Italian media). The government ceased to be viable after the withdrawal of the Northern League, a pivotal rather than a "surplus" member of the coalition whose votes were essential to its survival. Facing a motion of no confidence that he would surely have lost, Silvio Berlusconi resigned in late December 1994. (For more information on the rise and fall of this government, see Ignazi.)

TYPES OF GOVERNMENT IN MODERN EUROPE

Although the preceding case studies can give us a feel for the government-formation process in modern Europe, they cannot give us a systematic picture of the types of government that form. This picture is provided in Table 12-2, which summarizes the types of government that have formed since World War II in a wide range of European countries.

Looking first at the bottom line, we see a wide diversity of government types. Only 11 percent of governments are single-party majority administrations, with most of the cases in this category supplied by Britain, Ireland, and Norway. About one-third of the large number of governments analyzed were minimal winning coalitions, and this type of government can be found in virtually every European country. Taking these two government types together, therefore, well under half of European administrations are "conventional" majority cabinets, in the sense that the government controls a parliamentary majority but includes no "surplus" members whose votes are not needed for this. Conversely, well over half of the governments analyzed either had too few parties to control a majority, or had more parties than they needed to do so.

About 30 percent of postwar European cabinets were minority administrations. The body of the table also shows that minority governments tend to be especially common in certain countries, in particular in Scandinavia and Italy. We have already explored

TABLE 12-2   TYPES OF GOVERNMENT IN MODERN EUROPE 1945–1998

Country	Single-party majority	Minimal winning coalition	Surplus majority coalition	Single-party majority	Minority coalition
Austria	4	15	1	1	
Belgium	3	24	5	1	2
Denmark		4		14	12
Finland		6	21	4	7
France		7	39	4	5
Germany		16	5	1	
Iceland		19	1	2	
Ireland	7	7		4	3
Italy		2	29	11	9
Luxembourg		16	1		
Netherlands		8	9		
Norway	6	3		12	5
Sweden	3	5		15	2
UK	19			1	
Total	**42**	**132**	**111**	**70**	**45**
Percentage	*11*	*33*	*28*	*18*	*11*

Source: Woldendorp et al., 1998, updated with annual Data Yearbooks of the *European Journal of Political Research,* and authors' calculations.

the reasons for this, which may well have to do with the impact that opposition parties can have over government policy. Another pattern that emerges is that single-party minority governments are far more common than minority coalitions. This gives some support to the view that many minority governments may be formed around particular "strong" parties, whose position in the party system means that even though they do not command a majority on their own, they do not need coalition partners in order to be able to form a government.

Table 12-2 shows that surplus majority governments are also very common in modern Europe, although such governments tend to be concentrated in a small number of countries, notably Finland, France, and Italy. Just under 30 percent of cabinets are oversized, containing more members than they need for a majority. Many of the French oversized governments occurred during the French Fourth Republic, when party discipline was notoriously poor and governments needed a wide margin of legislative safety to be able to govern. Low party discipline may also account for many of the Italian oversized governments.

Overall, however, Table 12-2 sends a very clear message that although cabinets do need to be able to win the support of legislative majorities to govern in a parliamentary democracy, the government parties by themselves do not need to control a majority of seats. Both oversized and minority cabinets are clearly quite normal results of government formation in modern Europe. Stable governments can form with less than a majority of the legislative seats. And there may be incentives for governments to keep adding members even after they have passed the majority threshold. Above all, it is important to note that when a minority or surplus majority government is formed, it need not be seen as the result of some sort of failure in the political process. While most people understand that single-party majority government is the exception rather than the rule in modern Europe, fewer realize that "bare majority," or minimal winning, government is also far from being the normal outcome of government formation when no party wins an overall parliamentary majority.

All of this has important consequences for those who seek to understand the party composition of European governments. It is not at all unusual to find dominant parties forming single-party administrations even when they fall quite a long way short of a legislative majority. In the same way, it is quite common to find apparently weak parties being taken into government, despite the fact that their votes could be lost without danger to the government majority. Such parties can make a contribution to the stability of a government, even when their votes are not arithmetically necessary. These conclusions do, however, depend upon taking policy seriously when thinking about the making and breaking of governments. If, on the other hand, we assume that politicians set out to negotiate their way into cabinets with no other objective than to enjoy the perks of office, then the pattern of government formation in Europe leaves a number of unsolved puzzles. In other words, the relative frequency of minority and surplus majority governments is a clear indication that policy is indeed important for the politicians who bargain with one another over the formation of modern European governments.

BOX 12-1

CABINET TYPES

France

Government formation in France is complicated by the powerful role of the president of the republic both in dissolving the legislature and in nominating potential prime ministers. France was governed by a right-wing coalition from the start of the Fifth Republic in 1958 until 1981. This was sometimes just short of a parliamentary majority, but was able to govern as a result of divisions within the left. Sometimes the government was a minimal winning coalition, and sometimes it controlled a surplus majority (notably after a Gaullist electoral landslide in 1968). Since 1981, French governments have alternated between right-wing coalitions and left-wing socialist administrations. The latter have sometimes been minority cabinets needing support from either communists or centrists.

Germany

For most of the postwar period, German politics revolved around three parties that at some stage formed every possible two-party minimal winning coalition. In the early postwar period, the Christian Democrats (CDU/CSU) took other parties into surplus majority governments, despite controlling a legislative majority on their own. There were coalitions between the large CDU/CSU and the much smaller Liberals (FDP) formed between 1957 and 1966, after which a "grand coalition" of the two big parties—CDU/CSU and Social Democrats (SPD)—formed. This was followed by a coalition between SPD and FDP. After 1982, a coalition between the FDP and the CDU/CSU remained in place until 1998, surviving the first all-German elections in 1990. In 1998, a "Red-Green" coalition between the Social Democrats and the Greens replaced what had become one of the most stable party combinations in postwar Europe. The overwhelming norm in modern Germany has been minimal winning coalitions.

Italy

One of the most striking features of postwar Italian politics was that the Christian Democrats (DC) were never out of office until they finally dissolved in the wake of the corruption scandals of 1993. Sometimes they were in coalitions, often surplus majority coalitions, and sometimes they formed single-party minority governments. The new electoral system introduced in the wake of the corruption scandals provides strong incentives for coalitions of parties to fight elections as prospective governments. Since 1993, the winning electoral coalition, whether from the right or from the left, has typically gone on to form the government. Such coalitions have tended to be short-lived, however, as postelectoral legislative politics remove the incentives for the preelectoral coalition to stay together, and there has been considerable movement of legislators between parties.

Netherlands

Superficially, government formation in the Netherlands appears to involve an immense number of possibilities, given the large number of parties in the Dutch legislature. In practice, only a few of these have any real bargaining power, and government formation has revolved around four key players: the Labor party (PvdA), Liberals (VVD), Christian Democrats (CDA), and, since 1994, Democrats'66 (D66). Until 1994, the Christian Democrats were a member of every postwar Dutch government, in alternating partnerships with either the left or the right. They were excluded from office for the first time in 1994 by a "purple" coalition combining the Labour Party on the left, D66 in the center, and the right-wing Liberals. Despite appearing to combine quite disparate parties, this combination provided stable government, and was reelected in 1998.

Spain

Spain since Franco has been very strongly characterized by one-party governments, with or without a parliamentary majority. The first five of these were rather short-lived one-party minority administrations controlled by the right-wing Union of the Democratic Center (UCD), which was just short of a parliamentary majority and held office from 1976 to 1982. From 1982, when the Socialist Party (PSOE) won an overall legislative majority, until 1993, Spain was governed by one-party majority socialist cabinets led by Felipe González. After the 1993 election, in which the socialists lost their majority, González led a minority government. The end of this long era of Socialist one-party government came after the elections of May 1996. The Socialists were defeated and a right-wing minority one-party government formed, led by José Aznar of the Popular Party.

Sweden

For most of the postwar era, Swedish politics has been dominated by the Social Democrats, who typically have not won an electoral majority but have been able to form reasonably stable minority cabinets with the support of either the more left-wing communists or the more centrist Center Party. Since 1976 there has been some alternation in office, as the Center Party usually has been the swing actor in the legislature. Center-right coalitions formed from 1976 to 1982, sometimes very far short of a parliamentary majority (the smallest controlled only 11 percent of the seats but nonetheless lasted one year). A series of single-party minority Social Democratic governments held power after 1982. These were followed by a "bourgeois" coalition of center-right parties in 1991, but the Social Democrats regained control of Swedish government in 1994.

United Kingdom

The British first-past-the-post electoral system almost invariably ensures one-party legislative majorities, and hence one-party governments, which have been alternating between Labour and the Conservatives since World War II. After the February 1974 election, the only one in the postwar era in which no party won an overall majority, a Labour minority government formed with Liberal support and lasted until October of the same year. From 1976 to 1979, the Labour cabinet under James Callaghan lost its majority as a result of by-election defeats and continued in office as a minority government, with support first from the Liberals and then from assorted nationalists, before being defeated in 1979. After a very long period of one-party Conservative rule beginning in 1979, the "New" Labour Party under Tony Blair won a landslide victory in the 1997 election. While the new government investigated the possibility of electoral reforms that might make future coalitions more likely in Britain, no reform is likely until after a second successive Labour victory. Elections using proportional representation to the new Scottish Assembly in Edinburgh resulted, in 1999, in the formation of minimal winning coalition between Labour and the Liberal Democrats to control the Scottish Executive.

THE ALLOCATION OF CABINET PORTFOLIOS

As we saw in Chapter 3, the cabinet is the key organ of government in most European countries, acting both as a committee for making decisions in the name of the entire government and as a collection of individuals with responsibility for making and implementing policy in particular areas. It may come as something of a surprise to people who focus on elections and parliaments as being at the heart of representative democracy to realize that most important policy decisions do not require the direct assent of the legislature. Rather, as we have seen, it is the legislative vote of confidence or no confidence in the executive that gives parliament technical control over the government in all matters: legislators can instruct the government to act in a particular way, on pain of defeat in a confidence motion. In practice, however, the threat of such a dire sanction is a constraint on executive action only if the issue is one that a majority of legislators feel very strongly about, strongly enough that they actually would bring down the government. When legislators do not feel this strongly, then having at their disposal a threat to bring down the government gives them a sledgehammer with which to crack a nut. As a result, cabinet ministers in practice have considerable autonomy in relation to most aspects of public policy that fall within the jurisdiction of their portfolios.

We saw earlier in this chapter that the motivations of the politicians who bargain over coalition formation are the key to understanding the party composition of governments in most European states. Some might be most interested in changing public policy; others may be most interested in consuming the spoils of office. Whatever their motivations might be, however, the politicians who do the bargaining are the very same people who actually get to consume the spoils of office if they are successful. If they manage to negotiate their party into government, then most of them will also get their feet under the cabinet table, enjoying considerable control over government policy as well as the lifestyles of important public figures.

Notwithstanding the control over public policy that can be wielded by cabinet ministers and the evidence that policy is important in government formation, therefore, we should not be too quick to ignore the perks of office. To win a seat at the cabinet table is, after all, the pinnacle of a career in politics for most European politicians. The job brings public recognition, power, patronage, and many other pleasant trappings of success. We should not be surprised to find that many politicians dedicate their political lives single-mindedly to the pursuit of these coveted positions.

Thus, following from the two basic drives that we might assume to motivate politicians—the desire to consume the benefits of office and the desire to influence public policy—there are two basic ways of interpreting the political value of getting into the cabinet. On one hand, cabinet seats may be seen as political trophies to be distributed among members of the winning side. On the other hand, they may be seen as the vital levers of power with which to control the direction of government policy.

Proportional Cabinet Payoffs in France

If cabinet portfolios are seen as political trophies, then we can easily observe how these are divided up in different European countries. The patterns that we see are quite striking. Cabinet portfolios tend to be distributed among government parties in strict proportion to

TABLE 12-3   ALLOCATION OF CABINET SEATS IN FRANCE, JUNE 1997

Party	Number of parliamentary seats*	Proportionate contribution to cabinet's legislative majority (%)	Number of cabinet portfolios	Share of cabinet portfolios (%)
Communist Party	37	12	2	12
Socialist Party	246	79	12	71
Movement for Citizens	7	2	1	6
Left Radicals	13	4	1	6
Greens	8	3	1	6

*Winning threshold: 289 seats.

the number of seats that each party contributes to the government's legislative majority. As an example, consider the coalition cabinet that formed in France in June 1997, details of which are given in Table 12-3. This cabinet was formed after an early election called by President Jacques Chirac in what some saw as an attempt to preempt the possibility of a left-wing victory if the parliament had run its full term. If this was the intention, it failed, however. The incumbent right-wing government was defeated at the polls. The Socialist Party and leftist allies made strong gains, but did not win quite enough seats to govern alone. Accordingly, when President Chirac asked Socialist leader Lionel Jospin to form a government, Jospin invited both the Communists and the Greens to join him.

As Table 12-3 shows, Jospin formed a surplus majority coalition; only one of the three smaller parties was strictly needed for the government to control a majority. (For more information on the formation of this government, see Ysmal.) Nonetheless, what is striking about the figures in Table 12-3 is the close way in which the sharing of cabinet portfolios matched the proportion of seats that each party contributed toward the government's majority in the legislature. Clearly this situation did not arise by accident. When the government was being formed, it was taken more or less as a given that each party was due a certain number of cabinet portfolios by virtue of the number of seats that it had won in the election. This was despite the fact that some of the parties might well have been able to use their bargaining power to win more portfolios than their "fair" share.

Bringing any party into the cabinet involves giving it at least one cabinet portfolio; in this case, one cabinet portfolio was 6 percent of the total. Without sawing politicians in half and appointing a half politician from each of two parties to the same portfolio, this was the smallest payoff that could be given to any government member, despite the fact that each of the three smallest parties only contributed between 2 and 4 percent of the government's total legislative representation. The largest party underwrote this inevitable "overpayment" to the small parties, while the medium-sized Communist Party got a precisely proportional payoff.

This example is very typical of the pattern to be found elsewhere; Browne and Franklin demonstrated that a "proportionality norm" such as this is a very good predictor of the allocation of cabinet portfolios. This research also found a tendency for very small parties to be "overpaid" and for larger parties to underwrite this—almost certainly because of the "lumpy" nature of cabinet payoffs which means that even the smallest cabinet party cannot be given less than one portfolio. Browne and Franklin's findings, which have been confirmed by a number of more recent studies, are based on empirical analyses that explain about 90 percent of the variation in the allocation of cabinet seats in the real world, and as such they have gone down in the annals of political science as some of the most dramatic nontrivial empirical relationships thus far encountered. The facts suggest strongly that European politicians treat the allocation of cabinet portfolios very seriously indeed. This is hardly surprising, because, as we have argued, a cabinet portfolio represents the ultimate ambition for most of them.

Qualitative Portfolio Payoffs in Germany

Although the quantitative proportionality of portfolio payoffs is quite striking, these findings do not undermine the assumption that many European politicians participate in politics to have an impact on public policy—the interpretation that fits squarely with the facts on the frequency of minority and surplus majority governments. Being in command of a cabinet portfolio, after all, is the best means for a European politician to have an impact on public policy. This means that we must do much more than count portfolios when we analyze coalition outcomes. The allocation of particular portfolios to particular parties is a vitally important matter.

Consider the German example described in Figure 12-4. This describes the key players in the government-formation process in early 1991, after the first all-German elections

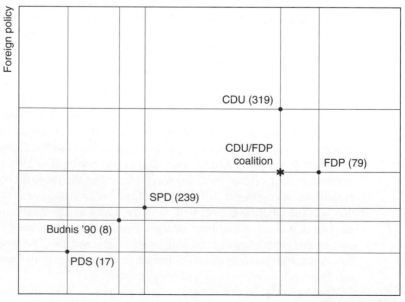

FIGURE 12-4   The allocation of cabinet portfolios in Germany

of December 2, 1990. The figure shows the five German parties that won seats in the 1990 election, describing them in terms of their positions on two key dimensions of politics. The first is economic policy, seen in terms of the conflict between taxation and public spending. The second is foreign policy, which at that time could still be seen in terms of attitudes toward the then-disintegrating Soviet Union. (Positions are once more taken from Laver and Hunt, except for that of the PDS, which has been estimated by the authors.) From left to right on economic policy—shown as the horizontal axis in Figure 12-4—are the former East German Communists (PDS), the East German Greens (Bundnis,'90), the Social Democrats (SPD), the Christian Democrats (CDU), and the Free Democrats (FDP). From left to right on foreign policy—shown as the vertical axis in Figure 12-4—are the PDS, the Greens, SPD, FDP, and CDU. The number of legislative seats won by each party, out of a total of 662, is shown in parentheses in Figure 12-4. From this it can be seen that the party at the median position on economic policy was the CDU. Counting from either left or right on economic policy, the CDU's votes turn a minority into a majority. Similarly, the party with the median position on foreign policy was the FDP.

The horizontal and vertical lines in Figure 12-4, which form a sort of lattice, show what each party might be expected to do if put in charge of the policy area in question. Thus, the vertical line through the CDU position shows what would happen if the CDU were put in charge of economic policy. We would now know what economic policy was likely to be, although, without knowing who was in charge of the foreign affairs portfolio, we could place foreign policy anywhere on this vertical line. In the same way, the horizontal line through the FDP position shows what would happen if the FDP were put in charge of foreign policy. We would now know what foreign policy would be, although, without knowing who was in charge of the finance portfolio, we would have to concede that economic policy could be anywhere on this horizontal line.

If we knew who controlled both cabinet portfolios, of course, we could forecast government policy on both policy dimensions. Thus, if the CDU were in charge of economic policy and the FDP were in charge of foreign policy, then we would know that what would happen would be on both the vertical line through the CDU position and the horizontal line through the FDP position. The policy that is on both lines is situated at their intersection, marked with a star in Figure 12-4. This is in fact the government that formed on 18 January 1991. Theodor Waigel of the Christian Democrats became minister for finance and Free Democrat leader Hans-Dietrich Genscher became minister of foreign affairs. Note that the government that formed was forecast to implement median policies on both the economic and the foreign policy dimension; this is quite often the most likely type of government to form in European coalition systems (Laver and Shepsle, 1996). This policy coalition, indeed, with the Christian Democrats in charge of economic policy and the Free Democrats in charge of foreign policy, was one of the more enduring governments in postwar Europe. Under the leadership of Helmut Kohl, it governed Germany from 1982 until 1998, winning five general elections in the process.

Cabinet Portfolios and Government Policy

Looking in more general empirical terms at the qualitative allocation of cabinet portfolios, we note a general tendency for parties to be rewarded with the ministries that are crucial in the policy areas of special interest to them (Budge and Keman). There is a very strong tendency for agrarian parties to get the agriculture portfolio, for example, and there are weaker but still distinct trends in relation to other portfolios.

This means, as we saw in the German case, that the allocation of cabinet portfolios is not just the handing out of a set of spoils to senior politicians who have managed to take control of the government; it is also a very important way in which the policy profile of any new government is defined, because allocating a cabinet portfolio to one senior politician rather than another makes a big difference to the expected policy output of the government in question. It also means that cabinet "reshuffles"—changes in the precise allocation of cabinet portfolios—are more significant than many commentators have realized.

Indeed, one account of government formation sees the allocation of cabinet portfolios as a fundamental defining characteristic of any government, since a cabinet minister is not just a member of the government, but has considerable discretion over government policy in particular areas (Laver and Shepsle, 1996). Thus, a minister of health, for example, has huge influence over public policy in the area of health; a minister of education has tremendous power over education policy; and so on. This implies that if you want to know a government's policy position on any issue, you do not necessarily take official policy statements at face value: these may well be unreliable "cheap talk." Rather, you might do better to look at the policy preferences of the politicians who have been given the relevant portfolios, as well at what these people actually do when in office. When all is said and done, these constitute the most credible signals about the effective policy positions of a government.

This approach also allows us to look inside parties at the role played by senior politicians in government formation. A particular government may be made possible by a particular cabinet appointment. The appointment of a hard-line defense minister or a liberal minister for justice, for example, may make all the difference to the political viability of a given administration. This phenomenon can even be found inside single-party majority governments with huge majorities. This is because the position of a single-party majority government depends crucially upon its ability to hold together and maintain party discipline. In one sense, for example, the British Conservatives under Margaret Thatcher enjoyed some of the most secure government majorities in postwar Europe. Yet the unity of the Conservative Party during this era had to be maintained in the face of deep internal divisions, especially over policy towards the European Union. "Euroskeptic" Conservatives were deeply suspicious of any move towards closer integration with Europe, while pro-European Conservatives were just as deeply committed to forging closer links. Feelings ran so deep that the party always had the potential to split on this issue, losing its huge majority. This meant that Conservative leaders making cabinet appointments to cabinet portfolios with an important role in European policy had to take care that these did not aggravate the potential for party splits. Even single-party governments can often usefully be seen as coalitions of factions, and this is why the allocation of cabinet portfolios between party factions is always a politically important matter.

Overall, there can be no doubt that the cabinet is a vital institution in European parliamentary democracy. In theory it is permanently beholden to the legislature, which can evict it at any stage by a vote of no confidence in the executive. In practice, however, the considerable autonomy of cabinet ministers to set public policy in their respective areas of jurisdiction means that the cabinet is much more independent than formal constitutional theory might suggest. This means that the question of who gets into the cabinet, whether he or she is motivated by the desire to change the course of public policy or by nothing more elevated than the desire to be a big shot, should be seen as one of the fundamental political questions with which party competition in each European system is concerned. In the last analysis, voters choose between alternative sets of politicians; these politicians bargain over who gets what in the cabinet. The ideological complexion of the cabinet that they form represents the most important single way in which party politics in general and the voters in particular can be said to have an impact on what European governments actually set out to do.

THE STABILITY OF EUROPEAN GOVERNMENTS

Some European countries have much more stable governments than others. Taking the average life expectancy of a cabinet as a measure of government stability, we can see this quite clearly in Table 12-4. The final column of this table ranks countries according to the average duration of their cabinets, in days, for the period from 1945 to 1998.

TABLE 12-4   AVERAGE DURATIONS, IN DAYS, OF DIFFERENT GOVERNMENT TYPES IN MODERN EUROPE 1945–1998

Country	Single-party majority	Minimal winning coalition	Surplus majority coalition	Single-party minority	Minority coalition	Mean duration
Luxembourg		1180	466			1136
UK	1038			227		995
Austria	1424	763	1420	548		933
Ireland	861	1006		872	732	901
Netherlands		1200	942			879
Iceland		876	1202	224		830
Norway	965	960		777	235	757
Sweden	493	708		816	802	752
Germany		815	703	501		660
Denmark		807		567	674	641
Belgium	464	644	316	134	35	511
Finland		507	548	494	140	404
France		363	323	585	303	334
Italy		347	360	285	351	331
Mean duration	**953**	**814**	**462**	**601**	**410**	

Note: Table excludes caretaker and nonpartisan cabinets.
Source: Woldendorp et al., 1998, updated with annual Data Yearbooks of the *European Journal of Political Research,* and authors' calculations.

At the more "stable" end of the spectrum we find Luxembourg, Britain, Austria, and Ireland. At the more "unstable" end of the spectrum, with the shortest average cabinet durations, we find Italy, France, Finland, and Belgium. Countries with stable cabinets have governments that last, on average, about three years. Those with unstable cabinets have governments that tend to last about a year or even less.

The stability of governments is obviously an important matter for all who are interested in politics, and considerable intellectual energy has been devoted to interpreting the patterns highlighted in Table 12-4. Before we move on to explore these patterns, it is worth commenting on one unexpectedly tricky matter, that of deciding when a government has actually come to an end. Unfortunately, different researchers have looked at this in different ways. To begin with the easy part, all researchers agree that one government ends and a new one takes office when the party membership of the cabinet changes. If a party leaves, or if new parties join, then there is effectively a new government. Some commentators take this as being the only definitive sign that a government has changed. Others regard a new government as having formed after every new election, even if exactly the same parties and the same prime minister resume control. They do this on the grounds that every new legislature represents a completely new bargaining environment, and so explaining what might appear on the face of it to be the "same" government presents a new problem.

A further important matter concerns the overall "turnover" of cabinet ministers from one government to the next. After all, if a government changes its prime minister and even its party composition, but most of the cabinet ministers remain the same, then it could be argued that it has not really changed very much. This argument is particularly important when one is evaluating the apparent instability of governments in, for example, Italy. While, on most definitions, postwar Italian governments have been very short-lived, it is also the case that there has been a limited turnover of Italian cabinet ministers from one government to the other. Thus, a certain stability of senior personnel underlies the apparent instability of Italian cabinets (Mershon, 1996, 2000).

All of this shows that the question "how long did this government last?" is more complicated than it appears at first sight. The figures given in Table 12-4 are based on data from Woldendorp et al., who have a "permissive" definition of the end of a government. They see a wide range of factors (elections, new party composition, new prime minister, resignation of incumbent prime minister even if she or he resumes office) as marking the end of a government's life. Obviously, this tends to show cabinet durations as being shorter than if the sole indicator of the end of a government were a change in its party composition. However, Lijphart has shown that different definitions do not make too much difference to the relative durations of different types of cabinet in different countries.

Most studies of the duration of European cabinets concentrate on two things. First, cabinets themselves may possess certain features that lead some to be more durable than others. It is widely believed, for example, that coalition governments are more unstable than single-party governments, and that majority governments are more stable than minority governments. Second, there are features of the bargaining environment in which a government must survive. Some of these may tend to encourage, or discourage, stability. A fragmented party system with many small parties, for example, or a party system with a powerful anti-regime party, may lead to greater cabinet instability.

Cabinet Attributes and Cabinet Stability

Several researchers have confirmed the expectation that single-party governments last longer than coalitions and the expectation that majority governments last longer than minority governments. These patterns can be seen by looking at the bottom line in Table 12-4. On average across the whole of Europe, single-party majority governments last about half a year longer than minimal winning coalitions, about a year longer than single-party minority governments, and more than twice as long as minority coalitions. Minimal winning governments, in turn, last much longer than minority or surplus majority governments. Single-party minority governments, on average, last longer than minority or surplus majority coalitions.

Broad European averages are a crude measure of the durability of different types of government, however, and the body of Table 12-4 shows that the pattern is more complex than it seems at first sight. Some general patterns hold when we compare different types of government within individual countries, but others do not. For example, minority coalitions are almost invariably less stable than majority governments, regardless of country. In most countries, single-party minority governments are also less stable than majority governments. Majority status does tend to extend government stability in all political systems.

Comparing the stability of minimal winning coalitions with that of single-party majority governments is instructive, however. With the exception of Austria, there is no evidence that minimal winning coalitions are less stable; indeed, in those countries that experience both types of government, minimal winning coalitions are likely to be as stable as single-party majority governments. The reason the European average makes single-party majority governments look more stable seems to be that these tend to be found much more in countries where the stability of *all* types of government is higher.

Moving beyond size, policy differences between members of a coalition cabinet can have a big impact on government stability. This has been shown most clearly by Warwick, who measures the ideological diversity of coalition cabinets along three important policy dimensions: the traditional left-right dimension; a dimension contrasting proclerical and secular ideologies; and a dimension that captures the extent to which party policy is "anti-system." Warwick shows that increasing cabinet diversity on any one of these three dimensions reduces the life expectancy of the cabinet, presumably because of the greater possibility for policy disputes.

Not all sources of government instability come from within the cabinet, however. Table 12-4 shows large differences between countries in government durability, even when we take account of the different types of cabinet that form. Minority governments are much more stable in Ireland, Sweden, and Norway, for example, than in Italy and Belgium. Minimal winning coalitions are much more stable in Luxembourg, Ireland, and the Netherlands and much less stable in France and Italy. Thus, the party system in which a government is set, as well as the type of government itself, appears to have a major impact on government stability.

System Attributes and Cabinet Duration

One of the patterns to emerge quite clearly from Table 12-4 is that countries in which governments are more short-lived tend to be those with larger and more complex party systems. This should not surprise us, because it is precisely in these more complex systems that small changes in the bargaining environment within which a government must exist may destabilize an existing equilibrium and bring the government down. Obvi-

---

BOX 12-2

GOVERNMENT STABILITY

France

The extreme and notorious government instability of the Fourth Republic, with an average government duration of well under one year, was one of the main reasons the constitution was revised to create the Fifth Republic in 1958. Since then, French cabinets have tended to be rather stable. However, when a president was elected who belonged to a different party from that of the prime minister, this was often followed by an immediate dissolution of the legislature, as the president hoped to be able to nominate a prime minister of the same political complexion.

Germany

German coalition cabinets are very stable, tending to endure for the natural life of a full parliament. Only once in recent times, in 1982, has a government been brought down between elections. As a result, the average duration of German cabinets, at around three years, is on a par with that to be found in countries, such as Britain, with mainly one-party majority cabinets.

Italy

Italy is often taken as the classic example of a European coalition system with very unstable cabinets; indeed, the average duration of Italian cabinets is the lowest in Europe, at less than one year. Minority governments in particular are very short-lived. Quite often, however, the same key people have filled the same key portfolios across a series of cabinets. This low turnover of cabinet ministers implies that Italian politics are more stable than simple cabinet durations alone might suggest. Recent electoral reforms have produced much more turnover of cabinets, but—contrary to what some had hoped—no noticeable increase in cabinet durations.

Netherlands

The average duration of Dutch cabinets is towards the top of the range found in continental European coali-

tion systems, excluding short-lived and clearly transitional caretaker cabinets that hold office during the negotiation of more permanent governments. Having typically taken a long time to negotiate, the coalition cabinets that eventually form tend to be quite stable in European terms. This stability is especially striking given the large number of parties represented in the Dutch parliament.

Spain

A number of rather unstable right-wing minority cabinets formed and fell in the immediate post-Franco period. Since the Socialists gained a single-party legislative majority in 1982, however, Spanish governments have been very durable, typically running for the full interelectoral period. This stability has carried through into the minority right-wing governments forming after the end of the era of Socialist government.

Sweden

Although Sweden has had a large number of minority governments, the average cabinet duration is very typical of that in continental European coalition systems. Indeed, minority governments in Sweden, particularly minority governments in which the Social Democrats have received legislative support from the Communists, have been more stable than other government types. The Swedish case thus suggests strongly that minority governments need be no more unstable than others, provided they are solidly based.

United Kingdom

Governments in the United Kingdom are among the most durable in Western Europe. Single-party majority governments tend to last for more or less the full legal period allowed between elections, though there is a very strong tendency toward the end of this period for governments to watch opinion polls closely and call an election when they hope to maximize their vote. It seems very likely that if it were not for intervening elections, many British governments would have been in a position to last much longer.

ously, a government is likely to be more vulnerable and short-lived if even a small change in its overall political environment can destabilize it.

In Finland, to take just one example, the set of potential governments that can form often depends upon details of the precise distribution of legislative seats between parties. Small changes in this seat distribution can have big effects on the balance of power. This means that even minor political shocks, causing unanticipated small movements in opinion polls, for example, may have important consequences for bargaining. This is so because even small opinion shifts may give some parties an incentive to pull the plug on the government and provoke an election that improves their bargaining position.

In Luxembourg, in contrast, almost no election result that can realistically be forecast is likely to change the power structure in the legislature. After any election, the situation that is likely to prevail is that any two of the three main parties will be needed to form a government and that the large centrist party, the Christian Social Party, is going to be very difficult to keep out of office. Because no election result is likely to change these facts of political life, the incentives to try to bring down the government and force an election are minimal.

Differences between countries in terms of the complexity of their bargaining systems, in short, seem to have a major bearing on government stability. Those with short-lived cabinets (Italy, Belgium, Finland, for example) all have large and complex party systems. Those with long-lived cabinets (Luxembourg, Britain, and Austria, for example) all have small and "simple" party systems—whether or not the typical election result gives one party an overall parliamentary majority. These conclusions are reinforced by extensive cross-national empirical analyses of factors affecting the stability of cabinets (King et al.; Warwick; Diermeier and Stevenson). These show that government duration is significantly affected by two factors that contribute directly to bargaining complexity: the fragmentation and the ideological polarization of the party system. The more fragmented the party system is, and the greater the ideological polarization of the parties, the less conducive is the political environment to durable cabinets.

Government Stability and Political Shocks

The "political science" approaches to the stability of European governments that we have just discussed appear to stand in stark contrast to the approaches typically adopted by political journalists and practicing politicians. Those who are deeply involved in the rough-and-tumble of day-to-day politics are apt to see the defeat or resignation of any government as the direct product of a particular sequence of events. When a government falls, therefore, newspapers and TV current affairs programs are typically full of chronologies that set out the "critical events" that led to its demise. Even governments that seem very durable can sometimes, it seems, be ambushed by events that are largely beyond their control. Table 12-4 shows very clearly that there are strong general patterns in the stability of European governments. Even so, we should not ignore the clear possibility that many governments might have lasted longer had circumstances been more propitious. A government that seems, on the face of it, to be rather durable can slip on a political banana skin—a scandal, perhaps, or the death of a key political figure—and be destroyed quite unexpectedly.

For example, an unexpected turnaround in opinion poll ratings may modify the expectations of politicians about the outcome of an upcoming election. This may provoke a reallocation of power within the incumbent government, or may even destabilize a sensitive bargaining equilibrium and bring the government down (Lupia and Strom). More generally, a wide range of different types of political shock may put pressure on the government. As well as "public opinion shocks," there may be shocks to the political agenda, arising when unexpected and quite possibly unwelcome issues simply must be decided. Perhaps an oil tanker strands on the coast—forcing hard decisions on environmental policy. A major company may go bankrupt—forcing unwelcome decisions on industrial policy. To this can be added unexpected ministerial departures, as a result of death, ill-health, or scandal. Laver and Shepsle (1998) set out to classify different types of political shock, and explore the types of effect that these might have on government stability.

When we set out to predict the durability of any particular government, therefore, we are talking only about the *probability* that it will last for a specified time. A government has a certain durability, arising from the factors that we have discussed, but it also must exist in an uncertain political world, bombarded by a stream of potentially destabilizing events. Any one of these events may be a bullet with the government's name on it. A fuller account of the life cycle of governments must take account not only of the key "stability-inducing" attributes of cabinet, but also of the possibility that even an apparently stable government can be shot down out of a clear blue sky by an unexpected event.

The 1985 football riot at Heisel Stadium: this completely unexpected event brought down a Belgian government. © Photo News/ Liaison Agency

Using appropriate statistical assumptions to model the impact of random events, it is possible to combine both approaches into a single account of government duration in Western Europe. Recent analyses by King et al., and by Warwick, do this; as mentioned, they underline that the complexity of the bargaining environment has an important impact on government stability. In the more complex and sensitive bargaining environments that are found in the "larger" party systems, smaller political shocks seem more likely to be fatal. In the less complex environments of the "smaller" party systems, it takes a larger shock to destabilize the government.

The statistical techniques used in these studies also allow them to "remove" the effect of holding scheduled elections on the life span of governments. This allows analysts to estimate what the durations of particular governments would have been, had they not been brought to an end by the constitutional requirement that elections be held every specified period. In this way, for example, King et al. found that scheduled elections have little effect on the duration of governments in high-turnover systems such as Finland and Italy. In contrast, if it were not for scheduled elections, governments in Britain would last even longer, on the average, than they do at present. In other words, there is evidence for the more stable cabinet systems that such turnover in governments as does exist is more a product of the constitutional requirement that elections be held at regular intervals than it is of forces at work in the party system. In more complex party systems, a high turnover of governments seems guaranteed as a result of instabilities in the bargaining environment, even without a constitutional limitation on their tenure.

The same statistical techniques also allow analysts to estimate whether or not a government faces increasing risks of termination as it goes farther into its term of office. Intuitively, this seems plausible. As a new government takes office, it might seem strong and more able to withstand large shocks than it will be after it has been under attack for a year or two by the slings and arrows of political fortune. The model of cabinet termination put forward by Lupia and Strom, furthermore, predicted that the risk of termination—or "hazard rate" as it is usually referred to—should rise during the lifetime of a government. For them, this is reasonable because with less time to go before the next constitutionally mandated election, the incentives for coalition partners to renegotiate their deal in the face of unanticipated political shocks will be less. Indeed, if some surprise event were to ambush a government shortly before an election was due to be held anyway, there might be no point in trying to renegotiate the deal. While initial research tended to confirm this intuition, careful recent work by Diermeier and Stevenson distinguishes between cabinet terminations brought about by early dissolutions and those brought about by the fall of a government between elections. They found that the risk of a government's being replaced *between elections* tended to be constant throughout its life, but the risk of a government's ending *as a result of an early election being called* typically did rise significantly during a government's life. This is a very important consequence of the fact that, as we have seen, many European prime ministers do have strategic control over the calling of elections. At a more informal level, it also confirms the instincts of many political observers that as the next election appears on the horizon, this has a destabilizing effect on the incumbent government, since the coalition partners begin to calculate ways in which they might leave the government and force an election on terms that will be to their advantage.

CONCLUSION

The formation of European governments has been more extensively studied than many other aspects of the political process. Although there is always more work to be done, our conclusions on this important subject can nonetheless be rather firmer than those we have drawn on some of the other important matters we deal with.

First and foremost, we reemphasize that the normal situation in modern Europe is for no party to have a legislative majority and for legislative coalitions to be needed in order to keep any government in power, given the system of parliamentary government. *Legislative* coalitions will always be needed in such cases if the government is to gain and retain office. But it is by no means always necessary that there be an *executive* coalition of parties. If a single-party "minority" cabinet can find favor with a majority of legislators, then it can form and maintain a viable government. Such minority cabinets are very much part of the mainstream experience in Europe. Minimal winning coalitions, albeit common, do not account for the majority of governments that form, notwithstanding the preconceptions of many of those who write about the government-formation process.

Second, the details of the composition of the cabinet are a matter of vital political interest. The proportional allocation of cabinet portfolios among parties is clearly a very firmly established norm in most European systems. This does not mean, however, that the allocation takes place according to a sterile political formula. What it means is that the real political action is concerned with which particular politician gets which particular portfolio; the end product of this process determines the fundamental character, and the likely policy outputs, of the government.

Third, certain types of coalition systems do indeed generate more unstable cabinets than others, with Italy, Finland, and Belgium being the obvious examples. Other coalition systems—those of Austria, Germany, and Luxembourg, for example—seem to be more or less as stable as the atypical one-party government system found in Britain, where government stability is often put forward as the main advantage of maintaining a non-PR electoral system. These stable coalition systems have provided some of post-war Europe's most successful governments.

Putting all of this together, the politics of coalition in Europe provide the vital link between legislative politics, on which citizens have at least some small impact when they vote for their legislators, and what the government actually does, over which voters have no formal control. The patterns that we have seen in this chapter show us that the politics of representation does not stop when an election result has been declared, but continue into the making and breaking of governments. The policy outputs of coalition cabinets are affected by politicians who do their deals while thinking about the possible results of the *next* election. The substantive effects of this can be seen in the way in which the policies of coalition cabinets tend to converge upon the center ground—and in this way to please the maximum number of voters.

REFERENCES

Baron, David: "A Spatial Bargaining Theory of Government Formation in Parliamentary Systems," *American Political Science Review,* vol. 85, 1991, pp. 137–65.

Browne, E., and M. Franklin: "Aspects of Coalition Payoffs in European Parliamentary Democracies," *American Political Science Review,* vol. 67, 1973, pp. 453–69.

Budge, I., and H. Keman: *How Party Government Works: Testing a Theory of Formation, Functioning and Termination in 20 Democracies,* Oxford University Press, Oxford, 1990.

De Vries, Miranda, Daniela Giannetti, and Lucy Mansergh: "Estimating the Positions of Political Actors in the Netherlands, Italy and Ireland," in Michael Laver (ed.), *Estimating the Policy Positions of Political Actors,* Routledge, London, 2000, forthcoming.

Diermeier, Daniel, and Randy Stevenson: "Cabinet Survival and Competing Risks," *American Journal of Political Science,* vol. 43, 1999, pp. 1051–69.

Farrell, Brian: "The Formation of the Partnership Government," in Michael Gallagher and Michael Laver (eds.), *How Ireland Voted 1992,* Dublin and Limerick, Folens and PSAI Press, 1993.

Garrett, Geoffrey, and George Tsebelis: "Why Resist the Temptation to Apply Power Indices to the European Union?", *Journal of Theoretical Politics,* vol. 11, 1999, pp. 291–308.

Grofman, Bernard: "Extending a Dynamic Model of Protocoalition Formation," in Norman Schofield (ed.), *Collective Decision-Making: Social Choice and Political Economy,* Kluwer, Dordrech, 1996, pp. 265–80.

Holler, Manfred, and M. Widgren: "Why Power Indices for Assessing European Union Decision-making?", *Journal of Theoretical Politics,* vol. 11, 1999, pp. 321–30.

Huber, John: *Rationalizing Parliament: Legislative Institutions and Party Politics in France,* Cambridge University Press, Cambridge, 1996.

Ignazi, Piero: "Italy," *European Journal of Political Research,* vol. 28, 1995, pp. 393–405.

King, G., J. Alt, N. Burns, and M. Laver: "A Unified Model of Cabinet Dissolution in Parliamentary Democracies," *American Journal of Political Science,* vol. 34, no. 3, 1990, pp. 846–71.

Laver, Michael: "Party Policy and Cabinet Portfolios in Ireland 1992–93: Results from an Expert Survey," *Irish Political Studies,* vol. 9, 1994, pp. 157–64.

Laver, Michael: "Models of Government Formation," *Annual Review of Political Science,* vol. 1, 1998, pp. 1–25.

Laver, Michael, and W. B. Hunt: *Policy and Party Competition,* Routledge, New York, 1992.

Laver, Michael, and N. Schofield: *Multiparty Government: The Politics of Coalition in Western Europe,* University of Michigan Press, Ann Arbor, 1998.

Laver, Michael, and Kenneth A. Shepsle, *Making and Breaking Governments,* Cambridge University Press, New York, 1996.

Laver, Michael and Kenneth A. Shepsle, "Events, Equilibria and Government Survival," *American Journal of Political Science,* vol. 42, 1998, 28–54.

Lijphart, Arend: *Patterns of Democracy: Government Forms and Performance in Thirty-Six Countries,* New Haven: Yale University Press, 1999.

Luebbert, G.: *Comparative Democracy: Policy Making and Governing Coalitions in Europe and Israel,* Columbia University Press, New York, 1986.

Lupia, Arthur, and Kaare Strom: "Coalition Termination and the Strategic Timing of Elections," *American Political Science Review,* vol. 89, 1995, pp. 648–65.

Mershon, Carol: "The Costs of Coalition: Coalition Theories and Italian Governments," *American Political Science Review,* vol. 90, 1996, pp. 534–54.

Mershon, Carol: "Party Factions and Coalition Government: Portfolio Allocation and Italian Christian Democracy," *Electoral Studies,* 2001, forthcoming.

Müller, Wolfgang, and Kaare Strom (eds.): *Policy, Office or Votes? How Political Parties Make Hard Choices,* Cambridge University Press, New York, 1999.

Narud, Hanne-Marthe: "Norway," *European Journal of Political Research,* vol. 34, 1998, pp. 485–92.

Nurmi, Hannu, and Tommy Meskanen: "A Priori Power Measures and the Institutions of the European Union," *European Journal of Political Research,* vol. 35, 1999, pp. 161–79.

Riker, W.: *The Theory of Political Coalitions,* Yale University Press, New Haven, 1962.

Schofield, Norman: "Political Competition and Multiparty Coalition Governments," *European Journal of Political Research,* vol. 23, 1993, pp. 1–33.

Schofield, Norman: "Coalition Politics: A Model and Analysis," *Journal of Theoretical Politics,* vol. 7, 1995, 245–81.

Strom, Kaare: *Minority Government and Majority Rule,* Cambridge University Press, Cambridge, England, 1990.

Warwick, Paul: *Government Survival in Parliamentary Democracies,* Cambridge University Press, Cambridge, 1994.

Woldendorp, Jaap, Hans Keman, and Ian Budge: "Party Government in 20 Democracies: An Update (1990–1995)", *European Journal of Political Research,* vol. 33, 1998, pp. 125–64.

Ysmal, Colette: "France," *European Journal of Political Research,* vol. 34, 1998, pp. 393–403.

13

FROM GOVERNMENTS TO PUBLIC POLICY

One of the main reasons many people are interested in politics at all is because they have a general sense that politics should, and indeed does, make a difference. In the context of European parliamentary democracy, this can be translated into a feeling that election results and government formation should, and indeed do, have at least some effect on how a country is run. Different election results and the formation of different governments should cause things to be done differently. Otherwise the whole edifice of parliamentary democracy is no more than a facade.

Some, however, argue that politics, at least national politics, is making less and less of a difference in an era of increasing "globalization" that more and more constrains the freedom of governments to take independent lines and implement distinctive policy positions. Thus, as we have seen when discussing the role of the European Union, many aspects of economic policy that would once have been the exclusive preserve of national governments are now decided at the European level. A striking example can be found in the drive towards a common European currency, agreed on in the 1991 Maastricht Treaty. European countries that are part of the process of European Monetary Union have given up control of many of the levers of traditional macroeconomic policy making that previously had been central to how they had run their economies. Not only are their currencies locked together into a single unit, the euro, but this also removes all local freedom to set interest rates and print money. National governments can no longer try to cool down potentially inflationary booms by raising interest rates or choking off the money supply, can no longer stimulate their local economies out of recessions by lowering interest rates. EU competition policy has also increasingly constrained governments in their ability to pump money into loss-making public enterprises if they choose to do so. Moves towards a common foreign and security policy put mounting pressure on member states to agree to a common line on these matters too. And all of this comes on top of a general development of the world economy characterized by increasingly free and rapid movement of capital that makes it ever harder for any national government to buck world trends. In the face of all of this, it might well seem that most European governments are far less free these days to do what they want. As a consequence, it might also seem that the scope for politics to make a difference is far narrower than it used to be.

Let us set against this point of view the fact that even in an era of rapidly expanding international travel, most people in most countries are not very mobile. The vast bulk of European populations are born, live, love, work, and die in a single country, speak a native language that differs from that of people in other countries, define themselves in large part as "German," "French," "Italian," "Greek," and so on, and do not expect things to be any different. Land is not mobile. Housing is not mobile. Hospitals, schools, roads, railway lines, airports, police and fire stations are not mobile. For the most part, labor is not very mobile. Social values may be changing, but there are still very wide variations across countries in attitudes to matters such as abortion, euthanasia, single-parent families, the role of women in the workplace, and many other matters besides. Even in the area of socioeconomic policy, different core values translate into the very different welfare systems that we find in different European countries. The net result is that even if some of the key levers of macroeconomic policy have indeed been pried from the hands of European governments, the big public policy differences that we still find between states, and the big public policy shifts that we sometimes observe within states, imply that politics might well still make a difference. (For an overview of the main contributions to this debate, combined with an excellent bibliography of it, see Schmidt, 1996.)

Even if we strongly suspect that politics does make a difference, the practical job of investigating the real-world impact of elections and governments on how things are done presents us with some almost impossible tasks. To assess the impact of any given government, for example, we need to know what *would* have happened if a different government had been running the country in its place. The need to face up to this task, however, is common to all policy evaluations in both the public and the private sector. Thus, to come to a view on whether the effective decriminalization of soft drugs in Amsterdam has increased or reduced the usage of hard drugs in the city, we need to know how many people in Amsterdam would have been using heroin if the Dutch police had adopted a much tougher policy on marijuana. We will never really know what would have happened in this "counterfactual" situation, but we can make educated guesses on the basis of careful research. The fact that it is in theory impossible to get a perfect answer to such a question does not mean that in practice we cannot get any answer at all. Furthermore, although it can be difficult to decide whether a particular government did make a difference to a particular policy area on a particular occasion, there is an accumulating collection of comparative studies that does throw considerable light on whether politics, in general, does make a broad difference to the real world of public policy.

Researchers who have tackled this problem have approached it from several different directions. Perhaps the most traditional approach has been to develop case studies of major government policy interventions, such as the comprehensive program of privatizing state assets implemented by British Conservative governments during the 1980s. The logic of such studies is quite straightforward. A dramatic policy initiative is launched with the intention of bringing about a major change in the state of the world. If this intended change does in fact occur, then we might conclude that the policy initiative was the cause of this. In effect, we assume that the world would not have changed in the same way without the policy initiative. When changes of direction are really dramatic, as with the British and French privatization programs we will consider, then this logic seems quite plausible.

Such dramatic changes, of course, are rather rare in European politics. We must look beyond these if we wish to find evidence that politics does in general make a difference. A second approach has been to compare what government parties promised voters during the previous election campaign with what they set out to do once installed in office. During election campaigns, of course, parties are trying to get as many votes as possible and may well pitch their policy promises to maximize electoral advantage. If politics makes a difference, however, policy promises made during election campaigns should have an impact on the policies of the governments that follow. We can study this by comparing the election pledges of the winning party or coalition with what the government says it will do during its term of office, once it has succeeded in getting into power.

A third strategy for determining whether politics makes a difference is to look at the actual fulfillment of campaign pledges and programs by governments. The theory of representative government is, after all, based on the premise that at least some of the pledges made to voters at election time are actually redeemed. Evidence on this is far skimpier, for a number of reasons. Often a campaign pledge is so vague that it can be almost impossible to decide whether it has been fulfilled or not. Some pledges, furthermore, are not fulfilled for reasons that are quite beyond the control of the government. A flood or an earthquake may strike without warning, for example, destroying a communications infrastructure that the government had promised to improve. There may be a stock market crash in Hong Kong, Tokyo, or New York that leaves a government's economic policy promises in tatters. Some other critical event completely outside the control of politicians may fundamentally change the political universe. Although it is no easy task to define the set of campaign pledges that in practice could have been redeemed but in the event were not, some progress has been made on this in recent years.

A fourth strategy for investigating the impact of politics on public policy is to look at patterns of public spending. Of course, some of the most important policy decisions to face postwar Europe have been only vaguely related to public spending. These have included matters of social policy, including AIDS, capital punishment, and race relations; matters of economic management, such as deregulation and free trade; and matters of foreign policy, including wars in Bosnia and Kosovo, or the enlargement of the European Union (EU). On top of this, patterns of public spending are very "sticky" in the sense that much of the public money that is spent—on education, pensions, and welfare, for example—is committed over a very long term. Such patterns can be changed only very slowly.

Furthermore, many of the changes in spending patterns that we do observe are the result of changes in the size of various "client" groups—the young, the old, and the unemployed, for example—and are certainly not the result of conscious spending decisions by the government. There is considerable variation in the proportion of the population in each country that is of school age, for example, with Ireland having the highest proportion in Western Europe and Germany one of the lowest. It is hardly surprising, therefore, that public spending on schools, as a proportion of national income, is higher in Ireland than it is in Germany. The age structure of the population, rather than anything to do with public policy, may well explain this difference. A more striking example concerns public spending on unemployment assistance. Governments that set out to cut public spending, as the Conservatives did in Britain between 1979 and 1997, often increase unemployment in the process, at least in the short run. They certainly do not set out to increase public spending on unemployment assistance, but such an increase is the unsought consequence of policy changes in other areas.

Notwithstanding these important complications, governments often promise voters that if elected, they will make dramatic policy changes with a significant impact on the direction and flow of public spending. Furthermore, the allocation of public spending among different policy areas is a very visible indicator of government policy, one that can reflect an explicit set of priorities argued and decided on at the cabinet table. This allows us to argue that if politics does make a difference, then different types of government should be associated with different patterns of public spending. In particular, we might expect that changes in government will be associated with changes in public spending flows.

A fifth strategy for determining whether politics makes a difference involves looking over a long time period at large-scale macroeconomic variables such as the overall size of the public sector and the extent of the welfare system. If politics does make a difference, then different types of party systems should be associated with major differences in key macroeconomic variables.

In the rest of this chapter we examine these five general ways of looking at how politics might make a difference. At the end of it all we still cannot get around the fact that we have no way of knowing what would have happened in a particular country if the particular government for a particular period had been different. But the accumulated weight of evidence we assemble by the end of this chapter, on the basis of the five different approaches we explore, will leave us in little doubt that politics does make at least some difference in what goes on in the real world.

TWO CLEAR-CUT CASES OF POLICY IMPACT: PRIVATIZATION IN BRITAIN AND FRANCE

British and French conservative governments during the 1980s and 1990s introduced comprehensive programs of selling public assets to the private sector, programs designed to "roll back the state" in major and readily observable ways. In each country, there were subsequently large-scale sales of public assets to the private sector. Few would argue with the conclusion that politics made a difference in these dramatic cases.

To get a feel for the magnitude of such policy initiatives, consider Michel Bauer's description (p. 49) of the political impetus toward privatization in France during the period from 1986 through 1988, following the defeat of the outgoing Socialist administration and its replacement by a right-wing coalition government.

The government, which had fought its electoral campaign on privatization, took office on 20 March 1986. On 6 August a law initiating the privatization programme was passed. By 24 October the implementing decrees were in the *Journal Officiel*. It took only seven months to move from the programme of an opposition party to a set of legal rules specifying the aims and methods of privatization. . . . These legal texts envisaged and facilitated the biggest redrawing of the boundary between the public and the private sector yet seen in the West. They applied to 66 firms . . . with a workforce of about 900,000. This involved capital estimated at the time at 300 billion francs, a figure to be compared with the total capitalization of the Paris Bourse [stock exchange] at the same date: 1200 billion francs. In seven months the government thus provided for the privatization of the equivalent of a quarter of the firms quoted on the Paris Bourse.

This is a clear-cut example of how politics can make a difference, in the right circumstances. The incoming government had fought an election on the basis of a clear-cut policy of privatization. It won the election, took office, and immediately set about implementing the policy in a most comprehensive fashion. (As an aside, it is worth noting that several of the firms scheduled for privatization had originally been nationalized by de Gaulle himself. The policy thus represented quite a considerable volte-face for the Gaullists, traditionally committed to a strong state.) What is more, the policy of privatization in France was not just retained as a piece of legislation on the statute books; it was actually put into practice. Within a year, one-third of the five-year privatization program had been enacted, and the result was a series of stock market flotations valued at a total of 100 billion francs. The number of small shareholders in France rose from 1.5 million in 1985 to 8 million in 1987 (Bauer, pp. 51–54). This explosion in "popular capitalism" was so dramatic that the Bourse was simply not able to cope with the increase in business, much of which was siphoned off by the London Stock Exchange (Cerny, pp. 184–85).

Helped by the steadily rising stock markets of the mid-1980s, many small investors bought and sold shares in formerly public companies and made healthy profits. The end of the era came equally quickly in France, however. The world stock market crash of October 1987, sparked off on Wall Street, badly burned many French small investors. These, coming to share ownership during a bull market, had made a lot of what seemed like easy money and learned the hard way that what cynics had described as "casino capitalism" involves losing as well as winning. Against this backdrop, the right lost both the presidential elections of May 1988 and the subsequent parliamentary elections, and the privatization program was "stopped in its tracks" (Vickers and Wright, p. 21). A change of government thus led to another major policy shift.

The program of privatization in Britain can also be traced directly to the policies promoted by a particular political party. The program provides another example of a very clear-cut discontinuity between the actions of an incoming government and those of its predecessor, one of the most dramatic such examples in postwar European politics. The Conservative government that took office in 1979 had not fought the preceding election on the basis of a comprehensive set of manifesto commitments on privatization, which had been only a "minor theme" in the campaign (Heald, p. 32).

The process started more slowly than in France, with the denationalization of a series of profitable companies, such as British Aerospace and Britoil, easy to sell at discounted flotation prices in a robust bull market. Once the program of privatization began, however, it rapidly acquired momentum and probably went farther than the Conservatives themselves had initially envisaged (Kavanagh, p. 221). The success of early privatizations fed back into Conservative policy and encouraged the party to boost the role given to privatization in the party manifesto. Thus, the 1983 election was fought and won by the Conservatives on the basis of a much more ambitious privatization program, extending not only to massive public companies such as British Telecom, British Airways, Rolls-Royce and the Rover group, but also to enterprises that had previously been thought of as "untouchable" basic services and natural monopolies: electricity, gas, and water services, for example. Within seven years, about fifty state corporations—that is, about half of the total state sector—had been sold to private investors. The shareholding population in Britain had increased threefold to almost 10 million people, and many billions of pounds sterling had been raised for the government by asset sales. By 1992 it is estimated that total privatization proceeds in Britain totalled 12 percent of British GDP. (Boix, 1998: 86. Boix provides an extensive discussion of the economic policies associated with this era of Conservative government in Britain.)

Britain and France are not, of course, the only European states that have implemented programs of privatizing the public sector in recent years. Privatization has taken place on a more limited scale in Greece, Portugal, Germany (Esser), Italy (Bianchi et al.), the Netherlands (Andeweg), Belgium (Drumaux), and even Sweden (Pontusson) and Austria (W. Müller), to take just a few examples. But in each case, the program has not been associated with unequivocal doctrinaire commitments on the part of the incoming government, and has been much less radical in its extent. There has undoubtedly been a general trend in Europe toward privatization of the public sector, and such privatizations are less likely when socialist governments are in power (Boix, pp. 88–89). By any account, however, the privatization programs of right-wing governments in Britain and France involved a massive partisan redirection of public policy that would not have taken place under most conceivable alternative administrations. Politics, without any doubt at all, made a big difference in these cases. (For a general comparative discussion of major shifts in policy regimes, see Notermans.)

PARTY MANIFESTOS AND GOVERNMENT POLICY PROGRAMS

The idea that what governments do is affected by which parties get into office is what makes sense of the notion of representative democracy. If government policy does not respond to the intentions of elected government members, then why have elections in the first place? We have just seen two dramatic examples of cases in which almost everyone would agree that politics made a big difference. The important question, of course, has to do with the extent to which we can generalize from this experience.

The first step along the rocky road from what is promised at election time to what is actually done by governments in office is to compare parties' election manifestos with the policy positions of the governments they join. The latter are recorded in the official policy programs typically published by newly formed governments as part of the investiture process, and in the formal statements of official government policy that are typically issued at the beginning of each new session of parliament.

In order to compare election manifestos with published government policy declarations, we need to have a systematic way of describing both of these. We can do this by using the technique of "content analysis," which involves classifying the entire content of each relevant policy document, sentence by sentence, and placing each sentence into one of a set of categories that captures important features of party and government policy. A key area of party policy in modern Europe, for example, is the running of the economy. This, of course, generates many policy problems related to unemployment, inflation, exchange rates, investment, government spending, and so on. One general set of policy prescriptions for these matters can be characterized as the promotion of "free market economics." This is associated with the encouragement of private enterprise, private incentive structures, free trade, balanced budgets, and general economic orthodoxy, together with opposition to the expansion of the welfare state. The long-standing Manifesto Research Group (MRG) has analyzed party manifestos and government declarations using content analysis, assessing the relative emphasis that each policy document gives to free market economics and many other themes. (For updated descriptions of the type of approach used by the MRG, and of alternatives to it, see Laver, 2000.) To compare what *parties* promise voters that they will do with what, having taken power, *governments* containing those same parties promise to do, we can conduct a content analysis of party manifestos, and compare this with a content analysis of government policy declarations. A collection of analyses making precisely these comparisons can be found in Laver and Budge.

The general pattern of these analyses was reasonably clear. On one hand, there is a group of countries, for example Norway and Denmark, in which there has typically been a clear-cut alternation of power between coalitions or single-party governments of the center left and coalitions of the center right. In such countries, there is typically little overlap between the parties who are in cabinets of the center left and those in cabinets of the center right. And in such countries, we do tend to see significant shifts in the ideological complexion of government policy declarations, depending upon which parties are in power. In these cases, it is relatively easy to infer the party composition of a government just by looking at the government's published policies. When this happens, parties clearly make a difference.

On the other hand, there is a group of countries, Italy before 1994 or Germany before 1998, for example, in which a single party has been a more or less permanent fixture of government, with a changing set of coalition partners. The alternation of government parties between elections has typically also only been partial in a number of other European countries: the Netherlands, Luxembourg, and Austria, for example. Comparing party manifestos with government policy declarations in these cases, we should not be surprised to find that the more limited turnover in the partisan composition of the government is more difficult to track in the changing substance of government policy declarations. And this is indeed the pattern found by the MRG researchers.

Overall, therefore, the rather limited available evidence suggests that parties do make a difference to the published policy programs of European governments, but that this is far more clear-cut when the entire party membership of the cabinet is likely to change from one government to the next.

REDEEMING CAMPAIGN PLEDGES

It is one thing for a party to announce, when it has just formed a government, that it is going to redeem a particular election pledge. It is quite another thing actually to do so. The next major step on the path that takes us from the promises made by politicians in the excitement of an election campaign to what actually happens in the real world is the redeeming of campaign pledges. Before we can get down to the systematic analysis of this matter, however, we must deal with a number of tricky methodological problems.

First, we must decide in a systematic way what is a genuine pledge to voters and what is a piece of typical campaign rhetoric and hyperbole that no sensible person would take seriously. This, of course, is a highly subjective matter. It has to do with how specific the promise is, with how literally it is intended to be taken by those who hear it, and with whether it proposes real actions or merely expresses pious hopes. Thus, promises to "make this great country of ours a better place to live in" or to "banish hunger and poverty from the face of the earth" ought not to be seen as campaign pledges in any real sense of the word. They are either too vague to be taken seriously or no more than general aspirations.

Second, we must decide who is to blame when campaign pledges are not redeemed. Has the politician who promised to double the rate of economic growth broken that pledge to voters if he or she tries as hard as possible but fails to do this? Has that politician broken the pledge if he or she doesn't try at all? Has the pledge been broken if the politician doesn't try very hard? If we are going to excuse pledges that are thwarted for reasons beyond the control of the pledger, someone will have to call the score, pledge by pledge, on who was to blame for the breaking of each.

A third problem relates to the business of giving credit for pledges that do indeed appear to have been redeemed. After all, if I promise that the sun will rise tomorrow, and it does, is it sensible to give me credit for having redeemed my promise? Finally, there is the problem that many campaign pledges tend to be carried out a little bit; few are enacted in their full splendor. A little progress may be made on cutting public spending or reforming the tax system, for example. Unemployment may be reduced somewhat, quite possibly not thanks to the government of the day. Once more, to classify these as pledges broken or as pledges fulfilled is a matter of highly subjective judgment.

There are no easy answers to these problems. The solution adopted by most of those doing empirical research on the redemption of campaign pledges in Europe is to muse a little on the types of problems outlined above and then just get down to work and do the best they can. It is difficult to see what else can be done.

Much of the early work on the fulfillment of campaign pledges in Europe related to Britain. The first detailed study was conducted by Richard Rose, who compared the record of redeemed pledges for the 1970–74 Conservative government with that for the 1974–79 Labour government (Rose, pp. 55–73). His conclusion, confounding the skeptics, was that manifesto pledges do make a difference, that "Conservative and Labour governments act consistently with the Manifesto model of governing; in office they do the majority of things to which they pledge themselves" (Rose, p. 64). The skeptics might retort that this conclusion is a product of an exclusive concentration on manifesto pledges that Rose deems "doable." This problem is compounded by the fact that one of the reasons that the record of these parties seems so good is that they promise many things that are straightforward and uncontroversial. Rose finds that about half of all pledges are nonpartisan, representing a consensus between the parties (Rose, p. 69). Such pledges are easy to make and are much easier to carry out than others. Whether we should set much store by them when trying to decide whether politicians keep their promises is another matter.

Rallings applied the general features of Rose's analysis to the period from 1945 to 1979 in Britain and came up with similar conclusions. He found that about 70 percent of all manifesto pledges were implemented, though some types were much more likely to be implemented than others. "Clear promises to increase pensions and other benefits (often by a named amount) and to repeal ideologically unacceptable legislation passed by the previous administration, are almost invariably kept. . . . The pledges least likely to be fulfilled are the small minority where the government cannot ensure their passage or which involve the expenditure of large amounts of public money on electorally unappealing and/or low priority projects" (Rallings, p. 13). This approach has also been applied to analyze the record of the PASOK (Socialist) government in Greece from 1981 to 1985, and once more a pledge fulfillment rate of about 70 percent was found (Kalogeropoulou, p. 293).

Terry Royed extended this work to a comprehensive comparative evaluation of the role of campaign pledges in Britain and the United States, looking at the relative rates of fulfillment of pledges made by government and opposition parties. Using a more precise definition of a campaign pledge than earlier authors, she found that over 80 percent of pledges made in Conservative election manifestos were enacted by the Conservative governments of 1979–83 and 1983–87—a significantly higher rate than that found in the U.S. The high rate of pledge fulfillment by the government party in Britain compares with a much lower rate for the opposition party. (Opposition party pledges may be enacted if these make the same promises as those made by the parties that go onto government.) In fact, when government and opposition disagreed in Britain, Royed found that the opposition had almost zero chance of seeing its pledges enacted (Royed).

While most of the research on the fulfillment of campaign pledges has been conducted in countries where one-party government is the norm, a valuable recent study by Robert Thomson investigated the fulfillment of campaign pledges in the Dutch coalition system during the 1980s and 1990s. The expectation in a coalition system is that fewer pledges will be fulfilled, because of the policy compromises between parties that must be made in order to form a government. Not only must some pledges be dropped as part of the process of compromise, but the subsequent need to do deals with other parties also provides a ready-made excuse for the nonfulfillment of campaign pledges. Using comparable definitions of pledges in the Netherlands and Britain, Thomson found pledge fulfillment rates of close to 80 percent in Britain and of about 50 percent, or even less, in the Netherlands. He quite firmly concluded that "[p]ledges made by parties that go on to form Dutch governments are significantly less likely to be acted upon than those made by parties that form single-party governments in the United Kingdom." (Thomson, p. 202).

Coalition systems create a more complex environment for the fulfillment of campaign pledges than that created by single-party governments, and Thomson's work throws some useful light on this. He found, for example, that campaign pledges are significantly more likely to be enacted if the party that made them controls the cabinet ministry with jurisdiction over the policy area in question. He found that pledges are significantly more likely to be enacted once they have found their way into the formal agreement signed between the government parties. And he found that pledges are significantly more likely to be enacted if they represent a consensus between the government parties. When a single party controls all cabinet seats, these issues do not arise. When power is shared between parties, Thomson's work on the Netherlands suggests that the level of consensus between cabinet partners, the specific policy agreement between them, and the allocation of cabinet portfolios to different parties, all have an important bearing on the redemption by parties of pledges made during election campaigns.

Taken overall, the research that has been conducted to date does suggest that parties honor more of their campaign pledges than skeptics, rivals, and journalists typically give them credit for. This may, in part, be an artefact of the data, arising because researchers regard as firm pledges only proposals that can be carried out. It may also be a product of real-world party competition, if parties tend to promise a lot of easy and uncontroversial things, precisely so that they can go back to the voters and boast about how they fulfilled most of their promises. Parties may anticipate all the easy things that they can actually deliver and make a great song and dance at election time about promising to deliver them. Notwithstanding these reservations, however, the growing body of work on this topic suggests that parties do redeem campaign pledges to a greater degree than many cynics had previously thought, that politics does make a difference in this particular sense.

PARTY GOVERNMENT AND PUBLIC SPENDING

When public policy has a bearing on patterns of public spending, we can find at least one concrete indicator of what the government is actually doing. If a promise is made to do something that involves public spending, to build more schools, for example, then we can see whether or not spending on school construction does in fact increase.

Patterns in the flow of public expenditure, and the links between these and the partisan composition of the government, have been the subject of an increasing body of academic research. The problem has been approached from two basic perspectives. The first is to look at different countries in the same time period in order to establish whether countries with particular types of government have particular types of public spending patterns. The second is to look at the same country in different time periods in order to establish whether changes in spending patterns can be traced to changes in government.

Differences Between Countries

The basic patterns of public spending in modern Western European states can be seen in Table 13-1. The first two columns of data in this table give alternative indicators of

TABLE 13-1   RELATIONSHIP BETWEEN LONG-TERM IDEOLOGICAL COMPLEXION OF GOVERNMENT AND SIZE OF PUBLIC SECTOR

	Soc. dem. & left percentage of total cabinet seats	Mean left score of government	Govt. spending as % GDP	Govt. employment as % total employment
Year	*1950–94*	*1945–95*	*1996*	*1996*
Portugal	5.7	na	41.1	16.7
Ireland	9.7	1.5	36.3	12.6
Italy	12.4	1.6	49.4	15.8
Netherlands	18.6	2.0	49.9	13.5
Greece	19.7	na	52.1	na
Switzerland	23.8	1.9	33.9	14.0
France	24.5	2.0	51.6	25.1
Germany	24.8	2.0	45.8	15.3
Spain	26.0	na	41.1	15.3
Belgium	27.6	2.3	49.9	18.7
UK	28.1	2.3	41.4	14.1
Luxembourg	28.4	2.1	45.0	11.3
Iceland	31.7	2.3	34.0	19.8
Finland	33.6	2.8	56.2	25.1
Denmark	50.7	3.0	59.6	30.5
Austria	60.7	3.4	47.2	22.8
Norway	73.1	4.0	42.4	30.6
Sweden	76.3	4.1	62.9	30.7
Correlation with left cabinet seats			*0.41*	*0.80*
Correlation with left score			*0.46*	*0.82*

Sources: Cabinet seat share for left: Schmidt (1996, p.160). Scores for Greece, Portugal, and Spain recalculated to cover the entire postwar period. Left scores: Woldendorp, Keman, and Budge (1998) and author's calculations. Size of public sector: OECD.

the average ideological complexion of each European country's governments over the entire postwar period. The first column gives the average share of cabinet seats controlled by social democratic and other left-wing parties over the postwar period. The second column reports an index of the average ideological complexion of the government. This index would score 1.0 if a country had been governed by a right-dominated government for the entire period, and 5.0 if it had been governed by a left-dominated government for the entire period. Countries are ranked in the table according to the average ideological complexion of their governments. Ireland has experienced the least impact from having left-wing parties in government over the postwar period, Norway and Sweden the most.

The third column of data in Table 13-1 shows total public spending in each country, expressed as a percentage of the overall gross domestic product (GDP). From this we can see that the extent of left-wing participation in government does tend to be higher in countries that have a larger public sector, such as Sweden, Denmark and Finland. Conversely, where there is extensive right-wing participation in government, the proportion of GDP devoted to public spending can be low, as in Switzerland and Ireland. There are, however, some striking exceptions. France, Italy, and the Netherlands have experienced considerable right-wing participation in government during the postwar period, yet have relatively large public sectors.

Overall public expenditure, of course, covers a multitude of sins, from welfare schemes to weapons of mass destruction, from schools to pensions to prisons. Much public spending, furthermore, is determined by the need to provide for "demand-driven" welfare transfers, such as unemployment benefits or old-age pensions. These may have far more to do with the state of the economy, or the demographic structure of the population, than with any explicit public policy initiative. Each of these factors has little to do with the ideology of the government. It might well be argued, therefore, that the general level of public spending in a given country conceals as much as it throws light upon. For this reason, the final column of data in Table 13-1 shows the level of government employment as a proportion of total employment. This may well be a better indication than total public spending of a tendency towards "big government." It gives a measure of the size of the government as a player in the economy, and strips out the type of welfare transfer that might be driven as much by the level of demand as by policy. Here we see a much more striking relationship between the average ideological complexion of the government and the size of the public sector. Countries, such as Ireland, Switzerland and Germany, that have tended to have more right-wing governments have distinctly smaller public sectors. Austria and the Scandinavian countries, which have tended to have more left-wing participation in government, have a distinctly larger public sector. The correlation between this measure of the size of the public sector, and either measure of the average ideological complexion of the government, given in the final two rows of Table 13-1, is much higher than the correlation for public spending as a whole. Politics does seem to make a clear difference to the size of the public sector.

We now move on to specific policy areas that make up significant components of public spending, which we might also expect to respond to long-term ideological trends in the composition of the government. Table 13-2 shows a strong relationship between the average ideological complexion of the government and overall public spending in at least three key policy areas: social welfare, education, and overseas development aid. In each case, countries that have traditionally experienced more left-wing governments have significantly higher levels of spending than others, although at least part of this pattern is contributed by the very distinctive position of four Scandinavian countries: Denmark, Finland, Norway, and Sweden. For social welfare spending, the pattern is consistent with research by Hicks et al. (p. 423), who found that "welfare effort" (the proportion of national income devoted to welfare spending) is very "sticky" and hard to change, but nonetheless related to economic policy making (see also Hicks and Swank). For education, the pattern is consistent with research by Francis Castles, who

TABLE 13-2 RELATIONSHIP BETWEEN LONG-TERM IDEOLOGICAL COMPLEXION OF GOVERNMENT AND SELECTED PUBLIC SPENDING INDICATORS

	Soc. dem. & left share of cabinet seats	Mean left score of government	Social security & welfare as % GDP	Govt. spending on educational institutions as % GDP	Public-sector health spending as % GDP	Overseas development aid as % GDP
Year	*1950–94*	*1945–95*	*1996*	*1996*	*1996*	*1997*
Portugal	5.7	na	0.5	5.4	4.9	0.25
Ireland	9.7	1.5	na	4.7	5.2	0.31
Italy	12.4	1.6	0.7	4.5	5.5	0.11
Netherlands	18.6	2.0	0.7	4.6	6.2	0.81
Greece	19.7	na	0.3	na	5.2	na
Switzerland	23.8	1.9	na	5.5	7.1	0.34
France	24.5	2.0	1.5	5.8	7.3	0.45
Germany	24.8	2.0	3.0	4.5	8.2	0.28
Spain	26.0	na	0.8	4.8	5.8	0.24
Belgium	27.6	2.3	1.0	na	6.8	0.31
UK	28.1	2.3	1.9	4.6	5.8	0.26
Luxembourg	28.4	2.1	na	4.3	6.2	0.55
Iceland	31.7	2.3	1.7	4.5	6.8	na
Finland	33.6	2.8	3.5	6.6	5.8	0.33
Denmark	50.7	3.0	6.7	6.5	6.5	0.97
Austria	60.7	3.4	3.4	5.3	5.7	0.26
Norway	73.1	4.0	2.0	6.8	6.5	0.86
Sweden	76.3	4.1	5.7	6.6	7.2	0.79
Correlation with left cabinet seats			*0.70*	*0.67*	*0.34*	*0.60*
Correlation with left score			*0.62*	*0.75*	*0.12*	*0.56*

Sources: See sources for Table 13-1. Levels of public spending: OECD.

looked in the same way at cross-national patterns in education expenditure and found strong evidence of "the negative educational impact of right-wing political strength" (Castles, 1989, p. 441). Even holding constant a wide range of other factors, there is a strong link between education effort and partisan control of government.

The exception to the main pattern in the data in Table 13-2 concerns health policy. There seems to be a much weaker relationship between the ideological complexion of the government and the level of public spending on health services. There is not much variation in these levels, and such variation as there is does not seem to be affected by political factors.

BOX 13-1

PATTERNS OF SPENDING IN PUBLIC FINANCES

France

The dramatic program of sales of public corporations between 1986 and 1988, carried out by a conservative coalition, marked a break in the continuity of public finances. This raised considerable, though short-lived, nonrecurrent income for the state. Governed for most of the 1980s by a Socialist president in tandem with a Socialist prime minister, France had public expenditures, especially for social welfare, that were higher as a proportion of national income than in Britain, for example, or Germany or Italy. Although nominal income tax rates are low (and thus have in the past attracted rich residents from other European countries), other payroll taxes tend to be high in France. France thus remains very much in the European mainstream in terms of the share of national income absorbed by taxes.

Germany

The coalition of the center right that governed for most of the 1980s and up until 1998 pursued financial policies very similar to those of earlier center-left coalitions, as well as the Social Democrat–Green coalition that followed it in 1998. This is in large part because the power of German cabinets in the area of financial policy making is constrained by the powers of a relatively autonomous and very conservative central bank. (In 1990, however, the bank was forced to back down in the face of government pressure on the exchange rate for East German marks.) The financial policy pursued by most German governments, of whatever hue, has been to seek to maintain the value of the currency and keep inflation low. As a consequence, German budgets have been more or less balanced in recent years, and public debt as a proportion of national income is low in Germany in comparison with such debt in other European countries. German reunification has obviously had a major impact on German public finances, though the long-term effects of this are still working their way through the system.

Italy

The center-right Christian Democrats were a more or less permanent fixture in every Italian government of the postwar era, until the collapse of the entire party system in the early 1990s, in the wake of huge political and financial scandals. Changes in coalition partners traditionally produced little discernible effect on patterns in public finances. Taxation traditionally has taken a rela-

tively low proportion of national income in Italy, in part because of a very large "informal" economy in which taxes do not figure at all. Public spending, in contrast, is very much in the European mainstream: lower than in France, but higher than in Britain and Germany. It is not surprising to find, therefore, that budgets tend to be well out of balance. As a consequence, inflation has traditionally been high in Italy relative to its European neighbors. The strong desire of many Italians to join with others to create the common European currency, the euro, did, however, lead to considerable efforts to bring public finances under control, and Italy did meet the convergence criteria for membership.

Netherlands

The exploitation of offshore natural gas fields produced short-term windfall gains to the public purse in the Netherlands, and the gains were used during the 1970s to increase welfare benefits and certain other public spending programs. As gas revenues began to decline, however, public spending faced a squeeze, although it was politically difficult to reverse the extensions of state benefits, a syndrome that became known more widely as the "Dutch disease." Despite the relatively large part of the postwar period in which right-wing parties have been in office, the share of national income taken by taxes in the Netherlands is now one of the highest in Western Europe (equivalent to that in Norway and less only than that in Sweden and Denmark), whereas public spending remains higher than in almost all other European countries outside Scandinavia.

Spain

Before the death of Franco in 1975, Spain's public finances had been characterized by very low taxes, low or nonexistent welfare benefits, and very low govern-ment spending—very much what we might expect from a right-wing authoritarian regime. Since democratization, and particularly since entry into the EU, both taxes and spending have risen rapidly as the welfare system has been extended. These are still, however, at the low end of the European mainstream, although high levels of unemployment are making heavy demands on welfare spending. The share of national income absorbed by public spending as a whole is less than that in Germany and the United Kingdom, and the share taken by taxation remains low.

Sweden

Sweden, run by the Social Democrats for much of the postwar period, is known, along with most other Scandinavian countries, for having very high levels of taxation relative to other Western European states, with particularly heavy and steeply progressive personal income taxes. Public spending also amounts to a very high share of national income, although very low unemployment rates mean that resources devoted to unemployment assistance are relatively low. State spending applies to a wide range of areas of activity, contributing to a high "social wage" that is delivered in terms of services provided either free or at subsidized rates by the public sector.

United Kingdom

Right-wing Conservative governments between 1979 and 1997 made deep cuts in the social welfare element of spending that were offset by increases in police and defense spending, and by increases in the level of unemployment and hence in spending on unemployment benefits. These policies were in sharp contrast with the policies of preceding governments, both Labour and Conservative. By the end of the 1980s, the rate of growth (though not the level) of public spending was lower in Britain than in many other European countries. A program of cuts in nominal rates of income tax, particularly for higher income earners, was offset to a significant extent by increases in indirect taxation. Nonetheless, Britain is at the low end of the mainstream of European countries in terms of the proportion of national income paid in taxes. Revenue from taxes on North Sea oil and from the sale of public corporations represented very significant but "nonrenewable" sources of government income during the 1980s and early 1990s. The "New Labour" government that took office under Tony Blair in 1997 was elected on a middle-of-the-road policy platform that promised no major changes in the pattern of public spending.

With the exception of health spending, therefore, which seems to be driven by other factors, the data in Table 13-2 do provide evidence that politics seems to be making a difference to public policy outputs, despite the vast array of cultural and other factors that distinguish one European country from another. Comparing spending patterns in different systems, it does seem to be the case that countries with higher levels of spending on education, welfare, and development aid are those in which left-wing governments have been more common. It is dangerous to draw too many firm conclusions about cause and effect in patterns of public policy from cross-national data such as these, however. Stronger indications of what is going on can be gleaned from analyses of spending patterns within countries, the matter to which we now turn.

Differences Within Countries

One way to look for evidence of whether governments make a difference is to look at whether changes in the parties of government in a given country tend to be associated with changing patterns of public spending. Research on this matter must take account of the fact that patterns of public spending can be shifted only a little bit from one year to the next. Governments can in practice have an impact on spending patterns only at the margin, controlling year-to-year changes in spending flows much more than they control the overall scale of spending. The actual level of welfare or defense spending, for example, might be much higher in one country than in another not because of the current political situation, but as a result of the interplay of a complex set of historical and structural factors. What an incoming government can do in the short and medium run is to cut or boost welfare or defense spending. But even savage cuts and generous boosts do not, unless they are repeated year after year, have a huge impact on the overall level of spending in these areas.

Manfred Schmidt tackled this problem by analyzing the year-by-year changes in government spending in a wide range of countries, and relating this to the partisan composition of the cabinet, controlling for important economic variables such as the growth rate and changes in the level of unemployment. He found quite clear evidence that having left or center-right parties in office contributed to annual increases in the level of government spending, while having a right-wing party in government contributed to decreases in this. His conclusion was that "social democracy and christian democracy have been major political 'engines' in the growth of government . . . in contrast to this, conservative parties have been major inhibitors of the growth of government in modern democracies" (Schmidt, 177).

Looking further into the relationship between partisan control of the government and public spending, Andre Blais and his colleagues found that the majority status of the government was an important factor. First, they found that "parties do not make a difference when the government is a minority one" (Blais et al., p. 55). This is not surprising, given our discussion of minority governments in Chapter 12. Minority governments typically can remain in place because they are at the center of the political spectrum and opposition to them is divided. In a sense, they can govern precisely because they do not make a difference in the sense of imposing their will over the will of a majority of the legislature. As soon as a minority government begins to implement distinctive policies, it is liable to be defeated. In contrast, Blais et al. found that majority governments controlled exclusively by the left did increase overall public spending by a small but significant amount, relative to majority governments controlled exclusively by the right. As might be expected, the difference between left- and right-wing governments is greater for governments that have held office for five years or more. Thus, considering the overall size of the public sector, the conclusions of Blais et al. are that "governments of the left spend a little more than governments of the right. Parties do make a difference, but a small one. That difference, moreover, is confined to majority governments and takes time to set in" (Blais et al., p. 57).

Hicks and Swank also found that the partisan composition of the *opposition* can make a difference to public policy. Thus, a left-wing government facing a numerically strong right-wing opposition tends to spend less on welfare than one facing a weaker right-wing opposition. Hicks and Swank call this an "embourgeoisement" of the left party. Conversely, a right-wing government facing a numerically strong left-wing opposition tends to spend more on welfare than one that does not. They call this phenomenon "contagion from the left," and Petry has provided further evidence of it for a number of different spending areas in the specific case of the French Fifth Republic.

As Margaret Thatcher found in Britain, massive efforts of political will are needed to produce modest effects on public spending. It is not surprising, therefore, that we do not find public spending patterns changing dramatically with every change in government. In general, however, the accumulating evidence does suggest that parties do make a difference to patterns of public spending. The overall effects that we can observe on public spending are small. However, if we focus on particular spending areas or on the impact of long-serving single-party governments, the impact of parties on public spending becomes easier to see. All of this means that if we look carefully and know what we are looking for, we should indeed be able to detect a change in the party composition of governments by examining patterns of public spending—our acid test of whether politics does make a difference.

BEYOND PUBLIC SPENDING

There is, of course, much more to public policy than government spending patterns. Even in the realm of economic management, governments must have policies on matters such as industrial relations and income inequality, for example.

The extent of political control over national European labor markets is elaborated by Armingeon, who argued that the key precondition for political control of labor markets is the combination of a strong labor movement with a powerful social democratic party. One or the other of these elements, acting alone, does not seem to be enough to make a real difference (Armingeon, p. 234). If a strong social democratic party coexists with a strong union movement, however, this allows for the development of a set of policies on wage restraint, employment, the "social wage," and the role of trade unions. At one end of the scale, Armingeon places Austria, Belgium, Denmark, Finland, and Germany. In these countries, there is a strong social democratic–trade union nexus; in each, changes in the government are associated with changes in effective political control of wages. In Sweden, for example, the social democratic–trade union nexus was strong for much of the postwar era, though it became significantly weaker in the 1990s. Political control of wages has tended to be high relative to that other countries, although there has not been enough alternation in government to allow the impact of changes in party control of government to be estimated. At the other end of the scale are Britain, France, and Italy, where the social democratic–union nexus is much weaker and political control of wages is much less obvious.

Given that governments can attempt to modify the distribution of both wealth and income if they choose to do so, using the welfare and tax systems, it is interesting to explore the impact of parties on income redistribution. This can take place in two quite distinct stages. The first concerns gross income, the aspect of inequality on which trade unions can have the greatest impact. The second concerns net income, which reflects how actual take-home pay is affected by taxes and by transfer payments in the social welfare system. This is the aspect of inequality on which governments can have the greatest impact. The bigger the change in inequality between gross and net income, the greater the impact of public policy.

E. N. Muller conducted an extensive comparative analysis of the impact of politics on income distribution. Controlling for a wide range of factors and analyzing data from a long list of countries, he concluded confidently that politics makes a considerable difference to income redistribution. According to Muller's empirical findings, socialist governmental strength does depress the income share going to the richest 20 percent of the population and does narrow the income gap between the richest and the poorest 20 percent. Conservative governmental strength does increase the income share going to the richest 20 percent and does widen the income gap between the richest and the middle income groups (E. N. Muller, 1989, p. 394). He finds that the negative impact of conservative parties on income equality is greater than the positive impact of socialist parties and concludes, quite unequivocally, that "most of the cross national variation [in income inequality] is explained by the inegalitarian influence of strong conservative parties" (E. N. Muller, 1989, p. 396).

Turning to inflation and unemployment, we find further evidence of the policy impact of government composition. Warwick found that the average monthly increase in unemployment was noticeably smaller under left-wing governments than under bourgeois governments or those that "mixed" right and left. Conversely, he found that the average monthly level of inflation was higher under left-wing governments and lower under bourgeois or mixed governments. This pattern of party effects on inflation was strongly confirmed by Suzuki. Thus, in accordance with popular preconceptions, left-wing governments tend to deliver lower unemployment and higher inflation. Right-wing governments tend to deliver lower inflation and higher unemployment. According to these findings at least, governments that mix right and left tend to deliver the worst of both worlds, with higher unemployment as well as higher inflation. Thus we can extend our conclusions based on patterns of public spending to economic policy more generally. Most of the research that has been done to date does imply that politics makes a difference.

Moving beyond economic policy—to environmental or foreign policy, for example, or policy on social and moral issues—we might expect policy to be more responsive to politics, since shifting the dead weight of public finances is not involved. For a number of aspects of social policy, furthermore, particularly those involving the reform of existing social legislation, either action is taken or it is not. Thus, either the law on abortion, on divorce, on the status of women, or on capital punishment is reformed or it is not. Public policy is easy to see in these areas for particular cases, but there is unfortunately little comparative research assessing the impact of parties on them.

One area of growing international concern is environmental policy, for which it is indeed possible to assemble some comparative information. Table 13-3 shows the levels of emission of two types of polluting gas: carbon dioxide and various sulphur oxides.

The partisan composition of governments can make a difference to the length of dole queues—this one in Leipzig in 1997. © R Bossu/Corbis/Sygma

TABLE 13-3   RELATIONSHIP BETWEEN LONG-TERM IDEOLOGICAL COMPLEXION OF GOVERNMENT
AND SELECTED POLLUTION INDICATORS

	Left cabinet seats	Mean left score	Tonnes CO_2/capita	Kg sulphur oxides/capita
Year	*1950–94*	*1945–95*	*1997*	*1997*
Portugal	5.7	na	5.2	36
Ireland	9.7	1.5	10.3	46
Italy	12.4	1.6	7.4	25
Netherlands	18.6	2.0	11.8	9
Greece	19.7	na	7.7	52
Switzerland	23.8	1.9	6.3	5
France	24.5	2.0	6.2	17
Germany	24.8	2.0	10.8	23
Spain	26.0	na	6.5	53
Belgium	27.6	2.3	12.0	24
UK	28.1	2.3	9.4	34
Luxembourg	28.4	2.1	20.4	19
Iceland	31.7	2.3	8.9	32
Finland	33.6	2.8	12.5	20
Denmark	50.7	3.0	11.8	34
Austria	60.7	3.4	7.9	8
Norway	73.1	4.0	7.8	8
Sweden	76.3	4.1	6.0	11
Correlation with left cabinet seats			*−0.07*	*−0.48*
Correlation with left score			*−0.22*	*−0.43*

Sources: See sources for Table 13-1. Levels of emissions: OECD.

The picture here is mixed. The negative correlations at the bottom of the table show that levels of sulphur oxide emission do appear to be generally related to the ideological complexion of the government, with more left-wing governments tending to be some "cleaner" environmentally than more right-wing ones. This pattern is almost imperceptible for carbon dioxide emissions, however. There may be a number of reasons for this weaker partisan patterning of environmental policy. One may be that environmental policy is unrelated to the traditional left-right divide that has structured our investigation of partisan public policy effects, while, with the exception of the German government since 1998, Green parties have hardly been in government at all in modern Europe. Put crudely, left-wing parties, seeking to boost economic growth and increase the general level of social welfare, may be no more concerned with the effects of pollution than their right-wing rivals. Another reason may have to do with the fact that the major public

Mainstream party politics seems to make less of a difference to the environment—either to emission of noxious gasses (in this case in France) . . . © Leimdorfer/REA/SABA Press Photos

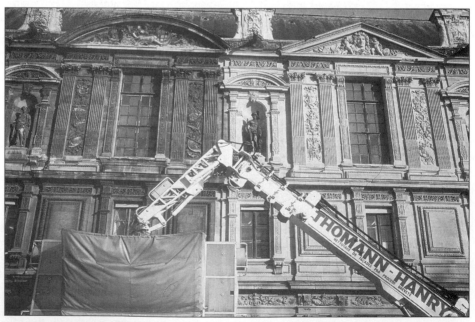

. . . or to cleaning up of the effects of industrial pollution—seen here in action on the Louvre in Paris. © Cuisset/REA/SABA Press Photos

and private investments required to have a significant effect on emission levels may be taking a long time to work their way through the system, and have yet to show up in the data. Overall, however, there is little evidence of mainstream partisan effects on environmental policy outputs, where these can be quantified.

SO, *DOES* POLITICS MAKE A DIFFERENCE?

It used to be fashionable to denigrate the impact of politicians on public policy, to argue that we have now reached the "end of ideology" and that politics no longer makes much of a difference. More recently, the steady globalization of economic policy has appeared to remove quite a lot of discretion from politicians. To counter this, we examined the self-evident impact made by particular parties on the ambitious privatization programs of the 1980s and 1990s. It is very hard to deny that politics made a difference in these cases. If we look at the problem more generally, furthermore, we see that almost all recently published studies conclude that party politics has a major impact on policy outputs in the real world.

It does seem to be the case that government programs tend to reflect the published policies of government members. At least in those countries in which there is a clear-cut alternation in the party composition of governments, promises made to the voters in the heat of an election campaign do seem to filter through to government policy. It does seem to be the case that parties enact their promises more often than the cynics would have us believe. In part this may be because many of the promises that politicians make are not controversial, but at least for one-party governments, pledge fulfillment rates of 70 percent or more have consistently been found. It does seem that changes in government spending flows can be partially predicted by changes in government policies, and in particular, by major changes in the partisan composition of the government. Spending flows are very sticky, but the evidence suggests that they can, from time to time, be shifted as a result of a major effort of political will. And it does seem to be the case that nonexpenditure aspects of economic policy vary according to the partisan composition of the government. Relative dominance by right-wing governments, in particular, is associated with significant variations in key socioeconomic variables.

Does all of this mean that politics makes a difference? The weight of evidence suggests that it does, at least in the economic sphere, which gives us all one respectable reason to get excited about the results of elections.

REFERENCES

Andeweg, R. B.: "Less Than Nothing? Hidden Privatization of the Pseudo-Private Sector: The Dutch Case," *Western European Politics,* vol. 11, no. 4, 1988, pp. 117–28.

Armingeon, K.: "Determining the Level of Wages: The Role of Parties and Trade Unions," in F. Castles (ed.), *The Impact of Parties,* Sage, London, 1982.

Bauer, M.: "The Politics of State-Directed Privatization: The Case of France 1986–89," *West European Politics,* vol. 11, no. 4, 1988, pp. 49–60.

Bianchi, P., S. Cassese, and V. Della Sala: "Privatization in Italy: Aims and Constraints," *West European Politics,* vol. 11, no. 4, 1988, pp. 87–100.

Blais, Andre, Donald Blake, and Stephane Dion: "Do Parties Make a Difference? Parties and the Size of Government in Liberal Democracies," *American Journal of Political Science,* vol. 37, 1993, pp. 40–62.

Boix, Charles: *Political Parties, Growth and Equality.* Cambridge University Press, Cambridge, 1998.

Budge, I., D. Robertson, and D. Hearl (eds.): *Ideology, Strategy and Party Change,* Cambridge University Press, Cambridge, England, 1987.

Castles, F.: "Explaining Public Education Expenditure in OECD Nations," *European Journal of Political Research,* vol. 17, 1989, pp. 431–48.

Cerny, P. G.: "The Little Big Bang in Paris: Financial Market Deregulation in a *Dirigiste* System," *European Journal of Political Research,* vol. 17, no. 2, 1989, pp. 169–92.

Drumaux, A.: "Privatization in Belgium: The National and International Context," *West European Politics,* vol. 11, no. 4, 1988, pp. 74–86.

Esser, J.: "Symbolic Privatization: The Politics of Privatization in West Germany," *West European Politics,* vol. 11, no. 4, 1988, pp. 61–73.

Heald, D.: "The United Kingdom: Privatization and Its Political Context," *West European Politics,* vol. 11, no. 4, 1988, pp. 31–48.

Hicks, Alexander, and Duane Swank: "Politics, Institutions, and Welfare Spending in Industrialised Democracies, 1960–1982," *American Political Science Review,* vol. 86, 1992, pp. 658–74.

Hicks, Alexander, Duane Swank, and M. Ambuhl: "Welfare Expansion Revisited: Policy Routines and Their Mediation by Party, Class and Crisis, 1957–1982," *European Journal of Political Research,* vol. 17, 1989, pp. 401–30.

Kalogeropoulou, E.: "Election Promises and Government Performance in Greece: PASOK's Fulfillment of Its 1981 Election Pledges," *European Journal of Political Research,* vol. 17, 1989, pp. 289–311.

Kavanagh, D.: *Thatcherism and British Politics: The End of Consensus?* 2d ed., Oxford University Press, Oxford, 1990.

Laver, Michael (ed.) *Estimating the Policy Positions of Political Actors,* Routledge, London, 2000, forthcoming.

Laver, M., and I. Budge (eds.): *Party Policy and Government Coalitions,* Macmillan, London, 1992.

Muller, E. N.: "Distribution of Income in Advanced Capitalist States: Political Parties, Labour Unions, and the International Economy," *European Journal of Political Research,* vol. 17, 1989, pp. 367–400.

Müller, W.: "Privatizing in a Corporatist Economy: The Politics of Privatization in Austria," *West European Politics,* vol. 11, no. 4, 1988, pp. 101–16.

Notermans, Tom.: "Policy Continuity, Policy Change and the Political Power of Economic Ideas," *Acta Politica,* vol. 34, 1999, pp. 22–48.

Petry, François: "Fragile Mandate: Party Programmes and Public Expenditures in the French Fifth Republic," *European Journal of Political Research,* vol. 20, 1991, pp. 149–72.

Pontusson, J.: "The Triumph of Pragmatism: Nationalisation and Privatization in Sweden," *West European Politics,* vol. 11, no. 4, 1988, pp. 129–40.

Rallings, C.: "The Influence of Election Programs: Britain and Canada 1945–79," in Budge, Robertson, and Hearl, 1987.

Rose, Richard: *Do Parties Make a Difference?,* Chatham House: Chatham, N.J., 1980.

Royed, T.: "Testing the Mandate Model in Britain and the United States: Evidence from the Reagan and Thatcher Eras," *British Journal of Political Science,* vol. 26, 1996, pp. 45–80.

Schmidt, Manfred.: "When Parties Matter: A Review of the Possibilities and Limits of Partisan Influence on Public Policy," *European Journal of Political Research,* vol. 30, 1996, pp. 155–83.

Suzuki, Motoshi: "Domestic Political Determinants of Inflation," *European Journal of Political Research,* vol. 23, 1993, pp. 245–60.

Thomson, Robert: *The Party Mandate: Election Pledges and Government Actions in the Netherlands, 1986–1998,* Thela-Thesis, Amsterdam, 1999.

Vickers, J., and V. Wright: "The Politics of Industrial Privatization in Western Europe: An Overview," *West European Politics,* vol. 11, no. 4, 1988, pp. 1–30.

Warwick, Paul: "Economic Trends and Government Survival in West European Parliamentary Democracies," *American Political Science Review,* vol. 86, 1992, pp. 875–87.

Woldendorp, Jaap, Hans Keman, and Ian Budge (eds.): "Political Data 1945–1990," special issue of *European Journal of Political Research,* vol. 24, 1993, pp. 1–120.

14

POLITICS OUTSIDE
PARLIAMENT

Most of this book deals with what we might think of as the "official" politics of representation in modern Europe. Until now, we have dealt with the national politics of choosing a legislature and an executive as well as with the public policy outputs that emerge from this process. While these vital matters are central to politics in any European country, they are only part of the story. A large part of the political representation of important social and economic interests inevitably takes place outside formal parliamentary processes, and there are big differences between European countries in the ways in which this happens.

Political scientists have spent a lot of time thinking about differences between countries in the ways in which key social and economic interests play a part in the decision-making process. This has led to two very different theoretical descriptions of how a wide range of formal and informal social groups, in what is often now described as "civil society," can have an impact on public decision making. One possible model for group politics, in which certain key groups are closely integrated into the formal political process, has become known as "corporatism." An alternative model for group politics, in which groups compete, in a political marketplace outside formal political institutions, to put pressure on decision-making elites, has become known as "pluralism." Having come to regard these distinctions as too stark to capture the complexities of politics in most real countries, many authors also now talk in terms of notions such as "social partnership" and "policy networks" that blend elements of the pluralist and corporatist models.

In the rest of this chapter, we explore how well each of these approaches seems to describe the politics of economic policy making, as well as the politics of decision making in some important non-economic spheres of activity. While policy making in any modern European state is a very complex process that certainly does not conform to any simple model, it is nonetheless useful to describe the essential differences between pluralism and corporatism, and to illustrate these with brief discussions of group politics in Austria and in Britain, the former typically seen as the archetypal corporatist system, the latter as essentially pluralist. We then discuss the ways in which the notion of a "policy network" might capture a number of the insights of both the pluralist and the corporatist models of politics outside parliament.

CORPORATISM

The Corporatist Model

Corporatism as we know it today has diverse sources in the political thought of the past hundred years or so. One important current that fed into modern theories of corporatist policy making was the fascism of the 1920s and 1930s. Fascist corporatism was a system of totalitarian state control of society based on an intimate interpretation of interest groups and the state. Domination of the major interest groups by the state was one of the main mechanisms of social control by the fascist one-party government, exemplified by Hitler's Germany, Mussolini's Italy, and Salazar's Portugal. Obviously, any form of thought even vaguely linked with fascism was totally discredited in Europe after World War II. This is the reason postwar theories of corporatism severed any association with fascism before being relaunched as "neo-corporatism" or "liberal corporatism."

A second intellectual source that flowed into modern corporatism was "Catholic Social Thought," especially influential during the early decades of the twentieth century. Roman Catholic church leaders became concerned that the role of the church was being undermined both by the growth of trade unionism and by what they saw as the relentless encroachment of the state into many aspects of social life. They mourned the passing of the medieval craft guilds and advocated an enhanced role for self-governing interest groups that constituted what they described as the "voluntary" sector. These groups would be intimately involved not only in the *planning* but also in the *provision* of major social services such as health care and education. What lay behind this was that in a predominantly Roman Catholic society, these groups would be made up primarily of Roman Catholics, so that public policy would be sensitive to the teachings of the church, despite a formal separation of church and state. These ideas were taken up in the early postwar years by Christian democratic parties (see Chapter 8), whose electoral success gave corporatism a further political impetus.

A third factor that contributed to the rise of neo-corporatism was the impulse for "national unity" that followed the destruction and trauma caused by World War II in many European countries. As we saw in Chapter 12, a number of states went through the immediate postwar period governed by coalitions of national unity encompassing both the right and the left. The sense that industry and labor had to work together in order to rebuild war-torn economies fostered tripartite cooperation in places such as Austria and Germany.

A fourth factor was the close relationship between the trade union movement and social democratic parties in several Western European countries (see Chapter 8). Many of these parties had grown out of the trade union movement and were still intimately connected with it. When social democratic parties were in power over long periods, notably in postwar Sweden and Norway, the relationship between trade unions and political parties became a relationship between trade unions and governments. Even in "pluralist" Britain, economic policy making came closest to being corporatist during the "Social Contract" between government and unions executed during the life of the 1974–79 Labour administration. Conversely, when social democratic parties move out of power, as in Sweden in the mid-1990s, decision making can look a lot less corporatist.

One of the problems with the concept of corporatism is that many different people have used it in many different ways. Some authors have used the term to describe what is little more than a system of centralized wage bargaining, in which government and the "social partners" of organized labor and business sit round a table and thrash out a national incomes policy. Others see corporatism as being rooted much more deeply in the policy-making system: as a set of institutional arrangements that entrenches major social groups in the overall management of the national economy and much more besides. In a recent and comprehensive review, which also provides an excellent bibliography for interested readers, Siaroff (pp.180–81) tabulates no less than twenty-four different working definitions related to corporatism used by authors writing between 1981 and 1997. (Wiarda also provides a recent review of this field. See also Cawson, 1986, and Lijphart, 1999.) On the basis of his review, Siaroff also offers a definition that he feels best captures the key ideas that most of these people are writing about. He feels that corporatism involves, "within an advanced industrial society and democratic polity, the co-ordinated, co-operative, and systematic management of the national economy by the state, centralised unions, and employers (these latter two co-operating directly in industry), presumably to the relative benefit of all three actors" (Siaroff, p.177).

Working from this general definition, Siaroff (pp. 177–79) breaks down the analysis of corporatist policy making into four general areas. These are the *structural* preconditions for corporatism; the *roles* within this structure fulfilled by key actors; the patterns of *behavior* that result; and the *contextual factors* that make corporatist policy making more likely to succeed.

The structural preconditions for corporatism are typically argued to include the following:

- most of the work force should be organized into a small number of powerful unions;
- the business community should be dominated by a small number of powerful firms, organized in a powerful employers' federation;
- wage bargaining between unions and employers should be centralized;
- a powerful state should be actively involved in the economy.

Both employers and unions in a successful corporatist system should have a fully institutionalized role in both policy making and *implementation*. The types of behavior by these actors that is held to be required to make corporatism work are these:

- a consensus on broad social values shared by state, unions, and employers;
- a preference for bargained outcomes, rather than those that are either imposed or won through conflict.

Corporatist industrial relations: The heads of Swedish trade union and employers' federations conclude a national wage agreement. (© Sven-Erik Sjöberg/Pressens Bild AB)

Among a range of interrelated contextual factors argued to make corporatism work more smoothly, we find these:

- a long tradition of social democratic rule;
- a small, open economy;
- high expenditures on social programs and low expenditures on defense.

The stress on policy *implementation* in this elaboration of the corporatist model is what sets corporatism fundamentally apart from other systems that involve interest and pressure groups in political decision making. The implications of this are far-reaching. For any particular decision-making regime accurately to be described as "corporatist," interest groups must be comprehensive in their representation of particular sectors of society and must be able to police their membership as well as represent their interests. This point is strongly emphasized by both Phillipe Schmitter and Gerhard Lehmbruch, two of the most influential political scientists associated with discussions of corporatism: "Corporatism is more than a particular pattern of articulation of interests. Rather, it is an institutionalised pattern of policy-formation in which large interest organizations co-operate with each other and with public authorities not only in the articulation of interests, but . . . in the "authoritative allocation of values" and in the implementation of such policies" (Lehmbruch, p. 150).

Many of the authors who have written about corporatism have gone on to produce rankings of countries in terms of how close they are to the idealized model of the corporatist state. Siaroff (p. 198) combined all of these into a single additive index of corporatism, the results of which are given in Table 14-1, with figures for the USA and Canada as a basis for comparison.

Table 14-1 groups countries crisply into three clusters. There are the "big three" corporatist countries (Austria, Norway, and Sweden) that are rated as being clearly more corporatist than all of the others. After these comes a group of countries that rank as moderately corporatist, with the Netherlands, Germany, Denmark, and Switzerland at

TABLE 14-1   CORPORATISM SCORES FOR EUROPEAN DEMOCRACIES

	Corporatism score	Soc. dem. & left share of cabinet seats
Austria	5.00	60.7
Norway	4.86	73.1
Sweden	4.67	76.3
Netherlands	4.00	18.6
Denmark	3.55	50.7
Germany	3.54	24.8
Switzerland	3.38	23.8
Finland	3.30	33.6
Luxembourg	3.00	28.4
Iceland	3.00	31.7
Belgium	2.84	27.6
Ireland	2.00	9.7
France	1.67	24.5
UK	1.65	28.1
Portugal	1.50	5.7
Italy	1.48	12.4
Spain	1.25	26.0
Greece	1.00	19.7
USA	1.15	
Canada	1.15	

Sources: See sources for Table 13-1; Siaroff (p. 198).

the more corporatist end of this group, and Luxembourg, Iceland, and Belgium at the less corporatist end. Finally, there are countries that are hardly corporatist at all, in which Britain and Ireland (as well as the USA and Canada) are joined by the "Mediter-ranean" democracies: Portugal, Spain, Italy, Greece, and France. Put crudely, those parts of Europe that are neither Anglophone nor from the Catholic south are likely to be at least somewhat corporatist in their policy-making style.

Table 14.1 also repeats information from Table 13-1 on the extent of left or social democratic control of government over the postwar years, and does confirm the view that this is indeed conducive to the development of a more corporatist policy-making regime. Four of the five most corporatist countries—Austria, Norway, Sweden, and Denmark—were also those with the most extensive social democratic control of their postwar cabinets. The striking exception is the Netherlands, in which Christian demo-cratic parties were dominant in the cabinet over much of the postwar era, yet which exhibits strongly corporatist tendencies. In this sense, the Netherlands is more like some members of the group of more moderately corporatist countries, notably including Germany, Switzerland, and Belgium. In these, a tradition of "northern European"

Christian democracy, combined with a need to reconcile fundamental religious or linguistic cleavages, has created an impetus to entrench extraparliamentary groups in the policy-making system. (On corporatism in the Netherlands, see Woldendorp.)

As we can see from Table 14.1, most authors agree that of all Western European countries, Austria exhibits the strongest form of corporatism. By looking in greater detail at the situation in Austria, therefore, we can gain some additional insight into what is involved in corporatist policy making.

"Corporatism" in Austria

Austria is usually taken as the classic case of a political system that is characterized by a very high level of corporatist policy making. Indeed, Marin has even argued that Austria is a "model-generator," one of a very few countries that theorists have in mind when they develop accounts of corporatism. This was possibly truer of the period up until the late 1980s than it is today, as the recent development of more confrontational party politics, combined with Austrian membership in the European Union, may have moved Austria somewhat closer to the European mainstream (Luther and Müller). Nonetheless, there can be little doubt that Austrian politics for most of the postwar period provided one of the main sources of ideas for those who have written at length about corporatism.

Perhaps the most striking and distinctive feature of Austrian politics in this regard has been the important role of the "chambers." These institutions were designed to provide formal representation for the interests, respectively, of labor, commerce, and agriculture. Although chambers (especially chambers of commerce) can be found elsewhere, the Austrian chambers traditionally have been much more important, given their statutory position and the vital role that they play in decision making. All working citizens in Austria are obliged by law to belong to the appropriate chamber. This requires the chambers to run their affairs in a manner that would withstand legal scrutiny—to make internal decisions and hold internal elections in a representative manner, for example. The chambers have the formal right to be consulted on and represented in a wide range of matters, as well as to nominate members to many other public bodies.

In addition to the statutory chambers, Austria has an extensive system of "voluntary" interest groups. These include a trade union movement organized under the auspices of the "peak" trade union organization, the ÖGB, and the League of Austrian Industrialists, the VÖI. The ÖGB, in particular, is a powerful independent actor in Austria, for a number of reasons. First, it is the main agency engaged in collective bargaining on behalf of its own members. The Chamber of Labor, by virtue of its statutory status, must also consider the "public interest" in its dealings. Second, the ÖGB is highly centralized: the member unions, legally speaking, are subdivisions of the ÖGB, rather than the ÖGB being a federation of autonomous unions. In addition, the level of trade union affiliation in Austria is relatively high, and unions tend to be organized on an industry-by-industry (rather than a craft-by-craft) basis.

Almost all observers agree that the three main chambers—the Chamber of Labor, of Commerce, and of Agriculture—and the ÖGB interact with one another as the four key players in the process of making and implementing economic policy in Austria, in a system known as *Sozialpartnerschaft,* or "social partnership." This system operates in parallel with, rather than in opposition to, the formal parliamentary system. Although the key interest associations are quite distinct from the political parties, the obvious political affiliations of their respective memberships mean that each association tends to be dominated by supporters of one or another of the main parties. This gives interest group leaders a very strong position. As might be expected, the Chamber of Labor and the ÖGB are dominated by the Socialists (SPÖ), and the Chamber of Commerce and Chamber of Agriculture are dominated by the conservative Austrian People's party (ÖVP). It is important, however, not to present relations between parties and interest groups in Austria as if these were in some sense exclusive entities. On the contrary, there has been an intimate interpenetration of interest groups and parliament, and this symbiosis has been identified by many as one of the strengths of Austrian corporatism. A steadily growing proportion of parliamentarians are also interest group representatives, and interest groups have played an important role in the selection of parliamentary candidates for the major Austrian parties.

The social partners in Austria traditionally have been concerned first and foremost with economic policy making, in particular with prices and incomes. The social partnership underpinning Austrian corporatism has thus involved both the negotiation and the implementation of policies on prices and incomes. This cooperation has been formalized in a powerful institution, the Joint Commission on Prices and Wages, representation on which has been governed by the principle of parity. Thus the representation of the Chamber of Labor and the ÖGB has equalled that of the Chamber of Commerce and Chamber of Agriculture, and the commission has often been referred to as the "Parity Commission." The concept of parity has been vital to the operation of Austrian corporatism, implying strictly equal membership for representatives of business and labor in all important economic policy-making bodies. The effect has been to force groups that might otherwise be antagonistic to cooperate with one another, as no effective decisions can be made unless they do. Thus, many important decisions have been "bargained out" by the interest groups before the government becomes involved.

As a system of economic planning, Austrian corporatism has been judged, especially during the relatively affluent 1960s and 1970s, to have been an outstanding success. The Austrian economy enjoyed steady growth and a record on inflation and unemployment that was much better than the European norm. More remarkable, however, was Austria's record in preserving many aspects of corporatism during the recessionary 1980s and early 1990s. While other countries came to exhibit some of the more visible institutional features of corporatist decision making during the 1960s and 1970s, an effective corporatist system involves far more than mere institutions. It rests on a history and culture of collective accommodation that cannot simply be invented as the need arises. Thus, "Austrians have internalized attitudes and values of social partnership and apply them even when they appear to or do actually contradict their individual and immediate interests. Austrians even consider that, in the long term and overall, social partnership optimally realizes their individual preferences by collective regulation" (Gerlich et al., p. 218). Full-fledged corporatism, therefore, is a comprehensive and deep-rooted decision-making culture rather than just a collection of superficial institutions.

Tripartism and Social Partners

The theoretical notion of corporatism describes an ideal type of decision-making regime, unlikely to be found in its pure form in any European country. The Austrian corporatist system that we have just described is probably the fullest practical implementation in modern Europe, to the extent that, as we have seen, some have described it as a "model-generator." At the same time, as we saw in Table 14-1, if we concentrate on the key area of economic policy, it is possible to classify European countries as being more, or less, corporatist in their decision-making ethos. To a large extent this classification depends upon the "tripartite" integration of the two key social partners—trade unions and employers' associations—with government in the management of the economy. This in turn depends upon the extent to which the social partners can speak and act authoritatively on behalf of those they represent.

Two of the key variables that affect the system of economic policy making are the level of trade union membership within the working population and the centralization of wage bargaining, or the extent to which the national peak organizations for labor and employers are involved in negotiations over wage levels. In general terms, European trade union membership is "densest" in Scandinavia, with membership rates of around 90 percent in Denmark, Finland, Norway, and Sweden. It is much lower than this in France, the Netherlands, Spain, and Switzerland. The centralization of wage bargaining is highest in Austria and Scandinavia and much lower in France, Switzerland, Britain, and Italy.

A highly unionized work force combined with a centralized trade union movement does not, however, guarantee an effective system of corporatist decision making. Thus, although it is true that the Austrian trade union movement is highly centralized (virtually all trade unionists are members of the main trade union federation, the ÖGB), the level of trade union membership in the work force is high but not especially high. Belgium, for example, has a much higher level of trade union membership and a moderately centralized trade union movement, but most people agree that it has a much lower level of corporatist decision making than Austria. The Netherlands, in contrast, which is generally held to be significantly more corporatist than Britain, has a much lower level of trade union membership.

Perhaps the most important condition for effective tripartite wage bargaining is that the social partners are able to rely upon strong and effective peak organizations. In Germany, for example, the peak organization for the trade union movement is the German Federation of Trade Unions (DGB), which represents over 80 percent of all unionized workers. On the side of business and industry, there are three different peak organizations, but these do not compete with one another. The Federation of German Industries (BDI) concentrates on the political representation of business. The Confederation of German Employers' Associations (BDA) deals with social policy and the labor markets, including collective bargaining. The Association of German Chambers of Industry and Commerce (DIHT), representing nearly 3 million companies, all of which are obliged by law to affiliate, deals with trade and commerce. Thus, the three peak organizations representing the interests of capital coordinate their activities and often function as one. This division of the employers' peak organizations, however, as well as the fact that the DGB can negotiate on general prices and income strategy but cannot bind individual member unions in its negotiations, means that Germany is probably better thought of as an example of tripartism rather than full corporatism.

It is also the case that the institutions of tripartism can rise and fall in significance over a period of time, even in the absence of a more fundamental corporatist culture. In Ireland, for example, economic policy during the 1990s was based upon a series of tripartite deals between government, employers, and unions—including the "Programme for Competitiveness and Work" (PCW) and "Partnership 2000." These involved agreements upon wage levels, productivity arrangements, aspects of employment conditions, and government policy in areas such as taxation, investment incentives, and the provision of certain social welfare benefits. Such deals were instituted at a time of economic crisis, when the public finances were in disarray, inflation and unemployment were very high, and large numbers of young people were leaving Ireland to seek jobs elsewhere. The resulting national agreements between what are explicitly referred to in Ireland as the "social partners" contributed to a far more stable economic environment. There are doubtless many reasons to explain the remarkable growth of the Irish economy in the latter part of the 1990s, projected to continue well beyond 2000. But the industrial relations environment produced by the partnership deals is certainly one factor that was used to explain the large inflows of foreign investment that fuelled this growth. At the same time there was a widespread perception among the trade union movement, by the time the Partnership 2000 deal was coming to an end, that the fruits of the economic boom had not been shared fairly by the employers; this perception the prospect of future partnership deals in jeopardy.

Successful tripartite negotiations between the social partners can therefore generate a number of the effects attributed to a more comprehensive corporatist policy-making regime. Nonetheless, as we can see from the collapse of the 1970s "Social Contracts" in Britain, there is a real sense in which tripartism is only as good as its last deal. It is far less deeply rooted than the type of corporatist institutions that are grounded in more fundamental social attitudes about the institutional roles of the key social partners.

The Decline of Corporatism?

Views about the likely spread of corporatism were modified by the 1990s, as the institutions of corporatism appeared to decline in a number of countries during the preceding years of recession. This led to an increasing tendency to categorize corporatism as a "fair-weather" phenomenon: a form of concerted action that tends to fall apart when resources become scarcer and interest groups must bargain more competitively to divide up a pie that is fixed rather than one that is continually expanding (Keman and Whiteley).

Two further trends may well be leading to a decline in the importance of "purer" forms of corporatism in modern Europe. The first has to do with the ever-expanding role of the European Union in major economic policy making, particularly after the Maastricht Treaty cemented an agreement to develop a common European monetary system. As we have seen, the need for a "convergence" of European economies to underpin a common European currency, the euro, implied the need for participating

European governments to surrender some of the autonomy they had at least in theory traditionally employed to manipulate key instruments of macroeconomic policy, such as interest rates, exchange rates, and budget deficits. In addition, many other formerly national levers of economic policy have increasingly come under the auspices of the EU, including state supports to industry, competition policy, and regional policy.

As we saw when discussing EU decision making, national governments remain very important in this process, via their role in the European Council. Thus, traditional economic groups still set out to influence economic policy making at the EU level, one stage removed, by influencing national governments. But the traditional institutionalized channels of influence used by such groups have been undermined to the extent that decision making is moved to EU institutions in Brussels. Interest groups have not sat around twiddling their thumbs while this has happened, however, and many have set up very effective Brussels-based organizations designed to work directly on EU decision-making elites. Key groups may or may not have become more influential as a result of all of this, but the traditional corporatist model—entrenched as it is in what is essentially a national decision-making system—has undoubtedly been undermined.

A second important trend that may well have weakened traditional corporatist arrangements has to do with the very steady shift in the sources of wealth generation in European economics towards the service sector, in line with trends in all affluent countries. This has been accompanied by a weakening of the power of the traditional trade union movement. Modern high-tech and service industries have created an increasingly white-collar work force, a much more rapid turnover in employment histories, and new patterns of work, that have combined to undermine the industrial power of trade unions.

Notwithstanding these important trends, however, Siaroff's recent survey shows that even in the 1990s, there were still big differences between European countries in the extent of institutionalized involvement of the main social partners—especially employers and trade unions—in the process of managing national economies. This is especially true in relation to the involvement of the social partners in policy *implementation,* as well as policy making, which is, as we have seen, one of the key defining characteristics of corporatist systems.

PLURALISM

Like corporatism, pluralism has tended to occupy an uneasy no-man's-land between being a "normative" theory of how politics *ought* to be conducted and a "positive" theory of how groups *actually do* operate. As a normative theory, pluralism is one of the underpinnings of traditional liberal democracy, perhaps best summarized by Dahl (pp. 4–33). But this is not our main concern here. As a descriptive scheme, pluralism typically has been used to characterize interest group activity in systems such as Britain (and, for that matter, Canada and the United States), where groups put pressure on political elites in a relatively disorganized and competitive manner. This is in contrast to the well-ordered and co-operative interaction between groups and elites that is implied under pure forms of corporatism.

Even though pluralism has been criticized for being a vague and incomplete theory of politics (Jordan, 1990b), it does nonetheless have a set of striking features that allow us to regard it as a distinctive description of political decision making. Pluralism can be distinguished from corporatism in a number of respects. The most important of these is that pluralist interest groups have no formal institutional role in the allocation of resources and the implementation of policy. A second fundamental difference is that interest groups in a pluralist system are assumed to be self-generating and voluntary. This implies the existence of a range of different groups, typically competing with one another to represent the interests of the same classes of people in a given sphere of economic or social activity. A further assumption in much of pluralist theory is that although not all groups have equal levels of power or resources, it is nonetheless relatively easy for people to form an interest group and thereby gain at least some access to the levers of political power (Smith, p. 309). This suggests that many of the salient social interests in a pluralist system will be represented by the set of competing interest groups. New interests that might emerge, for one reason or another, can be represented in the political system as a result of the capacity of existing groups to adapt, or as a result of the relatively unhindered formation of new groups. (Good introductions to modern pluralist theory can be found in Jordan, 1990a and b, and in Smith.)

The basic process by which pluralist theorists assume popular interests to be represented in decision making involves groups influencing the output of the executive branch of government by applying "pressure" on political elites. Different groups compete with one another for the ear of decision makers, who are pressed in many different directions at the same time. Those groups that apply pressure most effectively (possibly because they have the most public support, but quite possibly also because they have the most resources or the most privileged access to elites) have the greatest success in bringing public policy closer to their own preferred positions.

Despite allegations made by some naive critics, few pluralists assume that the resources available to different groups are in any sense equal, or that different groups have equivalent access to key political decision makers. Most pluralists accept that the market in political influence is far from perfect, containing actors with very different capacities to affect important political decisions. In particular, many pluralists accept that business interests are often in a highly privileged position and that the state is far from neutral, favoring business interests or, indeed, favoring the particular interests of the bureaucracy. A clear statement of this "neopluralist" position can be found in Charles Lindblom's influential book *Politics and Markets.* For Lindblom, there are some "grand" issues that are effectively removed from public debate by the combined power of business interests and the state. The effect of this is that conventional pluralist politics operates most effectively in relation to what can be seen as "secondary" issues (Lindblom, p. 142). Even reconstructed pluralists are thus distinguished by their assumption that there is at least something important left to be contested in the accessible political arena, and that such contests take the form of applying political pressure to decision-making elites.

Political pressure can be applied in a number of ways, although these are not always very clearly specified by those who write about pluralism. In the sphere of prices and income policy, however, the process is relatively clear-cut. Policy is set on the basis of bargaining between groups, backed up by the threat of the economic sanctions that each group has at its disposal. In the last analysis, trade unions get their way in a pluralistic system not because they are in some sense integrated into the political process but because they can go on strike and thereby inflict damage on the employers or the government with which they are dealing. Similarly, employers have power because they control the means of production and can inflict pain by engaging in sackings, lockouts, and plant closures if they choose to do so.

Perhaps the single most distinctive feature of the pluralist account of decision making, therefore, is that it is characterized by conflict rather than consensus. Of course, conflict will not always manifest itself in the shape of strikes, lockouts, and so on. Rather, it is the threat of such sanctions, whether explicit or implicit, that underpins pluralist bargaining. Indeed, if the various actors are rational and equipped with perfect information, they will anticipate the outcome of any potential conflict and settle their differences before overt hostilities can begin. Actual observed conflicts—real-world strikes and lockouts—are, according to this view, the product of imperfect information. They are what happens when competing groups test each other's strengths and weaknesses. For all this, however, the outcome of political activity in a pluralist system is assumed to be the product of the balance of forces between the various groups involved. And this balance of forces is determined by the anticipated outcome of head-to-head confrontations over essential conflicts of interest.

Most people see pluralism and corporatism as being at opposite ends of a spectrum describing types of group politics. For this reason, studies that describe different countries as being more, or less, corporatist are also making judgments about the extent of pluralist decision making. Thus Table 14-1 is also, in the minds of most authors, a ranking of European countries in terms of the extent to which they have a type of group politics that can be described as pluralist. As we have already seen, a striking regularity in Table 14-1 is the tight cluster of the Mediterranean and English-speaking European democracies at the "pluralist" end of this spectrum. This group accounts for the seven countries reckoned by a large variety of authors to be the most pluralist. None of these countries has a long tradition of social democratic government in the postwar era, and all seem to be characterized by a more market-oriented style of interaction between the main social partners.

"Pluralism" in Britain

As we have just seen, Table 14-1 shows us that Britain is a key member of the "pluralist" cluster of modern European countries. During the 1970s, when the interest of political scientists in corporatism was at its zenith, even Britain was diagnosed as moving toward the corporatist model. This had much to do with the emergence of the "Social Contract" between the Labor government of the day; the main British trade union federation, the Trades Union Congress (TUC); and the main employers' federation, the Confederation of British Industry (CBI). This era was, however, short-lived. For most of the postwar era in Britain, "competitive" rather than "cooperative" has been the best way of describing interactions between the main social partners in Britain. Trade unions themselves have set great store by their right to "free collective bargaining," backed up by a right to strike that is often exercised. Even more than the unions, British employers have also been willing for the most part to take their chances in the rough-and-tumble of the labor market rather than getting involved in institutionalized collaboration with the unions.

This mode of economic policy making conforms closely to the model of a pluralist system based on a political market in which self-generating interest groups compete freely with one another to influence the flow of public policy. The argument that Britain is decidedly not a corporatist system thus rests on two important phenomena. The first is the general lack of integration of both unions and management into the policy-making process. The second is the apparent preference of both sides for confrontational methods of settling their differences.

The fragility of what appeared to be moves toward tripartite decision making in Britain, with the "Social Contract" of the mid-1970s, can be seen clearly from the speed with which confrontational bargaining was restored after the introduction of government-imposed wage ceilings in 1977. Equally striking is the success of the Conservative attack on trade union rights and privileges after Margaret Thatcher's election victory in May 1979. As early as July 1979, the Conservatives proposed a series of restrictions on trade union power. These included the banning of "secondary" picketing (that is, picketing away from the main scene of an industrial dispute); the restriction of closed shops (which oblige all who work in a particular employment to join a particular union); and the requirement that unions hold secret ballots of those involved before calling strikes. A series of laws restricting trade union power was passed shortly afterwards. Confrontation between government and unions came to a head in a long and very bruising miners' strike that began in March 1984 and that soured

Relations between the state and the labor movement turn violent in Britain as police in full riot gear confront striking miners, October 1984. (© *Alain Noques/Corbis/Sygma*)

industrial relations in Britain for some time afterwards. The Thatcherite approach to economic policy making in Britain was thus to use legislation to weaken the power of trade unions and then relegate these to the position of "mere" economic actors with no formal political role. These attacks on the trade unions were defended on the grounds that trade union power hinders the free play of market forces. A strong belief in the effectiveness of the market left no room for tripartite economic planning, involving agreements between government, employers, and unions.

In this regard, not a lot changed after the landslide election in 1997 of a Labor government under Tony Blair. The Conservatives complained during the 1997 election campaign that "New Labor," in order to be reelected, had taken over many aspects of Conservative economic policy. This is confirmed by research into the British party manifestos of 1997, which for the first time show that Labor was no longer the most left-wing of the mainstream British parties and had moved sharply towards the Conservatives on economic policy (Laver and Garry, 2000). Certainly, having taken office, Labor did not demonstrate a dramatic rolling back of the Thatcherite trade union legislation, or a conscious attempt to forge a new social contract between the social partners, or any real indication that Britain was likely to move away from an essentially pluralist form of interest group representation.

Pluralism in Action: The Women's Movement

While the corporatist model of interest group politics explicitly refers to the management of the economy, and to the role of unions and employers in this, the pluralist model is entirely open as to which particular interests might put pressure on the decision-making system. Indeed, one of the virtues claimed for pluralism by its champions is that a "free market" in influence can adapt to changes in society and allow new groups into the decision-making loop. Whether or not this claim is justified, changes both in the structure of society and in social attitudes do have the potential to change the focus of interest group politics. This can be seen quite clearly in the rise to prominence over the latter postwar years of both the women's movement and the environmental movement.

As we have seen in Chapter 11, women are systematically underrepresented at virtually every level of politics in virtually every European country. This underrepresentation arises not only within political parties and bureaucracies, but also in the peak organizations of the social partners (there are relatively few senior women among trade unionists or business leaders) and in entrenched economic and professional interest groups such as churches, farmers, and doctors. The political underrepresentation of women arises even in Scandinavia, where the women's movement has made more progress than anywhere else.

It is not surprising, therefore, that groups promoting women's interests may be forced to operate outside the traditional institutional structure. Of course, women's issues have also been pursued within existing organizations, be they trade unions or political parties. Those promoting women's issues inside such organizations have often met with limited success, however. Almost invariably, women's activists have found themselves in the role of "ginger groups" within organizations, from which position they have applied internal pressure for change with varying degrees of success. One of the best examples of this is the way in which many European trade unions have now been convinced—often not without a struggle—to campaign for equal pay and conditions for women who do the same jobs as men. Such intra-institutional campaigns for women's rights have had most success inside established public organizations in Scandinavia and the Netherlands. Here, successful policies of "mainstreaming" gender issues have resulted in a situation in which many traditional bodies are now sensitized to the need to offer equal opportunities to women.

However, campaigners for women's rights are also prominently involved outside traditional organizations, in single-issue pressure group politics of particular relevance to women. Obvious examples include abortion (Lovenduski and Outshoorn), divorce, domestic violence, and a range of equal rights causes (Dahlerup). A recent striking example has been the role played by the Women's Coalition at stages in the Northern Ireland peace process. In almost all cases, women's groups have found themselves outside traditional institutional patterns of influence, and their "outsider" status has meant that they have had to fight very hard for every centimeter of ground won since the 1960s. At the same time, however, activism by women's groups has probably forced at least the public face of many mainstream organizations to take women's issues more seriously than they did before. This is a good example of the way in which issues forced up the political agenda by one group may provoke changes in the issue positions of a range of other groups in a pluralist system— producing indirect rather than direct results from that particular interest group's activity.

Pluralism in Action: The Environmental Movement

The environmental movement in Europe has adopted a very different strategy in its attempt to have an impact on public policy. The effects of this can be seen in the rise of Green parties in many European countries, a phenomenon discussed in Chapter 8. Green parties tend to look quite unlike traditional political parties. Rather, they share many of the features of new social movements, described in the following section, with views that cut across traditional ideological lines, and very ambivalent attitudes towards the need for strong party leadership. This tendency is reinforced by the fact that only one Green party has been in a position of power at national level, and that only quite recently: the German Greens took cabinet seats in a coalition with the Social Democrats following the 1998 election. Indeed, with this exception, few Greens have ever had any real bargaining power in the formation of national governments, and the movement typically remains divided over even the merits of seeking power. The main impact of the Greens on environmental policy, therefore, has been indirect—in the "greening" of their main opponents, who adopted more environmentalist policies once it became clear that Green politics could attract votes. Many European party programs have become "greener" in response to this potential challenge.

Notwithstanding the electoral role of the Green parties, there are many other active environmental groups in Europe, most of which use more direct political strategies. The Greenpeace organization, to take just one example, has engaged in a series of effective and headline-grabbing campaigns, blocking an outfall from the British nuclear reprocessing plant at Sellafield and placing Greenpeace members in rubber dinghies between whaling ships and whales in the Antarctic or in the way of ships dumping toxic wastes in the North Sea. Many of these campaigns as a result generated dramatic newsreel footage, and Greenpeace's membership underwent dramatic short-term growth as a result.

Most environmental groups have almost no institutionalized access to power and are thus forced to rely on more direct forms of pressure. When state agencies are established to deal with environmental issues, for example, prominent individuals associated with environmental causes may be selected for some role or other, but there are very few examples in Europe of environmentalist groups being given formal consultative status. In part this may be because the more successful groups, such as Greenpeace, have been quite militant and have deliberately distanced themselves from the political establishment. In part it may be because established parties and other organizations have identified the politics of the environment as something that they can annex for themselves. They are therefore unwilling to allow environmentalist groups to use Green politics to gain any sort of foothold within the established system.

New Social Movements

The examples typically used to distinguish corporatist from pluralist decision-making systems tend to deal with the relations between the social partners representing organized labor and management. Major entrenched interest groups such as these are but a tiny fraction of the vast range of groups, with women's and environmental groups providing just a few examples, that can be found in every European country. In particular, there is a cluster of groups and organizations, together with more loosely defined structures that we might think of as "movements," that appear to have a fair amount in common with one another. As well as women's and environmental movements, almost all European countries now have active anti-racist, anti-war, or anti-colonialist groups, gay rights groups, animal rights and anti-nuclear groups, and groups promoting a range of more or less radical single-issue causes. Many of these share a number of features that, taken together characterize them as what have been called "new social movements" by political scientists (Jahn; Kriesi et al.; Rucht; Schmitt-Beck). They are seen by some as "postmaterialist" or "postmodern" successors to traditional political parties and entrenched interest organizations.

The "membership" of a typical new social movement—though this may well not be formally defined—tends to be rather fluid, with people drifting in and out of affiliation with a movement or cause on a rather casual basis. The "leadership"—though some of these groups are actively opposed to any notion of formal leadership—often cut its political teeth during the period of student radicalism of the late 1960s and early 1970s. The views these movements represent tend to cut across traditional ideological lines. Thus, those who support the women's movement or the environmental movement may have views on other matters that might put them on either the traditional right or the traditional left of the political spectrum. Indeed, they may have views that combine elements of what traditionally has been thought of as right- or left-wing thinking. Radical feminists may favor censorship of what they see as pornography just as strongly as those who promote traditional family values. Radical environmentalists may promote what conservative farmers would defend as traditional farming methods, and so on. It is fair to say, however, that in general these groups would typically be seen to align much more with the left than with the right of the traditional ideological spectrum.

In terms of internal organization, those supporting new social movements tend to feel strongly in favor of active participation and group democracy, rather than the more passive membership and hierarchical decision-making structures of a traditional political party, trade union, or interest group. Some new social movements, as we have seen, may even refuse to acknowledge that they have any "leadership" at all. When it comes to intervening in the political process, they tend to work outside traditional institutional channels. Demonstrations, boycotts, and other forms of direct action are preferred to lobbying, letter writing, petitions, and more conventional pressure tactics (Dalton, 1996). Direct action such as this serves a number of purposes for new social movements. It mobilizes and engages members who would otherwise be alienated from the political process; it forces new issues onto at least the media's political agenda; and it maintains the group's status as a radical outsider, rather than as a co-opted part of the traditional establishment. For all of these reasons, new social movements fit more easily with a pluralist than with a corporatist view of the world of political decision making. Indeed, new social movements, particularly when these meet with some success, might even be considered as advertisements for the pluralist model, which holds the notion of an open and accessible market in political influence as one of its central normative justifications.

THE NEW PLURALISM? POLICY NETWORKS

As we have seen, political scientists increasingly have come to see the "pure" corporatist and pluralist models as being too simplistic to handle the complex ways in which the social actors of civil society influence decision making in modern Europe. The concepts that have emerged tend to blend aspects of the entrenched integration in policy making implied by corporatism, with aspects of the informality and practical power politics implied by pluralism.

Two very important and related political developments that are leading to changes in the ways that interest groups do their business derive from the general "globalization" of economic life and the continual accumulation of functions by the European Union. Both have the effect that key decisions are increasingly made—and thus must be influenced—at the supranational level. The European Union is itself a quite distinctive decision-making system, quite unlike any single national government and blending elements of pluralism and corporatism in its decision-making style. For many interest groups, it is very important to influence EU decisions, since these may bear far more upon their interests than any decision taken by a national government. For European farmers, for example, EU agricultural policy has a direct and vital bearing upon how easy it is for each of them to earn a living.

In response to this development, we have seen the growth in importance of European "peak" organizations that reflect interests (of farmers, for example, or trade unions) at a supranational level. These peak organizations do have direct access to EU decision-making elites. This means that it is possible for a national interest group to bypass its national government completely, and to attempt to influence EU decision making either directly, or through its European peak organization. Alternatively, or indeed at the same time, a national interest group may put pressure on its national government in an attempt to influence EU policy via the government's role in the Council of Ministers. (For an analysis of the various channels open to those trying to influence EU agricultural policy, see Pappi and Henning, 1999.)

This system of "multilevel" governance has created a very complex environment for the exercise of group influence on key decisions. Many actors are trying to influence one another and are exploring different routes through a complicated system of interactions. One way of trying to make sense of such a complex system of links, whether within the EU or elsewhere, is to see them as a network. This has led to a distinctive way to study the paths that interest groups use to influence policy, which is to describe and analyze the entire system as a "policy network." David Knoke (p. 508) captures what most writers mean by a policy network as "a heterogeneous set of persons or organizations, linked by one or more relationships into an enduring social structure with the potential to influence public policy decisions of interest to the network's members."

The key relationships behind the idea of a policy network are those of mutual interdependence, and therefore of exchanges, between key actors in the policy-making system. These relationships are important because, as König and Bräuninger (p. 448) put it, "no one actor is capable of deciding public policies in western democracies." Since all policy influence involves interaction with others, when a public or private actor interacts over and over again with the same set of other actors, both sides steadily learn about each other and begin to develop well-defined mutual interactions. Thus, farmers' organizations these days deal repeatedly with their national Department of Agriculture, with farmers' organizations in other countries, with European "peak" organizations for farmers, and with particular offices of the European Commission. Each has information the other values. Each may be helpful to the other in some part of the process of either making or implementing policy. Thus, relationships between the various actors, including both private actors and agencies of national or supranational government, come to be conducted according to clearly understood informal rules of the game that can be as potent as formal institutions. This set of established interactions can be thought of as a policy network. (For thorough introductions to the literature on policy networks, see Thatcher (1998); Pappi and Henning (1998). For a skeptical view, see Dowding.)

Policy networks differ from corporatist decision-making structures in the crucial sense that a network of relationships between key actors is not hierarchical (van Waarden). Corporatist decision structures are pyramid-shaped and are organized from the top down. Policy networks, on the other hand, look like spiders' webs. The notion of a policy network might in this way seem to bridge the gap between pluralist and corporatist models of policy making. However, we still need to know which actors have the power to influence which decisions in which political arenas if we are to tell an accurate story about how any particular policy dispute is settled.

Policy Networks in Action: Doctors

Physicians are typically organized as members of a self-governing profession. This provides an important basis for the exercise of political power on behalf of sectional interests. The key powers associated with the professional status of physicians derive from the fact that health care is an expert service, one that cannot properly be evaluated by its consumers or even by non-specialist political elites. This gives doctors the more or less unchallenged ability to define and defend professional standards of medical practice and therefore to control medical training and licensing—and hence access to the profession. This control is typically exercised by a powerful guild-like medical association to which all licensed physicians must belong. The medical association typically also plays a vital policy implementation role, besides controlling professional ethics and standards (and thus practice) via a system of peer review. Politicians can make all the policies they want on health and medicine, but they cannot implement such policies effectively without the cooperation of the medical profession, organized by the medical association. This gives the medical lobby a very powerful position in the policy process.

The control of highly specialized information by the profession, and the need for the cooperation of physicians in the effective implementation of policy, form the basis of an exchange relationship between physicians and decision-making elites that can very usefully be thought of as a policy network. In practice, European medical associations are incorporated into political decision making in ways that vary somewhat from country to country. In Germany, for example, the process of making health policy has taken on a decidedly corporatist flavor since the establishment of a Concerted Action organization in 1977. This has a sixty-member council, with representatives of medical associations, hospitals, insurers, and government, that makes annual recommendations on health care spending and doctors' pay (Altenstetter; Dohler).

> Despite some attempts by governments to clip doctors' wings, the autonomy of German physicians remains unchallenged. . . . On the macroeconomic level, their participation in a corporatist negotiating institution serves as a buffer against possible threats to professional autonomy . . . [facilitating] package deals between government and physicians, such as moderate fee increases in return for restricted access to medical schools. On the regional and local level the extensive self-governing authority, which is legally as well as structurally established . . . makes changes in the power structure extremely difficult to implement. (Dohler, pp. 186–88)

The situation in Sweden is rather different, despite the existence of the centralized Swedish Medical Association (SLF), which represents about 90 percent of all Swedish physicians (Dohler, p. 193). The SLF has monopoly bargaining rights in negotiations over pay and conditions, but the effectiveness of such an apparently powerful position was undermined by the decentralization of the responsibility for health care provision to Swedish local councils (Lane and Arvidson). What the Swedish example teaches us is that a powerful and hierarchical medical association can have a major impact on national policy making at an elite level, but its ability to influence a much larger set of local policy makers may be much weaker. At the local level of politics, the electoral concerns of politicians are more likely to prevail over sectional interests, and policy makers seem less likely to be co-opted into the received wisdom of what is good and bad about medical policy.

Overall, however, the Swedish case seems to be the exception to the European norm. When health policy is made at the national level, medical associations in Europe appear to be able to exploit with potent effect their ability to monopolize the market in expertise—a situation also found in the United States, given the political role of the American Medical Association. And the exercise of this monopoly inevitably gives them both control over vital information and a key role in the implementation, as well as the making, of health care policy. This creates the type of mutual interdependency between decision makers and interest organizations that can fruitfully be seen as a policy network.

Policy Networks in Action: Farmers

There is a strong tradition in Europe for farmers' groups to be very well integrated into the political system, wielding disproportionately more influence over policy makers than many other types of economic actor—the consumers of farm products, for example, or the unemployed. A succession of wars in Europe has led governments to cultivate indigenous food producers very carefully and set up a policy-making regime based upon assumptions of mutual interdependence between decision makers and interest groups—in other words, to set up a policy network. As a result, there has been a long tradition of farm support programs, typically involving government intervention in agricultural markets at guaranteed prices, to protect the interests of farmers. For those countries in what has become the European Union (EU), this tradition was enshrined in the Common Agricultural Policy (CAP), with its system of intervention prices and consequent "mountains" of stored butter or grain and "lakes" of surplus wine or milk. Payoffs for farmers have been immense (see Chapter 5). The very generous terms of the CAP, for a long time the most important and expensive feature of EU economic policy though its importance has been declining in recent years, are a testimony to the key role of the farmers' lobby in each of the member states.

It is probably fair to say that the prominence of the CAP from the early days of European integration has meant that agricultural policy making was one of the first to involve a very explicit and effective policy network that operated at a supranational level. Farmers' organizations quickly learned that they needed to pile on the pressure in Brussels as well as in their national capitals, and quickly adapted to take account of this. This was made easier because the power of the farmers' lobby is usually exercised, even in pluralist systems such as Britain's, in a very institutionalized way. Farmers' organizations, such as the British National Farmers' Union (NFU), have traditionally had consultative status with ministries of agriculture on many matters. Farmers and civil servants have tended to settle matters between themselves and to exclude other interest groups if at all possible (Smith, p. 313). It has been quite common, furthermore, for farmers' groups to be involved in policy implementation, especially in relation to the distribution among individual farmers of the official national and regional production quotas for particular agricultural commodities. (Such quotas tend to go hand in hand with above-market intervention prices, which would otherwise lead to massive overproduction.)

BOX 14-1

ECONOMIC POLICY MAKING

France

The low level of unionization, divisions in the French labor movement, and the fact that the left did not come to power in France until 1981 have led most people to characterize economic policy making in France as confrontational and pluralist rather than corporatist. A small number of big labor unions have been important, each traditionally associated with a political party rather than with a trade or an industry. Thus, political divisions have been reproduced in the union movement, which has rarely been a united, monolithic bloc working against either government or employers. When there have been income policies—for example, in the early 1980s—these have not been based on tripartite agreements between the social partners. Instead, they have been imposed by the government. Both unions and employers are unwilling to sacrifice their autonomy, and even during periods of socialist government, relations between unions and government have not been particularly close.

Germany

Although the level of unionization is not high, unions are organized on an industry rather than a craft basis, and so all employees at a particular facility belong to the same union. The German Federation of Trade Unions (DGB) represents the vast majority of unionized workers; it deals with union-government relations, while individual unions take care of collective bargaining over wages and conditions. Different employers' federations coordinate their actions rather than compete with one another. There have been periods of explicit "concerted action" when the social partners negotiated an economic program of prices and incomes that was implemented by the government. In general, the social partners in Germany have been oriented toward negotiation rather than confrontation in economic policy making. Some sections of the union movement became more confrontational during the 1980s and 1990s, at least partly in response to economic problems arising from reunification.

Italy

Italy is characterized by a set of labor unions divided on political lines rather than in terms of crafts or industries. Despite the relatively low level of unionization, there are three competing union federations—the CGIL, the CISL, and the UIL—confronting a single employers' federation, the Confindustria. Despite this, there have been periods during which the social partners attempted to emulate the concerted action arrangements found in northern Europe, notably the period of "national solidarity," from 1977 to 1979, when wage restraint was traded for a program of legislation on matters ranging from youth employment to pension reform. Also notable was the Tripartite Agreement of 1983, which traded wage restraint for an improvement in the conditions of service for employed workers. Deals such as these have not expanded into more broadly based tripartite arrangements, however, and relations between the social partners have remained essentially market-oriented and pluralistic.

Netherlands

Economic policy making in the Netherlands has proved hard for political scientists to classify. The level of unionization is low by European standards, and the major trade union federation does not have a high share of trade union membership. Yet, economic policy making has a broadly cooperative style. Unions have engaged in centralized bargaining with the government, though a strong bureaucratic tradition in the Netherlands has tended to mean that such negotiations are usually dominated by the state. Dutch unions, compared with unions in most other European states, have placed a heavier emphasis in their dealings with government on the development of an extensive system of welfare benefits. In this regard, they have been quite successful, and levels of welfare benefits in the Netherlands are among the highest in Europe. The economy of the Netherlands is one of the most open in Europe, with very high levels of foreign investment. This tends to restrict the impact of indigenous employers on the economy and hence their role as social partners.

Spain

Spain under Franco was a totalitarian state, with government domination of all aspects of economic life over a very long period. In post-Franco Spain, as in France and Italy, unions are organized along political lines, and the level of unionization is relatively low. Nonetheless, there has been a series of pacts between government, the two key peak organizations of unions (the CCOO and the UGT), and a single peak employers' federation (the CEOE), beginning with the Moncloa Pact of 1977. These pacts dealt with wage restraint, on the one hand, and a restrained approach to the problem of rectifying public finances, on the other. Although unions and employers were involved in the negotiation of the pacts, which have continued under both bourgeois and socialist governments, they had little formal role in their implementation.

Sweden

After Austria, Sweden is typically regarded as one of Europe's classic cases of corporatist policy making. The level of trade union membership is the highest in Europe, and unions are incorporated in an executive role in the administration of labor market policies. Swedish industry tends to be export-oriented, concentrated, and strong, and there is a traditionally powerful state. For most of the postwar period, Swedish politics has been dominated by the Social Democratic Party, giving the Swedish unions much more sustained access to political elites than unions in most other European countries. All of this has contributed to a situation in which each of the social partners has felt able to negotiate with the others from a position of strength. Unions have accepted relatively lower wage increases in exchange for stable, full employment and a high level of welfare benefits. Employers have conceded high levels of job security for wage restraint. There were some signs, however, that the "Swedish model" was beginning to break down by the 1990s, as inflation in Sweden rose well above inflation in Sweden's European trading partners and employers' groups, and conservative politicians increasingly promoted more liberal free market policies.

United Kingdom

Often cited as one of the classic examples of a pluralist rather than corporatist system, the United Kingdom has a relatively decentralized system of wage bargaining. Wage negotiations are conducted by a large number of trade unions and are organized on a craft basis rather than on an industry basis, and so many unions may well be involved in simultaneous negotiations with a single employer—a car manufacturer, for example. Most but not all unions are affiliated with a relatively weak national federation, the Trade Union Congress (TUC), and the proportion of the work force belonging to trade unions is about average by European standards. For a brief period during the mid-1970s, there was a "Social Contract" between unions, employers [represented by the Confederation of British Industry (CBI)], and a Labor government. This collapsed after unilateral action by the government, however, and has not since been renewed. Relations between unions and government have been essentially confrontational since then, and a substantial package of anti-union legislation introduced by Margaret Thatcher's Conservative government has been left largely unchanged by the Labor government that took power in 1997.

The political clout of farmers is not confined to the corridors of power, however, and farmers' groups have a long tradition of direct action, including large-scale demonstrations and blockades. A recent example can be found in skirmishes on the fringes of the 1999 "beef war" between Britain and France, provoked by France's continued refusal to import British beef, after an international team of vets had decided that Britain's epidemic of "mad cow" disease was largely under control. Threats of a reciprocal measures against French beef in Britain (on the grounds that French cattle were being fed, among other things, with products derived from animal and human excrement) provoked a brief blockade of the channel ports by tractor-driving French farmers. This was the latest in a series of disputes between Britain and France in which policy disagreements between politicians had quickly filtered down to local farmers' organizations and French farmers had taken direct action on the streets in support of policy objectives shared with the French decision-making elite.

France and Britain are by no means unique. The access of farmers' groups to policy-making elites is very good indeed in many European countries. This close cooperation between the farmers and the civil service might on the face of it look almost corporatist. However, the lack of any formal role in the political equation for any other "social partner" identifies this type of decision-making arrangement as being more like a closed policy network than an example of full-fledged corporatism.

CONCLUSION

Most recent developments in both the theory and the empirical analysis of interest representation imply that we are asking the wrong question if we ask whether a particular political system as a whole is characterized by corporatist or pluralist policy making. Political scientists these days concentrate much more on policy making within particular sectors. Corporatists see this as "sectoral corporatism." Pluralists make a distinction between sectors characterized by particular "policy networks," which include some groups and exclude others, and those in which there is a more traditionally free-for-all pluralist competition between groups.

Even in a country such as Austria, the "model-generator" that all commentators agree has provided the clearest example of corporatist decision making in modern Europe, corporatism is concerned mainly with economic policy, especially with prices and income policy. A great many groups that represent important political interests have nothing to do with corporatist decision making. At the other end of the scale—even in Britain, cited by most as having a very clear-cut pluralist decision-making regime—there is an officially established state church, there are self-governing professions in the key areas of law and medicine, there is very close interaction between farmers' groups and the relevant government department, and there has been a major experiment with "contracts" between the social partners over prices and incomes.

The parallel development of the pluralist notion of a policy network and the notion of sectoral corporatism highlights the fact that as each approach has come to terms with the other's arguments, the two approaches have grown together. Nonetheless, given the vital importance of economic policy making and the role of employers and trade unions in this, it does still make some sense to classify countries in terms of the extent to which the economic policy arena, at least, is characterized by corporatist or pluralist institutions. In some countries, the ones that we might think of as being more corporatist, a small number of powerful, authoritative, and centralized "peak" organizations monopolize the legitimate right to participate in the policy making and implementing of economic policy. In other countries, which we might think of as being more pluralist, trade union and employers' federations may well get their voices heard, but only if they make an explicit and often divisive political effort to do so. And these groups rarely participate in policy implementation.

In all countries, however, the only recourse for groups outside the political establishment—and these are inevitably the vast majority of groups anywhere—is the traditional portfolio of techniques that characterize pressure politics. In most European countries, we can find a range of groups sharing features of organization, membership, and strategy that identify them as new social movements. These groups provide a medium of interest representation quite distinct from traditional parties, unions, and interest organizations. Whenever groups operate outside the political establishment, however, the fact remains that policy outcomes are determined, as often as not, by the different access of different groups to resources and threats, as well as to efficient, effective, and well-connected members.

REFERENCES

Altenstetter, C.: "Hospital Planners and Medical Professionals in the Federal Republic of Germany," in G. Freddi and J. W. Bjorkman (eds.), *Controlling Medical Professionals: The Comparative Politics of Health Governance,* Sage, London, 1989.

Cawson, A.: *Corporatism and Political Theory,* Basil Blackwell, Oxford, 1986.

Dahl, R. A.: *A Preface to Democratic Theory,* University of Chicago Press, Chicago, 1956.

Dahlerup, D. (ed.): *The New Women's Movement: Feminism and Political Power in Europe and the USA,* Sage, London, 1986.

Dalton, Russell: *Citizen Politics,* 2d ed., Chatham House, Chatham, New Jersey, 1996.

Dohler, M.: "Physicians' Professional Autonomy in the Welfare State: Endangered or Preserved?", in G. Freddi and J. W. Bjorkman (eds.), *Controlling Medical Professionals: The Comparative Politics of Health Governance,* Sage, London, 1989.

Dowding, Keith: "Model or Metaphor? A Critical Review of the Policy Network Approach," *Political Studies,* vol. 43, 1995, pp. 136–58.

Gerlich, P., E. Grande, and W. Müller: "Corporatism in Crisis: Stability and Change of Social Partnership in Austria," *Political Studies,* vol. 36, no. 2, 1988, pp. 209–23.

Jahn, D.: "The Rise and Decline of New Politics and the Greens in Sweden and Germany: Resource Dependence and New Social Cleavages," *European Journal of Political Research,* vol. 24, 1993, pp. 177–94.

Jordan, G.: "Sub-governments, Policy Communities and Networks: Refilling Old Bottles," *Journal of Theoretical Politics,* vol. 2, no. 3, 1990a, pp. 319–38.

Jordan, G.: "The Pluralism of Pluralism: An Anti-theory?" *Political Studies,* vol. 38, no. 2, 1990b, pp. 286–301.

Kavanagh, D.: *British Politics: Continuities and Change,* 2d ed., Oxford University Press, Oxford, 1990.

Keman, H., and P. Whiteley: "Coping with Crisis: Divergent Strategies and Outcomes," in H. Keman, H. Paloheimo, and P. Whiteley (eds.), *Coping with the Economic Crisis: Alternative Responses to Economic Recession in Advanced Industrial Societies,* Sage, London, 1987.

König, Thomas, and Thomas Bräuninger: "The Formation of Policy Networks: Preferences, Institutions and Actors' Choice," *Journal of Theoretical Politics,* vol. 10, 1998, pp. 445–71.

Knoke, David: "Who Steals My Purse Steals Trash: The Structure of Organizational Influence Reputation," *Journal of Theoretical Politics,* vol. 10, 1998, pp. 507–30.

Kriesi, H., R. Koopmans, J. W. Duyvendak, and M. G. Giugni: "New Social Movements and Political Opportunities in Western Europe," *European Journal of Political Research,* vol. 22, 1992, pp. 219–44.

Lane, J. -E., and S. Arvidson: "Health Professionals in the Swedish System," in G. Freddi and J. W. Bjorkman (eds.), *Controlling Medical Professionals: The Comparative Politics of Health Governance,* Sage, London, 1989.

Laver, Michael, and John Garry: "Estimating Policy Positions from Political Texts," *American Journal of Political Science,* vol. 44, forthcoming, 2000.

Lehmbruch, G.: "Liberal Corporatism and Party Government," in P. Schmitter and G. Lehmbruch (eds.), *Trends towards Corporatist Intermediation,* Sage, London, 1979.

Lijphart, Arend: *Patterns of Democracy: Government Forms and Performance in Thirty-Six Countries,* Yale University Press, New Haven, 1999.

Lindblom, C.: *Politics and Markets,* Basic Books, New York, 1977.

Lovenduski, J., and J. Outshoorn: *The New Politics of Abortion,* Sage, London, 1986.

Luther, Richard, and Wolfgang Müller (eds.): *Politics in Austria: Still a Case of Consociationalism?* Frank Cass, London, 1992.

Marin, B.: "From Consociationalism to Technocorporatism: The Austrian Case as a Model-Generator?" in I. Scholten (ed.), *Political Stability and Neo-Corporatism: Corporatist Integration and Societal Cleavages in Western Europe,* Sage, London, 1987.

Pappi, Franz, and Christian Henning: "Policy Networks: More than a Metaphor," *Journal of Theoretical Politics,* vol. 10, 1998, pp. 553–76.

Pappi, Franz, and Christian Henning: "The Organization of Influence on the EC's Common Agricultural Policy: A Network Approach," *European Journal of Political Research,* vol. 36, 1999, pp. 257–81.

Rucht, D. (ed.): *Research on Social Movements: The State of the Art in Western Europe and the USA,* Campus Verlag and Westview Press, Frankfurt and Boulder, Colo., 1991.

Schmitt-Beck, R.: "A Myth Institutionalised: Theory and Research on New Social Movements in Germany," *European Journal of Political Research,* vol. 21, 1992, pp. 357–84.

Siaroff, Alan: "Corporatism in 24 Industrial Democracies: Meaning and Measurement," *European Journal of Political Research,* vol. 36, 1999, pp. 175–205.

Smith, M. J.: "Pluralism, Reformed Pluralism and Neopluralism: The Role of Pressure Groups in Policy-Making," *Political Studies,* vol. 38, no. 2, 1990, pp. 302–22.

Thatcher, Mark: "The Development of Policy Network Analysis: from Modest Origins to Overarching Frameworks," *Journal of Theoretical Politics,* vol. 10, 1998, pp. 389–416.

van Waarden, F.: "New Dimensions and Types of Policy Networks," *European Journal of Political Research,* vol. 21, 1992, pp. 29–52.

Wiarda, H. J.: *Corporatism and Comparative Politics,* M. E. Sharpe, New York, 1997.

Woldendorp, Jaap: "Neo-corporatism as a strategy for conflict regulation in the Netherlands," *Acta Politica,* vol. 30, 1995, pp. 121–51.

15

BUILDING REPRESENTATIVE GOVERNMENT IN POSTCOMMUNIST EUROPE

Up to now we have been dealing in this book with the politics of relatively long-established democracies, and we have been writing about how the process of representative government actually works. In this final chapter, which goes beyond Western Europe and looks at the experiences of four postcommunist democracies in East Central Europe (ECE)—Hungary, Poland, and the formerly federated Czech and Slovak republics—we are concerned with problems of a wholly different order, as we are dealing with countries that, following decades of authoritarian communist rule, have been engaged in the very building of representative government (for a general overview, see Ágh, 1998).

At the same time, however, none of these four countries is totally without experience in this task. Czechoslovakia, for example, which was created as an independent state in 1918 through the merger of Bohemia, Moravia and parts of Silesia, and Slovakia, had been one of the very few countries outside the West to maintain throughout the interwar years a system of parliamentary democracy. This system lasted until the invasion by Germany in 1938, when the country was effectively divided, with the Czech lands—Bohemia and Moravia-Silesia—being absorbed as a German "protectorate," and Slovakia being governed by a pro-Nazi puppet regime. Czechoslovakia was liberated in 1945, and its first postwar elections in 1946 recorded a narrow victory for an alliance between Communists and Social Democrats. Two years later, in 1948, this brief restoration of democracy was ended when the communists seized power on their own in a coup d'etat, forcing the country into the Soviet bloc. A Soviet-style constitution was adopted, in which the leading role of the Communist party was guaranteed.

Twenty years later, with the advent to power in January 1968 of a new Communist party leader, Alexander Dubcek, and in what was to become known as the "Prague

Spring," the regime began to be liberalized both economically and culturally. It was to prove a short-lived experiment. Dubcek, who was a Slovak, was deposed following a military invasion by Warsaw Pact forces in August 1968, being later expelled from the Communist party, and the country was brought fully under the control of the Soviet Union. Thereafter, with an ostensibly federal structure that granted limited autonomy to the Czech Republic and to Slovakia, it remained an orthodox communist regime, which was completely loyal to Moscow and which proved extraordinarily resistant to change. As Musil has noted; "In hardly any country of the Soviet bloc was the official doctrine after 1968 more devoid of ideas, more sterile and irrelevant for solving the important issues of society and state" (p. 177).

Hungary also emerged as an independent state in 1918 following the dissolution of the Austro-Hungarian empire at the end of World War I. Hungary was unlike Czechoslovakia, however, in that democracy failed to take root; the regime that developed during the interwar years took the form of a right-wing dictatorship under the leadership of Admiral Horthy. Horthy allied Hungary with the German forces during World War II, until it was eventually taken over by Soviet forces in early 1945. The first free elections were also held in 1945, in which the conservative agrarian Small-holders' party received an overall majority of the vote, with the Soviet-backed Communist party polling some 17 percent, and the Social Democrats 7 percent. The latter two parties then merged to create the Hungarian Workers' party (later renamed the Hungarian Socialist Workers' party) in 1948 and seized control of government, banning all other political formations and bringing Hungary firmly within the control of the Soviet bloc. A failed uprising against communist rule in 1956 led to several years of repression before the regime itself began to liberalize in the late 1960s, introducing quite widespread free market reforms in the economy while remaining fully committed to Soviet leadership in the foreign policy domain.

In the Polish case, the establishment of an independent republic in 1918 also led to a brief period of democratic rule, albeit one characterized by profound political instability. The democratic system was fatally undermined in 1926, following the installation of an increasingly authoritarian regime under the leadership of Jozef Pilsudski, a former army commander and leader of the Polish Socialist party (Rothschild, pp. 26–72). The invasion of Poland by Germany in 1939 led to the incorporation into the Nazi Reich of the west of the country, while the east was essentially colonized by the Nazis until it was overrun by the advancing Russian army in 1944. The Russians immediately established a communist-led coalition government in the liberated part of the country, and following the final defeat and expulsion of the German forces in the rest of Poland in 1945, the communist forces also proved the dominant element in the new all-Polish government. In 1947, communist-backed candidates secured an overwhelming majority in what was the first, but at the same time heavily manipulated, postwar election, and the new government went on to declare the creation of a "People's Republic." In 1952, the ruling Communist Party introduced a Soviet-style constitution, and thereafter, despite persistent waves of popular protest, strikes, and demonstrations in 1956, 1968, 1970, and 1976, which twice forced the replacement of the Communist party leader, Poland remained fully absorbed within the Soviet bloc.

THE RULES OF THE GAME: MAKING NEW CONSTITUTIONS

Prior to the eventual collapse of communist rule in 1989, each of these countries had therefore experienced at least four decades of authoritarian government, and each was therefore obliged to build a new system of representative government more or less from scratch. In so doing, and as is the case in all newly established democracies, the constitution makers were faced with a series of fundamental choices regarding the type of democratic regime that they were to construct (Lijphart, 1991, 1992; Zielonka).

Executives and Legislatures

Among the most crucial alternatives that they confronted was the question of whether they should operate within a primarily presidential system, as in the United States, where the executive is elected independently of the parliament and does not depend on support from within the parliament in order to remain in office, or should aim more toward a parliamentary system, like most of the countries that we have discussed in this book, where the executive is elected by and is responsible to the legislature (see Chapters 3 and 4). In the event, as we shall see, they all opted for parliamentary systems, although in Poland, following closely the French model, the government appointed by parliament was to share executive authority with a separately elected and quite powerful president. In addition, in 1998, the Slovak constitution was also amended to provide for the direct election of the president, although in this case the powers of the office are more ceremonial than substantive.

Another crucial choice they faced was how to manage the building of new democratic institutions. The first step was relatively easy: the immediate removal of the communist bar on competitive multiparty elections. To this was usually added a commitment to help fund the emergence of new political parties. Thereafter, it was a question of whether to sit down immediately to draw up a complete constitution for the new regime, or to proceed in a more piecemeal fashion through a series of amendments to the already existing communist constitution. Both the Czech and Slovak republics opted for the former strategy, and once it was known that the former Czechoslovak federation would dissolve, they devised their new rules in a matter of months (Kopecky). In fact, they had little choice in the matter. Apart from the change in regime—from a communist to a democratic system—they were also confronted with a change in the form of the state, from a federation to two separate republics. Simply to amend the existing constitution would therefore have been inadequate. In Hungary and Poland, on the other hand, reform proceeded through a series of stages. Poland initially worked with an amended version of the existing rules, and then adopted a new and more limited set of rules known as the "Little Constitution" before finally, in 1997, adopting a completely new constitution (Meer Krok-Paszowska). Hungary also proceeded to build democracy by amending the existing rules, and has not yet succeeded in adopting a wholly new constitution (Körösényi).

Even when definitive rules and institutions were finally agreed on, however—and in the Polish case in particular this involved a prolonged and sometimes very intense political debate—their implications in practice remained sometimes uncertain. It was one thing to specify on paper the different roles of the prime minister and president, for example, but it was quite another to work out a proper *modus vivendi* between the two officeholders in practice. This would take time, and, as we shall see, it is still far from settled.

Hungary   The Hungarian political system that was constructed following the collapse of the communist regime is a straightforward parliamentary system, with a powerful executive and yet with a relatively powerful and independent parliament. The constitution itself derives from a series of amendments to the former communist constitution that were passed by parliament both before and after the first multiparty election in 1990. Prior to this election, constitutional amendments had required a two-thirds majority in parliament, and in the immediate aftermath of the election the leader of the opposition Alliance of Free Democrats (SZDSZ) agreed with the new government not to stand in the way of further changes as long as this two-thirds rule was maintained for future constitutional amendments; the rule was extended to include other special legislation, including laws governing the press and the media; and parliament would also elect the president, the head of state. The SZDSZ in particular had been concerned that a system of popular presidential elections might have led to the election of a candidate from the reformed communist party, the Hungarian Socialist party (MSZP). In August 1990 the parliament elected Arpad Göncz, a member of the SZDSZ, as Hungary's first postcommunist president.

The parliament itself is unicameral and is responsible for electing the prime minister. As is also the case in Poland, the prime minister can be dismissed by the parliament only through a "constructive vote of no confidence," which requires the parliament to achieve prior agreement on the election of a successor. This is the device originally conceived in the German Basic Law in 1949 in order to help ensure executive stability, and it was also adopted in the new Spanish constitution following the Spanish transition to democracy in the mid-1970s. In addition, the prime minister appoints the members of the cabinet, and these cannot be dismissed by parliament unless parliament first dismisses the prime minister. They are accountable only to the prime minister.

Although these provisions might suggest that the executive can operate quite separately from the legislature, the system in fact places a lot of weight on the independent power of parliament. Executive authority is limited first by the "two-thirds" rule, whereby key decisions have to be agreed on by a two-thirds majority in parliament. This obviously restricts the capacity for narrow majoritarianism. Second, the system limits the executive by denying the prime minister the right to dissolve parliament and call new elections. Parliament may dissolve itself, but it cannot be dissolved by the government. Nor does the president, who, as noted, is also elected by parliament, enjoy many formal powers. He or she may order the dissolution of parliament, but only in limited circumstances, such as when parliament has passed a succession of no-confidence votes in the government; he or she can also refer bills to parliament for reconsideration, but without any veto power. (In addition, the president may refer bills to the constitutional court, which is composed of ten judges who are elected by a two-thirds majority of parliament and who serve for a nine-year period.) The result, according to Körösényi's valuable overview (pp. 157–69), is an emphatically dualistic parliamentary system, in which both parliament and the executive may work quite independently of each other, but in which they are also obliged to cooperate in order to ensure stable government.

Almost from the very beginning of the new democracy, however, ambiguities in the wording of the constitution, together with political conflicts between the SZDSZ and the then leading government party, the Hungarian Democratic Forum (MDF), provoked concern about the effectiveness of the new political structures and about the division of competencies between the president and the prime minister. In early 1991, for example, a dispute arose about whether Hungary should be represented by the president or by the prime minister at a crucial international summit involving the then Czechoslovakia, Hungary, and Poland; eventually, both politicians attended. Soon after this, a row developed over whether the government had the right to reorganize the military without first consulting the president. Still later, the president refused to confirm the government's nominees to senior positions in the Hungarian television network on the grounds that they were partisan appointments. In each of the latter disputes, the constitutional court was called on to resolve the dispute, and in both cases it came down largely in favor of the government (Oltay).

Since then, the constitutional court has been involved in a large number of key disputes between the different political institutions, such that it has become one of the most central actors in the new Hungarian democracy. Indeed, anyone reading through the history of political developments in Hungary during the 1990s could be forgiven for concluding that the court is almost the only actor that counts. According to Körösényi (p. 273), for example, it is a court that "possesses considerable *political* power . . . [and] has become the most important political institution for the defence of the constitutional state." One reason for this, of course, is that this constitutional state itself has been created simply by a series of amendments to the former communist constitution rather than being devised as a complete and coherent system in its own right. In other words, Hungary has still not managed to adopt a wholly new constitution, and the continuing wranglings among the parties concerning the exact provisions that a constitution should contain are such that it is unlikely that any agreement will be reached in the near future. In December 1997, for example, a draft constitution that had been in preparation for eighteen months was rejected by parliament in the face of opposition from the MDF, the Independent Small Holders party (FKGB), and the Christian Democratic People's party (KDNP) (see "Constitution Watch" in the *East European Constitutional Review* (henceforth cited as *CW-EECR*), Winter 1997, p. 15).

Poland   As is the case for the majority of new democracies in Eastern Europe (Lucky; Lukashak et al.), the four countries we are discussing here have tended to follow the conventional Western European path in favoring the establishment of parliamentary regimes, albeit with a presidential head of state. Poland comes closest to being an exception here, in that the president is elected by popular vote, as in France, and enjoys the right of veto over parliamentary legislation. At the same time, however, Poland has also instituted a system of strong prime ministerial and cabinet government, answerable to parliament, in which the president's nominee for prime minister may be rejected by a majority vote in the Sejm (the lower house). Poland therefore may be said to approximate the French model of "semi-presidential" government, although the new Polish president cannot so easily dismiss parliament and call for new elections.

As in Hungary, albeit only initially, the new Polish democracy operated under a series of amendments to the pre-existing communist constitution. In 1992, parliament adopted the so-called "Little Constitution," which was intended to operate until such time as a comprehensive new constitution could be agreed on. Its provisions also were restricted largely to defining the relations between executive and legislature (for a comprehensive overview, see van der Meer Krok-Paszowska). No provision was made for a new constitutional court, for example, and Polish democracy in the 1990s developed under the guidance of the pre-existing Constitutional Tribunal, which was first established under communist rule in 1982 and whose twelve members were elected by the Sejm for an eight-year period. In the event, it was not until 1997 that the new comprehensive constitution was drafted to the satisfaction of the various political parties involved, and then accepted narrowly by the people (on a 43 percent turnout in the May 25 referendum, the majority in favor of the new constitution was just 54 percent). Although one of the advisors to the committee drafting the new constitution had hoped that such a lengthy drafting process "would become an occasion for the public's civic education," he also admitted regretting having adopted this procedure, since he found that "a majority of politicians will use every available opportunity for enhancing their political careers or securing some other personal benefits. They have no desire to educate the public," he added, "and the arrogance stemming from the possession of an elected office, a 'democratic mandate,' makes many of them incapable of learning" (Osiatynski, p. 67).

Under the terms of the Little Constitution, Poland retained a bicameral parliament, with both chambers elected for a four-year period on the basis of the electoral system adopted for the 1993 election (discussed later in this chapter). Although most legislative power was to rest with the 460-member Sejm, bills were also subject to the approval of the 100-member Senate (the upper house), whose amendments could be overturned only with a two-thirds majority in the lower house. The position of the cabinet was also strengthened, with provision for rule by decree in the event of legislative deadlock. As noted earlier, the constitution also followed the German and Spanish examples by introducing a version of the constructive vote of no confidence. If the Sejm passed a vote of no confidence in the government and at the same time elected a new prime minister, then the president would be obliged to approve the change. If, on the other hand, the vote of no confidence were passed without the election of a new prime minister, the president then would have the option either to dismiss parliament and call new elections or to ask the parties to try to form a new government (Garlicki, p. 84).

The president, who was to be elected by popular vote for a five-year term, was accorded significant but at the same time limited powers. He or she had the right to nominate the prime minister, but this was subject to the approval of the lower house, which could reject the presidential nominee and appoint its own candidate without first seeking presidential approval. Prior presidential consultation was required for the appointment of the ministers of defense, internal affairs, and foreign affairs, and the president had to approve all other cabinet appointments. The president also could dissolve the Sejm in special circumstances, including those in which parliament was unable to approve the state budget or when parliament had passed a vote of no confidence in the prime minister without being able to agree on a successor. Finally, although the president also had the right to veto legislation passed by parliament, this veto could then be overturned by a two-thirds majority in the Sejm.

The new constitution adopted in 1997 retained many of these core institutional features, albeit with some modifications (Jasiewicz and Gebethner; see also Letowska; Garlicki;). The Sejm now may overrule the Senate with an overall majority, rather than requiring a two-thirds majority. It also now may overrule a presidential veto with a three-fifths rather than a two-thirds majority, while the presidential veto cannot be used at all with regard to the budget. Moreover, the president is now given no special role with regard to defense, security, and foreign affairs in the new constitution, thus strengthening the position of the prime minister's side in this dual executive. In general, the major effect of the new constitution was to sort out the ambiguities that had surrounded the dispersal of authority under the Little Constitution and to strengthen the position of the cabinet and prime minister with respect to both the Sejm and the president. According to Jasiewicz and Gebethner (p. 504), the new constitution also enhances the position of the prime minister in particular, who now is "no longer *primus inter pares,* but has a role comparable to that of the chancellor in the German system."

Whether these last changes will make for the smoother exercise of executive power in the future remains to be seen. For most of the 1990s, Poland was marked by quite severe rivalries between prime minister (and government) and president, a rivalry that stemmed partly from the uncertainties regarding the division of competencies between the two offices, and partly from more strictly political differences. Indeed, for much of the 1990s, Poland experienced what the Americans define as "divided government" and what the French refer to as "cohabitation": alternative political majorities in the two key governing institutions (see Tables 15-2 and 15-3 later in this chapter). The election of Lech Walesa to the presidency in 1990, for example, was followed by frequent conflicts between his office and the various fragmented coalitions that governed Poland on the basis of vulnerable parliamentary majorities through to 1993. Although many of these governing parties had emerged out of the same broadly based Solidarity movement that Walesa had originally led, divisions within this movement had sharpened in the years immediately following the defeat of communism (Jasiewicz; van der Meer Krok-Paszowska). Inter-executive conflicts became even more pronounced after 1993, when the former communists and their allies came to government and were obliged to share power with Walesa. In 1995, this period of divided government was brought to a temporary close when the former communists also won the presidency, but returned again—albeit in a less conflictual form—following the parliamentary elections of 1997.

The Czech and Slovak Republics   In the case of the former Czechoslovakia, it was not just the character of the new constitution but also the nature of the state itself that was to prove an acute problem (see Kopecky, who also provides the most comprehensive analysis of the politics of both republics during the 1990s). In the wake of the collapse of communism, tensions had begun to escalate between the two parts of the federation, with the Czech leaders attempting to hold on to the federal solution, and the Slovak leaders pushing for greater regional autonomy and also seeking to block progress on economic and social reforms until the broader constitutional issues could be resolved. Slovakia was the less wealthy part of the federation and had remained heavily dependent on aging heavy engineering and arms industries. Slovakia was also the smaller of the two countries, accounting for only one-third of the overall population, and included within its borders a sizeable Hungarian minority (some 11 percent of the Slovak population) that was increasingly concerned about the protection of its rights should Slovakia go it alone.

Under the federation, each of the two "republics" had its own National Council—a unicameral parliament, with two hundred deputies in the Czech Council and 150 deputies in the Slovak Council—and each also had its own government. The federal parliament itself was divided into two chambers, a House of People with 150 deputies (of whom roughly two-thirds were Czech), and a House of Nations, which included seventy-five deputies from each of the two areas. Because constitutional change required a two-thirds majority in the House of People as well as in each of the national delegations in the House of Nations, it was therefore possible for a minority of Slovak deputies in the upper house to block any proposed amendments.

The federation was eventually dissolved at the end of 1992, after both republics had already adopted new constitutions. The new Czech constitution was approved by the National Council on 16 December, 1992, and involved the creation of a bicameral parliament in which the lower house (the National Council, now the Chamber of Deputies) would have two hundred members elected for a four-year term. The new upper House, the Senate, was to have eighty-one members elected for a six-year term, with one-third being elected every two years. The new Senate would have the right to delay, but not veto, legislation, and it was initially proposed that its first members would be drawn from among the Czech deputies who sat in the soon-to-be-redundant federal parliament. This proposal was eventually rejected, however, and partly because of continuing disputes about its composition and its constitutional function more generally, the Senate was not finally brought into being until 1996 (Olson).

The new constitution also provided for a president who would be elected by a majority vote in parliament (including, eventually, the Senate), and on January 26, 1993, the leading former dissident, Vaclav Havel, who had earlier been elected as the first postcommunist president of Czechoslovakia in 1990, was reelected to office, this time as the first president of the new Czech Republic. An earlier proposal to provide for the direct election of the president by the people was rejected for fear that this might lead to the accumulation of too much personal power by the incumbent. The president was given the right to dissolve the parliament under certain limited circumstances (such as when the government had been defeated in a vote of no confidence); to suspend but not veto legislation; and to appoint the prime minister and ministers, subject to their winning the approval of the House. The president also was given the power to appoint the fifteen members of the constitutional court, subject to the approval of the senate. (Members of the constitutional court were to serve for ten years.) The constitution was subject to amendment only with the approval of 60 percent of all members in the Chamber of Deputies and 60 percent of those senators present at the vote.

Although this new Czech constitution came firmly down in favor of a parliamentary system, the practice of politics as it developed in the first years revealed quite sharp tensions between the prime minister, Vaclav Klaus, who served from 1992 until late 1997, and his former ally in the pro-democracy Civic Forum movement, head of state Vaclav Havel. Relations between these two leading Czech politicians had never been easy (see Kopecky), and in spring 1997, following a severe budget crisis, Havel even went so far as to suggest that Klaus's government should resign. Klaus refused, and later won a confidence vote before eventually leaving office in November (*CW-EECR,* Spring/Summer 1997, p. 10). At the end of that year, in his State of the Nation address, Havel attacked the social and economic record of both the parliament and the outgoing government, to which Klaus's response was that Havel simply did not understand economics (*CW-EECR,* Winter 1998, p. 13). Such public disputes between the formally authoritative head of government and the formally ceremonial head of state are virtually unknown in most of the long-established parliamentary democracies, even those with a president rather than a monarch at their head. In postcommunist Europe, on the other hand, including in both the Czech and Slovak republics, they are not uncommon, reflecting a continuing uncertainty about the division of executive authority in everyday political practice.

In Slovakia, the constitution of the new republic was approved by the Slovak National Council on September 1, 1992. Here also a parliamentary system of government was adopted, with a president to be elected by parliament by a three-fifths majority of the 150 deputies. On 15 February 1993, following several rounds of voting in which the nominee initially favored by the prime minister had been rejected by the parliament, Michal Kovac of the Movement for a Democratic Slovakia (HZDS) was elected first president of the first Slovak Republic.

The Slovak parliament is unicameral and is elected for a four-year term. There is also a ten-member constitutional court appointed by the president for a seven-year term, although before the election of Kovac, and in the face of much opposition criticism, the first members were actually appointed by the prime minister. Under special circumstances, the president may dissolve the parliament, and the constitution specifies that this can be done if parliament fails three times in the first six months following an election to agree on the government program. More generally, the makeup of the new constitution has led some critics to suggest that "what prevails in practice is closer to raw majoritarianism, with little attention paid to the rights of minorities" (Bútora and Bútorová, p. 80). Indeed, the Hungarian deputies in the parliament actually boycotted some of the votes on the new constitution because they felt that it failed to protect their ethnic rights.

More than in any other of the four countries we discuss here, Slovakia in the 1990s has been characterized by continuing and often exceptionally bitter conflicts between the different institutional actors. Indeed, so sharp have these conflicts been that the integrity of Slovak democracy often has been called into question by outside observers, and the country was excluded from the first group of postcommunist polities to be invited to open negotiations for eventual membership in the European Union. It has now joined the second group of countries to be considered for possible membership, however, together with Bulgaria and Romania (as well as Turkey and Malta, among others). Much of the responsibility for the problems associated with the new regime has been laid on the shoulders of Vladimir Meciar, prime minister of the independent Slovak Republic from 1992 until March 1994, and then again from December 1994 until November 1998. Meciar always provoked strong criticism, and not only inside Slovakia itself. A relatively restrained example is the judgment of one observer that "Paradoxically, the major challenges to democracy in Slovakia came from the way the Cabinet and coalition parties exercised power with a secure, stable and disciplined majority in parliament" (Malova, 1996, p. 454).

Studies of the development of Slovak politics during the 1990s are replete with examples of the how and why of the various conflicts—conflicts between parties within parliament, on the one hand, and especially those between prime minister and president, as well as between prime minister and the Constitutional Court, on the other—and these need not be reviewed here. Two particular incidents are worth recording, however, in that they offer a useful flavor of the style of Slovak politics as it emerged under Meciar. The first occurred when the son of President Kovac was abducted in Bratislava on August 31, 1995, and later abandoned in Austria (Malova, 1996, p. 457). It was alleged that Kovac, Jr., had been involved in some fraudulent financial dealings, and an international warrant for his arrest had been issued in Germany. If he were forcibly transported to Austria, it was thought, the warrant could then be served, and it was alleged that the abduction had been arranged by the Slovak Intelligence Service in order to embarrass the Slovak president. The second incident was the so-called "clock incident" (Fish, p. 50), when Meciar ordered that a clock be mounted on a high building in Bratislava, clearly visible from the president's office, a clock that would not display the time as such, but rather would ominously count down the days remaining in Kovac's tenure as president.

In 1994 Kovac had delivered a speech that encouraged the opposition in parliament to vote down Meciar's then minority government. The enmity between the two politicians had hardened thereafter (Malova, 1996, p. 456). When Kovac's term in office eventually expired in March 1998, parliament proved unable to elect a successor: the election required a three-fifths majority, and while Meciar's incumbent coalition commanded enough seats to block any opposition candidate, its numbers were insufficient to elect a candidate of its own.

The biggest single change in the Slovak Constitution since democratization stemmed partly from the need to avoid any repetition of these difficulties. Thus, following Meciar's defeat in the 1998 elections and the installation of a new government, a constitutional amendment was adopted by parliament with the necessary three-fifths majority that provided for the direct election of the president in a double-ballot procedure. The amendment also increased the powers of the president to dissolve parliament in case of a failure by parliament to establish a working majority in support of a government (*CW-EECR*, Winter/Spring 1999, pp. 37–38). The first direct election of the president was held in May 1999, with Meciar himself, a late entrant into the contest, ending up in second place behind the eventual winner, Rudold Schuster, of the appropriately named Party of Civic Understanding (SOP) (*CW-EECR*, Summer 1999, pp. 32–33).

Electoral Systems

One of the most important questions that had faced the constitution makers in the new postcommunist democracies concerned the new electoral system that was to be adopted. Of particular importance was the decision as to whether this was to be a majority or plurality system, as in France, the United Kingdom, and the United States, or it should be more proportional, as in most Western European countries. In addition, if a proportional system were to be adopted, the question was also raised as to precisely how proportional it should be, and whether it should involve the imposition of thresholds that might prevent very small parties from gaining representation in parliament (see Chapter 11). In the end, the Czech and Slovak republics as well as Poland tended to follow the prevailing Western European pattern by adopting proportional electoral systems, with the complex Hungarian system being a partial exception to this pattern.

Hungary Elections in Hungary have been held on the basis of a complicated system that has mixed single-member districts in the U.S., British, and French style with a more continental Western European style of proportional representation and party lists, in which citizens have two separate votes (Körösényi, pp. 117–32). For the purposes of these elections, the 386 seats in the unicameral parliament were divided into three groups. The first group was composed of 176 single-member districts in which candidates were elected, as in France, on the basis of a two-ballot system. If any candidate received an absolute majority in the first round of voting, then he or she was declared elected—provided that the turnout exceeded 50 percent. If no candidate received an absolute majority, then a second round of voting took place two weeks later, in which the contest was restricted to the three leading candidates from the first round and any other candidate who had received at least 15 percent of the vote, with the winner being whichever of these candidates then won the most second-round votes—provided, in this case, that turnout reached at least 25 percent. Turnout provisions such as these are, in fact, quite common to a number of postcommunist electoral systems.

The second group consisted of a maximum of 152 seats that were allocated to the twenty regions of the country in multimember districts, ranging from the smallest, with four seats, to the biggest, with twenty-eight seats. These seats were awarded to regional party lists on the basis of a separate proportional representation (PR) election, with no party receiving any seats unless it gained a minimum of 4 percent of the total vote cast for regional lists in the country as a whole and unless turnout in the region itself reached at least 50 percent. Finally, there were a minimum of 58 "national seats" that were distributed to national party lists on the basis of votes won by the national parties in both the single-member and the regional districts that had not already been used to elect any candidates—in other words, on the basis of the "wasted" or "residual" votes. In practice, voting patterns were such that it did not always prove possible to distribute the full quota of seats to the regional lists, and the seats remaining were then added to the national seats (Election results during the 1990s are Summarized in Table 15-1.).

TABLE 15-1 ELECTIONS IN HUNGARY, 1990–1998

	1990		1994		1998	
	% list votes	Total seats	% list votes	Total seats	% list votes	Total seats
Hungarian Democratic Forum (MDF)	24.7	164	11.7	38	2.8	17
Alliance of Free Democrats (SZDSZ)	21.4	92	19.7	69	7.6	24
Independent Smallholders party (FKGP)	11.7	44	8.8	26	13.2	48
Hungarian Socialist party (MSZP)	10.9	33	32.9	209	32.9	134
Alliance of Young Democrats/Hungarian Civic Party (MPP)	9.0	21	7.0	20	29.5	148
Christian Democratic People's party (KDNP)	6.5	21	7.0	22	2.3	–
Workers' party (MP)	3.7	–	3.1	–	4.0	–
Agrarian Alliance (ASZ)	3.1	2	2.1	1	–	–
Hungarian Justice and Life	–	–	1.6	–	5.5	14
Others*	9.0	9	6.1	1	2.2	–
All	**100.0**	**386**	**100.0**	**386**	**100.0**	**385**

*Also includes joint lists involving parties already reported in this table.

Source: For all tables in this chapter, see *Political Data Yearbook* (published by the *European Journal of Political Research*), as well as Rose et al.; Kopecky and Mudde.

Poland   Despite some support for an electoral system that would include provision for single-member districts, the actual system adopted for the first fully democratic elections to the Polish Sejm in 1991 was a PR system, with 391 of the 460 seats to be distributed to the parties according to the share of the vote received in each of thirty-seven multimember districts. No formal threshold was applied. The remaining sixty-nine seats were to be distributed on a national basis in proportion to the share of the vote received by parties that had registered a national (as opposed to simply a local) list and that had received at least 5 percent of the nationwide vote, or whose candidates had been elected in at least five districts. These latter thresholds did not apply to ethnic minority parties, such as the German Minority party. This was clearly a very open system, and the elections resulted in a total of twenty-nine parties winning representation in the 460-seat parliament, with the biggest single party winning no more than 13 percent of the total number of seats. Elections to the Senate (upper house) were to be conducted on a first-past-the-post basis in two- and occasionally three-member districts.

In 1993, in an effort to avoid a repetition of the extreme fragmentation that had characterized the 1991 elections, and that had rendered coalition formation particularly difficult, parliament approved a new electoral law for the Sejm that imposed a nationwide threshold of 5 percent for individual parties in the distribution of the 391 district seats, and that imposed a separate 8 percent threshold for electoral coalitions. The sixty-nine "national" seats were now also to be reserved for distribution among parties and coalitions that had registered lists in at least half the districts and that had polled at least 7 percent of the national vote. Moreover, whereas in 1991 parties that wished to register at a national level (and thereby qualify for the national seats) had been obliged to collect signatures in only five districts, the new law required them to collect signatures in twenty-six districts, with those parties that already had at least fifteen sitting deputies being excluded from this requirement. As in 1991, ethnic minority parties were exempted from these thresholds. The system for elections to the Senate also remained unchanged.

In the event, the new system had the desired effect, with substantially fewer lists being registered for the election and with only seven parties eventually winning representation. At the same time, however, this also proved a costly strategy in representational terms, in that some 35 percent of the votes were cast for a variety of different parties that failed to reach the threshold and were thus excluded from parliament (see Table 15-2). These unsuccessful parties included two Catholic parties, Catholic Electoral Action (ZChN) and the party of Christian Democrats (PChD), which, in fear of the new 5 percent threshold, had formed an electoral coalition, Catholic Electoral Committee "Fatherland." The new alliance polled just 6.4 percent, however, thus falling short of the 8 percent threshold imposed on coalitions of parties. Although no changes in these electoral rules were included in the new Constitution of 1997—which, incidentally, enshrined the principle of proportionality in elections—a new Law on Political parties adopted by the Sejm in June of that year raised the minimum membership requirement for the registration of parties from fifteen to one thousand. At the same time, the new law made provision for the reimbursement of election campaign expenses from public funds for all parties that polled at least 3 percent of the vote nationwide (Jasiewicz and Gebethner). Small parties might still have little chance of winning representation, but their efforts to do so would now leave them less out of pocket.

The Czech and Slovak Republics Thresholds also had been applied in the proportional voting system in the first postcommunist election in the Czechoslovak federation in 1990, and these were reinforced by the time of the second election in 1992. In order to win seats in the federal parliament, individual parties were required to poll at least 5 percent of the vote in either the Czech lands or Slovakia, with a similar 5 percent threshold applying in the elections to each of the National Councils. (This had also been the case in the 1990 elections, with the exception of the contest for the Slovak National Council, where there had been just a 3 percent threshold.) As in Poland in 1993, even higher thresholds were imposed in the case of electoral alliances in the contest for both the federal parliament and the Slovak Council, with alliances of two or three parties being required to poll at least 7 percent of the vote, and alliances of four or more parties to poll at least 10 percent. In the case of the Czech National Council, two-party alliances needed 7 percent, three-party alliances needed 9 percent, and alliances of four or more parties needed 11 percent (Wightman).

One result of this, as in Poland in 1993, was that a substantial number of small parties failed to win representation, with many voters finding themselves effectively ex-

TABLE 15-2 PARLIAMENTARY ELECTIONS IN POLAND, 1991–1997

	1991		1993		1997	
	% votes	N seats	% votes	N seats	% votes	N seats
Independent Trade Union "Solidarity" (S)	5.1	27	4.9	–	–	–
Center Alliance (PC)	8.7	44	4.4	–	–	–
Agrarian Alliance (PL)	5.5	28	2.4	–	–	–
Electoral Action Solidarity (AWS)	–	–	–	–	33.8*	201
Polish Peasant party (PSL)	8.7	48	15.4	132	7.3	27
Democratic Left Alliance (SLD)	12.0	60	20.4	171	27.1	164
Democratic Union (UD)	12.3	62	10.6	74	–	–
Liberal-Democratic Congress (KLD)	7.5	37	4.0	–	–	–
Freedom Union (UW)	–	–	–	–	13.4†	60
Solidarity of Labor (SP)	2.1	4	–	–	–	–
Social-Democratic Movement (RDS)	0.5	1	–	–	–	–
For Wielkopolska and Poland (W)	0.2	1	–	–	–	–
Union of Labor (UP)	–	–	7.3‡	41	4.7	–
Union of Real Politics/Republic's Rightists (UPR)	2.3	3	3.2	–	2.0	–
German Minority§	1.2	7	0.7	4	0.4	2
Catholic Electoral Action (ZChN)	8.7	49	–	–	–	–
Party of Christian Democrats (PChD)	1.1	4	–	–	–	–
Catholic Electoral Committee "Fatherland"	–	–	6.4**	–	–	–
Confederation for an Independent Poland (KPN)	7.5	46	5.8	22	–	–
Polish Beer-Lovers party	3.3	16	0.1	–	–	–
Christian Democracy (ChD)	2.4	5	–	–	–	–
Coalition for the Republic (KdR)/Movement for the Reconstruction of Poland (ROP)	–	–	2.7	–	5.6	6
Self-Defense Alliance	–	–	2.8	–	0.1	–
Non-Party Bloc in Support of Reforms (BBWR)	–	–	5.4	16	–	–
Pensioners' party (KPEiR)	–	–	–	–	2.2	–
Others	10.9	18	3.5	–	3.4	–
Total	**100.0**	**460**	**100.0**	**460**	**100.0**	**460**

*electoral alliance of S, PC, and PL; also includes ZChN
†electoral alliance of UD and KLD
‡electoral alliance of SP, RDS, and W
§exempt from electoral threshold requirements because of status as national minority
**electoral alliance of ZChN and PChD

cluded from representation in the decision-making process (see Table 15-4). One of the Czech parties, for example, the Czech Democratic Alliance (ODA), fell short of the 5 percent threshold in the House of People elections by just 1,009 votes. Had it won this additional support, it could probably have counted on six or seven seats; falling short as it did, it failed to win any seats at all. More generally, almost 26 percent of

TABLE 15-3   PRESIDENTIAL ELECTIONS IN POLAND, 1990 AND 1995

1990 Candidate (party*)	1990, % votes		1995 Candidate (party*)	1995, % votes	
	1st ballot	2nd ballot		1st ballot	2nd ballot
Lech Walesa (Solidarity)	40.0	74.3	Aleksander Kwasniewski (SLD)	35.1	51.7
Stanislav Tyminski (Ind.)	23.1	25.7	Lech Walesa (Ind./Solidarity)	33.1	48.3
Tadeus Mazowiecki (UW)	18.1	–	Jacek Kuron (UW)	9.2	–
Wlodzimierz Cimoscewicz (SLD)	9.2	–	Jan Olszewski (Ind.)	6.9	–
Roman Bartoszczze (PSL)	7.2	–	Waldeman Pawlak (PSL)	4.3	–
Leszek Moczulski (KPN)	2.5	–	Tadeusz Zielinski (Ind.)	3.5	–
			Hanna Gronkiewicz-Waltz (Ind.)	2.8	–
			Janusz Korwin-Mikke (UPR)	1.4	–
			Others (N = 5)	3.7	–
Total	**100.0**	**100.0**		**100.0**	**100.0**
Turnout	**60.6**	**53.4**		**64.7**	**68.3**

*For party labels, see Table 15-2; "Ind." refers to Independent candidates.

TABLE 15-4   ELECTIONS IN THE CZECH REPUBLIC, 1992–1998

	1992		1996		1998	
	% votes	N seats	% votes	N seats	% votes	N seats
Civic Movement (OH)	4.6	–	2.1	–	–	–
Civic Democratic Party (ODS)	29.7	76	29.6	68	27.7	63
Freedom Union (US)*	–	–	–	–	8.6	19
Christian Democratic Union/ People's party (KDU-CSL)	6.3	15	8.1	18	9.0	20
Civic Democratic Alliance (ODA)	5.9	14	6.4	13	–	–
Social Democratic party (CSSD)	6.5	16	26.4	61	32.3	74
Communist party (KSCM)	14.1[†]	35	10.3	22	11.0	24
Republican party (SPR-RSC)	6.3	14	8.0	18	3.9	–
Liberal Social Union (LSU)	6.5	16	–	–	–	–
Association for Moravia & Silesia (HSD-SMS)	5.9	14	–	–	–	–
Pensioners' party (DZJ)	3.8	–	3.1	–	3.1	–
Others	10.4	–	6.0	–	4.4	–
Total	**100.0**	**200**	**100.0**	**200**	**100.0**	**200**

*Split from ODS
[†]Figures refer to the Left Block, which included the KCSM in 1992.

the Czech votes cast in the House of People elections in 1992, together with almost 27 percent of the Slovak votes, went to parties that failed to cross the threshold. The equivalent figures for the National Council—later, the national parliament—elections were close to 20 percent and 25 percent, respectively (see Table 15-4).

These Czechoslovak voting systems and thresholds were maintained when the National Councils became the parliaments (the lower house, in the Czech case) of the newly independent republics. Since then, however, various reforms have been discussed and proposed. In the Czech Republic, for example, Vaclav Klaus's Civic Democratic party (ODS), which led the government until 1998, once suggested the adoption of a simple plurality system in single-member districts, largely with the intention of reducing party fragmentation in parliament—and helping his own party become even stronger, of course. Another suggestion was to raise the minimum threshold for individual parties from 5 to 10 percent, with a corresponding increase for electoral coalitions. In May 1999, both the ODS and the then governing Social Democrats (CSSD) agreed to consider changes that would favor larger parties, including a proposal to increase the number of districts from the current eight, with twenty-five members in each, to thirty-six, with five or six members in each, so raising the district threshold in practice to some 20 percent (*CW-EECR,* Summer 1999, p. 10).

In Slovakia, reforms had also been proposed, not least in an effort to strengthen Meciar's position. The most recent change came just four months before the 1998 election, in what was clearly an attempt to weaken the smaller parties and the opposition (Election results in the 1990s are summarized in Table 15-5.). Following the changes pushed through by the government, each party seeking to nominate a candidate or even taking part in an electoral alliance was obliged to submit a declaration stating that it had at least ten thousand members. In addition, the 5 percent threshold applying to individual parties when contesting elections on their own was now also applied even to those parties taking part in electoral coalitions. Thus, whereas two allied parties would have required just 7 percent of the vote to win representation as an alliance in earlier elections, in 1998 they were each required to win 5 percent. Finally, it was also ruled that parties could no longer campaign in the private media—through advertising, etc.—but only in the state-owned, and government-dominated, media. Although these reforms were challenged in the Constitutional Court, no ruling was made before the election, with the result that they did in fact come into force (Malova, 1999).

Notwithstanding any partisan purposes that may have become involved at a later stage, the constitution makers in each of these postcommunist countries had clearly faced a difficult initial dilemma in designing their new electoral systems. On the one hand, a fully proportional system was likely to enhance the legitimacy of the new democratic order, and would also facilitate the representation and hence possibly the integration of national and other minorities. On the other hand, given the adoption of parliamentary systems, excessive fragmentation could result in weak and indecisive governments and could thereby slow down the much-needed process of reform. The solution that each of these four countries adopted was therefore to maintain a reasonably proportional formula while imposing quite strict barriers in the way of smaller parties.

TABLE 15-5   ELECTIONS IN THE SLOVAK REPUBLIC, 1992–1998

	1992		1994		1998	
	% votes	N seats	% votes	N seats	% votes	N seats
Movement for a Democratic Slovakia (HZDS)	37.3	74	35.0	61	27.0	43
Christian Democrats (KDH)	8.9	18	10.1	17	†	–
Party of the Democratic Left (SDL)/ Common Choice (SV)*	14.7	29	10.4	18	14.7	23
Slovak National party (SNS)	7.9	15	5.4	9	9.1	14
Hungarian Alliance (SMK)	7.4	14	10.2	17	9.1	15
Democratic Union (DU)	–	–	8.6	15	†	–
Association of Workers (ZRS)	–	–	7.3	13	1.3	–
Democratic party (DS)	3.3	–	3.4	–	†	–
Christian Social Union (KSU)	3.1	–	2.1	–	–	–
Communist party of Slovakia (KSS)	–	–	2.7	–	2.8	–
Green Party (SZNS)	2.5	–	*	–	†	–
Social Democrats (SDSS)	4.0	–	*	–	†	–
Party of Civic Understanding (SOP)	–	–	–	–	8.0	13
Slovak Democratic Coalition (SDK)†	–	–	–	–	26.3	42
Others	10.9	–	4.8	–	1.7	–
Total	**100.0**	**150**	**100.0**	**150**	**100.0**	**150**

*Common Choice was an electoral alliance of Party of Democratic Left, Social Democrats, and Greens in 1994.
†SDK was an electoral alliance of Christian Democrats, Democratic Union, Democratic party, Social Democrats, and Greens in 1998

But although these new rules have had the intended effect of reducing parliamentary fragmentation, they have also sometimes proved potentially damaging in other respects, particularly insofar as the strong thresholds have prevented large segments of electoral opinion from winning a voice in the new assemblies.

PARTIES, VOTERS, AND ELECTORAL ALIGNMENTS

One of the most important lessons that we have learned from looking at the development of parties and party systems in Western Europe is that the structure of mass politics takes time to stabilize. When mass politics begins, in other words, it is often unsettled. As was the case in Portugal and Spain in the late 1970s and 1980s, for example, as well as in the rest of Western Europe in the wake of full democratization in the early part of the twentieth century, the formative years of mass politics are often characterized by significant volatility and change. New parties emerge and then disappear. Parties fuse with one another and then split away again. And the process by which voters learn about the limits and possibilities afforded by new electoral systems, on the one hand, and about the constraints and opportunities imposed by the new structures of party competition, on the other, can often take years to develop. In postcommunist Europe, then, as well as in most other new democracies, we cannot expect to witness an immediate settling down into stable party systems.

There are three principal factors involved here, each of which sets the postcommunist experience off from that in Western Europe, and each of which was also likely to promote quite high levels of electoral instability at least in the short term (for a more extensive discussion, see Mair, 175–98; see also Tóka; Kitschelt et al.). First and most obviously, the path towards democracy in postcommunist Europe has been radically different from that taken in most of Western Europe. Not only are we talking here about a massive and quite overloaded process of transition—from communism to multiparty democracy, and from command economies to the free market—but we are also talking about a different mode of democratization. (The original distinction between paths towards democratization derives from Dahl; for a discussion of its application in the context of post-authoritarian party development in southern Europe in particular, see Biezen, pp. 32–37.) When most of the Western European polities democratized at the beginning of the twentieth century, the process involved opening up to the mass of new voters a regime in which political competition was already an accepted principle. In other words, the previously non-democratized regimes were competitive, but exclusive: they denied the mass of ordinary citizens the right to participate. Democratization, when it came, therefore involved enfranchisement, the advent of mass suffrage. In postcommunist countries, by contrast, the process occurred the other way around. The principle of mass participation had been accepted under communism—indeed, if the mock elections that took place under communism recorded turnouts of less than 90 percent, the regime took umbrage—but not the right of competition. Elections were held, but they were not free elections. Given these different paths to democracy, then, we should not necessarily expect that the resultant parties and party systems will prove easily comparable or that the newer ones will easily stabilize.

Second, the electorates in postcommunist Europe are different. One obvious difference in this regard is the absence of a long-standing cleavage structure (see Tóka), characterized by distinct social divisions, a strong sense of collective identity within different groups in society, and strong organizations to which citizens might feel a sense of belonging (see Chapter 9). Social divisions themselves are essentially fluid, with the transition from a command to a market economy initially breaking down those few lines of social stratification that previously existed. And although the newly installed market economy is beginning to lead to new and more conventional lines of stratification, these are emerging in societies that experienced through transition what Batt (p. 50) once tellingly described as "an unprecedented degree of social destructuring, volatility and fluidity." To be sure, identities other than those tied to the communist economic system have survived: national or ethnic identities in a number of the postcommunist states, and a religious, Catholic, identity in Poland in particular. But these are the exceptions. The emergence of cleavages is also hampered by the fact that the parties in these new democracies do not appear to be investing much effort in building a popular sense of identification and belonging among voters. In many cases, the party exists almost only in parliament (Lewis), with very little evidence of any organizational presence on the ground. For example, party membership accounts for only 4 percent of the electorate in the Czech Republic (half of this being due to the legacy of the former Communist party's organizational network), for 3.6 percent in Slovakia, for 2.4 percent in Hungary, and for just 1.1 percent in Poland (two-thirds of this being due to the reformed Communist party). (For details of membership figures, see Mair and van Biezen).

In other words, the electorates in postcommunist countries tend to be different in the sense that, as Rose puts it, they are demobilized: lacking in any strong affective ties to the parties that compete for their votes, and often skeptical about the idea of party itself. It is not so much that these voters are *de*aligned, as is perhaps increasingly the case in contemporary Western Europe (Chapter 9); rather, they are *not yet* aligned.

Third, the parties themselves are different. This is not so much a matter of differences in ideology or programmatic identity—although these are also important—as it is of organizational behavior and practice. In brief, parties in new democracies in general, and those in the postcommunist democracies in particular, are less frequently characterized by a sense of organizational loyalty and commitment. When conflicts arise inside a party, the solution is often to split the party apart, with the dissenting factions establishing their own separate alternative organizations. At the same time, when common interests are perceived among different parties, even in the short term, the decision is often made to merge the parties into a broad electoral or even organizational coalition. The result is a constantly shifting array of actors, with parties entering elections in one guise, and then adopting yet another in parliament itself, with relatively little continuity in alternatives from one election to the next.

To be sure, there is quite substantial variation among the postcommunist systems in this regard. At one extreme lies the Polish case, where the huge variety of party alternatives move in and out of diverse alliances from one election to the next (Table 15-2), and where, within the Sejm itself, there is a constant shifting between parliamentary fractions and clubs, such that it becomes almost impossible even to identify some of the individual parties and to pin them down to particular positions (van der Meer Krok-Paszowska). In Hungary, by contrast, the alignments at both the electoral and the parliamentary level seem much more predictable, although in this case electoral support shifts quite considerably from one election to the next (Table 15-1). The Czech and Slovak cases fall in between (Tables 15-4, 15-5), but in the Czech case the apparent continuities in voting support across elections disguise quite frequent reshuffling within the parliament itself. Indeed, most analyses of Czech election outcomes usually begin by devoting considerable attention to the realignment of parliamentary fractions that had taken place in the period since voters last went to the polls (see, for example, the contributions by Lubomír Brokl and Zdenka Mansfeldová to the various editions of the *Political Data Yearbook,* published annually by the *European Journal of Political Research*).

Even in Slovakia, where the overriding importance of the pro- versus anti-Meciar alignment might have been expected to stabilize patterns of inter-party competition, a complex process of fission and fusion is also evident, with existing parties merging into electoral coalitions at one election or the next (e.g., Common Choice in 1994, the Slovak Democratic Coalition in 1998), and with new parties breaking off or setting up shop for the first time and winning quite substantial support (e.g., the Democratic Union and the Association of Workers in 1994, the Party of Civic Understanding in 1998).

Such complex processes of party fission and fusion are very uncommon in long-established party systems, almost by definition. Indeed, were such organizational behavior to be a feature of these systems, then it would be almost impossible to speak of them in terms of party "systems" as such. For a system of parties to emerge in the first place, and for it to persist, it must necessarily be characterized by regularity and predictability. This is what any system entails. And this is also why it still remains quite difficult to speak of real party "systems" in a number of the new postcommunist democracies. Neither the parties themselves, nor their modes of interaction, have yet been fully regularized.

This sense of flux is also clearly compounded by unpredictability at the level of the voters themselves. Over and above the uncertainties that follow from the relative absence of affective loyalties to parties, as well as those that can be associated with the continuing institutional fluidity (see above), there are also uncertainties regarding how even short-term voter preferences will be reflected. Two factors are important here. First, and particularly in both Hungary and Poland, turnout levels are relatively low, and hence a lot of voters may not yet have become socialized into the electoral process. In this sense, they remain demobilized and unpredictable. Second, because of the high thresholds imposed by the new electoral systems, and because both the voters and some of the parties needed time to learn how to operate within the constraints imposed by these systems, a lot of votes in the formative elections were wasted by the failure of the parties concerned to win through to parliamentary representation (see above).

Putting all of these factors together, the picture that emerges is one of instability and flux among voters and their parties. This picture is summarized in Table 15-6, which reports levels of turnout and electoral volatility in elections in these four countries during the 1990s, and which offers a useful contrast with the patterns evident in the long-established Western European democracies during the same period (see Chapter 9). Across the four countries as a whole in the 1990s, turnout averaged 67 percent, almost 12 percent less than the record low witnessed in Western Europe during the same period. To be sure, there are sharply contrasting patterns recorded here, with average turnout levels in both the Czech republic and Slovakia approximating to the Western European levels, and with that in Poland falling below even Swiss levels. This alone might suggest that it is also difficult to generalize even among this limited set of countries.

Volatility levels also differ from country to country, and even within countries. Across all four postcommunist polities in the 1990s, however, the average level of volatility was almost 26 percent, more than double the national mean level recorded in Western Europe during the "peak" decade of the 1990s. Indeed, in Poland, an average volatility of almost 33 percent across the elections of 1993 and 1997 is close to the level recorded in 1994 in Italy, which itself is by far the most extreme case among the long-established democracies in Western Europe. In Hungary, where the continuity in party alternatives from one election to the next is relatively marked by postcommunist standards, average volatility was almost 27 percent. In the Czech Republic, where volatility proved the lowest of all four countries, the average of just over 19 percent in the

TABLE 15-6   AGGREGATE ELECTORAL CHANGE IN EAST CENTRAL EUROPE IN THE 1990s

	Election year	Turnout (%)	Electoral volatility (%)*
Czech Republic	1992	83.6	19.9[†]
	1996	75.8	23.9
	1998	74.0	14.2
Mean		*77.8*	*19.3*
Hungary	1990	67.1	25.0
	1994	67.9	24.1
	1998	56.3	31.7
Mean		*63.8*	*26.9*
Poland (Sejm)	1991	43.2	n.a.
	1993	49.8	31.4
	1997	46.1	33.9
Mean		*46.4*	*32.7*
Slovakia	1992	81.8	29.6[†]
	1994	74.2	22.2
	1998	84.2	20.3
Mean		*80.1*	*24.0*
Mean (N = 4)	**1990s**	**67.0**	**25.7**
Western European Mean (N = 16)	**1990s**	**78.6**	**12.0**

*For definitions and measure of volatility, see Chapter 9 and Table 9-10.
[†]Volatility in the Czech and Slovak elections of 1992 is measured with respect to the outcomes in the separate Czechoslovak National Council elections of 1990.

three formative elections of the 1990s is still well above that recorded in the same period in Western Europe in all countries other than Italy (see Table 9-10).

When turnout levels began to dip in Western Europe in the 1990s, and when levels of volatility began to climb, it suggested the onset of a new period of dealignment (see Chapter 9). Party systems and electoral support patterns had been frozen in the past, but they now appeared to be thawing out. With even lower turnout levels and even higher peaks in volatility now evident in postcommunist Europe, the interpretation must necessarily be different. These systems are not emerging out of a frozen landscape—at least as far as democratic party systems are concerned. Rather, they are being formed for the first time. But, as we suggested earlier, while the Western systems may be becoming dealigned, these postcommunist systems might now well be on the way to an initial alignment.

In this sense, we might wish to conceive of each set of systems as beginning from opposite ends of some notional continuum, in which the Western systems come from a point of stability and head towards a more uncertain and unpredictable future, while the postcommunist systems emerge from a point of total uncertainty and unpredictability—an inevitable characteristic of newly created party systems—and head towards a more stable future (see also Ágh, 1996). What we might see, then, is an eventual meeting in the middle, the convergence on a point that is neither wholly frozen nor wholly fluid, and where broad continuities combine with sometimes rapid and short-term change. What also follows from this, of course, and what may well be the most interesting aspect of this contrast between the two sets of systems, is not that the postcommunist countries are catching up with the already developed party politics of the West, as such, but rather that the patterns evident in the postcommunist countries may well represent one version of the possible future facing their Western neighbors (see Sitter).

For this reason it also becomes tempting to try to indicate some of the likely sources of future division in postcommunist party systems and to relate these to the traditional dimensions of competition that have helped stabilize the established party systems in Western Europe (Evans and Whitefield; Kitschelt et al.). Competition revolving around the core problem of church-state relations, for example, has already become apparent in Hungary and especially in Poland, and all four political systems have already given rise to significant parties that identify with the sort of policies pursued by Christian democratic parties in the West. Center-periphery problems are also apparent, with the position of ethnic and national minorities in particular providing the basis for tensions that may yet emerge to threaten the long-term stability of these new democracies. The Hungarian minority in Slovakia is especially relevant here, but problems have also arisen regarding the position of the Romany community in Hungary and especially that in the Czech republic. Urban-rural divisions are also pronounced, much more so than in the West, and agrarian parties are already proving to be important political forces in both Hungary and Poland. This particular issue partly derives from the legacy of policies pursued by the former communist regimes, but its roots also go back to the underdeveloped economies of the interwar years, and now, as Batt (p. 48) notes, it continues to be "one of the most potent divisions in postcommunist politics."

Evidence of conventional class oppositions, on the other hand, that have proved so important in the development of Western European party systems, are more difficult to characterize, partly because the class structure that has emerged from communism is itself so unsettled, with as yet little scope—or time—for the development of more typically capitalist class relationships (though see Mateju et al.). Nevertheless, even at this early stage, it is possible to identify the existence of a substantial conflict of interest deriving from the process of transition itself, with the more liberal reformers being pitted against those whose jobs and living standards are inevitably threatened by marketization, a conflict that also tends to overlap with the more fundamental urban-rural divide. In the beginning, this conflict is what appears to have sustained the appeal of parties such as the Hungarian MDF and the Slovak HZDS, with each mobilizing on the basis of a potent combination of conservative nationalism and religious identity.

More recently, and especially in Poland and Hungary, this conflict has served to create a major dimension of competition between the new liberals, on the one hand, many of whom have adopted quite right-wing economic positions, and the reformed communist parties, on the other, with the latter proving surprisingly successful in the Hungarian elections in 1994 (the MSZP-see Table 15-1) and in the Polish Sejm elections in 1993 (the SLD-see Table 15-2). Indeed, these parties not only came to office in both countries following these elections, but in Poland in 1995 the former communists also captured the presidency (Table 15-3).

These successes, even when only temporary, should not be read as reflecting a demand for a return to the old system, however. Whatever their past, these ex-communist parties are now genuinely reformed, and are committed to maintaining democracy. Where their appeal lies is in the demand to slow down the often rapid process of social and economic modernization, and to protect the interests of those citizens left most vulnerable by the sudden introduction of the free market. In all of these countries, as Kitschelt and his colleagues conclude on the basis of an extensive analysis covering Bulgaria, the Czech Republic, Hungary, and Poland (p. 306), this is a potentially enduring conflict that sets "social protectionist against market-liberal parties." It is also a conflict that goes some way towards explaining the gains recorded by the former East German communist party in the all-German elections of the 1990s (see Chapter 7).

EAST *VERSUS* WEST, OR EAST *AND* WEST?

Although parties and party systems in postcommunist democracies may not be stabilized by new cleavage structures—the consolidation of new cleavages is unlikely to prove possible in twenty-first century Europe—they may well be stabilized by persisting dimensions of competition. In other words, key issues and alternatives are likely to remain relevant for quite some time to come, even if the manner in which individual voters line up on these issues may reflect quite particularistic concerns. Tóka (p. 607), for example, offers a convincing argument to suggest that postcommunist alignments in the future will be likely to hinge on value preferences and on what he calls "value voting," with the important dimensions being those constituted by religion versus secularism, left versus right, and nationalism versus anti-nationalism. In contemporary politics, he notes, whether in the West or in the East, such values are likely to remain relatively independent of circumstances related to status and demography, and, when it comes to generating partisan commitment, they "are at least as effective as is the political mobilization of organizational networks. . . . Rather than stick with parties whose followers or leaders 'look like them,' voters are most likely to stick with the parties with whom they agree on major issue dimensions." Here too, then, we can see a possible convergence between the directions in which the Eastern and Western systems are heading, with both groups of polities experiencing the freeing of political preferences from long-term social determinants.

In this chapter we have offered a very brief overview that sets the experience of building representative government in postcommunist Europe against the more lengthy analysis we devoted to the working of representative government in Western Europe. As we noted in the beginning of this book, these two separate worlds are not easily integrated with each other. The Western polities have, in the main, more than a half century of democratic development already behind them. The postcommunist polities, on the other hand, have experienced a long history of authoritarianism, and only managed to effect a transition to democracy at the end of the twentieth century.

What this brief overview indicates, however, is that the evident contrasts between these two parts of Europe may not last for long. It is not that the postcommunist polities are necessarily "catching up" with their more long-established Western counterparts. That would leave a misleading impression. Instead, the politics of postindustrial society at the beginning of the new century, whether practiced in East or West, is sufficiently different from what went before that both sets of countries may now well be converging on a new equilibrium. In the end, what matters may be not the former contrasts between the traditional capitalist democracies and the new postcommunist democracies, but rather the difference between both sets of polities now, on the one hand, and the patterns that formerly prevailed through most of the twentieth century, on the other.

REFERENCES

Ágh, Attila: *The End of the Beginning: The Partial Consolidation of East Central European Parties and Party Systems,* Budapest Papers on Democratic Transition, Budapest, 1996.

Ágh, Attila: *The Politics of Central Europe,* Sage, London, 1998.

Batt, Judy: *East Central Europe from Reform to Transformation,* The Royal Institute of International Affairs/Pinter Publishers, London, 1991.

Biezen, Ingrid van: "The Development of Communist and Socialist Parties in Spain and Portugal," *West European Politics,* vol. 21, no. 2, pp. 32–62.

Bútora, Martin, and Zora Bútorová: "Slovakia after the Split," *Journal of Democracy,* vol. 4, no. 2, 1993, pp. 71–83.

CW-EECR (Country Watch-East European Constitutional Review).

Dahl, Robert A.: *Polyarchy: Participation and Opposition,* Yale University Press, New Haven, 1971.

Evans, Geoffrey, and Stephen Whitefield: "Identifying the Bases of Party Competition in Eastern Europe," *British Journal of Political Science,* vol. 5, no. 4, 1993, pp. 521–48.

Fish, M. Steven: "The End of Meciarism," *East European Constitutional Review,* vol. 8, Winter/Spring 1999, pp. 47–55.

Garlicki, Leszek Lech: "The Presidency in the New Polish Constitution," *East European Constitutional Review,* vol. 6, Spring/Summer 1997, pp. 81–89.

Jasiewicz, Krzysztof: "From Solidarity to Fragmentation," *Journal of Democracy,* vol. 3, no. 2, 1992, pp. 55–69.

Jasiewicz, Krzysztof, and Stanislaw Gebethner: "Poland," *European Journal of Political Research,* vol. 34, nos. 3–4 [*Political Data Yearbook*], 1998, pp. 493–506.

Kitschelt, Herbert, Zdenka Mansfeldova, Radoslaw Markowski, and Gábor Tóka: *Post-Communist Party Systems: Competition, Representation, and Inter-Party Cooperation,* Cambridge University Press, Cambridge, 1999.

Kopecky, Petr: *Growing Apart? The Institutionalization of the Czech and Slovak Parliaments,* Ashgate, Aldershot, 2000.

Kopecky, Petr, and Cas Mudde: "The 1998 Parliamentary and Senate Elections in the Czech Republic," *Electoral Studies,* vol. 18, no. 3, 1999, pp. 411–50.

Körösényi, András: *Government and Politics in Hungary,* Central European University Press, Budapest, 1999.

Letowska, Ewa: "A Constitution of Possibilities," *East European Constitutional Review,* vol. 6, Spring/Summer 1999, pp. 76–81.

Lewis, Paul G. (ed.): *Party Structure and Organization in East-Central Europe,* Elgar, Cheltenham, 1996.

Lijphart, Arend: "Constitutional Choices for New Democracies," *Journal of Democracy,* vol. 2, no. 3, 1991, pp. 72–84.

Lijphart, Arend: "Democratization and Constitutional Choices in Czechoslovakia, Hungary and Poland," *Journal of Theoretical Politics,* vol. 4, no. 2, 1992, pp. 207–23.

Lucky, Christian: "A Comparative Chart of Presidential Powers in Eastern Europe," *East European Constitutional Review,* double issue, vol. 2, Fall 1993, vol. 3, Winter 1994, pp. 81–94.

Lukashak, Alexander, et al.: "Survey of Presidential Powers in Eastern Europe," *East European Constitutional Review,* double issue, vol. 2, Fall 1993, vol. 3, Winter 1994, pp. 58–81.

Mair, Peter: *Party System Change: Approaches and Interpretations,* Clarendon Press, Oxford, 1997.

Mair, Peter, and Ingrid van Biezen: "Trends in Enrolment in Political Parties in European Polities, with Particular Reference to Youth Enrolment," paper presented to the Conference on Youth and Democracy, Stockholm, June 1999.

Malova, Darina: "Slovakia," *European Journal of Political Research,* vol. 30, nos. 3–4 [*Political Data Yearbook*], 1996, pp. 453–58.

Malova, Darina: "Slovakia," *European Journal of Political Research,* vol. 36, nos. 3–4 [*Political Data Yearbook*], in press.

Mateju, Petr, Blanka Rehakova, and Geoffrey Evans: "The Politics of Interests and Class Realignment in the Czech Republic," in Geoffrey Evans (ed.), *The End of Class Politics? Class Voting in Comparative Context,* Oxford University Press, Oxford, 1999, pp. 231–53.

Meer Krok-Paszowska, Ania van der: *Shaping the Democratic Order: The Institutionalisation of Parliament in Poland,* Ph.D. thesis, Leiden University, 2000.

Musil, Jirí: "Czechoslovakia in the Middle of Transition," *Daedalus,* vol. 121, no. 2, 1992, pp. 175–95.

Olson, David: "The Czech Senate: From Constitutional Inducement to Electoral Challenge," *East European Constitutional Review,* vol. 5, Fall 1996, pp. 47–50.

Oltay, Edith: "Towards the Rule of Law: Hungary," RFE/RL Research Report, vol. 1, no. 27, 1992, pp. 16–24.

Osiatynski, Wiktor: "A Brief History of the [Polish] Constitution," *East European Constitutional Review,* vol. 6, Spring/Summer 1997, pp. 66–76.

Rose, Richard: "Mobilizing Demobilized Voters in Post-Communist Societies," *Party Politics,* vol. 1, no. 4, 1995, pp. 549–63.

Rose, Richard, Neil Munro, and Tom Mackie: *Elections in Central and Eastern Europe Since 1990,* Centre for the Study of Public Policy, Glasgow, 1998.

Rothschild, Joseph: *East Central Europe Between the Two World Wars,* University of Washington Press, Seattle, 1974.

Sitter, Nickolai: *The East Central European Party Systems,* Ph.D. thesis, London School of Economics, 1999.

Tóka, Gábor: "Party Appeals and Voter Loyalties in New Democracies," *Political Studies,* Vol. 46, No. 3, 1998, pp. 589–610.

Wightman, Gordon: "The Czechoslovak Elections of 1992," *Electoral Studies,* vol. 12, no. 1, 1993, pp. 83–86.

Zielonka, Jan: "Institutional Uncertainty in Post-Communist Democracies," *Journal of Democracy,* vol. 5, no. 2, 1994, pp. 87–104.

KEEPING UP WITH CHANGES IN EUROPEAN POLITICS: INTERNET AND OTHER RESOURCES

Representative Government in Modern Europe is as up-to-the-minute as we could make it, but, inevitably, there are details that will be overtaken by events even while the book is being printed. Fortunately, readers wanting to monitor continuing political developments in Europe have a number of sources that they can turn to.

As well as the wide range of general political science journals, there are some that specialize in European politics. The *European Journal of Political Research,* in addition to its regular issues, publishes an annual "Data Yearbook" containing the latest developments from each of the countries that we cover in this book. *West European Politics* has many articles on European politics, as its name suggests, and also carries regular reports on the latest elections in Europe—as does the journal *Electoral Studies.*

Increasingly, the Internet is a valuable source of political data. Virtually every government department, every parliament, every political party, every interest group, and every major newspaper in every European country maintains its own site on the Web; many individual members of parliament have their own sites, complete with photograph. We have decided not to try to provide a comprehensive list of these sites. One reason, of course, is that this would require a huge effort on our part, but a more persuasive reason is that websites are inclined to come and go with alarming regularity, and any such list would itself soon become out-of-date.

So, instead, we are listing a small number of sites that have established themselves as reliable presences on the Web, and that either contain useful information themselves or have links to other sites.

The first (1) is a multiple prize-winning site maintained by a British political scientist. Although it does not hold any information itself, it contains links to a huge number of political sites around the world, and is organized very clearly so that users should have little difficulty in finding a site that is useful for their purposes. Site (2) contains some information on the IPU itself, and, more importantly, has links to all of the parliaments that are affiliated to it. In most countries, the parliament site itself contains other links: to the sites of individual MPs, political parties, and governments. Site (3) has links to parties and other political organizations around the world, and a data archive containing election results. Site (4) is the site of the European Union, and contains a great deal of information as well as links to all the EU institutions.

Sites (5) and (6) both contain many details of election results; site (6) also provides a daily news service with news of current elections. Site (7) is the Lijphart Elections Archive, housed at the University of California, San Diego campus, and is a research collection of district-level election results for approximately 350 national legislative elections in twenty-six countries.

Document	Web address
1 Richard Kimber's political science resources	www.psr.keele.ac.uk
2 The Inter-Parliamentary Union	www.ipu.org
3 General political resources site	www.agora.stm.it/politic/index.html
4 Welcome to Europe	www.europa.eu.int/index-en.htm
5 An elections site	ElectionResources.org/
6 An elections site	www.klipsan.com/elecnews.htm
7 Lijphart elections archive	dodgson.ucsd.edu/lij/

INDEX